A SAHAPTIN
B SPOKANE
C KALISPEL
D COEUR d'ALENE
E CAYUSE
F NEZ PERCE
G BANNOCK
H CHEYENNE
I HIDATSA
J MANDAN
K ARIKARA
L PONCA
M MENOMINEE
N WINNEBAGO
O POTAWATOMI
P E. OJIBWA
Q OTTAWA
R HURON
S SENECA
T CAYUGA
U ONONDAGA
V ONEIDA
W MOHAWK
Y MAHICAN
x Unoccupied areas
POLAR ESKIMO
EAST GREENLAND ESKIMO
WEST GREENLAND ESKIMO
EAST GREENLAND ESKIMO
IGLULIK ESKIMO
NETSILIK ESKIMO
BAFFINLAND ESKIMO
SALLIRMIUT
CARIBOU ESKIMO
QUEBEC ESKIMO
LABRADOR ESKIMO
Hudson Bay
NASKAPI
MONTAGNAIS
BEOTHUK
WEST MAIN CREE
EAST CREE
NORTHERN OJIBWA
MICMAC
MALISEET
LAURENTIAN
ALGONQUIN
SOUTHEASTERN OJIBWA
ABENAKI
PASSAMAQUODDY
SANTEE-SISSETON
ATLANTIC OCEAN
SAUK
FOX
IOWA
MIAMI
KICKAPOO

. . . so long as the waters shall flow
and the sun shall shine . . .

Also by Wendell H. Oswalt:

Mission of Change in Alaska
Napaskiak: An Alaskan Eskimo Community
Alaskan Eskimos
Understanding Our Culture
Other Peoples, Other Customs
Habitat and Technology
An Anthropological Analysis of Food-Getting Technology
Eskimos and Explorers
Kolmakovskiy Redoubt
Life Cycles and Lifeways: An Introduction to Cultural Anthropology
Bashful No Longer: An Alaskan Eskimo Ethnohistory, 1788–1988

THIS LAND WAS THEIRS

A Study of Native Americans

SEVENTH EDITION

Wendell H. Oswalt
University of California, Los Angeles

Boston Burr Ridge, IL Dubuque, IA Madison, WI New York
San Francisco St. Louis Bangkok Bogotá Caracas Kuala Lumpur
Lisbon London Madrid Mexico City Milan Montreal New Delhi
Santiago Seoul Singapore Sydney Taipei Toronto

McGraw-Hill Higher Education

A Division of The ***McGraw-Hill*** *Companies*

1 2 3 4 5 6 7 8 9 0 BAH/BAH 0 9 8 7 6 5 4 3 2 1

Library of Congress Cataloging-in-Publication Data

Oswalt, Wendell H.,

This land was theirs : a study of Native Americans/Wendell H. Oswalt.

—7th ed

p. cm.

Includes bibliographical references and index.

ISBN 0-7674-1347-4

1. Indians of North America I. Title.

E77.08 2001

2001030723

Sponsoring editor, Janet M. Beatty; production editor, Melissa Williams; manuscript editor, Elaine Kehoe; design manager and cover designer, Susan Breitbard; art editor, Robin Mouat; illustrator, Patty Isaacs; manufacturing manager, Randy Hurst. The text was set in 10/12 ITC Garamond Light by G&S Typesetters, Inc. and printed on acid-free 45# Chromatone Matte by Banta Book Group.

Cover: Netsilik woman (top) from *Narrative of a Second Voyage in Search of a North-West Passage.* John Ross, E. L. Corey and H. Hart, Philadelphia. 1835; Indian with headdress of feathers (top, right). An 1821 painting from *The Indians of North America, Vol. 1.* Thomas L. McKenney and James Hall. D. Rice and J. G. Clark, Philadelphia.; Man in car (bottom, right) William N. Fenton Photograph Collection, Negative #230. Courtesy of the American Philosophical Society; Chipewyan camp in 1880 (bottom, left), Courtesy of the Canadian Museum of Civilization, image number 74880. All other photos courtesy of Wendell H. Oswalt.

www.mhhe.com

In memory of
Edward H. Spicer
and
John J. Honigmann

Preface

The first edition of *This Land Was Theirs,* published in 1966, introduced a different approach to the study of Native Americans living north of Mexico. The emphasis was, and remains, on traditional and changing Indian lifeways. The tribes with chapter-length presentations represent culture areas and varying degrees of cultural complexity. The tribal accounts include scientific and humanistic approaches to anthropological data. Likewise, ecological, ethnohistorical, functional, structural, and other perspectives are included as appropriate. Thus no single orientation dominates.

The two opening chapters address questions commonly asked about Native Americans, such as their prehistory, history, and current issues, including Indian casinos. This and additional background material are followed by twelve chapters about specific populations. After brief introductions, most chapters begin with early ethnographic accounts. The Navajo chapter is an exception because most information available is ethnohistorical, and the Navajo emerged as a tribe in the comparatively recent past. Each chapter plots historical developments to the summer of 2000. The concluding chapter offers an overview of Native American life with emphasis on the present and the near future.

The tribal chapters reflect differences in sociopolitical life (band, tribe, chiefdom), and particular aspects of their lifeways are accented. The presentation sequence is as follows. The Netsilik (Eskimo, Inuit) of north-central Canada, with their dog teams, seal hunting, and snowhouses, represent a "classic" Eskimo group in the Arctic culture area. Considerable emphasis is placed on their material culture and the impact of food stress. The Chipewyan of northwestern Canada represent Subarctic hunters and fishers; their adaptations to the fur trade are highlighted. The Lower Kootenai in Idaho and British Columbia represent hunters and fishers in the Plateau culture area; they provide an opportunity to examine the impact of Canadian and United States policies on a single group. The Cahuilla, with an aboriginal economy focused largely on wild plant products, inhabit an arid sector of the California culture area. The circumstances leading to the vast present-day wealth of the Palm Springs group are reviewed. The Crow of the northern Plains represent foragers, and their historic emphasis on horse-related activities. The Yurok of northern California and the Tlingit of southeastern Alaska provide a comparison with salmon fishers in the Northwest Coast culture area. Their attitudes toward property and wealth are central in these chapters. The Hopi of the

Southwest, as arid-area farmers, in numerous ways typify the complexities of Pueblo Indian life. For the Navajo in the Southwest, historical roots are stressed. Their varied biological and cultural background and comparatively recent emergence as a tribe attract considerable attention. The Iroquois of the Northeast depended largely on domestic crops; their political life is featured. The Cherokee as farmers are one of the few major Indian populations that continue to occupy their homeland in the Southeast. Finally, the Natchez of Mississippi reflect one of the most complex lifeways among Indians north of Mexico. The stages leading to their demise receive particular attention.

In closing, it is gratifying to acknowledge a resurgent interest in Native Americans among non-Indians. Hopefully, this new edition will lead to further understanding of Indian life, *past and present*.

New to This Edition

Two major differences distinguish this from previous editions. First is the addition of a chapter about a "standard" Eskimo (Inuit) group, the Netsilik. Second, the Plateau culture area is represented for the first time in a chapter about the Lower Kootenai (the Kuskowagamiut and Mesquakie chapters of previous editions are deleted). Unlike previous editions, tribal history is presented more concisely and follows a baseline ethnographic account. The Navajo chapter represents an exception; these people are introduced with an ethnohistorical presentation.

For this edition the ethnic boundary and linguistic maps are revised. These new maps are based largely on those in the new *Handbook of North American Indians*.

Powwows, tribalism, and intertribalism receive greater attention than previously. In this edition for the first time the presentation includes such topics as urban populations, the taxation of Indians, and tribes not recognized by the federal government in the United States. Chapter 15 includes a new section, "Indians in the News."

College students typically are unfamiliar with traditional Indian artifacts. Thus line drawings of prominent tools and food-procurement types are included as Appendix I. Appendix II includes additional resources about Native Americans.

For most tribes presented at chapter length, comprehensive published accounts about contemporary life are unavailable. I therefore visited each tribe, except the Netsilik and remanent Natchez. My visits, especially in the 1990s, usually were short, but often repeated.

Acknowledgments

I am most grateful for the help of Sharlotte Neely, the coauthor for the fifth and sixth editions. Without her devotion, the fifth and later editions would not have appeared. Many thanks Sharlotte.

The following colleagues provided insightful prepublication reviews of the manuscript for this edition: Mary H. Helms, University of North Carolina; Alan Lamb, Northern Idaho College; Stephen Lensink, University of Iowa; Leslie Shaw, Bowdoin College; and Cristina Taylor, Suffolk County Community College.

Individuals who were especially helpful in providing specifics about particular tribes and topics for this edition are as follows:

Netsilik: Asen Balikci, David F. Pelly, Quinn Taggart

Lower Kootenai: Jackie L. Bacon, Velma Bahe, Paul Flinn, Bev Hills, Jack Nisbet, Joseph Pierre, Greg Sprungl, and Deward E. Walker, Jr.

Cahuilla: Lowell John Bean

Crow: Denis Adams, Tim Berbardis, Ann Bullis, and Kaneeta Red Star Harris

Yurok: Thomas M. Gates, Traci Melendy, and Roland Raymond

Tlingit: Wallace M. Olson

Hopi: Leigh J. Kuwanwisiwma and three anonymous tribal members

Navajo: Christine Wallace

Iroquois: Barbara A. Mann

Natchez: Jim Barnett

Current Realities: Helen Louise Oswalt

Janet M. Beatty, senior editor, at Mayfield Publishing Company has guided this book through four editions. I honor her insight combined with flexibility and firmness. Other members of the Mayfield staff who have been especially supportive include Melissa Williams, senior production editor; Susan Breitbard, design manager; Robin Mouat, art manager; and Elaine Kehoe, manuscript editor.

Unattributed photographs in the text are by Wendell H. Oswalt.

Contents

1 Questions about Native Americans

We ask only an even chance
to live as other men live.
We asked to be recognized as men.

Chief Joseph, Nez Perce Tribe, 1877

THIS ANTHROPOLOGICAL STUDY begins by focusing on general questions about American Indians living north of Mexico. How have we been influenced by Indians? Who is a Native American? How long have their ancestors been in the New World, and where did they originate? The answers to these questions and others are the subject of this chapter. They provide essential background for the next chapter about what happened as Indians became deeply involved with non-Indians.

The use of the word *Indian* requires initial comment. The term originated with Christopher Columbus, who thought he had reached the East Indies, islands off Asia. He called the people *los Indios,* and even after the error was realized, the Spanish continued to use the word *Indios* for all New World peoples; the word became *Indian* in English. Alternatively, the words *savage, heathen,* and *barbarian* became commonplace in the 1600s to identify Indians and to emphasize their "noncivilized" and "non-Christian" status. By the late eighteenth century, the "Noble Savage" designation became an increasingly popular way to glorify and romanticize traditional Indian life, especially in art and literature. By the early 1970s the word *Indian* was becoming politically incorrect in the United States, and the term *Native American* became popular. In this book the words *Indian, Native American,* and *American Indian* are used to refer to the aboriginal populations of the New World. Another alternative, favored by some Native Americans, is *indigenous people.* Indians often call themselves *Indian,* or *Skins* in casual conversation.

Indians in Popular Culture

Discomfort and ambivalence characterize the widespread views of Indians among white Americans. The European roots of their perspective have been nurtured for centuries in American soil. In straightforward language, Native Americans are most commonly judged "good" and "bad," as obvious stereotypes. Stereotyping is an important facet of popular culture and reveals deep-seated American values (a value is a shared concept of what is desirable or undesirable). Negative views of Indians are especially evident in numerous American English words and phrases. Early general examples refer to Indians as *barbarians, heathens,* and *infidels.* Subsequently arose such terms and phrases as *Indian giver, speaking with a forked tongue, squaw, wild Indian,* the racist designation *redskin,* and, finally, *lo! the poor Indian.* Notably ambivalent terms include *Noble Savage* and *good Indian.* Finally there is the positive term used in Canada, *First Nations,* and the widely popular label, *America's first environmentalists.* If you personally have mixed feelings about Indians, there are good historical reasons. Yet gross misrepresentations of Native Americans are both sad and real.

In a less prejudicial popular-culture context, non-Indian American understanding of Indians is affected by typically superficial presentation in schools. A prominent example is emphasizing Thanksgiving-feast foods introduced by

Indians, such as cranberries, maize (corn), pumpkins, and turkey. Stereotypes of Indians were conveyed in the once-popular radio and television shows about the Lone Ranger and Tonto. Boy Scouts, Girl Scouts, and Camp Fire Girls strive to mimic Indian arts, crafts, and dances. They may learn also that birch-bark canoes, moccasins, and toboggans first were items of Native American material culture.

Likewise, popular culture is evident in early American literature. No subject had greater appeal than the Indians, but their literary image has been far from uniform. The Indian entered into American literature through speeches recorded during treaty deliberations. The oratorical skills of Indians were appreciated, and the texts were printed for general circulation in the eighteenth century. Because Indians were close at hand in the eastern states and were an obstruction when whites coveted more land, they soon were viewed as foes. As the frontier expanded westward in the first half of the nineteenth century, the image of the Indian reverted to that of a nonantagonist, in fact to a romantic figure. Drawing on accounts about Indians, James Fenimore Cooper wrote his great novels and conceived the character of Leatherstocking, a white Indian without literary equal. Henry Wadsworth Longfellow's *Hiawatha* too is a literary monument of this era. The earliest play about Indians, *Metamora,* was first produced in 1829 by the actor–playwright John Augustus Stone, and it became one of the most popular plays for the remainder of the century. Playwrights have continued to build plots around Indians. Included in the first American opera, *Tammany,* performed in 1794, was a Cherokee melody, and the Indian exists in such American folk songs as Charles Cadman's "From the Land of Sky Blue Waters" and "Red Wing" by Thurland Chattaway and Kerry Mills.

By the 1810s, west of the Mississippi River, Indians began to be regarded as they had been in the East by non-Indian Americans who sought land. According to these settlers, the Indian impeded progress and was a form of vermin to be exterminated. Never mind that the settlers traveled west over trails and pathways established by Indians. After Indians had been defeated in skirmishes and wars and remnant Indian populations were confined to reservations, these people again could be viewed romantically; even before the West was colonized, the Indian was a figure in nearly half of the 320 dime novels originating in the 1860s. The Indian theme never died.

Indians played an important role in shaping the belief system of one of the few large and important religions originating in the United States, the Church of Jesus Christ of Latter-day Saints, or Mormons. *The Book of Mormon* relates that Indians originated from a Jewish population that entered the New World before Christian times. According to Mormon beliefs, Indians descended from the Lamanites; although these were thought to be a degenerate people, the Mormons have been inordinately kind in their dealings with Indians. As noted by A. Irving Hallowell (1958, 461), the inclusion of population theory in a religious dogma "could hardly have occurred anywhere but in early nineteenth-century America."

It may be asked why, from a global perspective, North American Indian cultures were comparatively less elaborate than those further south. It was not from any lack of intelligence among Indians but rather because of the nature of their environmental setting and its possibilities for development. The New World was largely devoid of animals with great potential for domestication, such as cows and pigs; nor did there exist such grains as barley and wheat. More important, in the New World the animals and plants that did have potential as domesticates were *not* concentrated in one restricted geographical area. A contrary situation existed in the Old World, in which the basis for most of Old World civilization emerged in the Near East about 8000 B.C. New World developments, however, are not to be cast aside as failures. One must recognize that in aboriginal Mexico and Peru, complex societies emerged with large populations and elaborate lifestyles; in these regions the environmental potential for indigenous cultural developments was far greater than in settings to the north.

Who Is a Native American?

In the sixteenth century, as ever-increasing numbers of European maritime explorers ventured to the Americas, there was no difficulty in establishing who was a Native American. The biological, linguistic, and cultural differences separating Africans, Europeans, and indigenous Americans were apparent to all observers. Indians spoke languages that differed widely from one tribe to another, but none could be understood by the explorers. Indians looked different, dressed in an unfamiliar manner, and their bodily adornments were unusual, if not bizarre, to a traveler from England, France, or Spain. Then, too, the main crops that Indians raised, maize and beans, were not cultivated in Europe. Thus the people of the New World stood in striking contrast to Europeans and their ways.

The problem of classifying a person as an American Indian became complex with the arrival of African slaves and European adventurers, fishermen, missionaries, settlers, traders, and trappers. Three conditions resulting from these contacts were important. First, outsiders mated with Indian women to produce persons of mixed genetic heritage; second, Indians sometimes captured blacks and whites and made them "Indians"; and third, some Indians lost their identity by assimilation into the intrusive society. To identify an Indian with clarity after the period of early historic contact, we must deal primarily with racial and sociocultural factors. Socially, we can imagine that foreigners who were assimilated into an Indian tribe became Indians, despite their genetic heritage. Likewise, Indians who disassociated themselves from other Indians came to be judged as non-Indian. For individuals of mixed Indian and white or black ancestry, the distinctions were clear as long as they consistently followed one lifestyle or the other. Such persons could, however, behave as Indian in one context and non-Indian in another, as Indian or non-Indian exclusively throughout their lives, or as Indian at one time in life and non-

Indian at another. The identification of a Native American has become a matter of definition and is most reasonably considered in a legal sense.

Before we consider Indian identity further, one point requires clarification. Non-Indians classify Aleuts and Eskimos* as separate from Indians because of their physical appearance and cultures. In biological terms, Aleuts and Eskimos are the most Asiatic of indigenous New World peoples, having been the last to arrive from Asia, and their economic adjustments stand apart from those of other aboriginal Americans. However, the cultural differences separating some Indian tribes from each other are greater than those that separate Aleuts and Eskimos from many Indians. Thus Aleuts, Eskimos, and Indians all may reasonably be called Native Americans. In Canada the preferred term is First Nations.

It merits note that in North America by the early seventeenth century, Native Americans commonly were called "blacks" or "negroes." Subsequently, Indians also might be termed "free people of color," in the manner of some blacks, or "mulattoes." Likewise, individuals of Native American and African ancestry could be called "negroes." In the 1980 U.S. census, a person who checked the "black" and "Indian" categories on the census form was counted as "black." Until recently the official classification of Native Americans and blacks clearly was a product of Euro-American racism.

In the history of United States Indian law, there has been no uniform definition of an Indian. In general, if a person is considered an Indian by other individuals in the community, he or she is an Indian. The degree of a person's Indian genetic heritage may be important, but under most circumstances it is secondary to sociocultural standing in the community in which she or he resides. Regardless of heredity, a person who "acts white" may not be regarded as a "real Indian" in a settlement. Examples will illustrate why there is so much confusion. If an individual is on the roll of a federally recognized Indian group, the person is Indian; the degree of Indian genetic heritage is of no consequence. On some reservations a tribal member is Indian even if records show that fifteen of sixteen immediate ancestors were not Indian. However, the real need for defining an Indian is with reference to a specific piece of legislation at a particular time. A person who is on the federal roll of a tribe and lives on a reservation clearly is an Indian; if that person moves from a reservation but remains on the roll, he or she continues to be an Indian. If he or she receives a clear title to allotted reservation land, he or she may or may not subsequently remain an Indian, depending on the circumstances. Indian status also is lost by voluntary disassociation from other Indians and by identifying with some other segment of society.

*Canadian Eskimos and numerous white Canadians are adamant that Eskimos be called Inuit, their name for themselves, and not Eskimo. In this book, *Eskimo* is used as the generic designation of these northern peoples because all Eskimos are *not* Inuit; many who live in Alaska and small numbers in Siberia are *Yuit,* a designation comparable to Inuit yet distinct from it. Therefore, to use the word *Inuit* for Eskimos in general is incorrect.

In the United States, all Native Americans did not become citizens until 1924, when the Citizenship Act was passed by Congress. Previously, about 250,000 Indians had become citizens by other means; the act made citizens of about 125,000 more persons. As early as 1817 individuals were granted citizenship under treaty arrangements if they met certain provisions, such as the acceptance of title to individual lands in contrast to living on tribal lands. For many years the prevailing opinion of the federal government was that Indians who followed tribal customs and were not under the control of the state or territory in which they lived could not be citizens. Becoming a citizen was given a different basis with the passage of the Dawes Act in 1887 (see Chapter 2 for details). In 1888 a law was passed making Indian women citizens if they married citizens, the assumption being that these women were following the path of "civilization." As noncitizens, Indians were not inducted into the armed services during World War I. However, those who volunteered were made citizens by congressional action. By 1938 seven states still refused to allow Native Americans to vote, and only in 1948 were voting rights granted to Indians in Arizona and New Mexico. Opposition to Indian suffrage was based on their special relationship to the federal government.

One provision in the Canadian Indian Act of 1876 was that any Indian who had a university education or its equivalent thereby became a citizen. In other instances an individual, or the band by majority vote, initiated enfranchisement proceedings; this method required a probationary period before becoming effective. When a man with a wife and unmarried minor children became enfranchised, his family was granted the same legal status. These provisions were not generally applied to the Indians of British Columbia, Manitoba, or the Northwest Territories. For the next fifty years Canadian Indian policy fluctuated between voluntary and forced enfranchisement. Finally, as a result of the Indian Act of 1951, Canadian Indians became subject to the same general laws that applied to other Canadians. They could vote in national elections and could consume intoxicants legally for the first time. In 1985 a dramatic change was made in Canadian Indian law. One result was that Indians who had become non-Indian could once again regain their Indian identity (see Chapter 2 for details).

Population Figures

At the time of early European contact, around A.D. 1500, estimates of the Indian population north of Mexico range from about two to more than four million people; the latter figure may be more accurate. The Native American population in the United States reached its lowest point around 1890, with about 240,000 people. By 1999, some 2.4 million people in the United States identified themselves as Native American. The Navajo, with about 212,000 people, are the most populous federally recognized tribe. Many people consider themselves American Indians but have no formal affiliation with any Indian community, organization, or tribe, and some cannot document their claim to be Indian. Most Native Americans in the United States live in urban areas. About 33 percent live on or near reservations or traditional lands. The states with the highest estimated Native American populations in 1998 were California (309,000), Oklahoma (263,000), Arizona (256,000), and New Mexico (163,000). Native Americans in the United States represent about 1 percent of the total population.

In Canada the First Nations (Native American) population reached its lowest point around 1900, with about 100,000 people. The First Nations population in 1996 was about 805,000; of these, 554,000 were North American Indians, 210,000 were Métis (persons of mixed heritage), and 41,000 were Inuit (Eskimos). About 70 percent of the First Nations people lived on or near reserves (reservations). The provinces with the largest populations were Alberta, Manitoba, and Saskatchewan.

Today, about 56,000 Inuit (Eskimos) live in Greenland, a province of Denmark, having recovered from a population low of some 10,000 around 1900.

Where Did Native Americans Originate?

Speculations about the origins of Native Americans have had lasting romantic appeal. Humanists, the general public, and scientists alike have long puzzled over the original Indian homeland. The theories advanced to explain their derivation involve something that is lost to modern times; thus the supportive evidence can only be indirect.

Conjecture about a lost continent of Atlantis (or Antillia, the word on which Antilles is based) predates the discovery of the Americas. After Europeans learned of the existence of Native Americans, the idea that Atlantis had been a stepping-stone for early migrants from the Old to the New World seemed logical. Atlantis was thought to be a vast island beyond Gibraltar on which a complex civilization developed before it was destroyed by a cataclysm. The idea lingered among the Romans and was accepted by some persons in medieval Europe. Christopher Columbus may have sailed toward its presumed position, and some people thought that the land he discovered was Atlantis. By the 1880s the island's disappearance was still being attributed to a major cataclysm that had occurred after the people destined to become American Indians had left its shores. Each author who supported the theory was struck by the cultural similarities between American Indians, usually those in Mexico, and some early Old World civilization, usually Egyptian.

Another theory proposed that Indians were descendants of the Lost Tribes of Israel. The evidence for this idea was summarized long ago by Samuel F. Haven (1856). According to this theory, ten tribes of Israelites, defeated by the Assyrians, became lost by wandering into Asia. They ventured to a point nearest the Americas, from which they crossed the waters into the New World. Other speculators have identified seafaring peoples such as the Carthaginians or Phoenicians as responsible for the original occupation. Cotton Mather, in colonial America, advanced a unique explanation for Indian origins.

He wrote that "probably the *Devil* decoyed those miserable salvages* hither, in hopes that the gospel of the Lord Jesus Christ would never come here to destroy or disturb his absolute empire over them" (Drake 1837, 9).

In 1570 the Jesuit missionary Father Joseph de Acosta went to Peru, and about 1580 he began to write his *Historia natural y moral de las Indias.* The book appeared in its first Spanish edition in 1590, three years after he returned to Spain. Acosta reasoned that because Adam was the original ancestor of humanity and because Indians were people, then they must have come from the Old World, which Adam's descendants had peopled. He reasoned that the New World and the Old World had been connected, or separated, by a narrow strait, because certain land mammals were the same in the respective hemispheres. He felt that people and animals alike had traveled along the same route. The human entry was visualized as having taken place slowly, caused by overpopulation, famines, or the loss of former living areas. Thus Acosta was the first to advance a land-bridge theory to explain why and how people entered the New World. He also theorized that the original occupants were hunters who later developed a more complex way of life. Therefore, any comparisons between New and Old World civilizations could not be very meaningful.

Modern anthropologists support the general thesis of Indian origins first advanced by Acosta. People did not evolve in the New World but migrated there. The bones of *all* the distant human ancestors that have been found are reported in the Old World. Bones that are clear markers along humankind's evolutionary trail have been repeatedly discovered in Africa. In the same context, the earliest human remains in the New World appear to date from at least 14,000 years ago and to belong to individuals who were essentially modern in physical appearance. From the fossil record, we must conclude that people entered the Western Hemisphere in comparatively recent times. Furthermore, geological evidence indicates that continents did *not* formerly exist in either the Atlantic or Pacific oceans.

The most popular theory contends that the first people arrived in the New World over a land bridge in the Bering Strait region. These migrants first lingered in Alaska, eventually followed western mountains southward into the western United States and Mexico, and continued on to South America. In recent years a competing theory has gained attention. It holds that varied maritime peoples, intermittently sailing from northeastern Asia, traveled along the west coast to populate the Americas.

The only pre-Columbian voyages beyond reasonable dispute are the ones made by Viking, or more properly Norse, explorers. Iceland was settled in the ninth century by Scandinavians, and within a hundred years Greenland had been discovered. After becoming involved in a series of homicides, Eric the Red was exiled from Iceland for three years. He spent the time, A.D. 982–985, exploring southwestern Greenland, and on his return he organized a colonizing expedition. It left for southwestern Greenland in 986, and additional

*Middle English spelling of "savages."

settlers arrived later. The Greenland colony was occupied by the Norse until about 1540 and had a maximum population of about five thousand persons. Given the turbulent weather in the north Atlantic, many ships heading toward Greenland were lost or blown off course. One vessel strayed to the coast of North America but did not land. About the year 1000, the son of Eric the Red, Leif Erikson, purposely sailed for continental North America. In the centuries to follow, a number of planned trips were made to northeastern North America from Greenland, especially to obtain building timber. The Norse appear to have settled briefly in northern Newfoundland at L'Anse aux Meadows, which was discovered and partially excavated by Helge Ingstad. Radiocarbon dates indicate that the site was occupied about A.D. 1000. The presence of a few Norse artifacts and wrought iron at the site leaves little doubt that these were Norse remains. However, no clear evidence exists to suggest that these Europeans had any influence on the cultures of aboriginal Americans.

If voyagers from the Old World, apart from the Norse, did arrive in the New World during pre-Columbian times, we might expect to find artifacts that they brought with them. Conversely, if travelers ventured in the opposite direction, we would expect to recover objects in the Eastern Hemisphere that were made in the Americas. Despite the thousands of excavations in which millions of artifacts have been recovered, not one such artifact has been found in a clearly valid context. Admittedly, these objects may exist in unexplored sites, and if any are found, our thinking will need to be revised or even reversed.

If there were substantial Old and New World contacts, we would expect to find evidence in linguistic ties. Relationships between languages cannot be postulated based on a small number of words with the same form and meaning, because such parallels may be accounted for by chance alone. To demonstrate historical connections between languages, clear phonemic (sound) and grammatical (structural) similarities, as well as numerous parallels among words, must exist. Is there any evidence of this nature to link pre-Columbian peoples of the two hemispheres? The answer is a cautious "yes." The Eskimo–Aleut language family that spans the American Arctic and the Chukchi–Kamchatkan family in northeastern Siberia are possibly related. The same is true for Nadene languages in North America and Yeniseian languages in Siberia. These and other language comparisons suggest Native American linguistic ties with peoples in northern Eurasia.

Expecting to find Old World artifacts in prehistoric New World sites may be unreasonable, if only because few objects probably survived long ocean voyages. Similarly, the speakers of Old World languages could have arrived, but their languages might have passed out of existence when the original migrants died. This raises the question of whether *influences* from the Old World reached the Americas. As we consider the question, we must first make one critical observation. Innumerable examples exist of people in one part of the world inventing artifacts similar to those independently conceived and produced by a distant people. Thus we must be cautious in deducing that a form had a single place of origin and spread from there. Furthermore, evidence that coherent *groups* of Old and New World artifacts are similar is of greater potential significance than are similarities between isolated artifact types or design motifs.

Perhaps the best evidence for prehistoric Old and New World contacts is the presence of certain Asian-like artifact types in sites along the coast of Ecuador, dating about 200 B.C. As Emilio Estrada and Betty J. Meggers (1961) noted, this cluster is largely restricted to Ecuador. Included are pottery models of houses with saddle-shaped roofs and columns, figures with one leg folded above the other, and the "coolie" yoke. These finds suggest that ocean voyagers from Asia landed in Ecuador and successfully introduced these and other novel ideas.

Another approach to the problem centers on evidence of a different nature: domestic plants and animals transported by pre-Columbian peoples to the New World. In a symposium that he organized, Carroll L. Riley and his associates considered cultigens. A quotation from their summary remarks follows (Riley et al. 1971, 452–453): "The consensus of botanical evidence given in this symposium seems to be *that there is no hard and fast evidence for any pre-Columbian human introduction of any single plant or animal* across the ocean from the Old World to the New World, or vice-versa. This is emphatically *not* to say that it could not have occurred." Thus the case rests on a largely negative note.

Precontact History North of Mexico: An Overview

The earliest human migrants to the New World came from Siberia, and they were hunters. These statements seem beyond reasonable doubt. By early historic times, Indians had made innumerable adaptations, depending on localized resources, contact with other Indians, and other factors. This section provides a brief synopsis of pre-Columbian cultural developments, with the emphasis on the regions north of Mexico.

PALEO-INDIANS Controversy surrounds the question of when the earliest migrants first entered the Americas. It is widely accepted that in the vicinity of the Bering Strait a land bridge existed from about 75,000 to 45,000 years ago. Yet there is no current evidence to suggest that this bridge was used by people entering the New World. In the same region, a land bridge was known to have been exposed from about 25,000 to 11,000 years ago, and it was during this time span that the earliest humans probably entered northern North America. During this and earlier cold periods, glacial ice covered large areas of the Northern Hemisphere, and worldwide sea levels were lowered by as much as 300 feet. In eastern Siberia and western Alaska, there were no major glaciers because conditions were unfavorable for their formation: the amount of annual precipitation was low, and the land was relatively flat. When the land bridge, called Beringia, loosely connected the continents, it served as a pathway and a cultural filter. Hunters who lived by killing large herbivores, such as bison, caribou, mammoth, and horses, were quite possibly the earliest migrants.

A critical year in the discovery of evidence about prehistoric humans in the Americas was 1926. It was then that J. D. Figgins, a paleontologist excavating a site in northern New Mexico, uncovered the bones of an extinct bison that was much larger than modern bison. The site had been located in 1908 by George McJunkin, an African American cowboy who was the foreman at the ranch on which the discovery was made; unfortunately, McJunkin died before the site was investigated. Ultimately, Figgins found four flint points near bison bones, and a fifth point was embedded *in* bone. This evidence has never been seriously challenged. The projectile points were named Folsom, after the discovery site, and date around 10,500 years ago.

Excavations at the Folsom site demonstrated that Native Americans had considerable antiquity in the New World. The next question was and remains: When did people begin to occupy the New World? Unfortunately, we do not know. Archaeologists are rather confident that the sporadic claims that some sites were occupied 30,000 years ago or in the even more distant past are incorrect. Pre-Folsom artifacts made from flaked stone occasionally have been found in the far north and relatively near Beringia. Widely accepted examples are artifacts from Bluefish Caves in the northern Yukon Territory, Canada, that date around 13,500 years ago; those at Dry Creek in the Nenana River valley of central Alaska date around 11,200 years ago. Much farther south, especially in Arizona, distinctive projectile points, termed Clovis, repeatedly have been excavated in association with mammoth bones and are now dated around 13,400 years ago. Finally, there is the Monte Verde site in southern Chile. The occupants hunted small game and collected plant products; they lived there at least 12,500 years ago.

Considering the location and earliest date for the Monte Verde site, if the ancestors of these Native Americans traveled by land from Siberia and Alaska, they probably arrived in the Americas much earlier than 12,500 years ago in order to reach southern South America by this time. One reasonable explanation might be that there are older and yet-to-be-discovered inland sites. Another, more speculative, possibility is that at least some early migrants traveled by water, not by land. In this context, it is widely accepted that the initial human occupation of Australia was by watercraft at least 40,000 years ago. Could it be that watercraft existed long, long ago along the eastern fringe of Siberia? The possibility exists. If so, early migrants may have boated along the Siberian coast, island-hopped along the north Pacific area of Alaska, and continued southward in the Americas.

THE ARCHAIC TRADITION As the West and the Southwest became drier, hunting diminished in importance. By about 6000 B.C. a way of life adapted to the western deserts had developed, one that has been termed the Desert culture. The primary foods were wild plant products and small game. As small groups of people moved about to exploit varied resources, they occupied open sites or camped in caves and rock shelters on an opportunistic basis. Grinding stones became key technological forms in processing seeds, nuts, and other plant or animal products to render them edible. Small animals were stunned with missile sticks or captured in fencelike nets, and spears harvested large game, such as antelope or bison. Basketry became important for winnowing wild seeds, for cooking foods, and for storage. This eminently successful lifeway, the Archaic tradition, persisted in many parts of the West until after the arrival of Europeans. The Cahuilla Indians (Chapter 7) represent one form of this lifestyle as it continued into historic times. In the northwestern Plains, Archaic tradition bison hunters persisted into historic times, but their lives changed dramatically beginning about A.D. 1730, when domestic horses, of colonial Spanish origin, were introduced from the south. The Crow (Chapter 6) represent one such people.

Along the northwest coast from the Gulf of Alaska to northern California, prehistoric maritime cultures emerged, probably from an Archaic base. By 1000 B.C. people hunted sea mammals and fished for salmon with expanding intensity. Woodworking tools were well established by about 200 B.C., suggesting the manufacture of plank houses and large dugout canoes. These developments provided the general background for the emergence of historic Northwest Coast Indian cultures such as the Yurok (Chapter 8) and the Tlingit (Chapter 9).

In the eastern United States and Canada, along rivers and coastal areas, Indians lived as hunters and gatherers from about 8000 to 3000 B.C. These Archaic economies varied widely because of differences in local resources. In some areas, shellfish, fish, or large game were the dominant foods, whereas in many others, wild plants predominated. The oldest sites had relatively brief spans of occupation, but by about 3000 B.C. some settlements, especially those along major rivers with abundant food resources, had been occupied for generations. These people are noted especially for their ground and polished stone woodworking tools, such as adzes, axes, and gouges. The technology of these people was far more diversified than that reported among Paleo-Indians.

THE NORTHERN HUNTERS The distant descendants of some pioneer hunters in the north remained hunters or became hunters and fishers. Early evidence about them is associated with inland areas and dates from as long ago as 13,500 years. Some reasonably early finds recall Archaic tradition artifact types. Other tools are similar to finds in Siberia and thus support an archaeological link with northeastern Asia. It is thought that the Nadene Indians, the northern hunters who were the ancestors of modern Athapaskan Indians, were living in interior Alaska and northwestern Canada by at least 5000 B.C. These distinctly inland people hunted caribou or moose, depending on the locality, and fished; for most of them, their fishing activities increased during times of food stress. The Chipewyan Indians (Chapter 4) are a historic example of Athapaskans who were hunters and fishers, and the Lower Kootenai (Chapter 5) employ that strategy much farther south. The Navajo (Chapter 11) were northern hunters before they entered the western United States, where they became part-time farmers in prehistoric times and herders during the historic era.

The oldest known maritime economy in the New World appears to have emerged along the northern and western Pacific coast of Alaska about 6000 years ago. Their probable descendants moved north in the Bering Strait area of Alaska some 3000 years ago and became Eskimos, who filtered eastward into Greenland. About A.D. 1000 other Alaskan Eskimos, identified with Thule culture, soon occupied the northern fringe of North America from Alaska to Greenland. The Netsilik (Chapter 3) are their direct descendants.

THE FARMERS Among Indians in many areas, the most radical prehistoric economic change occurred when hunting and gathering were replaced by a primary dependence on domestic plant products. Maize was domesticated in Mesoamerica about 4000 B.C.; the common bean may have been domesticated at about the same time in Peru, where squash could have been a cultigen somewhat earlier. By about 1000 B.C., the cultivation of maize had spread from the south into the American Southwest; later, beans and squash were planted there as the primary crops raised north of Mexico. Some western Indians developed more productive hybrid strains of maize that enabled them to become increasingly sedentary. In the Southwest this led to the Hohokam cultural tradition in the deserts of Arizona and the Mogollon tradition best associated with highland areas of Arizona and New Mexico. The Anasazi tradition represents the ancestors of modern Pueblo Indians such as the Hopi (Chapter 10) and arose primarily from various groups of gatherers identified with the Basketmaker culture. The Pueblo Indian cultures that emerged between A.D. 700 and 1400 are most often associated with pueblo-type dwellings, separate ceremonial chambers or *kivas,* and elaborate pottery.

In the eastern United States, some Archaic peoples became gardeners, and by 2000 B.C. they were raising sunflowers for food, as well as a variety of squash, maygrass, and sumpweed. By A.D. 100, maize was cultivated, but beans did not become evident until about A.D. 1000. The Woodland tradition began to coalesce about 1000 B.C., with its burial mounds and distinctive pottery. The Adena people, concentrated in the Ohio River drainage area, became prominent mound builders who flourished until about A.D. 100. They traded widely for raw materials and probably were well organized, possibly with chiefs as leaders of political and religious life.

In the same general area, the successors to the Adena people represented the Hopewell tradition that flourished from about 200 B.C. to A.D. 500. They were probably farmers living in relatively permanent communities, and they are famous for their elaborate earthworks. They were organized into distinctive social classes and accorded prominent attention to certain of the dead. We do not know why the Adena and Hopewell traditions declined rather abruptly at their centers, although disease may have been a contributing factor. Hopewell branches persisted in the Northeast, and one group probably provided the background for Iroquois Indian culture (Chapter 12).

Prehistoric Indian culture in the United States reached its greatest complexity in the Mississippian tradition, found in parts of the Midwest and Southeast from about A.D. 900 to 1500; their economy was based on the cultivation of maize, beans, and squash. The Mississippians probably were organized into complex social and political units, each with a clear sense of national identity. Social ranks existed, with priests and other elites topping the hierarchy. Their ceremonial centers must have required years to plan and construct, with the labor of many people required to build their elaborate terraced temple mounds, as well as the house mounds of the elite. The Natchez Indians (Chapter 14) represent a remnant population within the Mississippian tradition. It had spread widely in the Southeast, and a more peripheral manifestation led to the emergence of the Cherokee (Chapter 13).

SUMMARY This brief review of the prehistory of Native Americans north of Mexico should demonstrate that the original American Indian culture developed from that of Asian migrants who were hunters. Farming emerged much later and was based primarily on crops domesticated in Mexico and Peru. The diversity of American Indian life observed by early Europeans represented adjustments to different ecological and social settings as these groups occupied the continent. Eventually, hundreds of distinct Indian cultures appeared. Thus no fanciful lost continents, lost tribes, or large-scale shipborne migrations in prehistoric times are required to explain the presence and diversity of Indians in the New World.

How Have Native American Cultures Been Studied?

No matter where Europeans settled in North America, it soon became apparent that Indians were well entrenched and quite different culturally. Some Native Americans were primarily fishers, whereas others farmed and still others hunted or gathered. They spoke many different languages and organized themselves in diverse ways, ranging from small, mobile, autonomous communities to large, stable nations or confederations. To better understand this variability and how it has been described, it is helpful to introduce a number of concepts.

Any reasonably systematic account of the lives of a people is called an *ethnography*. Their artifacts, language, social and political organization, art, knowledge, and myths are each an ethnographic dimension. An ethnography is overwhelmingly descriptive and pertains to a brief period of time. In more exact terms, an ethnography is a descriptive framework for behavioral information about a population at a particular point in time. Ethnographic data are collected as systematically as possible and are checked for internal consistency; for these reasons, most accounts by explorers, travelers, or journalists do not qualify. There are two general categories of ethnographies: baseline studies made about life at the time of historic contact and others made for later points in time. A *baseline ethnography* describes a people before they had any significant contact with representatives of Western societies. Thus the data represent conditions *before* the people studied were influenced or disrupted by Europeans, Euro-Americans, or the members of other clearly foreign groups. In a strict sense, a baseline ethnography should be compiled before European trade goods or diseases of European origins prevail. Yet capable observers seldom were present to record a broad range of information about a Native American population in a systematic manner before their customs were altered by agents of Western culture. The first comprehensive ethnography of an Indian tribe, or of any aboriginal people for that matter, that made a significant impact on anthropology appeared in 1851. The author was Lewis Henry Morgan, and his study was of the Iroquois Indians in the state of New York. Thus ethnography as a distinct intellectual pursuit is comparatively recent in origin. When narrow or broad generalizations are drawn from ethnographies, the study is termed *ethnology,* which is the comparative analysis of ethnographic data.

Trained investigators did not begin making thorough studies of American Indians until around 1900. Usually they attempted to collect verbal information about Native American life at the time of historic contact, or at least for a period as far back in time as an informant could recall. An ethnographer talked with Indians about the past, observed current customs, and consulted written sources. By using these data he or she assembled a *reconstructed baseline ethnography.* The primary difficulty in such an enterprise was obtaining reliable information about the early historic period. Most ethnographies written by anthropologists about American Indians are reconstructions made long after the first historic contacts of the groups studied. A major problem was to validate informants' statements, especially when documentary sources had not been studied thoroughly, a typical failing of early ethnographers. The time factor often could not be held constant for the early historic period, and as a result many descriptions were actually composites of customs at various times. Traditional ethnographies began changing character by the early 1930s, but it was not until much later that most anthropologists realized what had happened. The long-term ideal of reconstructing aboriginal baseline accounts rarely could be realized after about 1940.

As the lives of Native Americans changed following prolonged firsthand contact with exotic complex societies, the Indians were said to be undergoing the process of acculturation; the end product was either stabilized pluralism or assimilation into the dominant society. Thus we may consider *acculturative ethnographies* as a type of ethnography. They present a description of life relating to a brief span of historic time, usually based on documents, observations, and interviews. Margaret Mead (1932) was the first person to focus a field study on contemporary Indian life. She worked among the Omaha Indians in

1930. This was a watershed in North American Indian studies and anticipated hundreds of broadly similar accounts about Indian acculturation. Over the years, as ethnographers became more methodologically sophisticated, the emphasis shifted further. Problem-focused studies began to dominate, with one or more aspects of Indian life identified for detailed attention.

Clearly, the data base of old has disappeared, and the study of urban Indians or certain aspects of modern reservation life, such as health or land tenure, has been one response. Other aspects of modern studies are presented in Chapter 2. Noteworthy here, however, is another approach, called *ethnohistory*. Favored by persons more interested in traditional Indian life, this is the study of pertinent historical documents, often with accompanying field studies for additional information, to plot changes in a people's lifeway. The study of historical records long has been the purview of historians, and some of them, such as William T. Hagan, Roy H. Pearce, Lewis O. Saum, and Wilcomb E. Washburn, have a keen understanding of the Indian in American history. For American anthropologists concentrating on Indians north of Mexico, an appreciation of historical developments has been comparatively recent. One of the earliest studies was that carried out in 1928–30 by Felix M. Keesing (1939) concerning the Menominee of Wisconsin. The next major work was by Oscar Lewis (1942) and dealt with Blackfoot culture change. Thus ethnohistory as an anthropological focus is a comparatively new development; *Ethnohistory,* a journal devoted to the subject, originated in 1954.

Ethnohistory has emerged as a significant focus among anthropologists. In addition to archival and library research, field studies often are recognized as valuable; some Native Americans clearly remember many customs and historical events that had never found their way into written records. The study of historical records has led to major revisions in our understanding about some tribes early in their history. It probably is true that every tribal ethnography for aboriginal or early historic times could be more accurate after a careful study of existing archival and published records. Thus superior accounts for many tribes are yet to be written.

Thus far the units for study have not been defined precisely, but their clear identification is desirable. Different groups of Indians usually are termed tribes, yet no one set of criteria for a tribe accommodates all North American Indians. The difficulties in deriving a concept that encompasses the diversity of social norms and cultural forms may be illustrated by a rather typical definition. Alfred L. Kroeber (1925, 474) stated that a true tribe "has a name, a dialect, and a territory." Yet among the nearly fifty major Indian groups in California, only the Yokuts of the San Joaquin Valley had all three characteristics. Most California Indians did not have a distinct tribal name; they identified themselves only as members of a particular community. Efforts to define a tribe on the basis of political cohesiveness are equally unrewarding. As John R. Swanton (1953, 1–2) pointed out, the variability seems to defy the use of a single label. The Creek confederation comprised dominant and subordinate tribes; the name Powhatan embraced about thirty tribes or subtribes united by conquest; the name Ojibwa (Chippewa) included small groups of people who had little if any sense of political unity; each Pueblo village governed its own affairs and was in a sense a small tribe.

Kroeber (1955, 303) attempted to bring some order to the terminological maze. He wrote, "What are generally denominated tribes really are small nationalities, possessing essentially uniform speech and customs and therefore an accompanying sense of likeness and likemindedness, which in turn tended to prevent serious dissensions or internal conflicts." Within such nationalities were smaller sovereign states, usually termed bands or villages, that were economically self-sufficient and had a recognized territory and political independence. Kroeber reasoned that a tribe was rather like a German state before the consolidation in 1871: each state functioned independently although they shared a common language, culture, and ideology. In the United States these Indian units were more properly regarded as nations in the seventeenth and eighteenth centuries. Actually, the concept of a tribe or nation most often was a product of white contact; government officials grouped tribes, bands, or villages so they could more conveniently negotiate treaties, arrange resettlements, and so on. Aboriginal decision making most often was at the band or village level, although some peoples were consolidated into larger political aggregates. In the subsequent chapters, the difficulties in defining a tribe are not overwhelmingly important, but the reader should be aware that the label *tribe* does not always mean the same thing when applied to different peoples. Those interested in pursuing the topic further are referred to a volume on the subject edited by June Helm (1968).

A recent example suggests the continuing problem in identifying a tribe. For legal purposes, in 1993 the U.S. government identified each of the Native American groups that it recognized. The total was 543 "Indian entities." The contiguous states were represented by 315 entities, most of whom were tribes or bands. In Alaska, however, the 228 entities were most often villages, and yet in a legal context these villages were comparable to tribes or bands.

Another aspect of studying Native Americans that has led to confusion because of its overall inconsistency is any attempt to view the time of historic contact collectively. Historic contact with Indians differed widely in time from one region to another. Many tribes in the eastern United States had been destroyed by disease and homicide or displaced from their lands before others to the north and west ever heard of white people or knew of the diseases that they carried. Historic contact began about A.D. 1000 in northern Newfoundland, whereas in the Southwest it was 1540, and it was 1885 in one sector of central Alaska. Thus no single decade or century represents the contact period. This means that there is a *sliding historical baseline* (chronological skewing) for the beginnings of Indian history on a regional basis. Swanton (1953, 3–6) has suggested that if A.D. 1650 is taken as a base date, it is possible to establish many indigenous Indian boundaries for the southern and eastern United States, as well as for eastern Canada. In the northwestern sector of the continent, no major relocations of peoples appear to have occurred between 1650 and the time of their actual historic contact, making it possible to tentatively include them under this date as well. For the balance of the continent north of

Mexico, the date of 1650 is less satisfactory. An adjustment backward in time to around A.D. 1540 might be more accurate to accommodate the peoples of the Southwest. The Plains area would require several dates over a considerable time span. The most important conclusion is that the boundaries and positioning of many tribes on standard ethnographic maps, including those in this volume, are not entirely accurate for any single time period. Instead, they attempt to represent the area of any particular tribe at the moment in history when it was surveyed and located on a map.

The endpaper maps in this book identify the general areas occupied by tribes after taking into consideration a sliding historical baseline. These maps are based largely on the monumental language classification by Ives Goddard (1996) that appears in volume 17 of the new *Handbook of North American Indians*. The tribal names and distributions reported in other volumes in this series, published by 1999, also were consulted. The endpaper maps do not include all of the smallest tribes nor the tribes about which little is known.

What Do We Know of Native American Languages?

By conservative estimates two million Native Americans lived north of Mexico at the time of Columbus, and they spoke about four hundred different languages. In some sectors, such as among Eskimos (Inuit) along the Arctic rim, the same language was spoken over a wide area. In other regions, as in northwestern Canada, people spoke different but closely related languages. Elsewhere, highly distinct languages might exist in a limited area. In California, for example, far greater linguistic diversity existed than is found in all of modern Europe.

European settlers could ignore Indian customs if they wished because they lived in separate communities, but they could not ignore Indian languages if they hoped to communicate with them. Because typical colonists felt superior to Native Americans, they seldom attempted to learn an Indian language; most often Indians or persons of mixed heritage became bilingual. Yet, for Christian missionaries intent on converting Indians, it was essential to learn the languages of peoples among whom they worked. The first landmark in American Indian linguistics was the publication in 1663 of a Bible translated into Massachuset, an Algonquian language, by the missionary John Eliot; in 1666 he published an Algonquian grammar.

The first prominent student of Indian linguistics was Thomas Jefferson. He was concerned that Native American languages were disappearing rapidly, and before he became president in 1801 he had collected considerable linguistic information. Jefferson (1801, 149) reasoned that preserving linguistic data from Indians in the Americas would make it possible to trace the relationships among these peoples. Subsequent linguistic studies by Peter S. Du Ponceau and Albert Gallatin enabled John Wesley Powell to publish a definitive classification of Native American linguistic families in 1891. Powell's classification was revised by C. F. Voegelin and F. M. Voegelin (1966) and more recently by Goddard (1996, 4). The major language families are those identified by Goddard, and they appear in simplified form as Figure 1-1.

By 1995 about forty-five of the nearly four hundred Native American languages north of Mexico in early historic times continued to be spoken by adults and learned by significant numbers of children. These included Chipewyan, Cherokee, Navajo, and Eskimo (Inuit and Yupik). Some ninety other languages were spoken by adults but few or no children, for example, Crow, Kootenai, Tlingit, and Iroquoian languages (Cayuga, Mohawk, Oneida, Onondaga, and Seneca). About seventy languages were spoken only by small numbers of older people; examples include Cahuilla, Yurok, and Tuscarora, an Iroquoian language.

For many tribes a rapid decline in the number of aboriginal language speakers is a pressing concern. A typical response is to launch an indigenous language program in the primary grades. These efforts have been successful only with adequate funding and devoted staff in immersion schools. Another program involves pairing an indigenous language speaker with a younger member of the tribe who does not speak the language. This method was set forth in 1992 by the Advocates for Indigenous California Language Survival. The program is an intense and demanding master–apprentice relationship involving as many as twenty hours each week. It appears to be promising. By 1999, sixteen California tribes had from one to fifteen master–apprentice teams to help ensure language continuity.

Radio broadcasts in tribal languages are increasingly common and provide another context for learning. News items about Native Americans have been broadcast since the early days of commercial radio in the 1920s, but regularly scheduled programs for Indians did not begin until the 1960s. Native-owned radio stations and noncommercial public and tribal stations began to appear in 1971. By 1998 in the United States there were thirty tribal radio stations, including eight in Alaska. Canada has about two hundred stations dominated by First Nations peoples. In Canada and the United States, many Indian-dominated stations air native-language programs. They increasingly broadcast programs that emphasize cultural revitalization. These developments also hold promise for greater Indian-language vitality.

Grouping Tribes

The relationships among tribal languages provide valuable insight into their linguistic evolution, yet tribes belonging to a single language family sometimes have contrasting lifeways. As a result researchers found it desirable to group tribes based primarily on nonlinguistic factors. Their goal was to classify some four hundred tribes into a small number of meaningful units. By 1896 Otis T. Mason had advanced a means for grouping all tribes by culture area based on environmental and cultural characteristics. A *culture area* is a geographical sector of the world whose aboriginal occupants exhibited greater

Figure 1-1 | The dominant Native American linguistic groups north of Mexico at the time of early regional contacts with Europeans. Hokan and Penutian represent superfamilies; they include nine and eleven language families, respectively. These superfamilies and the major families are presented in capital letters. Languages in upper- and lowercase type generally refer to fami-

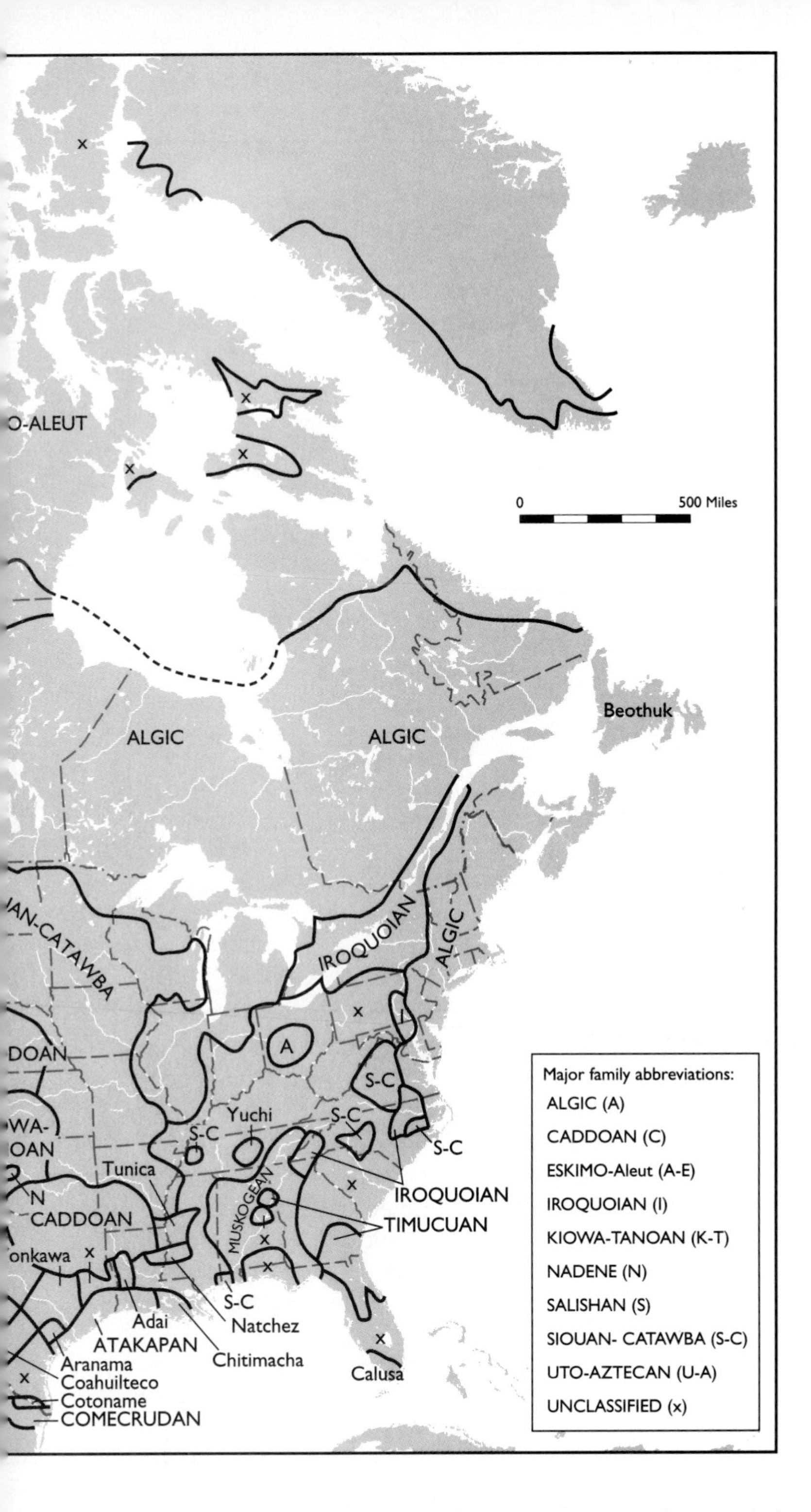

lies represented by a single language. "O" indicates an unoccupied or poorly known area. (Adapted from Goddard, 1996; Courtesy of the *Handbook of North American Indians,* Smithsonian Institution, Washington, DC.)

Figure 1-2 | Native American culture areas north of Mexico.

similarities with each other than with the peoples in other such areas. Ideally, culture areas are established from baseline accounts of each tribe within an area, considered on a sliding historical scale. The culture area concept was applied systematically to North American Indians by Clark Wissler (1938, 1942). We find, however, that one culture area may include peoples with different ways of life and that tribes along the boundaries may share the characteristics of two or more areas.

It is reasonable to assume that tribal names and their specific boundaries are well established. This is often, but not universally, the case, for multiple reasons. As European explorers or others entered a new area, they might learn the name of a particular tribe from the members of an adjacent tribe, and this name could be different from the target tribe's name for themselves. Likewise, the name of a target tribe might be mistranslated into a European language. Furthermore, a population initially identified as a tribe might prove to be a subtribe or band. Conversely, two tribes could later be combined on the basis of more complete information or, at times, for administrative convenience. In relatively recent years, some tribes have insisted on their original self-identification as their official name when it differs from their standard ethnographic name.

Tribal geographic boundaries may pose greater problems. The normal dynamics of tribal expansion and contraction meant that boundaries could have been unstable when non-Indians first appeared. And the indirect impact of European presence in a region could rapidly change aboriginal boundaries. For instance, prior to direct European contacts, the mortality rate from exotic diseases led to the contraction of some tribes, to the expansion of others, and to tribal extinctions. Likewise, early explorers typically had more on their minds than the distribution of tribes. Queries about boundaries could result in confusion from an inadequate understanding of an Indian language or from inaccurate translations by interpreters. Later, with systematic inquiries, aboriginal boundaries might be revised. Another widespread difficulty is that early non-Indians did not establish boundaries for many tribes. As a result, their aboriginal land holdings are uncertain and based on comparatively recent information. Additional cautionary observations are required. Although tribal boundaries for culture area maps are precisely drawn, they are not fully reliable for other reasons. The area between two tribes can be a contested "shatter zone," sometimes occupied by neither claimant. Finally, ethnographers may have honest but unresolved disagreements about some boundaries.

For aboriginal Native Americans living north of Mexico, ten culture areas are identified. They appear as Figure 1-2. The major sociocultural characteristics for each area are listed in Table 1-1.

Ethnographic Studies: An Overview

Early professional ethnographers (ca. A.D. 1900–1930) collected information from Indians with inordinate zeal because they thought that Native American lifeways would soon disappear. At least some Indians who helped them shared this dire perspective. Likewise, as products of their times, ethnographers were biased in how and what they recorded. For example, women's viewpoints and perspectives on sexual activities seldom were presented in a systematic manner. Subsequently, attention shifted to how Native American lifeways were changing in response to intensive contact with Euro-Americans and other outsiders. The 1930 study of the Omaha Indians by Margaret Mead is the best marker of this new approach. By the 1950s ethnographic studies of Indians typically had become narrower in scope, far more historical and problem-oriented, increasingly dependent on statistical approaches, and sometimes concerned with resolving Indian "problems."

By the 1990s a shift in emphasis and approach was emerging. By then it was abundantly clear that American Indians were *not* vanishing and that some tribes had retained aspects of their cultures with greater vitality than had

TABLE 1-1. Summary of characteristics of the ten culture areas

Culture Area	Languages	Subsistence	Descent
Arctic	Eskimo-Aleut	sea mammals caribou fish	bilateral
Subarctic	Nadene in west Algonquian in east	caribou moose fish	matrilineal in west patrilineal in east bilateral in both
California	highly varied	acorns mesquite beans game marine resources	bilateral
Great Basin	Uto-Aztecan	pine nuts rabbits antelope	bilateral
Plateau	Salishan	salmon game roots	bilateral
Plains	Siouan-Catawba	bison in west maize in east	bilateral patrilineal
Northwest Coast	Nadene in north Salishan in middle varied in south	salmon land mammals sea mammals	matrilineal in north patrilineal in south

Political Organization	Religion	Housing	Manufactures & Other
charismatic leaders bands	shamans good & evil spirits ceremonies in west	wood, stone, sod in east & west snowhouse in central area	tailored clothing elaborate harpoons umiaks, kayaks, dog-sleds sinew-backed bows feuds over women infanticide
charismatic leaders bands	shamans Nakani in west shaking tent divination in east	double lean-to & rectangular log-frame in west conical tent in east	semitailored clothing toboggans, snowshoes bark canoes deadfalls & snares birch-bark baskets cannibalism during famines spruce-root baskets in west hunting dogs in east
bands	shamans diverse supernaturals elaborate female puberty ceremonies	impermanent brush, bark, grass	developed basketry seed-grinding stones sinew-backed bows
bands	shamans elaborate female puberty ceremonies	impermanent brush, bark, grass	basketry seed-grinding stones sinew-backed bows nets for land mammals
villages	shamans diverse spirits	semisubterranean winter reed- or mat-covered summer	basketry important bark fiber clothing
bands band alliances military societies raiding important	vision quest guardian spirits emerging ceremonialism	skin tepee	developed bone & skin working dog-drawn travois game surrounds hide shields
villages	potlatch elaborate ceremonial round complex masks	rectangular, plank multifamily	elaborate woodworking dugout canoes social classes, slaves

TABLE 1-1. (continued)

Culture Area	Languages	Subsistence	Descent
Northeast	Algic Iroquoian	maize, beans, squash game fish	matrilineal patrilineal
Southwest	Nadene Uto-Aztecan	maize, beans, squash game	matrilineal bilateral
Southeast	varied	maize, beans game fish	matrilineal

been predicted. As a result, ethnographers are returning to Indian studies with a new respect for the "survival" of old traditions and customs. Indians sympathetic to a more accurate recording of their tribal ways can be quite knowledgeable, and they are numerous. As never before, Indians and ethnographers have become collaborators in data collection. Likewise, Indians are in a unique position when they hire anthropologists to work for them. This exciting development has a potential flaw: How accurate is a "remembered culture"? One study (Driver 1939) suggests that Native American memories about the distant past can be quite reliable.

Additional Sources

The best bibliographic sources by tribe are the fourth edition of the *Ethnographic Bibliography of North America* by George Peter Murdock and Timothy J. O'Leary (1975) and its 1990 supplement, by M. Marlene Martin and Timothy J. O'Leary. The best widely available anthropological and historical source about Native Americans is the new multivolume *Handbook of North American Indians* (Washington, DC) under the general editorship of William C. Sturtevant. The first of the proposed twenty volumes appeared in 1978. Brian M. Fagan's (1995) *Ancient North America* is an excellent source for North American prehistory. Jack Weatherford (1988) chronicles Indian contributions to the world, and Alfred W. Crosby, Jr. (1972) describes the impact of Old World diseases, animals, and plants on American Indian life. The book by Jack D. Forbes (1988) is the key source about black African and American Indian relationships. A volume edited by

Political Organization	Religion	Housing	Manufactures & Other
tribes confederations	developed ceremonial round harvest stress secret societies dogs eaten ceremonially	dome-shaped wigwam multifamily palisades	hide clothing bark canoes
villages	elaborate ceremonial round kiva masked dancers	pueblo-type	developed pottery & basketry cotton garments domestic turkeys irrigated farmland
tribes confederations warfare important	complex ceremonies sun worship priests	rectangular multifamily fortified	feathers over netting for clothing houselike storage facilities "black drink" emetic

William M. Denevan (1992) examines the difficult problem of Native American population statistics in 1492. A key and essential source about languages was edited by Ives Goddard (1996) as volume 17 of the new *Handbook of North American Indians.*

Selected Bibliography

Barth, Fredrik, ed. 1969. *Ethnic groups and boundaries: The social organization of cultural difference.* Boston.

Crosby, Alfred W., Jr. 1972. *The Columbian exchange.* Westport, CT.

Denevan, William M., ed. 1992. *The native population of the Americas in 1492.* Madison, WI.

Drake, Samuel G. 1837. *Biography and history of the Indians of North America.* Boston.

Driver, Harold E. 1939. *Culture element distributions: VII. The reliability of culture element data.* Anthropological Records, 1:205–19.

Driver, Harold E., and William C. Massey. 1957. *Comparative studies of North American Indians.* Transactions of the American Philosophical Society, n.s. 47, pt. 2. Philadelphia.

Estrada, Emilio, and Betty J. Meggers. 1961. A complex of traits of probable transpacific origin on the coast of Ecuador. *American Anthropologist,* n.s. 63:913–39.

Fagan, Brian M. 1995. *Ancient North America.* New York.

Forbes, Jack D. 1988. *Black Africans and Native Americans.* Oxford, England.

Fritz, Gayle J. 1994. Are the first American farmers getting younger? *Current Anthropology* 35:305–09.

Goddard, Ives, ed. 1996. *Languages,* vol. 17, *Handbook of North American Indians.* Washington, DC.

Hagan, William T. 1961. *American Indians.* Chicago.

Hallowell, A. Irving. 1957. The impact of the American Indian on American culture. *American Anthropologist* n.s. 59:201–17.

———. 1958. *The backwash of the frontier: The impact of the Indian on American culture.* Annual Report of the Smithsonian Institution, 1957–58, 447–72.

———. 1963. American Indians, white and black: The phenomenon of transculturalization. *Current Anthropology* 4:519–31.

Haven, Samuel F. 1856. *Archaeology of the United States.* Smithsonian Contributions to Knowledge, vol. 8, 1–159.

Helm, June, ed. 1968. *Essays on the problem of tribe.* Seattle.

Holmes, William H. 1893. The World's Fair Congress of Anthropology. *American Anthropologist* 6:423–34.

Jefferson, Thomas. 1801. *Notes on the state of Virginia.* New York.

Keesing, Felix M. 1939. *The Menomini Indians of Wisconsin.* Memoirs of the American Philosophical Society, vol. 10. Philadelphia.

Kinkade, M. Dale. 1991. The decline of native languages in Canada. In *Endangered languages,* R. H. Robins and E. M. Uhlenbeck, eds., 157–76. New York.

Kroeber, Alfred L. 1925. *Handbook of the Indians of California.* Bureau of American Ethnology Bulletin 78. Washington, DC.

———. 1955. Nature of the land-holding group. *Ethnohistory* 2:303–14.

Lewis, Oscar. 1942. *Effects of white contact upon Blackfoot culture.* Locust Valley, NY.

Mead, Margaret. 1932. *The changing culture of an Indian tribe.* New York.

Morgan, Lewis Henry. 1851. *League of the Ho-De-No-Sau-Nee or Iroquois.* 2 vols. New York. (Editions published in 1901 and 1904 were edited and footnoted by Herbert M. Lloyd and were reproduced in 1954 by the Human Relations Area Files.)

Murdock, George Peter, and Timothy J. O'Leary. 1975. *Ethnographic bibliography of North America.* 4th ed. (Supplement, 1973–1987 by M. Marlene Martin and Timothy J. O'Leary. 1990). New Haven.

Pearce, Roy H. 1965. *The savages of America.* Baltimore.

Powell, John W. 1891. *Indian linguistic families of America north of Mexico.* Bureau of American Ethnology, 7th Annual Report, 1–142.

Powers, William K. 1988. The Indian hobbyist movement in North America. In *History of White-Indian relations,* Wilcomb E. Washburn, ed., vol. 4, 557–61, *Handbook of North American Indians.* Washington, DC.

Riley, Carroll L., et al. 1971. *Men across the sea.* Austin.

Saum, Lewis O. 1965. *The fur trader and the Indian.* Seattle.

Swanton, John R. 1953. *The Indian tribes of North America.* Bureau of American Ethnology Bulletin 145. Washington, DC.

U.S. Department of the Interior. 1958. *Federal Indian Law.* Washington, DC.

Voegelin, C. F. and F. M. 1966. *Map of North American Indian languages.* American Ethnological Society.

Washburn, Wilcomb E. 1984. A fifty-year perspective on the Indian Reorganization Act. *American Anthropologist* n.s. 86:279–89.

Wauchope, Robert. 1962. *Lost tribes and sunken continents.* Chicago.

Weatherford, Jack. 1988. *Indian givers.* New York.

Wissler, Clark. 1938. *The American Indian.* New York.

———. 1942. *The American Indian and the American Philosophical Society.* Proceedings of the American Philosophical Society, vol. 86, 189–204.

Yarnell, Richard A. 1978. Domestication of sunflower and sumpweed in eastern North America. In *Early food production in North America,* R. I. Ford, ed., 285–99. Ann Arbor, MI.

Zepeda, Ofelia, and Jane H. Hill. 1991. The condition of Native American languages in the United States. In *Endangered languages,* R. H. Robins and E. M. Uhlenbeck, eds., 135–55. New York.

2 Indian–Non-Indian Relations

Don't you ever
you up in the sky
don't you ever get tired
of having the clouds
between you and us?

From a Nootkan song (Frances Densmore 1939, 284)

SOON AFTER DISCOVERY of the New World, a great debate raged in Spain about the humanness of Indians. Regardless of the manner in which the conquistadores were received, they argued that Indians were irrational, heretical, and tainted with mortal sin. This attitude served to justify inhumane treatment of Indians and seizure of their land or property. Francisco Vitoria, a professor at Salamanca and a founder of international law, argued against this thesis. He noted that in Europe heretics were privileged to own property and could not be punished for sins without a trial. Implicit in Vitoria's argument was the acceptance of Indians as human beings. When the exploiters of Indians maintained that the pope of the Roman Catholic church had granted title to all newly discovered lands to the kings of Spain and Portugal, Vitoria countered that the pope had no power over the aborigines and their land and that title by discovery could apply only to unoccupied lands. In a papal bull of 1537 Pope Paul III proclaimed "that the Indians are truly men and that they are not only capable of understanding the Catholic faith, but according to our information, they desire exceedingly to receive it" (Cohen 1960, 290). Considering Indians as human beings gave the church new millions of immortal souls to be saved. This acknowledgment of Indian humanness, combined with an acceptance of Native American land ownership, served as a guide for colonial governments in the Americas. In the years to come, the course of Indian–non-Indian relations was to take many twists and turns, as this chapter demonstrates.

Early Contact

European maritime explorers found the Indians fascinating because they felt that Indians embodied what people could be like when stripped of Christian and "civilized" behavior (see Figure 2-1). Indians were considered savages; although human in form, they were barely human in their customs, according to these biased observers. The land they owned was attractive, and many intruders felt that Indians were a blight on it. A brief review of early contact in different areas provides an overview of Indian–white relations that fosters greater understanding of the subsequent course of history.

The Virginia Charter of 1606 provided for bringing God to Indians because adopting Christian ways was equated with being civilized. Land was purchased from the Indians, and settlers were certain that they could live in harmony with Indians who would soon be Christianized. Before long, about fifty missionaries were sent to work primarily with children because it was felt that children would learn more readily than adults. The colonists were convinced that their efforts were succeeding, because there were no serious hostilities. Actually, the most powerful Indian leader, Powhatan, was waiting and hoping that the colony would fail, but the English grew more firmly entrenched with each year. In 1622 Powhatan's successor decided he had waited long enough, and attacked the colonists. Nearly 350 whites were killed, and the only reason the colony was not destroyed was that a Christian Indian warned the

Figure 2-1 | This 1493 woodcut accompanied the Italian printing of the first letter by Christopher Columbus about his New World discoveries. In the background is one of the earliest representations of aboriginal Americans. (From Winsor 1889.)

English at the last moment. To the colonists the massacre was clear evidence of inborn Indian treachery, and the settlers now felt justified in destroying these savages whom they no longer sought to understand. The Indians in Virginia were viewed as an impediment to the march of civilization, and within the next fifty years they were systematically destroyed or displaced. This pattern was repeated time and again.

"The Indian experience" of each colony was different because of the settlers' backgrounds and the Indians encountered. It might be anticipated that the Quakers, granted the land comprising Pennsylvania in 1681, would be more successful in making Indians into Christians, given their commitment to nonviolence and humanistic tolerance of others. The Quakers stressed the common denominators that unite all people and did not seek to identify differences between themselves and Indians. They offered the Indians love and peace; nevertheless, they were unable to win many converts. Moreover, the Quakers remained neutral when non-Quakers fought the Indians in their midst and at their frontiers.

The Puritans of New England believed that God would guide their affairs with Indians, who were viewed as fallen people in the grip of Satan. When many Indians died in a "wonderful plague" of smallpox, the Puritans saw it as God's way of furthering the goals of the settlers. The Puritans believed that Indian lands were intended for Christian English use. Nevertheless, to keep peace they purchased land from the Indians rather than taking it. On the other hand, they did not hesitate to initiate raids and wars against the Indians or to foster dissension for their own purposes. They also insisted that Indians should be "civilized." Missionaries like John Eliot began working among Indians in 1632, but the number of converts was small and success transient. Puritan efforts to integrate the Indians into transported Western European culture failed for obvious reasons.

The Spanish who first entered the Southwest in 1540 expected to find barbarians or savages and felt a strong obligation to civilize them. Church and civil authorities accepted this as their primary goal after realizing that the area was not going to yield great riches. The gross pattern of Spanish life was to be introduced, and the advance agents usually were Roman Catholic missionaries. They built churches and quarters near established pueblos, instructed certain individuals in Catholic doctrine, and soon recruited Indians as catechists and helpers. The missionaries especially were responsible for introducing new crops and novel crafts; their goal was to create self-sufficient Roman Catholic communities. The missionaries in New Mexico usually were accompanied by soldiers who reinforced Spanish authority; in general, the priests treated Indian transgressions harshly. Soon the Eastern Pueblos were paying tribute to the king of Spain, a good indication of the program's effectiveness.

Apart from the mission environment, Spanish frontiersmen impinged on the Indians of New Mexico through the policy of giving land grants to soldiers for services rendered. The great *encomienda* grants, made to Spanish colonists in New Mexico as a reward for services rendered, did not include any of the large pueblos; but the people who lived in the small communities in the midst of such grants were forced to work these lands for the Spanish, usually with little or no compensation. Before long, Spanish employees of encomenderos were marrying Indians and acquiring their lands. Abuses of the encomienda system engendered a great deal of hostility in some pueblos and eventually led to its abandonment. Spanish towns, with Santa Fe as the prime example, formed another setting for cultural contact, but because the Indians were drawn to them only for services, their impact was relatively minor.

When the Mexican War for Independence ended in 1821, Indians in the Southwest were granted the full rights of Mexican citizens. All persons born in Mexico became citizens, irrespective of their culture or race, and efforts were made to incorporate Indians into national life. This goal was not achieved in New Mexico, however. Anglo-Americans began to penetrate New Mexico in the 1840s, and their attitudes contrasted rather strikingly with those that previously had prevailed. The mission settlement had no place in their plans. They regarded the pueblo-dwellers as moderately "civilized" but considered most of the less sedentary Indians "wild." The American policy was to push Indians aside, either peacefully or by force, to facilitate westward expansion.

Effective Spanish intrusion into California in 1769 was guided by the same policies that the Spanish had introduced to the Southwest. A primary purpose of the Spanish colony in California was to Christianize Indians and to settle them at self-sufficient missions; thus Indians were very much a part of the economic order. Yet most of the people who were drawn to the missions, either voluntarily or by force, were unlikely to adapt to a sedentary life in crowded conditions with a rigid work routine. The experiment had clearly failed by the time the missions were secularized, beginning in 1834. Souls had been saved, but the cost in human life had been great.

In the northern portions of the continent, the English, French, and Russian ventures were of a different order. Here the fur trader, not the settler or missionary, usually was the most important advance agent of Western culture. Irrespective of their national origins and time of contact, fur traders viewed Indians very differently from most other white intruders. Indians and traders were *joined* by economic ties that profited them both. The areas where the fur trade dominated longest were those unsuitable for large settlements of whites, and thus the Indians' way of life was not disrupted by large groups of intruders. Furthermore, the fur trader and the Indian could maintain their relationship only as long as the Indians remained trappers and retained the essence of their aboriginal economy. Regardless of nationality, fur traders could be intolerant or tolerant, cruel or kind, depending on their personalities and their experiences with Indians.

Destruction and Displacement of Peoples

It seems likely that after initial historic contact far more Indians were killed by diseases introduced by whites than by bullets. It also appears that more Indians were killed by other Indians than by outsiders, although many such murders unquestionably were abetted by whites. Every tribe probably was subjected to at least one severe epidemic, and there were very few Indians whose way of life was not altered dramatically, or even destroyed outright, soon after contact.

Throughout this volume, the impact of disease on specific peoples is documented, and its disruptive force should not be underestimated. Certain diseases long prevalent among Europeans eventually became less virulent among them but deadly to a virgin population; measles and whooping cough are examples. Other diseases, such as malaria, raged through Indian and white populations alike. Tuberculosis was a dreadful killer of Indians but was less lethal among whites.

Records of tribes destroyed by diseases are not difficult to locate; one depressing example will illustrate the speed of impact. The Massachuset, with an estimated population of three thousand in 1600, were reduced to five hundred by 1631 as a result of a terrible epidemic, possibly smallpox. By 1663, when John Eliot published the Bible in their language, they were nearly extinct.

Even though an epidemic might not destroy a tribe, it could kill so many people that they could not defend themselves against outsiders or continue their cultural traditions. For example, a malaria epidemic struck in the Central Valley of California and along the Columbia River in the early 1830s. A mortality rate as high as about 75 percent made it impossible for the survivors effectively to resist subsequent white intrusions or to maintain their ways of old.

The extinction of a population unquestionably is tragic, but another consequence of white dominance was nearly as sad. Because of the intimate associations of Indians with their traditional homelands, their displacement to other areas was often heartrending. One example will suffice. In aboriginal times the Delaware lived in New Jersey and adjacent areas, but in the early 1700s the Iroquois dominated them politically and sanctioned their displacement by white settlers. Before long many Delaware settled in eastern Ohio, but only after wandering largely homeless for some time. By 1820 some lived in Arkansas, and others had ventured on to Texas. Some fifteen years later many of them had settled on a reservation in Kansas, from which they were moved to Oklahoma in 1867. Most of them remain there today, but Delaware Indians are scattered from eastern Canada to Montana, far from each other and from their eastern homeland.

The personal and cultural trauma wrought by purposely displacing a tribe from its home is tragic in itself. But the federal policy of moving all the Indian tribes from one vast area into another violates the very principles on which the United States was founded. Yet this happened, and the drama began to unfold with clarity about 1800. One overwhelming argument was advanced to justify assuming control of Indian lands, and it *never* has changed: Indians obstructed the progress of whites who could use land much more effectively, and thus it was the God-given right of the settlers or real estate promoters to obtain such ground. Displacement became a blanket policy with the Indian Removal Act of 1830. New England whites could deplore this policy elsewhere because they had long ago resolved their "Indian problem" by killing many local Native Americans, displacing them, or tolerating small remnant Indian populations. It was the residents of the southeastern states and settlers in the Midwest who became the wanton destroyers of Indian rights. Most surviving tribes with large landholdings east of the Mississippi River were bribed and intimidated into moving west. By 1831, the states of Alabama, Georgia, and Mississippi had forced the removal of the Choctaw, Chickasaw, and Creek. Cherokee resistance to removal was strong but largely unsuccessful (see Chapter 13).

Among the epic sagas of displacement, the Fox (Mesquakie) represent a fine example of tribal resiliency. One Fox homeland was in Wisconsin, where they were nearly destroyed by the French in the 1730s and from which they fled to Illinois. Here they clashed with white settlers in the early 1800s. The Fox received a parcel of land in Iowa, but most of them were forced to relocate to Kansas. However, in 1857 a small group *purchased* eighty acres of land near

Tama, Iowa, where they were joined by others. Gradually they bought additional land. By the early 1900s they were desperately poor and conditions did not change dramatically until 1992, when they opened a casino. From the profits the Fox were able to provide a substantial steady income to all enrolled members. Their land holdings now include about seven thousand acres. Although most Indian tribal governments in the east central United States disappeared long ago, the Fox are a notable exception; and the land is their own, not a reservation in the usual sense.

U.S. Treaties

Virtually all inhabitable land in North America was occupied by Native Americans when Europeans arrived. By the 1990s, Indian reservations in the United States represented about 2.5 percent of the country. A study of treaties reveals the changing nature of Indian and white relations.

Until the early 1800s, treaty negotiations were between governments, which established the basis for Indian laws and policies. The sovereignty of tribes was fully recognized by European colonial powers and, initially, by the United States. Negotiators sought to stabilize the white–Indian relationship through equitable treaties containing mutual accommodations. They established boundaries, often issued passports, and attempted to develop means to avoid military conflict. In the process, Indian conventions became a part of negotiations. A prime example was the ritual in which both parties smoked a peace pipe as a solemn gesture of trust. For at least some tribes, a treaty was more than a political document; it became a sacred text. The first treaty enacted by the federal government was with the Delaware in 1778. It provided that the Delaware and other tribes might form a state and have congressional representation, a provision that was never realized (see Table 2-1).

Between 1778 and the early 1800s, federal power over Indians expanded dramatically, especially in the eastern states. Eventually all tribes came to be regarded as quasi-sovereign peoples, not national equals. This view led to diminished tribal control over their destiny, their increasing exploitation, and federal paternalism. Tribes came to be regarded as dependent nations, and treaties were considered in the same light as other statutes of the U.S. Congress. It may come as a surprise that, despite military conflicts between the federal government and various tribes, the United States never formally declared war on hostile Indians.

Many treaty obligations continue to be met by the federal government, although no new treaties have been made with Indians since 1871. In later treaties the federal government reserved the right to regulate Indian affairs, and seldom was this right relinquished to a state. Once a treaty was negotiated and ratified, it could not be nullified by the Indians, even if duress, fraud, or improper Indian representation occurred during the negotiations. Treaties might be renegotiated by mutual federal and Indian consent. Treaties or treaty rights also have been repealed by Congress, with or without the consent, involve-

TABLE 2-1. Major events in Native American relations with the federal government of the United States

1778	The first U.S. treaty with Indians, the Delaware tribe
1824	The Bureau of Indian Affairs was created to "civilize" Indians
1830	The Indian Removal Act was designed to relocate southeastern Indians to land west of the Mississippi River; the purpose was to open the land to white settlers
1849	A Navajo treaty permitted the federal government, for the first time, to influence the internal affairs of a tribe
1871	The last treaties with Indians
1879	The Carlisle Indian School was founded and became the most famous Indian boarding school; its purpose was to acculturate children rapidly
1887	The Dawes Severalty Act was designed to allot reservation lands to individual Indians and thus break up reservations; "surplus" land was opened to Euro-American settlers
1934	The Indian Reorganization Act attempted to reverse the impact of the Dawes Act by restoring land to reservations and to encourage tribes to form federally recognized tribal governments
1946	The Indian Claims Commission Act was created to settle outstanding Indian claims as a step toward ending federal responsibilities to Indians
1953	House Concurrent Resolution 108 included a timetable for ending federal obligations to Indians; Public Law 280 transferred civil and criminal jurisdiction to select states as a major step in terminating federal responsibilities
1975	The goals of the Indian Self-Determination and Education Assistance Act were to foster tribal self-government and to transfer many of the functions of the Bureau of Indian Affairs to individual tribes
1983	President Ronald Reagan declared that the termination of federal responsibilities to Indians was no longer a goal and proposed greater funding for tribal self-government and resource development
1990	The Native American Graves Protection and Repatriation Act provided for the return of skeletal remains and artifacts by universities and museums to the tribes requesting them
1997	A proposal by Senator Slade Gorton (R-Wash.) would indirectly "tax" economically successful tribes and force a tribe to waive its sovereign immunity to receive Bureau of Indian Affairs funding; the proposal was rejected

ment, or agreement of Indians; this is called abrogation. Indian treaties, like all other treaties, have the same status as any other federal statute and can be repealed or modified by a later statute. Yet it has been a general policy of the government to interpret ambiguities in treaties in favor of Indians and to consider the circumstances under which a treaty was negotiated. The courts could not interpret a treaty in a manner not intended in the original wording, however.

Treaties with Indians were negotiated by the president of the United States and were binding when approved by the Indians and two-thirds of the U.S. Senate. It is important to note that a treaty could not provide funds for Indians; monetary commitments required separate congressional action. Nearly 400 treaties were negotiated. The greatest number, nearly 260, were arranged during the great westward expansion of white settlers following the War of 1812. The majority of these treaties, 230, involved Indian lands. A block of 76 treaties called for Indian removal from their lands and resettlement on other lands. Two tribes, the Potawatomi and Ojibwa (Chippewa), negotiated 42 treaties each, a record number.

The first treaty in which the federal government sought to control the internal affairs of a tribe was with the Navajo in 1849. It stipulated that the federal government could "pass and execute in their territory such laws as may be deemed conducive to the prosperity and happiness of said Indians" (U.S. Department of the Interior 1958, 163). By the mid-1800s, it was becoming apparent that treaties with tribes were unrealistic because of the increasing dependence of Indians on the federal government. Treaty making ended when the U.S. Senate and the House of Representatives could not agree on treaty appropriations.

Indians have land rights based on aboriginal possession, treaty, congressional act, executive order, purchase, or the action of some colony, state, or foreign nation. Reservations were created by treaty arrangements before 1871, by acts of Congress after that time, and by executive orders of the president. In almost every instance the federal government retained the title to reservation lands. Statutory reservations usually consisted of public domain or land purchased by the federal government for use by designated Indians. Reservations were created by executive order between 1855 and 1919. This practice met resistance from Congress, however, and was brought to an end except for the addition of some Alaskan reservations. From time to time Indians have purchased lands with their own funds for the group as a whole, and these properties have been supervised by the federal government (see Chapter 13). Because nearly all of the land that is now the United States was held earlier by European-based powers, the rights of Indians under British, Dutch, French, Mexican, Russian, and Spanish rule have been taken into consideration when a transfer of sovereignty has occurred. In each instance at least some recognition has been given to aboriginal rights of occupancy by the Indians.

Treaties with Indians after about 1800 usually were not negotiated in a meaningful sense. Representatives of a particular tribe or tribes were assembled, and a treaty was offered for their approval. The signers seldom had any realistic opportunity to modify the terms. Then, too, treaties often were made through "chiefs" who were sympathetic to the whites, and in certain areas of the United States it was not uncommon for intoxicants to be distributed freely at treaty-making sessions. In addition, the interpreters often could not or did not set forth the fine points of an agreement in true detail or spell out the implications of what the Indians were losing and what they were gaining.

Administration of U.S. Indian Affairs

In 1775 the Continental Congress created three agencies, on a geographical basis, to deal with Indians. Among the commissioners were Benjamin Franklin and Patrick Henry, an indication of the importance attached to Indian matters. The commissioners were to make treaties, to establish friendly relations with Indians, and to prevent them from aiding the British. In 1786 Indian administration was placed under the secretary of war. With adoption of the Constitution, the War Department maintained jurisdiction over Indians. The first Congress in 1789 appropriated funds for negotiating treaties and placed the governors of territories in charge of local Indian affairs. The next year Congress, in an important step toward federal control, began licensing traders among Indians. The Bureau of Indian Affairs (BIA) was created in 1824 within the War Department, and its administration passed into civilian control at the newly created Home Department of the Interior in 1849. Flagrant corruption and mismanagement within the bureau led to the creation of the Board of Indian Commissioners that functioned from 1869 to 1933. They oversaw the expenditure of funds and made policy decisions.

The BIA remains the federal agency most responsible for Indian affairs. However, bureau mismanagement again was endemic by the 1980s. A federal study in 1984 demonstrated that *two-thirds of the BIA budget was consumed by the bureau itself.* As a result of this finding and the excessive regulatory power of the bureau, administrative changes were launched. Despite revelations about inefficiency, by 1994 only an estimated twenty cents of each dollar received by the BIA actually reached the Indians for whom it was intended.

BIA mismanagement has yet another facet. The bureau is responsible for money held in trust for Native Americans by the federal government from Indian land sales and leases, grazing, logging, mining, and other agreements. The accounts of about 300,000 individuals are valued at about $500 million. There are also some 1,600 different tribal accounts. However, $3 to $10 billion is unaccounted for in tribal accounts; no one knows the real total. In 1994 a presidential appointee was placed in charge of the trust office to resolve the problem, but he resigned in 1999 because the bureau was not cooperative and pertinent records could not be located. Instead the bureau undertook to develop a computer system to collect and track each of the accounts, but it has estimated that the project will not be completed until 2004. In 2000, some Native Americans as individuals and as tribes did not trust the bureau to resolve the problems, and they planned legal action.

Canada, the First Nations

In recent years "First Nations" and "Aboriginals" have emerged as accepted terms for the indigenous peoples of Canada. The earliest significant grant of land to Indians was made in 1680 by the French to a band of Iroquois. The first large British grant was in 1784 to the Six Nations (Iroquois), who received about 675,000 acres in Ontario as a reward for their loyalty to the British during the American Revolution (see Chapter 12).

A cornerstone of British policy was embodied in the Proclamation of 1763. It included the guiding principles for Indian–white relations: Indians possessed the rights to all lands *not* formally surrendered; land could be surrendered only to the Crown; Indians could not grant land to individual whites unless it had been surrendered. Under these terms, settlers in what is now the

United States could not readily occupy Indian lands; this provision later emerged as a cause of the American Revolution. Large sectors of Canada have *never* been legally ceded by Indians to the Crown.

In the first series, eleven treaties were arranged between Indians and the British from 1781 to 1921. They involved relatively few tribes, and as a result the status of most land belonging to aboriginal Canadians is either unclear or unsettled (see also Chapter 4).

With the confederation of Canada in 1867, Indian administration passed to the Dominion of Canada, which became responsible for relief, education, health services, Indian-based farming, industry, and enfranchisement (full Canadian citizenship). Under the Canadian Act of 1871, reserve (reservation) land could be held by an Indian under an allotment system, with the allottee having the exclusive right to use and occupancy. An allotment could be passed on to heirs or sold to another Indian within the group. "Surplus" land could be sold by a tribe and the money received used for tribal welfare. Then, too, an Indian could obtain clear title to land by requesting and being granted enfranchisement. A Department of Indian Affairs, founded in 1880, underwent numerous administrative changes, and in 1967 the Department of Indian Affairs and Northern Development was created. It must be emphasized that Canadian provinces have far greater control over Indian lands than do states in the United States.

Canadians with European and Indian ancestry were treated differently from full-blood Indians in some contexts. In general, people of mixed heritage, or Métis, were given the rights of Indians, and those Métis who lived as Indians had the right to be treated as Indians. Efforts by the Métis to protect their land rights were partially responsible for the Red River Rebellion of Manitoba in 1869. As a result of this uprising, the rights of Métis were more fully recognized in that province. It was not, however, until the Canada Act in 1982 that all Métis obtained recognition comparable to that of Indians and Eskimos (Inuit).

When Bill C-31 became federal law in 1985, it embodied fundamental policy changes regarding the First Nations. Discrimination was largely removed by the bill, and each band controlled its membership. The process of enfranchisement was abandoned. For instance, the band membership of a woman who had lost her band status by marrying a non-Indian was restored by the government, but not necessarily by her tribe. The children of such a woman usually obtained band status. Subsequent legislation in the 1990s led to far greater self-government, in an administrative context, by select bands, and this policy is being expanded. The right of self-government does not include a right of sovereignty.

Another fundamental administrative change occurred in the eastern portion of the former Northwest Territories. In 1999 it became a separate territory, Nunavut (our land). The area includes about one-fifth of Canadian land, and the population was about 28,000, of whom about 85 percent were Inuit (see also Chapter 3). Significantly, the residents control the surface title to the land

and the subsurface title to a portion of it; the latter is important with respect to the development of mineral resources.

Canadian Indian efforts to obtain control of aboriginal landholdings are by far the least successful in British Columbia (see also Chapter 5). A small number of limited-scope treaties were negotiated in British Columbia before it became a province in 1871. From then until the present, the British Columbia provincial government seldom has acted in good faith with respect to Indians, despite intermittent pressure from the federal government during the past hundred years. The federal and provincial governments began serious negotiations with most tribes in 1991. A major development was achieved in 1998 with the Nishga (Nisga'a), a small tribe in northwestern British Columbia. A treaty involving a settlement of $253 million, about eight hundred square miles of land, and limited power of self-government was ratified by the Nishga and the legislature of British Columbia. It became binding in 2000, after approval by the Canadian senate. Fifty-one British Columbia aboriginal groups continue to negotiate with the province for settlements that probably will require at least ten years to complete. By 2000, however, some British Columbia bands had lost hope of ever receiving a just settlement from the provincial and federal governments. They were turning to the courts for adjudication. One major incentive was the 1997 Delgamuukw case in which the Supreme Court of Canada ruled that aboriginal title exists. Yet to seek a court settlement is a complicated, uncertain, expensive, and drawn-out process.

In 1999 the government of Quebec began serious negotiations with its Inuit population for the eventual creation of a new Native American government in northern Quebec, Nunavik. In the same year the federal government achieved an "agreement-in-principle" with the Labrador Inuit Association for self-government. In each instance, a final settlement probably is years away.

Greenland in Brief

Norse people, largely from Iceland, settled Greenland beginning in A.D. 986, but Eskimos had occupied portions of the island since at least 2000 B.C. The original Norse colony was neglected over the years and had disappeared by about 1540. Greenland began to be resettled in 1721 by Norwegian Lutheran missionaries; at that time Norway was under the political control of Denmark. Danish sovereignty over much of Greenland, however, was not established until 1921, and it was a closed country until after World War II. The Danes dominated most aspects of Eskimo life from the beginning and were concerned primarily with saving souls and with commercial profits. The deplorable health and living conditions of the Eskimos did not begin to be acknowledged in a realistic manner until 1953, when the colonial status of Greenland was abolished. In that year, Greenlanders became full citizens of Denmark, and their living conditions began to improve dramatically. Finally, home rule was extended to Greenland in 1979. Contemporary Greenland is occupied by about 56,000 Greenlanders, 80 percent of whom are Eskimo (Inuit).

Landmark U.S. Indian Policies

Indian tribes were relatively free and independent nations until the War of 1812 ended. Soon thereafter they became "domestic, dependent nations" and lost realistic control over their destiny. The Indian Removal Act of 1830 was a clear indication of the change in relations between Indians and the federal government. The end of treaty making in 1871 was another plateau, but the General Allotment Act (Dawes Severalty Act or Dawes Act) of 1887 had the greatest impact on changing Indian life.

THE DAWES ACT Under the terms of this act, the president was authorized to allot most reservation land to individual Indians. Indians were to select their acreage, and the federal government was to hold a trust title for at least twenty-five years, during which time the land could not be encumbered. Surplus reservation lands then were sold, and the funds derived were held in trust for the tribe, subject to use for educating and "civilizing" the tribe when Congress approved these uses. The Dawes Act was modified over the next ten years to allow allotted land to be leased. Indian education began to be stressed. Schools were provided, and the attendance of children virtually was forced; but federal support for church schools was withdrawn. An important supplement was made to the act in 1906 that permitted the president to extend the trust period for allotted lands. The aim of the Dawes Act was to bypass tribal organizations and make land allotments to individual Indians. The act was designed to *destroy* the tribes by doing away with the land base held collectively and, at the same time, to integrate Indians into the dominant society. Many whites who truly were concerned with Indian welfare felt that the sterile and depressing quality of reservation life should be destroyed and that the best means to accomplish this goal was to make individual Indians property holders and farmers.

THE INDIAN REORGANIZATION ACT (IRA) The goals of this act were the direct opposite of those of the Dawes Act. The IRA of 1934 was intended to end the alienation of Indian lands through the allotment process. In fifty years of allotments, Indians had lost nearly 90 million of their 138 million acres of land, and about half of the remaining land was desert. The most effective means to permit retention of the land base was to extend the period of trust holding, which the act did. Furthermore, the act acquired additional land for Indians, declared it exempt from taxation, and placed it under federal control.

Two guiding principles of the IRA were self-government with democratic ideals and parliamentary procedures and communal enterprises as the best avenue to bettered economic conditions. Tribes were encouraged to form chartered corporations and to operate essentially as local governments; revolving credit funds helped those choosing to incorporate. One key condition of the original law was that it would apply only to those tribes that by majority vote decided to come under its provisions. Initially, 181 tribes accepted and 77 rejected the IRA. Fourteen groups came under it because they did not vote, and the act was extended in 1936 to include Alaskan and Oklahoman peoples without their vote of approval. Because Indians in general had come to distrust the federal government, the Indian response to this enlightened legislation was not as positive as had been hoped for by its creators. Some tribes favored allotments and were able to obtain clear title to their land in spite of the IRA (see Chapter 7). Other tribes, such as those that stressed individual wealth, did not even agree with the principles behind the IRA.

World War II disrupted the implementation of IRA goals, and in the period between the end of this war and the late 1960s the federal government generally pursued policies designed to assimilate Indians into the greater American "melting pot." However, the IRA has remained the legislation with the most critical effect on reservation Indian life. As Wilcomb E. Washburn (1984) observed, acceptance of the IRA by reservation Indians in general over the years has led to the revival of tribal life or its creation among them. The act has contributed significantly to the vitality of tribal political structure. As will become evident in numerous chapters to follow, many tribes probably would have been destroyed by now had it not been for the IRA.

TAXATION HIGHLIGHTS A great deal of misunderstanding surrounds the subject of Indians and taxes; the topic merits review. In the United States, the taxation of Native Americans focuses on land identified as "Indian Country" by the federal government. *Indian Country* is defined as both reservation and nonreservation land owned by a tribe or its members and held in trust by the federal government.

By treaties and statutes, tribes cannot be taxed, and tribal members may not be taxed unless there are exemptions by treaty or statute. States, in theory, cannot tax in Indian Country. Tribes, as sovereign entities, have the inherent right to tax Indians and non-Indians in Indian Country, because the power to tax is an essential element for self-government (i.e., infrastructure). Tribes, just as all other units of government, are not taxable, nor are tribal businesses taxable by federal or state governments.

Specific examples illustrate application of the pertinent treaties and statutes.

When an Indian or tribe obtains a patent in fee to land (a clear title), such as under the Dawes Act, the land is subject to state property taxes. This does not apply to trust lands.

Tobacco products or gasoline sold at reservation businesses by Indians to non-Indians or nontribal members are subject to state taxes. This is an area of continuing conflict between tribes and states.

Indians, just as any other citizens, are subject to federal and state taxes beyond the boundaries of Indian Country.

Neither federal nor state income taxes apply to fishing rights set forth in treaties.

With reference to Indian gaming operations, the wages of *all* employees are subject to federal income taxes, but tribal members do not pay state income taxes. Winnings at an Indian gaming enterprise are taxable by the federal and state governments, except when a winner is a member of the tribe operating the establishment. Tribal governments do not pay taxes on earnings from gaming, but if they distribute a portion of the earnings to tribal members, they become subject to federal income taxes.

Tribes have been encouraged by the federal government to establish "industrial parks" on reservation lands, which may be an advantageous situation for non-Indian companies. A company is permitted accelerated depreciation rates on capitalized buildings and equipment.

FEDERAL INTRUSION AND INDIAN IDENTITY In the 1930s the concept of acculturation became prominent in anthropology. It came to mean the steps by which native peoples are gradually absorbed into the dominant sociocultural pattern. With assimilation, acculturation is complete. Yet few anthropologists are satisfied with the concept because it fails to define the stages leading to assimilation or to explain the persistence of tribal identity in the face of hundreds of years of pressures to negate it. Quite clearly, the idea of acculturation does not allow for the lasting quality of Indian identity. A bold and innovative approach to the general problem was articulated by Joseph G. Jorgensen (1971).

The central concept of Jorgensen's thesis is that tribes were assimilated into national economic and political life as soon as they came under U.S. control; Indian identity was strongest where federal intrusion was weakest. Jorgensen attributed the deplorable conditions on most reservations to what is essentially a colonial political system. The metropolis is the center at which economic and political power are concentrated. Thus the politically weak areas in which reservations usually are located are exploited by the metropolis for its own growth. Indians also are subject to the same laws that apply to everyone else, *in addition to* those imposed by federal control through the BIA. In the 1950s the BIA launched a program to "relocate" Indians to urban areas, and the program came to include vocational and on-the-job training. The goal was to force their assimilation into the mainstream national workforce. The BIA maintained that the program was voluntary, which was untrue; people were encouraged to participate and quotas were established for relocating Indians. By the mid-1970s the failings of the program and changing views of Indians by non-Indians led to an end of the experiment (see also Chapter 15).

Compatible with the goals of the relocation program, the federal government made a move to "get out of the Indian business" by settling old claims with the Indian Claims Commission Act of 1946. Then in 1953 a federal policy was launched that had a far more immediate impact—House Concurrent Resolution 108. It was designed with a timetable for ending federal responsibilities to Indians. As Randall H. McGuire (1992, 825) noted, "If Indian people would not vanish, then the Congress would terminate them." Termination of the Klamath and Menominee reservations was one result; these reservations included major stands of timber that were being sought by lumber companies. In addition, other reservations were terminated, such as those in western Oregon and in Nevada. For some Indians, Public Law 280 in 1953 transferred civil and criminal jurisdiction to select states, including California, Minnesota, Nebraska, and Oregon. Largely through efforts by the Menominee, the termination policy was itself terminated in 1974, and reservation status was restored to such tribes as the Menominee and Klamath.

Forces Fostering Native American Identity

Compared with European intruders, early historic cultural diversity among Native Americans north of Mexico was great. Indians not only spoke many unrelated languages and had varied social conventions but also reflected different social and political norms. By contrast, the cultural background of Europeans was homogeneous; their linguistic differences were minor, and social and political ideals were broadly similar. Thus, compared with Europeans, the Indians were fractured and fragmented along many dimensions. The agents of Western civilization often exploited these differences to divide Indians still further. In the face of European threats to their cultural integrity, Indians came to recognize what different tribes had in common and to develop a new sense of identity as Indians that transcended tribal lines.

PAN-INDIANISM This concept refers to a general sense of Indian cultural identity that unites the members of different tribes. *Pan-Indianism* is a term that gained prominence in the 1950s and was applied to a condition that had originated much earlier. More accurate designations might be intertribalism or pantribalism, because participation brings together Indians with different tribal backgrounds. Pan-Indianism began in the mid-1700s and eventually emerged as a movement that has become a primary source of Indian identity for many of its members. This has been true especially for those Indians with a weak sense of tribal identity, such as those raised off reservations, and for other persons who consider themselves Indian although they lack the customary biological or cultural heritage.

Varied factors contributed to the rise of pantribalism, especially the influence of Indian prophets who predicted what must be done to free themselves of control by whites. Prominent and relatively recent prophets are associated with the Ghost Dance. As Indians in the western United States came into increasing conflict with non-Indians, the first Ghost Dance was originated in 1869 but it did not have wide impact. The Ghost Dance of 1890 that originated with a Paiute from Nevada named Wovoka (Jack Wilson) became far more important. Wovoka reportedly died during an eclipse of the sun in January 1889 and went to heaven, where he saw dead Indians living in an idyllic state. God reportedly said that if Wovoka returned to earth and taught the people to perform the Ghost Dance, the dead and living would be reunited. He cautioned people not to fight with each other or with non-Indians; neither should they lie or steal. If these instructions were obeyed, there would be no more illness, old age, or death. Performing the Ghost Dance was to hasten the dawning of this new world. Although some tribes embraced the dance with fervor, it inevitably failed.

Much of the background for Pan-Indianism may be traced to Indian prophets, but there were essential non-Indian elements as well. The most important of these was the formal education process imposed on Indians. In government and mission schools instruction was in English, which became the language for communication between the members of different tribes. Boarding schools likewise had a profound influence. None was more famous than the Carlisle Indian School in Pennsylvania. It was founded in 1879 by Richard H. Pratt, an army officer, whose philosophy was encapsulated in his slogan, "Kill the Indian and save the man!" The school was organized along military lines and attended by the members of far-flung tribes. It was intended to be a way station between the reservation and assimilation. Carlisle often is thought of as a college because its football team played university teams, but it was largely a secondary school that stressed vocational training and the fundamentals of English. Indians who attended Carlisle and other boarding schools often had a difficult time readjusting to reservation life. Although some went "back to the blanket," meaning that they reverted to Indian ways, others were assimilated into the white world, and many worked for the federal government in Indian administration.

The boarding schools in the United States and residential schools in Canada were *the most powerful institutions for the systematic destruction of traditional Native American cultures.* The military model, with its repressive environment, is as sad as it was dreadful. Children, young and old, might be confined to a school for years on end. Furthermore, and of singular importance, many children were unable to learn the subsistence activities, social norms, or religious conventions of their parents. It appears that much of the social disorganization on contemporary reservations and reserves may be traced directly to these schools (see Chapter 12).

Christianity was an especially important influence on Indians in the late 1800s in a number of ways. Indians from different tribes came to be identified with each other because they were members of the same church denomination. Likewise, mission advocates helped foster Indian identity by working for their well-being. Missions maintained many schools, and diverse white organizations with Christian backing were concerned with Indian life. The members sought to *assimilate* Indians, and most of them had little tolerance for Indian customs. These white activists in Indian affairs supported the principles of the Dawes Act but deplored the injustices of its administration. As Hazel W. Hertzberg (1971, 22) has noted in the best study of this era, "All unwittingly the reformers—the Indians' chief friends in court in the white world—thus helped to break down Indian self-respect and Indian attempts at self-help." Many Indian leaders were Christian, but at the same time they often were unwilling to abandon their Indian heritage. They sought accommodation with Euro-American customs, and their general approach has endured among many

Indians seeking to retain their identity. For many others assimilation into white society was desired and realized.

Indians of many tribes with different historical backgrounds were drawn into Pan-Indianism through the peyote cult. The peyote plant, which grows in central Mexico, is a spineless cactus with "buttons" containing alkaloids that are stimulants or sedatives in varying proportions. When consumed, buttons produce a wide range of reactions. A common response to taking peyote is exhilaration and an inability to sleep for about twelve hours; depression and hallucinations, sometimes including color visions, follow. This non-habit-forming drug was consumed in Mexico in aboriginal times but was not widely used in the United States until more recently. It became popular among Indians of the southern Plains between 1850 and 1900 and spread to other western tribes. Early use in the Plains appears to have been associated with warfare, and it was taken only by men. Indians began using peyote more widely when they were suffering in the dismal aftermath of military defeat, physical displacement, and confinement to reservations. The Bureau of Indian Affairs, Christian missionaries, and white reformers all were actively opposed to the peyote cult, and its adherents were harassed. In spite of the oppression by whites and some Indians, there were about twelve thousand members in 1918. Efforts were made in 1916 and again in 1917 to pass a federal law against the use of peyote, but these bills failed. In 1918, as a response to white opposition, a group of participants incorporated as a formal religious institution, the Native American church. Although a number of states soon passed laws against the use of peyote (for example, Kansas, 1920; Arizona, 1923), seven states had chartered Native American churches by 1925. As members of a formal religious organization, Indians were afforded far greater protection from persecution than previously.

According to Hertzberg, the peyote religion had appeal because old tribal religions had lost their meaning and Christian teachings seemed remote from reality. Furthermore, this was an Indian religion that united members of different tribes in a common sense of brotherhood. Peyote often was considered a powerful medicine for the diseased, and the rituals also provided an opportunity for social gatherings. Some Indians, such as the Pueblo peoples, Five Civilized Tribes in Oklahoma, and Iroquois, were relatively untouched by the peyote religion, but it had become *the* religion for many Indians by 1934 (see Chapter 11).

The anthropologist James H. Howard (1955) was one of the first to identify the Pan-Indian movement and to define the traits associated with it. He identified the movement's roots as being in Oklahoma, especially among the small tribes originally from the East. Howard felt that racial discrimination against Indians was an important factor fostering solidarity among them. Coupled with poverty, apartheid tended to bind Indians of diverse backgrounds. Howard viewed Pan-Indianism as a breakdown of tribalism and a major step leading to the assimilation of Indians into the greater Euro-American matrix. As William K. Powers (1990) vividly conveys, empirical evidence does not support Howard's assimilation model. Instead, Powers suggests, tribalism

Figure 2-2 | This 1821 painting of Petalesharo, a Pawnee, is one of the first illustrations of a Plains Indian headdress (From McKenney and Hall 1933; Courtesy of the Historical Society of Pennsylvania.)

represents one dimension of modern Native American life and intertribalism another. The most important implication is that tribalism represents sociocultural continuity of the distant past *with and into the present,* as opposed to the slow death of tribal conventions. Widespread systematic studies about *modern* tribes are few.

THE INDIAN IMAGE The Plains Indian has come to symbolize Indians to most Americans, and we might take a moment to consider how it has happened that Indians in one sector of the country have become representative of all Indians.

Indians of the Great Plains were seen first by Spanish and then by French and English explorers, yet they were nearly unknown until after the Louisiana Purchase of 1803. In 1821 members of Plains tribes visited Washington, DC, and none was more popular than Petalesharo, the Pawnee who rescued a Comanche girl from being sacrificed to the Morning Star. In three paintings of him by different artists, he wore a flowing feather headdress (see Figure 2-2), and according to John C. Ewers (1965) this probably was the first pictorial record of the feather "war bonnet." Many other Indians in the same party had their

Figure 2-3 | The first illustration of a Plains Indian tepee to be published, appearing in 1823. (From Ewers 1965.)

portraits painted, and their exhibit long was a popular attraction in Washington. The earliest picture of a Plains tepee appeared in 1823 (see Figure 2-3), and the first illustration of a Plains Indian on horseback was printed in 1829 (see Figure 2-4). This beginning possibly never would have led to the emergence of the Plains tribes in popular fancy were it not for the efforts of Karl Bodmer and George Catlin, who painted Plains Indians in the 1830s. Catlin especially was important, for he not only painted many pictures of Indians but also exhibited his Indian gallery widely in the United States and then in London and Paris. His book *Manners, Customs and Condition of the North American Indians,* first published in 1841, had a wide distribution, and this two-volume work with over three hundred engravings was reprinted again and again. To Catlin the noblest Indians clearly were those of the Plains. His paintings and those of Bodmer were copied or modified and also inspired other artists to venture west to paint Indians.

The Plains Indian symbol crystallized in Buffalo Bill's Wild West Show, which opened in 1883. It was seen by millions of people in Canada, the United States, and Europe during its run of more than thirty years. William F. Cody, or "Buffalo Bill," was a colorful frontier figure who became the hero of innumerable dime novels. The show, a reenactment of episodes in Plains life, was highlighted by an Indian attack on a stagecoach and its dramatic rescue by cowboys led by Buffalo Bill. Other Wild West shows that imitated the original and Indian medicine shows intensified and spread the image of the Plains Indian. By

Figure 2-4 | Probably the first published illustration of a Plains Indian warrior on horseback, appearing in 1829. (From Ewers 1965.)

the turn of the twentieth century Indians all over the country were beginning to dress as Plains Indians for special occasions.

POWWOWS In Canada and the United States some two thousand major powwows are presented each year. For many non-Indians, powwows and reservations are prominent keys to modern Indian identity. *Powwow* is a Narraganset Indian word that originally referred to the activities of shamans; the earliest citation in English appears to date from 1624. By the 1950s the word became identified with an Indian ceremonial configuration of regalia, dance, and music among Oklahoma tribes. The regional styles in Oklahoma during the 1960s had essentially amalgamated by the 1980s and spread throughout much of Canada and the United States.

Powwows are hosted by tribes or organizations within tribes in association with Indian fairs, on patriotic holidays, and for other celebrations. Typically, a powwow committee organizes the event. A princess may be chosen, a convention dating from the 1960s. A paradelike procession of non-Indian origin introduces dancers to the performance area. Six major costume and dance styles are presented, three each for females and males. Performance contests for each dance style highlight a modern powwow. The two major types of dances are the relatively slow and dignified "straight" dances and the fast and furious "fancy" dances. Four-part songs, old and new, are sung repeatedly to the accompaniment of a drum. Participants consider the drum as the heart of dances, and a powwow is said to be only as good as the drummers. Songs may

Figure 2-5 | The Fancy Dancer, Wilber Bebee, a Canadian Blackfoot (Blood subtribe), at the Kootenai Casino Powwow, Bonners Ferry, Idaho, in 1999.

include words or be represented by sound combinations without meaning. In dance contests the performers must know the songs so well that they are able to stop dancing at the last drumbeat for a song.

For powwow visitors the most striking initial impression is the variety of colorful and elaborate costumes worn by the participants, male and female, young and old. The most popular dance style is the War Dance, especially the Fancy War Dance (Fancy Dance), which may have originated around 1920 for a Wild West show but has little to do with war. Men dominate as fancy dancers. The headdress, or roach, is of porcupine guard hairs and dyed hair from deer tails. Armbands, a choker, and moccasins are adorned with matched beadwork. Anklets have bells attached, important for keeping time to the music. The most spectacular features are the neck and back "bustles" dominated by turkey or eagle feathers (Figure 2-5). In dance contests a stick may be held in each hand and decorated with hair or ribbons. This dance, like all the others, is individualized, meaning that participants perform as they choose; thus the coordination of dancers and practice sessions are not required. Among the largest powwows is the one held at the Foxwoods Resort Casino in Connecticut. This four-day gathering is inspired by a traditional corn festival. In 1997 it attracted more than two thousand dancers.

For non-Indian observers, a powwow is highlighted not only by the dance performances but also by vendor sales of Indian arts and crafts. For Native American participants, a major highlight is the "giveaways." Individuals and families present gifts, sometimes quite valuable, to persons who had been helpful in particular contexts, an old convention among Plains tribes. Presents now acknowledge aid received at passage rites, notable leadership, and other events important in the lives of the givers. Among the Indians involved, powwows provide an opportunity to exhibit and strengthen their Indian identity in a public context.

Recent History

The feelings of non-Indians toward Native Americans seem to swing between sympathy and resentment. During the height of the civil rights movement in the 1960s and early 1970s, many Americans regarded Indians with sympathy, if not with compassion. Motion-picture stars, such as Marlon Brando, rallied to tribal causes; the depressed economy of Indians was the subject of television documentaries; and the Indian folksinger Buffy Sainte-Marie, who recounted old and new injustices, became popular. Members of the U.S. Congress less often urged Indian assimilation into the American "melting pot." Indians flexed their political muscles in an unprecedented manner: Native Alaskans formed an "ice block" in the statehouse, the Iroquois wanted their wampum back from museums, and Canadian Eskimos (Inuit) sought to establish their own political unit in the Arctic. Indian demands received more thoughtful attention from politicians and administrators than they had previously.

As the 1970s drew to a close, the civil rights movement had lost its thrust, and social justice diminished as a major American concern. With this new climate and a downturn in the economy, Native Americans and other minorities began to elicit more resentment than sympathy. One particular development in 1977 seems to have decreased American support for Indians. In that year a special White House study group issued a report about the land claims of the Passamaquoddy and Penobscot Indians of Maine. A settlement was proposed that would have given four thousand Indians millions of dollars and vast tracts of land. Officials in Maine labeled the proposal as "really outrageous" and "crazy." The suggested settlement received widespread and intense media attention, and many non-Indians shared the attitudes expressed by Maine officials. In the 1980 settlement, the Indians received $81.5 million from the federal government, a decision that elicited ill feelings toward Indians in general, especially among people not familiar with the merits of the case.

Anti-Indian feelings crystallized during this time, especially after other tribes realized that the Maine settlement represented legal precedent and pressed their own claims against illegal land seizures. Non-Indian constituents urged members of Congress to do something, and there was a serious proposal that the United States abrogate *all* Indian treaties. This approach failed, and in the 1980s a concerted federal effort was made to vitalize reservation life. The programs offered were complicated, expensive, and often misguided, and ultimately they have been relatively ineffective. By the mid-1990s, the widespread political discontent in the United States with the size, intrusiveness, and cost of federal programs was clear. Few federal agencies were regarded as sacred by politicians. For Indians, one result has been "termination by budget massacre." Barring a dramatic shift in federal goals, Indians must increasingly devise their own solutions for many problems facing reservation residents. One appealing option for numerous tribes has been to operate gaming facilities. Another trend, especially in the Southwest, has been for tribes to develop more effective means to profit from the millions of tourists who visit reservations each year. Indians have launched their own museums, more tourist-oriented businesses, fairs, and powwows to profit the tribes.

POLITICAL ACTIVISM The Pan-Indian movement of the 1930s appears to have been a source for the Red Power movement of the late 1960s. A major contributing factor was the impact of World War II and the Korean War on Indians who were members of the armed services and who afterward refused to fit back into the Indian stereotype. Some began to search for their cultural roots. College-educated Indians resented the way the BIA treated them. The most radical group to emerge was the American Indian Movement (AIM) in 1968; its goal was to seek equality for Indians in the civil rights arena. The most dramatic confrontation, and one that has stuck in the minds of non-Indians, began in 1973. AIM seized the small town of Wounded Knee on the Pine Ridge Reservation in South Dakota. (At Wounded Knee Creek, about 300 Siouan men, women, and children were massacred by U.S. Army troops in 1890; this episode and the site have long symbolized white injustice.) In a seventy-one-day standoff, between 250 and 400 Indians held out against 125 Federal Bureau of Investigation agents, 40 BIA police, and 150 U.S. marshals. The siege resulted in hundreds of arrests, and the two major leaders, Dennis Banks and Russell Means, spent fifteen years in court trying to vindicate themselves in politically motivated trials by the federal government. By the end of the 1970s, AIM had few members and diminished political impact. (In 1979 the Federal Bureau of Investigation files in Washington, DC, contained 17,725 pages of information bearing on the activities of AIM, which was said to be a revolutionary organization.) The Wounded Knee confrontation beginning in 1973 led to the conviction of Leonard Peltier, a Lakota Indian, for the premeditated murder of two FBI agents in the conflict. The prosecutor now admits that the government does not know who killed the agents. False testimony was made by government witnesses, and lab reports favorable to Peltier's defense were covered up. He has been in prison for some twenty-three years despite the fact that the federal government never proved that he was responsible for the deaths. Leonard Peltier is regarded by many people as the number one political prisoner *in the world.*

In 1978 Congress passed the American Indian Religious Freedom Act (AIRFA), which was designed to review and update federal policies so that Native Americans would have the legal right to practice their traditional religions, possess sacred objects, and gain access to sacred sites. Policies were reviewed, and several recommendations were made. However, in 1988 and again in 1990, the U.S. Supreme Court ruled that AIRFA is a policy statement and not law, and as such it does not afford rights to the protection of sacred sites or the religious use of peyote in the Native American Church. The Native American Graves Protection and Repatriation Act (NAGPRA), passed in 1990, was a notable exception.

NAGPRA requires that all federal agencies and all organizations receiving federal funds (most museums and universities, for example) conduct an inventory to determine what Native American skeletal remains and sacred objects are in their collections and which modern tribes are affiliated with the remains and objects. The tribes involved must then be consulted about what is to be done with the remains and objects. Although some groups have elected to leave items with museums and universities, others have requested their return for tribal museums or reburial.

TRIBAL SELF-DETERMINATION The current emphasis on greater tribal control over Indian lives may have been an indirect response to the civil rights movement, with its stress on ethnic diversity. In 1968 President Lyndon Johnson spoke of Indians as "The Forgotten Americans" and proposed changes in policies, including self-determination. Yet it is an old concept for Indians to manage their own affairs. Government-to-government negotiations took place in colonial times and in early U.S. history, when Indians had full jurisdiction over their internal affairs. As noted earlier in this chapter, tribal autonomy began to be eroded with a Navajo treaty in 1849. The current policy is set forth in the Indian Self-Determination and Education Assistance Act of 1975. It was designed to foster greater self-government and to free Indians from pervasive BIA control. A major barrier to self-determination had been the Alaskan Eskimo and Indian land claims that were resolved in 1971 (see Chapter 9). In 1983 President Ronald Reagan stressed that termination of federal responsibilities to Indians was no longer a goal, and he proposed that a greater percentage of the federal budget be earmarked for tribal self-government and resource development. However, the money for Indian programs actually was decreased.

The label "self-determination" is deceptive, because it does not mean that Native Americans are gaining unlimited control over their destiny. It does mean that the federal government has taken a somewhat more humane political attitude toward Indians. Again, the concept of "tribal sovereignty" is misleading. It is inconceivable that Indian reservations will become sovereign in a strict sense, despite a 1940 U.S. Supreme Court ruling that sovereign immunity is necessary for self-governance. Sovereignty really has come to mean that in some contexts Indians are regaining a degree of local autonomy at the state and federal levels. These changes, however, are set against a complex historical backdrop: there are nearly four hundred ratified Indian treaties; some five thousand federal statutes deal with Indians; and some two thousand court decisions have been rendered. The constitutions of tribes and lesser Indian political entities must be considered as well (see also Chapter 15).

Courtrooms increasingly have become a prominent Indian battleground, and sovereignty issues have been salient. In general, federal courts have been sympathetic to Indian rights, whereas state courts have been, and remain, largely anti-Indian. For example, in 1980 the White Mountain Apache in Arizona, together with a timber company, sued the state, maintaining that state motor carrier and fuel taxes did not apply on the reservation. The U.S. Supreme Court agreed on the basis that the federal government controlled such taxes on reservations. In 1996, the U.S. Supreme Court ruled that in Oklahoma tribal-owned service stations were exempt from paying the state gasoline tax. Thus federal court rulings have, on occasion, made non-Indians subject to Indian laws and regulations on reservations. Further examples are presented in later chapters.

A long-established aspect of sovereignty is represented by tribal courts that arose during the treaty-making era; initially they emerged from traditional Indian customs and laws for particular tribes. By the latter part of the nineteenth century, Indians on reservations were typically resolving their own internal legal disputes. In 1883 the BIA formally launched the Courts of Indian Offenses with Indian judges appointed by the federal government. These courts sometimes, possibly often, were used to suppress traditional Indian laws and were under the control of local Indian agents. The contemporary court system emerged in 1934 with the Indian Reorganization Act. This system was far more responsive to Indian customs and legal norms and was controlled by each tribe. These courts seek to resolve civil disputes and have limited jurisdiction over criminal law on reservations. Most cases seem to be alcohol-related or concerned with child custody and divorce. One recurrent problem is the difference between Indian customary law and the demands of the Euro-American legal system.

An unexpected and positive aspect of self-determination has been the emergence of tribal colleges. The Navajo Community College (now Dine College) was founded in 1968 because tribal leaders realized that formal education was one key to the future. Leaders were frustrated because many young people lacked the knowledge and skills to cope with Euro-Americans. Before long the federal government acknowledged the potential of Indian colleges, especially in the Tribally Controlled Community College Assistance Act of 1978. As a result, twenty-four tribal colleges were founded, most of which are in

Montana and the Dakotas. Typically, the libraries have relatively few books, most faculty are non-Indian, and the physical plants are inadequate. But because most reservations are located in rural areas with no ready access to four-year colleges, tribal community colleges provide an exceedingly valuable post–high school learning environment (see also Chapter 6).

INDIANS AND ALCOHOL Treaties and laws referring to Indians in Canada and the United States often made reference to the consumption of intoxicants. In Canada, Indians who were not enfranchised could not buy liquor legally for ordinary consumption until 1951. The Canadian Indian Act of 1951 permitted the provinces or territories, with the approval of the governor in council, to allow Indians to consume intoxicants in public places. This condition existed over most of Canada until 1958. Between 1958 and 1963 the restriction was lessened in most provinces and territories to permit Indians to buy alcoholic beverages in the same manner as Canadian citizens in general—that is, either in a public place or from a package store. A band has the option of prohibiting intoxicants on its reserve lands.

In the United States the first federal regulation of intoxicants among Indians occurred in 1802. The law was modified periodically to ease enforcement and to cover loopholes. The federal government did not repeal this law until 1953. Prohibition still was possible on any reservation under local option. Before Indians could consume intoxicants in some states, state laws against the sale of liquor to Indians had to be changed.

To Native Americans the right to drink has been important symbolically as well as literally. For hundreds of years whites have expressed the opinion that Indians have a tolerance of alcohol lower than their own. Some whites have gone so far as to use the stereotype of the drunken Indian to rationalize not attempting to resolve depressed social and economic conditions among Indians. The question of Indian tolerance of alcohol has been the subject of many studies, but the one by Lynn J. Bennion and Ting-Kai Li (1976) deserves particular attention. They compared the rate of alcohol metabolism in thirty whites and thirty full-blooded Indians who had had some prior exposure to alcohol. They wrote, "Since our study showed no significant difference between American Indians and whites in rates of alcohol metabolism, the conclusion cannot be drawn that racial variations in proclivity to alcohol abuse can be accounted for by racial variations in alcohol metabolic rates" (1976, 12). Subsequent comparable studies validate these findings.

Thus the effects of excessive alcoholic beverage consumption by Indians are best attributed to nonbiological factors, but, as Philip A. May (1994) has stressed, alcohol abuse by Indians is a complex issue. The most recent comprehensive studies date from the late 1980s, when about 18 percent of Indian deaths were attributed to alcohol use compared with 5 percent for the general U.S. population. As these percentages are compared, it is essential to be fully aware of the major contributing factors. First, the Indian population is quite young, with a median age in the early twenties compared with a median age in the early thirties for the United States in general. As in the general population, young Indians are the most likely age group to be risk takers and careless drinkers. Second, many Indians live in rural areas of western states, and when they are involved in accidents, aid often is delayed. Third, many Indians live in poverty, which makes them prime candidates for alcohol abuse that leads to accidents, suicides, and homicides. In addition, although broadly based statistics about Indian drinking suggest that the vast majority of Indians are heavy drinkers, this does *not* seem to be the case. The reason is that heavy drinkers inflate the apparent total number of drinkers in arrest and treatment records. That *non-Indians are probably heavier drinkers than are Indians* is suggested in one study: 52 percent of Navajo adults in 1984 drank, whereas at the same time 67 percent of adults in the United States in general drank.

The federal government has recognized the problem of Indian drinking, and by 1986 it had established more than two hundred programs in thirty-four states to combat it. Increasing numbers of these programs have been turned over to Indian management and adjusted to local conditions. Alcoholics Anonymous (AA) is a widely popular alcoholic therapy program for Indians and other U.S. citizens. However, by the late 1990s, there never had been a scientific study of the AA success rate; it appears that AA is no more successful in general than are other approaches to alcoholism.

RESERVATION GAMING OPERATIONS Although bingo is hardly an ancient American Indian game, it attracted intense Indian interest beginning in 1979 when the Florida Seminoles initiated high-stakes bingo. A 1982 U.S. Supreme Court decision held that reservation Indians could sponsor bingo if the game was permitted elsewhere in the state. There was no direct state or federal control over Indian gambling, nor were Indians subject to any taxes on gambling except those that Indians approved. As a result, the Indian gaming industry was born.

In 1988 Congress passed the Indian Gaming Regulatory Act (IGRA), which made Indian gaming the most rigidly controlled form of legal gambling in the United States. The act identified three categories of gaming that could take place on "Indian lands." Class I is regulated by a tribe and consists of social games or traditional forms of Indian gaming. Class II is controlled by the tribes and the National Indian Gaming Commission established by the act. It includes bingo and card games that are authorized by the state or legally played somewhere in the state and regulates hours of operations and bet or pot limits. Class III facilities are controlled by the tribes and the states in formal compacts. Included are all lotteries, card games, and games of chance apart from bingo. Class III operations are, in essence, casinos.

As Indian gaming expanded, opposition by non-Indians mounted. Some church groups and others objected that charity bingo games suffered. States objected to their inability to tax the operations. Gambling operators in Nevada and elsewhere objected to the competition from Indians. By 1999 the tribes with gaming operations numbered 198, and eight casinos accounted for

40 percent of the total income. The Foxwoods Resort Casino of the Mashantucket Pequot Tribal Nation in Connecticut is reported to earn more than $1 billion a year. (Under the IGRA, tribal earnings are not public information.) Indian gaming businesses nationwide employ at least 140,000 people, about 85 percent of whom are *non*-Indian. When it sanctioned Indian gaming, Congress stipulated that the revenues were to be used primarily for tribal programs or operations, general welfare, and economic development. At the same time some tribes, such as the Hopi and Navajo, have rejected gaming on their reservations based on moral grounds.

Most non-Indians do not realize that Indian gaming represents *less than 10 percent* of the legal gambling in this country. In addition, much misinformation has been spread about Indian gaming and taxes. Winnings in Indian casinos are taxable by the federal government, except those of members of the tribe that operates the casino. The federal government has the power to tax Indians on their lands; the states do not. All tribal employees in Indian casinos must pay taxes on their earnings to the federal government but not to a state government. When a tribe makes per capita payments from casino profits to its members, the money is taxed only by the federal government.

States, understandably, strenuously object to Indian gaming because they do not have the authority to tax their operations. Yet states have managed to tap Indian gaming profits. The Mashantucket Pequot agreed to pay the state of Connecticut $100 million a year *not* to permit slot machines elsewhere in the state. The Grand Ronde group of tribes in Oregon operates the Spirit Mountain Casino. Because a state lottery and video poker exist in Oregon, the state negotiated with the Grand Ronde to permit them to provide craps, roulette, and forms of poker not permitted elsewhere in Oregon. The state in turn receives 6 percent of the gaming profits, about $1.5 million in 1997. This "revenue-sharing" is a veiled tax. It is alarming that the Mashantucket Pequot and Grand Ronde have surrendered an aspect of their sovereignty to the respective states. The same is true for Indian casinos in other states (see also Chapter 15).

OUTSTANDING INDIANS At present and in the comparatively recent past, innumerable Indians have achieved prominence in many fields. It is feasible to include only a small cross-section of individuals here. (Indians who have been successful anthropologists are discussed in the next section of this chapter.)

Sherman Alexie (1966–), of Spokane and Coeur d'Alene ancestry, is a prominent young author. His books of poetry have been widely praised, and his collection of short stories, *The Lone Ranger and Tonto Fistfight in Heaven* (New York, 1993), and his novel *Reservation Blues* (New York, 1995) are both humorous and heartrending. In 1998 Alexie also wrote and coproduced the widely praised film *Smoke Signals*. Robert L. Bennett (1912–), an Oneida, was the BIA commissioner of Indian affairs from 1966 to 1969 and later became the director of the American Indian Law Center at the University of New Mexico. Benjamin Nighthorse Campbell (1933–), a Northern Cheyenne, is an artist, former judo champion, and politician. He is the only Native American in the U.S. Senate. The person of Native American heritage who achieved the highest political status in the United States is Charles Curtis (1860–1936). His mother was a Kaw (Kansa) Indian, and his father was white. He served in the House of Representatives and the Senate before becoming vice president (1929–1933) under Herbert Clark Hoover. Curtis believed strongly in the assimilation of Indians into the greater society.

Ada Deer (1935–), a Menominee, played a critical role in the restoration of the Menominee Reservation after it and other reservations had been terminated by the federal government. Her efforts led to the reinstatement of additional terminated reservations. She later became an assistant secretary of Indian affairs in the Department of the Interior. Deer is currently the chair of American Indian studies at the University of Wisconsin, Madison. Vine Deloria, Jr. (1933–), a Standing Rock Sioux, is possibly the most celebrated Indian writer. He is an attorney and professor best known for his book *Custer Died for Your Sins* (New York, 1969; reprinted Norman, OK, 1988), which includes a vigorous attack on anthropologists. Deloria is an author of ten additional books, and the ones that address the legal issues involving Indians are especially notable. Walter Echo-Hawk (1948–), a Pawnee, is a lawyer with the Native American Rights Fund, the most important advocacy group managed by Indians for Indians. Joy Harjo (1951–), a Creek, is most recognized for her award-winning poetry. She also is a screenwriter and plays saxophone with her band, "Poetic Justice."

Ira Hamilton Hayes (1923–1955), a Pima, was a U.S. Marine hero during World War II. He participated in the assault on the island of Iwo Jima and was one of the marines (in a famous photograph) who raised the U.S. flag at the summit of a volcano under heavy Japanese fire. William L. Hensley (1941–), an Eskimo (Inuit), was born in northern Alaska and played a significant role in resolving native claims in Alaska during the 1960s. He later served in the Alaska House of Representatives and remains an outstanding spokesman for native Alaskan issues. Russell Means (1940–), an Oglala–Yankton Sioux, is best known as one of the American Indian Movement leaders who confronted federal agents at Wounded Knee, South Dakota, in 1973. He also played a dominant role in subsequent confrontations while supporting Indian causes.

N. Scott Momaday (1934–) is a Kiowa raised in the Southwest who attended the University of New Mexico and became an outstanding novelist. His best-known book is *House Made of Dawn*. Momaday also is a widely respected poet. William Lewis Paul, Sr. (1885–1977), a Tlingit, became a lawyer and did more than any other individual to further Tlingit rights and those of other native peoples in Alaska. He was a pioneer in the 1920s in addressing civil rights issues.

William Penn Adair Rogers (1879–1935) was an Oklahoma Cherokee; known as Will Rogers, he was one of the most famous American humorists. He also was a prominent writer and actor. Buffy Sainte-Marie (1942–), a Cree, is an award-winning folksinger and a songwriter of note. She is an articulate advocate of Indian rights as well. Will Sampson (1934–1987), an Oklahoma Creek, was a notable motion picture actor best known for his role in the 1975 film *One Flew over the Cuckoo's Nest.*

James Francis Thorpe (1888–1953), a Sauk and Mesquakie (Fox) from Oklahoma, was regarded as the greatest athlete in the world after winning gold medals in the 1912 Olympics. Although he was later stripped of his medals on a technicality, they were restored posthumously. From 1907 to 1912, Thorpe played football for the Carlisle Indian School in Pennsylvania; at that time there were only about 250 students in the school old enough to play football. Carlisle football teams played against major universities and seldom lost a game. The teams of 1911 and 1912 were among the best in the history of football.

Native Americans and Anthropologists

American anthropologists have had a deep and abiding interest in American Indians for obvious professional and less obvious personal reasons. Because Indians in the United States and Canada have been quite accessible and usually considerate hosts, they have served as the subjects for thousands of ethnographic studies. A well-established tradition in cultural and social anthropology is the study of people in at least one other society as a part of professional training. In this manner the observer not only gains meaningful cross-cultural experience but also assembles a body of information that contributes to a broader understanding of humanity. The personal dimension is important because ethnographers typically develop a great affinity for the people among whom they work; they empathize with Native Americans in a way that most others do not. The field study of an ethnographer has two primary goals: to record the activities of people and to employ this information for the solution of theoretical or practical problems. Some Indians are resentful of anthropologists, and we need to ask: What do anthropologists do that may displease Indians?

Describing Native American life, the main purpose of ethnographers, would seem to be a relatively neutral activity. It is important if only because customs are reported that otherwise might go unrecorded and be lost to history. To preserve disappearing information has been a real concern of many investigators, especially those convinced that they were witnessing the rapid disappearance of aboriginal ways of life. Some ethnographers, especially those in the early 1900s, became secular crusaders who devoted their lives to recording cultural ways before they were gone forever. Surely this is a worthwhile, if not noble, goal.

With aboriginal customs as their focal point, many ethnographers recorded behavior that lived only in the memories of Indians. Counting coup (showing bravery by striking or touching a live enemy), scalping an enemy, bison hunts, and feather headdresses were given emphasis in descriptive accounts, conveying the impression that these forms and norms typified Native American life in the recent past. Modern Indians may justly object, because in their lifetimes or during the lives of their grandparents these customs no longer existed. Such ethnographers misrepresented Indians because they froze them in time; this was true of most pre-1930 studies. In retrospect, we can say that anthropologists did not lack compassion, but, unfortunately, they did produce a distorted picture of past practices lasting into the present.

Directly contributing to this misunderstanding is the fact that aboriginal or more recent Indian life often was described in terms of the "ethnographic present." This means that even though an ethnographer was describing extinct customs, the information was reported in the present tense as a literary technique to impart vitality to an account. Criticisms of this technique clearly are valid, especially because so much has happened to Indians historically and in the recent past. It distorts contemporary realities and contributes further to unrealistic views of Native Americans.

D'Arcy McNickle (1970) suggested that the use of the ethnographic present and the failure by ethnographers to present the *adaptive* changes in Indian lifeways has led to another unfortunate result, that of abetting the advocates of Indian assimilation. Acculturation studies became important in ethnographic fieldwork during the early 1930s, and usually stressed the negative aspects of reservation life. This hardly has been a criticism of the Indians involved, however, nor was it intended as a prop for assimilation programs. Instead it often was an expression of dismay about federal programs as they were administered at the time.

Older Indians often are quite sympathetic when an eager ethnographer arrives to collect information about the past, but younger ones often have neutral or hostile attitudes toward these efforts. The older people see what they regard as the essence of Indian life disappearing, and they are well aware that their children or grandchildren often have little or no interest in their cultural heritage as Indians. Thus an old man or woman finds it very satisfying to talk about the past to an ethnographer and have the conversations recorded with care. The attitude of many younger Indians about such information can be one of disinterest or of shame about old customs. If or when these younger people decide to learn about their past as Indians, it is probable that they will have to rely on the writings of the very ethnographers that they now resent.

In a discussion of anthropologists and Native Americans, it should be noted that a number of Indians have emerged as outstanding anthropologists with ethnography as a specialization. Anthropologists long have encouraged—and continue to encourage—Indians to join their ranks. Ethnographers are keenly aware that in many contexts a perceptive insider may be a better reporter and interpreter of Indian life than an outsider. The names of a number of Indian anthropologists come to mind. Francis La Flesche (1857–1932), an Omaha, first collected information about Indians with Alice Fletcher and then worked for eighteen years at the Bureau of American Ethnology. William Jones (1871–1909), of Mesquakie and white ancestry, earned a PhD at Columbia in 1904 and is noted for his research among Algonquian Indians. He was killed by the Ilongots on a field trip in the Philippine Islands. J. N. B. Hewitt (1859–1937), of Tuscarora and white ancestry, was an authority on the Iroquois. Edward P. Dozier (1916–1971), born at Santa Clara Pueblo, was noted for his writings about Pueblo Indians. Alfonso Ortiz (1940–1997) was a part-Hispanic member of the San Juan Pueblo and a specialist in Indians in the Southwest.

Prominent Indians today who are professional anthropologists are numerous. They include Edward D. Castillo (1947–), a Cahuilla and Luiseno, who holds a PhD in anthropology and is best known for his studies of California Indians. Nora Dauenhauer (1927–), a Tlingit, is recognized for her voluminous and insightful studies of the Tlingit. Jack D. Forbes (1934–), Powhatan and Lenape, earned a PhD degree in anthropology and is the chair of Native American Studies at the University of California, Davis. He is best known for his insightful historical studies of Indians. Shirley Hill Witt (1940–), a Mohawk, earned her PhD in anthropology and became a member of the U.S. Commission on Civil Rights. She has been especially active in supporting the rights of women. These are but a few examples.

An important question remains: If anthropologists know so much about Indians, why have they not played a more prominent role as "experts" on culture change among Indians? The basic reason is straightforward. For many years the guiding principle behind federal Indian policy in the United States was assimilation, the sooner the better—a position that anthropologists found distasteful. When the Indian Reorganization Act of 1934 became law, a number of outstanding anthropologists did work for the BIA to further the provisions of the act, because it was designed to restore vitality to reservation life. However, World War II diverted national attention from this program, and the early 1950s ushered in the termination policy, which found little support among anthropologists. In theory and in fact, the BIA was long committed to Indian assimilation, but like most bureaucratic organizations, it has in truth devoted a great deal of energy and funds to its own expansion. Furthermore, bureau personnel often regarded anthropologists as "Indian lovers" and neither sought nor welcomed their advice. Anthropologists in turn have had little sympathy with the bureau policies in general and have preferred not to become involved in most of their programs.

Anthropologists clearly have served Indians in useful and positive ways. They spoke out against the termination policy, although in retrospect not as strongly as they might have. They have worked to increase the effectiveness of health programs, given evidence to support Indian land claims and identity, testified in vigorous support of the Native American church, and often served as advisors to Indians in economic development programs. In recent years anthropologists have aided Native Americans in their efforts to obtain aboriginal resource utilization rights opposed by the federal and state governments. Furthermore, anthropologists have played an important role in interpreting Native American life to non-Indians, both in and out of the classroom.

Comparing Cultures

In each of Chapters 3–14, a particular tribe is discussed in detail. You will be reading about Indian conventions that seem quite ordinary, reasonable, and even self-evident. In these cases, your reaction no doubt will be one of appreciation and understanding, because you are familiar with these Indian ways; they will seem "normal." On the other hand, you will also be reading about Indian behavior that seems strange, bizarre, and possibly barbaric. In these cases, your response probably will range from negative to abhorrent. An additional cautionary note is fitting. Not infrequently we think that some types of human behavior, especially those associated with our biology, "occur everywhere." Yet this may not be true. An example is instructive. Youthful Navajo males stand to urinate while older men kneel on one or both knees. Young Navajo women squat but older women urinate while standing. Thus, something as basic and ordinary as urinating may, and sometimes does, vary from one culture to the next.

To better understand American Indians—or any other unfamiliar people—it is desirable to be as objective as possible. Three concepts are introduced for your consideration. The first is ethnocentrism, meaning that one's own lifeway is the basis for judging all other lifeways. This is a commonplace human reaction when exposed to persons in other cultures, especially those quite different from the one in which you were born and raised. Ethnocentrism is "good" in some ways; it gives you a strong sense of personal identity with a particular culture (or subculture). But ethnocentrism is "bad" in other ways; it fosters irrational prejudice, contempt, or hostility toward other peoples. The phrases "a good Indian is a dead Indian," "America right or wrong," and "ethnic cleansing" serve as examples. The "bad" of ethnocentrism overwhelms the "good."

The second concept is cultural relativism, which holds that human behavior always occurs within the context of a particular culture and should be considered within such a framework. Thus every culture has its own standards, attitudes, and particular logic. Stated differently, a culture is considered from an insider viewpoint. Examples illustrate the concept. We might say that the people in some cultures "smell bad," and we in turn may be accused of "smelling bad." There is no universally accepted standard for how people smell. Euro-Americans cut wood with a handsaw on the push stroke while the Japanese would cut with a handsaw on the pull stroke; the contrast represents different motor habits to achieve the same goal. The people in one culture may believe that "little people" inhabit a hinterland, whereas another people may label such an idea as "nonsense." Is one right and another wrong? No, because the ideas are culture-bound. Ethnographers embraced cultural relativism because it helped them avoid biases built into their own culture. However, as Paul R. Turner (1982) points out, the concept of cultural relativism is in essence ethnocentric.

Turner suggests a third approach. Universalism holds that certain categories of values are universal; they are found in all cultures. A value is a shared concept of what is desirable or undesirable by a people; when combined, all of their values provide a worldview. The universal value categories are the following:

1. power (participation in decision making)
2. enlightenment (access to information)
3. wealth (income, including goods and services)
4. well-being (health and safety)
5. skill (proficiency in any practice)
6. affection (love, friendship, and loyalty)
7. respect (recognition by others)
8. rectitude (ethical behavior)

With this list of value categories in mind, it becomes possible to view the behavior of people, any people, without reference to culture-specific standards. It encourages nonbiased comparisons. In sum, I would encourage you not to be ethnocentric as you read about Indian life. You may take a cultural relativist view, or, better yet, consider universalism as an approach to understanding human lifeways.

Additional Sources

The best widely available general source about Indians in historical perspective is volume 4 of the *Handbook of North American Indians,* edited by Wilcomb E. Washburn (1988) and published by the Smithsonian Institution. A brief but effective history about Native Americans is by William T. Hagan (1961). For the colonial era the best ethnohistory is by James Axtell (1981). The best presentation about treaties is by Robert A. Williams (1990). The Ghost Dance study by Alice Back Kehoe (1989) should be consulted for revitalization movements. The emergence of the Pan-Indian movement is detailed best in the volume by Hazel W. Hertzberg (1971). The wide-ranging study of dance, music, and powwows, with emphasis on the Plains, by William K. Powers (1990), is excellent. A relatively recent source concerning tribal government is by Sharon O'Brien (1989). The classic study of Indian law is by Felix S. Cohen, published originally in 1942 and republished by Lucy K. Cohen (1960) and Charles Wilkinson, editors (1982). An outstanding source about Indian law is by Vine Deloria, Jr., and Clifford M. Lytle (1983). The sovereignty issue in particular is addressed by Francis Paul Prucha (1985). Settlement of Passamaquoddy and Penobscot claims against the federal government is presented by Paul Brodeur (1985). Donald L. Fixico's book (1991) focuses on contemporary issues. The education of Native American children in Canada is presented in a volume edited by Marie Battiste and Jean Barman (1995). A book edited by David Alan Long and Olive Patricia Dickason (1996) examines diverse aspects of modern First Nations developments. W. Dale Mason (2000) provides a book-length presentation about Indian gaming.

Selected Bibliography

Axtell, James. 1981. *The European and the Indian*. New York.

Battiste, Marie, and Jean Barman, eds. 1995. *First Nations education in Canada*. Vancouver, British Columbia.

Bee, Robert L. 1982. *The politics of American Indian policy*. Cambridge, MA.

Bennion, Lynn, and Ting-Kai Li. 1976. Alcohol metabolism in American Indians and whites. *The New England Journal of Medicine* 294:9–13.

Brodeur, Paul. 1985. *Restitution*. Boston.

Brookings Institution. 1928. *The problem of Indian administration*. Baltimore.

Cohen, Felix S. 1960. *The legal conscience*. Lucy K. Cohen, ed. New Haven. Reprinted 1982 as *Felix S. Cohen's handbook of federal Indian law,* Charles Wilkinson, ed. Charlottesville, VA.

Cook, S. F. 1955. *The epidemic of 1830–1833 in California and Oregon*. University of California Publications in American Archaeology and Ethnology, vol. 43, no. 3.

Deloria, Vine, Jr., and Clifford M. Lytle. 1983. *American Indians, American justice*. Austin, TX.

Densmore, Frances. 1939. *Nootka and Quileute music*. Bureau of American Ethnology Bulletin 124.

Donaldson, Thomas. 1886. *The George Catlin Indian Gallery in the U.S. National Museum*. Annual Report of the Board of Regents of the Smithsonian Institution, 1885, pt. 2, appendix.

Ewers, John C. 1965. *The emergence of the Plains Indian as the symbol of the North American Indian*. Smithsonian Report for 1964, 531–44.

Fixico, Donald L. 1991. *Urban Indians*. New York.

Foreman, Grant. 1932. *Indian removal*. Norman, OK.

Hagan, William T. 1961. *American Indians*. Chicago.

Hearne, Samuel. 1958. *A journey from Prince of Wales's Fort in Hudson's Bay to the Northern Ocean*. Richard Glover, ed. Toronto.

Hertzberg, Hazel W. 1971. *The search for American Indian identity*. Syracuse, NY.

Howard, James H. 1955. Pan-Indian culture of Oklahoma. *Scientific Monthly* 81: 215–20.

Jorgensen, Joseph G. 1971. Indians and the metropolis. In *The American Indian in urban society,* Jack O. Waddell and O. Michael Watson, eds., 66–113. Boston.

Kehoe, Alice Beck. 1989. *The Ghost Dance*. Fort Worth, TX.

Kroeber, Alfred L., and Edward W. Gifford. 1949. *World renewal*. Anthropological Records, vol. 13:1.

La Barre, Weston. 1960. Twenty years of peyote studies. *Current Anthropology* 1: 45–60.

Long, David Alan, and Olive Patricia Dickason. 1996. *Visions of the heart*. Toronto.

Mason, W. Dale. 2000. *Indian gaming: Tribal sovereignty and American politics*. Norman, OK.

May, Philip A. 1994. The epidemiology of alcohol abuse among American Indians. *American Indian Culture and Research Journal* 18(2), 121–43.

McDonnell, Janet A. 1991. *The dispossession of the American Indian 1887–1934*. Bloomington, IN.

McGuire, Randall H. 1992. Archeology and the first Americans. *American Anthropologist* n.s. 94:816–36.

McKenney, Thomas L., and James Hall. 1933. *The Indian tribes of North America,* vol. 1. Edinburgh.

McNickle, D'Arcy. 1970. American Indians who never were. *The Indian Historian* 3(3): 4–7.

Mooney, James. 1896. *The Ghost Dance religion and the Sioux outbreak of 1890.* Bureau of American Ethnology, 14th Annual Report, pt. 2, 641–1110.

O'Brien, Sharon. 1989. *American Indian tribal governments.* Norman, OK.

Pearce, Roy H. 1965. *The savages of America.* Baltimore.

Powers, William K. 1990. *War dance.* Tucson, AZ.

Prucha, Francis Paul. 1985. *The Indian and American society.* Berkeley, CA.

Saum, Lewis O. 1965. *The fur trader and the Indian.* Seattle, WA.

Sorkin, Alan L. 1971. *American Indians and federal aid.* Washington, DC.

Spicer, Edward H. 1962. *Cycles of conquest.* Tucson, AZ.

Taylor, Theodore W. 1972. *The states and their Indian citizens.* Washington, DC.

Turner, Paul R. 1982. Anthropological value positions. *Human Organization* 41:76–80.

U.S. Department of the Interior. 1958. *Federal Indian law.* Washington, DC.

Washburn, Wilcomb E. 1984. A fifty-year perspective on the Indian Reorganization Act. *American Anthropologist* n.s. 86:279–89.

———, ed. 1988. *History of Indian–white relations.* Vol. 4, *Handbook of North American Indians.* Washington, DC.

Williams, Robert A. 1990. *The American Indian in Western legal thought.* New York.

Winsor, Justin. 1889. *Narrative and critical history of America.* Vol. 2. Boston.

3 The Netsilik: Seal Hunting and Snowhouse Eskimos

Life is so with us that we are never surprised when we hear that someone has starved to death. We are so used to it. It sometimes happens to the best of us.

(Rasmussen 1931, 134)

ESKIMOS* QUITE POSSIBLY are one of the most exotic peoples anywhere. In the widely accepted stereotype, they lived in a land of perpetual ice and snow, ate raw meat, wore skin clothing, built snowhouses, and sledded behind dog teams. They were a gentle and happy people who shared wives and never punished their children. Statements such as these are reasonably correct for some Eskimos but not for others who were equally noteworthy in less familiar ways. For instance, Eskimos along the Pacific littoral of Alaska usually went barefoot throughout the year, wore sleeveless garments, and took steam baths. They never saw a polar bear or "mushed" a dog team, and the wooden houses of some villages were backed by great forests. Sadly, perhaps, relatively few Eskimos lived in snowhouses. These observations have far-reaching implications. First, they indicate that Eskimos lived in more varied ecological settings and in different ways than generally recognized. Second, as suggested in Chapter 1, the culture area concept masks regional differences among the peoples within a single culture area. The failings of the classification are well illustrated by the Arctic culture area, which is occupied only by Eskimos. Typical conventions among some Eskimos are foreign to others. This chapter examines a "classic" Eskimo population.

One man, Robert E. Peary, an American naval officer and explorer, is most responsible for the view of Eskimos that prevails in the United States. Between 1886 and 1909 Peary repeatedly voyaged to a base camp in northwestern Greenland in his attempts to reach the North Pole, a goal that he claimed to have accomplished by 1909. For a U.S. citizen to become the first person to stand at the top of the world became a national obsession. Peary's efforts received intense press coverage for more than twenty years. The Polar Eskimos he encountered lived in snowhouses, hunted seals, and had dog teams. They provided Peary with essential help in his quest, and because so much was written about them most Americans came to regard the Polar Eskimos as typical of all Eskimos.

Of the nearly 52,000 aboriginal Eskimos, fewer than 5,000 lived as the Polar Eskimos did. The Netsilik (NET-silik) are one people who did. When discovered by Europeans, they possibly numbered 700. Their particular lifeway was one of the most remarkable sociocultural adaptations anywhere on earth.

Eskimo apparently means "eaters of raw flesh" in a language of Indians in northeastern Canada. *Netsilik,* or more correctly *Netsilingmiut,* means "the people of the ringed seal"; their name is largely an anthropological label. They

*The word *Esquimawes,* from which Eskimos is derived, was introduced into English in 1584 and thus is long established. Yet it is considered offensive among some present-day Eskimos because it is not their self-identification. Eskimos in Canada prefer the word *Inuit* or a variant, which means "people" in their language, whereas those in northern Alaska call themselves Inupiat. Greenlandic Eskimos call themselves Kalaallit, meaning "Greenlanders," not Inuit, although this term would be fitting. Most Eskimos in southwestern Alaska and others in Siberia call themselves Yuit or a variant, meaning "people" in their Eskimoan languages. Some Alaskan Eskimos regard themselves as Koniag, and others consider themselves Aleut. In sum, the only generic designation that embraces *all* of these people is Eskimo.

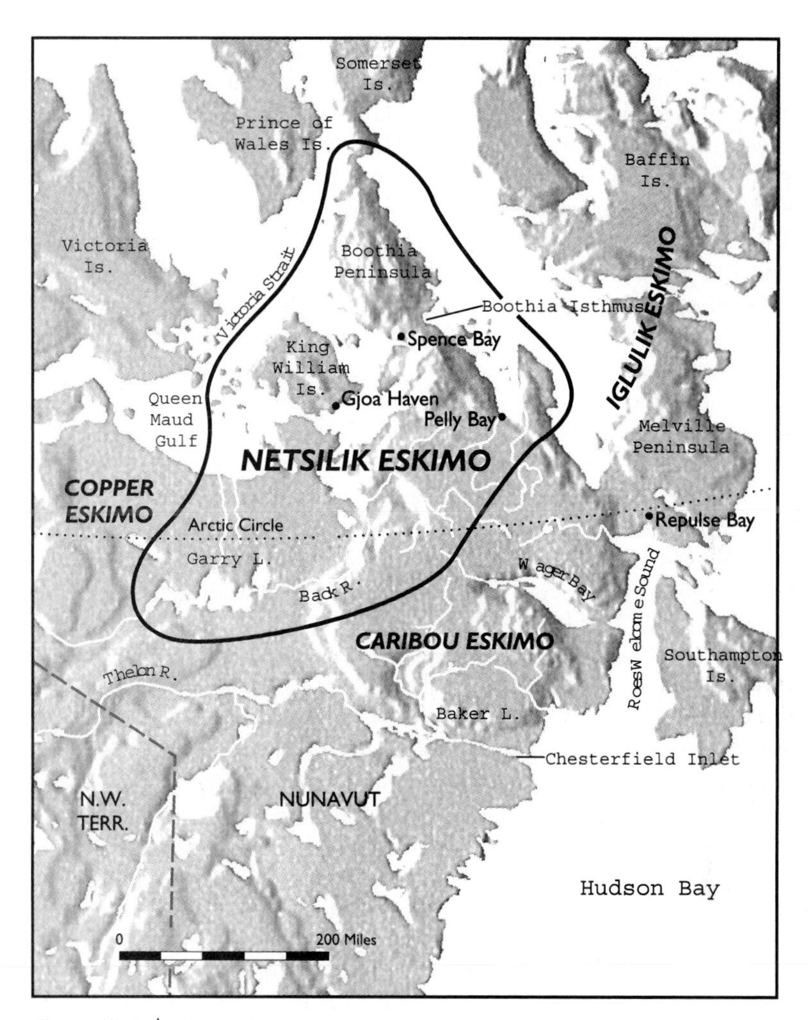

Figure 3-1 | The early historic Netsilik homeland.

spoke Inuit (IN-yoo-it), a language with sixteen dialects ranging from east Greenland to the Bering Strait area of Alaska. It is related to the Yupik (YOO-pik) language of Eskimos elsewhere in Alaska and eastern Siberia. Inuit and Yupik are distantly related to Aleut, the language spoken on the Aleutian Islands. These three populations make up the Eskimo–Aleut language family.

The Netsilik homeland is tundra country dominated by lichens, mosses, and other low-growing plants. The tree line is far to the south, a critical factor with respect to their material culture. Driftwood was their major source of wood; the people thought trees grew at the bottom of the sea and surfaced as driftwood after they died. The coastline of Netsilik country is convoluted with many inlets; rivers are common and lakes innumerable (see Figure 3-1). Virtually all of their domain is north of the Arctic Circle. Thus for part of each year there is no alternation between daylight and darkness. Instead there is continuous daylight in midsummer, and the darkness of winter is relieved only by moonlight and reflected sunlight. The winters are long and cold, with the mean daily temperature in January about −20°F; −40°F temperatures are common. On average there are twenty frost-free days a year.

The Netsilik spoke Inuit with minor local differences. They had neither a tribal name nor a clear sense of tribal identity. Instead, an individual was a member of one of nine named bands (a relatively small sociocultural group), each identified with a hunting area. Band membership was somewhat fluid, and rigid boundaries between bands did not exist; a sense of oneness among bands was lacking.

Eskimo biology is of interest, if only because of where they live. Compared with contemporary Euro-Americans, early historic Eskimos usually were of medium stature, not short, with large chests and relatively short legs. They were typically *not* fat, although their bulky garments and muscular build might suggest corpulence. Their heads and faces were relatively large, whereas their hands and feet were somewhat small. Eskimo physiological adaptations to the cold are evident in relatively recent studies. Their basal metabolism was elevated from 13 to 33 percent above the Du Bois (normal) standard and was highest among those living under essentially aboriginal conditions. Their higher metabolic rate was attributed primarily to diet, not to genetic differences from Europeans. Core body temperatures were much the same as among whites, possibly because Eskimo skin garments protected their bodies from extreme cold. When exposed to cold under test conditions, however, Eskimo finger and hand temperatures rose quicker than those of Europeans, and Eskimos had a greater cold tolerance at low temperatures. Their capacity to withstand low peripheral temperatures probably included a genetic factor. Summarily, Eskimos stand somewhat apart from most other peoples in their capacity to withstand cold. When genetic identity, language, and culture are weighed in combination, these Arctic peoples exhibited greater homogeneity than is known for any other North American culture area.

Aboriginal Life

In this and most other chapters about specific Native American groups, I follow much the same format. I first emphasize and present Indian life before intense contact with Westerners, followed by a relatively brief presentation of major historical changes. Each chapter concludes with an account of contemporary developments and issues.

Aboriginal Netsilik life was exceedingly different from contemporary American life. For example, a Netsilik lived all of her or his life with about fifty or fewer persons who were exceedingly well known to each other and usually related by blood or marriage. In a lifetime a person might never see more than two hundred other Netsilik at any one time and seldom had contact with non-Netsilik. Knowledge was self-gained or verbally transmitted across the generations; they were nonliterate, not illiterate. A family moved often from one camp to another and had no permanent home. A person could carry most of his or her belongings from one camp to the next. Furthermore, an individual wore one set of garments until they were outgrown or disintegrated. Illness was thought to be caused by evil spirits, and life expectancy may have averaged about thirty years. Intermittent hunger was a fact of life, and starving to death was an ever-present possibility. These realities should be considered as you read about their aboriginal lives.

ORIGIN MYTH Unlike most people around the world, the Netsilik did not have a unified account about the beginning of life on earth. Instead, a number of nonsequential myths addressed particular origins, and they did not attempt to reconcile inconsistencies or contradictions.

The earth always existed and was dark when the earliest people appeared; they survived without pleasure or suffering. Then people crossed a body of water on kayaks lashed together to form a raft. As they approached their destination, the children anxiously jumped into the water to go ashore. A little orphan girl was thrown into the water because she had no relatives. As she clutched a side of the raft, her fingers were cut off, and she disappeared beneath the water. Her detached fingers became alive, bobbed about, and turned into seals. The orphan girl emerged as the Sea Goddess who controlled everything on which the people depended for food. The Weather God was ill-disposed toward people and could, with his great power, produce storms to prevent men from hunting. The Moon God, the third major deity, was not especially powerful but was reasonably sympathetic toward people. The Sun and Moon were thought to be brother and sister who had an evil mother. She planned to kill them but they murdered her instead and became lovers who ascended into the sky.

In primeval times, spoken words produced immediate results. When the fox repeatedly said "darkness," it became dark, enabling him to raid human food supplies. The hare repeatedly said "day" to find a place to feed. Subsequently, darkness and light alternated. All animals and people died in a flood except for two male shamans. They copulated, and one man gave birth to males and to females.

MATERIAL CULTURE Among aboriginal North Americans, only Eskimos and some northern Indians wore tailor-made garments. Most Netsilik clothing was cut from caribou fur, an exceptional material for cold-weather apparel. Caribou fur is soft, light, and dense; each hair is hollow to provide excellent insulation. The caribou fur of a man's outer parka, worn for hunting and traveling, faced outward, and the fur on his inner parka faced inward. Parkas had hoods and sometimes front and back flaps with border trim. Decorative panels of light-colored fur adorned the arms and shoulders (see Figure 3-2). Inner and outer trousers reached from the hips to the knees, and two pairs of boots

Figure 3-2 | An engraving of three Netsilik. The man lost a lower leg in an encounter with a polar bear. The ship's carpenter on the Ross expedition in 1830 fitted him with a wooden leg. Note the facial tattoos of the women. (From Ross 1835.)

protected a man's feet. The fur of mittens faced outward; gloves were introduced to Native Americans by Europeans. A child wore a hooded combination suit that was put on and removed through a laced opening at the chest; this garment also had an opening at the groin for elimination.

A woman dressed much the same as a man, but a woman's garments were more bulky. A woman wore a single pair of trousers with boots attached that was held up with a belt. It is sometimes thought that a baby was carried in the hood of a mother's parka, but this was not so; a roomy pouch at the back of the parka accommodated an infant. On the outside of the parka, a cord that ran beneath the baby and over the mother's breasts held the infant in place. As a naked infant began to relieve itself, the mother quickly released the cord and rapidly removed the baby, holding it by its arms until it eliminated, irrespective of the weather.

Females were tattooed around the time of puberty and later, a painful process. Sinew threaded through an eyed needle was covered with soot and plant juice and laced beneath the skin. Alternatively, the skin could be punctured and the wounds rubbed with the tattooing substance to produce a blue color. Relatively simple facial tattoos were complemented by others on the hands, arms, and thighs that could be quite elaborate.

Two qualities in particular characterized Netsilik material culture: the limited nature of the raw materials available and the relative technological simplicity of the finished artifacts. The two major clusters of raw materials were flexibles (e.g., sinew and skins) and solids (e.g., antler, bone, snow, stone, and wood). In addition, the most valuable material of a plastic nature was a blood-based glue.

The preparation of skins was dominated by women and had emerged as the most integrated, complex, and time-consuming technological process. After a caribou had been killed and skinned by a man, the skin could be processed in varied ways. To prepare skins for inner garments, for example, a woman placed a raw skin on the ground with the flesh side down and anchored it with stones for preliminary drying. Subsequently, people slept with the underside of these skins around their naked bodies. In this manner skins were softened for scraping and stretching. A skin then was placed outside to freeze, and the subcutaneous (beneath the skin) layer was removed with a sharp-edged bone scraper. Finally, because of the strength required, a man thinned a skin with a scraper before it was cut and sewn by women.

Sealskin is more durable than caribou skin and has far greater resistance to water. A key use of sealskins was for kayak covers. A woman scraped the underside of these skins with a semilunar-bladed knife made from ground slate and set into an antler handle. She scraped the skin further and chewed it until all of the fat was removed. Skins were then rolled up and placed in a snowhouse on a drying rack that was suspended over a soapstone lamp fueled with seal oil. After a number of days the hair rotted and was scraped free. Kayak covers were stored in the snow until they were cut, fitted, and sewn over a kayak frame. Women used bone needles and thread made from caribou sinew. To make a waterproof seam, they used a blind stitch, one that was carried halfway through the skins; but for fur clothing a simple overcast stitch was satisfactory. Sealskins were the best not only for summer boots and kayaker parkas but also for tent covers, packsacks for dogs, and containers for oil or water. Sealskin thongs (*babiche*) served many purposes, especially as binders for composite tools and weapons.

Snow as a solid was a key raw material. It is often observed that Eskimos had many words for snow, depending on its particular qualities (e.g., snow in the air, soft and watery snow), an obvious indicator of its importance. The snowhouse unquestionably is the best-known Eskimo structure. It is widely thought that *igloo* means a snowhouse, but the word refers to any type of dwelling. The availability of snow, the nomadic nature of Netsilik life, and the scarcity of wood made snow an ideal building material. When constructing a house of snow, a man first tested a snowfield with a long, slender antler probe to make certain that the snow was sufficiently deep and of acceptable consistency. A large snowhouse, about fifteen feet in diameter, could be completed by a skilled craftsman in about an hour. The builder first drew a circle in the snow with his antler snow knife to outline the size and location of the structure. Enough blocks for the house could be removed from within the circle. Each block was about twenty inches long, twenty-five inches wide, and four inches thick. Lower blocks were cut with a basal slant to form a circular wall that spiraled upward as a dome. A long tunnel to trap cold outside air was added, as was a dome-shaped entryway. The builder shoveled snow over the new structure to fill cracks and provide additional insulation. He made a small ventilation hole in the ceiling and used a block of clear river ice to replace a snow block above the entrance to serve as a window. A sleeping platform was constructed of snow blocks at the rear of a dwelling, and another platform held a soapstone lamp with a drying rack suspended above it. The occupants of a snowhouse attempted to keep the temperature inside somewhat *below* freezing. Otherwise the snow froze on the inside and turned to ice, making the house colder.

Snow served additional construction purposes. Snow-block windbreaks protected men in the winter as they fished or hunted seals, and snow blocks piled on one another served as platforms for meat storage. In the fall, before satisfactory snow became available for a snowhouse, blocks of river ice were cut to form the vertical walls of a dwelling roofed with tent skins.

With the scarcity of wood, caribou antler emerged as a major raw material. Antler is relatively soft but strong and easily worked, and after being heated it may be bent into various shapes. Bone by contrast is hard, brittle, and more difficult to process. A primary tool for working antler or bone was an adz with a ground and polished stone blade lashed to an antler handle. The blade of an adz is set at right angles to the handle, whereas an ax has a blade parallel to the handle; greater cutting control is possible with an adz. To cut antler or bone into sections, a man fit a small stone blade into an antler handle. For refined cuts, an antler-handled knife was fitted with a stone blade in a groove near one end. Holes were made with a bow drill, and blood-based glue served to join two pieces of wood for tent poles and weapon shafts.

Another critical solid material was soapstone, available in one sector of their country. It is comparatively soft and was cut from the source with an ice pick and then shaped with an adz, drill, and knife. A soapstone lamp was about twenty inches long, oblong in shape, and had a flat bottom with low sides. The final key soapstone artifact was a woman's cooking pot, her most valued possession. It was rectangular, about twenty inches long, and steep sided, with holes in the corners for suspension over an oil lamp.

Technological ingenuity is in the eyes of the beholder, and most beholders would agree that the dominant Netsilik sled was an ingenious artifact. The first step in construction was to cut sealskins from a summer tent in half and soak them in river water to soften. Next, the two sections of skins were spread flat, and on each one overlapping fish were placed along one edge. The fish on each portion were rolled tightly, bound with thongs, flattened, turned up at one end, and left to freeze to form the runners. Caribou antler crosspieces were placed at right angles between the runners and bound in place with thongs

Figure 3-3 | A man completing a sled with runners of frozen fish wrapped in sealskins. The caribou antler crossbars are lashed in place with sealskin lines. (Courtesy Canadian Museum of Contemporary Photography, NFB Collection. Photograph by Doug Wilkinson.)

(see Figure 3-3). Crosspieces occasionally consisted of frozen meat. To protect the skin runners at the bottom, a thick mixture of moss, snow, and water was frozen in place. Finally, to make the sled shoes, a man squirted mouthfuls of water on a piece of polar bear fur and rubbed it on the bottoms of the runners to create a shoeing of ice that would slide freely over the snow.

Kayaks were narrow, about twenty feet long, and had round manholes. Frames preferably were made from driftwood, although components might be fashioned from antler. Bent sections of dwarf willow formed the ribs. Thongs joined the components, resulting in flexible joints that tended not to break with hard use. Each fall a kayak was stripped of its cover and cached (stored) on piles of stones near areas in which caribou would be hunted the following year. That spring women prepared and sewed new kayak covers.

As will become evident, the Netsilik were relatively mobile in their subsistence round. Although the foregoing inventory of artifacts is not complete, it does suggest that their material culture was limited. Most everything a family owned could be sledded from one camp to the next or carried in packs by dogs and people. The portability of their artifacts is remarkable, especially considering how and where they lived.

THE SUBSISTENCE ROUND A key to food-getting success for a family was to be at an optimal location at the right time to harvest edibles. This was a strategy of interception, as opposed to the pursuit of quarry. During a normal year the habits and availability of most key species could be predicted, and a man was free to hunt anywhere. Caribou migrated north from the tree line in the spring, and most of them returned south in the fall. Arctic char descended rivers to the sea each spring and returned in the fall. Seals do not migrate, and people began to hunt them after ice formed on the sea.

Localized food resources varied considerably; only the major subsistence methods are detailed here. Beginning in the fall as the weather turned cold and blustery, small groups of families moved to riverbank camps to fish for char. Because by then their tepeelike skin-covered tents were cold, men chipped blocks of river ice to form walls for houses roofed with tent skins. To fish, a man chipped a hole in the river ice with an ice pick and removed the small pieces of ice with an antler scoop. He knelt close to the hole, and with one hand he jiggled an ivory lure attached to a sinew line in the water. In his other hand he held a two-pronged leister (fish spear). As a char approached the lure, the fisherman impaled the fish on the leister. A man fished in this manner for hours, days, and weeks. Char provided daily food, and any surplus was stored in ice-block caches. By November, as the river ice thickened, this fishing method became unrewarding; families lived on cached char or previously harvested caribou meat until the sea ice thickened.

By January several scattered extended families sledded with their belongings from riverbank sites to camp on an expanse of sea ice. (An extended family consists of two or more consanguineal families spanning a number of generations; e.g., two brothers, their wives, and children.) The move by dogsled was slow and often arduous, especially over fields of broken ice. Only one or two dogs, with the help of people, pulled a sled; larger teams could not be fed. Very young children rode on a sled, while all others, young or old, walked. Women usually walked in front of a team to encourage and help guide the dogs. After reaching the sea ice, hunters searched for an expanse of flat ice likely to include a concentration of seal breathing holes. Families built their snowhouses nearby. Seals are active throughout the year and must maintain a series of holes in the ice to breathe through about every fifteen minutes. As the ice thickened, a seal scratched and gnawed the ice at a breathing hole to create a funnel-shaped opening. On the surface the hole was covered with snow and frost from seal's breath. Most important, a seal used numerous breathing holes over a comparatively wide area. It was strategically desirable for as many hunters as possible to be stationed at a cluster of breathing holes to increase the probability that a seal might be harpooned at a particular hole.

Hunting ringed seals at their breathing holes required skill and patience and was physically demanding. The most capable hunter at a camp decided where they would concentrate their effort. After a hearty meal the men set off, each with a dog on a leash (see Figure 3-4). Snow concealed the breathing holes, but dogs could sniff out their approximate locations. When his

Figure 3-4 | Men at a sealing camp on the sea ice in 1923 as they prepare to hunt seals at their breathing holes. Each man has a dog on a leash. (Courtesy of The National Museum of Denmark, Department of Ethnography. Photograph by Knud Rasmussen.)

dog had found such a spot, a man signaled to the others, who came running. Each man attempted to find the hole with a snow probe. The finder of the hole, irrespective of whose dog made the preliminary discovery, became the hole "owner," and with his snow knife he cut the snow away from above the hole. Using a long slender breathing hole probe of antler, he determined the hole's configuration so that he could launch his harpoon at a key point if a seal appeared. The small exposed hole was re-covered with snow to deceive a seal, and a seal indicator was placed in the hole. This indicator consisted of a split section of sinew attached to a sinew thread, with a small piece of swansdown tied at the end. When a seal entered the hole to breathe, the delicate indicator would move. After the indicator was in place, a man made as little noise as possible, because seals have a keen sense of hearing. To keep his feet warm and to muffle any sounds of movement, the man stood on the fur bag in which he had carried his sealing equipment. Next he stuck two peglike harpoon rests in the snow adjacent to the hole. Fur on the harpoon rests muted the noise as he lifted the harpoon to strike a seal. Bending slightly and leaning forward with his hands up his sleeves, the hunter waited with his eyes fixed on the seal indicator; and so he might remain, statuelike, for hours. According to one account, fifteen men bent over breathing holes for eleven hours and harvested a single seal.

If the seal indicator moved, a man grabbed his harpoon in one hand and held the coiled line attached to it in the other hand. He thrust the harpoon as hard as possible into the breathing hole, and the pointed bone harpoon penetrated the seal's body. A basal hole in the harpoon head was fitted to a foreshaft, which was designed to receive the impact of the thrust without breaking the harpoon head. The foreshaft was attached to a wooden shaft with an ice pick at the base. As a seal attempted to escape, the harpoon head toggled in its body in the manner of a button in a buttonhole. The harpoon head was attached through a hole to the handheld line, and the seal was played until it was exhausted. The last step was to enlarge the breathing hole with the ice pick and pull the seal onto the ice. Other hunters soon arrived, and, after making a cut in the seal's underside, the liver and some blubber were removed and eaten raw. After the incision was closed with a wound plug, dogs dragged the seal to camp. Each family shared in the catch. (Their elaborate distribution system is described later.)

Hunters sometimes discovered fresh polar bear tracks on the ice and anxiously followed them after turning their dogs loose. The dogs brought the bear to bay until the hunters arrived. If it was possible the men used a variety of weapons, including lances, bows and arrows, and harpoons, to dispatch the bear. Men and dogs alike were often maimed and sometimes killed. The man who actually killed a bear received the skin, and all of the others shared the highly desirable meat.

By late spring families abandoned the sea ice and sledded to the adjacent coast, where small groups camped together. After erecting their summer tents, they began sealing on the melting sea ice. By then the breathing holes of seals were large, and seals sunned themselves near holes for long periods. Under these circumstances, women and children stood at breathing holes and drove off seals as they surfaced to breathe. Thus hunters at other breathing holes were more likely to make a kill. This, the most rewarding sealing method, was employed as long as ice conditions permitted.

During the summer, and to a lesser degree in the winter, the subsistence pursuits varied depending on the edibles available to a particular band. Band members might collect seagull eggs, fish for lake trout with barbless hooks, fish for char with leisters at stone weirs (see Figure 3-5), hunt musk ox, and pick berries. Yet during the late fall, caribou hunting typically dominated.

As caribou congregated for their southward migration, they were hunted intensively because the animals were fat and their fur made prime garments. One prominent hunting method involved the cooperation of entire families. People camped on high ground near the narrows of lakes habitually crossed by migrating caribou. From a campsite they could see caribou far off and prepared to intercept them. As animals entered the lake water, concealed men launched their kayaks and paddled furiously to lance as many animals as possible. As frightened and wounded caribou approached the opposite shore, women and children appeared on the bank waving skins and imitating the cry of wolves. The confused caribou turned back, only to again face the kayakers. At the end of a hunt each man paddled to his kills, tied them together, and slowly made for the shore. Hundreds of animals could be taken in this manner. Soon after they were beached, children feasted on the eyes as adults ate raw meat. After butchering the harvest, everyone enjoyed cooked meat at leisure and cached excess raw meat beneath piles of stones.

The foregoing accounts of subsistence activities may suggest that these people thrived, especially considering the aptness of their technology, their

Figure 3-5 | Men and a woman fishing at a stone weir. Each person held a line in his or her mouth to string captured fish. (Courtesy Canadian Museum of Contemporary Photography, NFB Collection. Photograph by Doug Wilkinson.)

knowledge as hunters, and their persistence. But this was not the case. If for any reason migrating caribou did not appear at a lake crossing as expected, then the waiting families went hungry. With little or no food at hand, they might be unable to reach another hunting site, and to fish locally could prove unsuccessful. Likewise, when hunting seals on the winter ice, severe storms could force men to remain idle for long periods. If there were few seals locally, the families camped nearby were forced to scatter before they starved. When a family waited too long, a man might not have the strength to hunt at a new sealing site, or the site could prove unrewarding, and they starved. Around 1920, from a population of 259, 25 people starved to death within two years. Starvation led to cannibalism. "Hunger holds terrors; hunger is always accompanied by dreams and visions that may destroy even the strongest man and make him do things he would otherwise detest. So we never condemn those who have eaten human flesh; we have only pity for them" (Rasmussen 1931, 136).

DESCENT, KINSHIP, AND MARRIAGE Who are one's most meaningful relatives? This is a key question regarding one's kinship rights, duties, and obligations. In some societies the closest kinship ties (bonds based on descent) are traced primarily through females (matrilineal), whereas other peoples stress genealogical bonds primarily along the male line (patrilineal). Still others trace kinship ties through both females and males. This patterning prevails in the United States today and among the Netsilik; it is identified as a bilateral descent system. (The bilateral descent system in contemporary America must not be confused with our pattern of typically taking our father's surname. This practice may give added stress to the father's line, but a mother's line may be equally or more important in the lives of some individuals. The Netsilik did not have family names in early historic times.)

Among the Netsilik and contemporary Euro-Americans, close relatives belong to personal kindreds. A *personal kindred* consists of the consanguineal (blood) relatives of a person on his or her generational level, as well as junior and senior generations. In brief, blood relatives on both sides of your family to whom you trace step-by-step kinship ties represent your personal kindred. Significantly, *only* your siblings (biological brothers and sisters) share your personal kindred. The personal kindreds of your cousins differ from your own.

Why is a personal kindred important in many societies with bilateral descent? Most of all, it expands close kinship bonds beyond the nuclear family (a husband, wife, and their children) because it includes extended family members (minimally the families of two siblings). These family types provide a person with a network of meaningful relatives through the female and male lines for security in social, economic, and other contexts. As is typical for the Netsilik, members of one's personal kindred did not live together, nor did they usually assemble as a group. In addition, the members of a personal kindred with whom one never interacted were ignored. However, contrary to the definition of a personal kindred, some Netsilik relatives by marriage (affinal relatives) could be included when they lived with or had other close social ties with the kindred's members. In the Netsilik case, marriage was with a member of one's personal kindred.

We take our kinship terminology (the configuration of words used to identify relatives) for granted and may assume that peoples in other societies share our system. Some do, but most do not, as is evident in this and later chapters. If we begin by acknowledging that no particular kinship terminology is "natural" or "universal," understanding the differences among peoples is less difficult.

In a worldwide study of kinship terms, it was established that the words used by a male ego ("I") for female first cousins provides one useful guide for understanding a particular kinship terminology. A second, equally important, guide is provided by the terms used by a male ego for his parents and their siblings.

In the basic Netsilik cousin terminology (ego's generation), the term for "brother" was extended to all male first cousins, and the word "sister" included

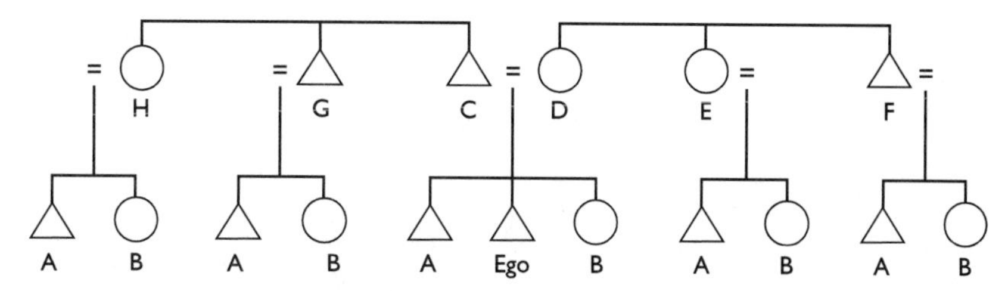

Figure 3-6 | The *basic* early historic Netsilik kinship terminology.

all female first cousins. Obviously, their sibling terms had broader meaning than ours do. In normal conversation a Netsilik did not distinguish between his or her brothers and sisters and cousins, but a person could identify these individuals precisely when necessary (e.g., my biological sister, my father's sister's daughter). Technically, the Netsilik cousin terminology is called Hawaiian because that patterning prevailed in Hawaii, and it came to be identified as a classic type in anthropological writings.

For the parental generation (the first ascending generation above ego), the Netsilik had separate words for mother, mother's sister, father's sister, father, father's brother, and mother's brother. The Netsilik system for the parental generation is termed bifurcate collateral, meaning that collateral lines are separated and termed differently.

The *basic* Netsilik system of kinship terminology appears as Figure 3-6. The symbols in this and all subsequent kinship diagrams follow the same pattern. A circle symbolizes a female; a triangle, a male. Short parallel lines represent marriage. The long horizontal lines and short vertical lines represent descent. The point of departure for examining a diagram is a male "Ego." Each letter represents a different kinship term.

The kinship terminology of these people was more complex than indicated in the figure, and all of the particulars need not be detailed. A number of observations, however, are pertinent. They identified older and younger sisters and brothers by different terms, depending on whether the speaker was male or female. They distinguished between blood relatives and those by marriage; once again the terms varied depending on the gender of the speaker. Nuclear family members were terminologically separated from other relatives except for cousins of the opposite sex, an important exception. We already have seen that uncle and aunt terms on each side of a family were different. Yet ideally a father's brother's relationship with this nephew was emphasized because the boy lived with or near both his father and his father's brother, who formed the core of an extended family. Likewise, relative age was important within an extended family, with younger persons deferring to older ones as reflected in the sibling and some cousin terms. Although it is not recognized in their cousin terminology, a Netsilik ideally married a first cousin. Thus for a man a "sister" became a "wife," and preferably she was a member of the husband's local group. Finally, a married couple typically lived with or near the husband's family (patrilocal marriage residence).

SOCIAL DIMENSIONS Eskimos may not have been the most congenial people in the world, but they had few serious rivals. For one Netsilik band, Jean L. Briggs (1970, 311–366) provided a preliminary review of emotional concepts and their social implications. Eskimos usually are judged as shy or nonaggressive, except for small children, and so it was with the group studied by Briggs. People tended to be bashful, withdrawn without being hostile. In fact, hostility in various forms was strongly disapproved, again with the exception of small children. Ill temper and aggression were associated with Euro-Canadians, who, like small Netsilik children, angered easily, became moody, and had strange ideas. Aspects of ill temper included jealousy, envy, and verbal or physical aggression.

Humor assumed many forms but may be best associated with pervasive laughter, either at oneself or someone else. The context in which people laughed varied, from behavior that was unacceptable or inappropriate to simply amusing. Eskimos who spoke a different dialect or the sounds of a foreign language caused laughter. The English word "affection" also had multiple dimensions. Its most crucial aspect was protectiveness; to feed the hungry, warm someone who was cold, or safeguard a person from harm were its manifestations. This rubric also was reflected in wanting to be with a loved person, as when a husband remained in bed with his wife because she was ill. Then there was happiness. To smile, laugh, and joke were personally satisfying and infectious for others. Happy experiences included play, telling stories, or sharing pleasant company. Happy individuals were worthy.

Given the texture of social life, emotional expressions such as these focused on a relatively small number of persons. The basic social unit was the nuclear family. The different and yet complementary work of women and men within a nuclear family is typical around the world. Netsilik men primarily obtained food because it would be unwise to expose women to the dangers of the hunt. Women cared for children, cooked the food, and processed skins for various purposes. Yet a nuclear family could not be self-sufficient for very long and was fully integrated into an extended family. In the Netsilik case an extended family usually consisted of an elderly father, his married sons, and their children—possibly fifteen individuals—who lived in adjoining tents or snowhouses and aided one another. A number of extended families occupied a winter sealing camp; as many as about fifty persons lived near one another.

At a large camp on the sea ice a dance house was often built, and it symbolized group cohesion. As snowhouses were constructed, four of them could be arranged as a square that became the base for a large, high-domed dance house that partially encompassed the original structures. As the central dome neared completion, portions of the inner walls of the adjoining houses were removed so that the activities of the occupying families were visible to one another at the periphery. The central dome area served as a community hall in which people danced, sang, and observed the seances of shamans.

The mutual dependency between hunters was institutionalized in a system of partnerships illustrated by the sharing of a seal at a large winter camp on the sea ice. In the snowhouse of the successful hunter, his wife butchered a seal into fourteen precise, named units that she distributed. The hunter received little meat but was given choice blubber. A man's sharing partner was unrelated, or distantly related, because to share with near relatives was a normal expectation. The choice of a partner was made by the parents of a boy, and sons tended to replace their fathers in particular partnerships. Thus dyadic (paired) socioeconomic integration spanned generations. A hunter addressed a sharing partner by the term for the portion of a seal that the partner received (e.g., my shoulder, my hindquarters). Behind this and other sharing was potential or real hostility felt toward persons outside of one's extended family. Partnerships tended to mute potential ill feelings between men and bound them to one another for food and thus for survival.

POLITICAL LIFE Concepts such as chief, honored elder, or judge were unknown. To write about Netsilik political life almost seems wrong. A more appropriate label could be "social control." In a strict sense each band was autonomous and had neither a formal leader nor a sense of political unity with another band. To the contrary, bands generally were hostile to one another. In late prehistoric times a state of "war" prevailed among bands that led to murders and massacres. The people were suspicious of strangers and would attack them when it seemed advantageous.

Within a band the leaders were older hunters who guided the activities of their extended families. Typically an extended family represented a bloodline of males, but it could be adjusted to include outsiders, especially by adoption. In this kin-based society, an extended family head was identified as "the one who thinks," but for important decisions the opinions of all adult males were welcome; a consensus was sought. In a decision age distinctions, specific kin ties, and the personalities of those involved were weighed.

Conflict between individuals took varied forms. A common means to express displeasure was to withdraw from a vexing situation and thereby avoid potential conflict. Gossip and ridicule also were powerful means to induce conformity, especially considering how few people lived together. Personal differences likewise could result in fistfights or in formal song duels (explained subsequently); in an extreme case, a deviant might be killed. The reactions of individuals varied widely in what appeared to be similar situations, such as a theft or an insult. One man could ignore such an episode, whereas another might contemplate the perpetrator's murder. In addition, a grudge could be harbored for many years before erupting. The cases that follow are drawn largely from the fieldwork of Geert van den Steenhoven (1959).

To avoid potential disharmony in a camp, newcomers were obligated to obtain permission to live there from those already established. This rule may have applied primarily to strangers. In one instance a man and his family from farther north moved near Pelly Bay. Although the residents distrusted outsiders, they permitted the family to remain there. They laughed at the man and abused him nonetheless. They knocked him over as he hunted at seal breathing holes. They poked fun at him for not having local relatives, and before long he and his family left. In his anger he performed sorcery to cause starvation at Pelly Bay, and many of those who had laughed at him slowly starved to death. As a postscript the sorcerer later died of starvation.

Songs were popular in many contexts. There were songs for hunting, joking, and magic; however, derisive songs were highlighted. The community hall at a winter camp typically was the setting for a derisive song exchange. A "song duel" could be either spontaneous or prearranged, with no clear-cut division between the two. One man sang and danced and might beat a tambourinelike drum as he poked fun at another man. The victim sang in response, and the man whom the audience applauded the most became the informal winner. To win approval, the text of a song might be based on fact, such as a theft, or on an accusation of avarice. Being henpecked was another subject for a song, as was murder. In addition to their value as pure entertainment, these exchanges represented social criticism and served to release tensions between individuals. At the same time, songs could mend ruptured friendships. But all exchanges did not end well; a "boxing" match might result. In this case the opponents faced one another and alternated in delivering blows, but neither man attempted to defend himself. The winner was the man who continued to strike blows longer.

The sanctioned murder of an adult resulted when band welfare was considered in jeopardy. In one instance an angry man killed another without provocation. Subsequently, he threatened everyone and wounded his wife with a knife. The man's instability posed a threat, and his logical executioner, in Netsilik thinking, was his brother, the oldest family member. The older brother told the murderer that he planned to kill him and asked how he wanted to die—with a knife or a bullet or by hanging. The victim chose a bullet and was shot to death (see Figure 3-7). Likewise, a sorcerer might be killed for common good. For killings of this nature, "execution" is an acceptable label. The most common cause for murder, however, was when one man desired the wife of another man and killed for her. A woman sometimes married two men (polyandry), and one husband might kill the other. Occasionally a woman killed her husband, in one case because the husband was hot-tempered. Surprisingly, in historic times the relatives of a murder victim did not seek blood revenge, but judging from legends that practice had prevailed in late prehistoric times. In sum, and admittedly the evidence is not the best, social control customarily was achieved by individuals and families, not by band members as a collective.

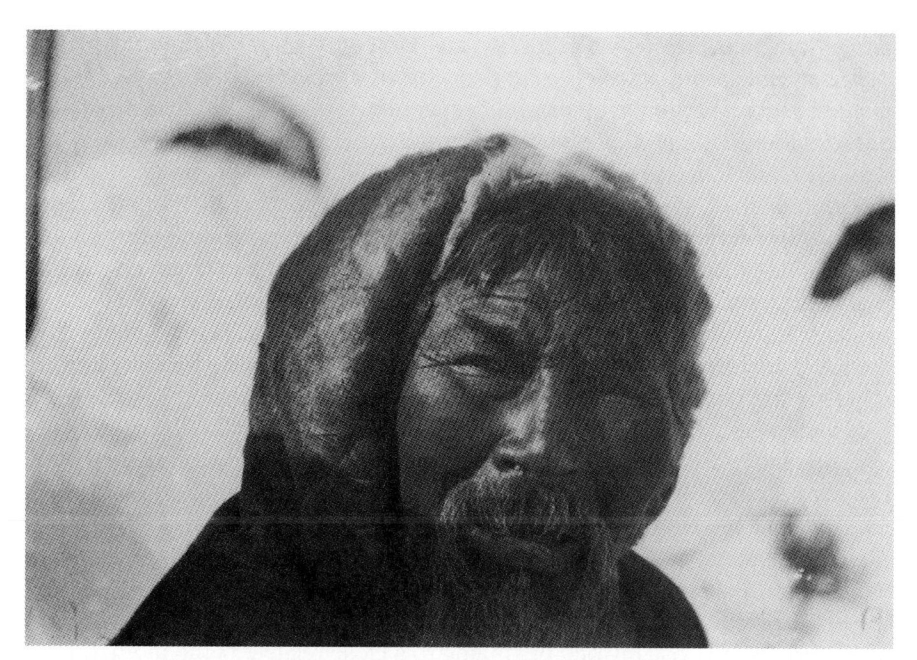

Figure 3-7 | This Netsilik man shot and killed his brother, who was a menace to the group. (Courtesy of The National Museum of Denmark, Department of Ethnography. Photograph by Knud Rasmussen.)

RELIGION A minimal definition of religion, "the belief in Spiritual Beings," was proposed by the first modern professional anthropologist, Edward B. Tylor (1871, 23). Among the many more detailed definitions, the one by Melford E. Spiro (1966, 96) is notable. He defined religion as "an institution consisting of culturally patterned interaction with culturally postulated superhuman beings." Within the parameters of either definition, Netsilik religion was quite different from what a modern Euro-American might expect. The Netsilik did not have an integrated body of dogma and ritual, structures devoted to religious purposes, or an annual calendar of ceremonial events, and priests (full-time specialists in supernatural matters) were unknown. Notwithstanding, religion was convoluted and complicated; it dominated their lives.

The conceptual basis for religion is encapsulated in accounts about the world's creation as summarized early in this chapter. In daily life the Sea Goddess, Weather God, and Moon God were the most powerful deities. Additionally, a host of greater and lesser spirits existed, and supernatural forces generally were hostile toward humankind. Fear more than solace characterized their religion. Amulets were thought to aid their owners, young or old, female or male, to gain protection from negative forces and thereby foster prosperity. Within each amulet resided a beneficial spirit force; the physical object was not important in itself. Amulets might be animal teeth, small bones, or miniature artifacts. They were attached to a parka or to an amulet belt. Some amulets were thought to produce hunting success and to promote physical skills. Others fostered personal well-being, and a third group protected one from evil and aided in shamanistic activities. One individual had eighty amulets. As Asen Balikci (1970, 203) noted, "[a]mulet spirits clustered around each person like a ring of supernatural protectors and helpers. They were individually owned and aided only their owner." Closely akin were magic words that were covert and highly personal and that worked to achieve a specific goal. These words were either learned from one's father or obtained by payment to a shaman. They could not be heard by anyone else and were said in secret or when alone. Such words helped to ensure success in caribou hunting or in fishing for a particular species.

A man derived his strength, health, and power from his immortal soul, usually conceived as an intangible replica of his physical body. Little information is available about the personal souls of women. Despite the positive qualities of a personal soul, it was vulnerable to evil forces. In one means used to avoid harm, a shaman would perform rituals at the time of a male's birth to remove his personal soul from his body. The soul was magically placed beneath a soapstone lamp, usually one belonging to a close relative of the mother. Here his personal soul remained and strengthened.

Each person, female and male, possessed name souls based on personal names; names were not identified with gender. The greater the number of sequential personal names, the greater the protection. The inventory of traditional names varied a great deal. Examples include "the unlucky one," "leister," "butterfly," "the round one," and "the one who just shit." Many names for males especially were thought to make them more manly, and for a woman they helped to ensure the health of her children.

Ordinary and extraordinary happenings in Netsilik life were bound by a rigid network of taboos. A *taboo* is something that is both sacred and forbidden. Taboos had become a major basis for the religious system. To ignore or to break a taboo invited disaster for individuals or potentially for an entire band. In the broadest terms, a land–sea dichotomy was fundamental and best reflected in the hunting of caribou as opposed to seals. To mix edibles from the land and the sea was antipathetical to the Sea Goddess and was surrounded by innumerable taboos. Taboos applied not only to people and animals but also to key localities in the subsistence round. A specific site for hunting caribou, or a stone weir for fishing, could be sacred and enveloped by restrictions that promoted successful harvests.

The rituals surrounding the harvest of a seal on the winter ice illustrate one set of taboos. The soul of a seal was thought to be highly sensitive to how its body was treated. To pacify a soul and help ensure its reincarnation into the body of another seal, a particular procedure was followed. Clean snow was placed on the floor of the snowhouse before a seal was taken inside for butchering. The animal was given a drink of water, and as long as it remained there adults were prohibited from most routine work. The skull of each seal was kept. As the people left the site, the accumulated skulls were faced in the direction that the people would travel. These and other conventions were rigidly observed. Innumerable taboos likewise were associated with caribou and polar bear kills. By observing taboos, some of the stresses in food-getting were reduced, but success was never assured.

Although adults in general had the individual ability to deal with supernatural forces, two major groups of specialized practitioners dominated. Those associated with lesser powers, head lifters, had no formal training. Their goals were to establish what taboo had been broken to cause illness in a family and to determine where game was located. Customarily a wife stretched out on her back, and her husband tied a thong around her head. He questioned the ghost (helping spirit) of one close relative after another to identify the broken taboo. The husband pulled upward on the thong. If his wife's head was "light," the answer to a particular question was negative; if "heavy," the head indicated a positive response. Thus evil spirits were forced to abandon a sick person, while helpful spirits aided in the food quest. This technique was used only when the aid of family ghosts was sought.

Shamans, as part-time specialists in supernatural matters, focused on spirits as individuals. Unlike all other persons, shamans integrated the natural and supernatural spheres at the highest level. A shaman's daily routine was the same as for other males, but he stood apart because of his superior abilities. A boy identified as having potential to become a shaman was instructed by a practicing shaman. The apprentice was constrained by many food taboos and prohibited from having sexual intercourse. As he began to receive visions of spirits, a snowhouse was built for his further instruction. Here he learned secret words from his instructor, and his parents presented him with a shaman's headdress and belt. The power of a shaman focused on one group of protective spirits that he attempted to control; such a spirit was called a *tunraq*. After completing his long and arduous training, the apprentice was given a tunraq by his teacher; but initially the spirit controlled the novice. He became a practicing shaman within a band only after he learned to control this spirit.

As a shaman aged, additional spirits came to his aid, and still others were gifts from other shamans. Some of these supernaturals were easily manipulated, whereas others were unreliable and potentially dangerous. The latter might rage out of control and in their fury cause illness and death. These dangers were real enough, yet another class of spirits were especially hostile toward people, the *tupiliq*. The tupiliq was round to the point of bursting its blood-filled body and was inherently evil. Thus the greatest challenges confronting a shaman were to cope with tunraqs gone astray and with tupiliqs.

One primary function of a shaman was to counteract hostile spirits after a broken taboo, which was viewed as the cause of all illness. His goal was to drive one or more evil spirits from the patient's body. Normally the rituals were held in the victim's dwelling with an audience in attendance. After the lamps were extinguished, the shaman covered himself with a caribou skin. He called for a protective spirit to enter his body through his mouth. After the spirit arrived, the shaman went into a trance. He began to speak in his secret vocabulary to remove the tupiliqs from the patient with the aid of his helpful spirits, but the tupiliqs hid outside. The audience lured them to return. When they appeared, the shaman fought them with a snow knife. He killed as many as possible, as evidenced by the blood on his hands. If the patient died, however, the reason was that the shaman had failed to kill all of the evil spirits. This became the explanation for failure to heal.

Miraculous travels to the underworld and to the moon and encounters with monsters provided evidence of a shaman's capacity to go far beyond the ordinary. Shamans also called forth their spirit helpers to attract game, to control the weather, and to avert famines. In situations such as these, as well as when curing, public confession of taboo breaking played an intimate part in shamanistic efforts to rectify the imbalance in nature or among people. Arbitration clearly was a shaman's major function. Another was to resolve differences between individuals, most often arising from envy and jealousy. Sometimes shamans used their power for personal goals and thus behaved in an antisocial manner. For example, a shaman who was sexually attracted to an unwilling woman might threaten her with illness to achieve his end.

To maintain and reinforce their positive authority, shamans singly or in competitions gave public demonstrations of their powers. To apparently wound oneself with a spear and thereby bleed or to suddenly grow a beard impressed an audience. And so it is elsewhere in the world when an audience does not know the basis for the trickery. Deception of this nature was real among the Netsilik, but to identify shamans as simply tricksters is mistaken. They believed in their powers, as did other Netsilik. In a sense shamans were incipient psychologists and scientists as they sought to understand cause and effect in the world.

LIFE CYCLE An ethnographic account of any people is enhanced by an overview of the lives of individuals. The transitions from one stage to the next deserve special attention. Passage ceremonies (rites of passage) in particular acknowledge changes in status that permanently alter the relationships of an individual with members of the greater community. Birth, puberty, marriage, old age, and death are prominent examples. As the Netsilik life cycle is compared with those of peoples described in later chapters, the differences in Native American lifeways will become abundantly apparent.

As the time of a birth approached for a pregnant Netsilik woman, a small snowhouse was built for her in which she remained alone for about four days. Isolated and unassisted, she gave birth on her knees. During an especially difficult delivery, she recited various personal names (name souls). When delivery followed the calling forth of a particular name, it meant that a specific name soul had entered the body of the newborn. The mother cut the umbilical cord with a special knife and cleaned the neonate with a special piece of skin that became a potent amulet. The baby soon was placed in the pouch at the back of the mother's parka. For the next month the mother and baby moved into a new snowhouse built for them. Sometimes she was visited by females, but she could eat only certain foods and had to observe many other taboos for the next year.

Female infanticide prevailed widely among Eskimos, but the Netsilik rate was unusually high. Apparently as many as half of the Netsilik females born were killed or permitted to die. An unnamed and unwanted baby girl might be suffocated, placed in the entrance of a snowhouse to freeze to death, or buried alive in a shallow grave. The name souls of these dead were thought to seek reincarnation. A baby named before or soon after birth was permitted to live. The father usually made the infanticide decision. An abandoned baby could be adopted by anyone who found it alive, and a newborn was not killed if the baby was promised in marriage.

Why was the rate of female infanticide so high? It was not because children were unloved, as will soon be apparent, or because these were a cruel and heartless people. One reason may be that women made no significant and direct contribution to food getting. Another is that local group solidarity increased if women did not become the wives of outsiders; first-cousin marriages and female infanticide strengthened a local group. Betrothing an offspring before she or he was born to a near relative likewise furthered group cohesion. Still other variables have been noted. Not only did girls not become hunters, but when a mother nursed a girl for the usual two or three years, the woman was less likely to conceive and was thus possibly unable to bear a male offspring. During famines families could not support a newborn. Likewise, when a starving family was on the move, any child, male or female, who could not keep up with the others was abandoned to die. More formal child killings also are reported. In one instance a mother in her fury stabbed her son after he broke her valuable soapstone pot; the child soon died.

Life and death decisions such as these were a family concern, not a matter of religion or morality. The physical survival of a family had precedence over the life of an individual. Thus there were many more boys than girls. Nonetheless, the adult sex ratio was nearly balanced. One major reason was that numerous men died in hunting accidents. Then, too, men were more likely to die from starvation or to commit suicide than were women.

An Eskimo stereotype is that small children were neither punished nor told "no," an exaggeration with more than a grain of truth. Briggs (1970) recorded many insightful particulars about traditional child rearing when she lived with a small isolated group of families in the 1960s. She found that young children often raged, screamed, cried easily, and were unreasonably demanding. The adult reaction was to appease them, to respond by amused laughter, but not to be critical. Little children had "no mind," meaning that they were incapable of reasoning. They began to gain this capacity as they learned to walk, to talk, and to remember. A child soon learned that a parent's raised eyebrows indicated "yes" or a wrinkled nose meant "no." As a child approached the age of six, an expanding ability to reason was expected. Instruction was by example, and to succeed or to fail in a task produced laughter from adults. Children and adults alike commonly used a phrase comparable to "just a minute," rather than saying no.

In the life of a small child, the birth of a sibling could be initially traumatic. To nurse on demand and to be carried in the back of a mother's parka had provided comfort and security. As a small child competed with a newborn, the mother distracted and comforted the child. The child in turn soon became more self-aware and self-sufficient. Maturing years brought absorption in solitary play and behavior comparable to "let's pretend." By the age of ten a girl helped her mother in meaningful ways, and by the age of twelve a boy was becoming a hunter.

A girl's menarche (first menstruation) involved innumerable taboos, as was the case for a woman in childbirth. Netsilik women did not have what modern Americans would consider a regular menstrual cycle. The reason was that a woman of childbearing age was usually either pregnant or nursing. When a woman did menstruate, she made the fact known to adults in a camp because she was regarded as impure. She stayed in her dwelling, avoided talking about game animals, and observed other prohibitions deemed essential for personal and community good.

In societies around the world, life tends to focus on birth, marriage, and death with differential emphasis. For the Netsilik, complications centered on marriage. Problems that contributed to the complexity were the scope of female infanticide, accidental deaths among adult males, deaths from starvation, low population numbers, and the physical proximity of a potential mate. Ideally a mother arranged a betrothal of a son soon after his birth to a young girl or to one as yet unborn. This was not always possible, and some marriages could not be arranged until a male was older. Additional alternatives existed. Widows and widowers were potential mates. Another man's wife might be stolen, or on rare occasions one man might kill another and take his wife. Plural marriages (polygamy), although uncommon, added another dimension of complexity. A woman might have more than one husband (polyandry) because of the scarcity of women, or an outstanding hunter might have more than one wife (polygyny); women were attracted to a man partially because of the security he provided as a hunter.

Marriages preferably were between first cousins, as described previously. A girl was expected to be married by the age of fifteen. For a male the age was about twenty because so many years were required for him to become a skilled hunter. A marriage ceremony did not exist, but a woman was expected to have property of her own, most important a soapstone cooking pot and soapstone lamp. The bride with her possessions customarily joined the family of her husband, or else the couple lived nearby (patrilocal marriage residence). Marriages were unstable until an offspring was born, and a woman could have had numerous trial marriages. A young husband continued to hunt and fish with relatives and friends in the same area in which he was raised, an obvious economic advantage.

A Netsilik couple was typically loving and caring, although having sexual relations outside of marriage was institutionalized. The arrangement was typically made by men who were friends or partners. Their presumption was that the wives would cooperate, which was usually the case. Concurrently, wives might informally arrange an exchange but leave the formalities to their husbands. Sexual desire may have produced many such arrangements, but a practical aspect existed. For instance, when a man planned a long trip and his wife was pregnant, he could arrange to take his partner's wife to perform womanly obligations on the trail. Wife exchange could be for a night or for a lifetime. A permanent exchange of spouses might result, or the practice might lead to jealousy, bitterness, and sometimes murder.

In the routine of adult life, food and children dominated, with the specter of death from starvation ever present. In this regard it is essential to realize that these people could not meaningfully stockpile food from one year to the next. As a result each subsistence year began anew, irrespective of how productive or poor the previous year had been. The trials of living did not lead to personal bitterness and dissatisfaction with life. Quite to the contrary, social geniality prevailed; warmth, good humor, and laughter dominated. Admittedly, jealousy, envy, and animosities could and did exist beneath the surface and could erupt in violence, to the travail of all.

As Knud Rasmussen (1931) noted, men dominated in marriages, but wives were not passive; quite the opposite. Wives not only were outspoken but also appear to have been more mentally agile in arguments. A couple did not customarily use given names when talking with one another. Pet names prevailed. These included "my new wife" and "my dear little elder brother." Likewise, children were called by names of affection, such as "my bit of a child," and children addressed their parents in a similar manner. In addition, an intimate sign of affection, nose rubbing, was a form of kissing between a man and woman or an adult and a child.

Living in a snowhouse or other structure was confining because the dwellings were small. Each person, young or old, was allotted a little space toward the back of a residence where people lounged and slept. Inside, at the rear of a dwelling, garments and equipment were stored. At the front were food and household items. As vividly conveyed by Briggs (1970), family members were inordinately considerate of one another, with the exception of small children. Bedtime was decided by the man of the house, who undressed and slipped into the sleeping skins, followed by all the others. This was the time when a man talked about the distant or recent past, times of trauma and times of joy, as family members fell asleep.

A death in a family could be planned, as in the case of infanticide, or it could be devastating, as when a hunter–husband–father died in an accident. Additionally, deaths of adult males from suicide were common. Balikci (1970, 163–172) examined thirty-five cases of suicide in a population of less than three hundred people. He found that there was about one suicide each eighteen months, an extremely high rate. Most suicides were committed by married men between twenty-four and fifty years of age who had children. A man was most likely to hang himself as a result of personal distress, such as the violent death of someone close to him, personal illness, or other misfortune. These data are contrary to the suicide pattern associated with Eskimos in which older people killed themselves because they felt useless; comparatively few Netsilik suicides were of this nature. Balikci suggests that Netsilik religious beliefs best explain most suicides. They believed that the manner of death influenced afterlife. The soul of a person who died a violent death, including suicide, dwelled in the most desirable afterworld.

After a person died the soul lingered with the body for a number of days, and household members were prohibited from normal work. They feared that the soul would become an evil spirit and do harm. During this period of mourning the people observed numerous taboos, such as not combing their hair or feeding dogs. In the winter, following the mourning period a body was sledded out on the ice by close relatives and left there without ceremony. During the summer a corpse was placed on the tundra with one stone at the head and another at the feet, and the person's earthly possessions might be left nearby. After disposing of a body, the people of a camp moved elsewhere. A soul was thought to be immortal, and it journeyed to one of three afterworlds.

The souls of notable hunters, especially those who died violent deaths, and of women who had suffered the pain of having large and beautiful tattoos went to a place high in the sky in which life was good and they never aged. Deep beneath the earth existed another favorable afterworld entered by the same persons, but here the seasons were reversed. Finally, women without exceptional tattoos and lazy hunters existed just beneath the surface of the earth, where they huddled with closed eyes and hanging heads and with only butterflies as food.

Historical Developments

History is young in the Netsilik region. Their homeland is in the far north, and the adjoining seas are ice clogged most of the year. The first European explorer to venture there was John Ross, the leader of a British expedition. In 1829 he set out to find a northwest passage to the Orient. He failed in this effort, although he did discover the magnetic pole and the Netsilik. The passage was first navigated by the Norwegian Roald Amundsen in 1903–1906, and he was the first person to describe the Netsilik in reasonable detail. By then Netsilik life had begun to change as commercial whalers ventured to northwestern Hudson Bay in the 1880s. Many Netsilik soon moved east from their homeland to Repulse Bay to take advantage of trading opportunities.

The people were amazed at the wealth of artifacts abroad the ships of explorers and whalers. Most of all, they coveted iron to replace the stone blades for their weapons and tools. The amount of wood on ships astounded them. In addition to iron and wood, they were anxious to obtain rifles and ammunition. Cloth was desired for summer garments, and tobacco and tea became desirable but previously unknown stimulants. Matches, exotic foods, kerosene-burning stoves, and metal containers likewise were greatly appreciated. As imports became widely available, the people gave up their traditional material culture with little hesitation. They were technological empiricists. By the early 1950s the Netsilik had abandoned their traditional way of life, and sooner or later all of the Netsilik were drawn into the fur trade.

Cooperative seal hunts on the sea ice declined in the 1920s as rifles became more readily available; a lone man with a gun could also harvest caribou throughout the year. The introduction of gill nets made fishing easier and more productive. A gill net looks rather like a tennis net with floats attached at the top and sinkers at the bottom. When a fish of appropriate size swam into a net, it was held in the mesh by its gills. Their traditional fish spear (leister) required the presence of a fisherman, whereas a gill net "worked" all of the time. With changes in hunting and fishing methods, food sharing was confined to near relatives. Likewise the earlier dependence on spirit aids, amulets, and magic in the food quest declined; hunting and fishing became mundane concerns. Yet to obtain rifles, nets, and other imports from the south, men were obligated to trap fur animals, especially white fox, and as a by-product of hunting seals for food, the skins were sold to traders. They obtained these animals on an individual basis, and each man kept his earnings.

Effective social control over the Netsilik by outsiders gained momentum in the 1930s. The Roman Catholics built a mission at Pelly Bay in 1935 that included a small store stocked with staples. It was not unusual for missionaries in isolated communities in the far north to operate trading posts. By the 1940s most Netsilik had become Christians. Missionaries were respected and were probably feared as rich and powerful white shamans. The conversion to Christianity was rapid and met no serious opposition. A major contribution of missionaries in the Canadian Arctic, beginning in 1876, was the development of an Eskimo (Inuit) syllabary. As a result literacy was rapidly achieved outside of a formal educational context. This syllabary in a modified form continues to be widely used in newspapers, as well as government and mission publications.

The Hudson's Bay Company established a post at Gjoa Haven in 1927, and a Royal Canadian Mounted Police (RCMP) station was founded at Spence Bay in 1949. In the early 1950s the Canadian government for the first time launched serious programs to maintain sovereignty in the far north. Concurrently, the influence of missionaries and company traders began to decline. Many Canadian outposts were centered at or near Distant Early Warning stations (DEW Line radar units). A radar station and airfield were built near Pelly Bay between 1955 and 1957. Local Netsilik built houses at Pelly Bay from materials retrieved from the DEW Line dump site. Likewise snowmobiles would soon replace dog teams; the "iron dog" only "ate" when it worked (see Figure 3-8). As a result, hunting pressure on caribou and seals declined as the need for dog food diminished.

By the early 1960s the people lived primarily at Gjoa Haven, Pelly Bay (Kugaaruk), and Spence Bay (Taloyoak). Canadian government programs began to make an expanding impact on Netsilik life. Each family with children

Figure 3-8 | A hunter from Pelly Bay (Kugaaruk) searching the sea ice for seals in June 1997. (Photograph courtesy of David F. Pelly.)

received monthly Family Allowance funds (now Child Tax Credit), depending on the number of offspring and their ages (see Figure 3-9). This was a major source of income for these cash-starved communities. In addition, anyone over sixty-five years of age received old-age assistance, and numerous welfare programs aided needy families. Schools, nursing stations, and family homes were built in the three major communities. Families also received electricity, heat, and water delivery and had waste facilities as municipal services at low cost. Jobs maintaining the infrastructure increasingly dominated the local economy, but most families continued to hunt, fish, and trap for a living. By the 1980s animal-rights advocates in Europe and the United States rejected the use of *all* animal pelts and skins in any context, a devastating blow to the local economy. Likewise Westerners successfully campaigned to stop the use of jaw traps because of the suffering of captured animals. With these developments, combined with the price fluctuations for pelts and skins, the people lost control of their economy in the world marketplace.

As aboriginal conditions and those in the relatively recent past are compared, one conclusion is self-evident: traditional artifact production as a means of making a living had nearly disappeared. Manufactured products from the "south" had won in the "north." The most important locally produced artifacts are for the art and tourist markets. If nothing else, this demonstrates modern Inuit technological adaptability. Before the arrival of whites, as mentioned previously, the Netsilik made cooking pots and lamps from a local source of soap-

Figure 3-9 | Spence Bay (Taloyoak) children in 1999. (Photograph courtesy of David F. Pelly.)

stone. It is the primary raw material for their art and craft productions. From 1948 to 1962, the Canadian artist James Houston encouraged the Inuit of the eastern Arctic to produce soapstone carvings for sale. Some Netsilik began to participate, although the effort did not have a major impact at Gjoa Haven until about 1970. By 1990 about nine hundred people lived there, most of whom were Netsilik. A few years later thirty-two men and seventeen women were soapstone carvers; for ten men it was a full-time occupation. To obtain soapstone located some ninety miles away required a number of snowmobile trips each year to the source, and men often attempted to combine quarrying with caribou hunts. Soapstone was processed with hand tools and electrical equipment. The inspiration for a carving was typically drawn from oral traditions, especially legends. Carvers attempted to impart the spiritual qualities of their subjects—human, animal, or the combination. Thus the basis for their art was intimately associated with traditional cultural knowledge. Carvings by the best-known Netsilik artists are in museum collections and are sold at galleries in Canada and elsewhere.

In numerous Canadian Inuit settlements, tourism makes a significant contribution to local economies. The three primary Netsilik communities, however, are among the most isolated ones in Nunavut, and they attract relatively few tourists because of the expense of travel. For instance, in 2000, a seven-day guided kayak tour at Pelly Bay cost about C$4000 per person, including air fare from Winnipeg (see Figure 3-10).

Figure 3-10 | The settlement of Pelly Bay (Kugaaruk) in 1997. (Photograph courtesy of David F. Pelly.)

Recent Changes

Historically the most momentous development occurred on April 1, 1999. It was then that the Inuit in the eastern portion of the Northwest Territories, including the Netsilik, obtained their own territory, Nunavut (our land). (A Canadian territory is subject to greater federal control than a province.) The Nunavut area represents about one-fifth of the Canadian land surface and in 1999 had a population of about 28,000, some 85 percent of whom were Inuit, who lived in twenty-seven widely dispersed communities (see Figure 3-11). The federal start-up costs were C$1.1 billion over fifteen years, beginning in 1993. This payment to the Inuit of Nunavut is part of the land claims settlement.

The creation of Nunavut was a long and involved process. The final result, however, produced the most just land claim settlement with an aboriginal population anywhere in the world. Nunavut was created by federal legislation and remains Crown land, but the residents will share in any royalties from gas, oil, and mineral development. The Inuit have the right to harvest wildlife throughout the settlement area, and they have comanagement rights with respect to wildlife. The territorial capital, with a population of about 4000, is at Iqaluit (Frobisher Bay). In February 1999, the first election was held for the new legislative assembly. Political parties do not exist; government is by consensus. Eighty-eight percent of eligible voters in the twenty-seven communi-

Figure 3-11 | Patrick Qaggutaq, a Pelly Bay (Kugaaruk) resident in 1997. (Photograph courtesy of David F. Pelly.)

ties turned out for the first election to select a nineteen-member legislative assembly. Eighteen men and one woman were elected. Paul Okalik, at thirty-four years of age, became the first leader of the assembly, the youngest premier to hold the office in all of Canada.

Skeptics doubt that Nunavut will succeed as planned. The overwhelming dependence of the new government on federal funds suggests that federal control may prove to be far greater than the Inuit anticipate. Most of the people have a relatively poor formal education, which leads to doubts about their capacity to manage the day-to-day administration for many years to come. The cost of living, unemployment rate, and suicide rates are higher than for any other sector of Canada. Then, too, drug and alcohol addiction rates are alarming—a contributing factor to high unemployment. Finally, teenage pregnancies are much higher than the national average. None of this bodes well for the future. The question is not whether Nunavut will succeed, but how much greater control the Inuit will have over the next decade.

A major and immediate problem confronting the political leaders is the allocation of economic resources. In the 1970s, as they began to negotiate a land claims settlement, it appeared that the exploitation of gas, oil, and mineral wealth was imminent in the region. The Inuit were deeply concerned about the environmental impact, and they built Inuit–government comanagement safeguards into their land claim administration. Substantial development of these resources have yet to materialize, but this regulatory aspect of land claims is expensive and necessary. Equally important, with the international economic downturn in the late 1990s, the Canadian government is unable to provide supplementary monies for all the provincial and territorial governments. Education and health care funding, for example, is barely adequate, and the unemployment rate is about 30 percent.

The standard of living declined in part because the animal-rights advocates in Europe and the United States destroyed the market for animal pelts and skins for the international market. Apart from local craft items for sale beyond the settlements, local pelts and skins were the primary marketable products for the greater Canadian and non-Canadian markets. By 2000 the situation was changing, as animal products again were becoming fashionable for garments on an international basis. One encouraging development for Nunavut residents is a recent agreement among the European Union, Canada, and Russia not to impose trade restrictions on fur-bearing land-mammal pelts. Presumably this will mean that Nunavut hunters and trappers will once again be able to market animal products and be able to live off the land more effectively than in the recent past.

Additional Sources

The best book-length presentation about the variability in aboriginal Eskimo culture unquestionably is by Edward M. Weyer (1932). The most durable popular and authoritative discussion of Eskimos is by Kaj Birket-Smith (1936, 1959, 1971 editions). Early accounts about Eskimos by explorers and others are examined in two editions of my book on the subject (Oswalt, 1979, 1999). The best overview about North American Eskimo prehistory, ethnography, and history into the early 1980s is the widely available *Arctic* volume of the new *Handbook of North American Indians* edited by David Damas (1984) and published by the Smithsonian Institution.

It was not until 1923 that Knud Rasmussen (1931), of Greenlandic Eskimo and Danish descent, compiled his wonderful, yet eclectic, baseline Netsilik ethnography. The second seminal study to focus on traditional life was by Asen Balikci (1970, 1989) based on fieldwork from 1959 to 1965. His book is a key source for the presentation in this chapter. Balikci's ethnographic films of the Netsilik are the best for any group of Native Americans. A third major study, based on fieldwork in the 1960s, is by Jean L. Briggs (1970), whose presentation about traditional family life is superior. The monograph by Geert van den Steenhoven (1959) is the best source concerning traditional Netsilik legal concepts. The key presentation about Eskimo kinship terminology is by Marc G. Stevenson (1997).

Selected Bibliography

Amundsen, Roald. 1908. *The North West Passage.* 2 vols. London.

Balikci, Asen. 1970. *The Netsilik Eskimo.* Garden City, NY. (Other edition: 1989).

Birket-Smith, Kaj. 1959. *The Eskimos.* London. (Other editions: London, 1936; New York, 1971).

Briggs, Jean. 1970. *Never in anger.* Cambridge, MA.

Damas, David, ed. 1984. *Arctic.* Vol. 5, *Handbook of North American Indians.* Washington, DC.

Oswalt, Wendell H. 1979. *Eskimos and explorers.* Novato, CA. (Other edition: 1999).

Rasmussen, Knud. 1931. *The Netsilik Eskimo.* Report of the Fifth Thule Expedition 1921–24, Vol. 7, pts. 1–2. Lincoln, NE.

Ross, John. 1835. *Narrative of a second voyage in search of a North-West Passage.* London.

Spiro, Melford E. 1966. Religion. In *Anthropological approaches to the study of religion,* edited by Michael Banton, 85–126. London.

Stevenson, Marc G. 1997. *Inuit, whalers, and cultural persistence.* Toronto.

Svensson, Tom G. 1995. Ethnic art in the northern Fourth World. *Études/Inuit/Studies* 19(1) 69–102.

Tylor, Edward B. 1871. *Primitive culture.* Vol. 1. London.

Van de Velde, Franz, Trinette S. Constandes-Westermann, Cornelius H. W. Remie, and Raymond R. Newell. 1993. One hundred and fifteen years of Arviligjuarmiut demography, central Canadian Arctic. *Arctic Anthropology* 30(2) 1–45.

van den Steenhoven, Geert. 1959. *Legal concepts among the Netsilik Eskimos of Pelly Bay N.W.T.* (Report no. NCRC-59-3.) Northern Co-ordination and Research Centre, Department of Northern Affairs and Natural Resources.

Wenzel, George. 1991. *Animal rights, human rights ecology, economy and ideology in the Canadian Arctic.* London.

Weyer, Edward M. 1932. *The Eskimos.* New Haven, CT.

4 The Chipewyan: Subarctic Hunters

Before the flood, caribou were easy to hunt with the bow and arrow, but after it the arrows could not pierce them: it was just as if they were nothing but bone. The hunters had to aim at their heads and hit a vein to make them bleed to death. Then the raven said, "We cannot kill the caribou because they are only bone," and while all others were asleep it stayed up and made magic all through the night. It was the raven that gave the caribou their present form with flesh on their bones, through which the arrows could go. After that they were easy to hunt. This is what we know about the raven.

A myth about caribou and the raven.
(Birket-Smith 1930, 88)

THE CHIPEWYAN HAVE been chosen to represent the Subarctic culture area for cultural, ecological, historical, and social reasons. They are one of the numerous Athapaskan tribes that inhabit interior Alaska and northwestern Canada. Most Subarctic peoples depended on caribou and fish for food, and the Chipewyan were reasonably typical in this respect, although caribou were far more important in their diet. We know more about them than about most other Northern Athapaskans largely because of historical chance. They were reasonably well described by Europeans soon after historic contact, and beginning in 1960 a thorough study was made of a modern community. Furthermore, there are comparatively recent ethnohistorical studies and additional field research among these people. We do not have information of comparable scope for any other Northern Athapaskan tribe. The sociocultural reasons for describing the Chipewyan are equally significant because their lifeway was considered one of the least complex reported for North American Indians. Typically described as a band-level society, they formed temporary groups of extended families and exhibited marked local variability in social organization. Furthermore, the Chipewyan provide an opportunity to analyze the impact of the fur trade, which changed them from caribou hunters to beaver and marten trappers.

Chipewyan (chip-uh-WI-uhn) is a Cree word meaning "pointed skins," a reference to the dangling point at the front and back of the poncholike garment worn by men. These people called themselves Dene, meaning "humans," and were unified on the basis of language and lifestyle. The major subgroups were territorial and based on the exploitation of regional caribou herds. By the time of contact with Europeans, the Chipewyan possibly numbered forty-five hundred, one of the lowest Native American population densities.

The Chipewyan language belongs to the Nadene linguistic family and the Athapaskan subfamily. The Nadene are concentrated from near the Bering Strait to the western shore of Hudson Bay. They were primarily inland peoples. Some Nadene spread south to form the Pacific group concentrated in sections of coastal Oregon and California. Another cluster settled in the Southwest. The close cultural and linguistic bonds between the Chipewyan and Yellowknife lead some modern ethnologists to consider them as a single people, as I do in this book.

The early historic range of the Chipewyan is shown in Figure 4-1. Chipewyan country is a vast expanse of tundra extending as much as seven hundred miles from east to west and nearly six hundred miles from north to south. The climate is continental, with long, cold winters and short, hot summers. The extremes range from the high 80s °F in summer to −60°F in winter. Everywhere networks of waterways—foaming as well as hesitant streams and rivers, great lakes, and countless smaller lakes—interlace. Barren rocks show obvious signs of glacial wear on their smoothed or striated surfaces. Results of glacial action are especially evident in the north, where rolling masses of bedrock give way to boulder-strewn valleys with adjacent lines of eskers. Lichens dominate the highlands, but valleys are covered with dwarf birch, mosses, lichens, and willows. This region is known to the Chipewyan as the Barren Grounds, a fitting

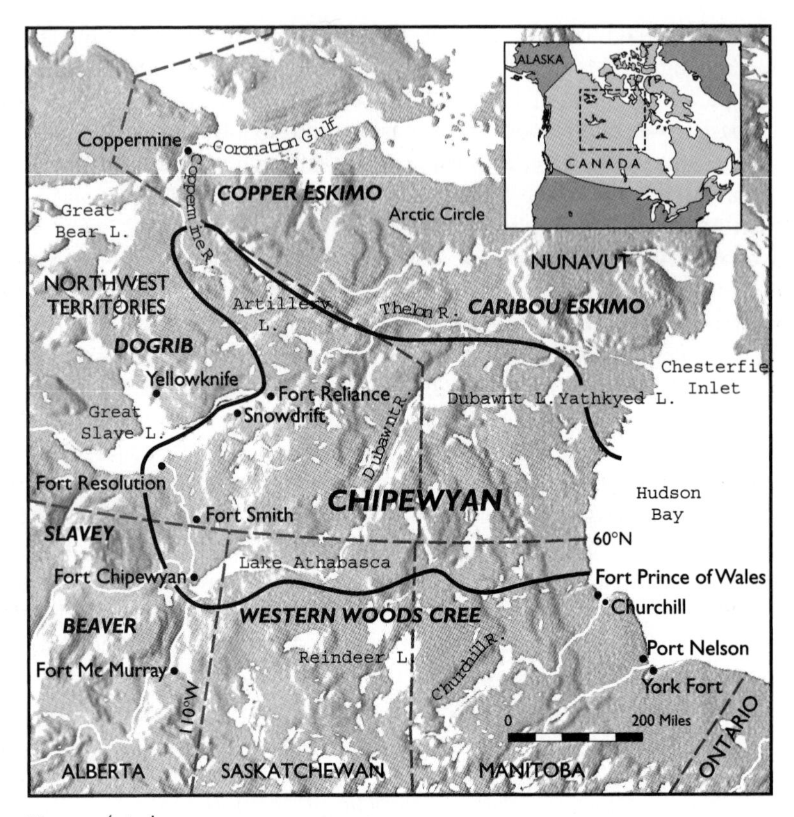

Figure 4-1 | Early historic range of the Chipewyan Indians.

term incorporated in geographical writings. Along river bottoms on the southern Barrens, stands of white spruce appear as outriders of their species; this is the taiga, where the tundra and northern forest meet. Still farther south the spruce are dense, and aspen, birch, and juniper stands are fringed by marshy bogs and upland tundras. The forested area was foreign to the aboriginal Chipewyan, but it became important to them in historic times. Above all, Chipewyan country was dominated by great caribou herds that meant survival for these Indians. Interestingly, and contrary to the title of this book, the Chipewyan maintained that they did not own the land but that the land owned them.

Aboriginal Life

When the Chipewyan first encountered Europeans, their economy, based on caribou and fish, was well established and probably had been much the same for thousands of years. The baseline ethnographic account that follows examines each major aspect of their sociocultural lives. Although much of the information is based on observations by Samuel Hearne, his findings are supplemented by those of later observers as they relate to aboriginal conditions.

ORIGIN MYTH The Chipewyan regarded the primordial world as centering about a woman who lived in a cave and subsisted on berries. As the myth unfolds, a doglike creature followed her into the cave to live with her. She thought that she dreamed this animal turned into a handsome young man who had sexual intercourse with her, but it was no dream, and the woman became pregnant. At this juncture a giant man approached; he was so tall that his head reached nearly to the clouds. With a stick he outlined the bodies of water and caused them to fill. The giant tore the doglike being to shreds and threw its internal organs into the water, creating fish. He tossed the flesh on the land in bits and it became land animals, and he tore the skin and threw it into the sky to become birds. The giant told the woman that her offspring would be able to kill as many of these creatures as they required and she need not worry about the animals' abundance, as it was his command for them to multiply. The giant returned from whence he had come and was never seen again. In this way, order in the world emerged, and the abundance of game was assured. This tale justified the Chipewyans' indiscriminate killing of game and led to a supernatural association with dogs, because the woman's human offspring were descended from a creature related to the dog. The creation myth was not only taught to children but also used to guide thoughts about the adult world.

CLOTHING Chipewyan garments were made from the skins of caribou killed in the early fall when the hides were strong and the hair dense but not long. Eight to ten skins were required to outfit an individual for winter. The upper garment of a man consisted of a loose-fitting, sleeved poncho with the hair side out and the skins cut to a point in front and back. He sometimes wore a fur boa when the temperature was low, and his ears might be protected by a fur band or cap. His ankle-length leggings were of dehaired skins, with moccasins sewn at the bottom. In severe weather he draped a caribou skin cape over his shoulders. The garb of a woman included a sleeved dress that reached her knees or ankles; to hold a long dress up from the ground she wore a belt around her waist. Her leggings reached from below the knee to the ankle and may not have had attached moccasins. She also wore a cape, and both sexes used mittens of double thickness. They could slip their hands out of the mittens without the chance of losing them because each was attached to a leather harness that hung about the neck.

SETTLEMENTS AND MANUFACTURES Habitations ranged from isolated family dwellings to clusters of as many as seventy units, but large aggregates usually were of brief duration. The size of a community depended on the time of year and the local availability of food. People lived in a Subarctic variety of the tepee best known from the American Plains. A Chipewyan tent was framed with poles set in a circle and bound near the top. The cone was covered with as many as seventy sewn caribou skins, and it measured over twenty feet across at the base. An opening at the apex of the cone permitted smoke from the central fireplace to filter upward. If spruce boughs were available, they were placed around the fire and covered with caribou skins; on these people relaxed, worked, and slept.

Most manufactures could be found in and around the tents. A well-supplied camp included tripods of poles from which hung caribou-skin bags filled with meat. Among the possessions of women were cooking and storage containers of birch bark or skin. The women commonly used a basket of folded and sewn bark for cooking by filling it with water, preheated stones, and raw meat. They probably had skin bags in which they kept sewing awls and thread of caribou sinew. The men's tool kits included antler wedges for splitting planks from logs; a crooked knife with a copper blade and antler handle, the most important form of knife; a curved, wooden-handled knife with a beaver incisor for a blade, another highly useful tool for cutting small sections of wood; and a hand drill with a copper bit and an antler handle, the only drill form known. Awls were of copper, and a copper ax head was hafted on a wooden or antler handle. These uses of native copper, and its use in icepick points, arrow points, spearheads, and spoons, reflect a reliance on this metal. The copper tools were made by pounding a raw lump of the metal into shape. These people never heated or smelted copper but processed it as they did stone.

CONVEYANCES The little that is known about aboriginal Chipewyan boats suggests that they had only small skin-covered canoes with wooden frames (see Figure 4-2). These vessels were used to hunt caribou as they swam across lakes, and canoes lashed together formed rafts to ferry people across rivers. The toboggan for winter transport was up to fourteen feet long and about fourteen inches wide. It was made from thin juniper planks that were steamed and bent upward at the front. The planks were joined to crosspieces, probably with thongs. Chipewyan men, or women if the occasion arose, pulled

Figure 4-2 | A man carrying a small birch-bark canoe in early historic times. (From Hearne 1796.)

the toboggans; they presumably did not use dogs as traction animals because of their supernatural associations. If wood was unavailable, the people could make toboggans by using sewn caribou leg skins as a substitute.

Snowshoes were essential for travel over deep snow, and men jogged along for hours on end at a pace faster than a walk. Snowshoes were made by lashing babiche through holes in birch-wood frames. A snowshoe had a slightly turned-up tip and was asymmetrical in outline; the outer edge flared, but the inner edge was relatively straight. Men prepared the frame, and women laced the babiche with an eyed snowshoe needle. Curiously, although women made snowshoe webbing with an eyed needle, they used awls to sew garments. This would appear to be an instance of "cultural blindness."

HOUSEHOLD LIFE In camp, women prepared meals and cared for children, as did their counterparts throughout most of the world. To these obligations was added one of their most important activities, the task of processing skins, particularly those of caribou. After a caribou had been killed by a man, his wife recovered it, skinned it, and removed bits of flesh and fat with a bone scraper. If the hair was to be removed, the woman propped a wooden beam obliquely in the ground, draped the skin over it with the hair side up, and removed the hair with a scraper. A dehaired skin often was smoke-cured by hanging it over a pole framework under which decayed wood smoldered. A skin to be used with the hair intact was scraped, softened in water, and wrung out and dried, and a paste of partly decayed caribou brains was rubbed on the inner surface. Later the skin was dried once again and finally scraped with a copper-bladed end scraper. The skin probably was rubbed by hand to make it pliable and relatively soft. This process of skin preparation was a key technological complex for the Chipewyan, who relied on caribou skins not only for clothing but also for bedding, dwelling covers, containers, and ropes. American Indians did not tan skins in the technical sense.

Favorite foods largely were caribou products: the head and fat from the back, a fetus, and grubs from beneath the skin. The Chipewyan did not consider steaks and chops luxuries. They ate caribou meat or fish both raw and cooked. In addition to boiling it in a birch-bark container, they roasted flesh over an open fire. The diet rarely included plant products, although a moss soup is reported and moss could season meat soup.

Although women prepared meals at camp, men ate first. This was customary because if men were not reasonably well nourished, especially in times of food stress, they could not hunt or fish as effectively. The women received what the men had not consumed, which might at times be nothing. However, because women typically prepared meals, we might assume that they ate at least some food in the process.

Pemmican was an important food in the Subarctic, although it usually is associated with Plains Indians. Pemmican, from a Cree word meaning "manufactured grease," was made from lean meat that had been cut into strips and dried by the sun or near a fire. The dry meat was pounded into a powder, mixed with fat, and stuffed into caribou intestines; this highly concentrated food was a favorite of travelers. Dried meat had the advantage of being light and portable. Many Chipewyan considered it more desirable than fresh meat.

SUBSISTENCE ACTIVITIES Aboriginal Indian life on the Barren Grounds probably would have been impossible without the presence of caribou as a basic food and an essential raw material for manufactures. The Chipewyan words for "meat" and "caribou" are quite similar, which is in itself revealing. Caribou migrating north in the spring were typically lean, and men hunted them largely as day-to-day food. In the early fall the herds began to wander south; at this time they were usually abundant with prime skins, a thick fat layer, and the most nourishing meat. That was the time for the most intense hunts. The subsistence cycle began anew in the early spring with caribou hunt preparations. Band members gathered at birch groves along the northern forest border, where tent poles were cut and canoes built for summer travels in the Barrens. The primary goal was to intercept caribou, and some people reported that they preyed on caribou in the manner of wolves.

As many as two hundred people might assemble for the trip north over the snows of spring. Women and young girls pulled the heavily loaded toboggans along the most direct route, and men and boys hunted on snowshoes adjacent to the toboggan trail. Dogs, burdened with parcels of tent skins, containers, and poles, accompanied the women. The female–male division of labor at this time might appear to have been more arduous for females, but this may not have been the case. Females pulled toboggans along the most direct route, and their noise scattered any game along the way. Men covered far greater distance in their pursuit of edibles. Thus a reasonable balance of energy expended may have prevailed between the genders.

In the eastern sector, winter and early spring camps were established on promontories along the forest edge, in localities frequented by caribou and near lakes containing fish. People moved only once or twice during the winter from an ideally situated camp, one accessible to lakes or wide rivers along which caribou normally passed. Here funnel-shaped caribou surrounds were built. Converging lines of brushy poles were erected, with poles at about twenty-yard intervals. When caribou approached the wider end of a funnel, they were unaware of the poles, which sometimes spanned three miles. As animals entered the surround, the women, boys, and some men appeared from behind to herd them. The caribou were driven into a trap, which was a large enclosure of branches at the end of the funnel, with snares set at narrow exits. After the entrance was blocked with trees, snared caribou were speared, and arrows were shot at loose animals.

In the fall, six hundred people might gather at well-known caribou crossings and camp in a single locality. Families seeing each other for the first time in months or years followed an established etiquette at their reunion. At first they sat apart from each other and said nothing. Then an older person of one party recounted all of their personal traumas since the last meeting, and women of the other group wailed on hearing of the misfortunes. The fate of the second party next was recounted and responded to. Men then greeted one another, and women exchanged presents as well as good news. When caribou appeared, their number might be truly fantastic. Sometimes so many were killed that only the skins, long bones, fat, and tongues were taken, and the carcasses were left to rot. As the caribou moved, the Indians followed, drying as much meat as they could conveniently carry.

When caribou rutted in October, a hunter sometimes attached lengths of caribou antler to his belt so that they rattled as he walked. A bull caribou in the vicinity would think he heard two other bulls fighting over females and would boldly approach, expecting to lead off the females. A bull could be killed more readily this way than by the usual method of stalking against the wind. At these times hunters used the self bow, a one-piece wooden shaft strung with babiche. Caribou-killing arrows had unbarbed bone or stone points and were vaned with feathers. An alternative and preferable fall hunting method was to drive large herds of caribou into water and kill them from canoes with lances.

When the snow was soft and deep, men, on snowshoes, sometimes tracked caribou. This meant following a single animal until it was exhausted from floundering in the snow. In the winter, the men might set gill nets beneath the ice of lakes or jig for fish through holes in the ice with hooks. In the western area of Chipewyan country, fishing was more important than among the eastern bands. Secondary means for taking game included the use of deadfalls for bear, marten, squirrels, and wolverine. The Chipewyan used nets for taking beaver in summer, but in winter, after they had broken open the beaver lodges, they took the animals from retreats beneath the ice along stream or lake edges. They set babiche snares to entangle hares or ptarmigan. Even though these Indians reached Hudson Bay at Churchill, they did not hunt the sea mammals abundant there at certain seasons.

It is important to note the advantage, in food-getting activities, of using devices that do not require the presence of a person. Set nets, snares, traps, and deadfalls are examples of "untended facilities" that operate when no one is present and no danger, waiting, or pursuit are required in their use. By contrast, lances and bows and arrows must be operated by hand and may be dangerous for the user—for example, against a bear. Thus, under most circumstances, it is preferable to use untended facilities when possible. Note that the Chipewyan used snares and deadfalls.

When the people could not harvest sufficient caribou, irrespective of the season or reason, they turned to their only other meaningful food source—fish, especially lake trout, northern pike (jackfish), and whitefish. Gill nets had emerged as the principal fishing method. The netting of babiche was strung with wooden floats at the top and stone sinkers at the bottom. Set across narrow streams, at river eddies where fish typically pause, and at spots in lakes, fish of appropriate size for a net were held by their gills. The people attached charms to nets designed to attract fish. Additional fishing methods included the use of dip nets that looked somewhat like our butterfly nets; fish trapped by weirs made from brush in shallow streams or rivers were caught with these nets. Likewise, men might shoot fish with barbed arrows from bows or impale them on leisters (fish spears) from canoes.

Additional details of Chipewyan hunting and fishing activities could be presented, but it already is obvious that caribou, and fish to a lesser extent, were the primary staples. Although recent studies suggest that the Subarctic may have been more productive than previously realized, relying on comparatively few species meant that food sometimes was scarce and that people might starve. At these times they ate berries, mosses, and other plant products and later consumed items of clothing; under extreme conditions they turned to cannibalism.

SOCIAL DIMENSIONS The Chipewyan were described in less than glowing terms by Europeans, who characterized men as patient and persevering but also as morose and covetous. The Chipewyan firmly believed that they were more intelligent than the intrusive outsiders. The Chipewyan were peaceful within their own community, at least in terms of not shedding blood. When angry with one another, the men wrestled, pulled their opponent's hair or ears, or twisted his neck. As far as honesty went, among the eastern tribes of the Northern Athapaskans, the Chipewyan were ranked as superior to all others; they abhorred a thief. However, they considered whites to be not quite human and did not really consider taking their property to be theft.

No description of these people would be complete without commenting on the status of women as recorded by Samuel Hearne, the first white explorer in the region. According to him, women were subordinated in every way, were treated cruelly, and were held in gross contempt by men. Female infants were occasionally permitted to die, a practice viewed by adult women as kindly. In fact, they are said to have wished their mothers had done it for them. Women were beaten frequently, and although it was considered an odious crime to kill a Chipewyan man, it was regarded as no crime for a man to beat his wife to death. We probably will never know whether this was typical behavior toward women, but we may suspect that Hearne exaggerated or that his description was based largely on the behavior of his guide Matonabbee. This man had six wives and was obviously a highly successful hunter and a charismatic leader; he unquestionably was a very powerful and self-centered person. The treatment of women as recorded by Hearne seems inordinately severe and out of character for Indians north of Mexico. Furthermore, a similar pattern did not exist among the Chipewyan in more recent historic times. Contemporary researchers have suggested that although women may have been devalued symbolically, in everyday life they had considerable influence and power (Sharp 1988).

As was typical for many collectors, fishermen, and hunters around the world, the constraints on individual behavior were defined largely on the basis of age and gender. Each household was self-sufficient and could exist in isolation until a member sought a spouse. Group responsibilities or community cohesion hardly existed, and individuals had a great deal of flexibility in their behavior. Environmental resources were open to exploitation by everyone on an equal basis; family hunting or trapping territories did not exist.

POLITICAL ORGANIZATION Aggregates of people structured in a formal manner and functioning as cohesive units did not exist among the aboriginal Chipewyan. Instead, as studies by James G. E. Smith (1970; 1976a; 1976b) and others have indicated, local groups were somewhat amorphous and highly flexible. In ecological terms, it is important to note that regional bands were defined largely on the basis of the separate herds of caribou exploited, and a regional group was divided further into localized bands of one hundred or more people who hunted together. Seasonally, when great numbers of caribou were available, several localized bands might assemble for a hunt. However, when caribou did not follow their expected migration routes, people divided into smaller hunting groups. Conditions influencing the movements of caribou included fires, weather variations such as sudden thaws or blizzards, and, in all likelihood, cyclical variations in their number. The most important observation about the nature of a band was its flexibility in number as a function of local food resources.

Families might unite under the aegis of a charismatic leader. Such a man was above all else an outstanding provider with an inordinate ability to take game and fish. Hearne's guide, Matonabbee, is an example. Once a man's reputation as a leader was established, fathers of marriageable daughters sought him as a son-in-law. This was to the personal advantage of the father-in-law because the pattern of marriage residence was for a husband to join his wife's natal household (matrilocal residence). Subsequent wives could be sisters (sororal polygyny) of the first, but other women could also be chosen. Such a man had to be physically strong because he was obligated to validate his claim to a wife, especially a younger wife, by wrestling if challenged by another man. Less successful hunters, relatives, and nonrelatives cast their lot with him for greater security. An important characteristic of this form of leadership was its transient nature. A man could keep his wives and other followers only as long as his powers of persuasion, hunting skills, and physical strength endured. As he began to fail physically, he sometimes could retain his position of authority by craft and intrigue, but this was only a temporary respite before he slipped into obscurity.

The Chipewyan were a tribe, but only in a general sense, and comparatively little political integration existed among the member bands. Conflicts with non-Chipewyan took the form of raids and generally were carried out by the members of a single band. An account by Hearne illustrates this type of hostility. He was accompanying a group of Chipewyan to the Coppermine River mouth when they raided an Eskimo (Inuit) camp. Matonabbee was the undisputed leader, and the raiders were unusually cooperative as they lent

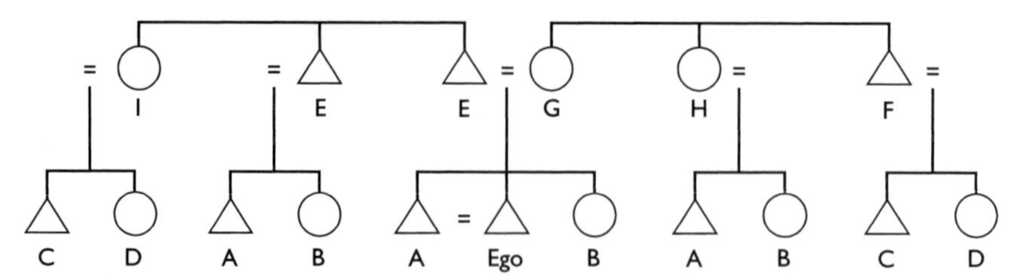

Figure 4-3 | The early historic Chipewyan system of kinship terminology.

equipment to one another. Beforehand each man painted his shield in black and red, adding one or more figures representing supernatural aids. They painted their faces red, black, or with a combination of these colors and took off most of their clothing or lightened it so that they could run fast. They launched the attack in the middle of the night and caught the Eskimos asleep. Once alarmed, the twenty or so Eskimos ran naked from their tents only to be speared to death by the attackers. Afterward the Indians plundered the camp and departed. As was typical among northern Indians, the Chipewyan attacked these Eskimos for individual prestige, plunder, potential glory, and tribal security; territorial gain was not a goal.

DESCENT, KINSHIP, AND MARRIAGE The Chipewyan calculated their ancestry through both female and male relatives (bilateral descent); the descent group (kindred) was like that which prevails in the United States today. When a man married, he attached himself to the household of his parents-in-law (matrilocal residence), and his ideal mate was his father's sister's daughter (patrilateral cross-cousin). In *recent* times at least some Chipewyan called a father's sister's daughters and mother's brother's daughters (cross-cousins) by the term for sweetheart, a convention that gives strength to the assumption of cross-cousin marriage. As the anthropologist Fred Eggan (1937) pointed out, a man relied on his son-in-law for support, and the son-in-law in turn was aided by his wife's brother's son. Although there was regional variation, it appears that, in general, in the aboriginal system of kinship terminology, the cousin terms were of the Iroquois type.

Their system of kinship terminology is diagrammed in Figure 4-3. Father's brother's children and mother's sister's children were termed the same as siblings, but different terms were employed for a father's sister's children and mother's brother's children. This terminology would be compatible with cross-cousin marriage. For the generation above an individual, the kinship terms for father and father's brother are alike (bifurcate merging), and mother's brother is distinct. Mother, mother's sister, and father's sister are all termed differently (bifurcate collateral). This terminology indicates that probably siblings and parallel cousins of the same sex (who were terminological siblings), particularly if they were males, extended mutual aid to one another and regarded their cross-cousins as possible mates. With the further presence of wife exchange, we find an integrated network of blood relatives on an individual's generational level. On the parents' generation the same social distance separated aunts and uncles from one another as from parents. The inference is that these individuals were not as important socially or economically as near relatives of one's own generation.

SUPERNATURALISM External threats to the Chipewyan came from the neighboring Cree and Eskimos. The hostility stemmed in part from the belief that the shamans of these people sent evil by supernatural means to cause illness. The Chipewyan believed that death or disease occurred from natural causes only among the aged. Thus in theory each physical disorder of a younger person resulted from the hostile activities of a foreign shaman. Chipewyan shamans attempted to negate the effects of such evil by acting through personal spirits that they controlled. When someone fell sick, a shaman sang and danced to summon his supernatural aids or "shadows," who were animal, bird, or imaginative familiars. He then sucked and tried to blow the intrusive disease substance from the patient. For serious cases a shaman treated an ill person in a special small square tent built with no opening at the top.

Death and disease led the Chipewyan to frequent hostilities with non-Athapaskan neighbors, and they made sporadic forays into the lands of their tormentors. In the raid on Eskimos reported earlier, the attackers carried wooden shields on which they had painted designs representing their individual guardian spirits. After the encounter the raiders observed numerous taboos to placate the spirits of those they had killed. A raid of this nature united the participants against a common enemy but did not require elaborate organization.

In the Chipewyan view of the supernatural world, spirits hovered about constantly; some more potent than others. Because the spirits of wolves and wolverine were considered dangerous, these animals usually were not hunted or killed. The bear, too, was considered dangerous; when one was killed, its skin might be burned and the large bones scattered in the four directions. A woman could not touch or step over a bearskin; thus, one placed before a door was a means of keeping women from entering a tent. The spirits of a shaman were powerful, and the spirit of an ordinary person was sometimes feared. Only a vague notion existed of a future life, a life like that on earth but free from cares, according to one observer. Not all accounts agree, however. One states that the Chipewyan believed that the soul of the deceased crosses a river and that if the individual has been good on earth he reaches an island on which life is free from worry. If he has been evil, he struggles in the river forever.

LIFE CYCLE The Chipewyan, like all other North American Indians, realized that conception resulted from sexual intercourse. As the time of delivery approached, a small tent or brush-covered structure was erected away from the main camp for a pregnant woman. Here she bore her offspring and remained apart from normal camp routine for about a month. Her isolation was enforced whether the group was traveling or at a relatively permanent camp. The mother was cared for by other women, but she had no contact with men. The father did not see his infant until the period of isolation had ended. Similar isolation was the norm for menstruating women and for girls at menarche. The blood associated with women at these times was considered antipathetic to fish and game, and men avoided contacts with females in these conditions. Apparently the women were successful in keeping the true nature of the menstrual cycle a secret from men. When a woman sought to avoid her husband, which might be several times in one month, she simply crawled out of the tent beneath a side, to indicate that she was beginning to menstruate, and went to the menstrual hut.

During the first year of life an infant was carried on its mother's back next to her skin; the baby was held in place by a belt that passed from the middle of the mother's back over her breasts. In this secondary "womb," a baby wore only a moss-padded diaper. A female infant was typically named after a form or characteristic of a marten, such as Marten's Heart, Summer Marten, or White Marten. The names for males were taken from the seasons, places, or animals. Unfortunately, little is known about the social environment of children. Males clearly occupied a favored position compared with their sisters, but children in general were treated as adults. Conversations in the presence of children were free and frank.

Childhood betrothals were customary, and parents were careful to prevent a girl from participating in sexual intercourse before she married. Matches were made by parents or other relatives; a girl had no choice. The usual marriage was between a pubescent girl and a man who was at least twice her age. There was no marriage ceremony; the man simply attached himself to his wife's household. A marriage assumed stability only after an infant was born. Offspring seldom were born during the early years of marriage, and from this it may be presumed that the young bride's adolescent sterility tended to delay conception. A nuclear family (a husband, wife, and children) was neither a stable nor a long-lasting unit. The possibility of death by accident, disease, or starvation always existed, and life expectancy was probably less than thirty years on an average. (High infant mortality rates often account for a statistic such as this one.) Dislike of a spouse could rupture a household, and the practice of wrestling to retain one's wife whenever challenged did not lead to familial stability. Skill in wrestling was developed during youth, and the rule was that the man first thrown to the ground was the loser. An opponent could be downed most readily by grabbing his hair—thus it was cut short—or by seizing his ears—so they were greased. The woman being fought over had no voice in these matters but was expected to follow the winner dutifully.

A wrestling match for a wife did not always end well. In one case the husband killed a potential rival. He and his wife then were forced to live in isolation, and whenever other Chipewyan happened on the couple, they would take everything they owned except their clothing. Women deserted their husbands, but because of the physical isolation of most camps this was a dangerous undertaking. The woman might be caught and beaten by her husband or seized by another man before she found safety with a man she desired. Men guarded their wives jealously, not allowing them out of their sight if the opportunity for adultery existed. Wives generally were faithful to their husbands, but a particular wife sometimes shared her husband with as many as seven co-wives. The exchange of wives for a night perhaps helped temper any urge to seize a woman for sexual purposes alone. Wife exchanges were made by men and had implications that were more economic than sexual. The bonds between men resulted in continuing friendship and mutual aid. If one of the men died, his partner assumed the responsibility, at least temporarily, of caring for the widow and her children.

Games and other forms of amusement were few, and the only dancing was a step borrowed from the Dogrib Indians. A widely popular pastime was the hand game, a guessing game in which two opponents sat opposite each other with ten to twenty counters beside them. One man had an object in one hand and, behind a skin, shifted it. His opponent then guessed the hand that contained the gaming piece. A correct guess gave the winner one counter, and the game was won when one man had all of the counters.

As individuals aged and became less capable of caring for themselves, they were regarded as a burden. Old people had the poorest of tattered clothing and were given the most undesirable food. When a camp was moved, they might be left behind in a small shelter where they would starve alone. The corpse of a person who had died in isolation was not buried when it was found, and the corpse of one who died in camp was simply placed on the ground. In both cases, the bodies were eaten by animals. Property of the deceased was destroyed, and immediate relatives also destroyed their personal property. A widow cut her hair short as a sign of bereavement, and the shorn hair might be placed beside the deceased. She wailed about camp, stripped of her clothing and other possessions, to be aided and soothed by relatives and friends but not to remarry for a year.

In drawing the Chipewyan life-cycle discussion to a close, it is appropriate to comment on the manner in which these people behaved toward one another, especially on men's treatment of women and the general treatment of the aged. We should realize fully that the area in which these people lived offered either feast or famine. It was one of the most difficult sectors of North America in which to live in aboriginal times because of food uncertainties. The men, as the hunters and primary providers, presumably were often anxiety-ridden about their capacity to feed their families. This at least provides a partial explanation for their harsh treatment of women and the aged. We also must recognize that early writers about the Chipewyan were European men whose own attitudes toward these segments of the population possibly colored their accounts.

Early History

According to nearly all standard sources, the Chipewyan lived in the northern forests at the beginning of their history and were driven into the Barren Grounds by the Cree after the latter received firearms. However, ethnohistorical studies by Beryl C. Gillespie (1970, 1976) have shown this was not the case. Instead, the Chipewyan lived in the taiga and tundra during early historic times and began to exploit interior forests only under fur traders' influence.

A Hudson's Bay Company post was built at Churchill along western Hudson Bay in 1717. From here agents launched the most important and lasting trading contacts with adjacent Northern Athapaskans. As Chipewyan began trading at Churchill, they told of a major copper deposit to the northwest. The Chipewyan, however, were making tremendous profits as middlemen in the trade with more distant tribes and were reluctant to guide company explorers. As a long-term Hudson's Bay Company employee, Samuel Hearne attempted to locate the copper deposit. In this endeavor his name became intimately associated with Chipewyan ethnography and with explorations in northwestern Canada.

Hearne made two abortive attempts to penetrate Chipewyan country and succeeded on his third effort. His ultimate success in this venture hinged on the Chipewyan guide Matonabbee, who had his own opinions about how to travel. The key to his plan was to take women along to relieve the men of the many burdensome chores. Matonabbee had six wives at that time. The trip to the Coppermine River and Coronation Gulf was completed successfully in mid-1772 and is one of the most noteworthy feats of individual exploration anywhere at any time. Hearne's maps were not accurate, and for this he has received periodic criticism, but, far more important, his book (1795) is a classic in exploration literature and the first comprehensive account of the Chipewyan. Hearne died a month after his manuscript was accepted by a publisher in October 1792.

The map Hearne prepared and his knowledge of the country facilitated further expansion to the northwest. The first trader to settle in the midst of Chipewyan territory was Peter Pond, who established himself near Athabasca Lake in 1778. The organization of the North West Company in 1783 introduced an era of fierce competition with the Hudson's Bay Company, and not until their amalgamation in 1821 did trading conditions become stabilized. The history of Chipewyan country centered about a failed quest for mineral wealth, the expanding fur trade, and disappointing searches for a water passage to the Pacific Ocean. Later, missionaries began the search for souls to save. In 1846 Roman Catholic missionaries founded a permanent mission at Lake Ile a la Crosse, and the Anglicans located at Churchill in 1912. Thus fur and souls attracted most outsiders to Chipewyan country.

As the people were drawn into the fur trade by the mid-1700s, some of them ventured south into the boreal forest, where they trapped beaver and marten to exchange for trade goods. The quest for beaver in particular led to a decline in caribou hunting, a major change from their aboriginal subsistence pattern. As contacts with Europeans intensified, the people were exposed to new diseases. A severe smallpox epidemic struck in 1781, and an estimated 90 percent of the people died. Although this estimate may have been exaggerated by whites who only observed Chipewyan living near the trading posts, there is no doubt of the horrendous effect of the 1781 epidemic. In 1819, another smallpox epidemic "carried away whole bands" (Simpson 1938, 81). Thus they had become a remnant people early in their history. With the emphasis they placed on trapping, they sometimes were unable to obtain enough food and faced starvation.

Famines made devastating inroads into the vitality of this society; although famines were not new, they now occurred more often. At Fort Resolution in 1833 some "forty of the choicest hunters" died in a famine (Back 1836, 209), and between 1879 and 1881 many people died of hunger.

The increased seasonal mobility required by the fur trade led to the construction of large birch-bark canoes to transport pelts and to obtain trade goods from Churchill or elsewhere. As the fur trade matured, a new leadership pattern emerged. Traders preferred to deal with representatives of a group, not with individuals, and this attitude led to the emergence of trading chiefs (see Figure 4-4). Traders strengthened a trading chief's standing by deferring to him and presenting him with clothing, medals, and a formal reception on his arrival at a post. By the late 1880s, the "chiefs" were distributing the meat of caribou and moose to whomever they chose, irrespective of the wishes of the men who killed the game, although the hunters personally kept the skins of animals. If this was the norm, we must conclude that a chief possessed authority and some form of power. By 1908 chiefs represented groups in dealings with officials of the federal Indian Affairs Branch, but, as we would expect, they were not very effective.

It is revealing to consider the changing status of dogs. Recall that a dog-like creature was thought to have fathered these people, and the dog, along with bears, wolves, and wolverine, had strong supernatural associations (Sharp 1988). In the 1820s the people were convinced by a powerful man that they should not use such closely related animals to do their work, and consequently they destroyed all of their dogs. For this reason, during the early period of contact the people had very few dogs or none at all. Apparently, dogs were not widely used as beasts of burden, nor did they pull toboggans, until sometime in the mid-1800s. Yet Hearne mentioned that in his time dogs hauled birch poles as hunters moved into the Barrens. Certain taboos still surrounded dogs in the early 1930s. For example, dogs were not shot, and to feed a dog a moose head or bear intestines was thought to bring ill fortune.

The unformalized supernatural system of the aboriginal Chipewyan population absorbed Cree concepts, and by the early 1800s they had borrowed the concept of manitou, a supernatural force that pervades the natural world.

Figure 4-4 | A 1913 photograph of Chief Squirrel, a Chipewyan trading chief. (Courtesy of the Canadian Museum of Civilization, neg. no. 26070.)

An evil manitou was blamed for sickness, disease, or bad luck. By 1908, some Chipewyan had learned Cree folktales, including tales that involved a trickster-hero. In these accounts, one animal tricks another, or a supernatural force creates something, and thus becomes a mythological hero. Christianity was introduced by Roman Catholic missionaries, and most Chipewyan became converts by the 1920s, at least in name. Yet many traditional supernatural beliefs continued to prevail; Catholicism was integrated with the old religion, a typical pattern among Indians.

In early historic references to caribou hunting, taboos were rarely reported. Later in history, caribou remained the key food, but numerous taboos surrounding them appeared. For example, in one area, if a woman's skirt were to pass over a hunting knife, there was fear that the caribou would not migrate in that direction during that year. A woman was supposed to pierce the caribou's eyeball before she butchered the carcass to prevent the spirit of the deceased animal from reporting its fate to others. The implication might be that these taboos emerged as caribou hunting became less dependable.

Becoming Modern at Snowdrift (Lutselk'e, Lutsel K'e)

1960 was a watershed year in Chipewyan history. It was then that a professional anthropologist, James W. VanStone, began his study of a contemporary settlement, Snowdrift. At this time also the people were just beginning to undergo the most dramatic changes since the introduction of the fur trade. To examine this transitional period provides insight into the nature of present-day Chipewyan life in one sector of their domain.

Snowdrift, along eastern Great Slave Lake, is a sparsely forested area that borders on tundra country. The people in the vicinity traditionally traded at Fort Resolution, founded in 1786, before a Hudson's Bay Company post was built at Snowdrift in 1925. In 1928 a devastating influenza epidemic struck the region, and families scattered widely in an unsuccessful hope of avoiding the disease. An estimated 20 percent of the regional population died from either influenza or pneumonia.

It was not until 1954 that most people began to settle there in response to pressure from the federal Indian agent. In 1960 about 150 people lived at Snowdrift, including 38 school-age children. The village consisted of twenty-six predominantly log houses, a Hudson's Bay Company store, a Roman Catholic church, and cabins of Euro-Canadian sports fishermen and mining enterprises. The commitment to settled village life represented a dramatic shift in residence pattern for these previously mobile hunters and trappers. With so many people in one community, it was difficult to obtain enough food locally. Their previous standard of living appears to have declined, and they came under far greater control by federal authorities.

THE PEOPLE AND THE SETTLEMENT In striking contrast with the not-so-distant past, clothing typically came from the local store. Most men wore imported shirts, trousers, underwear, and footwear. Older women wore imported underwear, stockings, dresses, skirts, sweaters, and shoes. Girls favored slacks, colorful lightweight jackets, brooches, earrings, finger rings, and curled hair. Younger males favored ornamental black leather jackets. The most important locally made items included skin moccasins for men and slippers for women as summer wear. Money obviously was required to purchase most clothing.

After 1950, with federal support, most families constructed substantial houses or renovated existing cabins. Some people participated with reluctance in the housing program because they hesitated to commit themselves to permanent village life. Most of the dwellings were one-room cabins with board floors and furnished with homemade beds, chairs, tables, and shelves. Light was supplied by kerosene lamps, and heat was furnished by wood-burning sheet-iron stoves. Trunks or bags for extra clothing and bedding, a battery-powered radio, a hand-operated sewing machine, and utensils were common household items. In nearby log storage sheds they kept frozen or dried fish, dog harnesses, outboard motor parts, traps, snowshoes, fishnets, and rifles. Quite clearly, with all of the new material goods, a family became far less mobile.

Each family owned a large imported canoe, an outboard motor, and a small canvas-covered canoe. A type of toboggan existed that was purchased from the store and that was more correctly a cariole with a rear panel and canvas sides. A family had about five dogs to pull its cariole. Dog teams and outboard motors unquestionably increased the mobility of a family in subsistence activities. The canvas-covered canoes were being replaced by aluminum boats that required a substantial cash outlay.

MAKING A LIVING Traditional Chipewyan economic life had centered about caribou and fish, and with the addition of trapping furbearers, these foci persisted. Although trapping was an important major source of cash, hunting remained a significant part of family welfare. Most men would abandon their traplines if caribou appeared in the vicinity.

Trapping was difficult and surrounded by uncertainties. To reach a trapline required one to three days of dog-team travel. Steel jaw traps or wire snares were set for the most valuable species: lynx, marten, mink, white fox, and wolverine. Wolverine sometimes ate the animals caught in traps or sprung a line of sets and ate the bait. Gray jaybirds or other creatures might also spring traps. A canvas trapping tent was small and impossible to heat for comfort, and men found it difficult to work alone for weeks on end. Previously the family of a man accompanied him on a trapline; this was no longer possible because school-age children were obligated to attend classes. Thus men tended to trap only for short periods in the late fall when the pelts of most furbearers were prime. The price of fur was not very high, and a trapper's average take was about C$320. Income from trapping remained the only source of cash for many families.

In the early 1960s dependence on caribou remained great, and the late summer hunt was of prime importance. A household head believed that he required about one hundred caribou per year, yet harvests of this magnitude were no longer realized. In the fall when caribou were absent locally, which usually was the case, families traveled in large canoes in search of game. Burdened by large amounts of equipment, they could not reach the best hunting grounds. Thus the rewards were meager. The meat they obtained was smoked, brought back to the village, and stored in the Indian Affairs Branch cold-storage unit. In 1960 nearly half of the households were unrepresented in the fall caribou hunt. For unsuccessful hunters and others, fishing with gill nets for lake trout and whitefish in the fall might be intense (see Figure 4-5). The catch was partially dried and stored as winter food for dogs and people.

Figure 4-5 | A Snowdrift man, Louison Abel, checking a gill net set beneath lake ice in 1960. (Photograph by James W. VanStone, © The Field Museum, Neg. no. A107886.)

Men began to prefer wage-labor employment, but jobs were few and usually temporary. As a result, making a living by wage labor was more uncertain than the subsistence pursuits of old.

Aboriginal foods were increasingly replaced by purchased edibles. People preferred fish and meat with every meal, but because these often were unavailable, the staple was bannock. This is an unleavened baked bread of Scottish origin, and it was usually made from barley or pease (peas). A variety of bannock ("fry bread" or "Indian bread"), the standard fare of poor Eskimos and Indians throughout Alaska, Canada, and elsewhere, is made from white flour and baking powder mixed with water into a paste and spread on a greased skillet to fry. Often this was the only food at a meal; bannock and tea are the bread and water of depressed Subarctic living. When families were able, they bought prepared foods from the store. The most desired imports were flour, sugar, tea, coffee, crackers, peanut butter, canned meats and fruits, evaporated milk, and seasonings.

SOCIAL DIMENSIONS Along with the changes in subsistence activities and material culture since aboriginal times, we likewise find significant differences in other aspects of living. The old attitudes and harsh treatment toward women described by Hearne were no longer reported. VanStone conveyed the impression that domestic harmony existed. Certain activities, such as food preparation and child raising, remained female obligations, but men performed these tasks as the need arose. Women could profit monetarily from their own labors. A woman who processed a moose or caribou hide or sewed skin garments for someone outside her family was paid directly and retained the profits. The favorable position of women at Snowdrift may have resulted from the fact that they were a distinct minority; for unknown reasons there were fewer young women than men. Because it was difficult to obtain a wife, she was treated with care (see Figure 4-6).

The people continued to trace their descent along both the female and male lines (bilateral descent), as they had in early historic times. Cousin terminology, however, was of the Eskimo type (similar to the current classification of cousins in the United States). Preferential cousin marriage no longer existed; in fact, people did not recall it as an aboriginal practice. The one hundred years of contact with Roman Catholic missionaries who spoke against cousin marriage probably had produced the change, yet premarital fornication between cousins continued.

When a person married, he or she was most likely to select a mate within the community (village endogamy), and immediately after marriage the couple lived with the in-laws who were best able to receive them (temporary bilocal residence). As soon as possible the couple built a separate dwelling and lived alone (neolocal residence). In 1961 most households were nuclear or nuclear core families, the latter comprising a nuclear family to which were added a near relative or two of the husband or wife. Plural marriages no longer existed, and capable providers did not attract followers who lived with them. The overall impression is that the nuclear family remained the most important social unit, although it was not as autonomous as before.

Social bonds beyond those based on kinship were new and of expanding importance. Village life produced feelings of unity, and people thought of themselves as economically, morally, and physically superior to persons in adjacent settlements. Other evidence of village cohesion was the widespread sharing of locally available foods. By the time a successful moose hunter beached his boat, he had given away most of the meat, and the same applied to a catch of fish. Food had been shared in aboriginal times, but apparently not

Figure 4-6 | A Snowdrift woman, Mary Louise Rabesca, sitting in front of a smokehouse in 1976.

in as pervasive or egalitarian a manner. Furthermore, an intensive pattern of reciprocal borrowing had developed, and this included major as well as minor items of material culture. These attitudes and their behavioral manifestations clearly were integrating the community on a social and economic basis.

Square dancing was a popular pastime. The people probably had learned the steps from commercial fishermen, who often stopped for a few days of relaxation during the summer. Men played guitars or violins and learned dance music by listening to village phonographs or broadcasts from the Yellowknife radio station. The square dances were called expertly by village men, and participation at dances was good. Less formal entertainment included nightly card games, which were extremely popular, particularly blackjack and gin rummy. Men and women often played together, and the stakes ranged from small change and ammunition to three-dollar hands in gin rummy games if men were affluent. While adults were playing cards, children sometimes gambled

Figure 4-7 | A summer card game at Snowdrift circa 1960. (Photograph by James W. VanStone, courtesy of the Field Museum, Chicago, neg. no. A107881.)

by pitching coins to a line. The hand game of old was known but seldom played; card games were considered more exciting (see Figure 4-7).

The consumption of alcohol was as much a ritual as a form of entertainment, and prescribed drinking patterns were rarely ignored. The only alcoholic beverage regularly consumed was home brew, produced from yeast, raisins, sugar, and water. It was made secretly by two or three men and allowed to age for about twenty-four hours. It was thought better if it aged longer, but anticipation negated the possibility. The men drank the brew in the home of one of the makers or in the brush during the summer; the object was to become intoxicated. A man would dip a cup into the three-gallon pail, drink the beverage, and pass the cup to the next participant. Normally, some brew was stored in bottles, to be consumed after the brew pail had been drained. When participants became reasonably intoxicated, they visited one house after another, regardless of the time, and drank as they chatted with their reluctant hosts. Sometimes they offered to share their brew, but this practice was not consistent. The conversations of intoxicated men were about village life, and they became more outgoing during drinking sprees than at any other time of their adult lives.

POLITICAL LIFE The Snowdrift Chipewyan were included in Treaty Number 11, which was signed by the Indians in 1921 and provided them with direct monetary and other benefits. The Indians gave up their aboriginal rights to the land but at the same time were protected in their exploitation of local resources. In exchange, they received tangible benefits such as formal education, health services, and material goods. Each year a band member received a cash payment of five dollars, the band chief received twenty-five dollars, and counselors, fifteen dollars each. The Indian Affairs Branch began to provide fishnets, ammunition, and items such as roofing and doors for house construction. Furthermore, families in need, as defined by the Indian agent, received a "ration" from the Indian Affairs Branch through the store. A national program of old-age assistance provided for the welfare of persons sixty-five years of age or older. Even more important was the "baby bonus," or Family Allowance, which was a national program. Every month, each family received six dollars for each child under ten and eight dollars for those ten through sixteen. The program was designed to improve child care, and it probably served this end at Snowdrift.

One result of living in a stable community was intensified contact with the Indian agent. Stationed at Yellowknife, he visited Snowdrift and called meetings on matters of villagewide concern. Attendance usually was poor, and it was difficult to conduct a general meeting because each Indian was inclined to raise issues of personal interest, usually specific requests for aid. Thus the process of democratic group action failed. Unity, when it was manifested, consisted of a stand against a proposal rather than any positive approach. The Chipewyan preferred to deal with the agent on a private, almost secret, basis concerning specific requests. They felt that an agent was in a position to grant favors, and for him not to do so was regarded as pure stubbornness.

Visits to the village by the Royal Canadian Mounted Police (RCMP) in the 1960s represented a show of federal power rather than a response to crime. Crimes in the Canadian legal system were rare and centered most on the manufacture of home brew. The people felt that it was wrong to appeal to Canadian legal authorities and rarely did so, although they might threaten such action.

In 1960 the bands of the region were reorganized, and the villagers received their own chief and two counselors. The people expected the chief not to interfere with village life but to adopt a stern attitude toward Euro-Canadians in general and the Indian agent in particular. An Indian agent, by contrast, expected a chief to be cooperative; if he was not, the chief was bypassed and the agent acted through the trader or teacher and thereby undermined Indian authority. During this period the federal government encouraged local band political development. Yet in 1969 governing obligations shifted to the Northwest Territories, whose representatives fostered the democratic process through local settlement councils in direct competition with the band organization. These competing institutions intensified local factionalism and divided the community politically.

THE BELIEF SYSTEM Villagers were participating but nominal Roman Catholics. A priest visited the settlement frequently and was always present during the Christmas and Easter seasons. Church dogma and beliefs were poorly understood, but attendance at ceremonies was high. In general, the Church was regarded as wealthy and as obliged to pay for labor performed on its behalf. Thus the feeling of belonging to a church and strengthening its purposes was not understood by the members. Interestingly enough, it was in the supernatural sphere that the Chipewyan admitted openly that they were different from whites.

The concept of a "bush man" prevailed here as among other Northern Athapaskans. In their conceptualization, this creature was a man who wore manufactured shoes and appeared at a distance during the summer. He kidnapped children, but apparently he did not harm adults as long as they remained beyond his reach. The Indians believed that certain supernatural beings could harm them but did not affect whites. They also held beliefs about trapping practices, but these were unknown by whites.

By the early 1960s, reliance on shamans as healers was declining. At least some people continued to believe in the power of spirit aids of shamans to cure illness and predict the future. As a secular cure, spruce gum may have been the dominant traditional medicine. Disease treatment was passing into the domain of the Indian and Northern Health Services and a lay dispenser, usually the Hudson's Bay Company manager. If a case was considered serious, the nurse at Yellowknife was contacted by radio, and she decided what course of action was to be followed. This nurse, sometimes accompanied by a medical doctor, visited the village at intervals. These Indians were concerned about their health but did not use patent medicines or turn freely to Euro-Canadians for aid. They seemed to enjoy talking about their aches and pains, but they sought treatment only when they were quite ill.

Contemporary Lutselk'e

Settled village life was above all else an artifact of federal policies, but the community had no realistic control over government decisions. During the early 1980s in particular the federal government launched innumerable programs to change the texture of village living. Homes were becoming better built, and water and fuel delivery were provided, along with sewage disposal, electricity, and roads (see Figure 4-8). By 1996 the 286 residents included 10 Euro-Canadians. With federal and territorial support, buildings had been constructed for band administration. There was a school that educated students through the ninth grade, along with a permanently staffed nursing station, a local RCMP office, and an airport with mail service six days a week (see Figure 4-9). Accompanying these developments, old-age assistance benefits were provided, in addition to varied forms of relief for the needy. The Child Tax Credit (previously Family Allowance) was a nationwide program to foster the welfare of children; the amount received depended on family income. Quite obviously, government policies and practices had dramatically altered what it meant to be a Chipewyan. In sum, the federal goal had been to recast the people into a generalized Euro-Canadian mold.

Figure 4-8 | The community of Lutselk'e (Snowdrift) in 1996.

Figure 4-9 | By 1996 Lutselk'e had mail service six days a week.

In the government effort to transform villagers into "standard" Canadians, the system of formal education became a major catalyst. In 1935 families began to be encouraged by the Indian agent to send children ranging in age from three to seventeen to a residential (boarding) school at Fort Resolution that was managed by Roman Catholic missionaries. Instruction was in English, and children were discouraged from speaking Chipewyan. Thus during their formative years these children spent only about two months at home each year. Residential schooling intensified after school attendance became compulsory in

1960. The fund of traditional cultural knowledge conveyed to a child depended to a great extent on his or her family background and ranged from being comprehensive to comparatively superficial. A federal village school was opened in 1960 that ended residential schooling for most young children. However, by 1996 a free high school education could be obtained only at the government residential school in Fort Smith; during that year, thirty-four high school students studied there. The school system in general, with its stress on Euro-Canadian values, did little to foster or sustain traditional Chipewyan life. A partial indicator is that most younger people do not speak Chipewyan.

For many, possibly most, adults, life had lost its purpose; they could no longer pursue their old ways, nor could they truly become Euro-Canadians. A widespread reaction was a pervasive dependence on the government to provide. A by-product of this situation was a growing dependence on the consumption of alcoholic beverages imported from Yellowknife. The situation became critical in the 1970s, and in 1980 the band council passed an ineffective prohibition law. In the 1980s multiple deaths and violence as a result of excessive drinking became alarming. By the mid-1990s intoxicant consumption had *decreased* significantly. By then about 25 percent of adults had been abstinent for about five years. During the first eight months of 1996, most of the police action cases involved alcohol, and about twenty individuals were the most frequent offenders. The following year a survey indicated that the community drug and alcohol counselor was regarded as helpful by numerous persons but of little value by others. There appears to be at least a short-term trend toward less social turmoil associated with intoxicants.

Recent years have introduced major changes in federal Indian policies. Greater administrative authority shifted to the local level, but not to local control. A number of examples are illustrative. In 1991 a symbolic but meaningful change was made. The official village name was changed from Snowdrift to Lutselk'e, Chipewyan words meaning "the place of small fish," a nearby locality. In that same year we also find that an effort was being made by the First Nations (Indians, Inuit, and Métis) in the Northwest Territories to renegotiate their treaty rights, including a transfer of land ownership to the indigenous peoples. The federal government has been reasonably sympathetic with these efforts, and a shift toward more administrative power is taking place. A major change in the local economy has already occurred. The Hudson's Bay Company store closed in 1973, and, after a brief period of private ownership and with financial assistance from the government, it became a member of a network of northern cooperative stores. Thus the people became the store owners. Management of the local school is supervised by a community educational authority that administers the budget and hiring. With respect to local government, a band manager was trained, and the band council has emerged as a municipal government with territorial funding and expanding administrative control over local affairs. The band council includes representatives from the major family groups, as well as women, and the council has been working together far more harmoniously than ever before. Likewise, a Chipewyan holds

Figure 4-10 | Lutselk'e men in 1996: Alfred Boucher (left) and his father, Joe Boucher.

the office of justice of the peace, and a local Dene was trained as a law enforcement officer. In sum, changes in federal policies have led to far more local responsibilities than would have been conceivable thirty years ago.

Socially, it is not insignificant that five white women had married Chipewyan men by 1996, and four Dene women once were married to white men. Furthermore, although we do not associate respect for most older persons with the early historic Chipewyan, the villagers of today appear to be changing their attitudes toward their elders (see Figure 4-10). Finally, the position of women is strong. This may be a product of a higher sex ratio for men, as in the early 1960s. More women than men have had post–high school training; one local Chipewyan woman earned a college degree.

By the mid-1990s local food resources remained of critical importance for many families. In the early 1960s game was scarce in the vicinity, and the area continues to be a "land of feast or famine." Since about 1980 the fall caribou migration has shifted to nearby localities and has included many animals; in addition, some caribou winter locally. Moose likewise have become more readily available as a source of meat. Coupled with an abundance of lake trout, this is a land of plenty, at least for the time being. Accompanying these increases has been a decrease in pressure on food resources from hunting and fishing in the settlement area from a generation ago. This is because a smaller number of families depend on these activities for their primary food supply. Others depend far more on federal and territorial monies, both earned and unearned. Historically, the harvest of furbearers was the major source of cash for the local people, but by 1996 trapping was a primary activity for only ten men.

Although employment opportunities were limited by the mid-1990s, the number of year-round jobs was far greater than previously. The band employed some twenty persons, including an elected chief, social worker, and a drug and alcohol abuse counselor. The cooperative store grossed about one million dollars a year and employed seven persons on a full-time basis. The school employed four teachers. To maintain the infrastructure, workers provided water and heating oil delivery and power plant and airport maintenance. In addition, summer construction projects were a source of employment, and ten men were available to fight forest fires. There previously had been commercial fishing at the eastern end of Great Slave Lake, but it was discontinued to help preserve the lake trout. Yet there were a number of local fishing lodges for sport fishermen, and some men in the community worked as guides for these fishermen.

Some cultural anthropologists have a reputation for emphasizing the changes in Indian life that were introduced by Westerners at the expense of traditional Indian culture. One reason is that the changes are often so overwhelmingly evident and important. One result of this focus has been to downplay or ignore the continuing vitality of traditional Indian ways that may be far less obvious. An example from Lutselk'e will illustrate the point. As a long-term observer of Athapaskan (Dene) Indians in the Northwest Territories, Father René Fumoleau, noted, "the most important thing in life is mobility." The capacity to move about remained a fundamental value in the 1990s, just as it was in much earlier historic times. To go to Yellowknife by airplane, boat, or snowmobile on the spur of the moment, to suddenly decide to hunt, fish, or visit someone, or to allow a child not to attend school on a particular day are part of this deep-seated pattern that remains Chipewyan, despite the span and intensity of Western influences.

Considering the near future, two closing thoughts appear relevant. In 1997, according to Brenda Parlee (1998, 16, 34), traditional foods, especially caribou, continued to dominate the diet of Lutselk'e residents. Concurrently, nearly two hundred community members reportedly had full- or part-time jobs, contracted work, or casual employment. With a Chipewyan population of about three hundred persons, this meant that most adults had at least temporary wage labor income, and most of them reportedly enjoyed at least some aspects of their work. Furthermore, recently developed diamond mines some 120 miles north of the community employed hundreds of Dene. Small numbers of Lutselk'e residents worked at the mines, usually as general laborers and housekeepers. Nevertheless, the procurement of local edibles has been and remains a defining characteristic of life among these people. If wage labor employment remains attractive and increasingly available, one would assume that "living off the land" will decline and thereby their unique identity as Chipewyan will be diminished.

Additional Sources

The best overview about Northern Athapaskans is the widely available volume edited by June Helm (1981) and published by the Smithsonian Institution. The best comparative analysis of Northern Athapaskan tribes is by James W. VanStone (1974) who also is the author of an in-depth study of Snowdrift (1965). Brenda Parlee (1998) conducted a "community-based monitoring" survey at Lutselk'e in the late 1990s. Her account consists primarily of quotations from residents about the past (e.g., "olden days") and contemporary conditions. Interpretive summaries supplement the quotations. For relatively recent and authoritative studies about the Chipewyan and their neighbors, the reader is referred to the selected bibliography that follows. The writings of Beryl C. Gillespie, Robert Jarvenpa, Henry S. Sharp, David M. Smith, and James G. E. Smith are especially important. For a conservative band of Chipewyan in the Barren Grounds, the key studies are by Sharp.

Selected Bibliography

Back, George. 1836. *Narrative of the Arctic Land Expedition*. London.

Birket-Smith, Kaj. 1930. *Contributions to Chipewyan ethnology*. Report of the Fifth Thule Expedition, vol. 6, no. 3.

Eggan, Fred, ed. 1937. *Social anthropology of North American tribes*. Chicago.

Gillespie, Beryl C. 1970. *Yellowknives*. Proceedings of the 1970 Annual Spring Meeting of the American Ethnological Society, Robert F. Spencer, ed., 61–71.

———. 1976. Changes in territory and technology of the Chipewyan. *Arctic Anthropology* 13:6–11.

Hearne, Samuel. 1795. *A journey from Prince of Wales's Fort in Hudson's Bay to the Northern Ocean*. London. (Other editions: Dublin 1796; Toronto 1911; Toronto 1958.)

Helm, June, ed. 1981. *Subarctic,* vol. 6, *Handbook of North American Indians*. Washington, DC.

Jarvenpa, Robert. 1976. Spatial and ecological factors in the annual economic cycle of the English River band of Chipewyan. *Arctic Anthropology* 13:43–69.

———. 1977. Subarctic trappers and band society. *Human Ecology* 5:223–59.

———. 1982. Intergroup behavior and imagery. *Ethnology* 21:283–99.

Jenness, Diamond, ed. 1956. The Chipewyan Indians: An account by an early explorer. *Anthropologica* 3:15–33.

Lowie, Robert H. 1909a. The Chipewyans of Canada. *Southern Workman* 38:278–83.

———. 1909b. An ethnological trip to Lake Athabasca. *American Museum Journal* 9:10–15.

Mason, John A. 1946. *Notes on the Indians of the Great Slave Lake area*. Yale University Publications in Anthropology, no. 34. New Haven.

Parlee, Brenda. 1998. *Traditional knowledge study on community health community-based monitoring*. The West Kitikmeot Slave Study Society.

Rich, Edwin E. 1960. *Hudson's Bay Company, 1670–1870.* 3 vols. Toronto.

Sharp, Henry S. 1975. Introducing the sororate to a northern Saskatchewan Chipewyan village. *Ethnology* 14:71–82.

———. 1977. The Chipewyan hunting unit. *American Ethnologist* 4(2) 377–93.

———. 1979. *Chipewyan marriage.* Mercury Series, Canadian Ethnology Service Paper, no. 58. Ottawa.

———. 1986. Shared experience and magical death: Chipewyan explanations of a prophet's decline. *Ethnology* 25(4) 257–70.

———. 1988. *The transformation of Bigfoot: Maleness, power, and belief among the Chipewyan.* Washington, DC.

———. 1991. Memory, meaning, and imaginary time: The construction of knowledge in white and Chipewyan cultures. *Ethnohistory* 38(2) 149–76.

———. 1995. Men and women among the Chipewyan. In *Women and power in native North America,* L. Klein and N. Ackerman, eds., 46–74. Norman, OK.

Simpson, George. 1938. *Journal of occurrences in the Athabasca department, 1820 and 1821.* Publications of the Champlain Society, Hudson's Bay Company Series, no. 1.

Smith, David M. 1973. *INKONZE: Magico-religious beliefs of contact-tradition Chipewyan trading at Fort Resolution, NWT, Canada.* Mercury Series, Ethnology Division Paper, no. 6. National Museum of Man, Ottawa.

———. 1976. Cultural and ecological change: The Chipewyan of Fort Resolution. *Arctic Anthropology* 13:35–42.

———. 1982. *Moose-Deer Island house people: A history of the native people of Fort Resolution.* Ottawa.

Smith, James G. E. 1970. The Chipewyan hunting group in a village context. *Western Canadian Journal of Anthropology* 1:60–66.

———. 1976a. Introduction: The historical and cultural position of the Chipewyan. *Arctic Anthropology* 13:1–5.

———. 1976b. Local band organization of the caribou eater Chipewyan. *Arctic Anthropology* 13:12–24.

Smith, James G. E., and Ernest S. Burch, Jr. 1979. Chipewyan and Inuit in the central Canadian Subarctic, 1613–1977. *Arctic Anthropology* 16(2) 76–101.

Tyrrell, Joseph B., ed. 1916. *David Thompson's narrative.* Publications of the Champlain Society, vol. 12. Toronto.

VanStone, James W. 1963. Changing patterns of Indian trapping in the Canadian subarctic. *Arctic* 16:159–74.

———. 1965. *The changing culture of the Snowdrift Chipewyan.* National Museum of Canada Bulletin no. 209.

———. 1974. *Athapaskan adaptations.* Chicago.

5 The Lower Kootenai: Plateau Fishers and Hunters

It was after the strangers came, more and more of them everywhere, that it [life] began to change.

(Elders of the Kootenai Nation 1990, 19)

THE PLATEAU CULTURE AREA is an inland sector of the Pacific Northwest in Canada and the United States in which Euro-American settlement has been comparatively recent. Of all the culture areas north of Mexico, the Plateau tribes probably are the least known. Unfortunately, yet typically, they were exposed to exotic diseases with devastating impact, both before and following the arrival of whites. In addition, after the boundary between the United States and Canada was determined in 1846, land-hungry white settlers soon began to pour into the Oregon Territory. Some tribes in the southern Plateau sector were nearly destroyed, whereas others were displaced or confined to relatively small tracts of land. As a result of new diseases and white intruders, their aboriginal cultures typically declined rapidly. More northern Plateau tribes, however, were affected somewhat later and less intensively by Euro-Americans. As a result, ethnographic accounts about some of these people are reasonably satisfactory. The Kootenai (Kootenay, Ktunaxa, Kutenai) are an example. Because they lived and continue to live on both sides of the international boundary, they also provide an opportunity to consider the national policies of Canada and the United States for a single Native American population.

These Indians had a number of names for themselves, but their self-identification is now *Kootenai* (KOOT-nee), a word of uncertain origin. No one knows their number in early historic times; two thousand may be a reasonable guess. They appear to have lived farther to the east before occupying their historic homeland. Their language is a "language isolate," meaning that it is not clearly related to any other linguistic group. The Kootenai are divided into the Upper (upriver) and Lower (downriver) dialect groups, depending on where they lived along the Kootenay River system. This geographical division is somewhat confusing; the Upper Kootenai occupy the eastern sector, and the Lower Kootenai are to the west and north of Kootenai Falls (see Figure 5-1).

The baseline ethnographic reconstruction presented in this chapter must be accepted with caution. Ethnographers did not begin to assemble comprehensive information about the aboriginal Kootenai until generations after historic contact. Investigators were forced to rely heavily on what people remembered about their earlier lifeway. The general tendency is for people to idealize their culture of old, and it can be difficult or impossible to verify what they remember. Life in the past no doubt seemed "good" to these people, especially in retrospect after outsiders had seized most of their land and had destroyed much of their culture. At least some of their oral history is questionable. Furthermore, verbal information about the past may produce contradictory statements. For instance, one person may report that a particular ceremony was aboriginal, whereas another person with a more recent knowledge base might deny that the ceremony existed. Contradictions of this nature produce interpretive challenges and may defy resolution.

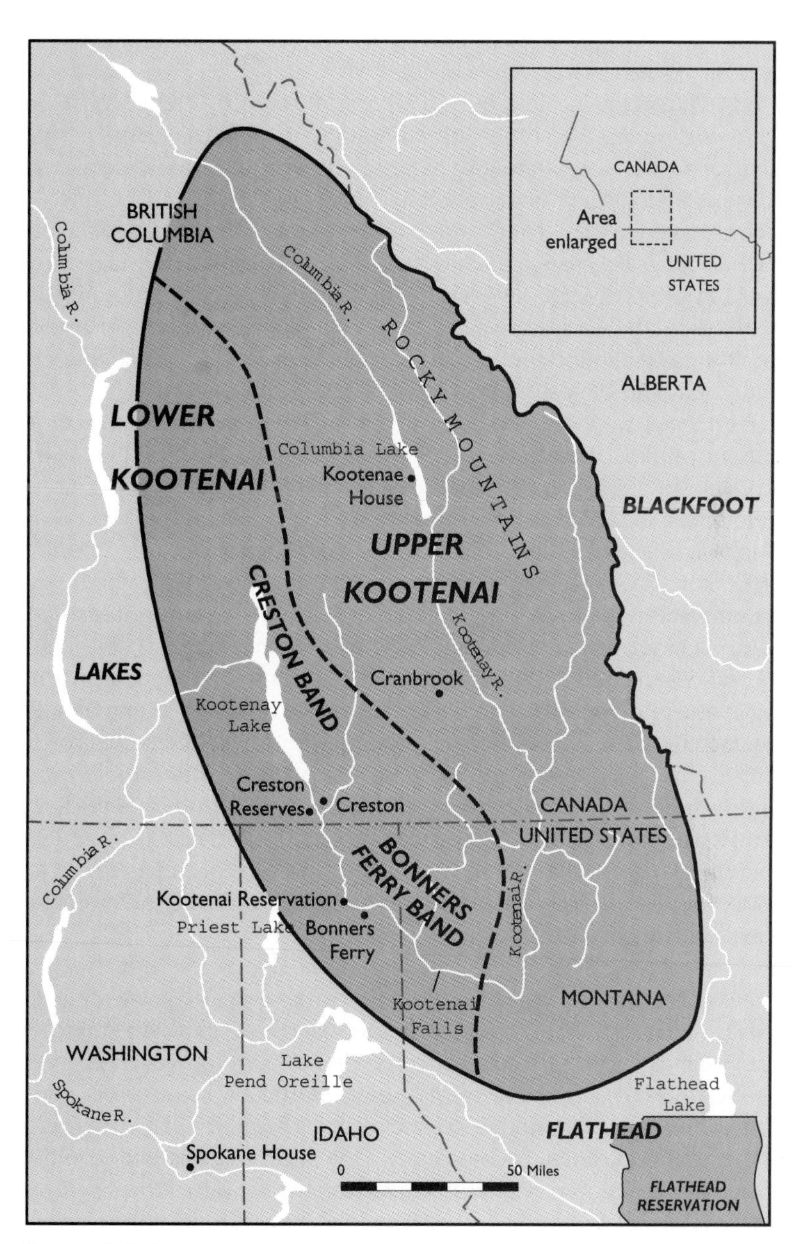

Figure 5-1 | Early historic Kootenai.

Aboriginal Life

This chapter, as far as the data permit, focuses on the Lower Kootenai. They are considered a subtribe by ethnologists, yet a case can be made for identifying them as a separate tribe. They occupied a clearly defined geographical area, spoke a distinct dialect, and had a separate economic base. The terms used to characterize the Lower Kootenai likewise are distinct. They include *Valley Indians, River People, Canoe Indians,* and their own traditional term, *Marsh People*. They were divided into two bands, the people of the modern Bonners Ferry area in Idaho and those of the Creston sector in British Columbia. The habitat was well suited to their economy, which was based on fishing, harvesting waterfowl, and deer hunting.

The Upper Kootenai to the east placed much greater emphasis on big game. Soon after domestic horses became available in the 1730s, providing greater mobility, big game became even more important. Furthermore, they expanded their hunting range eastward into the Plains, and bison became increasingly significant in their economy. This pattern did not prevail among the Lower Kootenai because bison did not frequent their area, nor were they readily accessible elsewhere. In brief, the Upper Kootenai became equestrian hunters in the manner of many Plains Indian tribes (see Chapter 6 on the Crow).

The Kootenay River and a fingerlike lake, Kootenay Lake, dominated the Lower Kootenai homeland. The valley bottom is relatively broad in the south and characterized by ponds, marshland, and meadows. The southern extreme is a forest of hemlock, cedar, fir, and pine. The valley narrows to the north and becomes a subalpine forest setting. Prominent trees include hemlock, fir, and spruce. Throughout the area winters can be cold, with deep snow and subzero temperatures, and the summers are typically hot. Average precipitation is about fifty inches a year. At the same time the climate is relatively mild, considering the geographical location.

ORIGIN MYTH The Kootenai did not have a specific account to explain their beginnings. Their rich and varied corpus of tales, however, does emphasize prehuman and humanlike animal spirits. Particular spirits produced an orderly world as precedent and as a model for human life. Some myths include specific creative episodes, such as when Doe and Lynx mated to produce two sons, the Sun and Moon. Numerous tales involve the adventures of Coyote as a trickster and transformer in his associations with various animals and birds. When humans emerged, spirit beings withdrew from the earth. Yet spirits continued to have a profound influence on human life, particularly as individuals obtained supernatural aid in personal vision quests.

APPEARANCE AND ARTIFACTS The Marsh People bathed often and favored perfumes produced from dried and crushed plants mixed with beaver

Figure 5-2 | A Lower Kootenai tepee covered with matting. (Courtesy of Glenbow Archives, Calgary, Alberta: neg. no. NA-1141-4.)

musk and grease. A woman parted her hair in the middle, with braids on each side. A man wore a braid on both sides of his head and had another at the back of his head and a braided scalp lock. Buckskin garments dominated. A woman wore a frock fringed at the bottom and leggings. A man's clothing included a breechclout, shirt, and leggings in cold weather. The people typically went barefoot in the summer, especially when working in wet areas. Otherwise they wore moccasins. Both sexes wore hats, mittens, and robes of fur in cold weather.

Summer dwellings accommodated small family groups. Mats sewn from rushes typically covered pole-framed tepees (see Figure 5-2). The winter home, termed a longhouse, accommodated multiple, closely related families. Paired poles bound near the top and spread at the base formed A-shaped frames arranged as an elongated triangle; horizontal support poles provided framework stability. Rush mats covered a longhouse, and the interior included a separate fireplace for each family.

A small, dome-shaped structure framed with bent saplings and covered with mats served as a sweat house. A pit dominated the interior. Stones, heated in a nearby fire, were transferred to the pit. Naked bathers sprinkled water on the hot stones to produce steam. People bathed for cleanliness, to cure illness, and, equally as important, to achieve or retain spiritual well-being. A small, probably mat-covered, conical menstrual hut completed the structures represented at a settlement.

Each family owned a number of dogs, their only domestic animal. Dogs guarded camps against intruders and served to drive big game toward concealed hunters. To train a hunting dog, a person might wrap a young puppy in the fresh skin of a big game animal, such as a deer, for a relatively brief period. In theory the puppy later became especially capable of pursuing that species. As families moved from one camp to another, dogs might serve as pack animals. A dog carried two loaded packs, one on each side of its back; binders beneath an animal secured the packs.

The most common tools included a variety of multipurpose knives with flaked flint blades, rodent-tooth knives, elk horn chisels, whetstones, and wooden wedges. They likewise had hafted and grooved stone axes and mauls of similar construction. To produce fire, a wooden fire drill was hand rotated on a fireboard made of a dry piece of poplar. Fungus on the board ignited, and dry grass caught the flames. The people attempted to keep at least one fire burning in a camp because of the labor required to produce a new fire.

Containers are a prominent cluster of artifacts. They fulfilled many functions, including collecting and processing plant products, cooking, serving foods, and storing edibles. The most common types consisted of folded sections of bark stitched to retain the vessel shape. A popular storage container, especially for fish and berries, consisted of a square cedar box with a lid. Foods stored in these boxes had a pleasing taste. Old containers of this type were torn apart by children and used as sleds. Deep coiled baskets were designed for food storage, and shallow ones were favored as plates. The bladders of big game held grease and oil. Note that most artifacts were highly portable and well adapted to a mobile way of life.

Skin processing by women had become the most integrated and complex technological process, just as among the Netsilik and Chipewyan. Women went to great lengths to whiten skins, as they were especially desirable for garments. After the preliminary preparation of a skin, it was soaked in a mixture of brains and water to remove blood stains, to break down the tissue, and to soften it. After this process was repeated as often as necessary, a skin finally was sun dried and scraped with a knife before being cut and sewn.

The Kootenai canoe is their most prominent aboriginal artifact type, primarily because of its distinctive outline. Canoes were indispensable in the lifeway of the Marsh People. The framework of a canoe consisted of cedar stringers some twelve feet in length and bent wooden ribs bound to the stringers with plant fibers. The vessel was covered with spruce bark, and pitch con-

Figure 5-3 | A Lower Kootenai bark-covered canoe. (Courtesy of Glenbow Archives, Calgary, Alberta: neg. no. NA-1141-5.)

cealed any holes in the bark. Wooden strips bound the gunwales to the cover, and a wooden crosspiece fitted across the top and middle of a vessel helped retain the shape. The beam was about thirty inches. A protruding ramlike bow and stern are the canoe's most distinctive features (see Figure 5-3). The leaf-shaped paddles lacked handgrips. To prevent leakage when traveling through ice, the canoer fitted the bow with a section of green hide.

SUBSISTENCE CYCLE Permanent settlements did not exist, and yet families generally camped at the same localities from one year to the next, depending on the availability of edibles. The primary staples consisted of fish, deer, and ducks, in that order of importance. The cooperative harvest of these edibles had emerged as most rewarding, and each major food source was under the supervision of a formal leader. Aided by a personal spirit, a leader had the reputation of being skillful and successful. Nonetheless, a fear of famine prevailed, and people depended heavily on the aid of spirits to obtain most edibles. This religious dimension suggests that food could not be procured on a reliable basis with the existing technology.

Cooperative fishing reportedly was most rewarding when supervised by a leader aided by either kingfisher or mink spirits; the mink spirit was classified as part fish and part clawed animal. The leader guided the activities of others in constructing weir-trap combinations, especially soon after the spring runoff. The weirs and traps were placed in streams and sloughs leading to the main river. At each fishing site ceremonial preparations spanned three nights. The fishing leader "divined for fish trap" to predict fishing success and foresee potential misfortune or deaths. First they prepared a weir, a damlike obstruction. Crotch-topped poles were cut and driven into the bottom of a water course. In the crotches they lashed long stringer poles. Next mats fashioned from fir boughs were lashed to the poles and stringers on the upstream side; three openings were left, one for each trap. In fast water they fashioned wickerwork weir sections from willow branches. A cylindrical fish trap with willow branch stringers was about nine feet in length, and the mouth was some two feet in diameter. The stringers at the opposite end were lashed together. Willow hoops bound around a trap helped retain the cylindrical design. At the trap mouth a funnel-shaped opening of willows was tied in place. Fish that swam into the funnel seldom could escape from a trap. After the weir-trap combination was completed, the fishing leader checked it each morning. He then returned to a camp to announce the number of men and canoes required to retrieve the catch. For supernatural reasons, fish could not be killed as they were removed from a trap. Trout, burbot, whitefish, or suckers were most often harvested, depending on the season. The catch was distributed to each family at a camp, irrespective of whether men from a particular family participated in the harvest. Fresh fish were placed in cedar root baskets with water and hot stones to cook. At the morning meal everyone ate together, whereas an evening meal was shared in small family groups. All fish bones were collected, saved, and returned to the river.

During the winter families fished especially for burbot, a large fish that was often plentiful. Traps and weirs for winter use were of heavier construction, and any ice that formed was crushed with a stone maul so that the traps could be set and tended from canoes.

A deer-hunt leader knew the habits of deer and the local terrain, and with the aid of spirits he reportedly could establish the location of deer. A hunt preferably was organized from a base camp in February following a heavy snow. On instructions from the leader, men and boys prepared their equipment, including small, round snowshoes of the bear-paw type. From high ground along each side of a stream at a hunting site, males yelled to drive deer into deep snow at lower elevations where the animals floundered. Self bows and arrows with needle-sharp heads dispatched the deer. Every effort was made to kill the lead deer first and thereby confuse the others. Following a harvest some meat was prepared for immediate consumption. The surplus meat was dried and cached on wooden platforms adjacent to large conifers to protect it from rain, snow, and predators.

A duck-hunt leader received spirit power from Two-Year-Old-Goose, and on summer mornings he supervised the harvest of ducks, swans, and geese. A twined bark net some twenty-five feet long and fifteen feet high was knotted with four-inch mesh to capture and hold ducks. Stretched between two stout poles with a rope arrangement, the net rested on the ground but could be raised abruptly by net tenders. Duck decoys were placed near the net, and a man imitated the cry of a feeding duck. If all went well, a flock landed nearby. The hunt leader watched the ducks until one of them stopped eating, an indication that they were preparing to fly off. The leader signaled the net tenders to raise the net abruptly as other men in strategic spots made a great deal of noise. After ducks flew into the net, it was dropped, and the net tenders broke the necks of the captives. Hunters hoped to harvest four flights in a morning. Larger-gauged nets served to tangle geese and swans. Waterfowl was processed soon after a kill for immediate consumption and storage because these birds spoiled rapidly. Some waterfowl nets could be converted into gill nets.

Women dug two species of camas (lily) bulbs as their primary contribution to the food supply. Before removing the bulbs with a fire-hardened digging stick, women recited prayers for a successful harvest. The bulbs retained their original flavor for a long while after being baked. A particular woman supervised the collection of salmonberries and huckleberries. Some berries were consumed fresh, and others were dried and stored for winter.

Tobacco was the only cultivated plant. A man dreamed that the Grizzly Bear, a supernatural, instructed him to sow the seeds and direct the plantings of others. Apparently the tobacco was harvested without ceremony. It was smoked in pipes during rituals, but not for pleasure.

Some families, apparently comparatively few, were known as "drifters." They were poor, had no fixed territory, and wandered about throughout the year in search of food. It would appear that they were not successful in enlisting the aid of spirits. They subsisted mainly by fishing with hooks and lines, and sometimes robbed the food caches of others. Such thefts were ignored, not punished.

These basic foods were augmented by a variety of others. For example, caribou provided a favorite meat and the best bedding. Mountain goats were difficult to hunt, but again the meat was appreciated, and the hides made fine robes. For sturgeon, a large and powerful fish, a baited hook was bound to a stout line. Finally, deadfalls served to trap furbearers.

Over the generations extended families typically exploited a particular locality for raw materials and edibles. Unclaimed land could be utilized by anyone. In at least some cases a particular spirit granted a man ownership of a specific locality in which he and his family might remain. A son or grandson who took care of his father or grandfather was likely to become the subsequent owner if the same spirit presented itself to that person.

DESCENT, KINSHIP, AND MARRIAGE The descent system of these people was bilateral, as has also been reported for the Netsilik and Chipewyan. Accounts about the traditional Kootenai kinship terminology are not consistent. The variations may represent local differences, historic changes, or a combination of these factors. Yet it is clear that numerous terms differed depending on whether the speaker was male or female (e.g., a woman and man used different terms for a younger brother). However, numerous terms were reciprocals,

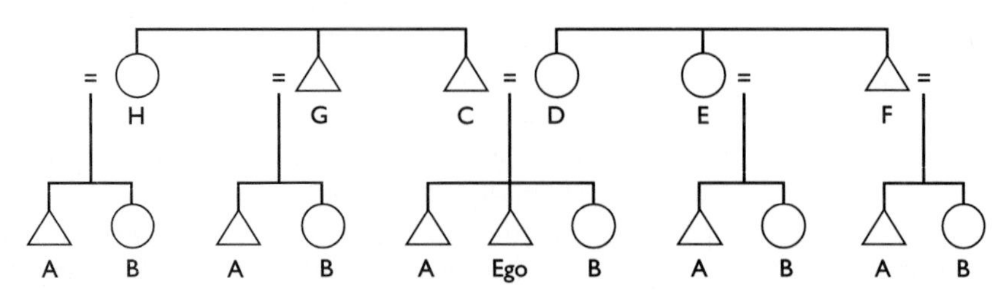

Figure 5-4 | Reconstruction of the basic early historic Kootenai kinship system.

meaning that they were the *same* for different sets of relatives (e.g., a grandparent and grandchild used the same word for each other). The brother and sister terms were extended to first cousins (Hawaiian cousin terminology) with obvious implications; cousins were treated essentially the same as biological siblings. With siblings and cousins termed alike, we would expect that the mother term would be extended to mother's sister and father's sister, but this was not the case. Instead separate terms existed for mother, mother's sister, and father's sister (bifurcate collateral parental generation terms). Presumably the basic terminology was changing when it was recorded (see Figure 5-4).

A newly married couple initially lived with the parents of the bride, and they later established an independent household nearby (matrilocal residence). The clearest joking relationship was between a man and his wife's sisters. Their jokes could be ribald, and sexually suggestive horseplay prevailed. This patterning was understandable because when a man's wife died it was customary for him to marry her oldest unmarried sister (the sororate). Similarly, a widow was expected to marry her deceased husband's brother (the levirate). In this general context, the death of a spouse tended not to disrupt the continuity of family life within marriages.

SOCIAL DIMENSIONS During the summer band members dispersed, and small family groups occupied tepees near one another. In the winter closely related families ideally lived in a single longhouse. By early historic times an estimated twenty families lived in the Bonners Ferry sector. The annual settlement pattern meant that comparatively few people lived in close contact with near biological relatives and in-laws. Yet in-law taboos prevailed. Parents-in-law did not directly address a son-in-law or daughter-in-law of the opposite gender. For example, a man never looked at his mother-in-law or communicated directly with her. When he had something to say to this woman in the presence of his wife, the message was conveyed by the wife. We also find that after puberty biological brothers and sisters avoided one another. These taboos may have emerged to prevent any hint of sexual relations that could disrupt the harmony within small, closely cooperating family groups.

Social bonds within a band found strength through male cooperation, with clearly defined subordinate and superordinate statuses, in key subsistence pursuits. In many social contexts, however, egalitarian relations prevailed. Young and old adults, as well as children, offered their opinions freely, without hesitation, and in straightforward language. Concurrently, people were exceedingly hospitable with other Kootenai and foreign friends. Families vied with one another to feed and lodge guests. It was rude not to offer someone food and in equally poor taste not to accept it.

Social control does not appear to have been a major problem, because band members were few and familiar with one another. Possibly the most powerful means of control was ridicule, as commonly is the case in small-scale societies. A persistently antisocial man might be ostracized until he conformed. Possibly the most disturbing situation resulted when one band member murdered another. Relatives of the deceased were obligated to seek justice. The murderer might be challenged to combat with an outstanding warrior, and whatever resulted could end the case, although enduring family feuds are reported.

If there was one Kootenai passion, it surely was gambling, and the hand game dominated; it was played separately by men, women, and children. Two players at a time were involved and backed by their supporters, who sang medicine songs for success and wagered on the outcome. A well-known gambler represented each side. The goal was to guess the hand that held a small white bone. Hand manipulations were extremely rapid, and ten counting sticks kept score until all were won or lost. When the stakes were high, a game might last through the night. Reportedly, in precontact times marten and fisher pelts represented the standard of wealth, especially for gambling. One might suspect that this emphasis on pelts was a product of the fur trade.

POLITICAL LIFE Early in their history, two Marsh People bands existed. A band of related families in a particular sector was presided over by a band leader. He was not the stereotype of a powerful "chief." Instead he possessed special rapport with spirits and represented moral authority. The people obeyed his decisions, not because of any threat but because he acted for the common good. A band leader was chosen by men who had achieved status through personal vision quests and had proven abilities. A band council consisted of leaders representing each of the three major subsistence complexes, a war leader, and the band leader.

When a band leader failed in his duties or died, an institutionalized procedure was followed. A new leader was chosen in council, but he could be a consensus leader before his formal appointment. A patrilineal emphasis prevailed in the selection, because the candidate seems most often to have been the wisest son of the previous leader. A candidate, irrespective of his background—or so it appears—went alone into the forest and sought spiritual instructions to become the successor. If he achieved his goal, he returned to camp singing a new song to validate his leadership role. He might then become the interim leader and the council-approved leader if the band thrived under his guidance. If not, the process was repeated until the council agreed on a replacement. The band leader alone officiated throughout the year.

The Marsh People are said not to have fought offensive wars. Their reasonably well-developed warfare complex was apparently a response to encroachments by other Indians. The Blackfoot were their greatest enemy. Campsites were chosen partially on the basis of defendability. The war leader for a band had proven abilities and spirit protection.

When preparing for combat, a warrior might wear only a breechclout and white body paint or body paint alone. Alternatively, he could wear an animal pelt with personal supernatural associations. A fourth possibility was to wear armor made from wooden slats bound tightly to protect the front and back of his body. Additional panels shielded his upper arms and lower legs. Over the body armor he could also wear a spirit-protected animal pelt. All of this variability was dictated by spirit aids. The primary weapon was the bow and arrow, but a war club or coup stick, used to touch or strike a live enemy, might be carried. In an open confrontation enemy warriors formed opposing lines, and a conflict began as they shot arrows at one another from a distance. Only the bravest warriors took quivers of arrows into battle. One such man after another approached the enemy, singing his protective song as he shot and dodged arrows. The most prestigious and dangerous form of combat was to strike an armed enemy with a coup stick and live to tell about the event. Dead enemies were scalped, but a scalp had no supernatural associations; it was a trophy. Ethnographic accounts suggest that counting coup and scalping were uncommon among the Lower Kootenai, unlike the Upper Kootenai, who were strongly influenced by the Plains Indian war complex.

RELIGION Earth, Water, and Sky represented the basic components of the natural world. Water with its aquatic life surrounded the Earth to sustain people, their artifacts, rocks, terrestrial plants, and animals. Sky was a dome occupied by avifauna; by the Sun, Moon, and other celestial bodies; and by natural phenomena such as thunder and lightning. Stars were human souls in the Sky, the Milky Way was the path of ghosts, and the Northern Lights represented the dead dancing. Each life form and every other earthly configuration possessed physical and spirit reality. A person became absorbed into the cosmological system through a vision quest.

Males and females alike sought visions, although those of males were judged more powerful. The people felt that a young person, ten years of age or somewhat older, possessed the potential for strong visions. To encourage a vision an object from the spirit (medicine, sacred) bundle of a relative might be taken on a quest. Yet the nature of spirit contacts was largely unpredictable. A father decided when a child would seek a vision, and preparations included purification with a smudge of dried juniper needles—the spirits were said to be attracted by the odor. A child sought spirit guidance at a body of water, in the mountains, or elsewhere. The successful novice had a vision, or less often a dream, in which an animal or sometimes a human spirit entered the person's body; supernatural power was conferred in a song. A particular spirit remained with an individual until he or she died. It then returned to the locality of its origin as a spirit ghost.

A successful quest by all men and many women was associated with a personal medicine bundle prepared under spirit guidance. An owner sang to his or her bundle and received instructions from it. A sacred bundle usually was buried with its owner. They thought that most people "only got cheap spirits," whereas those of shamans were powerful. Young people, female or male, could become shamans following an initial vision. Shamans served no apprenticeships, nor did they represent a distinct social group. Several shamans usually lived in a community, and each of them retained a respectful reputation as long as his or her spirit aids were successful in curing illness.

The major shamanistic ceremony was the curing ceremony, termed "putting-up-the-blanket," meaning that blankets were suspended from a rope across one section of a lodge where a juniper smudge burned for the evening event. In the darkened room a male shaman clad only in a breechclout sat with the blankets at his back facing the audience-participants. He beat a drum and sang a song to summon a spirit. After the spirit arrived, he went behind the blankets. The blankets began to shake, sometimes violently, and footfalls might be heard on the roof. After being tied up by a spirit, the shaman rolled out from behind the blankets. Someone placed a whistle in his mouth that was used to summon as many as four spirits, and he returned to behind the blankets. Next he appeared before the onlookers freed of his bonds. He again returned behind the blankets, from where a spirit was said to carry him off. The blankets shook so violently that the viewers could see that the shaman had disappeared. From behind the blankets spirits advised the audience in low and sometimes confusing voices. A seance ended when the shaman reappeared from behind the blankets in a dazed state. For his services in curing a patient he received no compensation. A number of shamans could perform in a single seance.

The most elaborate religious observance of the aboriginal Marsh People was the Grizzly Bear Ceremony. The veneration of bears prevailed widely among peoples of the northern forested regions in the northern hemisphere. A number of compelling reasons have been offered to account for this emphasis. Bears, like people, usually are omnivorous, they can stand on their hind legs, and they behave in other humanlike ways. Equally important, a skinned bear looks quite human. Bears can be dangerous, and their ability to hibernate is yet another impressive characteristic. Among the Marsh People black and brown bears had supernatural associations, but systematic ritual attention focused on the grizzly. They are impressively large, agile, and elusive; they maul or kill people when they feel threatened. People apparently hunted grizzly bears after a man dreamed that a friend or relative would be killed by a grizzly. If a shaman confirmed the dream, the dreamer sought to kill the animal. Dogs tracked the bear in the late fall or early winter, and they held it at bay for the hunter to make the kill with his bow and special magical arrows. Fresh bear meat was roasted over a fire, and any surplus was dried for the future; bear oil was valued as a condiment. Dogs were prohibited from gnawing on bear bones.

The grizzly bear was accorded special recognition in similar ceremonies held twice each year: before the bears emerged from dens in the spring and before they denned in the fall. The Grizzly Bear Ceremony "was characterized by petitions, propitiatory songs and mimetic dances, tobacco offerings, food sacrifices and other gifts made to the bear, with prayers by women that they not be molested during the root- and berry-gathering season, and by men that the spirit not be angry if one of its 'children' was killed, since the flesh was to be used as food" (Schaeffer 1966, 17).

The observances were held in an especially large tepee. Facing the entrance was the representation of a grizzly bear, possibly made from earth and including a bear skull. The male participants, and sometimes women with spiritual powers, appear to have had their medicine bundles included at the bear altar. The ceremony began with supernatural songs about the grizzly bear, other songs were sung in its honor, and some men and women danced for the same purpose. Gifts to the grizzly bear were made by the participants and accompanied by prayers. These presents were buried as offerings to the animal. The ceremony concluded with a feast of berries, a favored food of bears.

Sorcery also was associated with the grizzly bear and performed by shamans empowered by the bear's spirit. A sorcerer sent the spirit against a victim, and it reportedly entered a camp as a bear to seek the victim and attack him. A shaman-sorcerer also could cause illness, and the victim sought another shaman to sing over him; if he was cured, it was a sign that the malice of the shaman-sorcerer had caused the illness. The victim might in turn ask the helpful shaman to kill the evil one by supernatural means.

LIFE CYCLE A pregnant woman observed many taboos to help ensure the well-being of her offspring. She slept with few blankets, she could not pause in a doorway to look outside, nor could she break bones. These, plus many other prohibitions, set her apart from other women—in anthropological terms. Delivery occurred in her dwelling, where she knelt and held onto cords suspended from upright poles as a midwife supported her from behind. A midwife reportedly began her career following a dream in which she helped a particular woman. A midwife received no compensation. A shaman was called in for a difficult delivery; his aid appears to have been more supernatural than purely medical. After childbirth the mother wore a buckskin belt to bind her abdomen; she remained in the dwelling for ten days and drank through a drinking tube. For a month she was prohibited from having sexual intercourse. The major restriction of a husband was to drink through a drinking tube for that month.

A neonate was named at birth and usually retained the same name throughout life; however, names and the naming process are unclear. For a few days a new baby was wrapped in a robe and later carried in a cradleboard that hung from the mother's back; a piece of the umbilical cord was dried and sewn into a bag that was attached to the cradleboard. The inside of a cradleboard was lined with fur from which urine and feces could be removed. A baby initially slept between its parents, a symbolic prohibition against their sexual intercourse.

Indulgence characterized adult behavior toward small children, who were expected to speak Kootenai reasonably well at about fourteen months of age; soon thereafter she or he began to be taught. An emphasis on being silent and reserved prevailed; loudness was associated with antisocial behavior. Parents did not hesitate to spank their children, and older siblings disciplined younger ones, irrespective of gender. The following story for children appears to have been conceived to induce conformity: A brother and sister once lived as husband and wife, but their descendants became dullards and "wild people." Only their tracks were ever seen, and they became extinct. The story of these wild people appears to have been used as a "bogeyman" and may represent an effort to prevent brother-sister incest.

A small girl played with dolls and increasingly mimicked her mother's behavior. Thus the child learned to acquire womanly habits at a young age so that she could help her mother following the birth of a sibling. An eight-year-old girl was expected to be capable of preparing a simple meal. People likewise felt that a boy must begin to learn adult skills early in life. By the time he was six, a boy had his own bow and arrows. He was expected to kill birds and thereby make at least a symbolic contribution to the family food supply.

A child crossed a major threshold when he or she sought a lifelong protective spirit, as discussed previously. For a girl, her first menstruation represented another milestone. She was isolated under the supervision of an old woman and lived in a menstrual hut away from a camp. The girl drank little water and ate sparingly. Her hair was braided and painted red, and her face was painted the same color. When she itched, she scratched with a piece of wood. In the hut she sat on a low platform, and outside of it she walked over poles placed on the ground. Her ten days of isolation were followed a year later by the same set of conventions, but the isolation was for only five days. During subsequent menstrual periods she was not isolated. All of this ritual attention obviously separated her from other, more youthful, females and emphasized her new status as a woman. Comparable ceremonial involvement at puberty did not exist for a male. Yet as indicated earlier, a brother and sister avoided contact with one another upon reaching puberty.

Ideally a woman remained a virgin before marriage, and her close relatives attempted to prevent premarital sexual intercourse. Nonetheless, "mischief men" seduced maidens and then ridiculed them; rapes also occurred. Spirits reportedly ceased to aid such men. No stigma fell on a woman or her offspring if she conceived before marriage, and the biological father was responsible for supporting the child. The existence of such standards suggests that this pattern may have been relatively common.

Monogamy dominated in marriages, and a young couple had comparative freedom in making their own arrangements as long as the families involved did not strongly disapprove. A youthful male could take the initiative by composing and singing a love song for the one he desired. A young woman in turn could respond with a song if she looked favorably on the singer. Flute music likewise could be a part of courting behavior. Alternatively, if a girl desired a particular man and had the support of her mother, the older woman could initiate the arrangements. A few days following a marital agreement, the couple received gifts from each set of parents. No formal marriage ceremony existed, and a couple usually lived with the wife's family for a year or more to absorb the routine of adult life. Subsequently, they set up their own tepee in the summer near the wife's parents, and a feast was held to honor the couple, the only public recognition of their change in status.

Circumstances in all societies led to alternative marital arrangements. Among these Indians, for instance, an orphan girl could be taken into a family as a servant. A young man who desired her for a wife might creep silently at night into the dwelling where she lived. If the girl allowed him to remain, their cohabitation became a marriage. Divorce was common when a partner found the marriage difficult; this was a private decision, not a public concern, and children remained with the mother.

The concept of purity found prominent expression in the sweat bath, known to some people as Grandfather Sweat House. A person bathed for physical cleanliness, to obtain spirit blessing in prayers, to reinforce spirit songs, for gambling luck, and to cure illness under a shaman's supervision. In at least some bathing, a person with Sweat-House Spirit power put water on the hot stones. He dipped one handful of water at a time from a container and threw it on the rocks. Twenty-one handfuls produced so much moist heat that some bathers would be forced from a bathhouse.

Apart from shamans, female herbalists employed plant products under the guidance of spirits to cure physical ailments. Secular curers appear to have been instructed by spirits about how to use most plant products in this manner. Shamans, male or female, treated illness that was thought to be of supernatural origins. Their goal was to locate and remove a foreign substance from a patient's body by sucking.

It was anticipated that a fatally ill person could predict what would happen to the living. Following a death the body was attended by relatives and remained in the dwelling during the day of death, and that night all mourners were present. People cried and sang weeping songs. The following day the corpse was bathed and later removed from the dwelling headfirst. Burial was in a shallow grave and without ceremony. They had little interest in an afterlife.

ONE-STANDING-LODGE-POLE-WOMAN Early in Marsh People history, this woman unquestionably was the most famous individual in highly varied ways. She was a courier, guide, prophetess, warrior, shaman, peacemaker, and probably the only Kootenai female at that time to assume the role of a man. She was a transvestite, a woman-man, or berdache (meaning a woman-man or more often a man-woman). Firsthand accounts about her by white explorers and traders, as well as secondhand reports, are relatively numerous. She became famous from along the Columbia River to the sea.

As she matured, it appears that Lodge-Pole-Woman was large and heavy boned. She apparently had hoped to marry, but because of her size she could not obtain a Kootenai husband. Before long the first white traders appeared locally, and Lodge-Pole-Woman became the wife of one of them. They spent the winter of 1808–1809 at Kootanae House, where she appears to have learned to speak limited Cree. As a result of "loose" behavior, she was obligated to leave the trading post and her husband.

More than a year later she rejoined the Marsh People and told of her remarkable transformation. In dances she related that her former husband had performed an operation to change her sex—evidence for the great powers of whites. As a result of her sex change, she assumed a new name, Gone-to-the-Spirits. It was then that she began to wear a man's garments and carry weapons. She soon attempted to obtain a wife, but without success, despite her claim of supernatural powers. At this point people began to regard her as threatening, or possibly dangerous. Eventually Gone-to-the-Spirits began living with a woman abandoned by her husband. The woman-man beat her partner for having an open affair with a man, which led to their separation. Gone-to-the-Spirits, who was thought to have fashioned a leather phallus, subsequently had a sequence of wives.

In keeping with her male status, she became a warrior, although few details are known about this role. We do know that she accompanied her brother and others on foot to raid for horses. Whenever they came to a stream it was customary to cross it naked and to carry clothing on one's head. The brother noticed that his sister lagged behind the others at these crossings. On one occasion he saw his sister in the water below the waist and knew that she was not a man, but he said nothing. She apparently realized that her gender was now known to her brother and quickly squatted in the water, pretending to have turned her ankle. As a result of this feigned misadventure, she changed her name to *Qânqon kâmek klaúla* (Sitting-in-the-Water-Grizzly). Following the abortive raid she obtained a new wife and treated her poorly. During one noisy confrontation heard by the brother, he announced to the people of the camp that she really was a woman and that he would call her Qanqon, a derisive nickname, a reference to her squatting in the stream. Despite ridicule she continued to live with her band and obtained a new bride. Before long the woman was mistreated and threatened to use her supernatural powers against the woman-man. To test her power Qanqon shot the wife in the wrist with an arrow. The woman pulled out the arrow, rubbed the wound, and it reportedly healed immediately. She left Qanqon following this incident, but the woman-man treated subsequent wives with greater consideration.

In 1811, and with a new wife, Qanqon journeyed to Spokane House, a British outpost of the North West Company. Here she was asked by the trader to deliver a letter to a distant post. Qanqon and her spouse made a truly remarkable trip to the mouth of the Columbia River and the new Pacific Fur Company post at Astoria, an American enterprise. The contents of the delivered letter are unknown, and where it was to be delivered is confused. Nonetheless, Qanqon told the Astoria traders a great deal about the fur resources along the middle reaches of the Columbia. As a result a party of Astoria traders, loosely guided by Qanqon, was sent to build an inland post to rival Spokane House. As they traveled inland, Qanqon asked the whites to protect her because as a prophetess on the downstream trip she had predicted disease among the Chinook Indians, who feared a smallpox epidemic. The whites whom she guided assured the Chinook that they did not carry smallpox and probably saved Qanqon's life.

On the trip up the Columbia, Qanqon and her spouse pushed ahead of the whites as "bold and adventurous amazons." She claimed to be an advance agent of "the great white chief" (Schaeffer 1965, 206). She reported to Indians along the way that their desires for trade goods would be fulfilled, at no cost to them, by white men who were following her. By the time Qanqon and her wife were some distance up river, they had received twenty-six horses, many of them loaded with robes, and other spoils from foreign Indians. She had gained a reputation as a prophetess and was at least partially responsible for the Prophet Dance movement. It focused, as did the later Ghost Dance (see Chapter 2), on world renewal, a return of the dead, and a blissful life after a particular dance was performed repeatedly.

The next mention of Qanqon is in 1825, when she visited the Flathead Post and became "tipsy" on rum. Claude E. Schaeffer (1965, 214) suggested that by this time she was gaining a reputation as a shaman, possibly as a result of her transvestite status. Twelve years later, in 1837, she again emerges in history. By then she was about forty-seven years old and sought to make peace between the Blackfoot and Flathead. The same year she participated in an unsuccessful raid for horses with other Kootenai. According to Blackfoot and Kootenai oral traditions, the raiders were ambushed by a party of Blackfoot. A Kootenai who had lagged behind the others concealed himself before the attack. He heard one Blackfoot war whoop after another, indicating Kootenai deaths. He then heard a woman scream and knew it was Qanqon. Reportedly she was shot a number of times before being subdued in a sitting position. Blackfoot warriors slashed at her midsection with knives, but the wounds were said to close each time a knife was withdrawn from her body. One Blackfoot then cut open her chest and ate a piece of her heart, an ultimate tribute to a great warrior. She could not heal this wound, according to tradition, and died. Some time later when a Kootenai party located her body, they found that predators had not disturbed the corpse.

Historical Changes

Early in their history the number of Marsh People is uncertain. Before whites arrived, smallpox epidemics had struck repeatedly. Other early epidemics of exotic diseases in the region included whooping cough, a strain of cold or influenza, and probably measles; each could prove deadly to a virgin population. From the cumulative impact of these diseases, it is reasonable to assume that older people, infants, and children most often died. If so, this would mean that few elders survived to pass on cultural traditions and that relatively few children lived long enough to learn the old ways. Population numbers and cultural knowledge must have diminished a great deal within a few generations.

Two great fur trading companies dominated early explorations and control of the Plateau region. In the late 1700s North West Company agents reported that the Kootenai were attempting to reach their distant posts, but Plains Indians barred the way. The first local post was Kootanae House, founded in 1807. By then the Kootenai had few guns or ready access to other trade goods; they were delighted when this post was opened. The competing Hudson's Bay Company absorbed the North West Company in 1821 and controlled the region until after 1846, when the boundary between the United States and Canada was established. The international boundary divided the Marsh People into two groups: those around Bonners Ferry, Idaho, and others in the vicinity of Creston, British Columbia. Their total population in 1830 reportedly was close to three hundred, a third of whom were children. Oregon Territory was created in 1848 with Indian rights acknowledged but poorly respected. The major treaty with Indians of the region was the Hell Gate Treaty of 1855, but it did *not* involve the Lower Kootenai.

The earliest prominent historical leader among the Marsh People was Three Moons, their last great warrior and first "chief." He died about 1840. Three Moons had prophesied the arrival of men with light skin who would bring peace and salvation. His revelations, similar to those of other Indians in the region, resulted in the Prophet Cult movement. The earliest missionary was Father Pierre-Jean de Smet, a Roman Catholic. During an extended stay among the Lower Kootenai in 1845, he converted everyone to Catholicism and had a cross erected at the site that came to be known as Mission Hill near the future town of Bonners Ferry, Idaho.

The cosuccessors of Three Moons, christened Thomas and Moses, emerged as assertive Roman Catholic advocates. They sought to destroy the traditional religion. People who did not conform with Church teachings were confined to their dwellings or flogged, practices introduced by priests. Yet by about 1890 some people became disillusioned with the new religion. Successive chiefs vacillated between acceptance and rejection of Catholicism. The first church was built on Mission Hill in 1890, and people began to settle nearby. A new church was completed in 1907, but soon thereafter so many people were reverting to the old religion that the priests no longer visited them. The Marsh People obviously had mixed feelings toward the "strangers" among them.

THE KOOTENAI OF BONNERS FERRY, IDAHO This band of Kootenai emphatically and justifiably stress that they were not represented at the Hell Gate Treaty of 1855. As a direct result, these people had neither early nor formal recognition by the United States. Because their valley bottom land was prime for farming and grazing, it was coveted by white settlers and land speculators and regarded by the federal government as public domain. The Bonners Ferry Kootenai were strongly encouraged by federal agents to settle on the Flathead Reservation in Montana, and a small number of families relocated there. Those who refused to move finally were allotted the local land on which they lived by a presidential executive order in 1887. These holdings did not constitute a formal reservation but came to be regarded as the Kootenai Reservation.

The federal goal was to have families farm their allotments, but in the absence of any Kootenai farming tradition, most families continued to fish, hunt, and collect plant products on a miniscule and clearly inadequate land base. Nonetheless, a few men began to farm and raise cattle. Over the years, as the original allottees died, their plots repeatedly were divided by inheritance and became so small that a family could not farm even if they so desired. The federal government solution was to lease the land to white farmers. Oral tradition indicates that some "leases" negotiated by whites actually were bills of sale. Eventually the federal government leased most allotments to white farmers; band members received ⅓ of the lease profits.

By the early 1930s the people were largely landless, and addiction to alcoholic beverages had become endemic. (Indians in Idaho could not legally consume alcohol until 1955, when the state repealed their prohibition law.) In 1934 a federal response to their plight was to build new houses for families at Mission Hill. In another development the people sought compensation for land they had lost, and in 1960 they received a settlement of $425,000 based on the 1859 value of 125,000 acres in northern Idaho. According to the Elders of the Kootenai Nation (1990, 23–24), none of the money could be used to buy back land. Each person was to receive $4700 for the settlement, but they were obligated to put it in trust accounts to repay the state for welfare benefits, as was a common policy for states.

Pressured by the BIA, an elected tribal government emerged in 1947 as the Kootenai Tribe of Idaho. In anthropological terms, these people represent a band, not a tribe, but their identification as a tribe in this legal context is accepted in the following text. Tribal membership initially included all local Kootenai with at least one-fourth Kootenai genetic heritage who were not affiliated

Figure 5-5 | A war bond issued by the Kootenai of Idaho to help fund their confrontation with the United States in 1974.

with any Canadian Indian group. By 1999 nearly half of the 126 tribal members were under 18 years of age. About 90 tribal members lived either on their tribal lands or in the vicinity of Bonners Ferry. The same year, the tribe and its members held about 2,000 acres, most of which was leased to white farmers.

Dissatisfaction with their land settlement led to the next major development. In 1974 the tribe declared a "nonviolent war" on the United States, and in it they sought all of their rights to lost land. The single "battle" was a roadblock at Bonners Ferry. The Indians attempted to restrict access to one road and charged a toll of 10¢ per car from drivers willing to pay. The state responded by sending a large number of Idaho State Police to the town. The threat of arrest ended the roadblock. These Kootenai also issued "war bonds" to finance their cause (see Figure 5-5). In meetings with local, state, and federal represenatives, the confrontation was defused but not resolved, in part because the national press paid scant attention to their war. The people were awarded 12.5 acres at the Mission Hill site and assured that additional efforts would be made to obtain more land for them; by the late 1990s this promise had remained unfulfilled. The federal government did, however, build new houses for the people and a community hall. A state of war continues to exist with the United States.

The most positive change of recent years began in 1986 when the tribe opened a motel, the Kootenai River Inn, on allotted land in Bonners Ferry. More

Figure 5-6 | Paul Abraham, a Lower Kootenai, playing near his home on Mission Hill in 1998.

important, in 1993, they launched at the same site a gaming facility with bingo and pulltabs ("slot machines" that issue receipts for winnings as opposed to cash). By 1999 the inn and casino had 150 employees, of whom 4 temporary student workers were Kootenai; the annual payroll was $1.5 million. By then the inn and casino had become a major employer in Boundary County, Idaho. Each tribal member, irrespective of age, receives a significant quarterly income from the inn and casino investments. The earnings of underage members are held in trust (see Figure 5-6). They begin to receive their money at age eighteen if they graduate from high school or at age twenty-one for nongraduates.

Before opening the inn, it appears that most whites in Bonners Ferry were intermittently helpful and sympathetic to local Kootenai and quite willing to honor and to exploit them in promotional contexts (see Figure 5-7). In general, however, a socioeconomic chasm separated local Indians from residents of the town, and no Kootenai worked there. A widespread Indian stereotype prevailed. With some exceptions these Indians were characterized as lazy, unreliable, poor, and drunkards; they were most often to be pitied. Following the business acumen of the tribe in developing the inn and casino, the attitudes of

Figure 5-7 | A 1964 celebration at Bonners Ferry, Idaho, included Lower Kootenai participation. Chief Eneas Abraham posed on a horse. (Photograph courtesy of Paul Flinn.)

most townspeople changed, but not a great deal. The Indians continued to be regarded as lazy and unreliable but *rich*. In this sense Kootenai economic success became yet another *divider* between Indians and Euro-Americans. In a major effort to gain greater acceptance by local whites, a three-day Kootenai Casino Powwow was presented in June of 1999 as a part of the Bonners Ferry Centennial celebrations. The powwow attracted some 700 Indian dancers representing diverse tribes, and about 1,200 visitors attended the event. The tribe spent well over $100,000 on the powwow, which was considered by most whites and Indians as a great success (see Figure 5-8).

Casino profits earned by Native American tribes have been negatively labeled as a "quick fix" for their many problems, and this may be true. Yet it must be reemphasized that the Bonners Ferry Kootenai land holdings are minuscule and that they had no secure economic base. Likewise, their relationship with

Figure 5-8 | These dance participants are awaiting their turn at the 1999 Kootenai Casino Powwow.

all levels of the U.S. government has been disappointing at best. Yet the short-term positive benefits from inn and casino earnings are impressive:

1. Tribal members collectively have unprecedented economic security. How lasting it will be is unknown, especially considering continuing efforts in the U.S. Congress to tax gaming operations one way or another and/or to withdraw federal support from tribes with successful gaming operations.
2. The tribe now provides full college scholarships for eligible members.
3. The tribe helps fund the Indian Health Service for benefits received.
4. In 1997, when the county school district was in desperate need of funds, the tribe contributed $93,000.
5. They also have their own welfare program to aid members confronted by temporary economic adversity; the tribe receives neither federal or county welfare aid.
6. They contract with the county for general law enforcement.
7. To expand the land base, the tribe is buying back land that once was theirs.

8. The casino attracts local patrons and tourists alike to provide much needed economic vitality to the *town* of Bonners Ferry. This Kootenai contribution possibly amounts to millions of dollars each year.
9. Finally, the success of the inn and casino provide a newfound pride among tribal members as Indians, especially as Kootenai.

The "good" derived from the inn and casino operations understandably is accompanied by the "bad."

1. Historically, the Kootenai have been avid gamblers, a cultural focus that remains strong. As a direct result, for some members their income from the tribe has fueled their gambling passion. Thus a comparatively small number are worse off than previously. In addition, children and youth continue to be enculturated with a gambling emphasis. There is reason to believe that as adults at least some of them will become compulsive gamblers.
2. A county official familiar with the youth of the Bonners Ferry area reported that Indian and non-Indian youth have much the same rate of involvement with substance abuse. The motivation for individuals in both groups to obtain a high school education is mixed. Some youthful Kootenai see no reason why they should graduate from high school, acquire job skills, or attend college. They assume that as adults they will always have income from casino profits.
3. The long-standing historical pattern of heavy adult consumption of alcoholic beverages remains a major concern. For some adults among whom the problem was acute, it is now greater as a result of their economic security. The tribe employs a counselor who focuses largely on the excessive drinking of youth; adults usually have not been responsive to the program.

What did it mean to be an Idaho Kootenai in the late 1990s? A knowledgeable woman, a tribal leader, considered the question. She noted that about half of the adults continued to speak Kootenai and that about the same number were considered genetically as Kootenai. The vast majority of the tribal members lived nearby, and marriages to non-Indians were rare. Although most members were nominal Roman Catholics, the traditional religious system, although far from intact, was strong. This was reflected especially in the vision quests of some youths and a few adults. Likewise, for some persons the sweat bath remained a dimension of religious life. Their own brand of humor still prevails, along with an emphasis on gambling. She readily conceded as well that a few families had become Euro-American in their lifestyles.

THE CRESTON AREA KOOTENAI As indicated in Chapter 2, Native American administration in Canada has been quite different from that in the United States. The Canadian provinces have far more authority and power in dealing with Indians than the states of the United States. In theory, the major document regulating Indian affairs in Canada is the Royal Proclamation of 1763. It recognized exclusive Native American title to their land and declared that land could only be alienated with Indian permission and only to the Crown. For most Canadians of aboriginal ancestry, this document has proved meaningless, especially in British Columbia. A review of Indian policy in British Columbia is revealing.

The British North American Act, Canada's federal constitution, led to the creation of the Dominion of Canada in 1867, and the political status of British Columbia changed from a colony to a province in 1871. Apart from a relatively few small reserves (reservations) established on Vancouver Island in colonial times, the province denied the legal right of Indians to their land. An exception was for the Peace River area Indians in 1899. Despite intermittent efforts of other British Columbia Indians to have their claims recognized, they failed to gain a reasonable hearing until 1927. In that year a federal report responded to claims by declaring that Indians of British Columbia had *no* claims to their aboriginal land holdings! Separate legislation prohibited Indians from raising money to support their claims, and this prohibition was not lifted until 1951. Status (officially recognized by the federal government) and nonstatus Indians organized in 1969 and vigorously fought for their rights with some success. Village and tribal councils, with federal support in the 1970s, gained expanded control over the everyday administration of reserves.

Federal policy began to change from essential denial of the rights of First Nations to an acceptance of land claims in principle in 1972. Yet it was not until the Constitutional Act in 1982 that Native American rights received contemporary legal acceptance at the national level. The response in British Columbia in the 1980s was that a province had the right to deny special rights for Indians but that if these rights did exist, they were a federal, not a provincial, responsibility. First Nations goals were primarily to obtain land and its resources under their ownership, financial compensation, and self-government. Despite resistance in British Columbia, a treaty with the Nishga (Nisga'a) in the northwestern sector of the province was signed in 1998. Immediately thereafter the provincial government began to resist implementation of this treaty.

Traditionally, and at present, the Lower Kootenai near Bonners Ferry in Idaho and those in the Creston sector of British Columbia represent a single, integrated population. Admittedly, systematic ethnographic information about the Creston area people is not available, but the existing record strongly suggests that they have been and are similar to those near Bonners Ferry. The Lower Kootenay Indian Reserves (reservations) in British Columbia were created in 1877. They include about 7,000 acres in seven parcels along the Kootenai River. The land is held collectively by enrolled (status) Indians (see Figure 5-9). In general, historical developments for the Idaho and British Columbia populations are similar in numerous respects. White farmers and ranch-

Figure 5-9 | Headquarters in 1998 for the Lower Kootenay Indian Band near Creston, British Columbia.

ers obtained most of their land, and eventually small sectors were set aside for the Kootenai. With a much diminished land base, they could not continue to exploit their homeland in a traditional manner. Understandably, they had neither the cultural background, the skills, nor the motivation to participate broadly in the Euro-American economy. As a result their living standard diminished, and they became heavily dependent on indirect or direct aid provided by various levels of government.

In 1970 the Canadian Lower and Upper Kootenai formed the Kootenay District Council to advance their aboriginal land rights and gain self-government. In 1991 the organization expanded, and the name was changed to Ktunaxa/Kinbasket Tribal Council to consolidate their claims. (The Kinbasket are Shuswap Indians who had settled among the Canadian Kootenai.) Treaty negotiations began with the BC Treaty Commission in 1994, and an agreement in principle has been reached with the commission. If all goes well, it is anticipated that a treaty will be signed by 2003.

FURTHER COMPARISONS For the Lower Kootenai, the U.S. and Canadian boundary is artificial and troublesome. As the previous text demonstrates, the administration of Indian affairs in the province of British Columbia and the state of Idaho have differed, but not as much as one might imagine. Lower

Kootenai land was seized and settled by whites in both countries with explicit government cooperation. A major difference was that in Idaho land was allotted to families and divided repeatedly by inheritance; this was not so in Canada. As a result the Canadian land base has been more stable. In both countries, however, leasing farmland to whites continues to be the common practice with respect to arable plots.

Federal socioeconomic policies and programs in British Columbia have been far more liberal than they have for Indians in the United States. Thus the standard of living in British Columbia was higher than that of the Kootenai in Idaho. Casino earnings by the latter now make a major difference. In Idaho it is hardly conceivable that the Kootenai will obtain additional land from the federal government. On the contrary, the Creston area Kootenai will obtain additional land in the early 2000s as a result of pending treaty arrangements.

A dominant issue in the United States and Canada is the Native American quest for greater sovereignty, a special concern for the Lower Kootenai for obvious reasons. In the 1980s Creston-area Kootenai were arrested for crossing the international boundary without reporting to Canadian authorities. The Indians prevailed in a court case, which did not resolve the issue. Canadian and U.S. officials continue to delay and hassle the Kootenai, who insist that they have the legal right of free passage. The Indians especially object on religious grounds when customs officers prohibit the export or import of medicinal plants and animal parts used in ritual context. The Lower Kootenai on both sides of the border began exploring the concept of dual citizenship in 1998. If these efforts prove successful, they would represent a significant step toward Kootenai sovereignty. (The same problem confronts other Indians in the United States, such as the Yaqui and Kickapoo, who have close cultural ties with relatives in Mexico. Possible solutions for free passage include special visas or dual citizenship.)

Additional Sources

Unfortunately, an inordinate number of Kootenai studies are unpublished and not readily available. In addition, ethnographic accounts sometimes are contradictory, which makes it difficult or impossible to reconcile numerous differences. The best brief published report is by Bill B. Brunton (1998) and the best overview about tribes for the Plateau culture area is the volume edited by Deward E. Walker, Jr. (1998), and published by the Smithsonian Institution. Walker (1982), in his book about Idaho Indians, devotes considerable text to the Kootenai, and his material culture illustrations are superior. The major published Kootenai monograph is the reconstruction by Harry Holbert Turney-High (1941). Claude E. Schaeffer worked among the Kootenai intensively from 1935 to 1937 and continued his field studies among them into the 1960s. His major published contribution is about bear ceremonialism (1966). Schaeffer's field notes are a major source and were consulted for this chapter. An account of the "war" at Bonners Ferry in 1974 by Timothy R. Pembroke (1976) is excellent. Information about the Kootenai woman-man is based primarily on articles by O. B. Sperlin (1930) and Schaeffer (1965).

The best studies about Indian policies in British Columbia are by Forrest E. LaViolette (1973), Christopher McKee (1996), and Robert J. Muckle (1998).

Selected Bibliography

Baker, Paul E. 1955. *The forgotten Kutenai.* Boise, ID.

Boas, Franz. 1918a. *Kutenai tales.* Bureau of American Ethnology Bulletin 59. Washington, DC.

———. 1918b. Kinship terms of the Kutenai Indians. *American Anthropologist* n.s. 20:98–101.

Boyd, Robert T. 1998. Demographic history until 1900. In *Plateau,* Deward E. Walker, Jr., ed., vol. 12, 467–83. *Handbook of North American Indians.* Washington, DC.

Brunton, Bill B. 1998. Kootenai. In *Plateau,* Deward E. Walker, Jr., ed., vol. 12, 223–37. *Handbook of North American Indians.* Washington, DC.

Cassidy, Frank, and Norman Dale. 1988. *After native claims?* Victoria, BC.

Elders of the Kootenai Nation. 1990. *Century of survival.*

Garvin, Paul L. 1948. Kutenai I. *International Journal of American Linguistics* 14(1):37–42.

Lahren, Sylvester L., Jr., 1998. Reservations and reserves. In *Plateau,* Deward E. Walker, Jr., ed., vol. 12, 484–98. *Handbook of North American Indians.* Washington, DC.

LaViolette, Forrest E. 1973. *The struggle for survival.* Toronto.

McKee, Christopher. 1996. *Treaty talks in British Columbia: Negotiating a mutually beneficial future.* Vancouver, BC.

Muckle, Robert J. 1998. *The First Nations of British Columbia.* Vancouver, BC.

Nisbet, Jack. 1994. *Sources of the river.* Seattle.

Pembroke, Timothy R. 1976. *An anthropological analysis of conflict and confrontation among the Lower Kootenai of Bonners Ferry, Idaho.* Master's thesis, Washington State University.

Ray, Verne F. 1939. *Cultural relations in the Plateau of northwestern America.* Publications of the Frederick Webb Hodge Anniversary Publication Fund 3. Southwest Museum, Los Angeles.

Sapir, E. 1918. Kinship terms of the Kootenay Indians. *American Anthropologist* n.s. 20:414–18.

Schaeffer, Claude E. 1935–1969. Claude Everett Schaeffer Papers. Glenbow Archives, Calgary, Alberta.

———. 1965. The Kutenai female berdache. *Ethnohistory* 12(3):193–236.

———. 1966. *Bear ceremonialism of the Kutenai Indians.* Studies in Plains Anthropology and History, no. 4.

Sperlin, O. B. 1930. Two Kootenay women masquerading as men? Or were they one? *Washington Historical Quarterly* 21:120–30.

Turney-High, Harry Holbert. 1941. *Ethnography of the Kutenai.* American Anthropological Association Memoir 56.

Walker, Deward E., Jr. 1982. *Indians of Idaho*. Moscow, ID.

———, ed. 1998. *Plateau,* vol. 12. *Handbook of North American Indians*. Washington, DC.

Walker, Deward E., Jr. and Helen H. Schuster. 1998. Religious movements. *Plateau,* Deward E. Walker Jr., ed., vol. 12, 499–514. *Handbook of North American Indians*. Washington, DC.

6 The Crow: Plains Raiders and Bison Hunters

I wonder how my grandchildren will turn out. . . . They have only me, an old woman, to guide them, and plenty of others to lead them into bad ways. The young do not listen to the old ones now, as they used to when I was young. I worry about this, sometimes.

Observations by Pretty-shield, an elderly woman in the early 1930s. (Linderman 1932a, 23)

PLAINS INDIAN LIFE has long captivated Euro-Americans and Europeans, sometimes to the point of indifference to all other Native Americans. The image of warriors astride horses recklessly chasing herds of bison or enemies across the plains conveys a sense of daring and freedom. The Crow typify this life-style shared by other Siouans* and Algonquians, such as the Blackfoot, Cheyenne, and Gros Ventre. The Crow are presented because any book about American Indians would be incomplete without including a people of the Plains culture area. The Crow dramatically illustrate how a tribe could change rapidly early in their history.

Traditional Crow history relates that their ancestors and those of the Hidasta once lived together in the Lake Winnipeg sector of Canada. They moved south to establish earth lodge communities along the Missouri River, where they raised maize, beans, and squash. The planting of these crops was supplemented by hunting bison and deer. The Hidasta and Crow possibly separated in the early 1700s. In the early 1500s the Spanish introduced domestic horses in Mexico, and horses began to filter into the Crow area soon after 1730. Subsequently the Crow became highly mobile hunters and began to live in their historic homeland around 1750 (see Figure 6-1). By then the horse was becoming a catalyst for revolutionary changes in Crow life. For the next 140 years Crow culture was dominated by horses, bison, and warfare.

The Crow (KRO) call themselves Apsáalooke (Absaroka), commonly translated as "children of the large-beaked bird." The term probably refers to a "raven," however, rather than the "crow." A misinterpretation of this word by early white trappers led to the Apsáalooke being called the "Crow." About 1825 two rival chiefs, Arapooish and Long Hair, had a dispute, and the people separated into two subgroups. The Mountain Crow, followers of Long Hair, ranged south of the Yellowstone River in southern Montana. The followers of Arapooish, the River Crow, lived farther north, along tributaries of the Missouri River.

Early Historic Life

As Euro-Americans became familiar with the northern Plains in the early 1800s, the lifeways of local Indians already had begun to change as a result of indirect contact with outsiders. Pressures brought about by other Indians who were forced westward by whites were beginning to build, and the fur trade was making an impact in the region. The ethnographic account presented in this section attempts to describe Crow life before the direct impact of white influences became intense.

*The Crow are Siouan in the sense that they are linguistically related to the Sioux, the popular name for the Dakota Indians. The Siouan-Catawba linguistic family includes the Crow and Dakota, plus the Assiniboine, Hidatsa, Mandan, and Omaha.

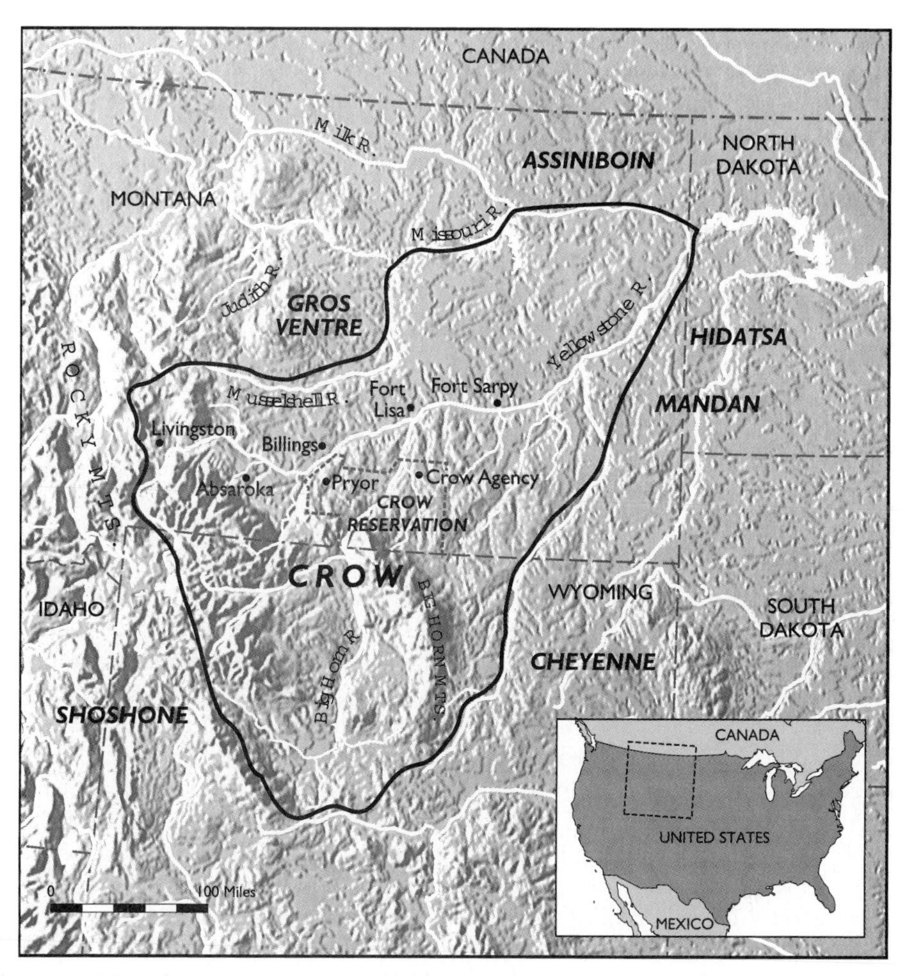

Figure 6-1 | Historic homeland of the Crow Indians.

ORIGIN MYTH According to the Crow, they originated with Old Man Coyote. While most of his adventures reflect his trickster character, Old Man Coyote also was the creator of the world. In the Crow origin account, there was first Old Man Coyote, who was traveling alone in a cold, wet world with no place to rest. He asked three species of duck to dive beneath the waters and bring up earth, but each failed. At last he asked a grebe to bring up some earth. The grebe dove deep, was down a long time, and surfaced with a small piece of mud. With this earth, Old Man Coyote was able to travel from east to west to make the land, its mountains and rivers, and its animals and plants and to give them life. The world remained a lonely place. So Old Man Coyote molded from the earth an image he liked and blew a small breath into it. The first man moved. Old Man Coyote still was not satisfied. He tried again and made an image he liked even more. The first woman moved. Now Old Man Coyote was no longer alone. He taught the people how to live and pray. He gave them their language and clans. Finally, with the help of mice, Old Man Coyote taught people the Sun Dance.

Additional names for Old Man Coyote include the One Who Has Made Everything, the First Doer, and the Maker. He was, and remains for many Crow, the ultimate supernatural. He directly or indirectly receives prayers, pledges, and requests and is instrumental in vision quests. He is "appropriately conceived as a pervasive agent, omnipotent over all natural forces, the ultimate life-force, and the perennial meaning in the cosmos" (Frey 1987, 63).

APPEARANCE AND CLOTHING To the Crow, a handsome man was tall and had a straight nose and a face free from blemishes or scars. The noble appearance and bearing of Crow men attracted favorable comment from most early travelers. Men greased their long hair and sometimes made it even longer by gluing on additional human or horse hair. One great chief, Long Hair, was inordinately concerned about the length of his hair because his inordinate abilities were attributed to his long hair. Thus he grew it to about ten feet in length. Men plucked their whiskers, and both sexes apparently removed axillary hair. Strings of ornaments hung from the hair on each side of a man's head, and his ears were adorned with abalone-shell earrings cut into angular designs. Men painted their faces red and highlighted their eyelids with yellow paint. Bear-claw and bone-disk necklaces, as well as bone pendants, were popular. Men in general, and young men in particular, were fastidious about their appearance. Men wore hair-trimmed leggings held up by tucking the tops into a belt. Other items of male clothing included a shirt, moccasins, and a bison robe.

Crow women were not pleasingly portrayed and were often reported as wearing dirty, greasy clothing. When they mourned the loss of a relative, which was often, their hair was cut short, and their faces were spotted with clay and dried blood from self-inflicted wounds. Dresses of deerskins or mountain sheep skins reached from the neck to mid-calf. The most distinctive characteristic of their dresses was that the fronts and backs were decorated with rows of elk teeth; openings on each side of a woman's dress were for nursing an infant. Women wore moccasins and leggings from their thighs to their knees. Young boys went naked until they were about nine and then wore the clothing of men; girls dressed in the manner of women.

SETTLEMENTS The Crow had no permanent settlements but moved from one campsite to the next in search of game. After so many people died from smallpox, most of the tribe camped together for protection against enemies. Camps were dominated by tepees framed with about twenty poles, each some twenty-five feet long, set in the form of a cone and covered with bison skins. An opening was left at the top as a smoke hole, and two external poles were attached to flaps at the top of the cover to open or close the smoke hole

Figure 6-2 | A Crow tepee, after a painting by Catlin. (From Donaldson 1886.)

(see Figure 6-2). Before the Crow had horses to haul tepee poles and covers, it appears that their dwellings were much smaller. There was a fireplace at the center of a tepee, and along the sides toward the back were hide mattresses beneath sleeping robes; the seat of honor was at the back and center. Other structures of importance were circular arbors with conical roofs made from boughs and used as sun shades and small dome-shaped sweat lodges where men bathed in a ritual context by pouring water over heated stones.

When a band moved, the caravan might extend for miles. Scouts kept a lookout for enemies, and hunters scattered in search of game. Men wore their best buckskin garments and carried their weapons in case of a sudden attack. Women rode astride horses, as did men, and from the saddle of a wife's horse hung her husband's shield and sword, if he owned one. Small children were tied to saddles, but five-year-olds rode alone. Meat, tools, utensils, and other property were packed in skin containers tied to horses. One horse carried a tepee cover and another dragged the poles. Some horses pulled pairs of tent poles with a frame attached to carry wounded or ill persons; this conveyance, a travois, was in earlier times pulled by dogs. The most important purpose of dogs appears to have been to warn of the approach of enemies or strangers.

HORSES Wild horses lived on the North American Plains during the Pleistocene era, but they disappeared about 8000 B.C. or perhaps in more recent times, possibly hunted to extinction by Indians. The domestic horses used

Figure 6-3 | A Crow woman on horseback. (Courtesy of the Field Museum, Chicago, neg. no. 2784.)

by Indians in North and South America all were descendants of those introduced by Europeans in historic times. The Spanish took domestic horses to Mexico in A.D. 1519, and by the end of the century large herds of domestic and feral animals ranged over northern Mexico. Thus North American Indians did not begin to use domestic horses until the early 1500s. The Crow had access to horses for about seventy-five years before they began to be described in reasonable detail by whites.

By the mid-1800s the Crow had more horses than any other tribe east of the Rocky Mountains. A poor person owned at least twenty animals, and a middle-aged man had up to sixty. Horses represented the major form of wealth and became a medium of exchange; a horse was worth from sixty to one hundred dollars. In a proper marriage, a groom presented horses to the bride's brothers. Personal conflicts in a camp, usually involving women, might be settled with horses.

Crow men, women, and children always were described as excellent riders who depended on horses so much that their ability to endure long periods of walking had diminished (see Figure 6-3). Their saddles were high in the front and back but were not used for hunts or during war. Most horses could be guided without a bridle. A rider leaned in the direction in which she or he wanted to turn, and the horse turned in that direction until the rider sat upright.

Horses were obtained in trade, but far more often they were seized in raids. When an enemy raid was expected, the best horses were tethered at the entrance of their owners' tepees so that riders could pursue horse thieves quickly at any time. Once it was realized that horses had been stolen, Crow warriors gave pursuit, each riding his fastest horse and leading another. They rode day and night, and when the first horse was exhausted they rode the other; when that horse gave out they might continue on foot. If they caught up with the thieves, they first attempted to recover their horses and then killed and scalped an enemy if it was possible to do so without the threat of losing one of their number.

SUBSISTENCE ACTIVITIES Part of the Crow habitat in the 1840s was described by Edwin T. Denig (1961, 139) as "perhaps the best game country in the world." He reported immense herds of bison from the Rocky Mountains to the mouth of the Yellowstone River and herds of hundreds of elk along the river, as well as many black-tailed and white-tailed deer. Antelope covered the prairies and badlands near the mountains, while in the mountains were many bighorn sheep and grizzly bears. The truly majestic Rocky Mountains, high valleys, fast-flowing streams and rivers, meadows, hot springs, and great forests characterized this idyllic land.

The Crow economy was based on hunting large game, especially bison, deer, elk, and antelope; in fact, they did not eat fish or berries. Except for the maize that they obtained by trading with the Hidatsa, the most important use of plant products was as seasoning for meat dishes. Cooperative hunts were the norm, and the purpose was to kill or maim herd animals by driving them over cliffs or riverbanks. Alternatively, animals were driven into a valley with a single narrow exit, and a fence was erected after the animals were confined. The planning and coordination required for large-scale hunts was supervised by the members of military sodalities, and hunting rituals were performed to further ensure success.

The bow and arrow was the primary weapon for the hunt or for war. The wood-shafted arrows were tipped with points of bone or stone. Bows were fashioned from horn or antler; pieces were cut, smoothed, spliced, glued, bound together, and then backed with sinew (composite, sinew-backed bow). Arrows were carried in skin quivers that were ornamented with porcupine quills.

A woman's life was physically demanding. She supplied the household with firewood and water, cooked the food, cared for children, collected plant products, and made and repaired all the clothing, skin containers, and tepee covers. Women were also responsible for erecting and taking down tepees. A woman groomed her husband, saddled his horse, and took off his leggings and moccasins in the evening. Women usually followed men on bison hunts and skinned the animals killed. One of women's most highly developed skills was working skins. Depending on the skin involved and the purpose served, hides or skins were dehaired, prepared on one or both sides, smoked or not smoked.

To break down its texture and make it supple, a skin was spread with a preparation made from bison brains and liver. In addition to processing bison hides for tepee covers and skins for clothing, women made small skin pouches for pipes and sacred objects. The best-known rawhide container, termed a parfleche, was folded, often painted with designs, and used primarily for storing and transporting dried meat or pemmican. Although other American Indians were skilled in basketry, pottery, weaving, and elaborate wood carving, the Crow did not practice these crafts.

For men, camp life was as leisurely as it was busy for women. They made tools and equipment, but these were not time-demanding activities. Some men were part-time specialists in making bows or arrows. The major pursuits of men, hunting and fighting, usually took place at a distance from a campsite.

DESCENT, KINSHIP, AND MARRIAGE Descent was traced through women (matrilineal system), since each person was identified primarily with the mother's clan (matriclan). Thus an individual was a member of the same clan as his or her mother, mother's sisters and brothers, mother's mother, mother's mother's brothers and sisters, and so on. The thirteen named Crow clans reported for both the Mountain and River Crow included Thick Lodge, Sore-Lip Lodge, Tied-in-a-Knot, and Bad War Honors. Clan members usually were dispersed over a broad area; in other words, Crow clans were not localized.

It appears that by the seventeenth century the Crow lived farther north, and their primary economic focus was on crops raised by women. Presumably the cultivated plots were relatively stable. Daughters learned horticultural skills from their mothers. In this reconstruction, women produced the food staples; when a man married he went to live with his wife. The resulting focus on the female line led to or sustained a matrilineal descent system with matrilocal marriages. However, as the Crow became bison hunters on horseback in the mid-eighteenth century, the emphasis dramatically shifted to men, and the Crow began to be patrilocal. Because whites were fast becoming a dominant force in Crow life, subsequent changes in their descent system and kinship terminology were forced rather than occurring naturally and logically.

Clans were grouped into two, or in one case, three units (phratries) that were not named; one of the two-clan clusters may have been a single clan. It was most common for a spouse to be from another clan (clan exogamy). Yet the bonds between some paired clans seem to have been so close that members could not marry each other (phratry exogamy).

The kinship terminology employed by the Crow came to be called the Crow type, and it is shared by other people around the world. The Crow termed father and father's brother alike and used a different word for mother's brother. Likewise, father's sister was termed differently from mother and mother's sister, who were termed alike (bifurcate merging). Furthermore, father's sisters' daughters and their daughters' daughters were termed as father's sister; the term really designated women of the father's clan from his generation down-

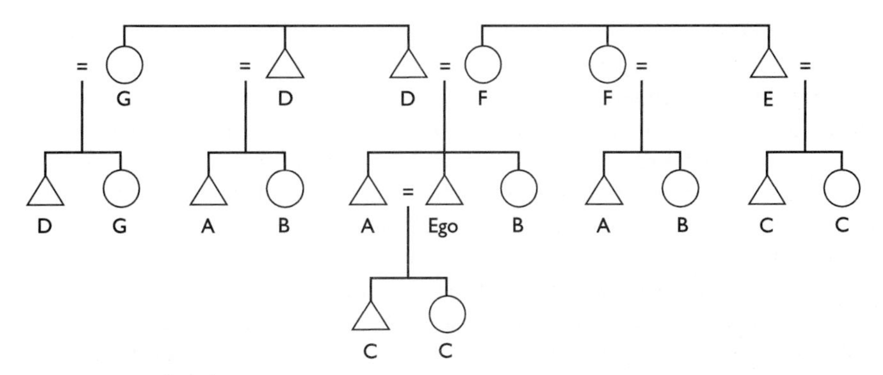

Figure 6-4 | The early historic Crow system of kinship terminology.

ward. The same logic applied when father's sister's husband was termed father, as was his son. The ignoring of generational distinctions in these contexts made clan members equivalents. In a like manner, the term mother was extended to her clan sisters (see Figure 6-4). The most rigid behavioral taboo prohibited a man from talking with or having any contact with his wife's mother or her grandmothers. Likewise, a woman did not interact with her daughter's husband or her daughter's daughter's husband.

SOCIAL DIMENSIONS The worst possible insult was for one Crow to say to another, "You are without relatives," meaning that the accused had no merit. Supportive relatives protected one from slander, came to one's defense in times of conflict with others, and provided material aid in times of stress. A matriclan was the largest integrated social unit, and one's obligations to it were great. Although members of the same clan do not appear to have camped adjacent to one another, they often ate together.

As Rodney Frey (1987) emphasized, clan solidarity represented the essence of social life. Their word for "clan" translates to "as driftwood lodges." The symbolism is telling. In a fast-flowing river a single piece of wood is battered, destroyed, or washed away. Along a riverbank, however, driftwood may accumulate in a compact, long-lasting mass. So it was with the Crow as individuals. Each person found security with other members of the same clan. Because the members of a single clan were dispersed, an individual was welcome among strangers belonging to the same clan. The bonds within a clan were most severely tested when a person from one clan killed someone from another clan. In these rare instances, the members of the murdered person's clan were obligated to kill either the offender or one of his clansmen. Despite their matrilineal focus, a father had close ties with his sons. When someone asked a special favor, a common phrase was, "By the love you bear your children, I beg you" (Lowie 1935, 18).

"Sodalities" are special-purpose groups in which membership might be either voluntary or required. Among the Crow most men were either Lumpwoods or Foxes. These were military sodalities into which young males were recruited by established members. Each sodality had distinctive adornments, dances, and behavioral characteristics.

In the fall after the first snow, Lumpwood men met and ate in the tepees of one member and then another. The membership was distinguished partially on the basis of age grades, and officers served for one year. The four pairs of officers were called elders, straight-staff bearers, hooked-staff bearers, and rear men. Being offered a pipe and smoking it were symbolic of selection and acceptance of an office. Men often were reluctant to become staff bearers because after a straight shaft was planted in the ground by its bearer during a battle he could not retreat from the spot unless another Lumpwood rode between him and the enemy. After a hooked staff had been placed in the ground, it could not be moved, and the bearer defended it until he was killed. Because of the danger involved, the bearers of these staffs counted a double coup if they struck an enemy.

Sodality members extended mutual aid to fellow members in stressful times; they sometimes fought together, and they honored by excessive mourning a member killed in battle. One Lumpwood behavioral peculiarity was that when a member mourned the loss of certain relatives, the other Lumpwoods had the right to make jokes about the loss to his face. This behavior would have been insulting to anyone else, irrespective of the circumstances.

The Foxes were organized much the same as the Lumpwoods, and competition between the two sodalities was keen. This was most dramatically expressed in the abduction of wives. In the spring either group could initiate the proceedings, and any man was free to abduct the wife of a member in the other fraternity if he had been her lover. Sometimes a woman was kidnapped without cause, and women sometimes hid to avoid abduction. A wife might also successfully plead with a potential abductor and not be taken away. Men who suspected that their wives would be abducted often made a point of being away because they had no desire to see their wives seized. Yet, if a man was present, custom dictated that he should make no effective effort to prevent his wife's capture. These women were paraded about and were received as brides by their abductors' families. A stolen wife could not return to her husband; a man caught sleeping with such a woman was tied up and smeared with feces. This period of license lasted about two weeks, and then the Lumpwoods and Foxes went on the warpath, each attempting to count coup (touch a live enemy) first so that they could ridicule their opposites. After the first snows fell the rivalry abated, only to surge again the next spring.

WARFARE The Plains Indian stereotype is that of a bloodthirsty killer for whom war was by choice a dominant cultural focus. Yet economic factors best account for the intensity of warfare on the plains and prairies. We find that the Crow rarely killed whites, even though they often had ample opportunity and just cause, especially for killing white trappers in their midst. This situation contrasted with the animosity between whites and the members of surrounding tribes. Furthermore, when the Crow were at peace with another people, they appear never to have initiated a new conflict. Their primary reason for launching a raid was to avenge the death of a Crow killed by the members of another tribe. Unlike most Plains Indians, the Crow killed men but usually captured women and children; the children were adopted and captive women worked beside Crow wives. An adopted boy who was raised as a Crow did not hesitate to kill men from the tribe of his birth. In rational terms, by not initiating a war and by assimilating captives, the Crow compensated for their relatively small number and their losses in war. They went to war most often for a combination of three purposes: revenge, glory, and horses.

The word translated as "chief" really meant "good, valiant," and to achieve this title a man had to perform four feats: lead a successful raid, capture tethered horses from an enemy camp, be the first to count coup, and take a bow or gun from a live enemy. Warriors who performed each of these deeds at least once were chiefs; but this did not mean that they were political leaders. The greatest living chief in 1910 was Bell-rock; he had led at least eleven war parties, taken at least two tethered horses, counted coup six times, and seized five guns. Such a man boasted of his achievements at public gatherings, depicted his brave deeds on a robe that he wore, and had distinctive adornments on his clothing. To take a scalp was important to the tribe but was not ranked as a major personal achievement, and when a man listed his war honors he did not mention scalps. It should be noted that scalping an enemy was especially widespread in the Northeast culture area (see Chapter 12).

The foremost weapon of war was the bow and arrow, but it soon was replaced by the gun. Spears sometimes were used, but they apparently were not very important (see Figure 6-5). For close combat it was customary to use a war club with a stone head bound at one end of a wooden shaft. The shields men carried had a purpose more supernatural than practical, except in defensive circumstances. These circular pieces of bison hide might have bird skins, feathers, or animal tails hanging from them. Either a shield or its leather case was painted with symbols or scenes revealed to its owner in a vision (see Figure 6-6). Men also went into battle with ornamental sticks used to count coup. These were tied together at intervals with skin strings ornamented with quills.

Ideally, each youthful male longed to achieve personal honor in battle and believed that the greatest glory was achieved by dying young in warfare. Yet every effort was made to prevent the death of a Crow in combat, and a war party was never considered successful if it lost a single member. Those who were fearless in battle were persons convinced of their invincibility on supernatural grounds or who were reckless by nature. Still, the positive value placed on an early death was a recurrent theme in Crow child rearing. Typically, a

Figure 6-5 | George Catlin (1926, vol. 1, 216) wrote of this painting of a Crow warrior, "I have painted him as he sat for me, balanced on his leaping wild horse with his shield and quiver slung on his back, and his long lance decorated with the eagle's quills, trailed in his right hand." (From Ewers 1965.)

young man eagerly sought his first opportunity to join a party of raiders. As a novice he performed menial tasks, such as carrying the meat supply and hauling water. He likewise was the butt of jokes as a part of his informal initiation into the life of warriors.

An attack was organized by a raid planner, who usually achieved his position after having a dream or vision that detailed the tribe to be attacked and the booty to be gained. An ambitious warrior not blessed with a personal vi-

Figure 6-6 | This is one of the finest Crow shields, and it was famous for its power. It belonged to the chief Arapooish and is said to represent the moon. Attached to the left side of the cover are the head and body of a crane. At the right is an eagle feather, and below it is a deer's tail. (Courtesy, National Museum of the American Indian, Smithsonian Institution, N29656.)

sion could turn to a shaman and succeed by following the shaman's instructions. Some warriors might doubt an announced leader's abilities and decline to follow him, but recruiting a war party does not appear to have been difficult, especially for previously successful war leaders. Raiders typically set off on foot with a supply of moccasins often carried by dogs. As they approached enemy territory, the scouts were especially watchful. Once an enemy camp was sighted, the war leader performed sacred bundle rituals. For example, the leader of a raiding party might place his sacred bundle on a rock, whistle or sing toward an enemy camp, and then relate how many enemy horses he hoped to obtain. To further ensure success, each participant attached sacred objects to his body and painted himself in an appropriate manner. One or two warriors were chosen to enter the enemy camp, usually late at night, and to drive off as many horses as possible without being discovered. The party made its escape by riding the remainder of the night, all the next day, and the following night before relaxing. As the warriors approached their home camp, they shot guns into the air and paraded the captured horses. The booty belonged to the raid leader, but he freely gave horses to the participants. These raids often were dangerous ventures. If a horse was not captured for each raider, some warriors were forced to return on foot and risked being overtaken by the pursuing enemy. Raiders sometimes went for days without food and rode so long and hard when attempting to escape that their "buttocks were worn out" (Lowie 1935, 222).

As warriors the Crow were daring and merciless enemies. In open battles, especially if a number of Crow were killed, they slaughtered every man and then tortured the wounded to death. Hands and feet were cut off, eyes gouged out, and intestines exposed to be pierced with sharp sticks. The brains and hearts of the dead were hurled in the faces of the living while the victors scorned their victims. It should be added that in defeat Crow warriors suffered a similar fate.

A newly taken scalp was the focus of a three-day celebration. Warriors carrying their weapons and wearing their finest clothing, their faces painted black, danced in a partial circle to the accompaniment of drums and rattles. The scalp was carried on a pole, and the warrior who had made the kill mounted a horse and was led by a chief in the midst of the dancers. That night young men walked around the camp, and at each chief's tepee they sang songs about his particular accomplishments. During the next day the scalp was tied to the bridle of a horse on which a young man rode while beating a drum and singing. When many scalps were taken in a battle, the celebration was far more elaborate and sometimes included a reenactment of the conflict.

Denig (1961) reported that a Gros Ventre girl was captured by the Crow at about the age of ten and became a great chief. As a child she preferred the activities of boys, and her adoptive father encouraged this behavior. She soon was playing with bows and arrows and riding fearlessly. As a youth she was trusted to guard horses. As an adult she always wore women's clothing. When her adoptive father was killed she became the head of his household. Later, in a raid against the Blackfoot, she killed and scalped one enemy and counted coup over another. She came to be known as Woman Chief after she consistently distinguished herself in other raids. Before long she sat as an equal in the council of chiefs. Woman Chief deplored the idea of doing woman's work and obtained first one woman as a "wife" and then three more. Thus she lived as an honored person for twenty years, until she tested a peace with the Gros Ventre and was killed by them after they discovered her origins.

When a man was killed by an enemy, everyone in the camp mourned as the body rested in state outdoors. The face of the corpse was painted; he was clothed in his best garments and was especially honored by members of his military society. They cried and sang over the body to the beating of drums.

They pierced their limbs and bodies with arrows or cut themselves with knives. These men also distributed the dead man's property. Relatives took the body to a tree or scaffold for interment and wept. Their period of mourning did not end until a member of the enemy tribe that had killed him was murdered. Thus, it was near relatives who most encouraged warriors to avenge deaths.

POLITICAL LIFE Control of the day-to-day Crow social unit or band was in the hands of a man who had performed each of the four honored deeds in war and had demonstrated the qualities of a leader. His authority expanded further if he was generous with booty, a shaman of note, and an able narrator of tales. Thus individual achievement, open to nearly all, was the avenue to honor and prestige in a political context. Tacit agreement determined who was to be band chief, and no formal installation ceremony existed. A band chief decided when a campsite was to be abandoned, where to move, and the placement of tepees. Yet he apparently had little control over people, since he neither judged nor punished in a manner often associated with chiefly powers. It appears that as long as the people who camped together enjoyed good fortune, their chief retained his office. When he failed, he was replaced quietly and informally. One of his most important duties was to appoint the members of a particular military society to take charge of the spring bison hunt. At larger camps the chief appointed an outstanding man as a crier; his duty was to ride among the tepees repeatedly making announcements about matters of public interest and making the chief's opinions known about matters of current concern.

Within a camp or band of the Mountain or River Crow, members of the thirteen clans formed the largest political entities. They dealt with each other as equals, and they recognized no superior authority to which they all were responsible. Feuds between clans were the greatest threat, but intermediaries attempted to settle conflicts as quickly as possible before they became emotionally charged and out of hand. Language, culture, and common social norms unified clans. Crow survival was partially contingent on cooperation among clans for the common good. If a segment of a clan separated from the main body, it could muster comparatively few warriors and would be destroyed by enemies. The tranquillity of camp life in tribal tradition was upset the most when an aggressive person with a small number of related followers became dominant. This was especially true of a person who was regarded as having powerful supernatural guardians. Such individuals might seize the horses or wives of others, but, as Robert H. Lowie (1935) pointed out, such a man was a de facto but never a de jure leader.

The members of the military sodality policing a bison hunt could and did severely punish nonconformity. The worst offense was for men to hunt bison alone or in small groups, because this scattered the herds and made it difficult for others to kill bison on the legitimate communal hunts. Likewise, on a group hunt, if a man broke and charged a herd prematurely, he might scatter the animals and ruin the opportunities of others. These nonconformists might be whipped, their weapons destroyed, and the kill seized. The warrior sodality in charge also had the right to prevent raiding parties from setting forth at inopportune times, and they attempted to settle differences between the people in camp peacefully, especially when a feud threatened to erupt between clans. Disagreements between members of different clans may have been reasonably common, but for one Crow to kill another was almost unknown. Any crime, except murder, could be compensated for with an exchange of property.

When the Crow split into two major bands, the River and the Mountain, it was Arapooish (Arapoosh, Sore-belly, Rotten-belly) who led the River Crow. A brief sketch of his life illustrates the qualities of leadership that he possessed. Arapooish was a retiring and even surly person who said little but spoke in an authoritarian manner. Although he was a relatively retiring shaman, he controlled powerful supernatural forces, and he apparently had many wealthy clansmen. He was fearless in battle. Time and again he successfully raided horses from enemies without any loss of Crow life. He saw to it that the Crow always were on the alert for enemies and that raiders who approached were killed. Arapooish was a confident aggressor and able tactician in the large battles that he planned. In a battle against the Cheyenne, more than 1,000 horses were captured, 200 Cheyenne men killed, and 270 women and children captured; the Crow lost 5 men. But Arapooish was a man possessed; when he charged a Blackfoot fortification in 1834 shouting, "One last stroke for the Crow Nation" (Denig 1961, 183), he was killed. Arapooish came to be known as *the* Chief.

RELIGION The basis for Crow supernaturalism centered on personal rapport with a guardian spirit. An unsought spirit aid might reveal itself, but far more often it was gained in a vision quest. All personal glory, power, and wealth ultimately were attributed to valid visions. Thus religion among the Crow was not a tightly integrated system of beliefs with accompanying dogma. In Crow linguistic expression, a vision or a dream of supernatural portent were the same. A youthful male sought a personal spirit aid as he began to emerge into the world of adults. If he was fully successful, he might never seek another vision in his life. Were he to do so, it might be to cure a sick child or in an extraordinary quest for vengeance.

The Vision Quest A vision seeker sometimes, perhaps most often, first purified himself by taking a sweat bath. Ideally he then went to a mountaintop, where he abstained from food and water and wailed. Lightly clad and covered only with a robe at night, he slept until the sun began to rise. The seeker next chopped off the final joint of his left forefinger, placed it on a buffalo chip, and held it up as an offering to the rising sun with an accompanying prayer for glory and success in life. As the blood flowed, he fainted and was unconscious until evening. He could not sleep because of the cold of night. Three nights passed; on the fourth one, with sleep coming late because of the cold, a vision came to him.

Alternative ways of obtaining a vision existed. One man might have another cut slits in his chest or back through which one end of a thong was passed, the opposite end being tied to a pole. The aspirant ran around the pole until he tired; he rested, only to run again and again. He might or might not tear the thong free in his quest. Another means to the same end was to pierce the back with two holes and tie a thong from them to a bison skull that was dragged about in the first stage of the search for power.

A supernatural visitant might assume the form of an animal such as a bear or bison, a bird, an insect, or the earth, moon, or stars. A person could be blessed by association with more than one such power, and literally anything might be revered by an individual. The Sun was the supernatural to whom a direct appeal was made, but it rarely was the source of power received; thus it was not a god worshipped in the usual sense. The supplicant might be taught a sacred song, learn of a symbol that could be represented graphically, or be instructed to follow certain taboos. A feather, a stone with a strange shape, a braided rope, or a weasel skin, among other forms, symbolized the receiver's power and formed the core of a sacred (medicine) bundle. A bundle and its power could be transferred to a near relative after proper instruction or purchased by a nonrelative; thus the control of supernatural forces could pass from one generation to the next. The degree to which any particular bundle was revered depended directly on the fortunes of its possessors.

Tobacco Ceremonialism The indigenous sacred tobacco known to the Crow as "Short Tobacco" (Lowie 1935, 274) was considered to have inordinate supernatural power. The Tobacco Society included many local chapters, each with distinctive rituals. Crow survival was intimately associated with the sacred seeds and harmony in the natural world. Potential members of a society chapter were instructed in the rituals and formally presented to the group. Typically a married couple was inducted together, and membership normally was for life. The tobacco planter played a key role, and his office was largely hereditary.

The yearly rituals of a chapter began with sowing the seeds in the spring. They built a huge tepee that could accommodate hundreds of people nearby and decorated the interior lavishly. Here the participants ate and danced for three days to music of bells, drums, rattles, and whistles, played in combination. The participants moved off only a short distance each day, indicating their reluctance to leave the sacred plants. To encourage the seeds to germinate, they placed a society member in charge of rainmaking, and he presented valuable property to the rain clouds as a sacrifice. If he was successful, the offerings became his property, and he gained great fame. If he failed, he blamed the other participants for improper behavior during the rituals. In late August members returned to the tobacco plot, harvested the crop, and collected the seeds.

Figure 6-7 | A Crow man in ceremonial costume smoking a pipe. (Courtesy of the Field Museum, Chicago, neg. no. A2790.)

Men alone smoked tobacco (see Figure 6-7). Smoking was most important when making peace with other tribes or during rituals, and shamans smoked when curing severe illness. Even when tobacco was smoked on less ceremonious occasions, the first puffs were dedicated to the earth, heavens, spirits, and the Sun. Each man present took four puffs and then passed the pipe on to the person on his left, because this was the direction in which the Sun moved. Furthermore, each man had personal smoking habits. One man would not smoke if a pipe had touched grass, another would not smoke if women were present, and another would insist on emptying his pipe on bison dung. These details were dictated by individual relationships with guardian spirits.

The Sun Dance The most sacred ceremony focused on the Sun, as a powerful and remote supernatural. A man pledged to perform the rituals following the death of a relative at the hands of an enemy tribe. To host the event involved a private vow to the Maker. The goal was to receive an extraordinary vision that would reveal how the killing was to be avenged. The personal commitment required to hold a Sun Dance was so great and rare that an elderly person may have witnessed only six such dances in a lifetime.

In early historic times the ceremony attracted all tribal members. The vow-maker, called the whistler, and a shaman who owned at least one sacred doll became the principals. A small wooden doll was the vehicle through which the whistler gained his vision. A doll with painted features and painted designs was dressed in skin with attached feathers. This type of doll reportedly led to success for war parties. Prior to the event the whistler fasted and became haggard. Preliminaries included the use of incense, ritual smoking, and the construction of a special lodge a few miles distant. The drama began as the whistler, painted with cross-shaped Morning Star designs and wearing a special kilt, held a wooden hoop with the doll attached at the center. He danced slowly to the lodge while blowing his whistle. Arriving there, he tied the doll at eye level on a lodge pole and neither ate nor drank water until after he received a vision. Other men likewise sought visions. Each such man cut slits in his chest or back and passed a skewer, attached to a line, through the slit and tied it to a lodge pole. Men pulled against the lines until they broke free. The whistler, who was not skewered, gazed intently at the doll and danced as chiefs successively recounted and acted out great deeds of personal valor. The whistler slept in the lodge. The next day he continued to dance before the doll, and he did so day after day until he obtained a vision that he customarily did not reveal. He next ventured forth in quest of the enemy.

Shamans Physical disabilities and death usually were attributed to supernatural causes such as ghosts or breaking taboos. One category of health care practitioners depended primarily on secular knowledge. They used plant products, lanced a swollen part of the body, or applied a poultice as ordinary treatments. A particular root that was considered a cure-all was rubbed on sores, placed on an aching tooth, or chewed and swallowed to cure a cold. The botanical pharmacopoeia was extensive and appears to have been applied most often in a secular context. Other curers, more properly shamans, had the ability to treat specific traumas because of revelations they received in visions. They might be able to cure snake or spider bites, wounds, or disease caused by a foreign object in a patient's body. Shamans were adept at sleight of hand; they appeared to transform bark into meat or mud balls into beads in either public or private performances. Competitive exhibits of their skills often were dramatic contests. These were men who had the most powerful guardian spirits, and it was primarily in this respect that shamans stood apart from persons who had less potent spirit aids.

Ordinary persons sometimes practiced sorcery to settle grudges against other Crow by supernatural means, but the practice appears to have been relatively uncommon. One technique was to draw the figure of an antagonist along a riverbank near the water's edge, burn incense, and blow smoke toward the figure. As the water washed the drawing away, the victim was expected to die. Other magical practices supposedly could cause lifelong disabilities in the target person. The only sure safeguard against sorcery was considered to be for the victim to have more powerful supernaturals working on her or his behalf.

LIFE CYCLE As the time for a birth approached, the husband, other men, and boys were excluded from a tepee, and the woman was aided by a male or female specialist who was well paid. The woman knelt over padding and grasped two sticks. To hasten delivery she might be given potions or her back might be rubbed with a special preparation. The particular aid used depended on the techniques that the birth specialist had learned in a vision or had obtained by purchase from someone else. A woman present at the delivery cut the umbilical cord, and part of it was encased in a container that hung from the cradleboard of a baby girl and later from the back of her dress. The new mother observed food and behavioral taboos for a brief period, but the father's activities were not restricted. Within a few days and without ceremony, a neonate's ears were pierced with a hot awl; the holes were held open with small greased sticks until earrings could be inserted. Offspring were placed in cradleboards and rocked to sleep with lullabies. Water was poured into the nose of a small child who cried often, and such a child soon learned to stop crying when someone said, "Bring the water!"

A few days after a birth an infant was named, but names were neither sex- nor clan-specific. The father asked a noted warrior to select a name based on one of the warrior's personal achievements and gave the warrior a horse in return. Names often were descriptive phrases; for example, a newborn girl might be named Captures-the-Medicine-Pipe or a boy His-Coups-Are-Dangerous. As a name was given, the infant was tossed into the air four times (four was a sacred number among the Crow), each time higher than the last. Women changed their names when someone with a like name died, and men assumed new names to commemorate brave deeds or to improve their fortunes. Nicknames, often based on unusual behavior, might be more commonly used than formal names. For example, a man who took an old dog with him to carry his moccasins on the warpath came to be called Old Dog as a result.

Adults placed few constraints on the behavior of children. Children might interrupt adult conversations at any time and typically were both forward and self-confident. The freedom of boys was especially boundless. Denig (1961, 154) wrote, "The greatest nuisance in creation is Crow children, boys from the ages of 9 to 14 years. These are left to do just as they please. They torment their parents and everyone else, do all kinds of mischief without either correction or reprimand." Boys swam and played water games, hurled sticks at each other with the ends covered with mud or mud and live coals. Individually or in teams they shot at targets with arrows, and the arrows were stakes for the winner. In the winter boys coasted down hills on toboggans made by covering bison rib frames with rawhide. Every youthful male ate part of a raw grizzly bear heart to bring him strength and a clear head in times of trouble. Thus he could say "I have the heart of a grizzly" in the face of adversity. When meat was plentiful in a camp, boys might cover themselves with mud so that they could not be identified and run into camp where meat was hanging to steal as much as possible before old women chased them away. The thieves cooked the meat away from camp, and the boy who had stolen the best piece ate the choice parts first. Boys hunted small game, and after a bison hunt they might ride out to kill the calves, bringing home the meat and giving the skins to girls for tepee covers. A pair of boys sometimes became close friends, and the bond could extend into adult life when they fought together and shared the same woman, either as a wife or mistress; these men referred to each other as "Little Father" and were closer than with any other persons.

At about the age of ten, boys and girls began imitating the camp life of adults, an activity called "calfskin tepee." Girls from affluent families had small tepees that they set up at a distance from the camps of their parents. Boys pretended to be their husbands and took food from their families for their "wives." The boys organized themselves in the manner of men, even to the point of kidnapping girls belonging to another group. When the boys killed a coyote or wolf, they returned in triumph with a piece of the pelt as a "scalp," and the girls danced with it in imitation of women dancing with scalps obtained by warriors.

Puberty went unacknowledged for males and females alike, although when a girl or woman menstruated she was prohibited from approaching sacred objects and avoided a wounded man or men preparing for a war party; most persons denied that women were isolated physically during menstruation. Girls appear often to have married before they reached puberty, and while marriage to a person in one's own clan was forbidden (clan exogamy), it also was considered in bad taste, at least in the eyes of some persons, to seek a spouse from the clan of one's father. To marry someone from a father's clan with whom no blood ties could be traced was acceptable although not desirable.

Marital arrangements varied, although the parents of a girl often seem to have had some influence, if only because a daughter was so young when she married. A man might meet a girl while she was alone and propose that they elope, offering her a horse for going off with him. A couple could summarily announce that they were going to live together, or a man might seek the aid of a go-between to make the arrangements. Young men seldom hunted before they married. They slept late and spent most of the day grooming themselves to show off on their horses. They courted girls with flute music and sometimes did not return home until daylight.

The most proper marriage proposal, especially for a woman of virtue, was for a man to offer horses to the girl's brother and meat to her mother; these arrangements produced the most lasting marriages. A man who had offered wealth for his bride had the right to claim her younger sister in marriage (sororal polygyny), and the girls' parents were likely to agree when the first daughter was well cared for. In the early 1800s perhaps half of the men had more than one wife, and apparently a few men had as many as twelve. They did not all live together, and some might simply have been betrothed to him. A woman could marry her deceased husband's brother (levirate), but she would not be forced into the union.

Crow sex life was free and open, especially for men, but women were far from pawns. Men and women alike might have many love affairs and made little or no effort to conceal their feelings and sexual activities; their philandering ways were often noted. When a married woman took offense at the affairs of her husband, she might hold him up to ridicule in songs about his behavior. Men and women alike hurled "a fine variety of beautiful epithets" at each other, according to Denig (1961, 151) and other observers. A woman could leave her husband and take her children, as well as her property, including horses, skins, and the tepee, with her; boys not fully dependent on their mother joined their father. Yet, after a couple had separated, irrespective of the reason, they could not live together again without bringing disgrace on them both. As noted previously, during a particular time each year, a Fox or Lumpwood could abduct and marry another man's wife if she previously had slept with him. If he did seize her, the woman could not return to her husband. Divorce was common, except among virtuous women, and could be initiated by either partner. Just as a marriage was without ceremony, so was a divorce. Men were expected to be unfaithful to their wives; in fact, for a man to keep the same wife for many years was considered unmanly and a source of ridicule. Yet some men were jealous of their wives to the point of always taking a favorite wife along on a hunt and strongly resenting it when she committed adultery.

Male transvestites, or berdaches, were reasonably common among the Crow and were not regarded as abnormal but as a third sex. According to Denig (1961), some boys preferred the company of girls in their preadolescence and eventually were dressed as girls by their parents. They then embarked on a lifetime of female activities and might "marry" a man. It also should be noted that there were sacred aspects of being a berdache. For example, in the Sun Dance certain rituals could be performed only by a berdache.

The hand game was a very popular form of entertainment, with garments and beadwork commonly bet on the outcome. A popular game called shinny (stickball) was played by women in the spring. The object was for the members of two teams to drive a ball to opposite goals by using curve-ended sticks. Another widespread game played by men was hoop-throwing, and they bet on the outcome. The object was to throw a dart through a rolling hoop that might have webbing in the middle. The man whose dart entered the hoop or passed nearest to it won a tally stick.

When someone died, the body was painted, clothed in fine garments, and shrouded in part of a tepee cover. The spirit was told not to turn back, and the body was removed under a side of the tepee to prevent further deaths in the household. Interment was either in the crotch of a tree or on a scaffold above four support poles. After the body had decayed, the bones were sometimes removed and placed in a rock crevice. Mourners from the immediate family pulled out their hair or cut it short, slashed themselves with knives, and often cut off finger joints. The practice of removing a finger was so common that scarcely a person had complete hands. However, men usually did not mutilate their thumbs or the fingers used to draw a bow or shoot a gun. The soul of a person was believed to first linger near the corpse, perhaps giving an owl-like cry, but to later go to the camp of the dead. The Crow had little interest in the fate of souls; although they believed that ghosts might return to harm the living, they also considered ghosts to be a source of helpful visions.

The expectation in this matrilineal society was for material property to be passed down along the female line, going to brothers, sisters, and their heirs rather than to a man's sons. But a dying man's request to pass his property to nonclan members was honored. A man could bequeath horses to his wife or sacred objects to an eldest son. Even when bequests were not made along the maternal line, they usually were made to an immediate family member.

Early History

The Crow soon gained the reputation of being clever, deceptive, and shrewd traders who disdained alcohol, which they called "white man's fool water." The first sustained contacts occurred in the early 1800s with the arrival of adventurous trappers and fur traders (collectively, "mountain men") in search of beaver pelts. Their influence was not great because the area was so inaccessible. A devastating result of visits by whites was the repeated epidemics, especially smallpox, that struck over twenty years beginning in the 1830s. By 1833 their population was about sixty-four hundred.

The rival chiefs, Arapooish and Long Hair, had a disagreement, and the people split into two groups, as previously noted. Just when the Crow were divided internally, the United States began to assert control over the region. A government agent was sent up the Missouri River in 1851 to negotiate the first Treaty of Laramie. Long Hair signed the treaty, but Arapooish refused. Treaty conditions included Crow recognition of the United States and of the federal government's right to regulate trade and intercourse. The Crow further agreed not to harm white Americans. By and large the Crow were faithful subjects, and the eventual protection provided by the U.S. Army probably saved the Crow from extinction at the hands of their Indian enemies.

Father Pierre-Jean DeSmet (1905) was the first Christian missionary to seek out the Crow. He visited them in 1840 and in 1842, being well received on both occasions. They were friendly and admired him, but he had no impact on their lifestyle. After hearing the tenets of Catholicism, one man responded that there were only two Crow men who would not go to hell for killing, stealing, and other non-Christian behavior.

In the first Treaty of Laramie, land was set aside for the Crow in northern Wyoming, southern Montana, and western South Dakota. By agreeing to the conditions of this treaty, the Crow and other tribes involved were granted annuities, and the federal government obtained the right to build forts and roads in the region. The second Treaty of Laramie in 1868 confined the Crow to a

Figure 6-8 | Crow schoolchildren. From left to right: unknown, unknown, Russell White Bear, Henry Shin Bone, Annie Wesley, Addie Bear-in-the-Middle, Fanny Butterfly, Kitty Deer Nose. (Courtesy of the Montana Historical Society.)

reservation south of the Yellowstone River in southern Montana; they have continued to live on a small portion of this area into the present. This treaty established a clearly defined reservation. The town now called Crow Agency became the administrative center of this community in 1884. From the beginning of the reservation period, the federal goal was to destroy the traditional basis for Crow life. Christian church services were to replace heathen ceremonies, the people were to wear "civilized" clothing and live in log cabins, the men were to become farmers, and the children were forced to attend school (see Figure 6-8). By treaty the Crow obtained highly specific yearly benefits for thirty years. For instance, each male older than fourteen years of age received "substantial woolen clothing, consisting of a coat, hat, pantaloons, flannel shirt, and woolen socks."

Within comparatively few years the Crow were dealt a number of crushing blows. They were forced to abandon the Big Horn Mountains by Indian enemies, and the presence of non-Indians was ever increasing. The most adverse calamity was a precipitous decline in the number of bison as a result of overhunting by whites for pleasure, hides, tongues, and, to a lesser extent, meat. Furthermore, many whites favored the destruction of bison to make way for cattle. By 1883 bison were nearly gone. An immediate result was privation. The people became dependent on Indian agents, who controlled food and goods that were assured by treaty and essential for survival. These agents were powerful and often corrupt, and they withheld aid to those Crow who were uncooperative with federal policies. The presence of whiskey traders nearby also contributed to declining living conditions. Within ten years of passage of the Homestead Act of 1862, whites were surging into Montana Territory seeking land. The new settlers resented the magnitude of Crow holdings. Under pressure from the homesteaders, Congress repeatedly reduced the amount of land designated for the Crow. Between 1882 and 1904, the size of the reservation was reduced three times. Congress liberalized lease laws and granted land for railroads and a dam. By 1968 two million acres remained of the eight million that the Crow had once occupied.

The disappearance of bison was not only an economic hardship but also psychologically traumatic. The cultural geographer John W. Stafford (1972, 132) summarized the prevailing white attitudes in terms of "good" and "bad" Indians. "The idea of a good Indian was nurtured. To the 'good' Indian who cooperated by cutting his hair, sent his children to school, and took up farming were given special monetary rewards, wagons, and cattle. Other 'good' Indians were given jobs in the agency. Leaders who cooperated were flattered with trips to Washington. On the other hand 'bad' Indians were threatened with loss of rations."

Later History: The Old and the New

The hallmark of Crow life in the twentieth century has been their resistance to assimilation. Despite pervasive changes, the essence of Crow culture remains. Their tenacity may be attributed, at least in part, to a pragmatic approach to Euro-Americans that began to emerge in the nineteenth century, as well as to their continuing sense of a separate identity. A prime illustration of this approach dates from 1857, when Plenty Coups, then nine years of age, had a vision that anticipated dramatic changes and provided guidance: learn from the mistakes of others and establish peaceful relations with whites. He foretold that the greatest defense of Crow culture would be achieved through education. By adhering to the Crow lifeway as much as possible while adjusting to Euro-American policies and practices, the Crow pursued and realized the vision of Plenty Coups.

THE OLD The "buffalo days" are long gone. Most traditional ceremonies have disappeared. Horses are plentiful, but their value is more symbolic than economic. Fewer people than ever speak the Crow language, and most of their material culture of old has given way to imported manufactures. The traditional foods are now served primarily on special occasions. Furthermore, in many ways, but certainly not all, Christianity has abridged the traditional religion. From the scope of these losses, one might assume that Crow culture is moribund, yet the evidence suggests otherwise.

A good indicator of their continuing identity as Crow is reflected in where they have lived in recent years. An estimated 75 percent of the enrolled tribal members continue to reside on or near the reservation. Why? An anthropologist familiar with the modern Crow, Timothy P. McCleary, responded to this question by saying, "The Crow like each other and they consider poverty [as]

Figure 6-9 | A Crow Sun Dance Lodge in the summer of 1994. (Photo by Rodney Frey.)

not having relatives nearby." In this context their traditional sense of solidarity continues to be reflected in the term for a clan, "as driftwood lodges." It well may be that kinship ties have gained even greater strength than in the recent past to compensate for other cultural losses. An individual continues to find social and spiritual comfort and security in kinship ties, especially with clan aunts and uncles. All male and female members of one's father's clan are considered clan aunts and uncles. They are to be respected, like "medicine," and acknowledged through gifts of blankets and food at giveaways held throughout the year. In turn, clan aunts and uncles bestow on each niece and nephew an Indian name that will protect the individual; sing praise songs for their accomplishments; and offer prayers for them before a meal, with a lit cigarette at sunset, or during a sweat bath.

A fine example of an old ceremonial complex that disappeared and that later was revived is the Sun Dance. The last traditional Crow Sun Dance was held in 1875, but by the 1940s they were once again being held (see Figure 6-9). Fred Voget (1984) documented the introduction of the Wind River Shoshoni Sun Dance to the Crow. Two individuals were key to the revitalization. William Big Day became disillusioned with the Roman Catholic church. He traveled to Wyoming in 1938 and witnessed the Wind River Shoshoni Sun Dance. Later at one of these dances Big Day reportedly was cured of chest pains by John Trehero, a supernatural specialist of Shoshoni and Mexican ancestry. Big Day pledged to hold a Sun Dance if his adopted son, Heyward, survived a desperate illness. The boy recovered. Trehero helped the Crow reintroduce the dance by giving them his medicine bundles, songs, and the right to hold the dance. As a result, Big Day organized a Sun Dance on the Crow Reservation in 1941. Subsequently over the years the Crow held the dance on numerous occasions. In 1991 Heyward Big Day held a fiftieth-anniversary Sun Dance in honor of his father.

The Shoshoni–Crow Sun Dance became fully integrated into Crow religious life and is now identified as the Crow Sun Dance. It has emerged as a cornerstone for Crow spiritual expression, as from 40 to 120 men and women dancers participate in three or four Sun Dances each summer. Dances typically last three days, and participants offer collective morning prayers for the welfare of all peoples and other prayers especially for family members. In addition, the ill are treated by curers, and individual dancers may receive visions.

THE NEW In 1904 an Indian agent launched the Crow Agricultural Fair to encourage farming. Over the years, the Crow Fair, as it is now called, became primarily a showcase for expressing cultural pride rather than an exhibition of agricultural produce. Eventually "powwow culture" was introduced in the context of these fairs. For six days each August, a host of Crow families and many Indians from Canada and elsewhere in the United States attend the fair in what is known as the "Tipi Capital of the World." Furthermore, the event attracts thousands of Euro-American visitors. The fair includes Indian dances, an all-Indian rodeo, dance parades, and family reunions. At the parade each morning two Crow veterans of U.S. wars lead the procession as clear recognition that warrior status continues to be respected. Parade participants wear their finest beaded garments as a symbol of their Indianness. The last day of the fair includes a "giveaway" in which individuals at a public ceremony present gifts to clan aunts and uncles.

The horse remains a focus of cultural identity. Photographs of family members on horseback are often seen on the walls of homes (see Figure 6-10). During the Crow Fair, horses are adorned with the finest beadwork and ridden with pride during the parades. Certainly the horse is no longer economically pivotal, nor is it a clear marker for male prestige. (The last bison hunt was in 1883, and the last coups were counted in 1886 during a Piegan and Siouan raid.) Nonetheless, by 1900 the Crow had approximately forty thousand horses. In 1919 the federal government instituted a livestock reduction policy, and horses were either shot or railed to canneries. By 1921 an estimated one thousand horses remained to the Crow, yet in recent years the number of horses has rebounded considerably.

Traditional tribal government prevailed into the 1930s, when the federal government strongly encouraged tribes to organize under the provisions of the 1934 Indian Reorganization Act. The Crow resisted this effort, but in 1948 they developed their own constitution, amended in 1961, which did *not*

Figure 6-10 | Kevin (Crow Boy) Old Horn in 1985.

include most provisions of the reorganization act. They established a distinctive general-council government in which every adult member of the tribe is a council member and entitled to vote at the council meetings. In turn, the council elects four officers: a chair, vice-chair, secretary, and vice-secretary, who each serve two-year terms. The council also established committees that are responsible for specific activities such as education, housing, industrial development, land purchases, and tribal enrollment. Council meetings are usually held quarterly and deal with issues of tribal concern. Along with the tribal court, the council governs the internal affairs of the tribe not under the jurisdiction of the BIA.

By the 1960s the negative impact of the 1887 Dawes Act (see Chapter 2) had become disastrous. A primary reason was the fact that when a Crow obtained title to an allotment, he often sold the land to a white farmer. Few Crow were willing to become farmers, and they sold their land because they were so poor. Furthermore, a man usually did not have the resources to farm or to raise stock. By 1960, if a man kept his allotment, he was likely to lease it to a white to farm or raise cattle. The federal government began to prohibit the sale of reservation land to outsiders; between 1961 and 1968 the tribe bought back about fifty-five thousand acres that previously had been purchased by whites.

The allotment process was a gross intrusion on the integrity of the Crow tribe—as it was meant to be—but the problems created for later generations were overwhelming. A basic problem was the failure of the federal government to make reasonable allowances for birth, death, and population growth rates. No land was set aside for future generations, as was the pattern in some Canadian treaties. An extreme case will illustrate the problem. One 160-acre allotment made in 1887 had passed to 245 heirs before 1967, at which time it was consolidated into 86 claims. Of these claims, the largest was for about 11 acres, and the smallest was for 0.0014 acre! The land was not divided physically, but all the heirs held an interest and shared any income derived from it. Most land with multiple owners was leased by the BIA, and the annual payments were made to the heirs. At a rent rate of fifty cents per acre, the yearly profit for the person owning the 0.0014 acre previously mentioned would be less than one cent. The same conditions held for leasing both dry farmland and small parcels of irrigated land.

The leasing arrangements finally became an administrative and financial burden for the BIA and an absurdity for the Crow. Federal legislation beginning in 1983 eventually led to the consolidation of fractionated leases. The end result was that, when more than five Crow owned a lease, it was consolidated; if the owners could not agree on the terms, the land reverted to the tribe. These arrangements seem reasonable and should resolve a long-standing problem.

For about forty years the Crow have fought vigorously for their legal rights. A major land claim settlement was made in 1961, when $9.2 million was awarded to the tribe. They also received $2 million for land sold to the federal government for the construction of the Yellowtail Dam and Reservoir, completed in 1965.

As recently as the 1970s the Crow language was spoken by about 90 percent of the people. The language continues to be used on a daily basis by many adults at various meetings, family gatherings, and church services. However, a 1989 survey found that only a third of Indian students under the age of ten who lived on or near the reservation spoke Crow. In more recent years, efforts to introduce the Crow language in grade schools have had limited success. Although far fewer children than in the recent past learn to speak Crow at home, nevertheless the language maintains a vitality that comparatively few other tribal languages can match.

The Recent Past

The reservation now includes somewhat more than two million acres, and most of the land is held in trust by the federal government. The acreage leased to whites for farming or grazing has declined to about 35 percent of the total. It is particularly important that the tribe has the first right of purchase when land that once had been a part of the reservation comes up for sale. In 1996, for example, some 62,000 acres were added to the reservation in this manner; but at the same time about 1,000 acres of fee patent land owned by individual Crow were sold to outsiders.

By the late 1990s local job opportunities were few, and the unemployment rate on the reservation ranged from about 70 to 80 percent. The major employer was the tribe, with about 600 permanent and temporary employees. The Indian Health Service hospital employed about 250 people, and the BIA had some 120 employees. Furthermore, the Crow casino employed about 65 people, the Little Big Horn College employed 30, and local businesses had hired a comparatively small number of additional persons. In each instance, most of the workers were Crow. It might appear that there were many jobs on the reservation, but such was not the case; nearly half of the Crow had a living standard beneath the national poverty level.

The 1990s and 2000

Thanks to Tim Barnardis (forthcoming), we have an excellent overview of reservation life in the 1990s. By 1998, the reservation included nearly 2.3 million acres, of which some 1.5 million acres were trust land allotted to individual Crow or held by the tribe. Most of the remaining land was owned by white farmers and ranchers who had purchased allotted land (fee deeded) from individual Crow. In addition, white farmers and ranchers leased reservation land, in part because individual Crow holdings usually were small parcels held as inherited allotments and could not be economically utilized as farms or ranches. *About two-thirds of the reservation was either owned or leased by whites,* and virtually all of the private businesses were owned by whites.

In 1998 enrolled tribal members numbered nearly 10,000, and about 40 percent were under eighteen years of age. Nearly 75 percent of the enrolled members lived on or near the reservation, an unusually high residence rate for reservations nationwide. In economic terms the unemployment rate in recent years has varied from 40 to 50 percent, and most people had low-paying jobs. The major employers in 2000 were the tribe itself (about 1,000 people), the Indian Health Service hospital (about 300 employees), the Bureau of Indian Affairs (about 150), and Little Big Horn College (about 40).

The relative isolation of the reservation made it difficult for most young people to obtain a post–high school education. To help remedy this situation, the tribe chartered Little Big Horn College as a community college in 1980; major funding was provided by a Congressional act in 1978 to support Indian education. In 1999 the college had nearly 170 full-time students, virtually all of whom were Crow (see Figure 6-11), and 17 individuals received Associate of Arts degrees that year. The requirements for graduation included courses on the Crow language and Crow studies. In 1999 the college launched the first phase of a $15 million program to construct new campus facilities. The college president, a Crow, Janine Pease-Pretty on Top, received a MacArthur Foundation grant in 1994.

For tourists the major local attraction is the Little Bighorn Battlefield National Monument (the Custer Battlefield until 1991), which is adjacent to Crow Agency. The battlefield is visited by about 400,000 people each year and pro-

Figure 6-11 | India Hill was a Crow student in general studies at Little Big Horn College in 1996. American Indian history was her major interest.

vides income locally from tourist dollars. The only other major attraction for outsiders is the Crow Fair in August, which is attended by as many as 30,000 visitors. To draw visitors to the reservation, the Crow launched the Little Big Horn Casino in 1994. It has poker and keno machines, but because these forms of gambling are widespread in Montana, casino profits have been modest.

In recent years, the Crow finally have gained political power in Big Horn County, Montana. This development is partially a result of a county redistricting of voting areas that had favored Euro-American voters. As a result of the change, two of the three county commissioners were Crow by 2000. In many ways the Indian majority is more symbolic than anything else, but it does have practical aspects. For instance, county roads to Indian households are now more likely to be comparable to the roads that lead to the farms and ranches of whites.

Another development has been a partial resolution of the "107th meridian" problem that resulted from an inaccurate survey of the eastern reservation boundary and that deprived the Crow of about 46,000 acres of land. The Crow, state, and federal government negotiations began in 1996 and may be entirely settled in 2001. It involves complex land exchanges, including the transfer of some 34,000 acres of state land within the reservation to the federal government, who will turn it over to the Crow. The land received includes major coal deposits, and the development of a mine was widely anticipated. However, the price of coal is not high, and to open the mine is not realistic at present. As a part of the settlement, the Crow are to receive a trust fund of as much as $85 million. The interest will be used for such purposes as education, land acquisition, and economic development.

Traditionally, Crow rights and those of other Montana Indians have been given short shrift by the state. An example is the severance tax on reservation coal commercially mined in the 1970s and 1980s; the tax was collected by the state. The Crow fought the decision in the courts but without resolution. In addition, the Crow had unsuccessfully attempted to obtain water rights to the Big Horn River as it flows through the reservation. In 1999 the Crow agreed to drop their legal battle over the coal severance tax in return for the disputed water rights. A special 1999 session of the Montana Legislature approved the Crow proposal to control these rights for Indians and non-Indians alike on the reservation. The tribe is to receive $15 million from the state over ten years to develop water and other public projects. The likewise seek from the federal government the revenue from electricity generated by the Yellowtail Dam on reservation land, which may amount to as much as $20 million a year in tribal income. However, the federal government and tribal membership must approve this legislation before implementation.

To increase reservation funding, the tribe imposed a 4 percent tax on gross revenues in 1995 for some sixty tourist-related businesses, such as stores, campgrounds, and fishing lodges. Numerous business owners refused payment and challenged the tax in state courts. In 1998 the Montana Supreme Court ruled that the tax was invalid because the tribe was immune to suit in a state court. Another somewhat similar case in federal courts involving the Navajo was resolved in favor of the Navajo. If challenges to that decision are denied, the Crow probably will be able to collect business taxes.

As is commonplace elsewhere, Crow reservation politics is contentious and includes deep-seated factionalism. A major split among the Crow developed in the 1950s between those who favored Yellowtail Dam construction and those who opposed it. This situation led to considerable political instability until Clara Nomee emerged as the first woman elected as the tribal chair in 1990. Soon after gaining office, she was granted broad and unprecedented authority by the tribal council to conduct tribal business between council meetings. The tribal chair is elected every two years, and Nomee was returned to office for an unprecedented five terms. In 2000 she ran for a sixth term. Her opposition, two male candidates, cited a pending case against her for the misuse of tribal monies as one major reason why she should not be returned to office. Her ten years as chair put her in a powerful position, because she controlled about 800 tribal jobs on the reservation. In this general context, she was accused of making appointments to gain and sustain her power base. In the May election, Nomee was decisively defeated by Clifford Birdinground. During the campaign he said he would not fire the current tribal employees and would stress tribal economic development. In July he fired about 130 tribal employees.

A declining number of Crow speak their language fluently. By 1995, 85 percent of the Crow speakers were forty years old or older, whereas about 25 percent of persons between three and eighteen years old spoke Crow as their primary language. Efforts to teach Crow in schools have had limited success. Yet a study by Bernardis (forthcoming) suggests the vigor of many traditional Crow ways in the 1990s. A key example is the enduring strength of the clan system. For most Crow, clan relatives dominate the core of social life. Younger people commonly request the prayers of clan elders and seek their advice when confronted with problems. Clan-based gift exchanges (giveaways) are prominent in social and ceremonial life, as are the feasts hosted by individual clans. In a broader context, an average of five Sun Dances are held each summer. The Tobacco Society, seemingly moribund not so long ago, is being revitalized as expanding numbers of new members are inducted into the society. Taking sweat baths and fasting for spiritual purposes, medicine bundle ceremonies, and participation in peyote ceremonies represent other examples. In addition, the collection of plant products as food or for ceremonial purposes continues, and their tradition as hunters remains strong.

There can be no doubt that traditional Crow material culture has disappeared. Horses, which were so critical early in their history, now have largely symbolic value. The inroads by Christian religions, formal Euro-American education, and the loss of the Crow language each challenge the vitality of their culture. Despite the high unemployment rate on the reservation, the rate of out-migration is low. A reasonable conclusion is that the Crow continue to value each other far more than they do the material well-being that non-Indian Americans have. "As driftwood lodges" endures as a key value among the Crow.

Additional Sources

The ethnography by Robert H. Lowie (1935, 1956) is the standard Crow source, and the ethnohistorical study by Frederick Hoxie (1989) is outstanding. The *Plains* volume (13) of the new *Handbook of North American Indians,* William C. Sturtevant, general editor (Washington, DC, forthcoming) provides an overview of Crow life and includes a wealth of information about the Plains Indians. Reliable early historic accounts by fur traders are by Edwin T. Denig (1961) and Zenas Leonard (1959). Outstanding historical discussions of the Crow include a book by Charles Bradley (1991) and a monograph by C. Adrian Heidenreich (1971). Joseph Medicine Crow was the first Crow to graduate from college, and he is the tribal historian. In a 1992 study, he combines oral traditions and written records to present an insider view of Crow life. The Shoshoni–Crow Sun Dance presentation by Fred Voget (1984) includes excellent biographical sketches of the key individuals involved. Thomas Yellowtail (1991) writes about his life, with particular emphasis on the Sun Dance. A primary contemporary researcher among the Crow is Rodney Frey (1987); in this important work he emphasizes worldview in modern life. Dale D. Old Horn and Timothy P. McCleary (1995) present a brief and notable account of social life, past and present.

The massacre of Lieutenant-Colonel George Custer and his command at Little Big Horn in 1876 is of some interest in Crow history because Custer's scouts were Crow. A great deal has been written about the Battle of Little Big Horn; the events leading up to the massacre are well described in the journal of Lieutenant James H. Bradley, edited by Edgar I. Stewart as *The March of the Montana Column* (Norman, OK, 1961).

Selected Bibliography

Bernardis, Tim. (forthcoming). The Crow people in the 1990s. *Plains,* vol. 13, *Handbook of North American Indians.* Washington, DC.

Bonner, Thomas D. 1972. *The life and adventures of James P. Beckwourth.* Lincoln, NE.

Bradley, Charles. 1991. *The handsome people: A history of the Crow Indians and the whites.* Billings, MT.

Catlin, George. 1841. *North American Indians.* 2 vols. London. (Later editions in 1880, 1903, 1913, and 1926.)

Crummett, Michael. 1993. *Sun Dance: The 50th anniversary Crow Indian Sun Dance.* Helena, MT.

Denig, Edwin T. 1961. *Five Indian tribes of the upper Missouri.* John C. Ewers, ed. Norman, OK.

DeSmet, Pierre-Jean. 1905. *Life, letters and travels of Father Pierre-Jean DeSmet, S. J., 1801–1873,* vol. 1. Hiram M. Chittenden and Alfred T. Richardson, eds. New York.

Donaldson, Thomas. 1886. *The George Catlin Indian Gallery in the U.S. National Museum.* Annual Report of the Board of Regents of the Smithsonian Institution, 1885, pt. 2, appendix.

Ewers, John C. 1965. *The emergence of the Plains Indian as the symbol of the North American Indian.* Smithsonian Report for 1964, 531–44.

Frey, Rodney. 1987. *The world of the Crow Indians: As driftwood lodges.* Norman, OK.

———. 1995. *Stories that make the world: Oral literature of the inland northwest as told by Lawrence Aripa, Tom Yellowtail, and other elders.* Norman, OK.

Heidenreich, C. Adrian. 1971. *Ethno-documentary of the Crow Indians of Montana, 1824–1862.* PhD dissertation, University of Oregon.

Hoxie, Frederick. 1989. *The Crow.* New York.

Larocque, François A. 1910. *Journal of Larocque.* Publications of the Canadian Archives, no. 3, L. J. Burpee, ed.

Leonard, Zenas. 1959. *Adventures of Zenas Leonard, fur trader.* John C. Ewers, ed. Norman, OK.

Linderman, Frank B. 1930. *Plenty-Coups.* London.

———. 1932a. *Pretty-Shield: Medicine woman of the Crows.* Lincoln, NE.

———. 1932b. *Red Mother.* New York.

Lowie, Robert H. 1912. *Social life of the Crow Indians.* Anthropological Papers of the American Museum of Natural History (APAMNH), vol. 9, pt. 2.

———. 1917. *Notes on the social organization and customs of the Mandan, Hidatsa, and Crow Indians.* APAMNH, vol. 21, pt. 1.

———. 1918. *Myths and traditions of the Crow Indians.* APAMNH, vol. 25, pt. 1.

———. 1919. *The Tobacco Society of the Crow Indians.* APAMNH, vol. 21, pt. 2.

———. 1922a. *The religion of the Crow Indians.* APAMNH, vol. 25, pt. 2.

———. 1922b. *The material culture of the Crow Indians.* APAMNH, vol. 21, pt. 3.

———. 1922c. *Crow Indian art.* APAMNH, vol. 21, pt. 4.

———. 1924. *Minor ceremonies of the Crow Indians.* APAMNH, vol. 21, pt. 5.

———. 1935. *The Crow Indians.* New York. (Revised, 1956.)

Maximilian, Alexander P. 1906. *Travels in the interior of North America.* In *Early western travels, 1748–1846.* Reuben G. Thwaites, ed., vols. 22–24. Cleveland.

Medicine Crow, Joseph. 1992. *From the heart of the Crow country: The Crow Indians' own stories.* New York.

Nabokov, Peter. 1967. *Two-Leggings: The making of a Crow warrior.* New York.

Old Horn, Dale D., and Timothy P. McCleary. 1995. *Apsaalooke social and family structure.* Crow Agency, MT.

Stafford, John W. 1972. *Crow culture change.* PhD dissertation, Michigan State University.

Thwaites, Reuben G., ed. 1905. *Original journals of the Lewis and Clark Expedition, 1804–1806,* vol. 5. New York.

Voget, Fred. 1984. *The Shoshoni–Crow Sun Dance.* Norman, OK.

Wildschut, William. 1960. *Crow Indian medicine bundles.* Contributions from the Museum of the American Indian, Heye Foundation, vol. 17.

Yellowtail, Thomas. 1991. *Yellowtail: Crow medicine man and Sun Dance chief: An autobiography as told to Michael Oren Fitzgerald.* Norman, OK.

7 The Cahuilla: Gatherers in the Desert

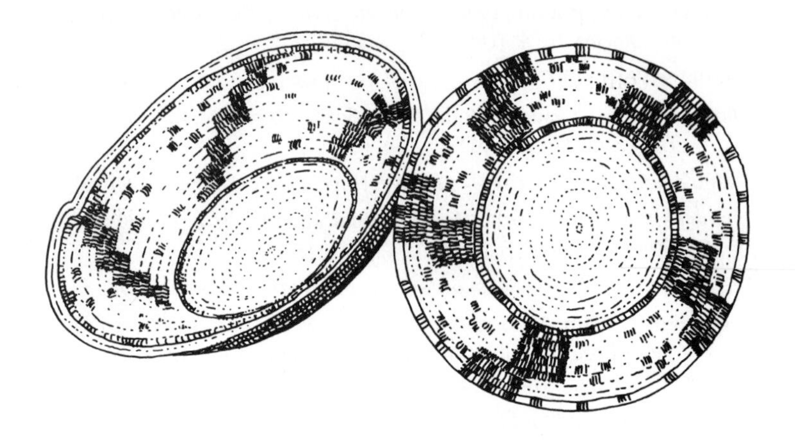

His food gave out, his water gave out,
Leave him now, go away from him:
Isilwelnet. [enemy name]
[repeated as many times as desired]

Bury him now, plant him now:
And then they buried him, and then they planted him:
Pehuetematewilwish.

There stands the whirlwind, there stands the whirlwind
Where they burned him, where they burned him:
Puchueulchalmalmia.

Three "enemy songs" among the Desert Cahuilla
collected by Lucile Hooper. (1920, 345)

A MAJOR REASON for selecting the Cahuilla to represent the California culture area is the quality of the information available about them. Yet it must be stressed that tremendous variability existed in California Indian lifeways; no individual tribe was "typical." Not only is the ethnographic and historical data about the Cahuilla superior, but over the years they have attracted inordinate Anglo-American attention. In historical context, the Cahuilla gained literary recognition in the novel *Ramona*. Once exceedingly popular, it depicts the life of a Cahuilla woman. Its author, Helen Hunt Jackson (1884), brought southern California Indians to national attention. The Palm Springs group (Agua Caliente Band) have been the focus of attention of bankers, land speculators, lawyers, municipal officials, and judges, especially in the resort city of Palm Springs; this interest has been, above all else, monetary.

Considering the course of Native American history, it might be expected that the Palm Springs Band of Cahuilla are relatively disadvantaged, but nothing could be further from reality. The land allotted to individual band members is valued at *billions of dollars*. In addition, the band owns a casino, spa hotel, and other tribal operations. The total assets of the nearly three hundred band members are astronomical. "Lo! the poor Indian" clearly is not a phrase that applies to these people.

Three Cahuilla subgroups are recognized: the Desert, Mountain, and Pass populations. In this chapter, the emphasis is on the Desert Cahuilla, who lived in the vicinity of Palm Springs. However, it was not always possible to determine from a source whether a specific trait was expressed in both the general desert area and at Palm Springs. As is true of most ethnographic reconstructions, this chapter does not apply in detail to a single community, but it does represent a composite for the desert dwellers.

Six thousand, or possibly fewer, Cahuilla (kuh-WE-uh) lived in the interior of southern California (see Figure 7-1). They are included in the Uto-Aztecan linguistic family, which is widely represented in the western United States and Mexico. The Cahuilla also are members of the Takic subfamily of languages.

Aboriginal Life

Cahuilla tradition states that they originally lived in the desert but were forced to flee to adjacent mountains by a great flood, a probable reference to the emergence of the inland sea that once covered much of the present lowland and subsided about five hundred years ago. The San Jacinto and Santa Rosa mountains where they sought refuge consist of steep granite ridges and barren tablelands at medium elevations, but higher up are streams, open meadows, and forests of oak and pine. After the flood subsided, the Desert Cahuilla moved into the Coachella Valley, a desert environment in which cacti, mesquite, and screw beans were economically important plants. The region has very little precipitation, and summer temperatures may reach 120°F. Precipitation, when it does come, is often torrential and causes widespread erosion.

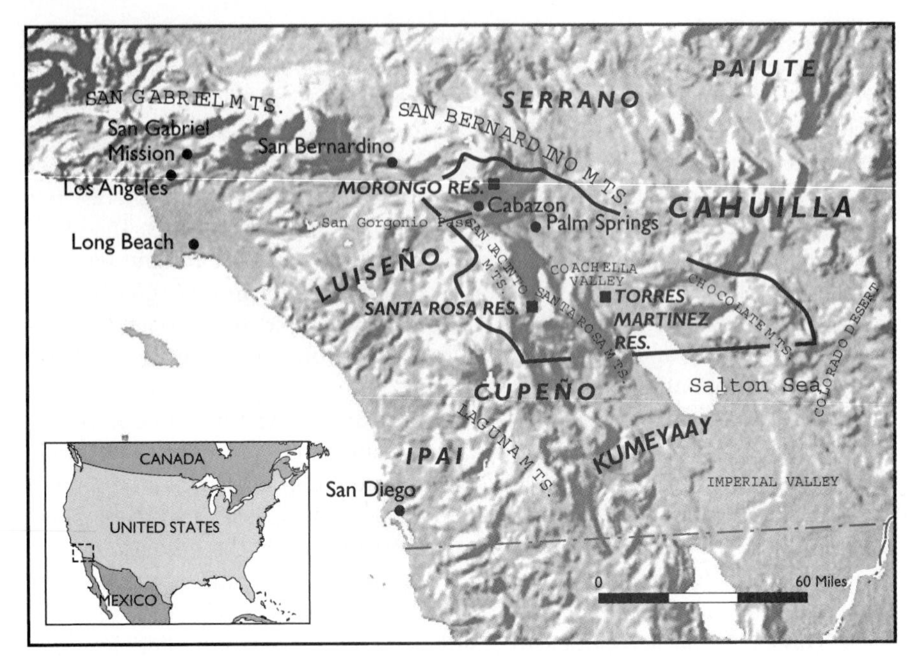

Figure 7-1 | The Cahuilla area with major reservations indicated.

Furthermore, severe dust storms may whip across the valley. Some sectors, particularly in the eastern part of the Desert Cahuilla range, are devoid of vegetation. The Pass Cahuilla occupied the country surrounding San Gorgonio Pass; here were open grassland and some oak groves, as well as desert areas.

ORIGIN MYTH In the Cahuilla culture, ties with the mythological past were very important. Their well-developed origin myth is as follows. In the beginning, there was no earth or sky or anything or anybody; only a dense darkness in space. This darkness seemed alive. Something like lightning bolts seemed to pass through it and meet each other once in a while. Two substances that looked like the white of an egg came from the lightning bolts. They lay side by side in the stomach of the darkness, which resembled a spider web. These substances disappeared. They were produced again, and again they disappeared. This was called the miscarriage of the darkness. The third time they appeared, they remained, hanging there in this web in the darkness. The substances began to grow and soon were two very large eggs. When they hatched two men emerged, Mukat and Tamaioit. They were grown men from the first and could talk. As they lay there, both at the same time heard a noise like a bee buzzing; this was the song of their mother, Darkness (Hooper 1920, 317).

With this great event the natural world began to emerge as an orderly system; at least this was said to be so by the Iviatim, the descendants of Mukat and Tamaioit, who have come to be known in the ethnographic literature as the Cahuilla (Coahuillas, Kawia), a word that may have meant "masters."

Once the twin creators existed, Mukat reached into his mouth and then into his heart to remove a cricket, another insect, a lizard, and a person. These creatures were charged with driving away the darkness, but they failed. From their hearts the creators removed tobacco, pipes, and a coal to light one pipe. Mukat and Tamaioit argued over which one was born first and which was the more intelligent. Mukat became associated with making things black, and Tamaioit made forms that were white. Together they created the earth, ocean, sun, moon, people, and some plants and animals. Finally Mukat and Tamaioit disagreed so violently that Tamaioit disappeared beneath the ground, taking with him many of his creations. It was then that mountains emerged, the earth quaked, and water from the ocean overflowed, forming streams and rivers. After this Mukat lived in a big house with people and animals who had human qualities. The moon was there as a lovely female who instructed women about marriage, child rearing, and both menstrual and pregnancy taboos. Mukat, who had created her, desired to make the moon his wife. She knew this but said nothing. Since she could not marry him because he was her father, she traveled to her present home in the sky. When she was asked to return, she said nothing; she only smiled. One day, while in a humorous mood, Mukat caused the people to speak different languages. As the sun grew hot, some of these people sought shelter and were transformed into different plants and animals. Those who stayed with Mukat remained human. He told the people how to make bows and arrows and how to shoot at each other, which led to the first deaths. It was about this time, too, that the sun turned people different colors. Those people who were nearest the sun's rays became black people, those who were far away stayed white, and the Indians turned brown because they were in between.

The people became angry with Mukat after he had caused a rattlesnake to bite a friendly little man, the moon woman to leave, and people to kill one another. They decided to kill Mukat but did not know how to do it. Mukat lived in the middle of the big house and only went outside to defecate when everyone was asleep; this a white lizard discovered. One night a frog caught the feces of Mukat in his mouth, and Mukat grew ill. The shamans pretended to try to cure him, but Mukat became sicker. As he was dying, he sang songs and told the people how to conduct a mourning ceremony in memory of the dead each year. After his death, Mukat was cremated, the big house was burned, and the essence of the world was established.

MANUFACTURES AND SETTLEMENTS In aboriginal times, clothing seems to have been nonexistent, although it is possible that women wore short skirts of plant fiber and men wore breechclouts. A more certain item of apparel was

Figure 7-2 | Palm Springs Cahuilla homestead, ca. 1900. (Courtesy of the Southwest Museum, Los Angeles. Photo #33934.)

footwear, which consisted of sandals made from mescal fiber pads. Women sometimes wore flat-top basketry hats. They were tattooed on the chin, and certain men, most likely leaders, had their nasal septums pierced and a deer bone inserted in the opening. Males and females wore strings of beads in their pierced earlobes. The beads were thin curved and circular pieces of shell received in trade from the coastal regions of southern California.

Cahuilla villages usually were located near canyon mouths or in a valley where flooding was unlikely. Where water was scarce, settlements clustered near water holes or hand-dug wells. Their dwellings were substantial rectangular structures with fork-top corner posts to receive roof beams. Along the sides and on the beam tops were arranged lengths of brush held in place with horizontal poles (see Figure 7-2). On some houses the brush was smeared with mud, and a layer of dirt was added to the roof. At the front of a house was a ramada or porch constructed like a house but walled only on the windward side. A settlement included a post-and-pole bathhouse built in a shallow pit and probably covered with brush and a layer of earth. A fire was built in the fireplace, and smoke drifted from the doorway until the people were ready to bathe. Cahuilla caches were distinct. They usually were raised above the ground on a pole platform and were made by intertwining small branches; they looked very much like birds' nests some two to four feet high and were used to store plant products (see Figure 7-3). The only other structures were a brush enclosure used for ceremonies and a large enclosure walled on three sides and attached to the house of a male leader. Among the Palm Springs Cahuilla in 1925, the social and ceremonial leader occupied the dance house, which was

Figure 7-3 | A 1907 Desert Cahuilla granary. (Courtesy of the Phoebe A. Hearst Museum of Anthropology, University of California at Berkeley.)

about forty feet in diameter with walls of fitted boards and a palm-thatched roof. At the back was a room where the sacred (medicine) bundle was kept; in front of the structure was a fenced enclosure.

An aboriginal house remained relatively cool even in the hottest weather. The inside was dark from soot on the walls, and natural light filtered in only through the doorway. On one side of the entrance were a woman's food-grinding stones. People the world over who collect seeds as food often used a set of stones to crush the shells. The Cahuilla spread seeds on a flat or slightly concave stone called a milling stone (metate, quern) and pulverized them using a smaller stone called a hand stone (mano, rubbing stone). On the other side of the doorway was a pottery water vessel. Toward the center of the room, fire-blackened cooking pots encircled the fireplace; at the back of the house, blankets and animal skins served as mattresses. Attached to the roof beams or in the thatch were bundles of plants or dried meat for future use. Near every house a section of log set vertically into the ground served as a mortar: the top was flat except that the center was hollowed out a foot or more in depth. A smooth pole some two feet long served as the pestle. The combination was designed to pulverize mesquite beans, an important item in the diet.

Most artifacts around a settlement were made from plant fibers. Baskets, usually fashioned by coiling, often had black geometric designs woven on the sides, the most varied cluster of forms. Among the more common styles were globular baskets used as utensils or containers for small objects and round forms for food or seed storage (see Figure 7-4). Mescal fiber nets used as carrying baskets looked like small hammocks and had loops at each end for cinching cords. A woman carrying a basket passed the cord over her forehead and rested it against the front of her basketry hat.

Figure 7-4 | A Cahuilla woman, Louisa Costa Rice, making baskets for the tourist trade in 1938 at the Soboba Reservation. (Photograph by Maxine and Gerald A. Smith, courtesy of the San Bernardino County Museum and A. K. Smiley Public Library, Redlands, CA.)

The only domestic animal, the dog, served as a pet and watchdog rather than an aid in hunting. The dog was not an ordinary pet because it was believed to possess certain supernatural powers. According to Cahuilla belief, dogs could understand human conversation but could not speak, and like people, they had souls. In the origin myth, at the time of Mukat's death, the people had only one dog, and among the modern Desert Cahuilla, some dogs still were named after the first dog. Other dog names referred to their appearance or to some behavioral characteristic.

SUBSISTENCE ACTIVITIES The Cahuilla identified three primary seasons: the budding of trees, hot days, and cold days. Some persons divided the year into eight more specific seasons, each associated with the development of mesquite beans. The beginning of a season arrived when a particular star appeared; this was a moment for rejoicing and a time to make preparations for an appropriate collecting activity. Star watching was especially important in the spring when food supplies might be low and edible plants were ripening. It is estimated that 80 percent of all edibles were harvested within five miles of a village.

The Desert people relied on mesquite beans as their primary staple. The most productive stands flourished near streams and along washes, but the productivity of trees varied by year, and the beans of some trees were favored over others because of their taste. Entire families participated in a harvest, with children climbing trees to dislodge bean pods from high branches. People gathered ripe pods from the ground and artificially ripened immature pods in the sun. They used upright wooden mortars with wooden pestles to grind fresh pods and produce juice for a beverage. The bulk of a harvest was cached and processed later in the year with mortars and pestles or on milling stones. Dried meal, moistened and pressed into cakes, became snacks or food for travelers. Pottery and basketry containers held loose meal that could be processed as a beverage or, more often, be prepared as a mealtime gruel. Screw beans, as an important but secondary staple, grew under the same general conditions as mesquite beans and were processed in the same manner.

Accounts about aboriginal California tribes justly identify acorns as a key staple, but they were comparatively unimportant among the Desert Cahuilla. Patriclans (families related along the male descent line) controlled acorn harvests, and specific families owned particular trees. In the fall, men climbed the trees to dislodge the acorns. Women cracked the acorns between two stones, spread the kernels out to dry for several weeks, and then pulverized them with pestles in stone mortars. To remove the bitter tannic acid, they spread the meal on a loosely woven basket or in a depression made in sand. In either case, grass or leaves were placed in the leaching basin to prevent the meal from washing away. Then they poured water repeatedly over the meal and stirred the mixture. The domestic capabilities of a woman were gauged by her skill in leaching and grinding acorn meal. Finely ground meal was made into cakes and baked in hot coals, while coarse meal was made into a gruel. Acorns that were not ground at gathering time were stored in platform caches.

In addition to the three plants cited, they harvested over one hundred additional plants as edibles. A number of specifics illustrate the diversity. A species of *Chenopodium* grew in well-watered localities. The seeds were collected, ground, and baked in cakes. One of the most important seed-producing grasses was chia, a member of the sage family. A seed beater dislodged the seeds from the whorls onto a flat basket. They were parched and ground to be baked into cakes or mixed with water to make a nourishing drink. When the century plants or agave of the canyons produced stalks, the stalks and "cabbages" were roasted in sand pits heated with stones. To this list of foods could be added many others, but the examples cited suggest the broad range of plants collected and the varied means of food preparation.

Contrary to expectations, the overwhelming emphasis on plant foods did not mean that hunting was neglected nor that the inventory of weapons and traps was impoverished. Adult males trapped animals and also stalked, chased, and intercepted them. The principal weapon was a shaft (self) bow with a plant fiber bowstring. The arrowshafts were vaned with split feathers, and shafts simply sharpened at the point probably were meant for birds and small game. Arrows with cane shafts and wooden arrow points probably were used against large game and enemies; some arrows apparently were tipped with poisons made from rattlesnake venom and other toxic substances. Another weapon was the nonreturning boomerang, commonly called a throwing stick when reported in western North America. It was a flat, curved piece of wood thrown at birds and small game. Hunters also used calls and decoys to lure game near enough to kill with arrows. Additional facilities for taking game included nets set along trails, deadfalls, and snares. Hunting was surrounded by numerous restrictions. For example, the Desert Cahuilla regarded mountain lions and grizzly bears as having powerful spirits and avoided killing them. When a mule deer was killed, people gathered to sing all night and eat the deer the following morning. In general, a man or boy did not consume any of the animals that he killed. Rabbits, squirrels, and wood rats taken by a young boy in a communal hunt usually were given to his mother's family. The kills of an adult male were given alternately to his own family and to his wife's family.

DESCENT, KINSHIP, AND MARRIAGE Many people around the world placed particular stress on either the male *or* female lines to identify their nearest relatives (unilineal descent). As noted in the previous chapter, the Crow emphasized descent traced through females (matrilineal descent). The Cahuilla, however, stressed the male line (a patrilineal descent system). A married couple resided with or near the husband's family (patrilocal marriage residence). A typical Cahuilla settlement centered around a group of males who traced their descent to a *known* common ancestor (patrilineage). Closely related patrilineages with a *presumed* common ancestor composed a larger unit (patriclan), which was the landowning political unit.

In the kinship terminology, a male individual distinguished among his older and younger male and female siblings and made similar distinctions between his father's brothers and mother's sisters. He employed still other terms for his father's sisters and mother's brothers; these did not take relative age into consideration. A male individual referred to his father's older brother's and his mother's older sister's son and daughter by the same term as for his older brothers and sisters. Similarly, he referred to the son and daughter of his father's younger brother and mother's younger sister by the same terms as for his younger brothers and sisters. In essence, parallel cousins (children of father's brother and mother's sister) were termed the same as siblings, with the same age distinction as for siblings. For cross-cousins (father's sister's and mother's brother's children), the male–female kin terms were the same but different from those for siblings or parallel cousins. This cousin terminology is of the Iroquois type, while the terms on the first ascending generation are bifurcate

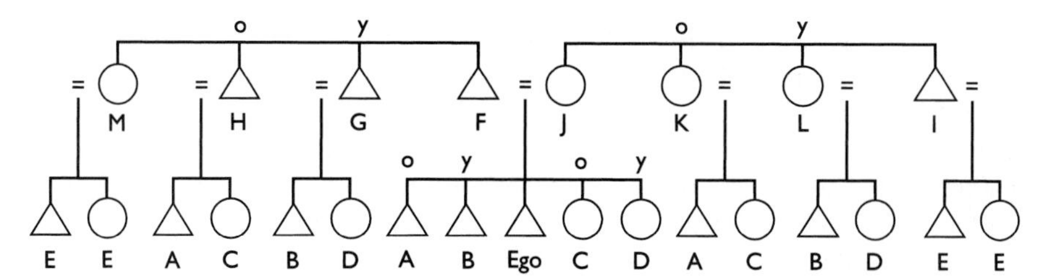

Figure 7-5 | The early historic Cahuilla system of kinship terminology.

collateral. The Iroquois cousin terms make particular sense since moiety exogamy (marriage outside each of the two basic tribal subdivisions) existed. Thus certain near relatives, such as father's brother's children and mother's sister's children, were of one's own moiety and reasonably called brother and sister. Cross-cousins, on the other hand, were of a different moiety and termed differently, but in spite of the terminological difference one could not marry a cross-cousin (see Figure 7-5).

SOCIAL DIMENSIONS In the Cahuilla origin myth, Mukat and Tamaioit were associated with the wildcat and coyote, respectively, and all Cahuilla identified with one or the other of these groups (moieties). Among the Desert Cahuilla, the Wildcat moiety included eight clans, and the Coyote moiety consisted of ten clans. In aboriginal times the members of each clan theoretically occupied a single settlement, but in actual fact, persons from a number of clans might live in one settlement. We may presume that at one time all the members of a patriclan lived in a single village. As their number increased and they could not support themselves at the village site, the surplus, most likely members of a junior patrilineage, formed a new village or joined another clan at its settlement. A clan section or patrilineage founding a new village might eventually become so populous that it qualified as a clan, with its own name and leader, or clan "chief," called a *net.* The office of net usually passed from father to eldest son (primogeniture), and it included extremely important obligations. Nets lived in dwellings with dance houses attached and were the trustees of sacred clan bundles. A net directed subsistence activities, settled conflicts between members, represented the clan before other clans, and was responsible for the correct performance of ceremonies.

In sum, the core population of a village consisted of small family groups related through male lines descending from a known common ancestor (patrilineage). In the same settlement might be the members of other patrilineages assumed to have had a common male ancestor (patriclan). Moiety exogamy prevailed, which meant that a Wildcat was obligated to marry a Coyote and vice versa. Persons in opposite moieties maintained a joking relationship and friendly rivalry, along with economic and ritual obligations.

POLITICAL LIFE Hereditary leaders did not exist above the clan level, and in instances in which the activities of one clan impinged on those of another, the differences were resolved by the nets in council. Decisions of a clan as a collectivity were made by the net, who ideally was a man of exceptional abilities. A net was required to know the boundaries of all clan lands, all clan traditions, and a broad range of esoteric facts important to the clan's viability; he also was expected to be a good orator and fair-minded. He did not possess more material property than anyone else, but families presented him with the initial harvest (first fruit) of any plant, which was partial compensation for the time he devoted to clan activities. At the rear of the net's house was a small room in which sacred objects, termed the "heart" of the clan, were kept. Eagle, hawk, and owl feathers were a vital part of each sacred bundle. Clearly, the net, as conveyer of clan knowledge and guardian of the most sacred clan objects, was the paramount leader.

A second important political and religious functionary was the *paha*. His role existed only in certain localities, and his exact duties have not been reported in detail. Apparently, where the office existed, the paha was primarily responsible for ceremonial preparations and the maintenance of order on such occasions. In addition, he was a leader of hunting parties and a spokesman and messenger for a net. Upon his death he was replaced by a son or another close male relative.

Formalized warfare or even feuds with neighboring ethnic groups were rare. To the east the desert area had no permanent occupants as far as the Colorado River; here the aggressive Mohave and Yuma lived. The Cahuilla feared these tribes, although trade with them was limited. The intervening desert was an effective barrier to intensive contacts. The Chemehuevi, who lived to the east along the Colorado River and into the deserts of California, were friendly with the Desert Cahuilla. The southern neighbors of the Desert Cahuilla were the Kumeyaay, but contacts with these people have not been described in any detail and are assumed to have been infrequent.

RELIGION Shamans were responsible for dealing with intermittent disaster and personal trauma, while the net and paha guided ceremonies focusing on the life cycle and belief system. The Eagle-Killing Ceremony belongs to the latter category and was a highlight in religious life.

The Eagle-Killing Ceremony symbolized the continuity of a lineage. According to Cahuilla belief, the eagle was one of the species originally created by Mukat. It was said that the eagle lived forever, and by permitting itself to be "killed" by people it assured them of life after death. Thus, although lineage members died, the lineage would continue as had the eagle as a species. Furthermore, the flight of the eagle symbolized the magical course of shamans when they led human souls to the land of the dead. The ceremony also provided a means of obtaining eagle feathers, essential for replacing ceremonial artifacts that had worn out, been destroyed, or exchanged in previous rituals.

In the higher country controlled by some clans, eagles' nests were closely watched by a clan member. This person notified the others of the clan when the eggs had been laid. A feast was then held, and after the nestlings were well feathered, one was removed and raised in a cage by the net's family. After the bird had grown, festivities were held with the members of a neighboring clan or clans as guests. At the appointed time, special songs were sung about the death of eagles, and dances were performed. The climax came after the eagle was rolled into a ceremonial mat held by the close family members of the net. They danced with the encased eagle and at dawn the bird screeched and died; it probably was gradually squeezed. The bird was skinned, and the net kept the feathered skin in the sacred clan bundle. Some feathers might be made into a ceremonial skirt, and others were kept to adorn images during the Mourning Ceremony.

Among the Desert group the status of a shaman was not hereditary, and a number of practitioners might belong to a single clan. A shaman often was a man who had been ill frequently as a child, and the healer who treated him had become aware of the child's potential as a curer, magician, and seer. As a young man the novice dreamed of a song that became a tangible manifestation of his inordinate powers. Mukat was responsible, in Cahuilla belief, for implanting the dreams and guardian spirits identified with shamans. A novice danced before the people of his clan for three nights and afterward was qualified to pursue his calling. In his dreams, and from other shamans, he eventually learned additional songs, dances, feats of magic, and bewitching methods. In his dreams, too, a shaman learned of herbal cures for particular ailments or, at other times, of harmful or curative spells. Certain creatures, such as the coyote, fox, hummingbird, and owl, were considered to be messengers who brought shamans warnings of impending illness. When not drawing on his pharmacopoeia, the shaman attempted to cure by sucking on the afflicted part of a patient's body. Reputedly, he removed the disease object without breaking the skin. Only a few plants were used in curing, despite the Cahuilla's extensive botanical knowledge and their many uses of plants as food. As a youth a shaman did not receive compensation for his services; but as he grew older and became established, he would charge a fee.

If a shaman became malevolent, he posed a threat to the community. In the latter part of the nineteenth century, one old man was considered the world's most powerful shaman. When shamans exhibited their skills, he always performed last and challenged the others to kill him. None was able to do so because he was protected by spirits on all sides. Finally, the old shaman was told by a man of a different clan to stop killing people. The man who gave the warning was soon struck by a "pain" that no shaman could remove, and he died. Everyone knew that the old shaman was responsible. A man from the shaman's clan and men from other clans met and decided that he must be killed. The executioner was to be the net of another clan because he was strong and brave. This man and another visited the sorcerer and were invited to spend the night. After everyone else was asleep, the net crushed the old man's skull with a stone pestle. At the head of the victim's bed were found a variety of small feathers and the skin of a gopher snake, objects used by the old man to make pains. As they were trampled into the ground, a thunderlike sound was heard. In the morning people came to view the body, and later the same morning the body and the house were burned. This is one of the rare recorded instances in which collective action was taken for the good of all the people.

LIFE CYCLE At critical times during an individual's life, he or she followed numerous rules, and one of these periods was pregnancy. A future mother refrained from eating any more than necessary; she drank only warm water, ate very little meat, and consumed no salt. In Cahuilla belief, if a pregnant woman ate fruit pecked by a bird, her infant would have sores; if she ate meat from the legs of game, a breech presentation would result; but if she was industrious when pregnant, her offspring would be energetic. These were but three of the rules to insure a safe delivery and a normal offspring. As soon as a woman gave birth and expelled the placenta, she lay in a specially prepared trough dug in the floor of a house. The depression was lined with hot sand, and after the woman stretched out, more hot sand was piled over her body. Here she remained for about ten days, leaving the trough only to urinate and defecate, to have the sand reheated, and to be bathed with hot water each morning. During the month following parturition, the mother remained subject to food taboos, and the father could eat no foods containing salt. A nursing mother did not have sexual intercourse with her husband, for to do so was thought to spoil her milk. She was the object of teasing if she weaned her infant early.

The naming of a child was enmeshed in ritual. After a number of children had been born into a clan, the parents began accumulating food and wealth for a formal naming ceremony. This meant that a child was between four and twelve years of age before he or she was named. A child who had not been named by the age of thirteen would always be known by a nickname. The ceremony was in the father's clan dance house with the couple's clans represented. Female names most often referred to plants or artifacts, whereas males tended to be named after animals, birds, or insects. Amidst singing and dancing, the net held up a child and shouted his or her name three times; the name was repeated by the audience. To prevent an "enemy" clan from learning a child's true name, a disgraceful revelation, and incorporating it in their songs, a net might not say the child's real name. In these instances, a false name would be shouted and the true name revealed in secret. After the namings, food and gifts were distributed to the guests to conclude the ceremony.

When a Desert girl approached adolescence, she was tattooed by her mother's sister as guests from the operator's clan watched. The tattoos were made with cactus thorns pricked in straight or angled lines from the lower lip to the chin, and black paint was rubbed into the wounds. At this time the earlobes of a girl were pierced. When a girl menstruated for the first time, the net summoned the clan of the girl's mother to a ceremony that began in the evening. A fire was built before the net's house to heat the ground, and afterward a trough was dug. The girl was placed in the depression, and her body was covered with hot sand. Throughout the night the members of the girl's clan danced and sang around the pit. In the morning the girl was removed, bathed in warm water, and her head covered with a white paint. For the next three weeks she was subject to food taboos very much like those surrounding pregnancy. The girl stayed in or near the house, and she scratched her head with a special implement rather than her fingernails to prevent her hair from dropping out. Subsequent menstrual periods were surrounded by the same taboos, and in addition, a married woman was forbidden to touch her husband when she was menstruating. The good health of a couple supposedly depended on how well the woman obeyed these rules.

Some Desert Cahuilla do not appear to have initiated adolescent males, but an appropriate ceremony occurred at Palm Springs. Boys between the ages of ten and eighteen were selected by elders for initiation and taken to a brush enclosure outside the dance house. The boys were secluded there for five days and saw only those persons who brought them special foods. Throughout three nights the old people danced until morning. The climax came on the fourth night when the initiates were brought out and given a drink of cooked jimsonweed, or *toloache* as it is known in Spanish. After taking it, the boys danced briefly, but they became dizzy and were placed in a corner while the older people continued to dance. The following evening the effects of the jimsonweed had worn off, and for the next five nights the boys were taught how to dance, sing particular songs, and behave correctly as adults. This ceremony seems to have symbolized the initiates' death as children and their rebirth as knowledgeable adults. The only forms of body mutilation among males were piercing the ears and the nasal septum. The latter operation was not common and was performed only on young boys with promise as leaders. In the opening at the base of the nose pieces of deer bone were inserted.

When members of different clans assembled, especially for the tattooing of a girl or the piercing of a boy's nasal septum, songs known as enemy songs might be sung. Between clans, especially those geographically removed from one another, a rivalry of unknown origins existed. Members of competing clans composed derisive songs in which they incorporated the personal names of individuals in rival clans. These names had been bestowed by a net in secret, and the fact that they were known to the members of other clans was shameful. First one clan performed and then the other, with victory going to the side mentioning the most names of rivals and heaping the greatest abuse or to the clan whose members were physically able to sing longer. Enemy songs were an obvious means for giving vent to aggressive behavior in a socially approved manner. (These were not comparable to the dueling songs sung by two hostile Eskimos in some sectors of the Arctic.) The joking relationship between moiety members served the same purpose in a friendlier atmosphere.

The Desert Cahuilla marriage pattern included not only moiety exogamy but a prohibition against seeking a spouse from known relatives on either side of the family. Since genealogies were remembered for about five generations, one could marry a distant cousin in the opposite moiety. A thirteen-year-old girl was most likely to wed a man of eighteen from a nearby community. The match was arranged by parents, and after the formalities had been settled, the bride was led into the groom's house (patrilocal residence). She sat facing a corner with her back to the assembled relatives of the groom. The groom then sat next to the girl, and the couple was given food as the boy's relatives ate. When the feasting was over, the couple was considered married, and that night the newlyweds were given a single blanket with the theory that if affection did not bring them together the cold desert night would. A girl who was unhappy in the home of her in-laws might return to her mother's home, but if she did this repeatedly, the presents that had been given were returned and the marriage considered dissolved. The groom and his parents had the right to expect the bride to bear an offspring within two or three years. Failure to do so might annul the marriage and again mean a return of the wedding presents. A man could, if the woman's parents agreed, receive a younger sister of his wife if the latter died (sororate). It was less common for a woman to marry her deceased husband's brother (levirate). Among these people monogamy was the prevailing form of marriage, and familial relationships appear to have been quite stable.

Of all the forms of entertainment, the hand game, called *peon,* played at secular gatherings and during ceremonies was most popular. A team from one village competed against one from another settlement. The goal was for a member of the opposite team to guess which clenched fist held a small bone. Bets were made, and shamans aided their respective sides while women sang at certain times during the game. A mediator kept a fire burning by which the game was played, held the stakes, and settled disputes. A particular game ended when one side had lost all the peons of the four players or had won a series of tally sticks. Then a new game was started, and new stakes were put up. Peon was frequently played throughout the night, and as one player tired, he was replaced by another.

Other games included races between two groups of men. Each group kicked a wooden ball for several miles and then back again to the starting point. The men on each team took turns kicking the ball, and the team that finished first was the winner. Another race took place on the night of a new moon. The first boy to see the moon would call the others, and they would race to a spot where they could swim. After swimming they raced home, and by so doing they supposedly brought good luck in the coming month. Cat's cradles were made by persons of both sexes. This skill had supernatural implications, since the people believed that before a person's spirit could pass into the world of other spirits, it was required to make string figures.

In the routine of adult life, a woman was the outsider in the extended family household of her husband. The husband and wife were expected to be

Figure 7-6 | Pasqual, a Cahuilla man said to be ninety years old, circa 1890. (Courtesy of the San Bernardino County Museum and A. K. Smiley Public Library, Redlands, CA.)

reserved in the presence of others, and the wife generally was retiring when with her in-laws or around men. Ideally, younger persons were thoughtful and unselfish in their dealings with older persons; these values were instilled in children when they were small. Young boys who hunted or collected the first plant products of the season were expected to take them to the aged (see Figure 7-6). The most respected men were nets, pahas, shamans, and outstanding hunters. Women gained the greatest recognition by being curers and as efficient workers.

In early times, death brought immediate destruction of a Cahuilla household: on the morning following the death of a person, the body of the deceased and the house in which the death had occurred were burned. In later times, however, this pattern was modified. When an individual died, the members of his or her and other clans assembled, bringing presents. The body was washed, dressed, and taken to the clan dance house of the deceased. Here the assembled mourners sang over the body throughout the night. If a man had died, the creation narrative was sung; for a woman, a song about the moon was sung, since it was the moon who had originally instructed women. The body was burned the morning following death, and within a week the person's house and possessions were burned.

In the Cahuilla life cycle, a ritual focus on death dominated, not for the cremation of a body but in an annual Mourning Ceremony, their most notable religious observance. In the fall or winter each clan held a seven-day ceremony for persons who had died after the ceremony of the previous year. Months of

Figure 7-7 | A Cahuilla shaman, Salvador Lopez, with a live coal from a wood fire in his mouth, photographed in 1963. (Courtesy of the Phoebe A. Hearst Museum of Anthropology, University of California at Berkeley.)

preparations by a clan net, paha, and other members preceded the event, especially to accumulate food and gifts for the guests. Relatives of a specific clan related to the deceased by marriage arrived, bearing gifts, on a particular night to avoid overcrowding. The commemoration included a narration of the origin myth in which Mukat described the creation of the world and the proper death rituals. During the opening three nights, shamans of the host and other clans sought to communicate with the spirits of the honored dead. In this context a performing shaman commonly placed live coals in his mouth and appeared to swallow them (see Figure 7-7). Throughout the next two nights, the singing of clan songs dominated.

The following night, singers, aided by relatives of the deceased, prepared images of the dead. Nearly life-size figures of reed mat construction were adorned with deerskins. A female figure included baskets decorated with eagle feathers. A male image required an eagle-feather headdress and a bow and arrows. At sunrise on the final day, guests ate and received presents from their hosts. The rituals climaxed in a procession by surviving relatives, who carried the images to a spot near the clan dance house. Somewhat later the images were burned, releasing the souls of the deceased and ending the period of mourning; the names of the honored dead ceased to be used. The rituals concluded as each guest received a string of shell beads from the hosts.

The evidence for the presence of human souls took varied forms. They believed that souls found expression in dreams, and when someone fainted, they inferred that that person's soul was wandering. Similarly, a person might become ill if his or her soul became wayward, and the intervention of a shaman became necessary to return the person's soul to the body. They also believed that the soul left the body months before death. After death a spirit or soul sought passage between the clapping mountains created by Mukat and was questioned by a deathless guardian. The spirits of those who had lived by Mukat's rules passed unharmed beyond the clapping mountains. Those who failed became bats, butterflies, trees, or rocks.

Historic Changes

The Cahuilla are often classified as Mission Indians, which is not an entirely accurate label. They were not subject to the mission environment in the manner of coastal Indians in southern California, and most Cahuilla had only indirect contact with Roman Catholic missionaries. Neither Pedro Fages in 1772 nor Juan Bautista de Anza in 1774, the first Europeans in the region, made any known impact on these Indians. In 1819 a mission outpost (*rancho*) was founded in the San Bernardino area, but it was not until Mexico secured independence from Spain in 1821 that the interior of southern California began to attract attention. After the San Bernardino rancho was secularized in 1834, it passed into the private ownership of ranchers. The rancho was sacked and burned by marauding Mohave, Paiute, and Yuma in raids on the cattle and horses of the ranchers. Cahuilla participation appears to have been minor. Then in 1847 the United States acquired California. Mormon settlers and Anglo ranchers soon became the dominant outsiders. The Cahuilla were left largely to themselves. Continuing raids for livestock by other Indians, however, led to general hostility among whites toward all Indians of the region.

In 1850 the U.S. Congress sent a special commission to California to negotiate treaties with Native Americans and assign them lands. A treaty arranged in 1852 set aside an area about forty miles long and thirty miles wide for the Cahuilla. The U.S. Senate, however, refused to ratify any of the eighteen treaties with California Indians. Congressional resistance stemmed from a number of factors: the commissioners had committed the government to spend a great deal of money; white Californians vigorously opposed the treaties; and it was thought that some of these lands might contain gold.

In 1852 Edward F. Beale was appointed superintendent of Indian affairs in California, and a report about Indians in the southern part of the state was prepared, possibly by Benjamin Hays. The report noted that numerous members of other nearby tribes were living among the Desert Cahuilla. The elders and many others spoke Spanish by this time. The Indians worked as underpaid laborers and domestics on the ranchos of whites and were frequently intoxicated. The report pointed out that under Spanish law the Indians had rights to their settlements and pasture lands, and in theory the State of California recognized Indian land rights. The report characterized state laws as "*All* punishment. *No* reform!" With congressional authorization in 1853, Beale established a small, short-lived reservation at Tejon between the San Joaquin Valley and Los Angeles. This appears to have been *the beginning of the modern reservation system.* It was not, however, until 1858 that setting land aside for Native Americans became a general federal policy.

In the mid-1850s, Cahuilla men reportedly numbered about thirty-five hundred, including many non-Cahuilla Indians, but they far outnumbered the local white settlers. At the same time leaders among the Cahuilla strived to protect tribal interests in dealing with whites. Leaders such as Juan Antonio and Cabeson, for example, represented their people in the failed treaty of 1852. These Indians were discontented after the federal government failed to set land aside for their exclusive use; they complained that they had not received farm equipment as promised and that whites were trespassing and squatting on traditional Indian lands, as well as taking water and wood. Then in 1863, and again in 1870, devastating smallpox epidemics struck, killing a large but unknown number of Cahuilla. These epidemics destroyed their previous cultural vitality at a time when whites were becoming far more numerous among them and increasingly dominant. Throughout the latter part of the nineteenth century, some Cahuilla worked on the ranches of whites, the men often as cowboys and the women as domestics. The men also tended orchards and vineyards, cut mesquite wood, and labored at salt works. When the Southern Pacific railroad was being built through the area in the 1870s, they were employed as laborers. They continued to collect products of the desert and farmed some of the better-watered localities.

By the 1870s the cultural norms of the people were moving in new directions. The rule of moiety exogamy declined, and money was substituted for the gifts formerly presented to a bride's family. A girl's family received thirty dollars around 1900, but a generation later a female infant scornfully was termed "a paper," meaning a marriage license that no longer brought a gift. By 1925 clan ownership of farmland remained the rule, but the amount of arable land was small because water was scarce. Changes in dwelling forms were notable because frame houses had replaced the aboriginal type; a frame house was not burned until three members of a household had died. In the desert, a clan dance house continued to be occupied by a net and his family, but it looked different from the houses of old because the roof now was pitched like that of a shed.

Ceremonial life reflected reintegration during the same period. A major shift occurred as unrelated ceremonies were combined with the Mourning Ceremony into a fiesta week. For example, among the Pass Cahuilla in the late 1880s, the Eagle-Killing Ceremony was joined with the Mourning Ceremony; the eagle feathers were used to decorate the images, which were burned two days later. In aboriginal times the people had cremated their dead; under Spanish, Mexican, and Anglo-American influence, they began to bury the dead. Interment sometimes included placing food, clothing, and bedding with the body in the hope that these things would be useful to the spirit if it did not soon find a permanent resting place. Changes in the Mourning Ceremony included dressing the images in manufactured clothing, such as hats and veils. Indian-owned lunch counters sold food and coffee to participants and observers. By 1931 the Mourning Ceremony at Palm Springs had become biennial and was held by alternating clans for the dead of the two previous years. Among the Desert Cahuilla, one of the last nets died in 1958. He had directed local ceremonial life, but when he died, the ceremonial structure, his house, and all of the ceremonial equipment were burned, an end not only to his life but also to the net ceremonials. Today most Cahuilla are Roman Catholic. Funerals continue to be an important rite of passage, however, and at death some personal possessions of an individual are burned as traditional Cahuilla songs are sung.

In the 1990s reservation lands best symbolized Cahuilla identity and their Indianness. In a broader cultural context, some Cahuilla, possibly most youth, were not taught traditional cultural ways, and many were uninterested in their Native American background. Those elders who have such an interest find it difficult to convey to the younger generations. Most Cahuilla no longer speak their language. Their distinct craft skills have declined, but a revival may be emerging. They have not had a ceremonial house since the early 1960s. The last shaman died in 1984, but one woman had learned the ceremonial songs, and she carries out part of the old religious tradition into the present.

The Agua Caliente Band

In the course of Desert Cahuilla history, especially for the Palm Springs Band, land rights have been a dominant theme since the late 1860s. In 1875 the Agua Caliente (Palm Springs) and Cahuilla reservations were established as slight yet meaningful recognition of the plight of these and other Indians in southern California. In 1881 Helen Hunt Jackson published a book entitled *A Century of Dishonor,* a scathing indictment of the treatment of American Indians. Because of her crusading interest in Indians, she was retained to report to the commissioner of Indian affairs about the Indians of southern California. She conducted her study with Abbott Kinney, and their report, partly a chronicle of wrongs against Indians and partly a series of recommendations, was submitted in 1883. This study did not make the impact on Indian policy that Jackson felt was essential, and so she decided to write a novel about the plight of these people. As a novel, *Ramona* was highly successful. It has appeared in at least three hundred English editions. Yet it failed to bring about the reforms Jackson advocated, although it called attention to much that was wrong and helped stimulate reforms in the 1890s (see Figure 7-8).

EARLY LAND DISPUTES The problem of Palm Springs Indian land rights is complex, and the most critical legal developments must at least be summarized. The modern reservation, created in 1896 under the Mission Indian Relief Act of 1891, set aside thirty-two thousand acres in essentially a checkerboard pattern in and around the town of Palm Springs. The act was based on the

Figure 7-8 | The Cahuilla woman Ramona Lubo at her home, probably photographed around 1900. Her life was fictionalized in the novel *Ramona* by Helen Hunt Jackson. (Courtesy of the Southwest Museum, Los Angeles. Photo #24329.)

Dawes Act of 1887, and the keystone of this act was the allotment of reservation lands to family heads. After twenty-five years an allottee could in theory receive a fee patent to the land and become the legal owner. Allotments were first issued in 1923, and the land per family was limited to 160 acres. Allotments were made irrespective of whether or not the band members agreed with the idea of dividing land into individual parcels. Furthermore, the allotments were not of comparable value. In 1927 allotments were made only to Indians who requested them; nearly half of the members made requests. These allotments consisted not of 160-acre parcels but of packages of a 5-acre parcel of irrigable land, a 40-acre parcel of dry land, and a 2-acre lot in the town of Palm Springs. The 1927 allotments were not approved by the federal government. Meanwhile, the Indian Reorganization Act of 1934 opposed allotments, and the Indians took legal action in the 1930s to force allotment approval. The Indian legal battle reached the U.S. Supreme Court, and in a subsequent decision in 1946 allotments were declared valid. Some allotments were approved in 1949. The ones that were unapproved involved conflicting claims; finally, however, selections were approved for the entire band.

One of the suits involving allotments resulted in a 1950 court decision that allotted lands should be of *approximately equal value,* since this was the original intent of the law. The allotment values, based on 1949 estimates, ranged from about $17,000 to $165,000, with a total value of lands allotted and pending allotment being about $7.4 million. To equalize the allotments, the BIA proposed that a tribal corporation be created and all tribal assets conveyed to it. A bill in 1957 before Congress in essence established a liquidation corporation that could have ended the tribal identity of the Cahuilla involved. It was rejected by Congress.

In 1959 two new bills were introduced in Congress, and these became law. The major provisions of one of them, the equalization bill, were that (1) allotments would be made to all band members who had not received them, but no future-born members would receive allotments; (2) equalizations would be made on the basis of 1957–58 appraised land values, and the cemeteries, Roman Catholic church, hot springs, and certain canyons were to remain tribal reserves not subject to allotment, but all other lands were to be allotted regardless of prior acreage limitations and in proportion to the highest monetary value of the prior allotments. The second bill provided that reservation lands could be leased for a period not exceeding ninety-nine years except for grazing land, which could be leased for not more than ten years. The 1957–58 allotment appraisals ranged from approximately $75,000 to $630,000, in contrast with the 1949 appraisal range of $17,000 to $165,000. Obviously, the land was rapidly becoming fantastically valuable. Even with the passage of the first bill, it was impossible to equalize the allotments fully. Some 80 percent of the band obtained allotments valued at not less than $335,000; the remaining 20 percent of the allotments had values in excess of $335,000. Most of the land was still in trust status by 1962 and thus was not producing income. However, changes in leasing laws made it likely that over the next ten years individuals would derive considerable profit from it. The first large leasing enterprise was the Palm Springs Spa complex at the hot springs. The spa was completed in 1960 at a cost of $1.8 million, and an adjacent hotel, also on Indian land, was completed in 1963. In 1961 the City of Palm Springs purchased lands allotted to eight Cahuilla adults and twenty-two Cahuilla children for $2,979,000, which was shared by the allottees.

WOMEN'S LEADERSHIP ROLE A notable aspect of all the Palm Springs land disputes is the leadership role assumed successfully by women. When the issues were coming to a climax in 1957, the band included only thirty-two adults and sixty-four minors. At that time there were ten adult men and twenty-two women; of the men, two were in the U.S. Navy, two were over seventy years of age, and two were incapable of handling their own affairs. At this point only two courses of action were possible: either the band could trust the BIA and its lawyer to handle its business affairs completely or the women could assume the role of leaders. The Cahuilla decided to pursue the latter alternative. Aboriginal sociopolitical life had set no precedent for female leadership, except that a woman did occasionally hold an office in trust for a son and old women sometimes were very active in clan ceremonies. The net was always a man, and in the early historic period whites appointed some Indian men to act as intermediaries and later as reservation leaders. These persons often seem to have been clan leaders. A differential rate of adaptation for women and men appears to have developed. Many of the men continued to follow a "collecting" pattern in their economic activities; they worked only sporadically as grape pickers, cowboys, woodcutters, or railroad laborers. In their jobs they interacted most often with other Indians, not whites. Women, by contrast, often worked as domestics in the homes of whites and therefore became much more familiar with the new ways. This was possibly an important reason why women could become the stable core around which the society was reorganized. In 1935 a woman became secretary to the band business committee, and by 1954 an all-woman tribal council had been elected, with Vyola Olinger as chairperson. Mrs. Olinger, who was an active member of the band, was an apt choice. She was intelligent, articulate, and hardworking. Although distrustful of the bureau agents, she managed to work successfully with them. Under the tribal council of women the major land disputes were resolved. In 1961 a young man was elected to the council, and this brought an end to the era of all-female political dominance, but it was the women who had handled the vital issue (see Figure 7-9).

ISSUES IN THE 1960S By the early 1960s a small group of determined Indians had gained a settlement, and seemingly the avarice of whites had become just another episode in our blemished past; justice had prevailed. Alas, it was not to endure. In 1967, George Ringwald, a reporter for the *Daily Enterprise* of Riverside, California, wrote a series of articles about the administration of Palm Springs Cahuilla lands and funds. He demonstrated beyond any doubt that greedy whites still were taking grossly unfair advantage of Indians. Among the individuals involved in the immoral and often illegal handling of Palm Springs Cahuilla affairs were BIA personnel, a Superior Court judge, a municipal judge, a former mayor of Palm Springs, a Palm Springs real estate broker, and a host of attorneys-at-law. As a result of Ringwald's journalism the BIA was forced to conduct an investigation into the system of court-appointed guardians and conservators for Indians. It was demonstrated, for example, that a municipal judge and one attorney had, over a seven-year period, collected $485,000 in fees. From 1956 to 1967, approximately 40 percent of the $10.8 million received by eighty-four estates had gone to conservators, guardians, or their attorneys under the supervision of the Riverside County Superior Court. Congressional action in 1968 put an end to the conservator and guardian management of these valuable lands.

A fair-minded person would hope that Palm Springs Indian problems with the BIA, some local developers, and city officials would have ended by the 1960s, but such was not the case. When Palm Springs incorporated as a city in 1938, its governing body included Indian land as part of the city without

Figure 7-9 | The all-woman Palm Springs Tribal Council in 1955. From left to right are Eileen Miguel, La Verne Saubel, Gloria Gillette, Elizabeth Monk, and Vyola Olinger. (Courtesy of the Agua Caliente Cultural Museum.)

consulting the Indian owners. The city passed zoning ordinances and a master plan that included control over Indian land in the city. The Palm Springs Indians in turn formed a zoning commission and prepared their own zoning ordinances that did not agree with those of the city. In 1966 the Indians won a judgment against the city with reference to zoning procedures, but by 1972 the city had not made the required modifications. The Indians initiated further zoning litigation, in which they accused the city of preventing the development of Indian land and thereby decreasing its value. The issue finally was settled in 1977 when the U.S. Supreme Court decided, in another case, that neither the state nor its political subdivisions could regulate Indian trust lands.

THE MODERN SCENE To enhance the value of the land owned collectively by band members, the Agua Caliente Development Authority was formed in 1989, a major administrative innovation. BIA managers in Palm Springs play a major role in leasing land belonging to the band. Their office was the only one in the country funded entirely by the Indians involved. It supervises residential and commercial leases, as well as the development of Indian land, which comprises about ten square miles in scattered plots within Palm Springs—more land than is held by any other single landowner in the

Figure 7-10 | The Spa Hotel & Casino of the Agua Caliente Band in Palm Springs as it appeared in 1999.

city, about 6,700 acres. Yet the Indians remain confronted with a major problem: allotments and their equity. After allotments were made to 131 band members, the available land for allotments was exhausted. As a result, those band members born after 1959 have no land allotments except by inheritance. Their greatest hope for financial gain is to share in the profits from the development of land held by the band collectively. By the 1980s most original allotments had been sold or subdivided among heirs, so that individual plots tended to be small and scattered. Since developers prefer large land units, numerous owners of small adjacent allotments must agree to the joint lease or sale of their holdings.

By the late 1990s major developments built by the band in or near Palm Springs included the Marquis Hotel, Canyon Country Club, and their Spa Hotel & Casino, launched in 1995 (see Figure 7-10). The casino payroll in 1997 was $10 million, and it reportedly was the most profitable Indian casino in California by 1999. The band also provided major funding for the Canyon National Bank that opened in 1998.

The most innovative development in recent years was a 1999 cooperative management proposal by the Agua Caliente Band and the U.S. Department of the Interior. It called for the establishment of a new national monument consisting of 140,000 acres of federal land in the San Jacinto and Santa Rosa mountains. The project, however, requires federal legislation that may or may not prove successful. For the band the creation of this national monument would represent a major step toward reclaiming traditional lands that they lost in the 1870s.

The Palm Springs Cahuilla are proud of their cultural heritage, but it understandably has diminished significance in their lives. No band member speaks Cahuilla fluently, and the essence of their culture virtually has disappeared. They are at the same time highly protective of the scenic beauty of the palm-lined canyons that they own; in many ways these canyons best symbolize band identity. They have developed the Agua Caliente Cultural Museum Center and plan to build a much larger museum in the near future.

By 1999 there were about 356 enrolled Agua Caliente Band members, most of whom owned allotted lands whose total value was in the billions of dollars. The band understandably is unwilling to release figures about total band assets. At the same time, it must be noted that numerous band members do not have allotments, and therefore the money they receive from the band depends on the collective investments that they share. Thus, not all Palm Springs Cahuilla are wealthy. Some rich band members, however, share their riches with those who are less affluent. They may buy them new cars each year, provide them with money for vacations, and pay their medical expenses. The Agua Caliente Band reportedly is the most wealthy group of Indians in the United States. In 1999 they allotted over $1 million to local nonprofit organizations. From 1995 to 1999, the total amount was over $3.2 million. Included were donations to police and fire departments, public libraries, senior citizen and youth centers, and a film festival. Their wealth clearly benefits local Euro-Americans.

Additional Sources

Lowell J. Bean is the most prominent student of Cahuilla life. The best place to begin searching for information about these people is the book by Bean and Lisa J. Bourgeault (1989). The *California* volume (8) of the new *Handbook of North American Indians,* William C. Sturtevant, general editor (Washington, DC, 1978) includes a Cahuilla summary by Bean, and the volume provides a wealth of information about other California Indians. Bean's 1972 study is an insightful ethnographic reconstruction with considerable emphasis on worldview and values. Bean and William M. Mason (1962) examine Spanish influences in their presentation of the Romero expedition accounts. For traditional Cahuilla material culture, the monographs by Lucile Hooper (1920) and Alfred L. Kroeber (1908) are the best sources. A pioneering ethnobotany study was written by David P. Barrows (1900), and it is supplemented by an article published by Bean and Katherine S. Saubel (1961).

Selected Bibliography

Barrows, David P. 1900. *The ethno-botany of the Coahuilla Indians of southern California.* Chicago. Reprinted by Malki Museum Press, Banning, CA, 1967.

Bean, Lowell J. 1963. *Cahuilla ethnobotanical notes.* Archaeological Survey, Annual Report 1962–1963, 55–76. Department of Anthropology and Sociology, University of California, Los Angeles.

———. 1972a. *Temalpakh: Cahuilla Indian knowledge and usage of plants.* Malki Museum Press, Riverside, CA.

———. 1972b. *Mukat's people.* Berkeley.

———. 1991. *Cahuilla landscape.* Menlo Park, CA.

Bean, Lowell J., and Lisa J. Bourgeault. 1989. *The Cahuilla.* New York.

Bean, Lowell J., and William M. Mason. 1962. *Diaries and accounts of the Romero expeditions in Arizona and California.* Los Angeles.

Bean, Lowell J., and Katherine S. Saubel. 1961. *The aboriginal uses of the oak.* Archaeological Survey, Annual Report 1960–1961, 237–49. Department of Anthropology and Sociology, University of California, Los Angeles.

Beattie, George W., and Helen P. Beattie. 1951. *Heritage of the valley.* Oakland.

Ellison, William H. 1922–23. The federal Indian policy in California, 1846–1860. *Mississippi Valley Historical Review* 9:37–67.

Gifford, Edward W. 1922. *California kinship terminologies.* University of California Publications in American Archaeology and Ethnology, vol. 18.

Hooper, Lucile. 1920. *The Cahuilla Indians.* University of California Publications in American Archaeology and Ethnology, vol. 16, no. 6.

Jackson, Helen Hunt. 1881. *A century of dishonor.* New York. (An 1890 edition contains the *Report on the conditions and needs of the Mission Indians of California.*)

———. 1884. *Ramona.* Boston.

James, Harry C. 1960. *The Cahuilla Indians.* Los Angeles.

Kroeber, Alfred L. 1908. *Ethnography of the Cahuilla Indians.* University of California Publications in American Archaeology and Ethnology, vol. 8, no. 2.

Ringwald, George. 1967. *Riverside Press-Enterprise* and *Riverside Daily Press* articles.

Rush, Emmy M. 1932. The Indians of the Coachella Valley celebrate. *El Palacio* 32: 1–19.

Shinn, George H. 1941. *Shoshonean days.* Glendale.

Strong, William D. 1929. *Aboriginal society in southern California.* University of California Publications in American Archaeology and Ethnology, vol. 26.

Transmitting report by Subcommittee on Indian Affairs. State of California, Senate Committee on Rules, Resolution No. 8. Sacramento.

Wilson, Benjamin D. 1952. *The Indians of southern California in 1852.* John W. Caughey, ed. San Marino, CA.

8 The Yurok: Salmon Fishers of California

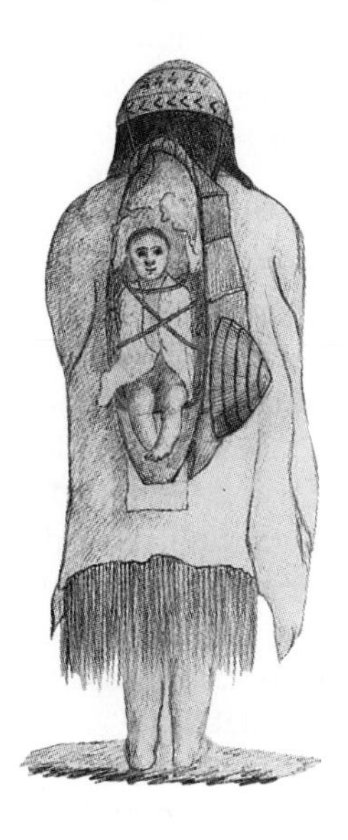

To make deer-hunting medicine, first you learn to see the bush that's in front of you, then the bush behind that bush, then the deer behind the bush behind the bush that's in front of you, then the spirit of that deer. Now you can call the deer, his spirit, and he'll walk up to you. The people with the strongest medicine learn to fly out, their spirits, and find the deer that way. A well-educated person learns to see two sides to everything while at the same time seeing the whole.

(Buckley 1979, 37)

A PLENITUDE OF SALMON enabled Indians of the Northwest Coast culture area to achieve greater sociocultural complexity than any other foragers (harvesters of wild species for food) described in this book. Northwest Coast Indians are most clearly identified with an emphasis on wealth and social standing, elaborate wood carvings, especially totem poles, and spectacular potlatches (giveaway feasts). Yet their distribution, extended some 1,500 miles from north to south, produced significant regional differences. This chapter and the next present tribes that illustrate the variability. The Yurok approached the southern limit for the distribution of salmon. They exhibit an amalgamation of the Northwest Coast emphasis on wealth and a material culture more typical of California and Plateau tribes. The comparatively unelaborate nature of Yurok technology and their complex social conventions make them worthy of attention.

The aboriginal Yurok (YUR-ahk) emphasis on aristocratic social standing and wealth is a fascinating aspect of their culture. As Arnold R. Pilling (1978, 141) noted, intriguing parallels exist between Yurok aristocrats and those of Europe in the comparatively recent past. The elite of both cultures accumulated family heirlooms as treasures and occupied named houses built on high ground. Each had special table manners, pride in an ability to speak another language, and a rich vocabulary. Ceremonial hosts and religious specialists emerged among them. These and other similarities provide an example of parallel social developments between cultures that otherwise contrasted with one another. In this general context, it must be noted that ethnographers among the Yurok usually associated with aristocrats and that their accounts tend to ignore life among the general population.

Yurok means "downstream" in the language of the Karok, their neighbors to the interior. The aboriginal Yurok population may have numbered about three thousand persons who occupied some seven hundred square miles of land dominated by Douglas fir and redwood forests. In early historic times most people lived along the Klamath River, although some coastal villages were relatively populous (see Figure 8-1). Their language is most closely related to that of the Wiyot to the south. These two tribes are members of the Algic language family and the Ritwan subfamily, but they are geographically removed from their linguistic relatives in the eastern United States and northeastern Canada.

Aboriginal Life

The Yurok view of the world was exact: the land was an essentially flat, circular expanse that rested on water and surrounded by it. As breakers rolled in from the sea, people thought they saw a gentle rise and fall of the land. Instead of designating regions, these people concentrated on naming particular localities or spots on the landscape. They had no name for the Klamath River. According to the Yurok, to traverse their country in a canoe along the Klamath River, a distance of about 150 miles, required 12 days. The center of the world

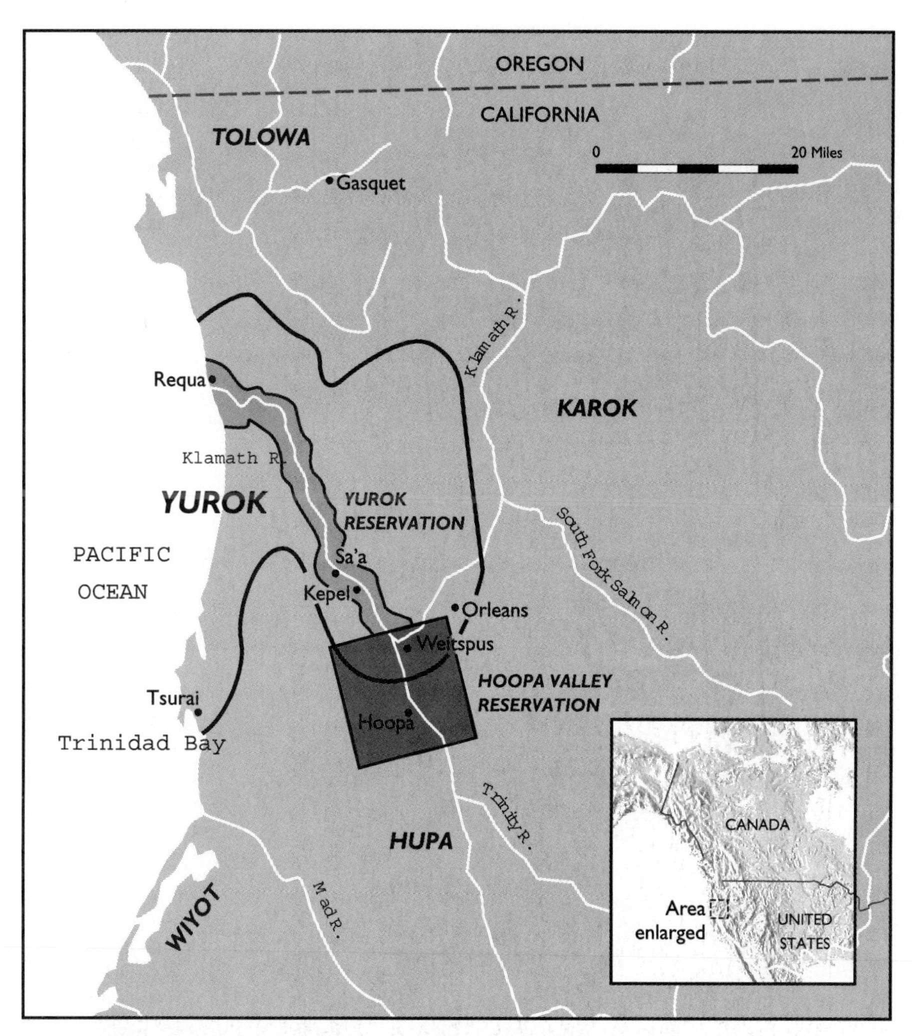

Figure 8-1 | Aboriginal range of the Yurok Indians.

was near the Klamath and Trinity river junction. As this worldview suggests, the Yurok were not great travelers; they had contact with their neighbors but apparently did not journey deep into the territory of other peoples. Not only did they refuse to go abroad, but they also regarded strangers as a threat, thinking that normal people stayed close to home with relatives and friends.

Directions were not conceived as cardinal points on a compass but in terms of water flow: there was an upstream and there was a downstream, and it did not matter to the Yurok if a river meandered in different directions. Calculating direction in terms of water flow also was applied to the coast, north being regarded as downstream. People usually traveled by boat, but they also maintained a well-developed system of trails. As Thomas M. Gates (1995, 393–423) has noted in his detailed analysis, trails served many customary functions. Trails provided access to settlements and a means to carry out subsistence activities or to trade and were used as paths to ceremonial events. Furthermore, trails were "like people" and had designated rest stops; to pause at a spot that was not a traditional resting place invited ill fortune.

ORIGIN MYTH According to the Yurok origin myth, the Widower across the Ocean made soil that he kept in a deerskin container, and by spilling it he created the firm earth of the world. Since he could not see his creation, he caused the sun to give light in the daytime and made the moon to give light at night. The earth was without life, and to replace the desolation he created the varied landscape, with streams flowing to rivers, and these emptying into the ocean. He made the forest and the animals. The first animal he created was a white deer, and then a red eagle to command the skies. After creating other animals and plants the Widower formed the first real man of soil and then created a woman to keep him company. This couple wandered from their home in the north and finally settled in the Klamath River valley.

APPEARANCE AND CLOTHING Yurok women wore basketry hats over their hair, which they braided and adorned with flowers. They pierced their ears for ornaments and had necklaces of bone, shell, or small pieces of fruit. A young girl was tattooed with three parallel bands from the lower lip to the chin to indicate she was marriageable. After a woman had children, and as she aged, additional lines were tattooed on her chin to produce a dark band. Women wore a short apron of skin with shells, nuts, and pieces of obsidian attached to the fringe. A longer skin apron was placed over the first and partly obscured the inner garment. On ceremonial occasions women wore elaborate shell-covered aprons and many strings of shell beads (see Figure 8-2). Little girls wore aprons after they were about two years of age, but boys went without clothing, except for furs worn during the winter, until they reached puberty.

Men wore their hair long and loose over the shoulders or else tied it in a knot on top of the head; in his hair a man might wear a garland of flowers or feathers. Facial hair was plucked with hinged mussel-shell tweezers. A man's earlobes were pierced to hold ornamental pins of bone or shell. Men painted their faces red to indicate joy and black for war. Several lines were tattooed on a man's arm to serve as gauges for measuring lengths of dentalium shells that were used as money. Most young men folded skins around their hips, but older males, as well as some younger ones, wore no clothing. When traveling overland a man wore skin moccasins, and when hunting in deep snow he wore

Figure 8-2 | A Yurok woman, Alice Frank Spott, dressed in her finest garments. (Photograph by Pliny Goddard at Requa, Del Norte County, 1901. Phoebe A. Hearst Museum of Anthropology, University of California at Berkeley. [15-3344].)

knee-length leggings and used snowshoes. During cold weather both men and women wore skin capes.

SETTLEMENTS Yurok villages were built along the Klamath River, bordering coastal lagoons or where streams and rivers flowed into the sea. Most settlements had three to seven houses, sweat houses, and menstrual huts (see

Figure 8-3 | Wahsekw, a Yurok village. (Photograph by Alfred L. Kroeber, 1907. Phoebe A. Hearst Museum of Anthropology, University of California at Berkeley. [15-1421].)

Figure 8-3). Each home was identified with a specific male line (patrilineage). Villages appear to have been abandoned often as a result of floods or disease; in addition, families might be forced to relocate because of quarrels with other families.

The rectangular, gabled, and post-framed houses were built in deep excavations and covered with planks. People entered a house through a round hole cut into a front wall plank at a gabled end. The outer entrance was paved with flat stones. An opening in the center of the roof allowed sunlight to enter and smoke from the fireplace to escape. The inside of a large house had partitioned rooms for firewood and equipment storage. These rooms provided entry into the living area, which was dominated by a fireplace some five feet

Figure 8-4 | A reconstructed Yurok sweat house in the foreground and a dwelling in the background; Patrick's Point State Park, California.

deep and ten feet square that had a notched log ladder descending into it. Over the stone-lined fire pit a pole frame was suspended from the ceiling for drying fish. Family members ate around the fireplace, while women and children usually slept there. Scattered about were wooden serving trays for meat, twined cooking baskets for preparing acorn meal, and similar but smaller baskets in which food was served. Spoons were made from antler, a mussel shell, or the top of a deer skull. Wooden bowls nearby were used for washing one's fingers after eating, and small redwood stools served as seats. At the side of a house sometimes was a lean-to of planks that served as a menstrual hut; in other cases, the menstrual hut was a separate structure built a short distance from a dwelling.

A sweat house served from one to three dwellings, and it was here that adult males lounged and men and boys slept (see Figure 8-4). No prohibition prevented women from being in sweat houses, and they sometimes slept there on cold nights.

A sweat house was rectangular with a gabled roof and was built largely underground of posts, beams, and planks. An old canoe was placed facing downward along the gable to prevent water leakage along the ridge. The floor of a sweat house was paved with stones or planked and was reached by stone steps or a rampway. Near the center of the building was a stone-lined fire pit. A small round exit hole was cut in one of the end wall planks. The only furnishings were pillows made from stone or blocks of redwood. Men collected the wood for a bath and sang songs of good fortune as they returned to the sweat house. The men built a fire, and after the wood was reduced to a bed of coals, they undressed and entered. They placed covers over the entrance and exit and sat in the intense heat for about half an hour. After crawling from the exit, they lounged on the stone paving and repeated the songs they had sung while gathering firewood. After cooling off, they swam in a stream and returned home to an evening meal.

CONVEYANCES The most time-consuming craft item to produce was a dugout canoe made from a redwood log. The log was split with antler wedges and stone mauls, and then a fire was built along the center of one section of the split log. The charred wood was removed with a shell- or stone-bladed adz until the vessel was hollowed. A typical canoe was eighteen feet long and three feet wide, with a rounded bottom and sides some fifteen inches high. At the front of a canoe on the inside, a small knob of wood was left, with a shallow hole in its center. This was the "heart" of the canoe, and without it a vessel was thought to be "dead." Pitch from conifers was used to caulk cracks in the wood, while crosspieces fore and aft prevented the sides from warping. These vessels were propelled by men standing in the front using poles or long-bladed paddles; a man seated in the stern used a shorter paddle as a rudder. Canoes were designed for river travel and drew as much as six inches of water when fully loaded. Given the rounded bottoms of these boats, a man sitting in the stern could quickly change course to avoid obstructions in the rushing water. When they traveled in the ocean, men sang songs and recited formulas to prevent their larger boats from capsizing and to keep the water smooth. Considering how ill-adapted such a vessel was to ocean travel, these precautions seem quite reasonable.

The only other manufactured form for travel was the snowshoe. Used by men hunting in deep snow, snowshoes were small with grapevine outer frames and wooden crosspieces.

SUBSISTENCE ACTIVITIES Salmon, the primary staple termed "that which is eaten" (Waterman, 1920, 185), far outranked deer, elk, acorns, and lesser edibles. Harvest success for any species depended to a great extent on exploitative site ownership. Examples included salmon fishing spots, oak groves, seed collection localities, and places to set snares along game trails. Salmon were harvested primarily with dip nets. These fish rest in eddies when ascending a waterway to spawn. A pole platform built above an eddy supported a man with a long-handled dip net, and a hundred fish might be taken in a single night (see Figure 8-5). From one to ten men owned a highly productive eddy, and fishing rights could be sold, bartered, or inherited. Eddies typically are not long lasting; they are destroyed with shifts in a river channel.

Additional means for taking salmon included gill nets and seines. Their netting, along with that of dip nets, consisted of knotted mesh fashioned from

Figure 8-5 | Umits, Yurok man of Sa'a, raising a dip net. Note the canoe in the foreground. (Photograph by Alfred L. Kroeber, 1906. Phoebe A. Hearst Museum of Anthropology, University of California at Berkeley. [15-2730].)

iris leaf fiber. They could likewise capture salmon with toggle-headed harpoons. A long harpoon shaft included two slightly diverging foreshafts bound in place with a harpoon head at the end of each foreshaft. After a salmon had been struck with a harpoon head, the attached handline provided the means of retrieval. Fishweirs represent another major means for taking salmon, and the most elaborate one was built at Kepel along the Klamath River. The ceremonial aspects of Kepel weir construction and use are presented later as an aspect of religious life.

Alfred L. Kroeber (1925, 87) wrote with economy and precision, "Acorns were gathered, dried, stored, cracked, pulverized, sifted, leached, and usually boiled with hot stones in a basket." Large baskets stored in houses held unshelled acorns. As needed, shelled nuts were converted into meal on a stone slab with a stone pestle. To remove the natural and bitter tannic acid, they placed the meal in a sand basin and poured hot water over it. When cooking

Figure 8-6 | A young Yurok man with bow and arrows for hunting land animals. The swordlike object in his right hand probably is an obsidian blade. (Drawn by Seth Eastman form a sketch by George Gibbs in 1851. Courtesy of the Smithsonian Institution, National Anthropological Archives, neg. no. 2854-F-27.)

acorn meal in a basket with water and hot stones, they stirred the mixture with a spatula to prevent the stones from burning the basket. The basket weave was close and expanded with the water to become essentially watertight.

Land mammals provided meat and raw materials for artifacts. Deer and elk might be driven with dogs and killed by hunters using a wooden bow strung with sinew cord and backed with sinew strips (sinew-backed bow); the feathered arrows had wooden foreshafts tipped with stone arrowheads (see Figure 8-6). In all likelihood, snares set in game trails had become the most reliable means to take deer and elk. A taboo prevailed against eating reptiles or dogs, regarded as poisonous. In Yurok thinking, when they secured fauna as food, the physical form of a species was captured but the spiritual essence of each animal endured. The feelings of some species, especially deer, required particular accommodations. Deer were attracted to places where people were living, and when eating deer meat the Yurok took care to avoid dropping any of it on the floor to be trampled. Success in obtaining deer resulted from these and other taboos, not from the skill of a person. The people felt that with proper human behavior, deer would remain plentiful. Restrictions surrounding salmon are considered later.

Tobacco was their only domestic crop. A tobacco grower harvested the leaves and dried and pulverized them to store in baskets for personal use or for sale. But they were careful not to harvest any feral tobacco plants for fear that they had grown over a grave. The smoke from a tubular pipe, usually made of wood, was inhaled. Men most often smoked only just before bedtime, although some old men were addicted to tobacco. Female shamans appear to have been the heaviest smokers; other women did not smoke.

MONEY AND WEALTH In the broadest sense, money is a divisible and portable class of objects having a standardized value and acceptable in exchange for goods or services. In terms of this definition, money clearly was important among the Yurok, and dentalium shells were the most widely circulated form. These small mollusks had tusk-shaped shells that ranged up to about three inches in length. They were most abundant in the coastal waters off British Columbia and were collected there with a rakelike device that was thrust into the sandy ocean bottom to impale as many dentalia as possible. In western North America the shells were traded throughout the area from the subarctic to southern California. Among the Yurok, as with most Indians, the shells were named and graded according to size, with the largest shells having the greatest value. An eleven-shell string, with each shell 2½ inches long, was valued at about $50 during the early American period; a string of the same length with fifteen 1⅞-inch shells was worth only about $2.50. Other monetary units included redheaded woodpecker scalps that ranged in value from 10¢ to $1.50 each. Ordinary deerskins, after being prepared for ceremonial use, were worth from $50 to $100; skins of albino deer were valued at from $250 to $500, although they were never sold. Blades flaked from black obsidian were worth $1 for every inch in length until they reached a foot; blades longer than this were worth a great deal more.

Many, if not most, items of material culture were scaled in value against dentalium shells. Around 1900, a small dugout canoe was worth a thirteen-shell string or three large redheaded woodpecker scalps; a house was valued at from three to five strings of shells; an oak grove from one to five strings; a fishing spot from one to three strings; a shaman's fee from one to two strings; a slave one string; and a woman's basketry cap filled with tobacco one small shell. A few items were so valuable that they normally could not be exchanged but were passed along a patrilineage. These were most important as exhibits during ceremonial occasions. Fine albino deerskins with transparent hoofs and huge obsidian blades nearly a yard in length were among these treasures.

The preceding account of money is a traditional one that is not incorrect, but it fails, as John and Donna Bushnell (1977) have noted, to take into account the overwhelming symbolic importance of wealth among the Yurok.

The ownership of wealth not only indicated social worth but symbolized the presence of those spiritual qualities needed to acquire it. Furthermore, the land of dentalium shells, called Dentalium Home and supposedly located across the ocean, was a supernatural figure sometimes regarded as a creator. Therefore, the shells and other highly valued objects, according to the Bushnells (1977, 128), "are intimately linked to the world of immortals and characteristically emit supernatural power that redounds to the good fortune and wealth of those who possess them."

LEGAL SYSTEM Yurok customary law was based on the idea that wrongs were committed against individuals. Disputes ranged in intensity from minor to major in highly varied contexts. Efforts to resolve lesser differences before they expanded typically involved rock-throwing episodes between disputants. Rock throwing was institutionalized and surrounded by numerous conventions, including songs, procedures for selecting rocks, and magical means to make them strike their target. Yurok stories often included accounts of rock throwing. More serious offenses were settled with the exchange of specific forms of property.

Any major deviation from a behavioral norm necessitated a compensatory settlement, and extenuating circumstances were rarely considered. The age, sex, and previous behavior of an offender were unimportant, but his or her wealth was relevant. Finally, once a dispute had been settled, no further recourse was possible. The major grounds for claims were murder, seduction, adultery, saying the name of a deceased person, trespassing, or a shaman's refusal to treat a person who was ill. Failure to ferry someone, even an enemy, across a river led to a claim. If someone injured himself while on the land of another, the owner was responsible for compensation. This was true even of a trespasser, but in such cases the landowner would likely press a counterclaim for trespassing. If a shaman refused to accept the responsibility for treating a patient and the person died, the shaman was liable. To pass before a village by boat when a family in the village was mourning a death from natural causes was grounds for a claim. If a person became hopelessly in debt because of some drastically antisocial act, he could, in lieu of payment, become the slave of the one he had offended. For example, if a poor person struck the son of a rich man, he could settle his debt through "debt-slavery" of himself or one of his female relatives. "Slaves" were never killed or abused but performed the more difficult subsistence tasks. A slave owner was free to integrate the individual into his household or to maintain his or her status as a slave. Foreigners or prisoners from raids were never made slaves. The former always were killed if they arrived unannounced, and prisoners were held for ransom.

DESCENT, KINSHIP, AND MARRIAGE In the Yurok social system the most important ties were those along a line of males. It is tempting to regard the descent system as strictly patrilineal, and unquestionably a man was most con-

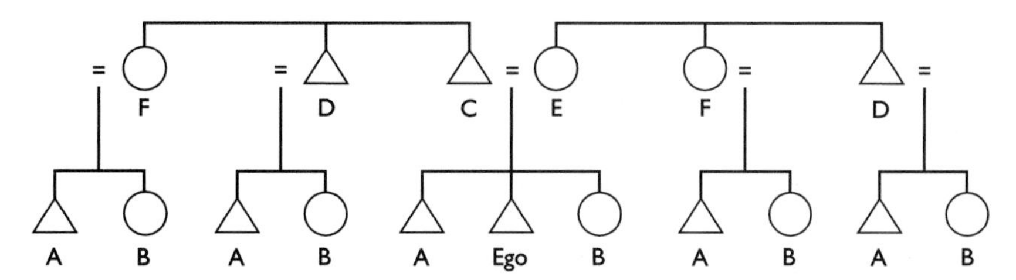

Figure 8-7 | The early historic Yurok system of kinship terminology.

cerned with his relatives along a male line. Still, there was ample recognition of a wife and her relatives in calculating social ties. Perhaps it would be best to characterize these people as patrilineal with a distinct and recognized tendency to consider relatives on both sides of a family as important (bilateral descent).

In the kinship terminology, a man referred to his father by one term; for his father's brother and his mother's brother, he used another term. For the mother's side of the family, the terminology was comparable to that on the father's side (lineal terms). Thus the Yurok employed terms for the parental generation that are of the same type as those used in the United States today. In an individual's generation, the term for sister extended to all female first cousins, and the word for brother extended to all male first cousins (Hawaiian cousin terms). It would seem that if cousins were called brother or sister, the parents of these individuals would be referred to as mother and father, but such was not the case (see Figure 8-7).

The only bar to marriage was the prohibition against taking a spouse from among near relatives. An individual in a small settlement was obligated to seek a mate from elsewhere, since all the occupants were near relatives; but a partner could be found easily in another village or another tribe. At the same time the tendency in large settlements was to find a mate in one's home community (village endogamy). It has been reported also that men tended to seek their wives from downstream settlements. Ideally, the couple lived in the settlement and house of the groom (patrilocal residence), but alternative arrangements were not unusual. Were a man's wife to die before she bore three or four offspring, the woman's family was obliged to offer one of her sisters or female relatives to replace her (sororate). Conversely, when a married man died, his brother was expected to marry the widow (levirate).

SOCIAL DIMENSIONS Personal ambition and extreme individualism dominated Yurok social life. The core members of each community were persons who traced their descent along the male line to a known common ancestor (patrilineage); within this unit were lines of familial authority, with a wealthy old man most likely to have jurisdiction over other members of the unit. A hamlet contained one or more patrilineages, each structured as the other, but no organized system of villagewide authority existed. An individual also was bound in a network of kinship ties with persons in other settlements through bonds of blood and marriage.

The Yurok also were grouped into five political units that became known as "districts." Each was headed by an especially well-educated aristocratic leader, sometimes referred to in English as a "real man." A well-educated person was considered to be one who knew a great deal about the law. Although the available information is not the most reliable, it suggests that real men mediated major disputes before important ceremonies were held each year; this procedure became a means of resolving differences before they exploded. Furthermore, a village or village cluster cooperated in rivalries with other villages or village clusters. In sum, while individualism dominated, it was constrained by allegiances based on kinship and residence.

Within a patrilineage and beyond it, worth was based on ownership of material property, and families were rich, well-to-do, or poor. It was difficult to move up in social standing, since everyone coveted wealth and was reluctant to part with it; but the possibility of a poor boy acquiring riches through persistence and supernatural aid did exist. The Yurok believed that constant thoughts about money led to its acquisition. Meditating about wealth when preparing for, taking, or resting after a bath was thought to be most propitious. An ambitious young man was urged to fast and work hard for ten days while concentrating on dentalium shells. When he gathered wood for the sweat house, he collected it from the upper branches of trees where he visualized the dentalia to be hanging. As he bathed, he thought of shells, and when peering intently into the river, he imagined that he saw huge dentalium shells. Such a person would say to himself, "I want to be rich," and he would make a tearful invocation for wealth, but not to any particular spirit or supernatural. Most importantly, however, according to Gates (1995, 464–65), visions of this nature "were not of the items of wealth, but are feelings of what lies behind the items; what the wealth items indicate. That is, consciousness focuses on the richness of the land and good feelings that come from participating with paradise in a centered way." Women were viewed as a complication in a male's quest for this richness. A young man seeking wealth was warned not to have anything to do with women, and an adult man was not to copulate with his wife in the house where his wealth was kept.

The nature and texture of life varied widely from one Yurok family to another. An almost insurmountable social barrier separated very rich, aristocratic families from the poor, and poverty was thought to have a genetic basis. A person supposedly was poor, lazy, and ill—except for instances of sorcery—because these conditions prevailed in his or her family line. The economic distinction was apparent in various dimensions of life. The speech of aristocrats was different from that of commoners, and the rich were wary and guarded in what they said. Rich people were "high class" and lived "clean" lives. An aristocrat knew the law and adhered carefully to its letter, while poor persons were far less familiar with it and also were careless and unclean and lacked social graces. To prevent an ambitious commoner from reaching a position of power, wealthy men practiced sorcery to dissipate the commoner's wealth or cause deaths in his family. Thus social distinctions ran deep throughout a Yurok's life, and to improve one's condition was quite difficult.

As would be expected, formal warfare did not exist in this society in which political ties were muted. Conflicts between families might develop into small or great feuds, depending on the size of the families involved, their wealth, and how quickly a settlement could be arranged by men identified as "judges." Fighting was with bows and arrows except for hand-to-hand combat, when short stone clubs were used. Protective armor was made either from elk hide or vertical wooden rods bound together, and it seems to have been worn only during prearranged battles. Murders, committed either in the heat of anger or by sorcery, could set off serious feuds and prompt the near relatives of the dead person to seek revenge. They might approach their enemy's village secretly and attack before the defenders could rally, or they might ambush the offending family on the trail. Following a successful raid or ambush, the contending parties might negotiate a meeting to settle their differences. The two sides armed themselves, painted their faces, and formed lines separated by the distance an arrow could be shot. They sang songs and performed a dance of settlement; at this point fighting might resume if the arrangements broke down. Otherwise, negotiations continued uninterrupted. The contesting parties carried with them the full amount of property necessary for a settlement. The side that had killed the most people and destroyed or seized the greatest amount of property was the "winner" but was at the same time required to relinquish the most property. This pattern represents a southern extension of the Northwest Coast Indian potlatch system (see Chapter 9). The items to be distributed were placed in baskets and held over a fire as songs were sung and a dance performed. This ritual was to cast away any feelings of hostility and to make any lasting feelings of vengeance the responsibility of the other party. If all went well, the settlement was made, and neither side could make further claims or hold a grudge.

RELIGION AND SUPERNATURALISM The only time that diverse Yurok families cooperated fully was in fulfilling ceremonial obligations. Collective rituals were held to renew and perpetuate the natural world with its resources as an orderly system. The principal ceremonies were performed to prevent disease, famine, and cataclysms such as earthquakes and floods. The ceremonial procedures supposedly were based on precedents set by immortals before the present race of people occupied the country, and the formulas recited concerned these immortals. Ceremonies were fixed calendrically and usually were held at the spots where they reportedly had been enacted for the first time. During certain ceremonies men displayed their wealth and greatest treasures, and Deerskin and Jumping Dances might be held.

Ceremonies The most elaborate Yurok ceremonial cycle was associated with a fishweir at Kepel along the Klamath River. Here the river was wide and shallow and had a gravel bottom, an ideal place for weir construction. Beforehand, a ceremony was performed at the mouth of the Klamath River to remove a prohibition against eating salmon caught that year. The designated weir chief dominated both the ceremonial and technical aspects of weir building and its use. He achieved his position by learning the formal recitations required; this knowledge was passed on to one of his sons. The weir chief wore a special deerskin robe throughout the ceremonies and, with the aid of a man and woman as assistants, became deeply involved in the ritual obligations. The chief and his assistants visited sacred places, burned incense, fasted, recited formulas, and bathed in a special manner. Five days were devoted to the preparation of materials for the weir. After this work was completed, they joked with one another for the remainder of the day. No offense could be taken at jokes at one's own expense, irrespective of how abusive they may have been.

On the sixth day, following prayers by the weir chief, construction began. Ten wooden fish traps were built on the downstream side of the weir. Each trap was about twelve feet long and fourteen feet wide with a moveable opening at each end. The hazel shoot mats were fitted in place along the weir to complete construction. An opening was left near one riverbank so that boats could pass by and some salmon could escape upstream.

On the tenth day, boys, girls, and the female assistant participated in a set of competitive rituals. This was followed by the male assistant removing the first salmon caught. The salmon was taken by the female assistant as her evening meal, but it was not until the following day that others could begin eating freshly caught salmon.

The catch from three traps was reserved for the principal participants and their relatives. Salmon were removed from the traps each morning with dip nets, and fish not taken in this manner from a trap were allowed to escape. Great numbers of salmon were harvested at Kepel and processed for future consumption.

The next event was a Deerskin Dance held nearby; a similar dance was held farther downstream. A Deerskin Dance was a colorful event, with each male dancer wearing the skin of a civet cat or deer around his waist. The dancers were not clothed above the waist, but around each man's neck hung massive strings of dentalium shells. Each man's head was adorned with a fur browband and a stick on which eagle or condor feathers were arranged to appear as one long feather. Each dancer carried a pole with a stuffed deer head at the top and a deerskin hanging loose that swayed back and forth as the pole was moved. A singer and assistants provided music as a line of dancers performed. Two other men paraded before the dancers, blowing crane bone whistles and holding obsidian blades. During a Deerskin Dance, as at ceremonies in general, members of the host community danced and were followed by performers from each represented village. Morning and evening dances were given by each group for a twelve-day period. On the final day, men danced with their finest white deerskins, and others displayed their most beautiful obsidian blades.

Figure 8-8 | Jumping Dance performers, circa 1900. (Courtesy of the A. W. Ericson Collection, Humboldt State University Library.)

Formal ceremonies at the Kepel fishweir ended with the performance of a two-day Jumping Dance held near Kepel. Dancing men wore a double layer of civet cat skins about their hips and many necklaces of dentalium shells. Each man wore a deerskin headband covered with woodpecker scalps and trimmed with a white band of deerskin; a white plume extended above his head on a stick. From the sides of his headpiece hung long skin flaps that swung rapidly as he performed. In one hand a dancer carried a cylindrical basket with an opening along one side (see Figure 8-8). Two steps were performed in the Jumping Dance; both involved hopping or jumping as the baskets were lowered.

After this final ceremony, most of the participants in the fishweir returned to their homes. Only the weir chief and his male assistant remained until the weir was destroyed by rushing water, about two or three months later.

While the Kepel fishweir ceremonies were the most elaborate, portions of the Yurok population participated in other ceremonies as well. At the junction of the Trinity and Klamath rivers in a community called Weitspus a ceremony was held to renew the world each September. It was designed specifically to avert natural disasters and disease. At two coastal villages, a village at the Klamath River mouth and another a little less than halfway between the Trinity junction and the sea, four other world-renewal ceremonies were held. Yurok participation in these and other ceremonies produced a form of integration along sacred, not secular, lines.

Another popular celebration, called the Brush Dance by Anglo-Americans, was held to treat an ill child, but it also served as entertainment for most participants. The event was held in a dwelling from which the roof and part of the sidewalls had been removed. On the first night a formula was recited for the ill child, and men danced about the fire holding boughs. Nothing took place the second night, but on the third and fourth nights the Brush Dance continued until dawn. On each night a series of three dances was performed by competing sets of dancers. The sick child was integrated into the performances with the recitation of formulas and the waving of torches above him or her.

Formulas were very important in the Brush Dance, as well as in calendrical ceremonies, and they also served individual needs under other circumstances. Some formulas involved the recitation of a list of sacred spots that someone long ago had visited to accomplish a particular purpose. Others were recitations or prayers, including the spirit responses. Offerings of tobacco and the use of plant products were associated with the formulas.

Curing Among the Yurok, women were the primary shamans (called "spiritual leaders" by the Yurok). Such a woman usually acquired her power in a dream, either unanticipated or sought after, about a dead shaman. From this deceased curing specialist the potential shaman obtained a "pain," considered a tangible object that entered her body and became the nexus of her power. Once she had acquired power, the next step was to bring it under control by fasting and dancing in a sweat house for ten days under the supervision of other shamans. The goal was for the novice to be able to vomit her pain and to swallow it again. As a further step the aspirant and a male relative visited a supernatural spot on a mountain for one night during the summer. On the mountain the woman recited a formula, smoked, and danced near a fire. Another ten days in the sweat house, performing as before, was followed by a dance around a large hot fire to bring the pain fully under the woman's control. This dance was the final step in becoming a shaman.

When a woman was asked to heal a patient, she negotiated the amount of payment with the relatives of the sick person before she attempted a cure. A female curer's equipment consisted of a pipe, two strings of feathers in her hair, and an ankle-length skirt. She effected a cure by chanting over the patient, smoking, and dancing for as much as six hours. A long session sometimes was necessary to see into the body of the patient and to locate the pains that caused the disease. The pain, or pains, were then removed by sucking. If the shaman was unable to remove the pains, she referred the patient to another curer. If a patient died, the shaman returned her fee.

In a secondary category of curers were men who probably did not acquire their power from supernatural sources but intensified it by supernatural means. They visited mountaintops, recited formulas, bathed ritually, and smoked in order to reinforce their power. These men relied on a pharmacopoeia consisting of plant and mineral products. This knowledge and the position were passed from father to son or to another close male relative. Like a female shaman, the male was paid before he attempted a cure and returned the payment if he was unsuccessful. Among the illnesses treated were wounds, snakebites, and chronic diseases, as well as other forms of unidentified sickness. One source states that male curers served as a check on the ambitions of female shamans. Apparently, the duties of female and male shamans were distinct, females handling cases of psychological ailments with supernatural cures and males treating physical disabilities due to natural causes.

Sorcery Some female shamans had the reputation of using their powers for antisocial purposes, the motivation being material profit. These shamans allegedly made a person ill and then collected a fee to cure her or him. Another technique was to leave one of multiple pains in the body of a person who was treated in order to be called back when this pain became troublesome. Other persons were more truly "devils"; they reportedly acquired a malignant object by purchase or special knowledge and used it to kill individuals. If the possessor of such a power went out at night, the power was thought to appear as sparks or as a bluish light. It could be placed on the end of a miniature arrow and shot from a small bow at the home of the victim. It was thought that the victim would die if not treated by a shaman. A person also could be harmed by a poison made of crushed meat from a dog, frog, rattlesnake, or salamander. After the poison was added to a victim's food, the individual would supposedly remain healthy for a year but then become ill and die if not cared for by a very powerful shaman.

When a person's rights were violated and just compensation could not be obtained by legal means, the only alternative was to turn to a sorcerer. These usually were men, and they customarily charged as much as a bride price, which meant that their services could be commanded only by aristocrats. A sorcerer was either of high social standing or was attempting to achieve higher status. He owned two to twelve "poisons" that ranged in effectiveness from very mild to lethal; each strength was represented by a different miniature arrow. The mildest form was said to produce a headache or cold and the middle level to cause chest pains that led to the victim's confinement. From the eighth level upward, all were lethal and were associated with behavior while sleeping. Once the fee and the degree of illness to be induced were agreed upon, the sorcerer went outside the victim's house disguised as a dog. He shot the mildest arrow from a miniature bow and returned at specified intervals to shoot arrows until he reached the level of illness desired. When the victim showed symptoms of illness, a shaman was hired to extract the "pains," but very few shamans had the power to remove lethal arrows. If a shaman could suck the pain from a victim, she spit it out of her mouth, and the arrow supposedly rose into the air and flew back to its maker, with only the shaman seeing the return. It was essential for a sorcerer to handle the objects of his power with great care. When not in use, they were buried in a cache of stones, but it was necessary for the owner to use the force of the poison at least once a month. If he did not, it was thought that the power would harm his children, or himself if he was childless. This form of sorcery possibly developed during the early historic period when the economic position of aristocratic families was threatened by white intruders who began to control key economic resources.

LIFE CYCLE The first time a woman conceived, her offspring was born after ten months, according to tradition, but later births followed nine-month pregnancies. Most births were in the spring, but not because a mating season existed, as was once suggested. The reason is that a man stored his material wealth in his house, and riches were believed to be diametrically opposed to sexual activity. To have sexual intercourse in the house was to invite poverty, and thus couples were most likely to copulate in the summer when sleeping outdoors. A pregnant woman worked hard, ate little, and was concerned about how her physical actions might affect the fetus. For example, she worried that she might bear a large neonate if she ate too much and slept excessively.

In giving birth, a woman rested on her back with her feet braced against a midwife and her arms bound with leather straps suspended from the ceiling. During labor the midwife told her when to lift herself with the thongs. The newborn was steamed over wild ginger, and a preparation made from ground land snail was applied to the navel. The severed cord was put inside a pine tree branch that had been split to receive it. Because these people thought that the colostrum from the mother's breast was harmful to ingest, an infant was fed hazelnut soup for the first ten days and then was nursed. After twenty days a grandmother, probably most often the paternal grandmother, began to massage the infant's leg muscles to encourage it to crawl. Between the time of birth and the healing of the navel, parents observed food taboos, and they were prohibited from having sexual intercourse until the baby crawled. Cradleboards ("baby basket" is the term used by the Yurok) were made in such a manner that the infant sat with its legs hanging free (see Figure 8-9). The baby could move its legs at any time, which was in keeping with the desire to have it crawl at a tender age. Many, if not most, aspects of rearing an offspring were designed to encourage self-reliance. This attitude clearly was reflected in the practice of weaning at one year, which was earlier than among most American Indians.

A child was named when he or she had clearly demonstrated a systematic recall capacity, probably at about eight years of age. The names for males were selected by fathers, and for females by mothers; each family seems to have had its own set of personal names. Nicknames of girls often contained

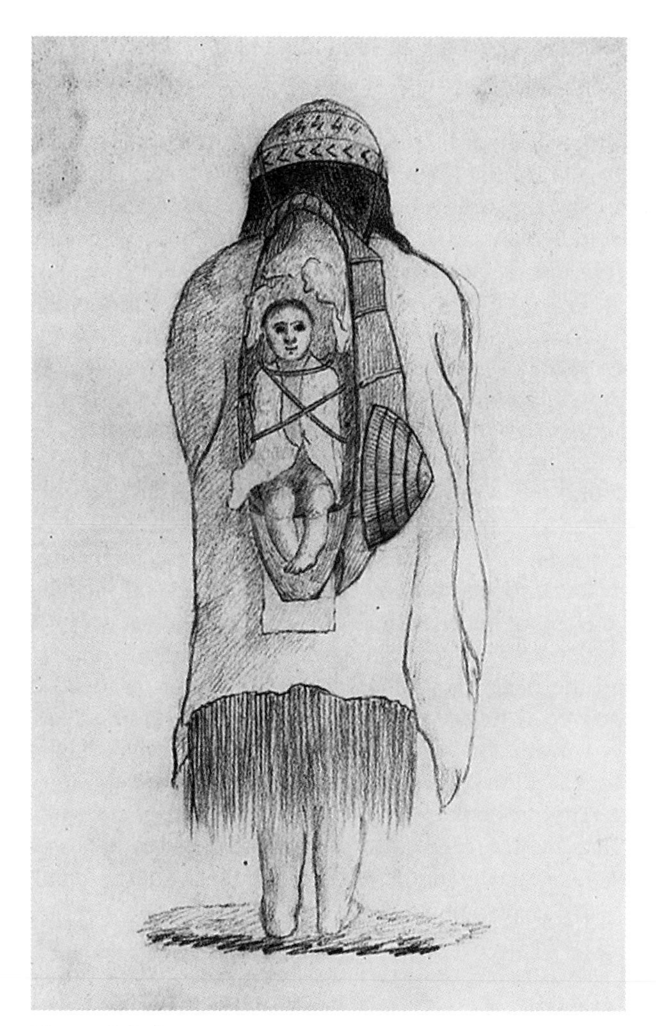

Figure 8-9 | A woman with her child in a baby basket (cradleboard). (Drawn by George Gibbs in 1851. Courtesy of the Smithsonian Institution, National Anthropological Archives, neg. no. 2854-F-21.)

some reference to their marriage, such as Married a Rabbit. Personal names were used in referring to or addressing individuals, but they were dropped when someone married.

The Yurok believed that each child had a unique personal spirit derived from the energy of the Universe, which acted against itself and sent its waves through everything. According to Thomas Buckley (1979), an ethnographer of the Yurok, this infusion of energy was thought to occur ten weeks after conception. At an early age a child was not considered capable of learning systematically. His or her readiness to learn was based on a capacity to remember, not on chronological age; the process of learning began as she or he matured.

At this time each child was taught on an individual basis, since each one was viewed as different from the others. The information taught primarily involved ways to think and behave in particular situations. It was uncles and aunts who taught children; parents were considered too close to them, while grandparents were too emotionally involved with grandchildren to be routine teachers.

A child was taught comparatively little in a formal way; the Yurok felt quite strongly that an individual could learn only by experience. For example, aristocratic families placed an inordinate emphasis on table manners, and a child was expected to learn the proper etiquette by observing others. If a maturing offspring seized food greedily, ate greedily, ate rapidly, and did not chew thoroughly, his or her meal basket was turned upside down as an indication of parental disapproval. It was up to the child to determine what she or he had done wrong and to correct this behavior. Some instruction was formal, however. A child might be shown rocks shaped like figures and told they formerly were persons who did not follow social norms. One rock in particular was pointed out as once having been an errant child. Animals and birds, too, were the subjects of stories about proper behavior. One particularly vivid tale concerned the greedy buzzard who put his entire head in his soup while it was still hot. He scalded the top of his head and henceforth could eat only old, rotten food. Another dominant concern of parents was to ensure that a child learned not to offend the dead. Any direct statement about the dead or reference to items associated with death was considered a form of swearing. A rude gesture used as a means of swearing was to hold out one's hands with the fingers outstretched and the thumbs together, since this was thought to be how the dead swore. The probable reason for disapproving of such behavior was that it led to claims by the relatives of a deceased person. To discourage words or gestures of this nature, a mentor placed nettles against a child's lips or hands, a very effective punishment.

A child sooner or later came to understand what the people conceived of as the law; everything was subject to this law. The essence of the law, which was above all else an expression of the Universe, was *truth,* because it was correct and proper at all times. As Buckley (1979, 30) has noted, "All education and training must move in respect of each unique person's individuality while, at the same time, insuring the success of the results as far as this is possible. That is, the interface between individual and society is specified by culturally defined truth expressed in a legal idiom." An individual who learned a great deal of the law was called a "well-educated one," which was an exalted achieved status. The key to education was to learn to perceive "facts" in perspective. In this context, objects as well as behaviors, thoughts, and feelings were objectified as *things* to be seen and understood. A child first learned to comprehend the nature of material things as an essential step toward understanding things that were nonmaterial. To draw distinctions between the two, such as between a tree in a physical sense and a spiritual one, a child was encouraged to be reflective and was given clues, not answers, by instructors. Youths were encouraged to be contemplative, to do their own thinking, and especially to be true to themselves. This was how they not only became upright adults but acquired the spiritual power that brought them both wealth and inner contentment.

The most important skill to be acquired by a young girl was basket weaving, since a great deal of prestige accrued from making excellent baskets. After watching older women make baskets for years, a girl attempted to weave her first one when she was about six years old. She tried a simple form, and often after the first few rows were completed, her mother ripped out the poor weave and gave the basket back to the girl to do again. The learner received little credit for "trying" because a basket either served its purpose or it did not. If a girl's interest and abilities were sustained, a skilled basket weaver instructed her informally. Only one set of weaving techniques existed, and therefore all baskets were similar, differing only in quality and to a lesser degree in design elements. Not all girls became good basket weavers.

When a girl first menstruated, she spent most of ten days sitting silently in a corner of the house, facing away from the fire. Whenever she needed to scratch, she used a special stick, and she wore a skirt of inner bark like that of a female shaman. The girl moved about as little as possible but brought in a load of firewood each day. For at least the first four days she ate no food, under the assumption that the longer she fasted the more wealth she would accumulate later in life. When she did eat, it was at the bank of a roaring river where she would hear no sound but the water. Each night she bathed the number of times equal to the days of her confinement, except that on the ninth night she bathed ten times. At dusk of the tenth day each small child living nearby washed her back. Finally, her mother or another woman told her she would have ten boys and ten girls.

The preceding account is based on traditionally accepted writings about the initial menstruation of Yurok females, which imply that during their first and subsequent menses women were isolated because of their capacity to contaminate anything with which they had contact. For a menstruating woman to seduce an unknowing man was considered odious; thus the impact of menstruation on women and men alike was interpreted largely negatively. However, a field study among the Yurok by Buckley in 1978 (Buckley 1982), coupled with his examination of unpublished field notes collected by A. L. Kroeber in 1902, leads to a reevaluation of published accounts about menstruation and sheds new light on Yurok social and religious life. Buckley emphasizes that the data are not the best and that his reconstruction of the menstrual complex is tentative, but his nonetheless is an important interpretation to consider.

On her "moontime," as the Yurok called menstruation, a woman was isolated from males for ten days and ate separate meals prepared in particular containers. Furthermore, men were expected to refrain from hunting or participating in ceremonial activities when their wives or daughters were menstruating. One rationale for isolating women at this time was negative: menstruating women were considered highly polluting. Yet a positive reason existed as well:

a menstruating woman was thought to be at the height of her power because the flow of blood purified her. This was why she refrained from ordinary tasks and concentrated instead on the purpose and meaning of her life. The Yurok drew a clear analogy between the purification men sought in their sweat houses and that sought by women in menstrual isolation. Men seeking wealth secluded themselves in a sweat house, avoided contact with fertile women, and ate special foods for ten days. In a similar fashion, Yurok women during their menses attained purification and supposedly had the greatest capacity to attract wealth.

From these data it becomes obvious that if the women of a household menstruated at different times, the normal household routine frequently would be disrupted. Buckley suggests that this may not have been the case because of a menstrual synchrony among the fertile women in a household group. (Menstrual synchrony is widely recognized as occurring among women who interact frequently, such as in college dormitories. A female pheromone can diffuse through a large room with sufficient strength to synchronize the menstrual cycles of women who customarily occupy the room.) Presumably, the women in a Yurok household, or in clusters of closely related households, interacted often. Furthermore, it may be, as Buckley cautiously suggests, that Yurok women synchronized their menses by being exposed to the full moon. (It has been demonstrated that the exposure of a woman to light while she is asleep may affect the onset of menstruation.) The lunar cycle was known to be highly significant among the Yurok in calculating time, and this awareness of lunar change may have led them to use photic stimulation to influence the onset of menstruation as required for synchrony. In any case, the menstrual synchrony that apparently existed meant the absence of all fertile adult females from the household at one time, which may have been more advantageous than constant disruptions of routine.

A maturing girl of good breeding was watched carefully by her parents to make certain that she did not fornicate. The prohibition was not so much a matter of morality as to prevent the girl from becoming pregnant and thereby decreasing the amount of bridewealth she would bring. A girl who conceived before marriage attempted to abort by placing heated stones on her abdomen; if successful, she threw the fetus in the river.

Property exchanges at marriage were critical because a person's social standing depended on the amount of bridewealth offered at the time of his mother's marriage. At the bottom of the scale was a nonlegitimate offspring who had no formal standing. Next was a poor person, whose father had offered little for his wife; he in turn could provide his son with very little bridewealth. A third level of prestige was achieved by persons whose fathers had offered substantial wealth. Finally, some persons' rich fathers provided far more wealth than was necessary to consummate a marriage. Marital arrangements were not a simple offering of a given amount of wealth to the bride's family; instead there often were manipulations and compromises. According to the ideal, a man with wealth suggested a suitable amount of material goods to the girl's relatives, had it accepted, and took the girl to reside in his settlement (patrilocal residence). Such was a "full marriage." Any particular groom was unlikely to possess enough wealth of his own to satisfy the girl's relatives, but his father or father's brothers ideally gave the young man the necessary balance. The bride of a wealthy man brought with her a considerable amount of property, which partially offset the outlay of the groom and his relatives. A girl of high social standing might bring ten baskets of dentalia, otter skins, a canoe, deerskins, and other small assorted valuables. It was possible also for a man with a small daughter to be deeply in debt to a man with a young son and to offer the girl in marriage when she was quite young. In this case, the girl would grow up in the household of her prospective in-laws and would marry the boy after puberty. Sometimes a father was so covetous of his wealth that he refused to give his son a sufficient amount for a full marriage. If the son worked hard, sweated often in the sweat house, cried for wealth, and fasted, after about four years the girls' relatives might feel sorry for him and permit a full marriage.

Another form of marriage was "half marriage," which meant usually that the groom could not accumulate the necessary wealth to make a full-marriage payment and was forced to be content with lower social standing. He offered his potential father-in-law all the wealth he possessed and went to live in the girl's village, either in the same house or in a nearby house (matrilocal residence). In a typical marriage of this sort, the children of the couple were affiliated with the wife's family, and the bridewealth given at the marriage of their daughter went to the wife's kinsmen. Furthermore, the woman in a half marriage could correct her husband openly and supervise his subsistence activities, while the children were under her direct control even concerning their marital arrangements. A half marriage sometimes was negotiated quickly if a girl was pregnant, to prevent the social stigma of bearing a bastard. Finally, a greedy father of a girl who was a successful shaman might force a half marriage upon her to continue his claim on her earnings. In a record of 356 marriages, 25 percent were half marriages, indicating that either the number of persons with little wealth was small or that extenuating circumstances often were involved in a marriage. At the same time, full marriages were not all equal, for very rich men would offer far more than the minimum amount of wealth necessary in order to acquire increased prestige for themselves and their children.

Possibly the most common grounds for divorce was failure of the wife to conceive, and if she could not be replaced by a kinswoman, the bridewealth was refunded. If a man abused his wife in a full marriage so much that she returned home, the husband was obligated to pay the woman's family an additional amount before he could receive her back. If he did not do so, the girl's family probably would return part of the bridewealth, and the couple was considered divorced.

Following a death, the corpse was washed, but it was touched as little as possible. The deceased was painted, clothed, wrapped in a skin, and placed on a plank for twenty-four hours. Mourners wailed before the body, and then it was removed from the house through an opening made in the wall and buried near the house. During burial the mourners wept, sang appropriate songs, and said good-bye to the deceased.

The spirit of a good person was believed to travel a narrow, winding trail north until it climbed a ladder into the sky to a peaceful afterlife. The soul of an unworthy individual supposedly traveled a broad trail to a river where an old woman and a dog lived. Sometimes the dog drove the soul back into the dead person's body, and he or she came to life again. This was rare, and if it did happen, the person was not happy and would meet a sudden death. When the old woman had control of the soul, she sent it across the river in a waiting canoe of the Yurok type but without a "heart" near the bow. A young man propelled the canoe and landed the soul in a damp, depressing land where food, although plentiful, was unpalatable. As described, these beliefs about the fate of souls sound as if they might be of Christian derivation.

Historical Developments

A shipborne Portuguese explorer visited coastal Yurok country in 1595, but the region did not become reasonably well known until the coastal fur trade emerged from 1818 to 1848. Intense contacts with Euro-Americans began in 1849, when placer gold was discovered along the Trinity River. Although the Yurok equated foreigners with enemies, they appreciated the local availability of manufactured goods from traders. Intoxicants also were sold in stores and contributed to confrontations with outsiders. Conflicts between local Native Americans and whites led the federal government to establish the Klamath Reserve in 1855 along the lower Klamath River; eventually, in 1988, this land, plus the Hoopa Valley Extension, became the Yurok Reservation. The Hoopa Valley Reservation was created farther inland by Congress in 1864, an area occupied in part by the Yurok (see Figure 8-1).

Ethnohistorical information about the changes in Yurok life during most of the 1900s is sketchy. However, fieldwork in 1965 by Cynthia Burski and Dorothy Hosler made a significant contribution. The same is true for the work by Buckley and the Bushnells in the 1970s and by Gates in the 1990s. In combination, these studies suggest that what it meant to be a Yurok remained reasonably strong in numerous contexts. Old religious life began to decline in the 1920s, when the Indian Shaker church began to have a local impact. Becoming members of this and other Christian churches resulted in major belief system changes. The traditional world-renewal ceremonies had ceased long ago, but a Deerskin Dance was held in 1955. The same year much of the ceremonial equipment for this dance was destroyed in a fire. The next such dance was held in 1964, and it was soon followed by a severe flood along the Klamath River that destroyed thirty-five Yurok homes. Some people thought that the flood may have resulted because a truck, contrary to tradition, sprinkled water on the dance area before the event. Then too one man refused to display his wealth at the dance, which again invited disaster. The people were distressed also because cemeteries were washed away by the flood and the bones of the dead were exposed. The tradition-oriented Yurok explained the continuing rains of January 1965 as being caused by the exposure of bones of the dead; they thought the rains would continue until the bones once again were covered.

The views of many local whites about these Indians were stereotypic and fell into an expectable pattern. The Indians were considered drunkards with little or no respect for the law; dirty, irresponsible employees; and generally unreliable. Unquestionably, the opinions of the whites had a certain amount of truth to them, for the consumption of intoxicants did seem to be important to many Yurok, and the attitudes of many of them toward wage labor were not shared by whites. The Yurok considered whites to be greedy and felt that they looked down upon Indians. More important to the Yurok were their specific complaints against the Hupa, who they felt were unjustly favored by the BIA, and against BIA officials for both real and imagined injustices.

Yurok social life still was built on the nuclear family residence unit, but Yurok of both sexes showed a striking tendency to marry whites. Yurok clothing did not differ from the garments of whites in the area, since both men and women wore store-bought clothing exclusively. Yurok homes were large, rectangular frame dwellings with four or more rooms. One characteristic of households was their cluttered appearance, the result of a great accumulation of material goods. Household furnishings included both expected items, such as refrigerators, stoves, tables, and chairs, and many seemingly useless items. The clutter apparently was compatible with older housekeeping norms. Houses contained collections of baskets, an overt sign of their Indian heritage. Production of baskets was limited, since few women retained the skill to make them, and they were sold primarily to Yurok. The sweat houses, which once were so extremely important, had largely ceased to function. Stools, which were one of the few items of aboriginal furniture, were occasionally seen in the dwellings, but they were regarded more as heirlooms than as furnishings. The traditional forms of Yurok wealth, such as elaborate ceremonial costumes, dentalium shells, and white deerskins, existed as treasures.

Subsistence fishing for salmon had become less important, although certain family fishing spots were owned, and trespassers were prosecuted. The timber industry was the primary source of employment, followed by road construction. During the summer months, numerous men served as hunting and fishing guides for tourists. In the mid-1960s, working in the timber industry much of the year was a major source of employment, supplemented by unemployment insurance and food stamps when there was no work.

In more recent years, the concerted attention of the Yurok and nearby Indians focused on a long-standing conflict with the federal government over the Gasquet-Orleans (G-O) Road in the Six Rivers National Forest. The road's purpose was primarily to provide access to timber for logging, and it was later to become a scenic drive for tourists. By 1974 the road was completed except in the vicinity of Chimney Rock, a sacred place for local tribes. Native Americans went there when they were "called." Apprentice female shamans went there to acquire power, and men visited its sacred places to experience the power, beauty, and essence that represented a core of their traditional religious life.

In a federal court suit to halt completion of the road, Indians and environmental groups joined forces. Years of complex litigation culminated in 1988, when the U.S. Supreme Court ruled on the basis of the First Amendment to the Constitution, the free exercise clause. The court determined that despite the religious importance of the area to Indians, the government *could* permit road construction and timber harvests in the area. However, the decision became moot with passage of the California Wilderness Act of 1984, which precluded building and use of roads in the area. Subsequent legislation protected the area from exploitation; entrances to the road are blocked by locked gates to prevent its use. Thus the Indians "won," but in essence were denied federal protection of religious sites on federal lands.

The Recent Past

For decades the most contentious issue was a Yurok–Hupa legal battle. The Hoopa Valley Reservation contained valuable timber, and in the 1940s the BIA permitted the harvest of trees, with profits going to the Hupa. The reservation, however, had been established for local Indians, not exclusively for the Hupa. The Yurok contended that they deserved compensation from the sales. This led to a suit, filed by Jesse Quinn McCoy Short, for a share in timber sale profits; she was one-quarter Yurok and one-quarter Hupa. This case was one of the most drawn-out litigations in American legal history, lasting for thirty-two years. A complication was that the Yurok had never officially organized as a tribe, and therefore they found it difficult to act against the Hupa. For the Yurok not to have organized was in keeping with their strong sense of individualism and the factionalism among powerful family lines.

In 1973 the U.S. Supreme Court ruled that the Yurok had a legal claim to the profits from the Hupa timber sales. A 1987 court decision stated that the legitimate Yurok claimants were owed timber-harvest payments and the interest from these monies dating back to 1958. The timber sales dispute led to the Hoopa–Yurok Settlement Act of 1988. In 1991 about thirty-five hundred Yurok were judged eligible for individual payments of between four and fourteen thousand dollars in a complex distribution arrangement. The final payments were made in 1996.

The settlement act authorized the Yurok to organize as a tribe under the amended Indian Reorganization Act, which led to the creation of the Yurok Reservation. A Yurok committee drafted a constitution that was adopted by the tribal members in 1994, and a tribal council became their governing body. In some ways the Yurok were advantaged by their relatively recent organization as a tribe. One compelling reason is that as a result of federal legislation in 1975 the BIA had been turning their administrative functions over to local Indians. By 1996 the Yurok had become deeply involved in self-government, enabling them to help guide their destiny to a far greater extent than ever before. They have been able to achieve expanded control over Indian law enforcement, the development of tribal courts, a greater share in forest management, and a more dominant voice in fishing regulations—the latter having been a long-standing conflict with the federal and state governments. These developments represent positive strides toward Yurok autonomy, even partial sovereignty. Yet their future, like their past, is linked to federal Indian policies, to their funding, and to the general political climate, none of which can accurately be anticipated.

When looking at a modern map of California that includes Indian reservations, their size may appear to be reasonably impressive. So it is with the Yurok Reservation, incuded in Figure 8-1 in this chapter. Their aboriginal land base consisted of about 320,000 acres. The land set aside for them by the federal government amounted to about 56,000 acres. By 1999, however, timber companies owned about 40,000 acres *within* the modern reservation, and thousands of additional acres were owned by non-Indians. The core of tribal land held in trust by the federal government included 3,300 acres, plus some 3,500 acres purchased by the Yurok in the 1990s. Land allotted to Yurok and other Indians on the reservation and owned by them by fee simple patent amounted to about 1,800 acres. State laws apply to patented land (e.g., taxes, logging, and road construction). Thus the Yurok actually own or control only a small percentage of reservation land, and the same is true on numerous other reservations.

Many Yurok stoutly maintain that allotment holders have been repeatedly swindled out of their land, in part because they were nonliterate. The most recent cases were in the early 1950s, when BIA personnel and timber company agents visited allottees with timber holdings. The whites claimed that the timber was needed for the Korean War effort and that it would be unpatriotic for the Indians to hold on to their timber. This convinced numerous persons to sell what they *thought* were timber rights; in fact, they also were selling their land. The courthouse in which the records of these transactions were kept subsequently was destroyed by fire.

As the land base has declined dramatically over the years, there has been a corresponding significant decrease in the resident reservation population. By 1996 residents numbered about 750. However, their unemployment rate has been estimated at about 85 percent because so few job opportunities exist. This may help explain why an additional 1,900 Yurok live in the general area where logging service jobs offer greater employment opportunities. At the same time, the definition of a Yurok has changed over the years, so that a person with one-eighth Yurok genetic heritage may now be on the tribal roll. The loss of genetic identity suggests that numerous tribal members have abandoned their sense of being Yurok except in select contexts.

The diminished scope of traditional Yurok culture is readily apparent. Fewer than twenty individuals fluently speak their aboriginal language. Traditional dances are still performed, but the last Deerskin Dance to be held in its appropriate context was in 1906. They continue to make old-style baskets and

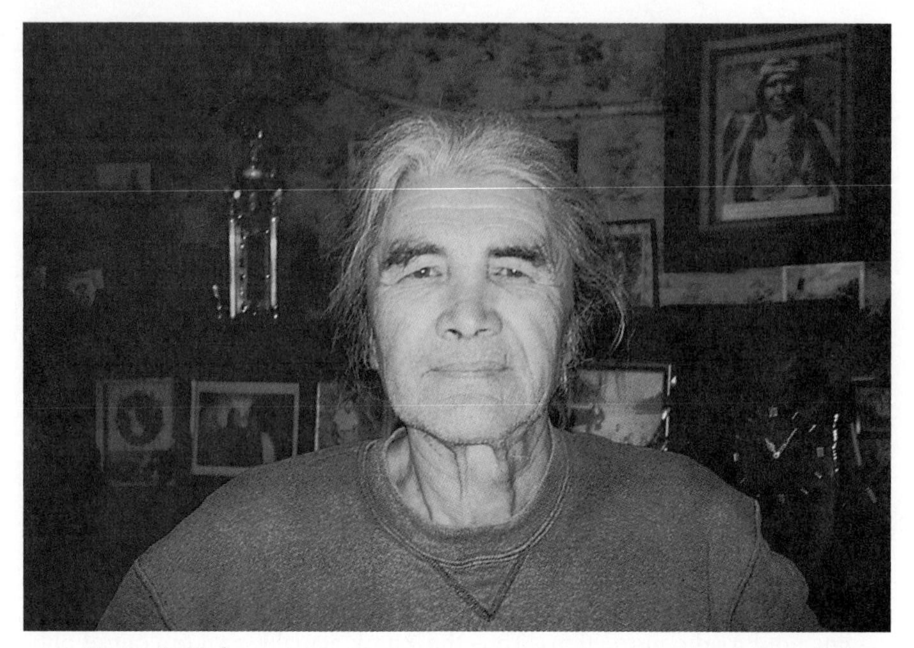

Figure 8-10 | Desmond (Merk) Oliver, in a 1996 photograph, a Yurok living at Requa.

other craft items, but these efforts do not seem to be an important part of life. Female shamans, who once played a central role in curing, have nearly disappeared. One woman remains a practicing shaman; she has a few apprentices who seek to become practitioners.

Despite these examples of eroding continuity with the past, for numerous, perhaps many, Yurok the sense of tribal identity remains strong and appears to be becoming stronger. Influential factors unquestionably have been settlement of the Jessie Short case in their favor and their recent organization as a tribe. The latter is especially critical because the Yurok are now able to control their own destiny in critical issues more than ever before; such issues include fishing regulations, forest management, and tribal courts. The fact that traditional Yurok ways have tenuous continuity may not matter all that much when they confront the modern world as reservation Indians (see Figure 8-10).

Since organizing as a tribe, the Yurok have devoted appreciable attention to the revitalization of traditional culture. To focus this effort, they formed a tribal cultural committee and hired a cultural anthropologist, Thomas M. Gates, PhD, who administers the Tribal Heritage Preservation Office. This office assumed the responsibilities previously held by the state. A major effort has been made to pinpoint and document pertinent archaeological and ethnographic information about sites in traditional Yurok country. The cultural committee likewise has been developing other programs, such as one to revive Yurok as a spoken language. The devotion of the cultural committee to encouraging the furtherance of their traditions is clear.

Additional Sources

The Yurok article by Arnold R. Pilling in the *California* volume (8) of the new *Handbook of North American Indians,* William C. Sturtevant, general editor (Washington, DC, 1978) provides an excellent overview of these Indians and neighboring tribes. The best general ethnography is by Robert Spott and Alfred L. Kroeber (1942). The book by Lucy Thompson (1916), a Yurok woman, is an exceptional narrative by an Indian about her people. Superior presentations about particular aspects of Yurok culture are: material culture, Kroeber (1925); personality, Erik H. Erikson (1943); basketry, Lila M. O'Neale (1932); and placenames on the land, Thomas M. Gates (1995) and Thomas T. Waterman (1920).

Selected Bibliography

Buckley, Thomas. 1979. Doing your thinking. *Parabola* 4(4)29–37.

———. 1982. Menstruation and the power of Yurok women. *American Ethnologist* 9:47–60.

Burski, Cynthia, and Dorothy Hosler. 1965, January. Field notes.

Bushnell, John, and Donna Bushnell. 1977. Wealth, work, and world view in native northwest California. In *Flowers of the wind,* Thomas C. Blackburn, ed., 120–82. Socorro, NM.

Erikson, Erik H. 1943. *Observations on the Yurok: Childhood and world image.* University of California Publications in American Archaeology and Ethnology, vol. 35, no. 10.

Gates, Thomas M. 1995. *Along the ridgelines.* Ann Arbor, MI.

Gifford, Edward W. 1922. *California kinship terminologies.* University of California Publications in American Archaeology and Ethnology, vol. 18.

Heizer, Robert F., and John E. Mills. 1952. *The four ages of Tsurai.* Berkeley.

Kroeber, Alfred L. 1925. *Handbook of the Indians of California.* Bureau of American Ethnology Bulletin 78. Washington, DC. (Reprinted 1953, Berkeley.)

———. 1976. *Yurok myths.* Berkeley.

Kroeber, Alfred L., and Edward W. Gifford. 1949. *World renewal, a cult system of native northwest California.* Anthropological Records, vol. 13, no. 1.

O'Neale, Lila M. 1932. *Yurok-Karok basket weavers.* University of California Publications in American Archaeology and Ethnology, vol. 32, no. 1.

Pilling, Arnold R. 1978. Yurok. In *California,* Robert F. Heizer, ed., vol. 8, 137–54. *Handbook of North American Indians.* Washington, DC.

Spott, Robert, and Alfred L. Kroeber. 1942. *Yurok narratives.* University of California Publications in American Archaeology and Ethnology, vol. 35, no. 9.

Thompson, Lucy. 1916. *To the American Indian.* Eureka, CA. (Reprinted 1991, Berkeley.)

Valory, Dale K. 1970. *Yurok doctors and devils*. PhD dissertation, University of California, Berkeley.

Waterman, Thomas T. 1920. *Yurok geography*. University of California Publications in American Archaeology and Ethnology, vol. 16, no. 5.

———. 1938. *The Kepel fish dam*. University of California Publications in American Archaeology and Ethnology, vol. 35, no. 6.

Waterman, Thomas T., and Alfred L. Kroeber. 1934. *Yurok marriages*. University of California Publications in American Archaeology and Ethnology, vol. 35, no. 1.

9 The Tlingit: Alaskan Salmon Fishers

Tlingit rattle (from Lisianskii 1814)

The world is rolling around for all the young people; therefore let us not love our life too much, hold ourselves back from dying.

A song about the earth composed by Dry Bay George. (de Laguna 1972, 792)

WE PROBABLY HAVE more information about the Tlingit from early historic to modern times than we have for any other Northwest Coast salmon fishers. The Tlingit are an excellent example of a people in a land of plenty who stressed wealth as well as social achievements within family lines. Yet they were not politically organized at the tribal level; instead, narrowly defined bonds of kinship focused their economic, political, and social lives. Totem poles and potlatches, characteristic of Northwest Coast Indians in general, predominated among the Tlingit. Although Tlingit totem poles usually are assumed to have been an aboriginal characteristic of Northwest Coast Indians, this chapter shows that they were a relatively recent development, quite possibly stimulated by the fur trade. The Tlingit's complex social network and ceremonial life invite comparison with the Yurok. In addition, the Tlingit capacity to cope with Euro-Americans is notable.

Tlingit (TLING-kuht) means "the people." Their language belongs to the Nadene family of languages, and they may have numbered about ten thousand early in their history. Tlingit country is a mass of mountains that reach a sea marked by islands, deep bays, and glaciers. This verdant land with its tranquil and turbulent waters had rich exploitative potential. Along the northern third, impressive mountains abruptly meet the sea, and sheltering bays are rare. In the balance of Tlingit country innumerable large and small islands front a fractured coastline. The mild temperatures and heavy precipitation produce a lush and varied vegetation, including stands of red cedar and Sitka spruce. Considering the geographical configuration, it is understandable that travel by boat was far more important than walking, although trails to the interior existed along certain rivers and over low divides and were negotiated for trading or raiding ventures (see Figure 9-1).

Aboriginal Life

Among all the aboriginal peoples of the world who lived as hunters, fishers, and collectors, those of the Northwest Coast of North America achieved a high level of cultural complexity. Their lifeways were in many respects more complex than those reported among numerous aboriginal farmers. The Tlingit are reasonably typical of these Indians; as was true of other Northwest Coast populations, the richness of their culture was based on the abundance of salmon and the reliability of this major food source.

ORIGIN MYTH According to the Tlingit, the first people simply existed, and no explanation was sought for their origin. Among these people, according to one account, was a woman whose sons were killed by her brother. She decided to commit suicide, but an old man told her to swallow a heated beach pebble. The woman followed his instructions and became pregnant. She bore an offspring, who was Raven in human form. When Raven was older, he visited his uncle despite his mother's warnings that this man had killed his ten

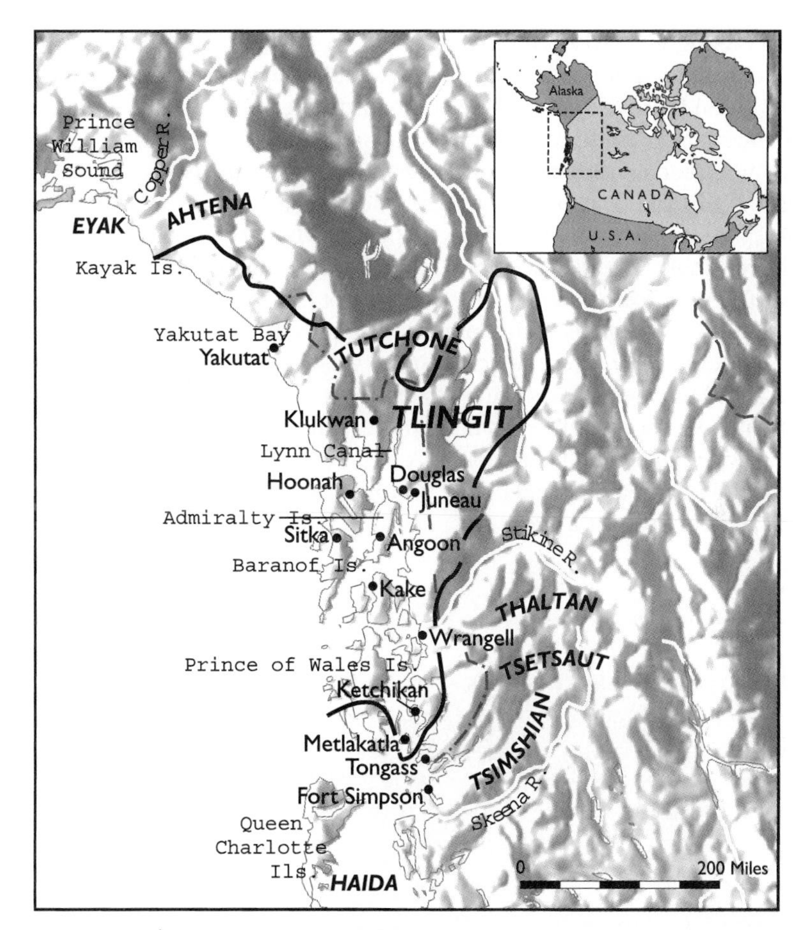

Figure 9-1 | Range of the Tlingit Indians.

older brothers. The uncle attempted to kill Raven, but because of his supernatural powers Raven saved himself. Finally, Raven caused a flood, and all the people perished except for Raven and his mother, who donned bird skins and flew into the air. Raven stuck his beak in the sky and hung there for ten days. After the water subsided, he fell to earth and landed on a heap of seaweed. Raven went to the house of Petrel, a man who had always existed. In a small locked box on which he sat, Petrel kept water, and when Raven was thirsty, Petrel gave him only a little. Raven tricked Petrel into thinking that he, Petrel, had excreted in his bed. While Petrel was outside cleaning his blanket, Raven drank more than his fill of water and then flew to a tree with pitch in it. Petrel built a fire beneath the tree, and the smoke turned Raven from white to black. Later the trickery of Raven released the stars, the moon, and finally the sun into the sky. Raven was a creator or releaser of forces in the world, a culture hero, and an inordinate trickster.

APPEARANCE AND CLOTHING The Tlingit were lean, medium to tall in stature, and had skins no darker than those of many persons in southern Europe. Women wore their hair loose and had striking adornments. From a woman's pierced earlobes hung ornaments of shell, stone, or teeth, and her nasal septum was pierced to receive a bone pin. Each woman also wore a large medial labret (lip plug) inserted through a hole beneath the lower lip (see Figure 9-2). The initial opening was made about the time of puberty and was fitted with increasingly larger labrets until the hole was as much as four inches across; as one observer noted, these women could not kiss. Men wore their hair loose and rubbed it with grease; although their whiskers were not numerous, they were nonetheless plucked. When a male was young, his nasal septum was pierced, and through the opening a small ring was suspended. Men wore ear ornaments like those of the women, and a man of great achievements might have bits of wool or small feathers stuck in several small holes around the outer edge of each ear. Facial paints were worn by men and women on special occasions and as protection from temperature extremes and insects.

Figure 9-2 | A girl in the Yakutat area with earrings, a nose pin, and labret. Sketched by Don Tomás de Suría in 1791. (Courtesy of the Beinecke Rare Book and Manuscript Library, Collection of Western Americana, Yale University.)

Adults of both sexes dressed in long-sleeved shirts of dehaired skin, over which they wore sea otter skin capes with the fur facing outward. The processed skin undergarments of women reached from the neck to the ankles. During severe weather they wore moccasins made by interior Indians or styled after their footwear. Tlingit hats, worn for hunting and ceremonies, were woven from roots or bark and were shaped like a truncated cone with a flat top. Their clothing hardly seems adequate to an outsider, but these people conditioned themselves to accept temperature extremes. They not only bathed in cold or icy waters but also lived in scorching houses.

SETTLEMENTS Winter villages were built along bays, inlets, or the lower courses of rivers, near good fishing grounds and where canoes could be landed safely. The square plank-covered houses had gabled roofs. At small villages, houses were built in a line facing the water, but the houses in larger settlements were arranged in rows. The plank-covered floor of the small dwellings was at ground level, but the central area of the larger houses was dug down about three feet. Along the sides at ground level were board- or mat-enclosed compartments for sleeping, bathing, or storage. Around the fire pit were stones to be heated in the fire and placed in containers for cooking food. Hunting and fishing devices were stored overhead along the beams, and fish might be hung from the roof beams to dry. Among the northern Tlingit, in particular, the house of a leading lineage was likely to have decorated wall partitions or panels called heraldic screens. It appears that behind a screen was the apartment of the house chief. Around the entry to a house, or even around an entire village, were palisades to protect the occupants. A bough-covered structure might be leaned against the outer wall of a house or built nearby for women during menstrual periods or childbirth. Pole racks for drying fish were scattered about a settlement, and a short distance away, either toward the forest or sea, were clusters of graves. At summer camps, where they caught their winter supply of fish, families lived in flimsy plank structures, some of which were walled only on the windward side.

MANUFACTURES AND HOUSEHOLD LIFE Tlingit artistic skills rank high among tribal peoples anywhere in the world. Their manufactures in bone, stone, and wood are justly famous. A wide variety of wooden containers filled a typical aboriginal household. One style was made from a thin plank of cedar that was steamed and bent into a rectangular form, then overlapped and sewn with root. A wooden bottom was fitted into place and a top sometimes added. Some of these boxes had bulging sides that were painted or carved. The largest and most elaborately decorated boxes were for the storage of valuables, and others were used for cooking or food storage. Another common wooden form was made from a single piece of wood and ranged from round to oval to rectangular in outline. To these basic forms were adapted various animal shapes, such as a beaver lying on its back, with its head at one end, legs on the sides, and tail opposite the head. Other household items included dishes, spoons, and ladles of mountain sheep or goat horn. Oval lamps of pecked and polished stone furnished light, as fish or seal oil burned on a moss wick.

Family members gathered around the fire pit to rest, eat, or work during the day. At the fireplace, they prepared meals at irregular times of the day for as many as thirty house occupants. They boiled foods in wooden or woven containers. They poured water into the containers and dropped hot stones in to simmer the meat or fish before putting on the lid. Fish were boiled, roasted, or dried and served as the principal food, supplemented by flesh from land and sea mammals. They also ate shellfish, vegetable products, and fruit, particularly a wide variety of berries. These foods were relatively unimportant; however, shellfish became important in times of food stress. Boiled foods were dipped from their cooking containers in large spoons, which served as plates, and people consumed large quantities of water at meals.

CONVEYANCES The most important Tlingit manufacture for subsistence activities was the canoe, normally built in the winter when unhurried production allowed men to make attractive and sound vessels. The best wood came from a straight-grained red cedar blown over by the wind or felled by building a fire at the base. A builder would hew and scrape the log with a stone-bladed adz. To spread the sides of the hollowed log he filled the cavity with water and dropped hot stones into it. As the log expanded, pieces of wood were wedged across the gunwales to give the sides the desired degree of flare. The outer sides might be painted with designs and the bow carved. A small canoe carried two or three persons, whereas larger ones held sixty persons and were forty-five feet long. They propelled canoes with paddles and used an extra-long paddle for steering. When not in use, a canoe was covered with mats or blankets to protect it from the sun, and water was sprinkled over the sides. A small canoe made from a cottonwood log was used for fishing and river travel.

Snowshoes were essential for overland mobility during the winter, especially among the Chilkat, who went inland to trade at this time of year. The maple or birch snowshoe frames were heated over a fire and shaped; the netting was made from rawhide thongs. The shoes were about four feet long and ten inches wide at their broadest point, with rounded toes that turned up at the front and pointed heels.

SUBSISTENCE ACTIVITIES Terrestrial fauna included black and grizzly bears, fox, wolves, wolverine, lynx, and deer on some islands. Scattered caribou herds occupied mainland plateaus, and mountain goats, as well as mountain sheep, frequented the coastal ranges. Smaller species included hare, squirrel, ermine, porcupine, muskrat, and a few beaver. Among the marine mammals were whales, hair and fur seals, sea lions, and sea otter. Of all the fish the most important were the salmon and candlefish (eulachon); halibut, haddock, trout, and herring also were caught. Along the edges of the sea were edible algae, crabs, sea urchins, mussels, and cockles. Avifauna included the bald eagle, raven, owl, and migratory waterfowl that summered in the area.

The subsistence cycle ebbed during the winter, and even March did not offer reliable weather for fishing. Nonetheless, it was during March that the subsistence year began anew. Men repaired canoes, readied fishing gear, and waited anxiously. In calm weather they fished for halibut along the coast fronting the Pacific Ocean. Two men fished from a canoe, maintaining about fifteen lines with baited V-shaped hooks and a wooden floater for each. When they hooked a fish, they paddled to the bobbing float, raised the line, and clubbed the fish to death as it was boated. Trout fishing with baited hooks also was important at this time. Following the breakup of river ice in March, women fished for trout with gill nets of rawhide with inflated bladder floats and stone sinkers. One woman usually paddled a canoe as a second handled the drifting net. They collected clams and mussels in large quantities and either dried and smoked them for future use or steamed them in a pit by pouring water over hot stones and applying a leaf covering. The pelts of fur animals were prime in March; fox, mink, wolf, and river (land) and sea otter all were sought. They trapped some of these animals in deadfalls but hunted sea otter with harpoon darts.

Candlefish were a rich source of the oil that was drunk during feasts but was more commonly served as a dip for dried salmon. These small fish were taken in traps or dip nets in the spring as they ascended rivers. The people began processing these fish by placing the fish and water in a canoe half-buried in the sand. They dropped heated stones repeatedly into the mass, and as the oil from the cooked fish surfaced, they ladled it into wooden containers. In mid-April herring spawned in shallow bays and were so numerous that they could be impaled on sharp tines set in the side of a pole. The tine-studded pole was drawn back and forth in the water, and the pierced herring were shaken off into the canoe. They either were eaten soon after being caught or were strung on ropes and dried.

Auke, Chilkat, and Stikine men traveled inland trading fish oil to Athapaskan Indians in exchange for caribou skins, moccasins, sinew, and lichens to be used for a particular form of dye. During the summer they paddled great canoes south to Haida and Tsimshian country, and in early historic times they ventured as far as Puget Sound in trading canoes. They carried copper from the Copper River and other local products to exchange for dentalia, haliotis, shark teeth, and slaves.

They usually hunted sea mammals with harpoon darts that had a line running from the detachable dart head to the shaft. When an animal was struck, the barbed dart head held beneath its skin, and the shaft was dragged through the water as the animal dove into the water. When it surfaced, the captive was harpooned again or killed with a spear or club. The most important species hunted were dolphin, seals, sea lions, and especially sea otter in early historic times. From the ethnographic accounts it seems that sea mammal hunting was not very important or that inland hunting was important at most settlements. If bears or mountain goats were pursued, they were cornered with the aid of dogs and killed with bone-pointed spears.

In the late summer people collected berries and stored them with candlefish oil in airtight boxes. Salmon eggs, oil, and berries were similarly mixed and preserved. If large land mammals were killed, their flesh usually was cut into strips and sun-dried or else boiled and stored in oil. Some foods were stored for winter at this time of the year, but it was not until September that the winter food supply became a major concern. They took diverse species of salmon during the summer but made no great effort to catch and dry quantities of them until September. The species available included dog (chum), humpback (pink), king (chinook), silver (coho), and sockeye (red), and these were taken from July through December. The principal salmon-fishing device was a funnel-shaped trap set with the mouth opening downstream. The stream was blocked with a weir, which opened only at the trap. Fish caught in September were cleaned and hung on racks to dry or were smoke-cured in the house. After being dried or smoked, they were bundled and stored. As soon as a house group had obtained enough salmon for the winter, the members left their fishing camp and settled down in their village until April. Very little food apart from shellfish was gathered during the winter months, for this was the season for rituals, feasting, storytelling, and recreation.

In subsistence activities men dominated as the procurers of edibles, and women played the key role in households. The principal wife of the Keeper of the House was responsible for allocating domestic female tasks. The capacity of these women to process food, especially salmon, was a critical factor in the prosperity of a household. As Frederica de Laguna (1983, 81) noted, "The whole Tlingit economy of subsistence and luxury wealth rests ultimately on the stores of dried salmon prepared by the women."

DESCENT, KINSHIP, AND MARRIAGE In social and political life the *kwaan* (kwáan, kon) represented a key geographical unit. It refers to the people who lived in a particular area. In many ways a kwaan is comparable to a tribe, in which case the Tlingit as a whole made up a "nation." Every kwaan included precise boundaries, and the members of each village controlled the portion its residents exploited. From north to south the first kwaan was Yakutat, with its most important settlement along Yakutat Bay. The most powerful kwaan was that of the Chilkat, with four major villages along the shores of the upper Lynn Canal. One of these, Klukwan, had sixty-five houses and about six hundred residents. The only interior group, the Inland Tlingit, lived around a series of lakes and occupied the largest area. The other kwaans, each of which had at least one large village, were the Auke, Taku, Huna, Killisnoo, Sitka, Kake, Kuiu, Stikine, Henya, Tongass, and Sanya.

The people of each kwaan were divided into two groups (moieties) that were traced through female lines (matriclans) and that were represented in each of the kwaans. The moieties were named Raven and Wolf, with the Wolf moiety called Eagle in the north; these were in turn divided into named matriclans. The Tlingit associated specific personality characteristics with the moieties. Raven people were expected to be wise and cautious, and the Wolves quick-tempered and warlike. According to Aurel Krause (1885), the clans of the Raven moiety included the Frog, Goose, Owl, Raven, Salmon, and Sea Lion. Clans of the Wolf moiety included the Auk, Bear, Eagle, Shark, Whale, and Wolf. These lists, although far from complete, identify the important clans in early historic times. An outsider, who was not a member of any clan, was addressed as uncle or son-in-law, reflecting his in-marrying status. Within each clan the lineage with the greatest wealth was most influential. Ideally, the leadership of a lineage was passed from a man to his sister's son. Each settlement with a number of clans represented had more than one "chief," but one dominated because of his wealth and personality. A person in one moiety was obligated to seek as a mate someone in the opposite moiety (moiety exogamy); further ramifications of marital arrangements are presented in the section about the life cycle.

Within a village the land was owned by groups of persons who traced their descent to a presumed common female ancestor (matriclan), and land was subdivided among house groups. Plots of ground near houses were owned by the adjacent households, but village paths were common property. Community members as a group cleared the trails, and everyone was free to use the beach. Within the domain of a village, each represented clan had particular localities defined as its own. Unclaimed sectors could be exploited by anyone. A clan, or portion thereof, owned fishing streams; land of a stream's drainage used for hunting; sealing islands; mountains inhabited by mountain goats; ocean banks; berry patches; and house sites. They conceived of ownership in terms of specific spots used rather than as geographical areas exploited.

Each clan recognized a particular settlement as the place of its origin. Although a clan was identified initially with a specific site, by the time of historic contact a number of different clans usually were represented in most villages. If a clan was large in a particular settlement, it was divided into lineages represented by house groups. In theory, the clans of each moiety possessed distinctive titles and associated design motifs that only members could use. These might be lent temporarily to or even usurped by a more powerful clan. Again in theory, only members of the Raven moiety had the right to the raven design, and only those of the Wolf moiety, the wolf design. House names usually were derived from a clan myth, from the clan's name, or by assuming the name of another clan's house for legendary or historical reasons. Moieties were each divided into a number of matriclans that in turn were divided into house groups composed of nuclear families, again related through females.

Nuclear family unity did not exist among the Tlingit because the parents were of different clans and moieties. Because various clans were represented in most areas, geographical groupings acted as a unit only in those rare instances when a feud affected all sections of the clan. A clan had no common leader or unified territory, and even crests were often identified with localized lineages rather than with the clan as a whole. Finally, each clan included persons ranked as nobles, "commoners," and slaves, depending on the social standing of particular lineages.

In the kinship system we find that a single term embraced all the people of the grandparent generation. To these persons the individual was attentive and respectful. The ties between a mother and her son were close even though the son might leave home to live with his mother's elder brother, who was for him the most powerful individual in Tlingit society and his authority figure. Fathers were considered too lenient to discipline their sons effectively, and of course a father did not belong to his son's clan or moiety. Parents were especially concerned about the welfare of a daughter, who would command a large bride price only if she were well mannered and a maiden; thus she always was watched by someone. A mother's sister was called by a term for diminutive mother and was treated as one's mother. The "little mother" term was extended to all the other women of her moiety in her generation. A mother was aided and advised in raising children by her sister. A father's sister was termed differently from mother and mother's sister, with the father's sister word extended to all women of her moiety in both her generation and descending generations. The father term was unique, whereas the term for father's brother was extended to the other men of his moiety of his generation, as well as the next lower one. A man treated his father's brother with respect, and on rare occasions a girl might marry her father's brother.

A man ideally married his father's sister, and because she was a potential mate, their relationship was always warm. At one's generational level a man distinguished between older and younger brothers, and these terms were extended to the other men of one's generation and moiety. Older and younger male sibling distinctions were highly important because an older brother had the first rights of inheritance, greater authority, and more ceremonial responsibilities. A woman made the same distinction among sisters. There also was a particular term for a man's sister and one for a woman's brother; these were extended to all the members of that sex of the individual's generation and moiety. Brothers were socially and physically close because they were of the same clan and lived in the same house; with a sister a man was supposed to be distant and withdrawn, although he was concerned for her welfare. A mother's sister's children were termed brother and sister, and the boys were raised in the same household as the mother's children. The terminology for the first ascending generation was essentially bifurcate merging, and the cousin terminology was of the Crow type (see Figure 9-3). One overriding principle governed the kinship terminology of the Tlingit: to separate blood relatives in one's

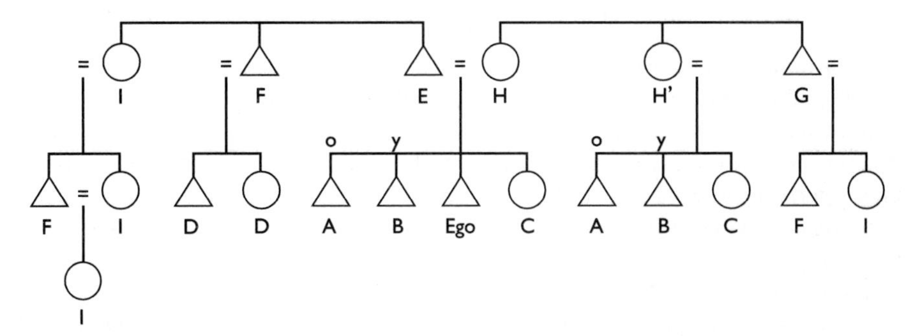

Figure 9-3 | The early historic Tlingit system of kinship terminology.

own moiety from those in the opposite moiety. The average adult avoided using relationship terms in direct address in everyday conversation for fear of offending someone, as a great deal of emphasis was placed on an exact ranking of individuals. Thus nicknames and given names were in common use. Relationship terms were employed primarily on ceremonial occasions.

SOCIAL DIMENSIONS The most important social and economic unit was the household, and it had a significant place in the ceremonial life of the clan and moiety. A house group ideally was composed of a male and his brothers, as well as his mother's sister's sons who were classificatory brothers, and the sons of the sisters of these individuals, plus the sons of the daughters of these sisters. All were members of one matrilineage, and there were additionally the in-marrying spouses. A household of this nature functioned as an economic unit, with members working for their common welfare. In particular it was brothers, led by the eldest, the Keeper of the House, who aided one another in feuds, potlatches, and other matters of house group concern. The importance of the Keeper of the House in directing house group life cannot be overestimated. He guided the economic activities of household members and was deferred to by the other men in his residence unit. The house group leader allotted items obtained in trade, was given choice foods, and was freed from any humble form of household labor. It was this man, the eldest brother, who represented the household in ceremonial activities, as well as in clan councils. Furthermore, when he died the rights to his position fell to the next oldest person called brother. In addition to the position of Keeper of the House, the wealthiest of the local household heads in any clan, and thus the ranking Keeper of the House, was designated Rich Man. These men more than any others were responsible for the fortunes of their clan units.

Within a household the Keeper of the House and his principal wife outranked all other members. Older brothers and sisters outranked younger ones, and bastards and slaves ranked lowest. The same system prevailed between the members of a leading lineage and of the secondary ones within a clan. The highest-ranking persons were aristocrats, chiefs, and the wealthy. Their status was based on birth, personal character, accomplishments, age, and either inherited or acquired wealth. "Commoners" as such did not exist; instead, most persons within lineages were junior members who could be ranked against other persons in broadly similar positions. Furthermore, just as households and lineages were ranked against one another within a clan, so it was among the clans of a moiety. The members of lowly clans were poor, whereas those of lofty clans were rich, hosted elaborate potlatches, and had splendid artifacts as clan heirlooms. The leading members of some aristocratic clans reportedly could not sleep at night because they thought so intently about their greatness.

Men clearly were the overt Tlingit leaders, but the importance of women behind the scenes was exceedingly strong, so much so that they may be considered the dominant gender. Judgments by women were critical in trading relations; they were the keepers of household wealth, and they made critical decisions in social life. The prominence of women was in keeping with Tlingit matrilineality. Thus, moiety, clan, and lineage matters were in their firm grasp. Unfortunately, however, their position is not well reported in the early ethnographic record.

In this social setting, based as it was on rank, classes did not exist. Instead, wealthy and prestigious households competed with one another within a clan and beyond it for high status that changed with the fortunes of these units. In the absence of social classes, the rank of a household, a clan segment, or a whole clan relative to another such unit constantly was being reassessed. The comparative wealth and prestige of these units was tested in numerous ways, such as in potlatches and, to a lesser extent, in the erection of totem poles.

CRESTS AND TOTEM POLES Among these people their most valued possessions were clan and lineage crests. Crests were represented on canoes, dishes, ceremonial garments, totem poles, and other artifacts. A crest ideally was carved by a member of the opposite moiety who held a rank equal to that of the individual requesting the item. By preference this would be a wife's brother; if such an individual was not a capable carver, he could hire someone else of either moiety to make the object. The man who was first asked to do the work paid the craftsman and in turn was paid by his brother-in-law. Carvings produced in this manner fulfilled ritual obligations, and the labor was ceremonial. The most important crests for Raven moiety were the raven, owl, and whale. Wolf moiety crests included the eagle, wolf, and bear. Crests represented Tlingit totems that were honored in ritual contexts, but totems were not worshiped.

No aspect of Northwest Coast Indian life has fascinated Westerners more than totem poles. Their size, boldly sculptured figures, and design motifs have

Figure 9-4 | The earliest illustration of a Tlingit mortuary pole and graves, 1791, for the Yakutat area. (From Malaspina and de Bustamante y Guerra 1885.)

made them memorable cultural monuments. Edward L. Keithan (1963), in a comprehensive account of Tlingit poles, identified six primary types.

1. The four main vertical support posts for a house usually were plain, but they might be faced with carved pillars (or panels) bearing clan crests that could include abalone shell inlays. *Carved house pillars* were one of the two prehistoric types.
2. The second prehistoric type was the *mortuary pole*. The pole body was plain. A box was set at the top of the pole in which were placed the cremated remains of the person honored. A crest figure might be carved on the upper portion of the pole. The earliest example was reported in 1791 (see Figure 9-4).
3. A *memorial pole* honored a deceased house group leader and was raised under the sponsorship of a younger brother or maternal nephew of the dead person. Such a pole usually was not erected at the interment site. Its purpose was to honor the deceased and, equally important, to validate the succession of the house group leader.
4. A *heraldic pole* was raised at the front and center of a house. A myth or tale associated with the house group was represented by the carved and painted pole.
5. The *ridicule pole* usually was raised to force another house group to settle a debt. One particular example was said to have been erected to shame a white trader for not repaying a potlatch held in his honor.

6. The *potlatch pole* was the most recent type to appear. They were raised to enhance the prestige of a family group that had accumulated and distributed wealth from the fur trade or by working directly for whites (see Figure 9-5).

Totem poles in general did not become commonplace among the Tlingit until the late 1800s. In 1881–1882 one pole was reported among the Chilkat, none among the Sitka or Killisnoo groups; however, they were numerous at one Stikine village. Some observers have suggested that great totem poles may not have been carved until iron-bladed tools became widely available as a result of the fur trade. Yet a well-developed woodworking technology predates the Northwest Coast Indian fur trade.

For the Tlingit, erecting a totem pole was an end in itself. A pole that was carved and raised for a particular purpose was thereafter unimportant as a physical object. As a pole tilted with age or threatened to fall, it was not supported in any manner. Restoration necessitated ceremonial involvements and an outlay of wealth equal to that expended when the original pole was raised, and therefore it was more sensible to erect another pole and bring even greater honor to the house group. Because poles deteriorated rapidly in this damp area and comparatively few new poles were raised after 1900, most have rotted away.

The totemic symbols exhibited on poles were associated with one or the other of the moieties, with clans, or with house groups. All of the Raven moiety members employed the Raven design as their primary symbol. The Wolf moiety had the Wolf as its chief totem in the south and the Eagle in the north. Not only the actual crests but also the names of animals associated with a clan were important, and their uses were validated through the potlatch system. These honorific names, often drawn from the clan or moiety totems, tended to pass from great-grandfather to great-grandson. The animals associated with a moiety could be killed and eaten by moiety members, however, and the uniform eating habits of all the tribe indicate no taboo on eating one's totemic species.

POLITICAL LIFE Conflicts between Tlingit moieties were common, and modern Tlingit liken these disputes to relations between European nations. For real or imagined injuries, either material goods were exchanged or a life was taken. The nature of a settlement depended on the ability of the guilty to pay and the power of the offended to collect. Minor conflicts eventually were settled at feasts that included property settlements. When a person was grievously offended, the only acceptable retribution was the offender's murder, but this was bound to lead to a retaliatory killing. If those murdered were of unequal rank, there was the further problem of establishing a value for each death. Sometimes when an individual felt badly wronged and had no means to retaliate, he committed suicide, and his relatives then pressed for compensation.

Figure 9-5 | Chief's house with painted front and totem poles in 1899. (Courtesy of the Smithsonian Institution, National Anthropological Archives, neg. no. 43,548-H.)

On occasion, clan disputes were settled by a duel between warriors who represented each group. Murders were committed by ambush, as were raids against other clans or tribes. The only crimes occurring within a clan were incest and witchcraft, each punishable by death. It should be stressed that overall political unity did not exist within a moiety, and some of the bloodiest feuds were between clans of the same moiety.

Clans conducted raids to avenge deaths and to obtain slaves. Preparations for impending conflict involved fasting and abstaining from all contact with women. In addition, a warrior conditioned himself for combat by bathing in the sea, even at the coldest time of the year, and by being whipped by an older man. As a raiding party traveled, it seized property from camps along the way irrespective of whether the residents were friendly or not. A shaman always accompanied the party and predicted events of the near future. Plans for an attack on an enemy community were kept secret, and the foray was launched at dawn. Rod or skin armor protected a man's body; his face was covered with a mask, and his head with a wooden helmet. All the enemy men who did not escape were killed with daggers; women and children were taken as prisoners. A reprisal attack would be expected to avenge the murders.

Copper-bladed daggers, spears, and war clubs appear to have been the most important weapons. Scalps were taken at times, and the scalped person's head sometimes was impaled on a stick and exhibited. The men in a war party sang of victory as they returned to their village, and the paddle of each warrior killed was propped up at the spot he had occupied in the boat. To bind peace, hostages might be exchanged and kept for a year or longer. Peacemaking followed a pattern of ceremonialism, which climaxed with the exchange of hostages, termed "deer" since they were to behave as timidly as these animals.

Most slaves were captured in raids or purchased from peoples to the north or south. Others were the children of indebted men who could find no way out of their dilemma except to offer themselves and as many of their children as necessary to cancel the debt. These slaves, unlike the captives, might be redeemed. Slaves usually were well cared for by their masters since they were a valuable form of property. Yet some reports picture the lot of slaves as extremely difficult. They performed all odious tasks and might at any time be killed at their owner's fancy. Sometimes slaves were killed to emphasize the importance of their owner—for instance, when he built a new house. To gain prestige one man might kill a number of slaves; his rival would be obligated to kill a greater number, and so it went until one contestant had no more slaves. The ownership of slaves apparently provided prestige more than economic gain. The proportion of slaves to free persons is not known, but ten slaves in a house was a large number.

RELIGION AND SUPERNATURALISM The Tlingit crystallized their knowledge about the natural world and integrated it into a loosely ordered system. They thought of the world as a flat expanse with the sky as a dome above the earth. They believed that everything that existed in all this space was alive: spirits lived on the sun and moon; stars were the lights of distant towns or houses. They sometimes named clusters of stars, and they identified Venus. A rainbow was thought to be the path of dead souls to the upper world, and the northern lights, human spirits playing. For the Tlingit, everything on earth was possessed by a spirit quality, which had subordinates or helpers; each trait, every fire, and everything that one did had its main spirit and helpers.

Tlingit shamans reputedly were the most powerful on the north Pacific coast, and their effectiveness came from the spirits they controlled. The usual manner in which a clan acquired a new shaman was for the spirit of the clan's shaman to leave his body at death and enter the body of an upstanding clan youth. Nephews who aspired to the position went into trances around the dead man's body, and the one who remained in a trance the longest was most likely to be named the successor. After this supernatural visitation the novice and certain near relatives went into the forest, ate little, and searched for a sign. The most propitious was to see a bird or an animal drop dead; the spirit of this creature henceforth aided the novice. After the young man demonstrated that he had his uncle's power, he inherited the ceremonial equipment.

Shamans controlled the spirits represented on their masks (see Figure 9-6), and although most spirits served specific clans, some could be controlled by any shaman. The latter category included a spirit associated with the souls of persons who were lost at sea or died alone in the forest. The primary protecting spirit was represented as the main figure on a mask, and helping spirits also might appear. A secondary spirit might be posed around the eyes of a mask, thereby increasing the vision of the primary spirit. A shaman neither cut nor combed his hair, and about his neck he wore a bone necklace and a small whetstone, the latter used for scratching his head. A shaman owned rattles that had spirit associations and were used in his performances. The split tongues of animals, especially the river otter, and the claws of eagles were sources of power; both appear to have been placed in sacred bundles of cedar bark, grass, and devil's club. After a shaman bathed, he rubbed himself with the bundle, and he used it in all his rituals. Among the spirit helpers were those of the sun, the sea, and the crest animals of the shaman's clan. After summoning his spirit helpers, a shaman cured an afflicted individual by blowing, sucking, or passing an object over the locus of the disease, which drew out the cause. Other services of a shaman included locating food sources and predicting the future. A shaman and his family usually lived in a separate residence, and in the forest near the house was his shrine. From time to time shamans retreated for extended periods to intensify their spirit relationships.

A number of charms appear to have been employed by ordinary persons. Made from parts of plants, they were used in such diverse activities as foreseeing the future, attracting a woman, making one wealthy, or improving hunting abilities. A few additional items seem to have served as secular cures, but these were rare and apparently unimportant. In general, it would appear that curing and supernaturalism were shamanistic matters. It is interesting that salmon, which were the all-important subsistence item, were not dealt with in a sacred manner. They simply were accepted as present and were caught and eaten. Even in Tlingit mythology, salmon play a relatively unimportant role; they seem to have been regarded as a constant part of the environment.

Figure 9-6 | Shaman's mask of painted wood. (Courtesy of the Field Museum, Chicago, neg. no. A98082.)

Witchcraft was most often performed by obtaining an item intimately associated with the victim and using it in a representation of the victim in the form desired. If a person became ill, the cause was attributed to sorcery, and the offender was named by the curing shaman. Persons accused of being witches usually were women, children, or slaves. They were tortured to extract a confession or killed if a confession was not forthcoming. An accused witch was bound by clan members and given no food or water for eight days or longer. If the person was a witch and did not confess, death was expected at this point; if the accused confessed, the object or objects used to bewitch a victim were scattered in the sea, and the individual presumably resumed an ordinary status.

LIFE CYCLE Childbearing was prohibited within the mother's home because it supposedly would bring ill fortune to the men of the house. Thus, a birth took place in a shelter never visited by men. During the birth, slaves and a midwife, always a member of the opposite moiety and preferably the woman's husband's sister, aided the woman. Inside the structure a pit was dug and lined with moss, and a stake was driven into the center of the hole. While giving birth, the woman squatted in the pit, holding the stake. After the birth the umbilical cord was cut and placed in a bag hung around the neonate's neck for eight days; the umbilical cord of a boy later was placed under a tree where an eagle had nested to make the boy a brave adult. To prevent a baby from crying repeatedly, the first cry was caught in a container and buried where many people walked so that it would be smothered as the baby grew. The baby was wrapped in skins, with moss for a diaper, and was tied to a board. The mother carried the cradleboard with her or hung it from a roof beam when she was in the house. She placed woodworm burrowings on her nipples so that as the baby nursed she or he would swallow the burrowings and would be neat in later life. A child was nursed for three or four years and was given its first solids after about a year. An infant born to a woman without a husband normally was suffocated. A baby was named after a maternal ancestor; the name itself was taken from an animal associated with the clan. With the birth of a son the parents referred to themselves by the son's name, as the father or the mother of the son (teknonymy).

Children were encouraged to behave in a manner appropriate to adults of the same sex. They were taught to restrain signs of emotion, to be dignified and aloof. They were expected to take cold baths daily from the time they learned to walk and were physically punished if they refused to bathe in the winter. When boys moved to the household of their mother's brother, they were whipped with a switch by this man after bathing and were forced to run up and down the beach. After this exercise, they were instructed by older men in the customs and history of the clan, and they learned certain skills by watching men perform routine tasks. As a boy grew, he came increasingly under the influence of his maternal uncle and performed tasks for this older man rather than for his father. A boy tended to gravitate toward a particular uncle whom he wished to emulate in his exceptional skills relating to carving, hunting, or the supernatural. The uncle gave honorific names to his young charges and taught them clan lore, but no secret initiations took place. The most important nephew was the oldest, for he would inherit from his maternal uncle not only material property and wives but titles as well. Even while young, boys were free to use a maternal uncle's tools with permission. If a mother died, the father was obliged to place the offspring in the custody of the mother's siblings.

When a girl first menstruated, she was confined to a brush-covered shelter or to a compartment in the house behind the heraldic screen. Her face was covered with charcoal, and she was attended by female relatives and a slave if her parents were wealthy. A high-born girl was isolated for a year, and one of lower birth was confined for at least three months. She drank water through a bird-bone tube and went outside only at night, even then wearing a broad-brimmed hat so that she would not taint the stars with her gaze. During isolation her mother instructed her about proper female behavior and taught her clan myths and songs. At the beginning of her confinement, her lip, nasal septum, and possibly her earlobes were pierced by a woman of the opposite moiety. When she came out of seclusion, she wore new clothing, and her slave attendant, if she had one, was freed. The girl would marry soon, and to ensure that she remained chaste she slept on a shelf above her parents' bed. The rank of a person was reckoned through both sides of the family and depended largely on the amount of bride price paid by one's father for one's mother; thus parents attempted to provide a daughter with all the advantages of careful rearing and wealth.

Moiety exogamy was strictly observed, and a match was initiated by the suitor, who used a go-between to approach the girl and her family. If favorably received, he sent presents to his future father-in-law. The most desirable marriage partners, in decreasing order, were a father's sister, brother's daughter, father's sister's daughter, and finally, mother's brother's daughter. In the ideal form of marriage with father's sister, the groom assumed the role of his mother's brother. However, the most common marriage was with a father's sister's daughter, and this was preferred by a young man. Marriage to near relatives served two important functions: to keep wealth concentrated and to provide spouses of nearly equal rank.

A wedding ceremony was held in the bride's house. Here relatives of the groom assembled as he sat in the middle of the floor wearing his most elaborate ceremonial garb. The bride was concealed in a corner of the house and was lured to sit beside the groom by the singing and dancing of the assembled group. The guests were feasted, but this was not a formal potlatch event. A month after the ceremony the couple was considered married. Marriage residence was with the family of either spouse (bilocal), depending on the wealth and standing of the principals. If the couple moved into the man's household, the bride's relatives presented him with property equal to or exceeding the value of that presented by his relatives. A man of wealth might have multiple wives (polygyny), with the first wife holding a rank superior to that of any subsequent spouses; five wives appear to have been the maximum. A woman sometimes had more than one husband (polyandry) but only if the second husband was a brother (fraternal polyandry) or near relative of the first. A widow customarily married her late husband's brother (levirate), and if the deceased husband did not have a brother, his sister's son married the widow. If neither category of individual was available, a widow could marry any man of her former husband's clan. If his mother's brother died, a man was obligated to marry the widow even though he might already have a wife, and he inherited his uncle's wealth. In spite of the ideal that a man should live in the house of his mother's brother, inherit his wealth, and marry his daughter or another person in this line, his father's clan attempted to lure him into its domain. This especially seems to have been true for a boy who had married into the community. When a married woman was seduced, blood revenge might be exacted by her husband, or the seducer might make a property settlement. If the seduction was by a near relative of the husband, the offender was expected to become the woman's second husband.

Gambling was an important pastime among adult Tlingit males, and some men were so addicted that they sometimes lost prized possessions, including wives. The most important form of gambling was a hand game in which one man guessed which hand of an opponent held a uniquely marked stick. The game was played by teams, but only one man of each team handled the sticks at any one time. Other adult diversions included dice games and a ball game in which the purpose was to drive a ball along the tidal flats to the opponent's goal. Boys played a game that involved throwing a stick at a rolling wad of grass. They also wrestled, hunted, and swam for entertainment. A favorite diversion among little girls was to arrange beach pebbles in the form of figures.

In the production of artifacts, the dominant materials worked by women were flexibles such as wool and cedar bark or the root fibers of spruce. Their most famous woven products were Chilkat robes, which were made from mountain goat wool with symbolic patterns produced by using wool dyed black and yellow. A single robe required six months or longer to make (see Figure 9-7). Women also wove baskets, making named patterns of geometric design. Men usually worked hard materials such as red cedar, copper that was pounced and incised, horn, and ivory. They often included symbolic patterns, especially clan crests, as decorative elements on their totem and house poles, canoe parts, and ladles.

To outsiders, the Tlingit (Koloschеs) were not likable. Physicians for the Russian-American Company at Sitka in 1843–44 described the people as follows (Romanowsky and Frankenhauser 1849, 35): "The Koloschеs are proud, egoistic, revengeful, spiteful, false, intriguing, avaricious, love above all independence and do not submit to force, except the ruling of their elders." Still, adults were patient and persistent; they never seem to have hurried; and they became angry only with provocation. During the fishing season they worked long hours, but winter was a time for leisure. During the winter women made their famous robes and baskets; in general, women appear to have had less free time than men. The social position and respect that a woman commanded depended on her personality and standing within her clan; a woman with abilities was listened to by men. Women had well-defined rights, and relatives were willing to come to their defense in case of any injustice from the husband's side of the family. An individual, whether male or female, was expected to behave in accord with his or her rank. Persons were of higher rank if their clan was large, wealthy, and powerful. Still, not all such persons were noble in their behavior, in which case they were treated as though they belonged to a lesser clan. Were a person from a high-ranking clan to behave coarsely as judged by fellow clan members, he or she might be killed by them.

Death, as a major aspect of the life cycle, was given elaborate focus in funeral ceremonies, memorial feasts, and especially memorial potlatches. Collectively, these involvements provide insight into the substance and symbolism of Tlingit culture. The conventions surrounding Tlingit dead in the nineteenth

Figure 9-7 | Chilkat woman weaving a dance robe. (From Krause 1885, vol. 1.)

century have been reconstructed by Sergei Kan (1983; 1986), who emphasizes the meaning behind the rituals and ceremonies.

A corpse embodied specific qualities and was considered dangerous to lineage members. The flesh was regarded as soft and wet compared with the bones, which were solid and dry. Bones were intermediate between the flesh and spirit; with cremation, bones, which were pure, found release from the polluted flesh. A ghost dwelled with the bones and, by cremation, became warm in the afterlife. The fireplace in a house served as the medium through which to communicate with the deceased of a lineage; burning food and gifts became a means for the living to provide for the dead.

Shortly after a death a body was prepared by members of the immediate lineage. The ghost of the deceased was thought to remain in the dwelling for four to eight days, while the body rested in state at the back of the house surrounded by personal wealth and by lineage and clan possessions. The principal mourners were closely related lineage members who painted their faces black, fasted, and observed other customs as they wailed and sang "crying songs." One important ritual was to burn food and tobacco in the fireplace as offerings to matrilineal ancestors. At this critical time, parental and affinal relatives (members of the opposite moiety) performed routine household activities to free mourners from ordinary and thus polluting concerns. Members of the opposite moiety also visited the mourners each evening to comfort them and received token gifts for their efforts.

Following a wake, the body was removed through a temporary opening made in the back of the house or through the smokehole above the fireplace. Males of the opposite moiety cremated the corpse, and some of the person's possessions were burned. Females of the opposite moiety collected the ashes and bones, which were put in a box and temporarily placed in a grave house. Afterward, the primary mourners bathed, dressed normally, and hosted the first of a series of small feasts for those who had helped them. At these events, food and tobacco again were offered to the matrilineal ancestors of the deceased. This series of small celebrations ended when the spirit of the deceased was believed to have entered the "village of the bones' people," the Tlingit term for a cemetery. The dead usually were buried behind the house of their clan, although the ashes and bones of aristocrats might be placed in mortuary poles. In their afterlife, the dead were believed to follow the lifestyle of their immediate descendants. Obligations to the recently deceased did not end until a new box, a repaired grave house, or a mortuary pole was provided for the remains. This was taken care of by the same group from the opposite moiety that had aided the bereaved relatives throughout the wake.

The memorial potlatch, for which extended preparations were made, was given to compensate moiety opposites for their help at the time of a death. A second purpose was to end the period of mourning, and a third one was to transfer the names and certain items of property of the deceased to a successor.

The word "potlatch" is of European and anthropological origins. The Tlingit word is *kueex,* meaning to call or invite to a ceremony that focused on marriage, death, or the investiture of an heir. The hosts sent delegates near and far to extend formal invitations to named guests. When guests arrived, songs and dances of greeting were exchanged and a mock battle enacted. Although a potlatch spanned only four days, the hosts entertained and fed their guests for about a month. The formalities began as the hosts cried and sang sad or "heavy" songs to indicate that their period of mourning was nearly over. Guests offered condolence speeches, followed by speeches of gratitude from the hosts. The hosts also placed food in the fire for the deceased, who were considered to be present. The tenor of the rituals then shifted, as the guests coaxed the mourners back to a normal state with jokes and "lighter" songs. The climax of the potlatch came when hosts transferred the titles and ceremonial objects of the deceased to his or her successor and to others in the maternal group. The hosts also ceremonially presented gifts to specific guests according to their rank; the number and quality of gifts a person received became a marker of his or her status. Some gifts were burned in honor of lineage ancestors, who were believed to receive the essence of the goods. When the potlatch ended, guests received any excess food and expressed thanks to their hosts (see Figure 9-8).

By the end of a potlatch, the bones and ghost of the honored dead were thought to be at home in the village cemetery, and the person's spirit had reached the "village of the dead." Another noncorporeal entity was believed to return to the living to be reincarnated in matrilineal descendants of the deceased, while names, ceremonial titles, and lineage or clan artifacts went to his or her immediate successor. Sergei Kan (1986, 198) writes, "The rebirth of the deceased and the death's failure to interrupt the continuity of the matrilineal group were dramatically expressed by addressing the new owner of the title or the regalia as if he were the deceased himself."

In analyzing Northwest Coast Indian potlatches, ethnographers often have placed the greatest emphasis on competitive aspects, both within the host group and between the hosts and their guests, as individuals or groups vied for rank, status, and prestige. Competition seems to have been most keen among host lineages of nearly equal rank in their efforts to "grab" a high-ranking name, rather than between hosts and guests. Although this element clearly was important, Kan emphasizes that among hosts and guests there also was a major stress on group or individual "love and respect" for ancestors. Finally, reciprocity in different forms was a pervasive aspect of potlatch traditions. Reciprocity between the living and the dead of a lineage or clan and reciprocity between hosts and guests were especially prominent. In sum, a potlatch fostered both competition, to separate, and cooperation, to unite, the participants.

Early History

As early as 1582 a Spanish explorer sailed along the Tlingit coast, but he apparently made no contact with the people. An expedition led by Vitus Bering sailed from Kamchatka in 1741 to determine whether the Asian and North American landmasses were continuous. The ship that Bering commanded anchored off Kayak Island, at the northern fringe of Tlingit country; and although the sailors saw no people, they found a camp with a burning fire. The commander of the other vessel, Alexei Chirikov, anchored off the southern shores of Tlingit country. He sent two boats to investigate the coast, but neither boat returned. Indians later paddled two canoes toward Chirikov's ship but withdrew before making contact. On the return voyage Bering and his crew were forced to winter on what came to be known as Bering Island off the coast of Kamchatka. Here Bering died, but his men returned to Kamchatka the next year with valuable sea mammal pelts. Russian adventurers hastily formed trading

Figure 9-8 | Two Tlingit men in ceremonial garments before 1895. The man on the left wears a painted hide tunic and wooden hat. The one on the right with a nose ring and facial paintings wears a woven dance shirt and holds a rattle. Both men are wearing leggings decorated with porcupine quills. Photograph by Lloyd V. Winter and Edwin P. Pond. (Courtesy of the Alaska State Library; PCA 87-296.)

and hunting expeditions and sailed to the Aleutian Islands in a quest for furs, especially for sea otter pelts, which were extremely valuable in China. Before many years passed, Russian fur hunters and traders had reached the Alaskan mainland. In the late 1700s competition between European and American trading vessels seeking sea otters expanded.

With increased competition, Russian merchants moved to gain firm control over the north Pacific trade. In 1799 the Russian-American Company was granted a monopoly by Czar Paul I. The company was dominated by one man above all others, Alexander Baranov, who had established the first permanent base on Kodiak Island in 1791. The major fort and trading post were built at Sitka in 1799. As long as Baranov was there, the Indians, who respected his bravery, were afraid to attack. When he left temporarily in 1801, the Indians destroyed the fort and killed the members of the small garrison. Baranov returned in 1804, and founded a hilltop settlement, New Archangel (Sitka). Following Baranov's retirement in 1818 relations with the Tlingit fluctuated with the abilities of the chief administrator. Sitka remained the primary trading center.

Russians and shipborne European or Euro-American traders were most eager to obtain sea otter pelts from the Indians, and they found the Tlingit to be cunning and dangerous hagglers. Furthermore, women were usually at the forefront of commercial transactions. As trade contacts intensified, the people were increasingly selective. They wanted woolen blankets because they were trading away their animal pelt clothing; they also desired firearms and were able to obtain them from non-Russian sources. Standard early trade items included axes, metal containers, tobacco, glassware, and clothing. The Russians never gained political control over the Tlingit. The Russians could only try to minimize the violence around the Sitka area.

Russian-era efforts to Christianize the Tlingit were not very successful because of the strong aboriginal religious system, the limited scope of Russian influence, and the scarcity of clergy. A Russian Orthodox priest made an unsuccessful attempt to vaccinate the people of Sitka against smallpox in 1834. In 1835 a smallpox epidemic struck. No Russians died, but nearly half of the Tlingit may have perished. When the Indians realized their shamans could not cure the disease, they turned to the Russians for vaccinations.

Later History

In 1867 ownership of Alaska was formally transferred from Russia to the United States. The ceremony took place at Sitka. The Tlingit were not permitted in Sitka for the ceremonies, but they watched from canoes in the harbor. Russians in Alaska had the option of either returning to Russia within three years or becoming U.S. citizens; nearly all of them left soon after the transfer. For ten years civil government did not exist, and the U.S. military garrisons at Sitka, Tongass, and Wrangell were more often a source of trouble than a means to establish order. The Tlingit clashed repeatedly with the military over Indian deaths that went uncompensated, which led to murders and the destruction or threatened destruction of Tlingit settlements. After the troops departed, the U.S. Revenue-Cutter Service vessels and the collector of customs usually represented legal authority. In 1880 gold was discovered near the present city of Juneau, which brought miners and confusion; still, it was not until 1884 that a civil government began to function in the more populous areas of Alaska.

By the early 1880s, the most obvious changes in Tlingit life were the changes in material culture. Women had stopped wearing the labrets that had begun to go out of fashion fifty years earlier. Bracelets and finger rings made from silver coins became popular. Skin garments rapidly were replaced by cloth clothing, and imported woolen blankets served as capes. The people raised vegetables, especially potatoes, which had been introduced by the Russians. Women were the gardeners. Intoxicants, unknown in aboriginal times, had become an important item of trade. A discharged American soldier taught the people to distill alcohol, and this drink, called hooch in English, became extremely popular.

Tlingit settlements became consolidated in the early twentieth century as a result of population decline, pressure by the federal government, and the availability of better boats with engines for greater mobility. Nuclear families increasingly built lumber houses, resulting in a shift away from house group and lineage solidarity. Women worked as domestics for whites and in salmon canneries. Men often became trappers or commercial fishermen or worked in local gold mines. As employees for whites, the Tlingit often found the working conditions intolerable. To be ordered around and required to work scheduled hours was insulting. Craft skills of old survived largely in response to the tourist trade.

Protestant missionaries usurped Russian Orthodox workers to become a powerful influence on Tlingit life. One of the problems faced by missionaries was the condition of slaves. With rare exceptions, slaves were not freed when Alaska was purchased by the United States because there was no effective federal agent to enforce emancipation. The missionaries likewise took a firm stand against cremation, shamans, the potlatch system, polygyny, and intoxicants.

Presbyterians established a mission at Sitka in 1878, and a school was founded in 1880. Missionaries found that Tlingit women were more receptive to Christianity than were men. Because women were influential in this matrilineal society, working through them became an important avenue of culture change. Girls attended school more often than boys and became interpreters more often than men, which gave them increased standing and influence. Certain biblical messages were readily understood. For example, the sacrifice of Jesus Christ for the sins of humankind was fully comprehensible in terms of compensation. A Tlingit also considered it much better to give than to receive, which again was a Christian ideal, although with a different meaning. They began to expect rewards for becoming Christian. When asked to attend church, an old Tlingit was likely to respond, "How much you pay me?" Parents also expected compensation for permitting their children to attend school. Presbyterian mission schools became widespread and a key institution for the introduction of systematic changes. Instruction was in English, and students were

Figure 9-9 | The totem pole erected at the town of Kake in 1971 is 136 feet high and is the tallest pole ever raised. (Courtesy of the Alaska Division of Tourism.)

punished for speaking Tlingit. It was through these schools that missionaries were most successful in winning converts.

Despite missionary pressures, the potlatch system continued with much of the pageantry and drama of aboriginal times. The predilection for borrowing and imitating the songs, dances, and costumes of foreigners continued. For example, some shipwrecked Japanese arrived at Dry Bay in 1908. The next year Tlingit women displayed a memorable imitation of Japanese clothing and hairstyles. Changes were also evident in the form that potlatch gifts took. Blankets from traders came to be more important than Chilkat robes; silver dollars were a favorite gift item, followed closely by store-bought food. Over the years, the tradition of erecting totem poles continued on occasion (see Figure 9-9).

Expanding Tlingit acceptance of Euro-American technology led to pervasive material culture changes, just as Christian missionaries altered the nonmaterial aspects of life. Russian Orthodox and Presbyterian missionaries alike sought to assimilate the people into mainstream Western culture. After converting people to Christianity, church-centered brotherhoods, as voluntary associations, became a major means to foster culture change. The strength of Tlingit traditions and the small number of Orthodox priests made their mission less than successful. Then too Orthodox influence declined after the sale of Alaska in 1867. The first Orthodox brotherhood was established in 1896, but again, with few church workers, they were unable to make significant progress. Following the Russian Revolution in 1917 most priests left Alaska. Orthodox failure paved the way for temporary Presbyterian achievements.

BROTHERHOODS Presbyterian Indian leaders strongly committed to integration into the greater society founded the Alaska Native Brotherhood (ANB) in 1912. By the 1920s chapters (camps) existed in most southeastern Alaskan Indian villages. The Alaska Native Sisterhood, created in 1923, became a parallel organization for women. Their official song was "Onward Christian Soldiers." Eligibility for membership was restricted to English speakers, and the constitutions were printed in English.

The ANB concentrated on gaining rights for Indians equal to those of whites. The Russo–American treaty for the sale of Alaska stated that uncivilized tribes, including most Tlingit and other aboriginal Alaskans, were to be subject to such laws as the United States might pass. With the purchase, no attempt was made to negotiate treaties or to establish Indian reservations, and therefore the citizenship status of aboriginal Alaskans remained unclear. They were not "wards of the government" in the sense of reservation or treaty Indians. They came to consider themselves as citizens, but the whites in Alaska usually regarded them in the same light as Indians in the United States. Until they were declared citizens, the Tlingit could not file on mining claims, a major cause of resentment. The citizenship issue was forced in 1922 by a Tlingit lawyer, William L. Paul, who was extremely active in brotherhood affairs. As a result of Paul's efforts, Alaskan Indians, in theory, had full voting rights before the federal government passed the Citizenship Act of 1924 granting full citizenship to all Indians who were not previously citizens. (In 1924 William Paul was the first Indian elected to the territorial legislature.) In 1945 the territorial legislature passed an antidiscrimination law.

The original brotherhood goal of doing away with aboriginal customs had been partially realized in the 1950s. The principal target, the potlatch, was regarded as heathen and was deplored; however, as Philip Drucker (1958) pointed out, it was primarily a social, not a religious, ceremony. In reality some potlatch customs emerged within the structure of the ANB. These included addressing persons of the opposite moiety in a ceremonial fashion; fining individuals for infractions; and gift giving by the family of a deceased person for burial services provided by the opposite moiety through the brotherhood. In one sense the ANB served as a new institution through which moieties reciprocated. Furthermore, although the ideal of speaking English continued, the meetings of local chapters sometimes were conducted in Tlingit, especially since the most active members normally were older and less likely to speak English with ease.

Despite Presbyterian missionary success and the neglect of the Tlingit by the Russian Orthodox church, Orthodoxy thrived. Two reasons may best account for this development. First, Presbyterians were aggressive in winning and keeping converts and were closely identified with the civil government of Alaska that the Tlingit justly regarded as unfair to them. Second, and in response to these circumstances, many Tlingit felt that if they were to become Christians, it was better to be Orthodox, because this church was more tolerant and traditional in its orientation.

LAND CLAIM SETTLEMENTS Following the 1867 purchase of Alaska, the federal government made no early effort to address Native American land claims. Finally in 1906 the people were permitted to claim 160 acres, but few did so, in part because the plots were so small in terms of their needs. When Alaska became a state in 1959, Native Alaskan rights to the land they occupied and used were acknowledged; however, no formal allowance was made for any settlement. The state was authorized to obtain title to 103 million acres of land from the public domain, with no consideration of Native American claims. The alarm over this situation led to the founding of the Alaska Federation of Natives in 1966 to press their claims throughout the state. Their first key victory was the federal "land freeze" on state selections. Finally after years of proposals and counterproposals, the Alaska Native Claims Settlement Act (ANCSA) was passed by Congress and became law in 1971. Two factors above all others produced the settlement. First, the federal government was, at that time, determined to "get out of the Indian business," and the last major block of land claims was in Alaska. Second, the construction of an oil pipeline from the North Slope to Valdez could not be built until title to the land involved was resolved. Thus the settlement act had little to do with a just resolution of Native Alaskan land claims.

The major provisions of the ANCSA were that Native Alaskans were to receive fee simple title to 40 million acres of land and that $962.5 million was to be paid to the Alaska Native Fund over a period of years as compensation for extinguished claims. The money was to come from congressional appropriations and 2 percent of the mineral revenues from certain federal and state lands in Alaska. U.S. citizens in or from Alaska of one-fourth or more Aleut, Eskimo, or Indian heritage were enrolled and became stockholders in regional corporations and usually village corporations as well. In general, the regional corporations held mineral rights to village lands. Payments were from the Alaska Native Fund to regional corporations on a per capita basis; the regional corporations retained part of the money and turned the balance over to village corporations and to individuals.

Prior to the ANCSA, because land and property rights were paramount in aboriginal Tlingit life, it is not surprising that the seizure of their lands by outsiders without compensation became a major issue. Originally, Euro-American settlement in southeastern Alaska was more widespread and intensive than elsewhere in the territory, and it seldom had clear legal justification. In 1935 the Tlingit and Haida in Alaska sued the federal government for land losses and sought a settlement of $80 million, but in 1968 the U.S. Court of Claims determined that they should be awarded only $7.5 million as compensation for the *sixteen million acres* of land involved.

The ANCSA included Tlingit claims not resolved by earlier court decisions. Under the terms of the act, the Tlingit and Alaskan Haida formed one of the original twelve regional corporations, the Sealaska Corporation. (The Haida Indians lived primarily on the Queen Charlotte Island of British Columbia, but some of them moved, chiefly to Prince of Wales Island in southeastern Alaska during prehistoric times.) Sealaska initially had about sixteen thousand stockholders, the vast majority of whom were Tlingit. Corporation assets were about $420 million in 1984, and revenues that year were $230 million. These statistics suggest that the shareholders were economically secure, if not wealthy; yet this was not the case. As far as a typical Tlingit was concerned, Sealaska failed them during the 1980s. Mismanagement to varying degrees by Tlingit and white employees caused substantial losses, which led to negative stockholder feelings. Not only were the well-paid managers a significant drain on corporation finances, but their lifestyles alienated stockholders.

By the late 1990s, most Tlingit remained unhappy with Sealaska management. As one Tlingit said, "Sealaska has no soul or spirit." Timber sales brought in revenues of $23 million in 1996, the major source of income. However, some eighty-five hundred acres of timberland were clear-cut, even though the corporation position was that they practiced "careful management." It may take as long as two hundred years for the trees of a clear-cut area to become harvestable again. Even with the timber revenues, profits for shareholders remained modest—in 1996 they received $4.98 per share. It does appear, however, that current management is more competent than that of the comparatively recent past. Nevertheless, most Tlingit identify far more closely with the village corporations established under the ANCSA than they do with Sealaska.

A VILLAGE CORPORATION No Tlingit village corporation is "typical," and Goldbelt Incorporated is less so than most others. It was created for the Auke kwaan ("tribe" in some contexts) in and around Juneau, the capital of Alaska and a major tourist stop. Goldbelt enterprises are increasingly tourist-oriented, but they do provide a good example of Tlingit adaptability to present-day realities.

Auke kwaan had little contact with colonial Russians or with agents of the United States until 1880, when gold was discovered in the Juneau area. The sudden influx of miners, prospectors, and others led the U.S. Navy to establish a local presence to contain white lawlessness. The federal government previously had identified the area as "Indian country," meaning that trade and intercourse laws, including a prohibition on intoxicants, were in effect. Naval officers in charge recognized some aspects of Tlingit customary law and were impressed by its sophistication. However, before long the Tlingit were restricted in where they could live and were forced to settle at the margins of white-dominated Juneau.

With ever-expanding white control in southeastern Alaska during the early decades of the twentieth century, Tlingit rights became a pressing issue. The Auke were a principal participant in the lawsuit that eventually forced the federal government into a partial settlement of Tlingit land claims in 1959. With the ANCSA of 1971, as revised, a village corporation was permitted to claim thirty-two thousand acres; but there was no block of land in the Juneau area for the Auke to claim. They became obligated to select acreage nearby. Initially they logged a great deal of timber from the area to pay stockholder dividends.

In 1998 Goldbelt corporation assets amounted to approximately $77 million, excluding the value of their landholdings. The board of directors included five men and three women. The corporation and its subsidiaries employed nearly five hundred shareholders from a total of nearly three thousand. Alaska has become an increasingly favored destination for cruise ships in the summer months, and Juneau is a major stop; in 2000 about 632,000 people were expected to visit there. Understandably, Goldbelt management has invested heavily in tourist-related businesses. They purchased a major hotel in downtown Juneau, and by 1998 they had four local cruise ships, including one that provided "soft adventure activities." Their wholly owned subsidiaries include tour and travel operations, docking facilities, and sales outlets for Tlingit crafts. In partnership with non-Goldbelt companies, it owns a tramway to the top of a mountain in downtown Juneau. Future economic prospects for Goldbelt and its shareholders appear to be bright.

Current Developments and Issues

For the Tlingit, as with many other tribes, the relative homogeneity of their aboriginal culture has disappeared. According to one observer, Sergei Kan (1989b), three largely generational subgroups have emerged: elders with a traditional orientation, progressive elders and middle-aged Tlingit speakers, and middle-aged to young English speakers. These shifting subgroups do not share a uniform sense of what it means to be Tlingit. Likewise, the capacity to speak Tlingit, and all that it implies, is a major divider. By the late 1990s the vast majority of fully fluent Tlingit speakers were over sixty-five years of age; they may have numbered five hundred in a population total of about fifteen thousand. Few individuals under 40 were fluent in their language. As Wallace M. Olson (1995, 71) noted, "there are many Tlingit who are more fluent in computer languages than they are in their traditional tongue." A logical conclusion is that as the number of older Tlingit speakers declines, many aspects of traditional Tlingit culture will become increasingly ephemeral.

Thomas F. Thornton (1998) justly maintains that "subsistence" has been the most contentious issue in Alaskan politics for over twenty years. Among

Native Alaskans the word refers not only to the local harvest of wild food resources but to their right to determine harvest levels and to exercise general control over their landholdings. Thus subsistence and "sovereignty" are intimately associated. In essence, subsistence issues pit people in rural areas, Native and non-Native, against urban Alaskans. Alaska is home to nearly 600,000 people, about 80 percent of whom live in urban areas. Of the 20 percent who live in rural areas, about half are Native and half non-Native. Therefore, urban Alaskans, who are primarily Euro-Americans, have the greatest political power. Two additional sets of statistics further suggest the scope of the conflict. In rural areas during 1994, the average harvest of local edibles was about 375 pounds per person per year, whereas in urban areas it was 22 pounds. Equally significant, 4 percent of the fish and wildlife harvests throughout Alaska in 1990 was for subsistence use; 1 percent was taken by sportspersons; and 95 percent went to commercial interests, meaning primarily the fishing industry. Clearly, subsistence takes represented a small fraction of the total harvest.

The legal and political battles over subsistence usage among all interested parties are convoluted. A brief summary will suffice. The ANCSA and the Alaska National Interest Lands Conservation Act of 1980 indirectly and directly support Native preference in subsistence matters; about *60 percent* of Alaskan land is under federal control, a crucial statistic. The state of Alaska has argued that it has the right to manage all of its fish and wildlife resources. The federal government agreed to state management of subsistence on federal and state lands *if* they complied with federal laws. The state has not complied, and the federal government has assumed the responsibility for subsistence management on federal lands. The federal government assumed control over subsistence fisheries management in 1999. In all likelihood, in 2000, the federal government will restrict commercial salmon fishing to ensure a more reasonable catch for rural residents. State officials are distressed over these developments, but resolution of the impasse remains elusive. The jury is out.

The Westernization of the Tlingit has been somewhat eased by what might be called the "Tlingit factor." This factor comprises three sets of unique circumstances. First is the sophistication of aboriginal Tlingit culture. The second is the fact that they remained essentially free of effective Euro-American political control until the early 1900s. The third is the traditional Tlingit emphasis placed on trade for economic gain; this key value fit comfortably into the Euro-American concept of capitalism. As a result of these factors, the Tlingit could be reasonably discriminating in their acceptance of Western innovations, and they were adept at fitting new ideas into traditional patterns. As a result, selective sociocultural continuity becomes evident (see Figure 9-10).

As previously discussed, the Tlingit people made numerous early adjustments, such as replacing Chilkat robes with imported blankets and using silver dollars in potlatch exchanges to partially replace craft items. The Orthodox and Protestant brotherhoods provide examples of compromises that furthered Tlingit values. For many Tlingit, clan affiliations have lost their meaning, but identity with a moiety remains strong. Kan (1989b, 406) noted that modern

Figure 9-10 | Tlingit art is especially apparent in Juneau, Alaska. The State Office Building includes the "Old Witch" totem pole made in the 1880s on Prince of Wales Island.

potlatches retain many essential elements of the traditional versions. Old age and ritual expertise are now more important to hosting a potlatch than rank status, as in the past. Participation in potlatches, however, has declined. Memorial potlatches to release the spirits of the dead persist and often are ecumenical. Traditional Tlingit, Orthodox, Presbyterian, and Salvation Army participation may all occur in one ceremony, with little or no conflict.

The regional geographical clusters, or kwaans, have retained selective vitality, due in part to their incorporation into the structure of the ANCSA. Thus corporations such as Goldbelt remain a central factor in assuring Tlingit identity. Similarly, we find that traditional Tlingit artifacts are important identifiers for some clans and house groups. For example, the Eagle Nest House at Sitka has a comprehensive inventory of traditional ceremonial artifacts, and six other clans or house groups have similar holdings. In addition, many craftspersons make Tlingit artifacts for sale to tourists. Some twenty-five highly skilled craftsmen contract with individual buyers to produce artifacts, such as masks, helmets, and house post facings. The best artists may charge as much as $15,000 for a mask, and many have a backlog of orders of up to four years. In this general context, some Tlingit singers and dance groups, especially the Naa Ka Hidi Theater, are widely honored for their performance skills, and recognition of these groups continues to expand. Thus Tlingit culture is far from moribund despite its losses.

Additional Sources

The best relatively brief overview about the Tlingit, past and present, is by Wallace M. Olson (1995). The best synopsis is by Frederica de Laguna (1990). The key general source about Northwest Coast Indians is edited by Wayne Suttles (1990) and published by the Smithsonian Institution. An excellent Tlingit ethnography for the late 1880s is by Aurel Krause (1885, 1956). The only comprehensive ethnographic reconstruction concerning a kwaan is for Yakutat by de Laguna (1972). Traditional social life at Klukwan is brilliantly described in a monograph by Kalervo Oberg (1973). The best discussion of Tlingit totem poles is by Edward L. Keithan (1963), and the best general work about totem poles is by Marius Barbeau (1950). Bill Holm (1965) provides the most insightful book-length discussion of Northwest Coast Indian art. The ethnohistorical studies by Sergei Kan are especially valuable for the Russian era and subsequent developments.

Selected Bibliography

Bancroft, Hubert H. 1886. *History of Alaska, 1730–1885. The works of Hubert Howe Bancroft,* vol. 33. San Francisco.

Barbeau, Marius. 1950. *Totem poles.* Ottawa.

Dauenhauer, Nora Marks, and Richard Dauenhauer. 1994. *Haa Kusteeyí, our culture: Tlingit life stories.* Seattle, WA.

de Laguna, Frederica. 1960. *The story of a Tlingit community.* Bureau of American Ethnology Bulletin 172. Washington, DC.

———. 1972. *Under Mount Saint Elias.* Smithsonian Contributions to Anthropology, vol. 7. Washington, DC.

———. 1983. Aboriginal Tlingit sociopolitical organization. In *The development of political organization in native North America,* 1979 Proceedings of the American Ethnological Society, Elisabeth Tooker, ed., 71–85. Washington, DC.

———. 1990. Tlingit. In *Northwest Coast,* Wayne Suttles, ed., vol. 7, 203–28. *Handbook of North American Indians.* Washington, DC.

Drucker, Philip. 1958. *The native brotherhoods.* Bureau of American Ethnology Bulletin 168. Washington, DC.

———. 1965. *Cultures of the North Pacific coast.* San Francisco.

Emmons, George Thornton, with Frederica de Laguna and Jean Low. 1992. *The Tlingit Indians.* Seattle, WA.

Holm, Bill. 1965. *Northwest Coast Indian art.* Seattle, WA.

Jonaitis, Aldona. 1986. *Art of the Northern Tlingit.* Seattle, WA.

Jones, Livingston F. 1914. *A study of the Thlingets of Alaska.* New York.

Kamenskii, Anatolii. 1985. *Tlingit Indians of Alaska.* Sergei Kan, trans. Fairbanks, AK.

Kan, Sergei. 1983. Words that heal the soul. *Arctic Anthropology* 20(2):47–59.

———. 1985. Russian Orthodox brotherhoods among the Tlingit. *Ethnohistory* 32: 196–222.

———. 1986. The 19th-century Tlingit potlatch. *American Ethnologist* 13:191–212.

———. 1989a. *Symbolic immortality: The Tlingit Potlatch of the nineteenth century.* Washington, DC.

———. 1989b. Cohorts, generations, and their culture: The Tlingit potlatch in the 1980s. *Anthropos* 84:405–22.

———. 1991. Shamanism and Christianity: Modern-day Tlingit elders look at the past. *Ethnohistory* 38(4):363–87.

———. 1996. Clan mothers and godmothers: Tlingit women and Russian Orthodox Christianity, 1840–1940. *Ethnohistory* 43(4):613–41.

Keithan, Edward L. 1963. *Monuments in cedar* (rev. ed.). Seattle, WA.

Krause, Aurel. 1885. *The Tlingit Indians.* 2 vols. Jena. Translated edition, Erna Gunther, trans., American Ethnological Society, 1956.

Lisianskii, Urey F. 1814. *A voyage round the world.* London.

McClellan, Catharine. 1954. The interrelations of social structure with northern Tlingit ceremonialism. *Southwestern Journal of Anthropology* 10:75–96.

Malaspina, D. Alejandro, and Don Jose de Bustamante y Guerra. 1885. *Political-scientific trip around the world* (translated title). Madrid.

Niblack, Albert P. 1890. *The coast Indians of southern Alaska and northern British Columbia.* Annual Report of the Smithsonian Institution, 1887–88, 225–386. Washington, DC.

Oberg, Kalervo. 1973. *The social economy of the Tlingit Indians.* Seattle, WA.

Olson, Wallace M. 1995. *The Tlingit: An introduction to their culture and history.* Juneau, AK.

Porter, Robert P. 1893. *Report on population and resources of Alaska at the Eleventh Census: 1890.* Washington, DC.

Romanowsky, S., and E. Frankenhauser. 1849. Five years of medical observations in the colonies of the Russian-American Company. *Medical Newspaper of Russia* 6:153–61. St. Petersburg. (Translated from German and reprinted in *Alaska Medicine* 4:33–37, 62–64, 1962.)

Suttles, Wayne, ed. 1990. *Northwest Coast,* vol. 7, *Handbook of North American Indians.* Washington, DC.

Swanton, John R. 1908. *Social conditions, beliefs, and linguistic relationship of the Tlingit Indians.* Bureau of American Ethnology, 26th Annual Report, 391–512. Washington, DC.

Thornton, Thomas F. 1998. Alaska Native subsistence. *Cultural Survival Quarterly* 22(3):29–34.

Veniaminov, Ivan. 1984. *Notes on the islands of the Unalaska district.* Lydia T. Black and R. H. Geoghegan, trans.; Richard A. Price, ed. Kingston, Ontario.

10 The Hopi: Farmers of the Desert

Your beautiful rays,
may they color our faces;
being dyed in them,
somewhere at an old age
we shall fall asleep old women.

Woman's prayer to the sun, for
a newborn girl. (H. R. Voth 1905, 53)

The Pueblo peoples of the Southwest may best typify Native American lifeways. Massive pueblos, painted pottery, colorful rituals, and kachina dolls characterize these people to most outsiders. Pueblo Indians, such as the Hopi of northeastern Arizona, continue to live in their desert setting, and most of them have clung tenaciously to their Indian identity. The survival of the Hopi as a people is remarkable in light of the forces that have been bent on their destruction over the centuries. As an example of the persistence of their culture, Christian missionaries began working among the Hopi in 1629, but by the 1950s fewer than 2 percent of the Hopi were practicing Christians.

There are additional reasons for devoting a chapter to the Hopi. Nowhere else are Indians so intimately associated with one locality. Nowhere else among Indians do the past and present blend into such a consistent whole. Furthermore, a wealth of information exists about the Hopi. They have long attracted the attention of ethnographers, resulting in excellent studies about their lifeways. The monograph titled *Old Oraibi* by Mischa Titiev (1944) is one of the best ethnographic studies of American Indians.

Pueblo peoples were distinguished from other Native Americans in the Southwest by their emphasis on maize cultivation, social and political complexity, and rich ceremonial life. Yet significant differences existed between the Eastern Pueblos, such as Isleta, Taos, and Zia, and the Western Pueblos that included Acoma, Hopi, and Zuni. Pueblo Indian linguistic diversity suggests that they had varied prehistoric backgrounds, and they differed by region in other ways. The Western Pueblo matrilineal stress contrasted with the patrilineal emphasis in some pueblos to the east. Western Pueblos were theocratic and less centralized than those to the east. Furthermore, kachinas (supernatural beings) were prominent in the west, whereas medicine societies tended to dominate in the east. Clearly it is incorrect to view Pueblo Indian cultures as uniform.

Hopi (HO-pee), the word that these people apply to themselves, is often translated as "good" or "peaceful." The Hopi language is in the Uto–Aztecan family, and the aboriginal population numbered about twenty-eight hundred. Their Arizona homeland is one of deserts and plateaus with sporadic and unpredictable rainfall (see Figure 10-1). Rainwater from the upland sandstone region seeps into a layer of shale and emerges at the ends of mesas as springs and moist areas. At higher elevations on the mesas, juniper and scattered pinyon grow. This flora is replaced by grassland nearer the valley floors, and in the lower areas desert vegetation, including saltbrush, greasewood, and sagebrush, dominates. In damp localities or along irregularly flowing streams, cottonwoods and willows grow.

Aboriginal Life

Unlike the peoples discussed in earlier chapters, the Hopi were sedentary farmers whose lives centered in small, stable villages. They, possibly more than any other Pueblo people, display an appealing continuity with the past. Their ancestors settled in northern Arizona at least a thousand years ago, and the

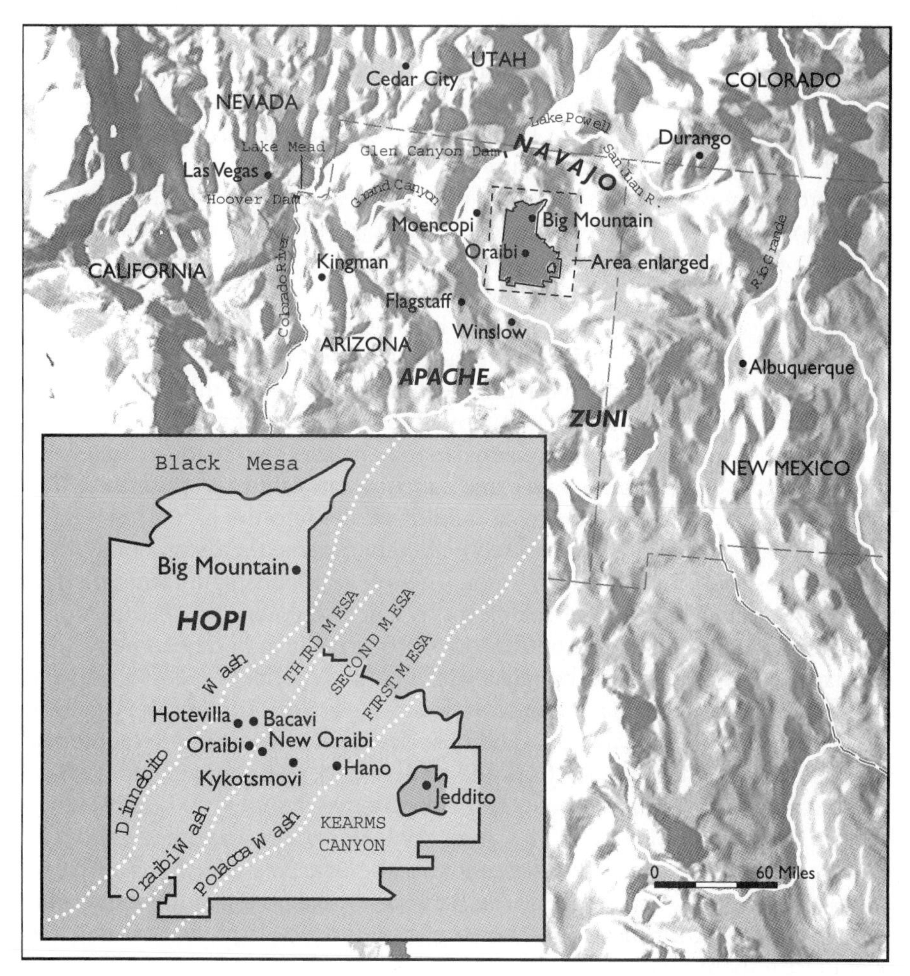

Figure 10-1 | The Hopi Reservation.

Hopi village of Oraibi (Old Oraibi) is one of the oldest continuously occupied settlements north of Mexico.

ORIGIN MYTH Each Hopi clan had its own version of a creation story. In primeval times, according to a myth recorded at Oraibi, there was no light or living thing on earth, only a being called Maasaw (Death). Three caves beneath the earth's surface likewise were engulfed in darkness. In the lowest cave people existed in crowded and filthy conditions. Two brothers, The Two, lamented the plight of the people and pierced the cave roof; they grew one plant after another, trying to reach the second world. After a particular type of cane grew tall enough, the people and animals climbed it to the second cave world. This level finally was filled with people, and they ascended to the third cave.

Here the brothers found fire, and the darkness was dispelled. Here the people built houses and ceremonial structures called *kivas;* but great turmoil developed when women began to neglect their duties as wives and mothers, preferring instead to dance in the kivas. Finally, the people, along with Coyote, Locust, Spider, Swallow, and Vulture, emerged at the fourth level, which was the earth. They wandered about with only torches to light their way. Together the people and the creatures with them attempted to create light. Spider spun a white cotton blanket that gave off some light. The people then processed a white deerskin and painted it turquoise. This skin was so bright that it lighted the entire world. The painted deerskin became the sun, and the blanket was the moon. Stars were released from a jar by Coyote.

Once the earth was lighted, the creatures realized that the land area was limited by surrounding water. The Vulture fanned the water with its wings, and as the waters flowed away, mountains appeared. The Two made channels for the waters through the mountains, and canyons and valleys were formed. The people saw the tracks of Maasaw and followed them to the east. They caught up with Maasaw, and a girl conspired with him to cause the death of a girl she envied. This was the first death among people, the conspirator was the first witch, and her descendants became the witches of the world. The dead girl was seen living in the cave world below the earth, which had become an idyllic place. The witch caused conflicts with people who had emerged on earth before the Hopi, particularly the Navajo and Mexicans. Another deity helped people by making their maize and other seeds ripen in a single day. Of the two brothers who led the people from the underworld, the younger brother was the ancestor of the Oraibi people. The older brother went east but promised to return when the Hopi needed him. After many generations and in accord with this promise the older brother's descendants, the Bahanas, were to return when the Hopi were poor and in need. The Bahanas would be rich and would bring food and clothing for the Hopi. The Hopi would reject them, but the Bahanas would treat them kindly.

APPEARANCE AND CLOTHING A Hopi girl wore her hair long until she passed through a puberty ceremony; it then was put up in two disk-shaped bundles ("squash-blossom hairdo"), one over each ear. After she married, her hair was parted in the middle and worn long again. A woman's clothing consisted of a wraparound cotton blanket that passed under her left arm and was fastened together over the right shoulder. This garment extended a short distance below her knees, and she wore leggings as well as moccasins. Men wore headbands to control their hair, which might be relatively short or long and knotted behind the neck. Everyday male clothing included a breechclout of deerskin or cotton cloth and a cotton cloth kilt, belted at the waist. A man also might wear deerskin leggings and moccasins or sandals.

SETTLEMENTS AND MANUFACTURES At the south end of Black Mesa are three tongues of land, and on the westernmost, called Third Mesa, the village

Figure 10-2 | The village of Oraibi, with melons and peaches drying on the roof in the foreground. (Courtesy of the Southwest Museum, Los Angeles. Photo # neg. no. 24007.)

of Oraibi is located (see Figure 10-2). This is the community where Mischa Titiev worked, and whenever possible the descriptions will focus there. The pueblo was laid out in a series of eight nearly parallel streets with scattered kivas and a plaza between two streets. In aboriginal times the square houses were made from stones dressed and set in place for the floor and walls by the men. The roof beams were placed on the uppermost course of stones, and the women for whom a house was being built prepared and applied a mud plaster to the inner walls. A woman and her friends completed the roof by adding brushwood, grass, and finally mud. Women owned the dwellings, and new ones were usually built next to the residence of a woman's mother or another close female relative. Houses were often windowless, and no doors opened on the street. They were often multistory, with access through an opening in the ceiling beneath which was placed a notched log ladder. Bin metates (milling stones) of different degrees of coarseness for grinding maize lined one side of a room (see Figure 10-3), and fireplaces completed the furnishings. Rooms without any outside opening were often used for storing food and material goods. A kiva (ceremonial structure) was a rectangular subterranean room entered by descending a ladder from an opening in the roof. The section of the floor where observers sat was slightly raised, and the remaining portion included a fire pit and sipapu, a hole in the floor through which spirits were

Figure 10-3 | A Hopi woman grinding grain in a bin metate. (Courtesy of the Southwest Museum, Los Angeles. Photo # LS. 6035-N42082.)

thought to enter. Along most walls were stone compartments that held sacred objects. At Oraibi there were about fifteen kivas, each owned by a matriclan.

The most elaborate manufactures were textiles, usually woven by men. They carded and spun cotton into thread and wove textiles on looms in their homes or in kivas. The fiber often was dyed black, green, orange, red, or yellow. On a vertical loom suspended between the ceiling and the floor they made square and rectangular cloth for blankets. Belts were made on a waist loom attached to a beam at one end and to the weaver's waist at the other, being held taut with his body. Women wove rabbitskin blankets on vertical looms. The most important textiles woven by men for women were for wedding robes, belts, dresses, and shawls. For themselves, men wove kilts and sashes for ceremonies, and blankets, kilts, and shirts for daily use.

Women made pottery, both undecorated ware for cooking and storage and polished and decorated forms for other uses. They collected clay from nearby deposits, soaked it, and kneaded it into a paste, adding ground sandstone to the paste of utility wares. Long coils were added to a flat clay bottom, and each seam was pinched to join the preceding piece and then obliterated by hand-smoothing. The completed containers were dried, and undecorated utility ware was fired without further processing. If a pot was to be decorated, the woman smoothed and thinned it after drying with a piece of sandstone.

Then she moistened and polished it with a stone in preparation for painting. Pottery was painted black, orange, red, white, and yellow, and the prevalent designs were quite similar to those used in early historic times, when old designs were revived after falling out of use. In 1895 an archaeologist excavated an abandoned Hopi pueblo. One of his Indian workmen was the husband of a woman who was widely recognized as one of the best Pueblo potters, Nampeyo. She found the beautifully executed, painted pottery unearthed at the site fascinating and studied the sherds to become familiar with the patterns. She developed a style based on these originals, and it became very popular.

SUBSISTENCE ACTIVITIES The Hopi farming year began near the end of February, when plots were cleared for planting. The time to sow was established by a Sun Watcher, who based his determination on the occurrence of the sunrise at a particular spot on the horizon. At the stipulated time, the men of a matriclan worked as a unit from planting through the harvest. A married man planted the clan land allotted to his wife and her immediate family. Men owned the crops until the harvest was taken to a wife's house, upon which the harvested food became her property. Farmland at the foot of Black Mesa was watered by ground seepage or from stream overflow (floodwater farming). A farmer prepared a plot by trampling the weeds or cutting them with a broad-bladed implement and breaking up the soil with a pointed stick. Maize, the most important crop by far, was planted in holes made with a digging stick. He dropped ten to twenty seeds into a single foot-deep hole; if a planting did not sprout in about ten days, he might reseed the plot. As plants grew, farmers weeded the plots and loosened the soil about the roots. Fields, about one acre in extent, were not rotated, nor was the maize hilled. They sometimes planted beans among the maize stalks but more often raised them in separate plots. Squash and cotton also appear to have been raised in separate acreage. During planting and harvesting, someone impersonating Maasaw, the God of Death, was usually present. Most other Hopi subsistence activities also were group endeavors, organized by individuals or societies to embrace some or all community members. One cooperative, communal task was to clear sand and debris from village springs that were owned by the Village Chief but used by everyone.

About forty plant species were cultivated in the 1930s. Of this number, five species were aboriginal (kidney and tepary beans, maize, cotton, and squash); four others may have existed prior to Spanish times but more likely were postcontact domestics (Aztec and lima beans, gourds, and sunflowers). Five species were introduced during the Spanish period (chili peppers, onions, peaches, watermelons, and wheat); all others were introduced by Mormon farmers or other Anglo-Americans. The Hopi cared for ten species of wild plants, but they apparently did not sow the seeds regularly. Seeds from two species of wild tobacco were sown when necessary to provide sufficient leaves for ceremonial uses. They used wild dock root for dye and sometimes planted the seeds. Fifty-four different wild plants were eaten, fifty were used to make or decorate artifacts, sixty-five were used medicinally, and forty had ceremonial or magical purposes. Although there is some overlap in these listings, the Hopi obviously used a wide variety of plant species. About two hundred wild flowering plants grew locally, of which half commonly were used.

The primary staple, maize, was the symbol of life to the Hopi, and they grew three varieties. In early historic times the flint variety was important because the hull of each grain was hard and not easily destroyed by weevils in storage. The flint variety was so difficult to grind, however, that it declined in importance. The most popular variety of maize in more recent times had been the flour type, which every farmer grew. They raised sweet corn of two named strains in small quantities.

They prepared maize for consumption in numerous ways. The harvested product was usually stored on the cob and shelled as needed. They made ground maize into gruel, dumplings, soups, and a breadlike product. Hominy was prepared by soaking shelled maize in a mixture of juniper wood ash and water, then boiling the grains and washing them to remove the hulls. Maize also was roasted on the ear, parched, or baked in pits. One important food made of maize, piki, was used as bread. They made it from a finely ground cornmeal mixed with water, using ashes as leavening, and cooked it on a special stone slab over a fire. The stone was heated and greased, and the bluish-gray liquid was poured onto it. After cooking, the piki was folded or rolled into "loaves" for later consumption. They often ate it by dipping one end into liquid food and biting off the moistened portion.

Compared with farming rituals, the ceremonial preparations for a hunt were elaborate. The most important species hunted were antelope, cottontails, and jackrabbits. They often hunted rabbits in the late summer, when crops did not require attention. A man organizing a hunt could be from any clan so long as he made prayer offerings to the God of the Hunt. A crier announced the details of the time for the hunt, and the next day the organizer performed further rituals. In the hunt, men formed a surround and moved in until they could kill the encircled animals with throwing sticks (boomerangs, rabbit-killing sticks) or with hurled clubs. The surround was formed repeatedly, and the game continued to be taken until the leader called an end to the hunt. When they returned to the village, each man gave his kill to his mother, sister, wife, or father's sister. The recipient made a ritual offering to the dead animal to restore the game to the God of the Hunt.

Before hunting antelope, deer, and mountain sheep, the organizer, as well as all the others in the party, made prayer offerings, and they practiced ritual smoking. The surround method was used to capture these animals in aboriginal times. The pattern seems to have been to run down and suffocate an antelope. A deer apparently was shot with arrows or clubbed to death but not stabbed. Once again, they made a ritual propitiation of the deceased animal. Coyote hunts were conducted by kiva members collectively, and as usual they employed the surround technique to catch and kill the animals. After a hunt

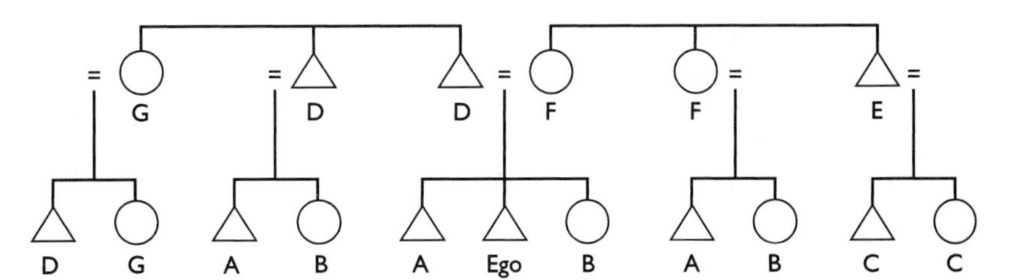

Figure 10-4 | The historic Hopi system of kinship terminology.

they took each coyote to a kiva, gave it a lighted corn husk cigarette to placate the animal's spirit, and spoke to it as a child before the owner took the animal home.

DESCENT, KINSHIP, AND MARRIAGE As already indicated, the Hopi traced descent through females (matrilineal), and grooms always joined the households of their brides (matrilocal). Matrilineages were very important in social terms, and matriclans were overwhelmingly important ceremonial units.

A male individual termed his mother the same as his mother's sister and did not distinguish between them in normal conversation. Father and father's brother were termed alike, but mother's brother was termed differently. The designations for females in the first ascending generation paralleled those for males, because father's sister was distinguished from mother and mother's sister (bifurcate merging terminology). This usage is reasonable as mother and mother's sister were of the same clan, and father was in the same clan as father's brother. In the cousin terminology, parallel cousins were termed as siblings, whereas mother's brother's children were termed as one's own children, and a father's sister's daughter was called the same as father's sister. Finally, a father's sister's son was termed father (Crow type cousins) (see Figure 10-4). The most distinguishing characteristic of the cousin term is the ignoring of certain generational distinctions. The kinship terminology provided the framework for lifelong responsibilities, with particular forms of behavior expected in each set of relationships. One of the most bitter overt displays of anger against a relative was to renounce kinship ties.

SOCIAL DIMENSIONS The Hopi knew of no term for household, yet this social unit dominated and guided the life of each individual. A child was born into this unit and retained a strong emotional identity with it throughout life. The household consisted of a core of women—grandmother, daughters, and daughters' daughters—plus unmarried sons and in-marrying husbands. All except the husbands belonged to the same matriclan; also members of the lineage were those males born into the unit but now married and living in the houses of their wives. When a household outgrew its space, a room was added on to accommodate the newer members. This adjacent household retained its ties with the parent matrilineage, held farmland in common, and worshiped a common fetish (sacred bundle). The lineage fetish was in the custody of the oldest female lineage head, and the associated ceremonies were conducted largely by the old woman's brother or son. These ritual obligations were passed down the most direct maternal line. Common lineage problems were discussed at the original lineage residence, and it remained the heart of the matrilineage, sometimes after it was abandoned as a residence. From a leading matrilineage, with the greatest rights and duties, subordinate (daughter) lineages developed. As a daughter lineage grew, it might become socially removed from the original group and lose the underlying ties. The distant lineages would become separate clans if they created new bundles and acquired distinct names. Members of a named group who traced their ties through the same bundle formed a matriclan even though they could not trace connecting genealogical ties.

By 1906, about thirty named matriclans existed at Oraibi, a number that represented splits as well as the possible settlement there of new clans. The names, including Bear, Bow, Butterfly, and Lizard, were linked with happenings in mythological times or referred to clan ancestors. These ancestors were termed *wuya* and might or might not be tangibly represented by a sacred clan bundle. A bundle sometimes included more than one wuya; this led to alternative names for the clan and probably represented the consolidation of two clans. Clans formed nine larger groups (phratries) that were associated with the mythological past but not named; clans of the same phratry possibly stemmed ultimately from the same lineage base. Members of the same phratry shared common ceremonial and landholding interests, and they could not marry within the group (phratry exogamy).

POLITICAL LIFE Overall village control was in the hands of the Village Chief and the War Chief. The Village Chief was from the Bear clan, and a sacred stone in his possession verified his authority. The stone reportedly was brought from the underworld by the legendary village founder. The stone was engraved with motifs, including human figures, and their interpretation was the basis for a division of lands among the clans. The stone was inspected as a part of each Soyal Ceremony that the Village Chief headed (see next section). The Village Chief had not only the greatest sacred responsibilities at Oraibi but important secular duties as well. He settled land disputes, the most important differences between villagers. His sacred duties, in addition to those dealing with the Soyal Ceremony, included offering prayers for village welfare. It was the Village Chief who remained up late each night smoking and musing about pueblo conditions after most people slept. For any critical community matter, his advice was sought, although he could not compel the actions of others. The office of the Village Chief was passed to a brother or to a sister's son after a long period of training. The Village Chief wore no badge of office, but he had a distinctive style of body painting for certain ceremonies and a sacred stick or cane of authority.

The only person at Oraibi with permanent power was the War Chief, who attained his position by being the most outstanding warrior. He had the right to inflict verbal or physical punishment for nonconformity. On occasion, when parties of men were organized for a community project, men as *kachinas* (gods) assembled the workmen and directed their activities. (See the section "The Kachina Cult" later in this chapter.) A lazy man might be reprimanded or in extreme instances beaten by a kachina. The authority and power of the overt leaders *never* extended beyond the village. No means existed for uniting the Hopi as a tribe; in fact, the only time they clearly joined in a common cause was during the Pueblo Revolt of 1680.

The Hopi prided themselves on being a peaceful people who disliked shedding blood, and yet they organized for armed conflict. They fought to defend their pueblo, and the role of a warrior was recognized as dangerous, important, and necessary. In primeval times, when the Hopi reportedly emerged from the underworld, the Kokop and Spider clans introduced a Warrior Society. Every man was a member, but not all were of the same rank. Members were divided into ordinary warriors and stick-swallowers. Boys were trained for warfare with a rigorous program of cold baths, races, archery practice, and early rising. The Warrior Society held a ceremony each fall, using the sacred equipment held by the Spider and Kokop clans. The two days of rituals involved making prayer objects, ritual smoking, offering prayers, and building altars. A war medicine was prepared and drunk, after which one branch of the membership gave exhibitions of stick-swallowing. For the real warriors, those who acknowledged killing and scalping an enemy, a special initiation that involved fasting and secret rituals took place.

Warfare was said always to have been defensive. Men went into battle clad in ordinary clothing but with the addition of caps made from mountain lion skin to which eagle feathers were attached. A warrior fought with a bow and arrows, stone club, spear, and throwing stick. Before a battle the men prayed to Maasaw and to long-dead warriors, and they sang songs to make themselves brave. Armed only with a stone club, the War Chief led them into conflict. A slain enemy was scalped to the accompaniment of a scalping song, and scalps were carried into the pueblo on poles. A Navajo scalp was considered worthless, but one from an Apache or Ute was valued. The permanent resting place for a scalp was in the home of its taker. A scalp was washed with yucca suds and intermittently "fed" by its owner.

RELIGIOUS SYSTEM The Hopi religious system was precise, the ceremonial round was exacting, and the kachinas played a vital ceremonial role. To maintain the balance in nature and to sustain human relationship with the gods, each individual was obligated to contribute to the best of her or his ability. Through this effort an individual expressed a desire to be *hopi,* or good, but being hopi involved more than goodness alone. A Hopi ideally was cooperative, self-effacing, and nonaggressive, and the particulars of such behavior were spelled out in detail. A Hopi had moral and physical strength and good health and accepted collective responsibilities while concentrating on good thoughts; this was the Hopi Way. Conversely, an evil or bad person was *kahopi,* with personality traits opposite those of the ideals.

Central Concepts The basic tenet of the Hopi religion was the continuing relationship between the living and the dead, a duality expressed in many ways. A person not only had a physical body but also a "breath-body," spirit or soul. At death a soul journeyed to the underworld and continued to exist as it had on earth, with the exception that souls consumed only the essence of food. Preparations for the burial of the dead were similar to those for a newborn Hopi: a corpse was sprinkled with cornmeal, bathed, and received a new name. Because of their weightlessness, a soul could rise into the sky, where it would become a cloud to bring rain to the living. Thus, the God of Death, Maasaw, was in essence a god of fertility. The Sun too was a god of fertility in intimate association with the dead: it spent half of its time in the underworld with the dead and half of its time over the earth. Prayers and offerings to the Sun and to the dead were thought to bring earthly blessings. Birth and death formed an endless cycle; in theory, death held no fears because it represented rebirth.

The Sun's daily and yearly cycle in some ways mimicked the human life cycle. Each day on earth began as the Sun left its eastern home in the morning and ended when it set in its western home; thus the Sun gave light to both the earth and the underworld. A yearly cycle began with the summer solstice around mid-June. The summer solstice began the winter season because it was then that the days began to shorten. Summer, quite logically, began about mid-December, as the days grew longer. Earth and the underworld were thought to mirror each other: a summer solstice in one realm was a winter solstice in the other. Furthermore, when a major ceremony was held on earth, a minor one was being performed in the underworld, and vice versa.

Ceremonies The Hopi religious system required a series of annual and biannual ceremonies hosted by particular religious associations. Each important ceremony was controlled by a specific organization that was linked to a different matriclan. Each association was headed by a male elder of the leading lineage in the clan; this lineage also owned a sacred bundle called the "mother" or "heart" of the clan, which consisted of an ear of maize, feathers, and coverings, as well as other sacred objects. Ceremonies were held in a kiva associated with the clan and at times established by phases of the Moon, the location of the Sun when it rose, or the number of days since a previous ritual had ended. The pattern for major ceremonies was similar. The rituals spanned nine days, during which kiva members were not permitted to eat fatty foods, meat, and salt. Sexual activities were restricted before, as well as during, these celebrations. The specifics of the ceremonies included the use of altars and associated wooden, stone, or clay tablets painted with motifs symbolic of animals, clouds, maize, and rain. Sand paintings and certain fluids with a water base likewise were important, and prayer offerings were left at the proper shrines.

The performance of each major ceremony was the responsibility of a secret society, and it was essential for each Hopi to participate actively in the affairs of one or more of these societies. At about nine years of age, boys and girls were initiated into either the Kachina Society or the Powamu Society, the latter being more restricted in membership. Within the next few years, girls also joined one of several women's societies, and boys joined those for men. Occasionally, a woman joined a man's society and vice versa to fulfill a particular role, but by and large the ceremonial societies were divided by gender. The organization of women's societies was similar to that of men's: they were controlled by a lineage in a particular clan, possessed sacred bundles, carried out secret rituals in a kiva, and performed certain ceremonies in public.

The ritual calendar may arbitrarily be considered to begin with the winter solstice or Soyal Ceremony. The Soyal was conceived around that mysterious moment each year when, in Hopi thinking, the sun rises at the same place for four days and the days are shortest. The principal purpose of the Soyal Ceremony, which was conducted by those males who had completed the Tribal Initiation, was to induce the Sun to begin the trip back to its summer home so that it would bring warmth enough for the crops to be planted. The ceremony had the complementary purposes of inducing fertility in women and plants, and participation was villagewide. The typical smoking and prayers were accompanied by the manufacture of a large number of prayer offerings of corn husks, feathers, and prayer sticks. The kachinas performed, and select men and women danced.

The Powamu Ceremony began with the new moon of February and centered on the forced growth of beans in the kiva of the Powamu Society. After the beans sprouted, they were presented by kachinas to the grower's uninitiated offspring, his ceremonial children, and favored relatives. A child to be initiated into the Powamu Society saw some of the sacred rituals for the first time. This new knowledge was not to be revealed, under threat of punishment by men representing kachinas. Initiated children were permitted to impersonate kachinas, to participate in kachina rituals, and to become kachina fathers (ceremonial sponsors). Children who were not inducted into the Powamu Society became members of the Kachina Society.

Another high point in the ceremonial round came in August of every other year when the Antelope and Snake societies joined for a major ceremony. Together they manufactured prayer offerings, then went to their respective kivas to perform secret rituals. Snake Society members collected snakes to become a focal point of a dance. A Snake man held a snake's head with his lips or teeth as he danced around the plaza several times. During the dance another man brushed the shoulders of the snake holder with a "snake whip," a short stick with eagle feathers attached. The man danced with each snake and then released it on the ground at the plaza. Afterward the snakes were gathered in a circle and sprinkled with cornmeal by women and girls of the Snake clan. Finally, younger men of the Snake Society picked up as many snakes as they could handle and took them to shrines in each of the four cardinal directions. The major goal of the ceremony was for the snakes to carry the message of the Hopi desire for rain to the underworld.

The public performances of Snake Society members have attracted more popular interest among Euro-Americans than any other American Indian ceremony. The reason is that the snake dancers carried prairie rattlers in their mouths as often as they did harmless species and did so with equal ease. Although prairie rattler bites could be fatal, illness or death from snakebite among the dancers was not reported. No evidence suggests that the handlers were immune to snake venom or that the snakes were charmed or drugged. Furthermore, laboratory tests showed that the Hopi did not have an effective antidote for venom. There appear to have been two reasons for Hopi success in handling rattlesnakes. In 1883 a herpetologist visited a kiva in which rattlesnakes were being kept for a dance; he inspected the fangs of one rattler and found them intact. After the dance he sent two of the rattlesnakes that had been used to the U.S. National Museum, and the venom glands were found to contain poison. Thus it would seem almost certain that the fangs were milked before the public ceremony. In 1932 and again in 1951, after a snake ceremony, herpetologists recovered rattlesnakes that had had their fangs removed. These studies suggest that traditionally the Hopi had milked the poison from rattlesnake fangs but that between 1883 and 1932, they began to cut away the fangs. Presumably, as Anglo-American (English-speaking whites) knowledge about rattlesnakes became known to the Hopi, they cut out the fangs to eliminate the risk of poisoning from bites.

The final ceremony of major importance was the Tribal Initiation. Controlled by the Agaves Society, it was held only when this society had at least one candidate for initiation. During this ceremony, adolescent males were initiated into one of four secret societies: the Agaves, Horns, Singers, or Wuwuchim. A male could not be a fully participating adult in Hopi society until he had passed through this initiation. The Tribal Initiation was the most complex of the ceremonies and a cornerstone of Hopi religion. It took place in November at a time established by the Sun Watcher. A new fire was made in the Agaves kiva by the kiva chief, and some embers were carried to the other participating kivas. A figure of Dawn Woman was brought from her shrine and exhibited on top of the kivas until the fifth day of the ceremony, when she was returned to her shrine after "delivering" her offspring. All candidates slept in their kivas. The dances performed on the third and fifth days were clearly associated with fertility; phallic symbols and simulated pregnancies were presented. These events, and many others, symbolized the ritual rebirth of male children into manhood and reaffirmed the integration between the living and the dead.

The Kachina Cult Once long ago, according to a Village Chief of Oraibi, after the Hopi had departed from the uppermost level of the underworld, they wandered on earth with their gods, the kachinas. They were attacked by Mexicans, and all the gods were killed. The dead returned to the underworld, and the Hopi divided their ceremonial paraphernalia to impersonate them. From then on, impersonations of kachinas formed the core of Hopi rituals.

When a man wore the sacred apparel of a kachina, he became what he impersonated, and his basketry or leather mask was the most sacred item of his dress. As masks wore out, became soiled, or broke, they were replaced or repaired; however, this did not detract from their sacredness. The chief kachina masks were the only ones reportedly not replaced or duplicated. It was possible also to vary a new kachina mask from the original without impairing its supernatural associations.

Participation as a kachina was open to all village men under the general sanction of the Village Chief, and the activities of the kachinas were under the control of the Badger and Kachina clans. Kachinas were present at Oraibi from the winter solstice until the summer solstice, after which they were supposedly in the underworld except for Maasaw Kachina, representing the God of Death, who was about the earth all year long. While a Hopi adult did not believe that an impersonator was a god but rather a friend of the gods, small children were told that these were actual gods.

Kachina "dolls" have attracted widespread attention from whites and have been collected avidly for many years (see Figure 10-5). These carvings are stylized renditions of the disguises worn by the men who portrayed kachinas. They are small painted and adorned wooden images usually made by men prior to kachina performances. The figures were presented to children by kachinas and were considered by them as gifts from the gods. These kachina images were hung from the rafters of the homes to familiarize the children with the many different forms. Although kachina figures frequently are called dolls, this is a misnomer. They were not toys but served mainly to instruct uninitiated children about one aspect of the religious system. The Hopi made more than 240 different forms of kachina figures; they fit into six groups, including chief kachinas, clowns, and runners. A figure was carved from cottonwood tree roots, shaped, and then smoothed before appendages such as ears or horns were pegged in place. A thin layer of white clay was applied, and the clay was painted in vivid colors, the same ones used for the body paintings of real kachinas. Finally, feather adornments often were added to complete the figure.

Sorcery To the Hopi, community-wide prosperity indicated that each individual had contributed his or her utmost, and the ideals of the Hopi Way thus were achieved. But what about failures? Why was it that during some years rain did not fall, winds dried the soil and blew seeds away, and the streams did not flow with water? Obviously, it was essential to be able to explain why nature sometimes did not respond to the complex ceremonies. The burden of failure

Figure 10-5 | Model of the Prickly Pear Cactus Kachina. (© The Field Museum, Chicago, Neg. A 95940.)

was said to rest largely with individuals, persons who were kahopi, thinking evil and doing evil; these persons were sorcerers (witches).

The origin of sorcery was traced to Spider Woman, who caused the first human death. Hopi have reported that they believed a typical village included more witches than ordinary people. Witches might be male or female and from any clan; no one was considered to be incapable of witchcraft. A Village Chief or ceremonial leader might be suspect simply because he held an important office. Any self-assertive person was open to the accusation of being a witch because such behavior was not hopi. One could become a witch either by voluntarily practicing sorcery or by having been unknowingly inducted into a society of witches as a child. In the latter instance, existing witches reportedly carried off a related child while it slept and inducted it into a secret society that followed the pattern of other Hopi secret societies. The initiate was taught the witches' art of assuming the shape of an animal to pursue their nefarious craft by night. The power of a witch was derived from association with an animal familiar, such as a coyote, owl, wolf, or small black ant, from whom the greatest forces of evil emanated; quite logically, sorcerers supposedly possessed "two hearts," their own and that of their animal familiar. Sorcerers reportedly worked evil by sending pestilence to the fields, by causing land erosion, or by driving off rain clouds and replacing them with a conjured windstorm. A witch was not content with destroying crops but killed people as well. Murder probably was the most important activity of a sorcerer because it was believed that he or she extended his or her own life by killing one relative each year. In Hopi belief, a relative was killed or caused to be ill when a sorcerer shot stiff deer hairs, ants, a bit of bone, or some other object into his or her body without breaking the skin.

Ordinary people believed they could best protect themselves against a witch, who was most likely a near relative, by wearing stone arrow points regarded as the ends of lightning flashes associated with the clouds. The Hopi did not attempt to interfere with the activities of witches because they believed that they would die prematurely or encounter misfortune. A witch's spirit supposedly thirsted and hungered for the underworld and approached it by one step a year. The sanctions against a witch were not in this world but in the underworld; when his or her spirit arrived there, it was supposedly burned in an oven and became a beetle.

Shamans Some persons harmed and killed people by supernatural means, but others, shamans, cured people through their special abilities. A society of Hopi curers existed in early historic times, but it became extinct before being reported adequately. In any event, curing specialists relied on pharmacopoeia and massaging techniques. Some shamans were secular healers; they set broken bones and prepared herbs for patients. Their rather complex body of knowledge required specialized training, and a secular shaman was likely to pass his information on to a sister's son. In another category were the shamans who performed supernatural cures. These "two-hearted" individuals were supposed to employ their powers only for curing illness caused by witches. Obviously, such a person would be suspect in a sorcery case and considered a dangerous individual in any event. He would chew jimsonweed root or some other plant to induce a vision that aided in diagnosing the source of a malady.

LIFE CYCLE As might be anticipated, the Hopi stress on fertility led to behavior considered conducive to pregnancy. A woman was supposed to pray to the Sun at each dawn and was thought to be most likely to conceive if she had sexual intercourse while menstruating. Pregnancy was recognized by failure to menstruate, and if a woman suspected that she was carrying twins, she sought a shaman's aid to make the twins one. To bear twins was considered difficult, and it was thought that if both lived one parent would die. A pregnant woman prayed to the Sun and sprinkled cornmeal while she prayed to ease the labor of childbirth. She was active during her pregnancy, and she, as well as her husband, observed diverse taboos.

A woman often gave birth in the same dwelling where she was born. She delivered in a squatting position over a layer of sand; the sand and afterbirth were covered with cornmeal and deposited in a special rock crevice. Following a birth the mother's mother cut the umbilical cord, and before long the father's closest female relative arrived to wash the head of the neonate. This woman was in charge until the naming ceremony twenty days later. Note that the relatives of both parents were involved with a newborn. The father was not present during the birth, and he usually lived in the kiva with which he was identified for forty days after an offspring was born.

An infant was nursed on demand and weaned after two to four years, sometimes longer. After a small child was able to walk, he or she was encouraged to urinate and defecate outside the home; if a child repeatedly defecated in a house, she or he might be scolded or slapped on the head. Because everyone slept in one small room, children soon learned about sex. Sexual activities, including masturbation by children, were accepted with casual regard. Small boys were taught jokes that we would consider obscene, and they told the jokes when performing as ceremonial clowns. Despite this casual attitude, young girls usually were shy, and a licentious person might be called "crazy."

Young children were taught that kachinas were gods, and in this role kachinas encouraged childhood conformity. Children were told that giants were coming to visit, and, if they had misbehaved, they were warned to prepare themselves. Girls were instructed to grind cornmeal and boys to trap small animals. A few days later, giant kachinas arrived at households wearing frightening masks and carrying weapons and baskets with which to carry off wayward children. The kachinas cited a child's specific transgressions—having been previously informed of them by parents—and threatened to seize particular children. Erring little girls offered the kachinas baked cornmeal; it was accepted, but the animals trapped by boys were rejected. Parents defended their children, and finally the kachinas left after receiving a gift of meat from the parents. Obviously the entire community was involved in childhood socialization. Children also had further contact with kachinas during formal ceremonies (see Figure 10-6).

There were no formal puberty ceremonies, but it was customary for boys in their early teens to begin sleeping in a kiva rather than at home. A girl was, however, expected to pass through a ceremony before she married. Each year girls between the ages of sixteen and twenty assembled at the house of a paternal aunt of one girl. The event usually was directed by a female who recently had passed through the rituals, and she was aided by two boys. For most of four days the girls ground maize in a darkened room; they observed food taboos and drank liquids only at midday. The boys organized a rabbit hunt on the third day, and the girls spent most of their time baking piki. Afterward, the girls appeared for the first time with new coiffures termed "butterfly wings" or "squash blossoms." A girl continued to wear her hair in this manner until she married. She was most likely to marry someone from within the community (village endogamy) soon after passing through this ceremony.

Premarital sexual relations between teenagers were expected and were formalized in the *dumaiya*. As a boy began sleeping in a kiva, he was free to roam the pueblo at night and did so wrapped in a blanket so that he could not be easily identified. As the members of his amourette's household slept, he

Figure 10-6 | Young children being introduced into the ceremonial round in a Flute Dance. (Courtesy of the Field Museum, Chicago, neg. no. 7020.)

crept in carefully to the side of the girl, who in a whisper asked who it was. The boy answered, "It is I," and from the sound of his voice, the girl identified her caller. If she were willing, which usually was the case since the boy went only where he thought he would be received, he passed the night with the girl, leaving just before daylight. A dumaiya supposedly was secret, but it could not remain so in a small community like Oraibi. The girl's parents did not interfere if they regarded the boy as an acceptable husband for their daughter. A girl was not likely to have only a single lover, and before long she might become pregnant. If this happened, the girl named the boy she liked best as the father, and the formalities of arranging a marriage were begun. It also was possible for a girl to propose directly to a boy during certain festive or ceremonial occasions. A couple did not court unless they stood in a proper social relationship with one another. A person could not marry another in the same clan or phratry and was not supposed to marry someone from his or her father's clan or phratry, but the latter rule was not observed with care.

After the relatives of a couple approved a match, the girl ground maize for three days at the groom's house to demonstrate her abilities as a homemaker. There was no comparable trial for the groom. While the girl was in the boy's home, his paternal aunts attacked the boy's mother and her sisters with mud and water for permitting the girl to "steal" their "sweetheart." An atmosphere of jovial hostility surrounded the fight. On the fourth morning the couples' hair was washed in one container by their respective mothers and female relatives. A mingling of their hair symbolized the marital union. Once again the paternal aunts of the boy attempted halfheartedly to disrupt the ritual. After their hair had dried, the couple stood at the mesa edge to pray to the Sun and later returned to the groom's home for a wedding breakfast. They were now man and wife, but they continued to live in the groom's house until the bride's wedding costume was completed by his male relatives and other men who offered to help. The men prepared the cotton and wove two sets of wedding garments, a small robe, and a white-fringed belt; in addition they prepared skins and sewed white moccasins and leggings. During the manufacture of these items the groom's family feasted the workers. After a month or more, the garments were completed; wearing one set and carrying the second in a reed container, the bride returned home. Her husband informally and unobtrusively took up residence in her household. The wedding garments were very important because they reportedly were required for entering the underworld after death.

All Hopi women appear to have married, but such was not the case for men. Indirect pressure was put on a girl by her brothers and her mother's brothers to bring another male into their economic unit. A boy's parents did not encourage him to marry because they then lost him as a productive family member. Any form of plural marriage was prohibited, but many unions were transient. It appears that over 35 percent of the people had from one to eight divorces. The most common grounds for divorce was adultery, followed by what we probably would call incompatibility. Divorce was a simple matter since it was only necessary for a man to rejoin his natal household or for a woman to order her husband from her household. The primary pressures against a divorce came from a girl's family, because they did not relish losing an economically productive male. The mother and her small children continued to reside in their old abode; an older offspring might join either parent.

The social core of a household consisted of a line of females. Within this setting the closest bonds were between a mother and her daughters. Daughters were destined to spend their lives in their mother's home or in an adjacent residence, and eventually they assumed their mother's role. From her mother a girl learned domestic skills and the norms of proper behavior. A mother guided the most important decisions in the ceremonial life of a girl and was likely to have a voice in the selection of her mate. As a girl's menarche arrived, she was instructed by her mother about caring for herself. The girl was not isolated at this time, nor at any other menstrual period; neither was she restricted from participating in ceremonies while menstruating. Were a mother to die, the mother's sister, who was called mother, replaced the biological mother in the girl's affection. Between a mother and her son the social bonds were not as close. A mother indulged an offspring of either sex, but a son in his early teens soon found his identity with a kiva group. A man's natal home remained the residence with which he felt most identified, however. He returned there if divorced and was a frequent caller in his mother's house. Like a girl, a man identified closely with his mother's sister, especially if the mother had died. A father was not overtly important in the upbringing of his children. A father took comparatively little active interest in a son until the latter's tribal initiation. Then the father selected the boy's ceremonial sponsor, which was an important decision. As a boy grew older, his father assumed a major role as his teacher. He imparted farming and ceremonial skills, as well as advice about being hopi (see Figure 10-7).

The maternal uncle of a young boy was the only male of his parents' generation who was of the same lineage and clan as himself. If such an uncle were a ceremonial leader, a boy might follow him in office, which called for systematic training of the youth. A mother's brother was likely to be the most important figure of authority associated with the boy's home, and he did not hesitate to apply discipline. A mother's brother was not all sternness toward his sister's children, however. He often told them myths or tales about their clan and occasionally presented them with gifts. One very warm relationship was between a man's sister and his son. As a small child, a boy soon learned that he was always a welcome guest in this woman's home. Here he received favored foods and frequent demonstrations of love and affection. As he grew older, he took game to his paternal aunt and exhibited his warm feeling toward her. Sexual relations with this aunt and her daughters were possible, and Titiev suspects that in the recent past a youth may have been expected to marry a father's sister's daughter.

As death approached it was said that a person's body became swollen. Youths as well as most adults left the house because they feared being present at the time of a death. The body and hair of a deceased person were washed, and then he or she was reclothed. After a man was wrapped in a deerskin or a woman in her wedding blankets, the corpse was flexed into a sitting position. Prayer offerings were fashioned by the father of the deceased or another male in his clan. A prayer feather was placed beneath each foot and in each hand, as well as over the navel, the supposed location of a person's spirit. The face was covered with cotton, symbolic of the time the dead become clouds, and food and water were placed with the body as sustenance on the journey to the underworld. The body was carried to the cemetery by men from the house of the deceased; here a hole had been dug just large enough to receive the bundled corpse, and soil was spread hastily on top. Men who attended the dead purified themselves afterward by washing in a boiled juniper preparation, and there was a ritual in the household of the deceased to protect members against spirits. The next day the man who had manufactured the prayer offerings took cornmeal and five prayer sticks to the grave. The prayer sticks were supposed

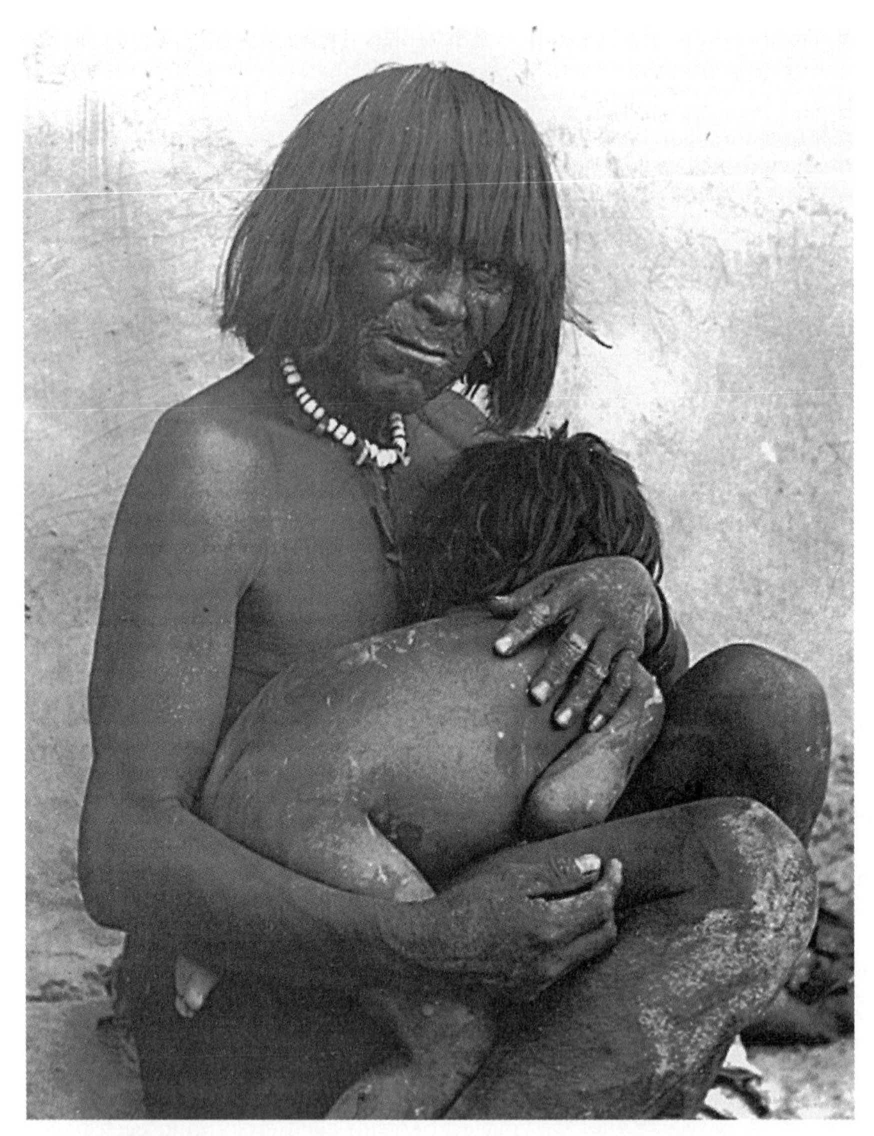

Figure 10-7 | An old man and a child. (Courtesy of the Southwest Museum, Los Angeles.)

to help the person on his or her travels to the land of the dead, and the food was to feed the spirit. A prayer was offered, and the spirit was told not to return for anyone else in the community. Later, household residents washed their hair and smoked themselves over hot coals on which pinyon gum had been placed. All possessions of the deceased were thrown away. A separate cemetery was provided for the stillborn, infants, and children. It was believed that the spirit of an infant did not travel to the underworld but lingered above the house, to be reborn again as a person of the opposite sex. The death of an adult was surrounded with misgivings and fear despite the fact that in Hopi belief most dead were to be reborn into a peaceful world that was an intimate part of the Hopi Way.

Early History

In July of 1540 the Hopi saw the first Spanish. A small group under Pedro de Tovar arrived from the pueblo of Zuni, where Francisco Coronado, the expedition leader, rested. When de Tovar arrived at an eastern Hopi settlement, he encountered hostility and attacked the village, defeating the Indians. De Tovar then peacefully visited the six other Hopi communities. More lasting contact was made by Juan de Onate in 1598 when the Hopi grudgingly submitted to the authority of the Spanish king. The Spanish hoped to make these people Christians, but Franciscan missionaries did not settle among them until 1629. Churches were built at three settlements, and two more missionaries joined the first three. The Franciscans reported great progress, but the poisoning of one of the priests in 1633 suggests that not all Hopi were contented charges. Vigorous Franciscan efforts to destroy the old Hopi religion led to cruel punishments for backsliding Indians. In 1655 a missionary caught a Hopi performing an "act of idolatry." The man was beaten severely in public and again beaten inside the church; turpentine was applied to his body and ignited, and he died. The missionary was relieved of his post, but no punitive action was taken against him.

In 1650 the Hopi refused to join the other Pueblo peoples in a revolt against the Spanish, but they fully supported the Pueblo Revolt in 1680. Their major contribution was to kill the four missionaries stationed among them. The Hopi indirectly aided the insurrection by accepting refugees from the Rio Grande pueblos when the Spanish struck back. The Hopi feared Spanish reprisals, and three villages were relocated on mesa tops that could be better defended than could their valley bottom settings. The Spanish returned in 1692, and when the Indians willingly swore to support the Spanish king, peace was established. By 1699 the Spanish were in firm control of the Rio Grande pueblos, and this led to a Hopi faction that favored Catholicism to request missionaries from the authorities at Santa Fe. A missionary visited, but after he left, the community was summarily destroyed by the anti-Catholic Hopi faction. The men who resisted were killed; their wives and children were scattered among the remaining settlements. Throughout the 1740s and early 1750s the Hopi thwarted Spanish efforts to bring them under effective control.

Beginning in 1755 the course of Hopi history gravitated increasingly toward accepting the Spanish. When a sequence of dry years exhausted their reserve of food, they were faced with hunger. By 1779 many of them had abandoned their homeland and moved among the Zuni to survive. The next year most Hopi were so scattered that the local population was reduced to about eight hundred persons. In the midst of this struggle came the smallpox epidemic in 1781. In this same year, however, rain was plentiful, and the bountiful crops made it possible for the population to reconsolidate. Pressures by marauding Navajos forced the Hopi to request aid from the Spanish in 1818, but the Spanish, who were faced with their own survival problems, were unable to help. The most striking characteristic of Hopi historical contact with the Spanish was the ability of these Indians to withstand Spanish sociocultural changes, especially in the religious sphere. Hopi resistance against the Spanish evidently was not unanimous, but the pro-Spanish faction seems to have been of minor importance.

Later History

The next serious problem was how to deal with another group of non-Indians who began to enter their country. Among the earliest Hopi and Anglo-American contacts was a conflict in 1834; white trappers raided Hopi gardens and killed about fifteen people. In 1850 the Hopi asked Anglo officials in Santa Fe for help in controlling Navajo intrusions on their grazing lands, but the authorities took no immediate action. Most Hopi took a cautious approach to Anglos. Everyone knew the origin myth in which an elder brother of the Hopi, a Bahana, departed and promised to return when the Hopi were in need. They reasoned that perhaps Anglos were the Bahanas, the prophesied whites; but no one knew for certain how to identify them.

THE RESERVATION The Hopi were recognized by the federal government in 1870 when the Moqui Pueblo Agency was established, and a mission school was founded in 1874. The Moqui Pueblo Reservation (later changed to Hopi Indian Reservation) was created by an executive order in 1882, but the land set aside was for Indian, not exclusively Hopi, use. The Dawes Act of 1887 resulted in federal pressures on the Hopi to shift from family and community landholdings to individual allotments. Conflicts with the Navajo over grazing lands intensified, as there had been no boundary survey when the Hopi Reservation was established, and Navajo encroachment on Hopi lands continued. Through a series of executive orders the Navajo Reservation came to surround the Hopi, and about 1937 the BIA reduced the area officially designated as Hopi land to about one-fourth its original size, or one thousand square miles.

CHANGES IN THE SUBSISTENCE CYCLE By the early 1900s, the Hopi economy had undergone major changes. Their primary reliance on maize, beans, and squash continued, but new crops and animals became increasingly significant. The most important new animal was the sheep, and virtually every man had at least a small flock by 1900. Each animal was individually owned, but men herded cooperatively. Sheep were held as wealth and were butchered only for ceremonial occasions. Surplus meat was dried as jerky or dried, pounded, and mixed with fat as pemmican. Cattle were less popular because of their initial cost and because the pattern of allowing them to graze freely led to the destruction of crops. Although people owned horses, they were difficult to maintain. They had to be rounded up each day for pasturing, usually at considerable distance from the village. Like sheep and cattle, horses were individually owned, but men often tended them jointly.

THE RUPTURE AT ORAIBI The Hopi population in 1890 was about twenty-two hundred, of whom some twelve hundred lived at Oraibi. Oraibi residents were divided into two major factions vis-à-vis Anglos in general and federal agents in particular. The antiwhite faction (conservatives or hostiles) categorically rejected Anglo ways. Their counterpart, the progressive (friendly) faction, made concessions to whites. One critical issue was whether or not the Anglos were the Bahanas, who were to aid the Hopi. The hostile faction claimed that the real Bahanas would speak Hopi and could produce a stone matching the one held by the Village Chief at Oraibi. Obviously the Anglos were not Bahanas, and if the progressives accepted them, the anger of a supernatural would lead to a flood that would end the world. The progressives, on the other hand, traced Hopi difficulties to the underworld and witchcraft rather than to Anglo-Americans. An individual's choice of sides in this conflict was influenced by such factors as clan and phratry ties and kinship links to the leaders of the factions.

In 1894 U.S. soldiers attempted to survey Oraibi land and were opposed by the hostiles, which resulted in the imprisonment of the leaders at Alcatraz from January to August of 1895 (see Figure 10-8). Additional factors contributing to the turmoil at Oraibi included disputes about clan farmlands that were being reduced by erosion, the continuing problem of Navajo encroachments on Hopi land, and a smallpox epidemic in 1897–98 in which many people died. Open factional conflict occurred in September 1906. The conservative leader drew a line in the ground and became the object of a push-of-war. Before the shoving began it was decided that the losers would leave the village. People pushed the man from behind and in front. The conservatives lost, and the same evening about three hundred of them abandoned the settlement with their belongings. They founded a new village, Hotevilla, about seven miles north of Oraibi.

Over the years Oraibi was virtually abandoned, in part because the Village Chief was an extremely quarrelsome and vindictive person. By 1933 only about 109 people remained there. Others founded New Oraibi on the nearby valley floor, or they settled at Moencopi. At Oraibi a complete ceremonial round could no longer be held, but the old Village Chief faced the situation calmly as he aged. He maintained that the time would soon come when everyone would abandon him, and he alone would carry on the Soyal. Then there would be a great famine, and following it, all of the old ceremonies

Figure 10-8 | The original caption on this picture reads: "Mosqui Indians Chief Lo-Ma-Hung-Yo-Ma, arrested at Oraibi, November 25th and 26th 1894, for seditious conduct and confined to Alcatraz Island, California, since January 3rd 1895." (Courtesy of the Southwest Museum, Los Angeles. Photo # 20086.)

would be reinstituted at Oraibi. Again the village would thrive in all of its colorful glory. The Village Chief waited and waited, and died still waiting.

Emergence of the Modern Hopi

By the 1940s about four thousand Hopi lived in fourteen settlements. Critical problems included greater soil erosion and a population increase on a land base made smaller by expanding Navajo encroachments. For years the federal government had encouraged herding, and sheep became an essential element in the economy. To remedy the erosion problem federal efforts centered on a dramatic livestock reduction program, which the people resisted, to no avail; and their diet became essentially meatless. Meals typically consisted of maize, beans, potatoes, sugar, and coffee. At Oraibi the kiva-centered life of males declined, and the significance of the nuclear family increased proportionally. This lessened the position of men and strengthened that of women. The net result was the fostering of a previously unheard-of male individualism. Because the Oraibi land base was not adaptable to the accumulation of farmlands or to male control of such lands, ambitious men moved toward wage labor. Another avenue open to individual men was political leadership; however, personal achievement remained disapproved.

One compelling reason why profound changes did not occur earlier and more rapidly among the Hopi was their remoteness from major Euro-American power centers. In sum, Hopi country was not readily accessible to outsiders for many years. Titiev (1972) proposed that abandonment of traditional Hopi life grew in intensity following the construction of paved highways linking Black Mesa with cities and towns in northern Arizona and New Mexico. No longer isolated physically, the Hopi turned outward to the white world. Many people bought automobiles or trucks, ending travel by wagon or on the backs of burros and horses. Men began commuting daily to jobs in nearby towns or weekly to more distant cities, returning to the village on weekends. Some of these men continued to farm clan lands but only on the weekends. Surplus crops now could be transported over highways to be sold at distant markets, and in times of local food scarcity, a staple such as maize could be imported. Good roads also brought increasing numbers of tourists, especially during ceremonies such as the Snake-Antelope Dance.

In its physical aspects, Oraibi underwent less profound but equally far-reaching changes. The number of occupied houses was about the same as in the early 1930s, but larger houses were being built. Cinder block and cement were replacing local stone and adobe as building materials (see Figure 10-9). Outhouses became common, and most people owned store-bought furniture and appliances. The matrilocal marriage residence pattern and clan ownership of houses continued, but a woman no longer shared a household with her mother. When a woman married, she wanted an official American civil or religious ceremony to document the event, because experience had taught that documents were required in any legal dealings with whites. Each bride, even if she married elsewhere, still received traditional wedding garments from relatives.

As is evident from the account of aboriginal Hopi political life, each village was autonomous; there was no tribal-wide political unit. The federal government strongly encouraged them to organize as a tribe under the terms of the Indian Reorganization Act of 1934 (see Chapter 2). Christian Hopi and those employed by the BIA voted to form a tribal governing body, whereas those opposed did not vote. As a result a Tribal Council was created in 1937, but for many years it barely functioned, if at all. By the 1970s, however, it had become increasingly accepted by many villagers.

The consumption of alcohol traditionally was shunned by the Hopi. But some veterans returning from World War II were heavy drinkers, and intoxicants became increasingly popular, with accompanying drunkenness. Social life changed in yet another respect because numerous clans died out and some others were represented only by males. They, too, will become extinct unless outsiders who are members marry into Oraibi. Political life assumed an unprecedented turn when a woman became the Village Chief because the people

Figure 10-9 | Hopi women cleaning corn. (Courtesy of the Field Museum, Chicago, neg. no. 368.)

could not agree on a male successor. Hopi religion has disintegrated, and the Soyal Ceremony is no longer performed. In 1955 at Oraibi the only remnant of this ceremonial event was that two men stayed up all night making prayer sticks for the Sun.

In 1969 the Hopi signed an agreement with the Peabody Coal Company to strip-mine coal on Black Mesa. Some traditionalists opposed the contract because it caused pollution of the earth. However, the Hopi had mined and burned coal as a fuel from the 1200s to the 1600s and may have been among the earliest coal miners in the world. Why they ceased is not really known. Under government pressure, most Hopi accepted the Peabody mine but were concerned about the air pollution from the generating plants. Equally or more critically, the Hopi were alarmed over the use of so much ground water to slurry coal from the mine to generating plants. A vexing problem was also that the federal government had forced them to accept royalties of mined coal that were well below market value. In 1982 the Hopi enacted a severance fee on coal mined from Black Mesa. The Assistant Secretary of the Interior for Indian Affairs vetoed the plan. By 1987, however, the tribal council negotiated a more favorable coal lease arrangement with energy companies that was far more environmentally responsible. By 1998, the revenue from coal mining provided about 80 percent of the tribal operating budget. However, a major environmental problem had become increasingly evident. Hopi and Navajo population growth in the area, plus the demands of coal mining and transport, had dangerously reduced the level of the water table. The Hopi, and other concerned parties, have proposed the construction of a pipeline to the area from Lake Powell, Arizona, to meet local Indian and mining needs. By 2000 this proposal remained in a planning stage.

Recent Developments

Another long-festering problem involves Hopi land rights and the Navajo. When the Hopi Reservation was created by executive order in 1882, the order did not specify that the land was for exclusive Hopi use. The Navajo who lived nearby grew rapidly in number and gradually came to occupy much of the land on the reservation that traditionally had belonged to the Hopi. In the 1930s about 1.8 million acres of Hopi land, from a total of 2.4 million acres, were made part of the Navajo Reservation. In 1962 the U.S. Supreme Court ruled that the land detached from the Hopi had in fact been set aside for both tribes; however, the Navajo continued their effective control. In 1974 the Navajo–Hopi Land Settlement Act was passed by Congress to separate the disputed lands, allotting one section for the exclusive use of each tribe. The act also created the Hopi Partitioned Lands, which led to the removal of some ten thousand Navajo from Hopi land and the relocation of about one hundred Hopi from Navajo land. The Hopi also launched a lawsuit for damage to their partitioned land, largely as a result of overgrazing by Navajo livestock. The suit was finally settled out of court in 2000 when the Navajo agreed to a $29 million damage settlement with the Hopi.

Recent accounts by Richard O. Clemmer (1995) and John D. Loftin (1991) examine modern Hopi developments in detail and with sympathetic insight. They each emphasize the conflict between the attraction of traditional Hopi life and the realities of dealing with the federal government in particular and Euro-Americans in general. Loftin (1991, 84–6) views the Hopi situation as "compartmentalization," a temporary suspension of old values while partaking of Anglo culture and adherence to traditional Hopi values in nontraditional ways. Clemmer (1995, 273) suggests that "segregative goals" characterize the Hopi as they try to maintain their unique identity while concurrently adapting Western institutions to their particular needs and desires. The approaches are complementary.

As the subsequent examples indicate, Hopi ambivalence toward Anglos is manifested in many ways. Fundamentally, the Hopi are opposed to tourists visiting their villages, especially during religious ceremonies, and they are distressed when tourists attempt to take photographs. But the Hopi know that tourist dollars improve reservation economic conditions. Therefore, in 1971, they opened the Hopi Cultural Center, which has produced substantial profits for the tribe by selling craft items to tourists. Furthermore, arts and crafts businesses owned by individual Hopi have flourished from the tourist trade (see

Figure 10-10 | A Hopi from Second Mesa, Alphonso Numkena, makes and sells traditional-style gourd rattles. This 1998 photograph was taken at the Hopi Cultural Center.

Figure 10-10). At the same time, because of pressure exerted by staunch traditionalists, villages and ceremonies periodically are closed to outsiders, only to be opened again by Hopi who seek compromise.

By 1986 about 80 percent of the Hopi lived on reservation land, and soon thereafter most homes had electricity from power lines. At Old Oraibi and Hotevilla, however, traditionalists resisted having power lines in their communities. One result was the installation of solar-powered electrical systems for some households. Whereas traditional houses were made from native sandstone and mortar, nontraditional building materials, especially cinder block, now predominate. Newer homes may look like the old type, but they are cheaper to build.

Religious ceremonies are now held largely on weekends because so many people hold wage-earning jobs during the week. In a religious context, the money earned from jobs has been important because food sharing and gift giving are an integral part of ceremonial life. The greater amount of available cash seems to be responsible for an increase in the number of kachina dances performed. Thus adjustments and readjustments continue.

One present-day facet of reservation life has crystallized—tribal political power. Their government is largely controlled by a small number of Hopi-speaking families and their allies. As the primary employer, with about four hundred workers, reservation government is the major source of steady employment. By dominating the administration, the leadership cliques are well entrenched. This means that potentially capable employees, especially educated younger persons who may not speak Hopi well, cannot obtain tribal jobs because they do not belong to the "right families" or have the "right connections." To obtain steady and rewarding employment they must relocate, usually to nearby cities, and moving away makes them "less Hopi." As a Hopi woman working in Phoenix said, "I want to go back; there is nothing out here for me." Yet the prospects for her return and those of many like her are not bright.

Are Anglos the Bahanas? The issue remains unresolved. Yet it is not clear whether prophecies, which are now prominent among the Hopi, were an integral part of their traditional culture or represent a comparatively recent development. Regardless, some Hopi, especially those on Third Mesa, contend that their actual white brother has not returned; Anglos are not Bahanas because they have not produced a stone to match the one at Old Oraibi. Hopi who subscribe to this position contend that the descendants of their *real* white brother have yet to appear.

By the late 1990s the Hopi tribal enrollment included about twelve thousand persons, most of whom lived on the reservation. Among them an old and contentious issue remains: Who is a real Hopi? Contemporary Hopi identity takes many forms, and individuals cannot be separated into the friendly and hostile factions of old. One good reason is that no modern Hopi follows the traditional Hopi Way in all its aspects, if only because a complete round of ceremonial and clan activities no longer prevails. Thus being Hopi is a matter of degree with countless variations. Can a Hopi also be a member of a Christian church? Are children, many of whom do not speak Hopi, destined as adults not to be "real" Hopi? Is an alcoholic fundamentally kahopi? In an official panel discussion, one man took a broad view of tribal identity: "First a Hopi is honorable, a virtuous person, has humility, possesses humbleness and values. Self respect, discipline and respectfulness to others by treating women and children with special compassion—these are all traits that embody a Hopi" (Martin, 1998). It would appear that a compromise of this order will prevail.

Additional Sources

Two publications in particular provide a good introduction to the Hopi. They are by Ernest and Pearl Beaglehole (1935) and Nancy Bonvillain (New York, 1994). The best works about a particular village are Mischa Titiev's studies made at Old Oraibi. Alexander M. Stephen's (1936) diary offers a wealth of information about most aspects of Hopi life, but it is difficult to use. The best biography of a Hopi man was edited by Leo Simmons (1942). The best ethnohistory is included in a book by Edward H. Spicer (1962), and Laura Thompson's (1950) work is a superior source of information about the emergence of the Hopi into modern times. One (vol. 9) of the two *Southwest* volumes of the *Handbook of North American Indians,* edited by Alfonso Ortiz (1979), includes a wealth of information about the Hopi and other Pueblo Indians in prehistoric, ethnographic, and historical contexts. The book by John D. Loftin (1991) is an exceptional account of contemporary Hopi religion. Richard O. Clemmer's book (1995) also is an excellent source about the recent past.

Selected Bibliography

Beaglehole, Ernest, and Pearl Beaglehole. 1935. *Hopi of the Second Mesa.* American Anthropological Association Memoir 44.

Bonvillain, Nancy. 1994. *The Hopi.* New York.

Clemmer, Richard O. 1995. *Roads in the sky: Hopi culture and history in a century of change.* Boulder, CO.

Colton, Harold S. 1949. *Hopi kachina dolls.* Albuquerque, NM.

Cushing, Frank H. 1923. Origin myth from Oraibi. *Journal of American Folklore* 36: 163–70.

Dozier, Edward P. 1970. *The Pueblo Indians of North America.* New York.

Eggan, Fred. 1950. *Social organization of the western Pueblos.* Chicago.

Forrest, Earle R. 1961. *The Snake Dance of the Hopi Indians.* Los Angeles.

Geertz, Armin W. 1993. *The invention of prophecy: Continuity and meaning in Hopi Indian religion.* Berkeley, CA.

Jones, Volney H. 1950. The establishment of the Hopi Reservation, and some later developments concerning Hopi lands. *Plateau* 23:17–25.

Loftin, John D. 1991. *Religion and Hopi life in the twentieth century.* Bloomington, IN.

Lomatuway'ma, Michael, Lorena Lomatuway'ma, and Sidney Namingha, Jr., with Ekkehart Malotki. 1993. *Kiqotutuwutsi: Hopi ruin legends.* Lincoln, NE.

Martin, E. Bradley. 1998. Cultural awareness activities. *Tutuveni* (Hopi newspaper), September 25, 1998.

Oliver, James A. 1958. *Snakes in fact and fiction.* New York.

Ortiz, Alfonso, ed. 1979. *Southwest,* vol. 9. *Handbook of North American Indians.* Washington, DC.

Sekaquaptewa, Helen. 1969. *Me and mine: The life story of Helen Sekaquaptewa.* Tucson, AZ.

Simmons, Leo W., ed. 1942. *Sun Chief.* New Haven, CT.

Spicer, Edward H. 1962. *Cycles of conquest.* Tucson, AZ.

Stephen, Alexander M. 1936. *Hopi journal.* Columbia University Contributions to Anthropology, vol. 23, 2 pts.

Thompson, Laura. 1950. *Culture in crisis.* New York.

Thompson, Laura, and Alice Joseph. 1944. *The Hopi way.* Chicago.

Titiev, Mischa. 1943. *Notes on Hopi witchcraft.* Papers of the Michigan Academy of Science, Arts, and Letters, vol. 28, 549–57.

———. 1944. *Old Oraibi.* Papers of the Peabody Museum of American Archaeology and Ethnology, vol. 22, no. 1.

———. 1972. *The Hopi Indians of Old Oraibi.* Ann Arbor, MI.

Voth, H. R. 1905. *Oraibi natal customs and ceremonies.* Field Columbian Museum, Anthropological Series, vol. 6, no. 2.

Waters, Frank. 1963. *Book of the Hopi.* New York.

Whiting, Alfred F. 1950. *Ethnobotany of the Hopi.* Museum of Northern Arizona Bulletin no. 15.

Yava, Albert. 1992. *Big Falling Snow.* Albuquerque, NM.

11 The Navajo: Transformations among a Desert People

Earth's feet become my feet, thereby I go through life.
Its legs become my legs, thereby I go through life. . . .
Long life-happiness I am wherever I will go.
Before me it is blessed wherever I will go,
Behind me it is blessed wherever I will go,
It has become blessed again, it has become blessed again!

A part of the Blessingway chant, the purpose of which is to restore harmony and heal. (Wyman 1970, 224–25)

THE NAVAJO are by far the most populous tribe north of Mexico to maintain the essence of a traditional lifeway. There are about 212,000 Navajo, most of whom speak Navajo; this is a good indicator of their cultural vitality. Equally significant, despite centuries of efforts by Christian missionaries, most Navajo still adhere to their own belief system.

The Navajo are possibly the tribe best known to non-Indians. Their blankets and silver jewelry have been appreciated and bought by generations of Anglo-Americans ("Anglo" refers to English-speaking whites). In recent years about one hundred films and videos have been released about the Navajo, far more than for any other tribe. They also have been studied by anthropologists more often than have any other Indians. Approximately 2,600 authoritative articles, books, and monographs (book-length technical reports) had been published about them by 1987. A Navajo family has sometimes been defined as "a man, his wife, their children, and their anthropologist"!

An additional compelling reason to include a chapter about the Navajo (NAV-uh-ho) is their remarkable cultural adaptability. For example, in the early 1860s the U.S. Army sought to subjugate and apparently to destroy them as a people. Soldiers herded most Navajo from their homeland to a distant fort, an infamous episode that the survivors termed the "Long Walk." During the course of their removal many people were purposely killed—including women in childbirth. When the surviving captives were released after five years, they had little more than hope and tenacity. Amazingly, despite continuing trauma, they not only persevered but began to thrive. One key aspect of Navajo history was their relative freedom from political control by Euro-Americans until the early 1900s. Another has been their capacity to adopt the ideas of other peoples and integrate them into their culture. In sum, the modern Navajo possibly are the most remarkable example of cultural adaptation and readaptation among Indians north of Mexico.

Navajo country has both inviting physical beauty and stark cultural reality. Year-round splendor is visible in the colorful canyons and mesas, rock spires, broad valleys, and mountains. Nonetheless, living there requires constantly shifting adjustments. The low and erratic rainfall, sudden torrents from occasional storms, windstorms, the possibility of heavy snowfall, the high salt content of most soils, and expanses with little vegetation posed cultural challenges. In the Navajo portion of the Colorado Plateau, the landscape is high, ranging from about 3,000 to 10,000 feet above sea level. At lesser elevations grama grass, a coarse western grass, prevails, but where there is water cottonwood and willows thrive. At higher elevations pine or pine and juniper dominate the mountainsides. A salient climatic feature is the low precipitation, sometimes as much as ten inches a year but more often considerably less. In the many small valleys, groundwater encourages the growth of tumbleweeds, which soon turn brown and blow away. This weed, a thistle, was accidentally introduced to the United States from Europe in 1873.

Fauna played an early and critical role in Navajo economic life. In addition to small game, such as cottontails and jackrabbits (actually hares), antelope and deer were important for food and hides. Bobcats, coyotes, black bears, and wolves were numbered among the predators. One touchstone of Navajo survival has been their capacity to exploit the resources in varied ecological zones.

This chapter is presented in a different format than are those about the other tribes for a number of reasons. First, and most important, the Navajo did not appear as a clearly distinct tribe until around A.D. 1725, some 185 years after the Spanish first arrived in the Southwest. Hence, we cannot examine aboriginal Navajo life in depth. Second, in their historical emergence the Navajo absorbed so many Indians from other tribes that they justly have been identified as "biological and cultural hybrids" by Garrick Bailey and Roberta Glenn Bailey (1986, 15). Third, in the process of assimilating foreign elements, both Indian and European, the Navajo reworked them into a distinct configuration. Their culture cannot be understood without an appreciation of these factors. Therefore, the Navajo are introduced in an ethnohistorical account to emphasize their cultural "layering."

The Background

The Navajo (Navaho) call themselves Dine, meaning "the people." They identify northwestern New Mexico, their original home in the Southwest, as Dinetah, or "land of the people." The word *Navaho* entered English from Spanish and is possibly derived from a Tewa Indian word that refers indirectly to cultivated fields. Despite a wealth of information about the Navajo, we know surprisingly little about their ancestors before they arrived in the Southwest. In linguistic terms, they belong to the Nadene language family and the Athapaskan subfamily. Most Athapaskans live and continue to live in a vast inland region of northwestern Canada (see Chapter 4) and interior Alaska. The close early historic association between the Navajo and the Apache as distinct populations creates confusion, yet they both entered the Southwest from the north and emerged as a distinct language subgroup, Apachean.

FILTERING SOUTH We justifiably think of human "migrations" as significant movements from one place to another. The migrants usually are numerous and their destination is known. In these terms, the Navajo and many other people did not migrate. Instead, small family groups or bands typically moved from one watershed to the next. They had no distant target destination in mind because they had no knowledge about far-off places. Why did they move? The reasons usually cited are food stress, overpopulation, disease, and internal or external conflicts. The northern ancestors of the Navajo may have responded to each of these conditions on their journey southward. They did *not* move south in search of a warmer land. They were as yet unaware that warmer land existed.

Neither the ancestral Navajo route to the Southwest nor the time of their arrival has been established with precision. When the precursors of the Navajo

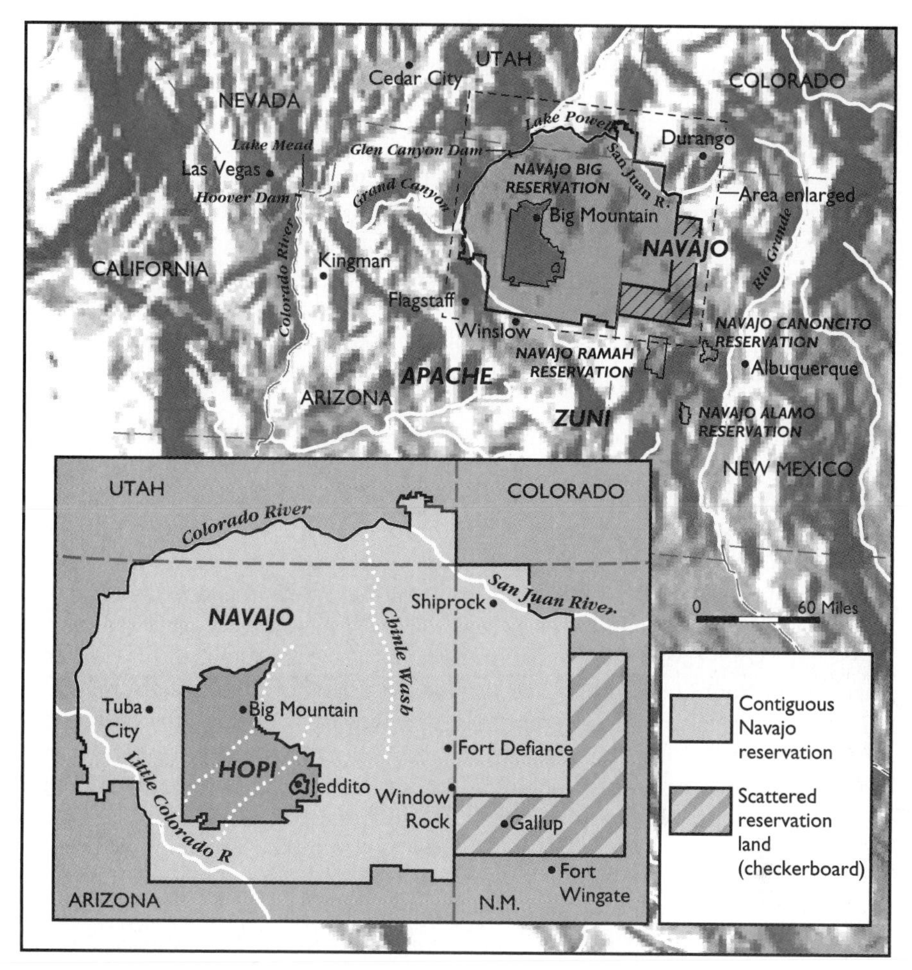

Figure 11-1 | Historic homeland of the Navajo Indians.

lived in the subarctic, they obviously adjusted to local conditions. Probable adaptations included a social life based on small family groups closely related by blood and marriage. Hunting dominated their economy, and their material culture included tailor-made garments and cone-shaped dwellings. They may have begun to leave the far north around A.D. 1000 and may have descended along the eastern flank of the Rocky Mountains. Along the way, perhaps in the Plains, they learned about farming. Shortly before A.D. 1600 they appear to have arrived in Dinetah as a populous Athapaskan group but not as a distinct Navajo tribe (see Figure 11-1). A competing theory suggests that the Navajo presence in the Southwest goes back further. They may have entered the area and intermarried with the Anasazi (prehistoric Pueblo Indians) before A.D. 1100. If so, the blending of Athapaskan and Pueblo cultures into the historic Navajo may have taken place earlier than is generally believed.

THE SPANISH AND PUEBLO IMPACT The Spanish era in the Southwest began with the Coronado Expedition of 1540 and ended in 1846 with the inception of the Anglo-American era. Reasonably clear evidence of direct Athapaskan–Spanish contact dates from 1582. Initially, relations were friendly, but soon conflict arose over the fate of captives held by the Indians. One of the markers of emerging Navajo culture became evident: they were aggressive and successful raiders for captives, edibles, and loot. Other early markers included trade with varied tribes and the cultivation of maize (corn) as an important food.

Spanish colonialism in New Mexico began in 1598, and Roman Catholic missions soon were established at pueblos; but missions to the Athapaskans failed. Athapaskans were soon raiding both Spanish and Pueblo communities for livestock, which they usually killed for food. In the Pueblo Revolt of 1680, the Spanish settlements were destroyed, some four hundred colonists were killed, and the survivors fled south. In 1692 the Spanish returned in force to reestablish themselves and seek revenge. The Spanish killed many Pueblo Indians and sold captives into slavery. At this juncture, thousands of Pueblo dwellers in New Mexico fled their homes, and most of them sought refuge in Dinetah. Athapaskan contact with these refugees was critical in the emergence of the Navajo. Pueblo refugees introduced weaving, possibly pottery, and a host of religious concepts, including ceremonial masks and sand paintings. Some modern Navajo clans originated at this time by assimilating particular Pueblo populations. From the Spanish they began to learn the complexities of herding goats, sheep, horses, and cattle. It also was from the Spanish that the proto-Navajo began to learn to process metal.

By 1696 the Spanish once again were entrenched in New Mexico, but Indians continued to raid their settlements. The Athapaskans in turn were raided by the Ute Indians, who drove them south and west from Dinetah. During these years, around 1725, Navajo tribal identity was emerging. By the late 1700s they had increasingly turned from hunting and raising maize at homesteads to a more mobile lifestyle, with herding as a major economic focus. The mobility inherent in a herding economy, especially after horses were captured and raised in quantity for riding, enabled the Navajo to become even more formidable raiders. Peaceful negotiations with the Spanish seldom lasted for long, and the same was true after Mexico won independence in 1821. Because the Navajo had no overall political unity, some bands would make peace with the Spanish and Mexicans, whereas other bands continued to raid. The Navajo had become an independent people.

ANGLO-AMERICAN CONTROL In 1846 the United States seized New Mexico and inherited confrontations with Navajo raiders. In the early history of Na-

Figure 11-2 | A watercolor portrait of Narbona made from a sketch on the day he was killed. (Courtesy of the Ewell Sale Stewart Library, the Academy of Natural Sciences of Philadelphia, Ms. Coll. 146, no. 44 Kern.)

vajo relations with Anglos, no date compares with August 31, 1849. An Indian agent, along with Colonel John Washington of the U.S. Army and his troops, met with a group of Navajo, including Narbona, a leader who sought peace with the Anglos. A disagreement arose when a Mexican man who was with the troops said he saw a horse that had been stolen from him. Washington demanded that the horse be returned to the Mexican. The Navajo refused and had begun to leave when the soldiers were ordered to fire on them. Seven Navajo were killed, including Narbona, who was shot in the back and scalped. No official action was taken against Washington, and Navajo mistrust of Anglos appears to have intensified. (See Figure 11-2 for a portrait of Narbona made on the day he was killed.)

In the first four years of Anglo-American control of New Mexico, an estimated 450,000 sheep were seized by the Navajo and Apache from Hispanic and Anglo settlements. Neither peace conferences nor military expeditions could stem the raids. The U.S. Army response was to build Fort Defiance deep within Navajo country in 1851. It was attacked unsuccessfully by the Navajo in 1860 and temporarily abandoned in 1861 at the beginning of the Civil War. Until the army returned there in 1863, the Navajo and other Indians, Anglos, and Hispanics fought for revenge, animals, slaves, and booty. By then the Navajo may have had 300,000 herd animals.

THE LONG WALK By the early 1860s the Navajo transformation from hunters and relatively sedentary farmers to mobile herders, raiders, and farmers was well developed. Most Navajo appear to have favored peace with the United States, but they were hostile to many other Indians in the region and to the Hispanics. Unfortunately, federal Indian policy was inconsistent and dominated locally by anti-Navajo military officers. One reason behind the periodic belligerence of the Navajo was that slave traders, including Hispanics, were seizing so many children. Brigadier General James H. Carleton, the commander of the U.S. Army troops, was determined to remove the Navajo from the 30,000 square miles they occupied and relocate them to Fort Sumner (Bosque Redondo) in New Mexico. The Long Walk of some 300 miles, beginning in 1863, was one of the most disreputable actions by the U.S. military against Indians. The army pursued a scorched-earth policy so that the Navajo had little food and few places where they could escape. They were herded to Fort Sumner. Those who could not keep up with the others were shot and killed, whether they were women giving birth, the ill, or individuals who paused to help another captive. About nine thousand Navajo were driven to Bosque Redondo. As many as two thousand Navajo may have avoided capture by the military, but some of them were found by slave traders and sold. At least another two thousand died during the Long Walk or at Bosque Redondo (see Figure 11-3).

Fort Sumner was located in an area without adequate food or water and ill adapted to farming, which was intended to help provision the prisoners. The army was poorly prepared to house and feed so many people in such a bleak setting. The prisoners were homesick; some became desperately ill, and some starved to death. They were raided by their enemies. Navajo boys reportedly went to where horses and mules were corralled, rooted around for undigested corn, and roasted it as food.

The army effort to transform captives into subsistence farmers failed. When they did plant crops, insects, disease, and drought led to repeated crop failures. As a result, the federal government spent more than $1 million a year to provision the captives, but the rations provided made many of them ill. Finally, the government decided to return the Navajo to their homeland because keeping them captive was a financial burden. A treaty was arranged with the cooperation of a prominent leader, Barboncito; it was ratified by the U.S. Congress in 1868. The return trip of the Navajo was not without hardships. Children rode in wagons, some adults rode horses, and others walked.

This is an appropriate context in which to consider Navajo "warfare" in brief. What has been called warfare among them should more properly be termed *raiding;* conflicts typically involved a small number of warriors who approached an enemy covertly to seize livestock. True battles were rare. Men developed many skills to become successful raiders. They became adept at handling bows, riding horses, tracking, controlling livestock, and performing the religious rituals associated with warfare. Men who aspired to be raid leaders underwent a prolonged apprenticeship under an older man who knew one or more highly complex war rituals. A leader organized a small group of fam-

Figure 11-3 | Navajo are guarded by a soldier at Fort Sumner following the Long Walk. (Courtesy of the National Archives: U.S. Signal Corps Coll.: 111-SC 87964.)

ily and friends to form a raiding party. As preparation, warriors often had a medicine man (a singer) perform an elaborate ceremony (a sing, or chant way) called the Enemyway. More often, an Enemyway was performed to purify returning warriors and to protect them from ghost sickness as a result of contact with the spirits of slain enemies. A large number of people from a warrior's clan would attend, requiring the warrior's family to slaughter many sheep as food. Outsiders referred to the Enemyway as the "Squaw Dance" because in the social dancing that accompanied the ceremony, women chose dancing partners from among the men.

A small party of raiders set out on foot, hoping to return in a few days with at least as many horses as raiders and driving home a herd of sheep. They never wiped out an enemy's herd, however, so that it would eventually be replenished for future raids.

RESERVATION HISTORY TO WORLD WAR I In their excellent study of the Navajo reservations up to 1975, Garrick Bailey and Roberta Glenn Bailey (1986) described the changes in insightful detail. The original reservation in northwestern New Mexico and northeastern Arizona, created by the treaty in 1868, included about 10 percent of what had been Navajo country before their confinement at Fort Sumner. Because their land base was so much reduced, federal administrators permitted Navajo to live in adjacent areas. The resettlement program encouraged Navajo self-sufficiency because the government feared that they would revert to raiding.

This is not to say that few problems existed along the way. Scattered over about 25,000 square miles, the federal government had little control over the people. The inadequate staff at the administrative centers of Fort Defiance and Fort Wingate led federal agents to appoint "chiefs" to act on their behalf. These charismatic leaders, known to the Navajo as "big men," became powerful because they distributed goods guaranteed by treaty. This arrangement, however, ended in 1879. When some Navajo resumed raiding, the government turned to the big men and hired tribal police to curb the raiders, a combination that was reasonably successful.

After resettlement the people survived by hunting and collecting plant products. Initially, they seldom killed domestic animals for meat. Before long, hunting and gathering depleted local food sources, and goats became an important edible. Goats, who often bore two offspring at a time, were a good source of milk, cheese, and meat. Sheep began to multiply and eventually became the key herd animal, providing meat and wool that was woven into blankets and garments to wear or to trade. Horses, mules, and burros were ridden and provided a source of meat, but cattle were unimportant.

Trade with other Indians and Hispanics flourished and expanded as Navajo blankets became a major item for barter. Trading changed in character once Anglo traders on the reservation were licensed by the federal government in 1868. Initially, the people were poor; annuity payments did not begin to meet their needs. At the same time, local resources were overexploited. A case in point is the supply of skins used for moccasins. The people traditionally killed deer and used these skins to make moccasins, but hunting pressure soon depleted the deer population. Neither goat nor sheep skins were acceptable substitutes. At this time, however, Navajo sheep herds were increasing rather rapidly, and as a result they were able to exchange sheep wool, both with other Indians and at trading posts, for buckskins. Around this time, too, the Anglo-American demand for wool was increasing, and the railroad, which reached western New Mexico in 1881, provided an economical means to ship raw wool east to be processed. Before long the wool trade expanded dramatically, and trading posts both on and near the reservation became numerous and relatively stable enterprises.

By the early 1890s the Navajo owned an estimated 1,700,000 sheep and goats; they were also considered the best weavers in the region. Their blankets had long been a premium craft item, but they also produced a variety of other woven products, such as ponchos, saddle blankets, sash belts, and women's dresses, both for their own use and for trading. They made use of changes in weaving materials and techniques introduced by Anglos, including commercial yarns and dyes and manufactured wool cards (to straighten tangled fibers and thus prepare the wool for spinning). These developments increased and modified the productivity of women, who were the weavers. A new market arose after a railroad was built through the southern sector of their country, thereby introducing tourists as customers for blankets and silverwork.

The Navajo learned the rudiments of silverwork from the Spanish, and the quality of Navajo jewelry grew in the 1870s as the inventory of production tools improved. In addition to and equally important as its appeal to the tourist trade, silver jewelry became a significant way for the Navajo to concentrate their wealth. In the 1880s they developed a pawn system with traders. Silverwork was pawned for goods in times of economic stress and was redeemed as individuals became more affluent.

Navajo assimilation into the greater Anglo-American society became a long-range federal policy. Under the terms of the 1868 treaty, schools were to be provided for children, but the dispersed nature of the Navajo population and the limited federal resources allotted made this goal unrealistic. The Presbyterians founded a day school at Fort Defiance in 1869, but it was a failure, as was a local boarding school. Only a small number of children attended the Carlisle Indian School in Pennsylvania during the 1880s, in part because the people objected to sending their children so far away. By 1892 there were about 18,000 Navajo, but less than one hundred children attended school. Around this time only about fifty Navajo spoke English, and fewer still could read and write. Formal education obviously had failed to this point.

In the late nineteenth century a multitude of events over which the Navajo had no control impinged on their lives. The federal government granted land to railroads in a checkerboard pattern, along a right-of-way in the vicinity of Navajo lands. The eventual illegal exclusion of Navajo from public lands, the arrival of Anglo and Hispanic farmers and herders in their midst, and an expansion of the cattle industry by whites each had negative consequences. Furthermore, an increase in the Navajo population, expansion of their herds, and overgrazing by Navajo and non-Navajo stock created environmental problems.

The last decades of the nineteenth century proved a disaster. With the national economic Panic of 1893, livestock and wool prices fell precipitously. Repeated dry years and heavy snowfalls in Navajo country led to an alarming decline in goat and sheep herds; droughts resulted in crop failures. Many Navajo went hungry or starved despite considerable government aid. These hard times continued into the early 1900s. Overgrazing and competition with outsiders for land meant that most Navajo could no longer depend primarily on herds as their subsistence base. They developed alternative economic strategies. Gradually they improved the breeding stock of sheep, intensified farming activities, and turned increasingly to wage labor as an income supplement.

Federal control over reservation life became far more intense in the late 1800s. The General Allotment Act (Dawes Act) of 1887, as discussed in Chapter 2 and elsewhere, was a concerted federal effort to destroy the reservation land base and assimilate Indians into the general population. The act had relatively little immediate impact on the Navajo, but federal domination increased as six regional administrative centers were created by 1909. Additionally, in the early 1900s the political appointees in charge of Indian reservations began to be replaced by career civil servants, who usually were more rigid in furthering federal policies. Federal agents sought to eliminate childhood marriages, plural marriages, and other "vices," but with poor results.

Navajo–Anglo conflicts varied from one sector of the reservation to another because of localized conditions. Throughout much of the reservation,

Indians complained about their inability to graze stock on public lands and their restricted access to water. They were also concerned that the size of the reservation was inadequate for their needs, especially compared with the areas traditionally exploited. Reservation crowding became more acute as the population increased; by 1900 there were about 21,000 Navajo. The land problem was partially and temporarily alleviated by repeated expansion of the reservation. By the 1910s some Navajo claimed land allotments under the Dawes Act despite strong opposition from local whites, who anticipated that one day the reservation would be abandoned by the federal government and they would be able to homestead most of the land. When Arizona and New Mexico became states in 1912, Anglo political power vastly increased at the expense of Indians.

As mentioned previously, Navajo blankets had long been a major craft item both for personal use and to trade with other Indians. Blanket designs include patterns based on Pueblo Indian, Spanish, and Navajo designs (see Figure 11-4). By the 1890s, with the encouragement of trading post owners, weavers began to produce textiles for the Anglo market. Rug weaving soon had a major impact on reservation economic life following changes in weaving styles. An early "rug" measured about four by six feet, and many actually were blankets or ponchos sold as rugs by traders. The Santa Fe Railroad and the Fred Harvey Company were instrumental in fostering the Anglo passion for Navajo crafts. Navajo rugs and, to a lesser extent, silverwork designed for the Anglo market began to be sold in stores that featured Indian crafts. In 1903 the Navajo may have sold as many as 50,000 blankets and may have earned as much as $350,000 from their sale. The market continued to expand until around 1920, then declined during the Great Depression.

| Traditional Life

The preceding summary of Navajo ethnohistory before World War I points up a major problem when attempting to describe their "traditional life." Over more than two hundred years of Navajo tribal identity, the people changed repeatedly and dramatically. First they were hunters, farmers, and raiders who shifted to herding and then to herding supplemented by wage labor, which becomes increasingly prominent. In becoming "Navajo" they were profoundly influenced by the Spanish, Pueblo Indians, and Anglo-Americans, as previously emphasized. No comprehensive Navajo ethnography appeared until after they began to be dominated by the federal government. Hence, a "typical and traditional year" cannot be presented. Instead, the account in this chapter represents a mixture of customs both old and relatively new. The emphasis in this ethnographic reconstruction is on the decades surrounding the year 1900.

ORIGIN MYTH Numerous varying Navajo accounts record their creation and emergence as a people. Narrators of and listeners to these tales accept the

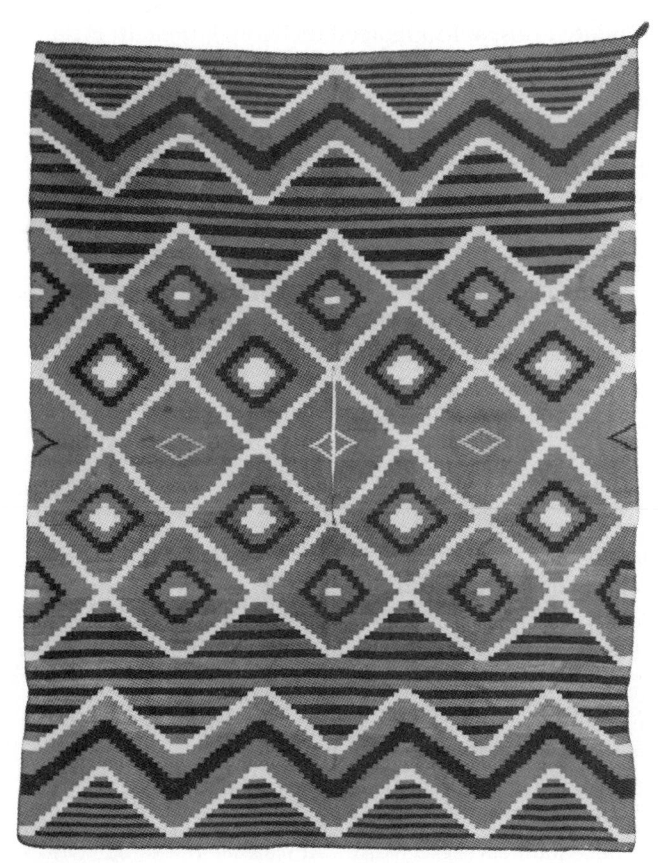

Figure 11-4 | This Early Classic–style poncho was made before 1860. A Navajo woman probably spent more than a year in its manufacture. (Courtesy of the Southwest Museum, Los Angeles, Photo #42671.)

legends as legitimate, despite the textual differences. The myth recounted here represents a composite and differs significantly from some versions. Initially, we should note that the word used by the Navajo for themselves, Dine, literally means "Earth Surface People." They contrasted with the Holy People, who once lived beneath the present earth surface. Holy People are termed Yei; they exist at the zenith and nadir of the celestial sphere and at points of the compass. The Yei are associated with many things: features on the landscape, the weather, plant life, and some animals. The Yei are not gods in our sense because they may either help or hinder the people; to control them in rituals is a cornerstone of Navajo religion, crystallized in the Blessingway.

In a series of twelve stratified worlds beneath the earth lived the Holy People, but discord, usually resulting form witchcraft, forced them into one higher world after another. At one point men and women could not reconcile their differences and lived separately, but finally they learned to live together.

In the last of the underworlds, a flood forced the Holy People to escape to the earth's surface. It was here that death originated.

The Yei created natural objects. They also originated the Earth Surface People, commonly referred to as "the ones with five fingers." The Earth Surface People were the ancestors of the Navajo and other peoples. The Holy People taught the Navajo how to live. The Holy People also were the parents of Changing Woman, the most prominent individual in Navajo mythology, who is identified with the earth itself. Changing Woman later conceived miraculously by the Sun and gave birth to two sons, the Twin Monster Slayers, who killed earthly monsters. The sites of these slayings are prominent features on the landscape. In this way the natural world was created.

APPEARANCE AND CLOTHING Traditionally the hair of adults and children was brushed back, folded, and tied in place. Men followed a newer custom of keeping their hair in place with a rolled handkerchief in which they carried small items, such as tobacco and coins. Adults wore large silver earrings and locally made necklaces of silver or turquoise beads; alternatively, they might obtain coral or shell beads from traders. Silver bracelets likewise were popular, as were belts made from heavy silver disks strung on leather straps.

Around 1900, new apparel styles were displacing older ones. However, low-cut moccasins with rawhide soles remained the universal footwear. White man's shoes were taboo; they could not even be touched. Similarly, some older people thought that garments manufactured by whites would produce illness if worn. This restriction began to disappear as factory-made yard goods, Pendleton blankets, and shawls became more readily available. Both sexes wore knit stockings. Navajo blankets were worn and used as bedding, but their use declined as blankets became a popular tourist item.

Traditional woolen dresses were being displaced by homemade calico dresses or hand-sewn blouses and skirts. On special occasions a woman wore a heavy knee-length woolen tunic with border designs and knee-length leg wrappings of goat or buckskin. The tunic was held in place with a woven girdle. Apparently, velveteen blouses and satin skirts did not become popular until the 1920s. Men wore pants of wool or calico, calico shirts, and leggings of dyed deerskin held in place with garters of woven thread. On special occasions their leggings or pants were trimmed with buckskin fringes and silver buttons.

SETTLEMENTS AND MANUFACTURES As the people became less mobile in the early 1900s, they created new dwelling types and modified old ones. The standard traditional winter house, or hogan, continued to dominate. It was cone-shaped and about fifteen feet in diameter. The frame consisted of three interlocking forked posts at the center that extended to the outer walls; a pair of additional posts and poles formed an entrance that always faced east. Pieces of wood and poles were placed against the frame, and the structure was covered with mud or earth. A shallow interior excavation became the floor, and a storage shelf extended around the inner walls. Smoke from a central fireplace escaped from a hole near the dwelling peak. Aboriginal American Indians did not make chimneys over fireplaces. Early in the 1900s an improvised metal flue began to be fashioned above a fireplace to draw smoke from the room. They also bought metal stoves from traders or fashioned homemade stoves from oil drums. A small number of houses included Anglo-style tables and chairs, but otherwise there were no furnishings. People worked and slept on sheepskins.

Another traditional hogan type had four interior posts to support cross-beams and a post and pole entryway. The frame was covered with small poles, bark, and, finally, packed earth. This flat-topped dwelling type was intimately associated with ceremonies. Hogans competed with new forms of housing that included log cabins, inspired by Anglos, and jacal dwellings of Hispanic origin; a small number of families occupied frame houses with either flat or gabled roofs.

Summer and temporary campsites consisted of improvised shelters. They included lean-tos, ramadas (open porchlike structures), and windbreaks, or tepee-style structures covered with canvas. Another prominent structure at a camp or winter settlement was a sweat house. This was a tepee-shaped structure with a pole frame covered with cedar bark and then with dirt. Rocks were heated in a nearby fire and transferred inside the structure for the bathers. A settlement also included wooden enclosures for securing livestock (see Figure 11-5). They also employed various items for the animals, such as saddles, quirts, lassos, and hobbles for horses and imported baby bottles of glass for feeding newborn lambs.

Imported artifacts were becoming increasingly popular. Iron axes had replaced those made from ground stone, and knife blades flaked from chert or chalcedony long ago had given way to imported metal knives. Near a homestead were looms on which women produced woven goods. Some people made and used clay cooking pots, but most containers were of metal and bought at trading posts. Locally made baskets and pottery were primarily produced for religious ceremonies, although some families continued to use relatively flat coiled baskets as food dishes.

Farming equipment of old, such as wooden digging sticks and wooden weed cutters, were being displaced by imported shovels and hoes. To harvest wild seeds a person might use a clublike wooden flail, and he or she could remove kernels of corn from a cob by striking one ear against another. For grinding corn and other grains, they used a lava slab metate and round stone mano. These, however, were giving way to the hand gristmills that traders stocked. Roasting pits provided a traditional means for cooking meat, ears of corn, and ground cornmeal products.

Horses and burros had become beasts of burden, but some people continued to use tumplines as an aid for carrying firewood, water containers, and other heavy loads. A tumpline was a strap made from buckskin or wool that could be slung over the forehead or across the chest of a male or female bearer

Figure 11-5 | A Navajo camp as it appeared in 1944. (Photo by C. E. Purviance. Courtesy of the Museum of Northern Arizona.)

to help support a burden. This form, however, appears to have been a relatively recent introduction. To carry water, they coiled sumac twig splints to form a somewhat globular basket that had loop handles near the top and that was covered with pitch. Goatskin water bags were a recent addition to their material inventory.

THE SUBSISTENCE ROUND By the 1910s the economic round continued to depend most heavily on herd animals. Wealth, prestige, and security were linked primarily to the ability to meet the needs of livestock. The insightful discussion of Navajo stock by James F. Downs (1972) based on his fieldwork in the early 1960s is the primary source of information about herding in earlier decades.

One characteristic of Navajo pastoralism was their dispersion into small family groups at homesites. But as the population expanded, pressure on grazing land intensified. A key to their success was an ability to meet the particular needs of cattle, goats, horses, and sheep in thoughtful combination. Efficient herding depended in part on having at least a few horses, and owning them increased one's social status. In practical terms, to keep at least one horse at a living site was highly desirable. A hobbled or tethered horse nearby provided immediate mobility for meeting various needs, especially for locating animals that had strayed. Yet keeping horses at hand meant that they must be fed and watered on a daily basis.

Sheep were most important as a food source, but they could also be converted into money, and they provided a major source of personal satisfaction. The care of sheep dictated the texture of Navajo life. Sheep required daily attention, but they also were the most domesticated and the least intelligent of the livestock raised. A herding instinct leads sheep to follow one another; a stray sheep is defenseless and will die of hunger, thirst, or predation, especially by coyotes. Sheep are nervous and react to the behavior of one another. To counteract this characteristic, a few goats usually were added to a herd because goats are more curious and self-reliant; they calmed and led the sheep. A small number, even hundreds, of sheep and goats could be managed by one person, adult or child, because after they were driven to grass the animals could be ignored. In sum, sheep required a great deal of care but were readily controlled.

Yet sheep herding itself was demanding. Herders typically moved their flocks to high country in the summer and to lower land in the winter, a pattern termed transhumance. A heavy snowfall forced a family to dislodge the snow so that animals could graze, and cold winds made it difficult to find grass. Spring lambing required careful attention. Lambs were separated from a herd and tended at a homesite to increase the survival rate. Sheep were grazed on open range, penned each night, and taken out to feed shortly before dawn. This pattern may have originated in years past when other Indians raided Navajo herds. In addition, most Navajo feared the dark because of religious beliefs. Sheep were also penned during the heat of the day because in hot weather they would stop and refuse to eat or move despite vigorous efforts by a herder. The proximity to water was another crucial factor in the tending of sheep. Finally, if nearby land became overgrazed, a family was forced to move at least temporarily to more distant pasturage.

During World War I, the sizes of sheep and cattle herds increasingly responded to the market demands for lamb and beef. Cattle were raised to sell. Most families owned a few animals, but they were rarely slaughtered as food. Those families that placed at least some emphasis on cattle were constrained by a number of factors. Most important, a single cow required about four times as much rangeland as a sheep or goat. A few cows could be grazed together with sheep, but herds of cattle tended to stray widely. Considerable effort might be required to locate such animals and to drive them back again, especially if a man did not have a horse. Considering the importance of sheep as food, the fluctuations in cattle prices, and the far greater emotional identification with sheep, it becomes clear why cattle assumed secondary importance.

The only other important domestic animal was the dog. Often, each family member owned a dog and viewed it with considerable affection. One practical reason for owning a dog was to help herd sheep. Dogs usually aided a herder moving sheep in a particular direction, but they were not trained in the manner of Anglo sheep dogs. Perhaps the most important role of dogs was to keep coyotes away from sheep. They also served as scavengers around a homestead. Dogs were hungry most of the time and contributed to sanitation around a home by eating cow, horse, and human feces.

The arid nature of Navajo country meant that it was ill suited for intensive farming. At reasonably well-watered sites, family members, especially women, were largely responsible for raising maize and squash as dietary supplements.

Alternatively, a family might exchange sheep or sheep wool at a trading post or with the Hopi for maize, flour, and fruit. Planted fields were preferably near a homesite, but might be several miles away when the distant land was better suited. Despite the labor expended on clearing land, planting seeds, and controlling weeds, crops often failed for lack of moisture; or the seeds might wash away with heavy rains. After a few years the yield of a plot declined abruptly, and the process was repeated.

In another context, maize cultivation served a critical need unrelated to food. Corn pollen was considered an exceedingly sacred plant product, an idea borrowed from Pueblo Indians. Pollen was placed in small bags and used to bless individuals, animals, and hogans; it played a crucial role in all religious rituals.

DESCENT, KINSHIP, AND MARRIAGE Descent was traced through females and included about sixty named matrilineal descent groups (matriclans). These clans in turn were grouped into about fifteen unnamed phratries. A primary purpose of the clan and phratry was to regulate marriage. No one could marry into one's own clan, the clan of one's father, or a clan in the same phratry. Members of the same clan tended to be widely dispersed, and, possibly as one result, neither clan chiefs nor clan councils existed. A prominent man in a clan might influence the lives of nearby clan members and persons representing other clans in the vicinity; thus his authority was territorial and not based on clan affiliations per se. Furthermore, when a person traveled to another part of Navajo country, he or she could expect food, shelter, and other forms of aid from members of the same clan, irrespective of whether or not the persons had ever met previously.

Navajo kinship terminology not only is changing but also varies from one segment of the population to another. The version discussed is possibly the most widely prevailing system. A child was "born in" the mother's clan and regarded all the females of the mother's clan as "mothers." Whenever necessary for clarity of meaning, a person would identify a biological mother as his or her "real mother." A child likewise was "born for" the father's clan, and the males of this clan were "fathers." In addition, those *born for* a father's clan were siblings, whereas those *born in* a mother's clan were children. Mother and mother's sister were termed alike because they were women of the same clan. Similarly, father and father's brother were termed alike. Different terms existed for father's sister and mother's brother. The terms for the first ascending generation are bifurcate merging.

For siblings and mother's sister's children, distinctions were made by age and gender, and all were termed alike (e.g., an older sister and mother's sister's older daughter were both in a sense "older sisters"). Cross-cousins were termed alike with no gender distinction, and parallel patrilateral cousins were distinguished by gender. The terminology for cousins is basically Iroquois (see Figure 11-6).

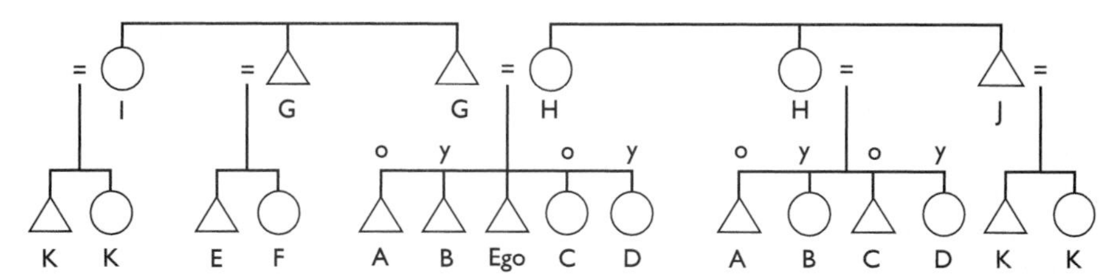

Figure 11-6 | The early historic Navajo system of kinship terminology.

The kinship terminology provided the framework for lifelong responsibilities, with particular forms of behavior expected in each set of relationships. Mother's brothers had important responsibilities toward their sisters' children, especially their sisters' sons, since many of the duties of raising children fell to the mother's brother. Adults who acted irresponsibly were said to bring shame on their families and, in fact, to act as if they had no families. Brother–sister relationships often overrode those of wife–husband in long-term importance.

Some relationships required polite, almost bashful, behavior, as was required of younger kin in dealings with older relatives. Women had high status and could address any man as "my son," whereas a man might address any woman by the more respectful term, "my mother." Daughters acted politely toward fathers. Intermediaries were often called upon to communicate with relatives who deserved extreme respect. When a brother married, his sisters might interact with him through their children or his wife. The social distance between a man and his mother-in-law was so great that a son-in-law was obliged to avoid her—he never spoke to her or remained in the same building or even in her vicinity. By contrast, relationships between a mother and her children were said to be "easy," warm, and affectionate. Sons enjoyed similar relations with their fathers. Some family ties were so familiar that joking was allowed, as between sisters and their unmarried brothers. In some relationships the joking could be of sexual content, as between cross-cousins or between a mother's brother and his sisters' sons.

A young couple was expected to live with the family of the wife's mother (ideally matrilocal residence). Despite this expectation, a newly married couple might live for a time with the husband's family unit (actually bilocal residence). Any number of factors determined the residence of a couple, such as whether a family could accommodate the newcomers or whether a family required the help of another male. For a couple to move back and forth before they settled down was not uncommon. As the population continued to grow, however, and the land base remained relatively stable, increasing numbers of couples lived apart from their parental families, especially when the husband had a wage-labor job.

POLITICAL LIFE The Navajo did not emerge as a distinct tribal entity until about A.D. 1725. Furthermore, incipient political integration was initially thrust upon them following the treaty of 1868. It was then that the federal government appointed charismatic leaders, Navajo "big men," whom the administrators called "chiefs." This effort was largely unsuccessful. These points were made earlier, but they bear repeating to introduce more recent political developments.

In 1899 the federal government began to create regional administrative centers on the reservation, and soon thereafter career civil servants began to replace political appointees in Indian administration. These changes, as mentioned previously, meant that the United States was in a better position to assert greater political control over the people. As in the past, men who were appointed as "leaders" were those who did not actively oppose federal policies. There were thirty such appointees in 1900. In some sectors of the reservation, councils were organized that functioned on an intermittent or regular basis, but they were above all else the tools of Indian agents. Yet some agents opposed Navajo councils and sought instead to deal directly with individual Indians. These devices prevented the people from developing a unified political base. Even when an elected Navajo Tribal Council was launched in 1923, the purpose was to serve the interests of oil companies in lease negotiations. Broader Navajo interests were not considered.

RELIGION The Holy People ("gods"), as Navajo precursors, have a dominant role in the mythology and belief system, as evidenced in their origin myths. As supernatural beings the Holy People are dangerous and powerful. Equally important, they are not especially sympathetic to people. Yet they may be induced to restore harmony in human life that results largely from inappropriate behavior. A major goal literally is to compel the Holy People to restore balance in the universe. The Holy People are not worshiped as gods in a Christian sense; instead harmony is regained after people meet their proper ritual obligations. This presentation of Navajo religion is in the present tense because most of the people continue to accept their traditional belief system.

As noted by Leland C. Wyman (1983) in a masterful synthesis of the Navajo ceremonial system, these people have neither a word nor phrase comparable to the English word "religion." And yet religion is the best English word for their configuration of beliefs and practices, which expands far beyond the usual definition. As Wyman (1983, 536) wrote, "[t]hey regard the universe as an orderly all-inclusive, unitary system of interrelated elements. The tiniest object, being, or power, even minute insects; the most stupendous, the great mountains that bound the Navajo country and the thunder and lightning that crash above them; and man himself—all have their place and significant function in the universal continuum."

In Navajo thinking, the natural and supernatural blend into one another. A key to understanding and dealing with the Holy People is embodied in an inherent conflict between evil and good. To achieve a balance in life by dealing with these forces simultaneously is a persistent goal. Many potential sources of evil prevail, such as whirlwinds, lightning, human ghosts, and particular animals, especially bears, coyotes, and snakes. Likewise, breaking taboos, excessive gambling or sexual activity, and out-of-the-ordinary behavior in general can disrupt balance and harmony. Therefore, the world is a dangerous place and every reasonable effort is made to avert contamination. Disharmony results in the anticipation of illnesses, or illness itself, and is to be avoided for the well-being of herd animals, farmlands, and other aspects of living.

One word, *hozho,* expresses the most fundamental Navajo value. Collectively hozho includes concepts of beauty, harmony, goodness, normality, and success. When disharmony or imbalance prevail, hozho is restored in varied ways, ranging from prayers to immensely complex ceremonial configurations. If hozho is not restored, it is a result of human failings. In broader context, and unlike the Pueblo Indians, the Navajo have neither religious societies nor a rigid ceremonial calendar to achieve and sustain general well-being. Instead the focus is on individual specialists with specific capabilities. They usually are men called *singers,* an indication of the emphasis on singing, a key activity in meeting ritual obligations. A singer's attention usually centers on a specific patient in a particular context. Any beneficial results aid not only the patient but also his or her family, a local group, or sometimes the Navajo in general.

A tyro (novice) singer typically serves an extended apprenticeship under the guidance of an older established practitioner. For a major "chant" a tyro must learn hundreds of songs precisely, long and involved prayers, the use of plant medicines, the preparation of drypaintings (sand paintings), and involved ritual procedures. A singer specializes in one or more chants because of the breadth and depth of knowledge required for a major chant; specific chants are identified as "chantways."

Major chantways are numerous, varied, and distinct in purpose and procedure. So much variability is involved that Karl W. Luckert (1979, 7) suggests that each chantway might be regarded as a "minireligion." At the same time, chantways share many common elements. Ideally they are held in a circular hogan with an entrance to the east—the direction from which good arrives. A smokehole at the center of the roof is for the exit of evil. A chantway is held for two, four, five, or nine nights. The sacred bundle of a singer may include rattles, whistles, fossils, animal claws, and many other forms, each with its particular significance. Maize pollen is an especially holy substance employed in many contexts. It is tossed in the air during prayers and applied to consecrate or sanctify people, artifacts, and animals. In a chantway drypaintings are likely to be included, and over five hundred highly symbolic designs have been reported (see Figure 11-7). Most of them illustrate two or more Holy People on rainbow-bars to represent their means of movement or on black bars representing the earth. A chantway ends with a prayer and song to negate the ill consequences of any errors in the rituals.

The Blessingway is one of the two cornerstones in the ceremonial system. Its goal usually is to promote harmony (hozho), achieve well-being, and result in a fruitful life. Blessingway rites include dedicating a new hogan, validating a marriage, aiding a woman in childbirth, and protecting livestock. This

Figure 11-7 | This Navajo drypainting (sand painting) was made ca. 1935–40. (Courtesy of the Southwest Museum, Los Angeles, Photo #42669.)

chantway usually begins at sundown and lasts two nights and one day. (Time is determined by nights, from sundown to sundown, not by days.) The opening night is devoted to songs and prayers by the participants while the person who is the focus of the rituals holds a medicine (sacred) bundle at his or her chest. The buckskin bundle includes small containers of earth from four sacred mountains, prayer sticks, and small packets of pollen. Additional songs and prayers are performed during the day, and the rituals end with songs during the final night.

The second cornerstone, originally designated the Enemyway, was designed to protect warriors from the ghosts of slain enemies. It evolved into a cure for illness thought to be caused by the ghosts of non-Navajo; it is grouped with Evilway (Ghostway) ceremonies. The Evilway is unusual because it spans from three to five nights, because it has more than one singer in charge, and because rituals are held in different localities.

As a cultural institution, traditional religion clearly was, and remains for many Navajo, a prominent aspect of life. Yet some people, possibly not very many, appear to achieve personal goals by witchcraft and sorcery. Inordinate envy of others may be the most prominent characteristic attributed to witches.

Likewise, a witch might seek vengeance for real or imagined wrongs, strive to obtain wealth beyond normal means, or seek to harm someone based on pure malice. Witches are feared and despised because they are presumed to cause illness, death, and disharmony. To combat their evil requires constant vigilance. Protection is gained in songs and prayers, in plant and animal substances, and especially in the ownership of ceremonial artifacts. Extreme care is required in disposing of any body substance (e.g., feces, urine, menstrual blood) or body materials (e.g., hair, nail clippings) that could be used in sorcery by a witch. Partial security is achieved by being among trustworthy relatives and friends. Caution is required in large crowds that include strangers. People also prefer to be in the company of others at night.

Witches are usually considered to be male, or sometimes a childless woman; they are intimately associated with death and the dead. Witchcraft is reportedly learned from a parent, grandparent, or less often from a spouse. A powderlike poison made from the flesh of corpses, which has the appearance of pollen, is said to be their primary weapon. Witches usually are thought to go forth at night in animal skins, especially those of wolves. A witch might drop poison through the smokehole of a hogan to infect a victim. Another possibility is to blow poison in the face of a person in a large crowd. Strange noises at night suggest the presence of a witch, and their tracks are said to be like those of animals, only larger; they might be traced a long way to a hogan.

Someone suspected of witchcraft could be called to a meeting by his accusers and led there, tied by a rope, for questioning. When confession was not soon forthcoming, he was tied down, deprived of food and drink, and not allowed to relieve himself. Confession meant recovery for the victim unless the person was near death. Within a year a witch was expected to die with the same symptoms as his victim. A witch who did not confess was killed as an approved form of capital punishment. When a witch went undetected, he eventually was expected to be killed by lightning.

Are Navajo witches real? The comprehensive study of their witchcraft by Clyde Kluckhohn (1944) addressed the question. In one sector of Navajo country nearly every family possessed medicine against witchery in the form of a specific antidote, animal gall. Individuals have been accused of witchcraft in private and in public; some people think they have been bewitched. If, in Navajo thinking, an illness is inexplicable, witchcraft is suspected by at least some persons. Witch fear is real, and accused witches have often been murdered. Kluckhohn concludes that witchcraft is practiced, but there is no certainty that all of the traits associated with witches exist.

When men take sweat baths, usually about once a week, two purposes are served: to cleanse one's body and to worship. The relatively small semisubterranean bathhouse at a homestead has a low entrance. Rocks are heated in a nearby fire and transferred on a shovel to a corner of the sweat house. Before entering a bath, naked adult males tie a string about their prepuce (foreskin); it is considered dangerous not to do so. It is an indication that a boy has gained adult status when his father or an uncle shows him how to apply the prepuce string. After bathers crowd into the room, the entrance is covered. The men begin by singing songs to bring good fortune in cycles of four, eight, or more depending on the bathers and their tolerance of the extreme heat. Women formally bathed after men, but this practice appears to have declined.

The formalities of chantways and their crucial role in dealing with the natural and supernatural realms represent one aspect of religious behavior. A second dimension pervades ordinary daily life. Each day the oldest male in a household group greets the rising sun with a sacred song and by dropping maize pollen in the four cardinal directions. As James F. Downs (1972, 98) noted, "[t]hroughout the day that follows, the routine is accompanied by endless and almost unconscious acts of ritual." The lives of these people are enveloped in songs with varying degrees of sacredness. The words might be barely audible or sung in a loud voice. Singing is common during such activities as driving sheep, doing farm work, collecting wood, and spinning, weaving, or cooking. In each instance the goals are to aid and to protect the singer, household members, and their possessions.

LIFE CYCLE Ethnographic gems are unusual, and a flawless one is exceedingly rare. The autobiography of Left Handed, a Navajo male born in 1868, is a stellar example. Compiled by Walter Dyk and published as *Son of Old Man Hat* (New York 1938), the book recounts the life of Left Handed from his childhood until after he married, at about the age of twenty. The narrative style is compelling, as are the particulars. Although it is rash to depend on one man's view of growing up, a number of examples from his account ring true and provide details usually unrecorded or muted in a standard ethnography. In addition, at least some Navajo had the capacity to remember the precise wording of conversations for many years and thus provide another dimension of reality. Some events from Left Handed's childhood are described later in this section.

Children were valued by the Navajo, but no elaborate ceremonies accompanied birth. Corn pollen was sprinkled over a baby's head immediately after delivery. The baby then was bathed, wrapped in a blanket, and "shaped" by a midwife's kneading and molding. Within the first day of life, his or her ears were pierced. The afterbirth and everything stained with blood was buried, burned, or wrapped in a bundle and hidden in a tree to prevent a witch from using these items to harm the offspring. The umbilical cord was buried in the sheep corral or somewhere else near a family home so that the person's mind would be rooted to the family land. Although children were named, they were typically addressed by kin terms. Babies could be several months old before a name was chosen. They were indulged and kept in close physical contact with their mothers to nurse on demand. A baby's mother, as well as the other members of a household, were responsive to his or her needs and cries, and the baby was often held and cuddled.

A neonate spent most waking hours strapped with cotton cloths to a cradleboard, which could be carried easily. After a few months, he or she spent less and less time in the cradleboard and gradually learned to walk. A baby's first laugh led to gift giving and was a sign that his or her time in the cradleboard had ended. The person who first made a baby laugh was responsible for organizing a celebration.

Children could breast-feed until they were three or four years old or a sibling was born. Toilet training was not begun until a child could talk and typically was a slow and gentle process. Children decided what and how often to eat and when or where they would sleep. It was not unusual for a family to rearrange its plans to accommodate a child's wishes. Children seldom, if ever, were spanked or reprimanded; instead they were encouraged and taught with stories. They grew up feeling confident, loved, and valued and soon learned to respect those who were older. Small boys and girls helped with camp responsibilities by hauling water or firewood. Lambs were often given to children to raise. It was while herding that a child learned to value some measure of silence and solitude.

Left Handed was raised by his mother's sister and her husband, Old Man Hat. The family initially had few sheep and moved often from one semi-isolated hogan to another in search of pasture for the animals. Thus in his formative years Left Handed was primarily under the direct influence of his sociological parents above all others. They often provided formal guidance about growing up. Left Handed was told repeatedly to run each morning for good health and a long life. Old Man Hat said time and again that Left Handed should go to bed late at night and rise before the sun. By the time he was twelve he ran early in the morning, at midday, and in the evening. He put sand in his moccasins so his feet would toughen and he would be able to run in sand or snow.

Left Handed's life centered on herding sheep, and he was introduced to the task while quite young. He herded in the morning and evening near the family hogan. Because he was afraid, he stayed in the middle of the herd where he felt safe. Before long he learned to avoid soft ground in which the sheep might sink and not to allow the sheep to stray. By the time he was about eleven years old, he had a large sheep herd and many horses under his care.

As a child the daily cycle of the sun puzzled Left Handed. He did not ask about it but reasoned that the sun came up and went down in the same pattern each day. He thought that where the sun set, there must be many suns, or else they melted and disappeared. As he thought about the seasons, he wished for summer when it was cold and for cold when it was hot. He reasoned that when it was cold where they were living, they should return to the place they had been when it was warm. Similarly, when he was young he heard about the concept of a year, and it troubled him (e.g., one year as opposed to many years). He came to think that a year must have a body like an animal and he wanted to see it, but he never was able to see a year.

Sex puzzled Left Handed as a young child. He wondered, for example, why a girl had no penis. Did their parents cut them off? He asked his mother, who said that girls and boys were born as they are. When out herding, he met girls who also were tending sheep, but his mother told him to stay away from them. She said that girls and women had teeth in their sexual organs and could bite off his penis. He knew this was not so for sheep and reasoned that it possibly was true only for human females. It might be noted that the idea of a toothed vagina occurs in the mythology of many different people around the world.

The *Kinaalda,* a Blessingway rite, honored a girl's transition into adulthood. During her initial menstruation she was especially vulnerable to adverse influences. For four days she was the center of ritual attention as relatives, friends, and guests gathered to sing and help ensure her success as an adult. Subdued and somewhat withdrawn, the girl remained in the family hogan, but left there to gather wood at dawn, run, and demonstrate the adult ethic of hard work. Her mother and maternal relatives prepared food, and on the fourth day the initiate distributed it to everyone and was congratulated.

A formal institutional means prevailed for a young woman to seek a husband following her Kinaalda. Loosely termed a "Squaw Dance," it originally was a part of the Enemyway chant. Usually held in the summer in comparatively recent times, the overt purpose was for a medicine man to treat an ill person. The patient's immediate relatives enlisted the aid of distant relatives to host the four-day event. Curing was thought to be most successful when many guests attended, and they sometimes numbered in the hundreds. An unmarried woman dressed in her finest garments and, wearing her best jewelry, selected a dance partner who could not easily refuse her and was obligated to dance with her on subsequent nights. This courtship pattern was accompanied by a great deal of joking, and a girl might elect to dance with a married man.

A woman clearly had considerable influence in the selection of a spouse but hesitated to ignore the feelings of her mother and other maternal relatives. When an agreement had been reached, livestock was presented to the family of the bride (bride price) by the groom's family. The wedding ceremony at the bride's hogan was simple and concluded with a feast for the guests. Plural marriages were also common. If a man had multiple wives, they most likely were sisters (sororal polygyny), and each wife had a separate hogan. The levirate and sororate also were customary.

Ideally, social and economic life centered around a "head mother," her stock, farmland, hogan, and the adjacent land that the family used. With her or close by lived her unmarried children, daughters and their husbands, and the children of these couples. Thus an ideal homestead consisted of matricentered hogans. The core residents were persons born into the matrilineage of the head mother. The stability of a homestead might be disrupted when the head mother died. In that case, her daughters might move away to found their own homesteads and in turn become head mothers. A less serious disruption occurred when an in-marrying husband was divorced by his wife or vice versa. In either case, the former husband left, usually to rejoin his mother's family at least temporarily; his children remained with their mother.

The nuclear family was the basic socioeconomic unit, and it was deeply enmeshed in kinship or marriage ties with other local families. A neighborhood ideally was dominated by extended family members of the core matrilineage. Additional matrilineage relatives probably lived at more distant localities. In combination, these matrigroups might form an "outfit." The term also has been applied to a more extensive territorial unit that did not have a strict basis in kinship; in this sense an outfit may be a comparatively recent development. In sum, social life focused on matricentered lineages.

Domestic tasks such as child care, cooking, and sewing occupied the time of women, who also were responsible for weaving blankets and rugs for household use, trade, or sale. Women, men, or children might herd sheep, but men focused on herding. Men not only had responsibilities to their children, wife, and wife's family but also to their mother's and sisters' families in which the men had grown up. As members of their own clans, sisters' children received special attention from the men. Men helped arrange the marriages of their nieces and nephews and instructed them in clan responsibilities and religion. Men usually were the ones who dealt with outsiders for the family. Few responsibilities fell to the nuclear family alone; parents were responsible for clothing their children, and fathers worked to build up herds of livestock for their sons.

Divorce was easy and could be initiated by either gender. Putting a husband's saddle outside the hogan indicated that a wife had terminated a marriage, and the man returned to his mother's home. A woman retained all property and custody of the children, since they were members of her clan. A decision to divorce was not difficult for Navajo women, who depended on their extended families, rather than their husbands. A woman could also rely on her brothers and other relatives to help raise her children.

The Euro-American stereotype of American Indians is that they are stoic and devoid of humor, but nothing could be further from reality, at least for the Navajo. In his study of Navajo humor, W. W. Hill (1943) found that it was rich and varied. A popular category of humor was based on accidental or ridiculous episodes. For example, a man might lie about his relationship with a woman, and she might accuse him of the lie in public. In another instance, a person caught stealing would have the stolen property in hand. Thus the offender appears ridiculous, and the episode might be told and retold to the enjoyment of the listeners. Practical jokes also were popular. For instance, when a horse race was scheduled for the following day, the horse that was a sure winner might be stolen the night before, ridden until it could hardly walk, and then returned to the corral of the owner. There also were what we might call "numbskull jokes." When a sheep was slaughtered, for instance, a man was told to obtain salt to process the meat; he might spend four days obtaining the salt.

Foreigners, especially Anglos, provided a basis for humor. When numerous Anglo tourists were watching a ceremony, a Navajo said he thought there must be many transvestites among whites since so many women wore trousers.

Although the Navajo did not ideally approve of sadistic humor, it nonetheless existed, especially with reference to individual physical or behavioral characteristics. Nicknames such as Ugly Woman, Scum of Coyote Ear, and Hunchback are examples. Vulgar humor was also common, such as asking a man with a big belly how long it had been since he had seen his penis. Institutionalized humor, including "joking relationships," a form usually noted by ethnographers, was well developed among the Navajo.

Humor provides a fitting context in which to consider personality differences. The Navajo are well known for their individualism and flexibility; ideally, each person spoke for herself or himself. This behavioral variation extended to all aspects of their culture. One woman, for example, might consider a joke laughable, while another could regard the same joke as vulgar if not obscene. Or one man might take offense and become violently angry if a practical joke was played on him, while another would regard the joke as very funny. Admittedly, within any particular culture individual personality differences would be expected; the Navajo represent an extreme in their individual behavioral differences.

Within a homestead and beyond it, respect for and deference to the aged, rich or poor, prevailed. Old persons with the greatest number of children and grandchildren were held in highest regard. As conveyers of complex socioreligious traditions across the generations, the aged fulfilled a critical role. The Navajo probably feared death no more or less than most peoples around the world. Although death was not a focal point of life, the dead were dreaded and feared. The ghost of a person embodied the evil aspects of his or her life, including ghosts of individuals regarded as good in life. Failure of the living to behave properly in any context invited a human ghost to enter the body of a living person to bring illness or other trials that upset the balance in life. Thus it was wise to have as little to do with the dying and dead as possible, be they relatives, friends, or enemies. To prevent contamination of a hogan a special structure might be built for a dying person; otherwise a hogan was abandoned. Quickly and without ceremony a dead person was buried with the artifacts that she or he valued in life. Ghosts were associated with darkness, and as a result the Navajo had a deep-seated fear of venturing forth at night.

The Comparatively Recent Past

As historical changes are considered further, one variable in particular merits attention: the proximity of Navajo and Westerners to each other. Navajo autonomy prevailed during the Spanish and Mexican eras because the people were so scattered and far from the administrative centers. And so it was during the early Anglo era. Anglo expansion became more persistent as wagon trails were developed and as railroads penetrated the region. Nonetheless, most of the reservation remained isolated. Much of the country was so rugged that most travel was on horseback. Remote sectors did not become accessible until adequate roads were built. In realistic terms, road construction began on a modest scale in the 1910s. As the network expanded, not only were Anglos able to reach distant places, but also local Navajo could travel afar with much greater ease. The popularity of wagons was followed by Navajo ownership of automobiles and trucks. Yet by the early 1930s many Navajo continued to depend on travel by horseback or horse and wagon.

Road access contributed to the construction of day schools in more isolated localities, and as the people came to realize that formal education for their children was desirable, school attendance was more regular. Proselytizing by Christian missionaries became more widespread, though ineffective. With increasingly dependable roads, greater numbers of men either sought year-round jobs at distant towns or expanded their pattern of seasonal work on distant farms and ranches owned by whites. Roads and highways thus became enablers and facilitators. Yet it was not until after 1950 that more remote sectors became accessible by paved roads or highways.

NEW TRAUMA: LIVESTOCK REDUCTION A number of environmental concerns began to arise in the early 1900s. Both the Navajo population and their herds were perceived as increasing at a dramatic rate, even though herd numbers probably were relatively stable. But because the Navajo eventually were forced from nonreservation public lands that they traditionally had exploited, the impression was created that the number of livestock was increasing. From 1900 to 1934 the reservation land base was expanded several times in an attempt to keep pace with this presumed growth. In terms of actual use, however, the land base had declined. Nonetheless, livestock reduction became a major federal goal.

Flocks, especially of sheep, were growing rapidly, and land erosion in the semidesert became alarming. The federal government began to encourage stock reduction in the mid-1930s and became coercive by 1937. By then most livestock was owned by comparatively few individuals, and they were the target of the most drastic reductions. One result was that livestock ownership by wealthy and poor persons alike suffered, and so it was into the 1940s. Thus wealthy individuals were unable to host ceremonies, and, equally as important, most people could not make a living from their livestock holdings. The herding economy was essentially destroyed, and people were forced to turn to wage labor jobs, which were few, and to depend heavily on government welfare programs. Most people were poor and felt helpless, and hozho clearly was out of balance, which was psychologically devastating.

WORLD WAR II The Navajo considered World War I to be a white man's conflict and assumed a passive attitude; no more than perhaps a dozen individuals served in the military during the war. They could not be drafted because they did not become U.S. citizens until a congressional act was passed in 1924. Early in World War II, many Navajo did not register for the draft because they distrusted the federal government; some people thought that registration had a connection to stock reduction. After the Japanese attack on Pearl Harbor, however, their attitude changed, and most of them supported the war effort. By the end of the war about 3,600 Navajo had served in the armed forces. About 15,000 others held war-related jobs locally and elsewhere. In 1945 the total Navajo population was about 59,000.

The most famous Navajo during World War II were the approximately four hundred "Code Talkers" in the U.S. Marine Corps. Searching for a code that the Japanese could not easily decipher, the military turned to Navajo servicemen. The code was used in Pacific-area campaigns largely to report the location of enemy artillery and to direct fire at it from marine positions. The code itself consisted of isolated Navajo words; the first letter of each word was translated into English to spell out the message in English. In the assault on Iwo Jima, over eight hundred transmissions were made without error. The Japanese were never able to break the code, and the success of the Iwo Jima campaign was attributed in large part to the Code Talkers. (During World War II, the U.S. Army had Choctaw and Comanche Code Talkers, and during World War I Choctaw speakers served the same purpose.)

World War II impinged on Navajo life in other ways as well. The federal government reduced its presence and influence on the reservation, and stock reduction programs were not enforced. More important, after the war, returning veterans and civilian war workers who held jobs off the reservation were far better able to cope with the white man on Navajo terms.

THE NATIVE AMERICAN CHURCH The Navajo began to participate in the "peyote cult" in the mid-1930s (see also Chapter 2). Its successful introduction was in part a reaction to the BIA livestock reduction program and a result of the growing hostility toward whites in general. Despite vigorous opposition from some Navajo, state and federal officials, and Christian missionaries, the church has thrived. Membership statistics are unreliable, but it appears that by 1951 about 13 percent of the people were church members. In 1972 from 40 to 60 percent of adults and children out of a population of about 130,000 were members.

A church leader is termed a Roadman (Road Chief, Peyote Chief). An aspiring Roadman is trained by an established one and begins to hold services when he considers himself capable. No formal creed exists, and there is variability in details of beliefs and rituals. An important prohibition, however, is the consumption of alcoholic beverages. Church members share a belief in the same supreme being and employ peyote for its psychotropic impact as a medicine and as a source of spiritual enlightenment achieved through prayer. (Peyote is not addictive, nor do users crave it.) The goals of a particular church service vary widely. Frequently a meeting is held to cure physical or psychological illness. Less often the purpose is to achieve economic success, counteract witchcraft, sanctify marriage, honor the dead, or celebrate holidays such as Christmas or the Fourth of July. A specific service is sponsored by someone out of harmony with the universe and with his or her spouse.

Services begin in the early evening and end the following morning. They are held in either a hogan or a Plains-type tepee. Prayers, smoking cigarettes, singing, and eating peyote are dominant, and in essence each represents prayer. Ritual equipment provided by a Roadman include an ornamental cane, eagle feather fans, a bunch of sage, whistle, and drum. An altar of sand is made with a crescent moon symbol of the Peyote Road of Life, and a four-stick fire is built at the center of the structure.

As David F. Aberle (1966), the foremost authority about the Native American church, repeatedly has noted, the church gained prominence as a reaction to long-term oppressive conditions of reservation life. Surprisingly, perhaps, the peyote church supplements the traditional religious system; the church represents a comparatively new means to cope with adversity. In many contexts, the Native American church supplements the goals of traditional Navajo religion.

THE NAVAJO NATION EMERGES Stock reduction and World War II provided a partial background for a virtual cultural revolution beginning in the 1950s. It was then that reservation mineral resources—coal, gas, and oil—began to be exploited intensively to supply power to the rapidly growing population centers in the west. By the 1960s the tribe was receiving an average of $14 million a year in bonuses, leases, and royalties from mineral resources, including uranium and vanadium (a mineral used in vanadium steel). The interest from tribal monies was more than $4 million in 1975.

The Navajo Tribal Council began to be controlled by the tribe rather than by the BIA in the 1950s, when it gained the right to allocate money earned from mineral resource development. The tribe likewise gained control over their police and the management of grazing land. Navajo court judges were elected rather than appointed by the BIA. Before long the council created its own infrastructure as a way to gain far greater authority over education, housing, and health services.

Following World War II people became increasingly mobile as better roads were built and motor vehicle ownership expanded. Wage labor, year-round and seasonal, off and on the reservations came to dominate the economy, together with a significant welfare supplement. Livestock ownership was becoming concentrated in the hands of fewer stockmen with larger herds, but there was no decline in the total number of animals. Rug production declined, while silverwork for sale to tourists remained modestly profitable. Before long the trading posts of old disappeared or became convenience stores.

Formal education developed so slowly that by 1945 the median attendance figure for adult schooling was about one year; understandably, most of these people did not have basic English skills. In the late 1940s a serious federal effort was launched to make schooling for children far more widely available. By the late 1970s reservation day schools, boarding schools, and public schools provided nearly all children with at least some formal education. Before 1950 few students had completed high school, but by the end of the 1960s the rate had improved, and higher education began to become available. The first Indian tribal college was launched by the Navajo themselves in 1968—the Navajo Community College (now the Dine College). Soon thereafter, universities in the region began offering programs to further Navajo higher education. By 2000 they had eight college campuses and tribal centers for higher education.

As is evident in this synopsis, Navajo culture became transformed in an erratic pattern. In the early 1900s direct control of the people and their lifeway diminished in fits and starts, depending on the degree of federal intrusion, national and regional economic conditions, and the accompanying Navajo responses. The extraction of reservation mineral resources beginning in the 1920s and the eventual control gained over much of Navajo life by the Navajo Nation president and the Navajo Nation Council heralded a new era that continues into the present.

Modern Developments

The capital of the Navajo Nation is Window Rock, Arizona. Reservation land includes about 17.6 million acres. It is dominated by the "Big Rez" in Arizona, New Mexico, and Utah. Additional holdings include the Alamo, Canoncito, and Ramah reservations in New Mexico. Despite the size of the land base, there are so many residents that the herding and farming economy of old supports relatively few families. Concurrently, the exploitation of mineral resources has become a major source of tribal income, but coal and uranium mining have also been disadvantageous. The lease and royalty arrangements were unfavorable, whereas open-pit mines and polluting power plants have been environmentally destructive. Another major problem has been a lowering of the water table to produce slurry to transport crushed coal to power plants. Uranium mining led to illnesses and deaths from radiation as a result of unsafe conditions. It was not until 1995 that the tribe gained greater control over mining operations, royalties, and related matters.

In 1990 the tribal government was reorganized to include executive, legislative, and judicial branches; the office of tribal chief was replaced by a president. A significant problem, before and after the reorganization, has been and continues to be corruption of tribal officers, resulting in resignations and displacement from office. Internal tribal politics likewise remained divisive in the late 1990s.

The land dispute with the Hopi, outlined in the previous chapter, continues as a source of conflict. As a result of a 1977 agreement, some two thousand Navajo families on the Hopi side of the dividing line were to leave their homes and be relocated (see Figure 11-8). By 1997 most families had signed accommodation agreements with the Hopi. The families who signed have the right to live on Hopi Partitioned Lands under Hopi and BIA administration for seventy-five years. About a dozen families refused to sign an agreement, and they were, in theory, to be evicted in the year 2000. Historically, the Navajo

Figure 11-8 | Jenny Manybeads was among the many Navajo to be relocated as a result of the Navajo–Hopi land dispute. (Photo by Paul Natonobah, 1993. Courtesy of the Gallup *Independent* newspaper.)

have been on friendly terms, both socially and economically, with the Hopi. One unfortunate result of the land dispute is that now there is a great deal of bitterness on both sides. The Navajo, however, do permit the Hopi to take eagles for ceremonial purposes from Navajo lands.

Major concerns in the late 1990s were economic and cultural. In 1998 the unemployment rate was about 52 percent, and the prospects for more jobs in the immediate future were dim. Some Navajo have long felt that to open a casino would help resolve their economic plight. In 1994 and again in 1997 the people voted against high-stakes gaming on the reservations. Some Navajo chapters (local government districts) favor casinos. A supportive resolution was passed by their national council in 2000 and later approved by the tribal president. It appears that there is no firm resistance against efforts to attract tourists in greater numbers for economic gain. By 1998 arts and crafts sales reportedly approached $20 million a year (see Figure 11-9). Tribal leaders have begun to actively develop programs to foster tourism; tourists are regarded as a largely untapped "gold mine."

In a 1999 address, Kelsey Begaye, the Navajo Nation president, expressed concern about the future of tourism, and he outlined other plans. Prominent among these were the possibility of launching a Navajo bank, instituting an income tax for everyone working on Navajo land, and taxing gasoline sold on

Figure 11-9 | David Tsinnie, in this 1998 photograph, is a Navajo artist living in the Coconino District of Arizona.

the reservations. To achieve far greater self-sufficiency obviously dominated Begaye's vision of the future. The problems, however, remain formidable. The unemployment rate in 1999 was 46 percent, the poverty rate was 56 percent, and tribal earnings from natural resources fell by 25 percent in 1998.

Acceptance of many Anglo institutions has led to questions about their appropriateness in terms of Navajo traditions. The Navajo Nation Zoological and Botanical Park at Window Rock, Arizona, is an example. The zoo began in 1963 as a place for young, injured, and old animals from the area. Navajo children in particular enjoyed and appreciated the zoo. However, Milton Bluehouse, the outgoing president of the nation, ordered the zoo to close in 1999 and the animals to be freed. A primary reason behind the closing order was that two women reported to Bluehouse that the Holy People were disturbed because the balance in nature was being upset by keeping animals in cages. Children especially objected to the closing. The incoming president, Kelsey Begaye, allowed the zoo to remain open pending further review. The ultimate fate of the zoo is to be decided not by politicians but by medicine men.

Additional Sources

Peter Iverson (1990) provides a brief book-length historical and ethnographic overview, whereas James F. Downs (1972) describes life in one community. Longer standard works are by Clyde Kluckhohn and Dorothea Leighton (1946) and Ruth Underhill (1956). The best ethnohistory is by Garrick Alan Bailey and Roberta Glenn Bailey (1986), and Gladys A. Reichard (1950) is the standard source about religion. The second *Southwest* volume (vol. 10) of the new *Handbook of North American Indians,* edited by

Alfonso Ortiz (1983) and published by the Smithsonian Institution, includes excellent chapters about most historical and ethnographic aspects of Navajo life.

Selected Bibliography

Aberle, David F. 1966. *The peyote religion among the Navaho.* Chicago.

———. 1981a. Navajo coresidential kin groups and lineages. *Journal of Anthropological Research* 37:1–7.

———. 1981b. A century of Navajo kinship change. *Canadian Journal of Anthropology* 2:21–36.

———. 1993. The Navajo–Hopi land dispute and Navajo relocation. In *Anthropological approaches to resettlement: Policy, practice, and theory,* 153–200. Boulder, CO.

Adair, John. 1944. *The Navajo and Pueblo silversmiths.* Norman, OK.

Bailey, Garrick Alan, and Roberta Glenn Bailey. 1986. *A history of the Navajos: The reservation years.* Santa Fe, NM.

Benedek, Emily. 1992. *The wind won't know me: A history of the Navajo–Hopi land dispute.* New York.

Bingham, Sam, and Janet Bingham. 1984. *Between sacred mountains: Navajo stories and lessons from the land.* Tucson, AZ.

Brugge, David M. 1994. *The Navajo–Hopi land dispute.* Albuquerque, NM.

Downs, James F. 1972. *The Navajo.* New York.

Dyk, Walter. 1938. *Son of Old Man Hat.* New York.

Dyk, Walter, and Ruth Dyk. 1980. *Left Handed: A Navajo autobiography.* New York.

Frisbie, Charlotte J., and David P. McAllester. 1978. *Navajo Blessingway singer: The autobiography of Frank Mitchell.* Tucson, AZ.

Henderson, Eric. 1989. Navajo livestock wealth and the effects of the stock reduction program of the 1930s. *Journal of Anthropological Research* 45:379–403.

Hill, W. W. 1943. *Navaho humor.* General Series in Anthropology no. 9.

Iverson, Peter. 1990. *The Navajos.* New York.

Jett, Stephen C., and Virginia E. Spencer. 1981. *Navajo architecture: Forms, history, distributions.* Tucson, AZ.

Kelley, Klara B. 1993. A rebuttal to some negative stereotypes of Navajos and misconceptions about Navajo history and Navajo–Hopi relations. Typescript. Window Rock, AZ.

Kelly, Lawrence C. 1968. *The Navajo Indians and federal Indian policy: 1900–1935.* Tucson, AZ.

Kluckhohn, Clyde. 1944. *Navaho witchcraft.* Papers of the Peabody Museum of Archaeology and Ethnology. vol. 22. Cambridge, MA; reprint 1967, Boston.

Kluckhohn, Clyde, and Dorothea Leighton. 1946 and 1974. *The Navaho.* Garden City, NY.

Kluckhohn, Clyde, W. W. Hill, and Lucy Wales Kluckhohn. 1971. *Navaho material culture.* Cambridge, MA.

Lamphere, Louise. 1977. *To run after them: Cultural and social bases of cooperation in a Navajo community*. Tucson, AZ.

Luckert, Karl W. 1979. *Coyoteway*. Tucson, AZ.

Lynch, Regina H., and the Rough Rock Demonstration School Navajo Curriculum Staff. 1993. *A history of Navajo clans*. Chinle, AZ.

McNitt, Frank. 1970. *Navajo wars*. Albuquerque, NM.

Ortiz, Alfonso, ed. 1983. *Southwest,* vol. 10, *Handbook of North American Indians*. Washington, DC.

Parmon, Donald. 1976. *The Navajos and the New Deal*. New Haven, CT.

Reichard, Gladys A. 1928. *Social life of the Navajo Indians*. New York.

———. 1950. *Navaho religion: A study of symbolism*. New York.

Spicer, Edward H. 1962. *Cycles of conquest*. Tucson, AZ.

Tamir, Orit. 1991. Relocation of Navajo from Hopi partitioned land in Pinon. *Human Organization* 50:173–78.

Underhill, Ruth M. 1956. *The Navajos*. Norman, OK.

Walters, Frank. 1950. *Masked gods: Navaho and Pueblo ceremonialism*. Chicago.

Witherspoon, Gary. 1975. *Navajo kinship and marriage*. Chicago.

Wyman, Leland C. 1970. *Blessingway*. Tucson, AZ.

———. 1983. Navajo ceremonial system. In *Southwest,* Alfonso Ortiz, ed., vol. 10, 536–57, *Handbook of North American Indians*. Washington, DC.

12 The Iroquois: Warriors and Farmers of the Eastern Woodlands

Great Spirit, who dwellest alone, listen now to the words of thy people here assembled. The smoke of our offering arises. Give kind attention to our words, as they arise to thee in the smoke. We think of thee for this return of the planting season. Give to us a good season, that our crops may be plentiful.

A portion of the Planting Ceremony speech of the Seneca that is typical of ceremonial prayers. (Morgan 1954, vol. 1, 188)

ANTHROPOLOGISTS HAVE LONG HAD a special fondness for the Iroquois, and not without good reason. They were the subject of the first essentially modern account of an aboriginal people, written by the Jesuit missionary Father Joseph F. Lafitau and published in 1724. However, because this work first appeared in French, it did not make an immediate impact on Americans. Then in 1851 Lewis Henry Morgan published a book about the Iroquois that became a model for ethnographic reports.

The Iroquois have also been of special interest because they played a prominent role in shaping the North American colonial empires of the British and French. From colonial times to the present, distinguished members of Iroquois tribes have been known to the people of Canada and the United States. During the colonial period, Hendrick was an outstanding Mohawk military leader and warrior, Joseph Brant was a Mohawk warrior and politician, and Red Jacket, a Seneca, was a great orator. Kateri Tekakwitha, a Mohawk born about 1656, was canonized as a saint in the Roman Catholic church in 1980. General Ely S. Parker, a Seneca, served as secretary to General Ulysses S. Grant and drafted the terms of peace at Appomattox, Virginia, that ended the American Civil War. Jay Silverheels (Harold I. Smith), a Mohawk, was better known as Tonto of "Lone Ranger" fame, and the famous runner Tom Longboat was an Onondaga. The Iroquois, famous in war and politics and representative of the Northeast culture area, have retained their identity with a rare resilience, but now their battles are most often fought in courtrooms.

The Iroquois (IR-uh-kwoi) are considered a tribe or as nations. The original "Five Nations" were the Cayuga, Mohawk, Oneida, Onondaga, and Seneca. The Tuscarora in North Carolina spoke a closely related language. Following wars with white settlers, they moved north to join the other Iroquois in 1722 or 1723 to form the "Six Nations."

The origin and meaning of the word *Iroquois* is unknown. The aboriginal core population lived largely in northern and western New York State, where each tribe occupied an oblong strip of country (see Figure 12-1). Collectively at the time of early historic contact, they may have had a minimum population of ten thousand. The Iroquois belong to a distinct language family, Iroquoian, and each of the Six Nations has its own language. The Cherokee language belongs to the same family.

Early Historic Life

One major difficulty in assembling Iroquois sources is to separate ethnographic information about the Iroquois in general from that about a single tribe. The problem cannot be successfully resolved because we do not have parallel information about all of the tribes. The descriptions to follow represent a composite view stressing the Mohawk and Seneca. A second major problem is that systematic ethnohistorical accounts date largely from the nineteenth century into the present. Therefore, it is difficult to place early Iroquois history in an acceptable perspective.

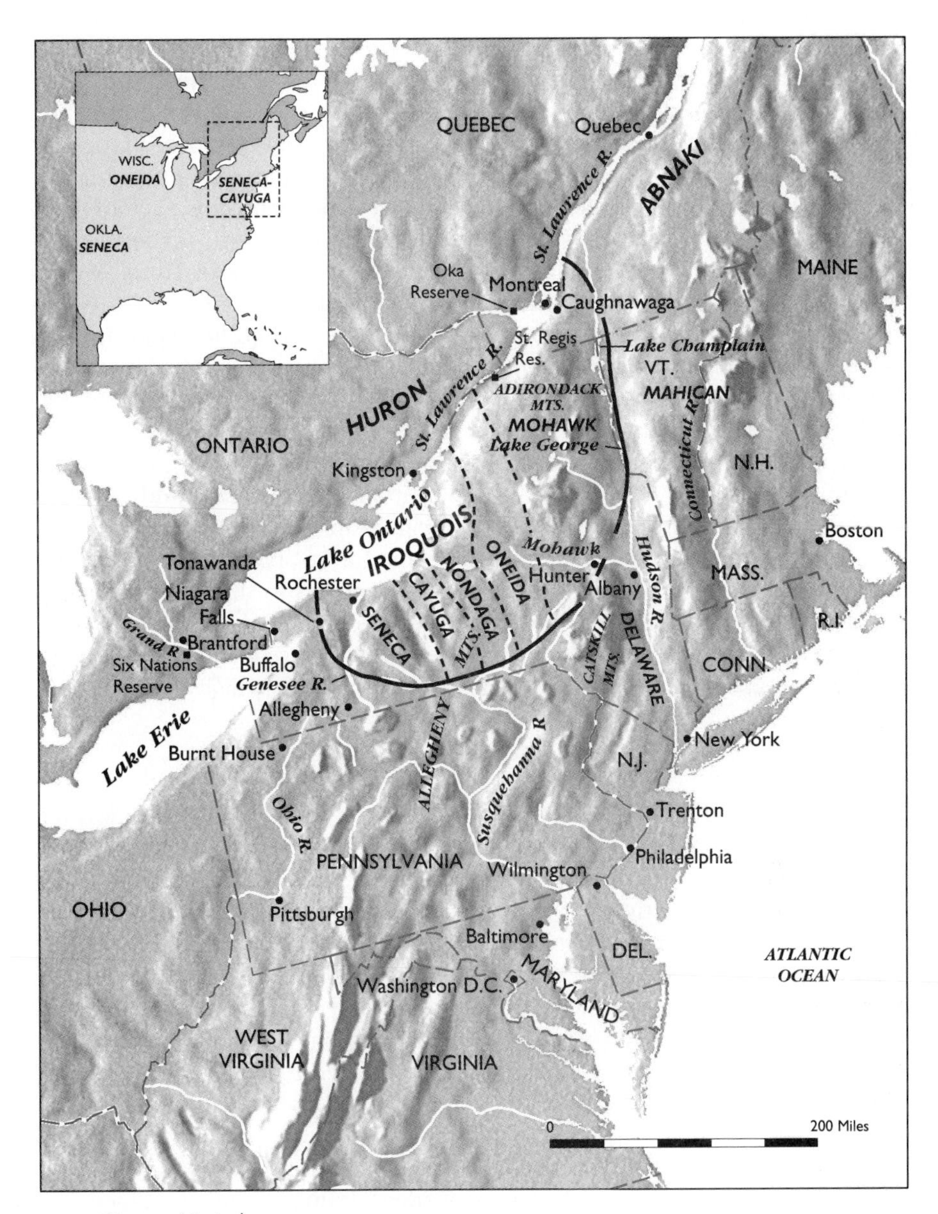

Figure 12-1 | Area of early historic Iroquois occupation.

ORIGIN MYTH Iroquois origins are reported in at least forty accounts, most of which were recorded in the comparatively recent past. The content exhibits considerable variability, although the overall plots are reasonably consistent. The account to follow is a composite synopsis.

The primeval world was a sea of water, enveloped in darkness. Aquatic animals represented the only form of life. The earliest humans lived in a sky dome among the clouds, where a great tree grew that always bloomed. Their lives mimicked later life on earth. The pregnant daughter of the Great Chief, Sky Woman, was told by her father to follow the tree roots to the world below and establish the earth. Fire Dragon in the sky hole gave her maize, a mortar, a pot, and a firebrand so that she could cook food. Sky Woman dropped through the hole. Various aquatic species dove in the sea to find land, and each of them failed until Muskrat was successful. He brought soil to the surface that expanded to become the earth that was supported on the back of Turtle. Waterfowl flew up from the water to cushion the fall of Sky Woman. The earth was small, but by walking about, she caused it to grow beyond her sight. In time she bore a daughter who soon matured, and Sky Woman was visited by a man. He placed two arrows over her, and she subsequently gave birth in a normal manner to a male, Sapling (Older Brother, Good Twin). His twin, Flint (Younger Brother, Evil Twin), emerged from his mother's armpit, and she died as a result. In his grief, Sapling created the sun from his mother's face and obtained the moon and stars from her breasts. Sapling created mountains and rivers in an orderly pattern, he created earth people and forests, planted crops, and became the source of well-being. Flint created darkness to drive the sun westward, jumbled the mountains, and made the rivers crooked; monsters, weeds, and species to attack plants were included among his creations. Eventually, Sapling defeated Flint, who lives in a vast cavern from which he persists in sending forth evil.

SETTLEMENTS AND MANUFACTURES In the early 1600s the Iroquois occupied ten major towns. These settlements, joined by major and minor trails, clustered along an east–west line. After about ten years, communities were relocated as the productivity of nearby farmland declined, firewood became scarce, and the dwellings began to decay. Palisades enclosed a settlement (see Figure 12-2). The well-known longhouse, up to 130 feet in length and 16 feet wide, had a framework of poles and a dome-shaped roof, and overlapping sections of bark covered the basic structure. At each end of a longhouse a bark door hinged at the top provided access. A partitioned section adjacent to each entry contained maize and other provisions. Small matrilineal families occupied as many as twenty apartments in a large longhouse, and each family had a fireplace. An apartment included high and low platforms covered with bark, reed mats, and skins on which people worked, lounged, and slept (see Figures 12–3 and 12–4). Oblong openings at intervals in the roof admitted light and allowed smoke to escape from the fires; bark slabs covered these spaces during storms. Additional village structures included underground caches for maize or dry meat, and temporary tepeelike dwellings had bark covers.

These people wore deerskin garments sewn with bone awls (not needles) and sinew thread. A woman wore a waist-to-ankle underskirt highlighted along the lower border with porcupine quill designs. Over the skirt was a long dress

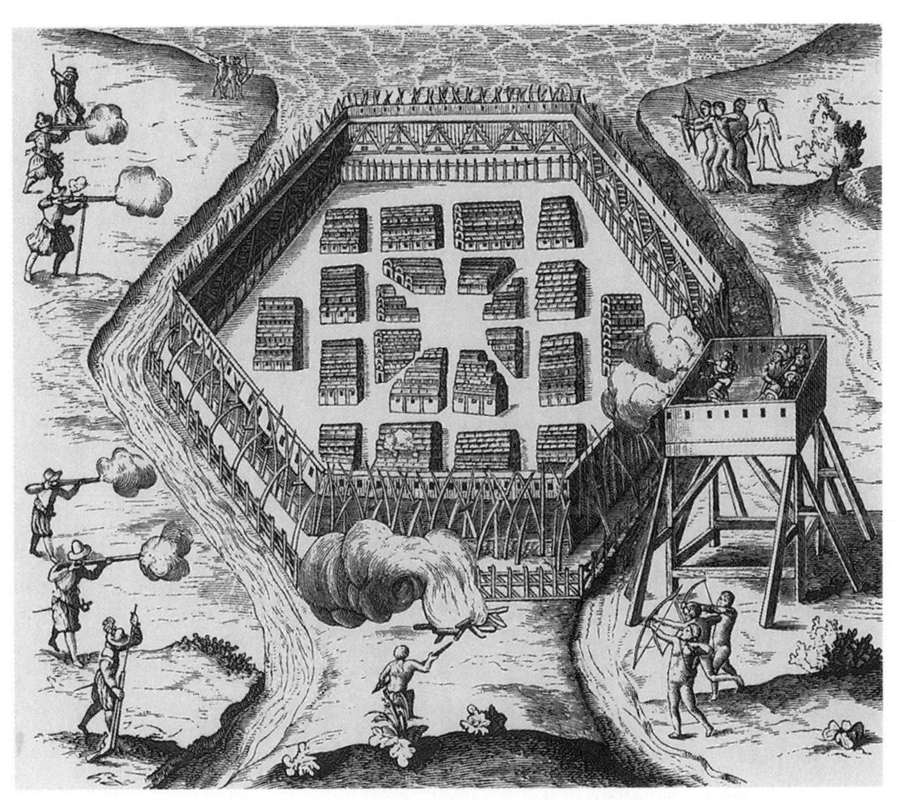

Figure 12-2 | This engraving of the principal Onondaga community in 1615 withstood attack by Samuel de Champlain and his Indian allies. Located between a pond outlet and streams for defense, a series of palisades, some as high as thirty feet, provided further protection. The settlement covered some six acres, with the longhouses arranged in blocks. (From Morgan 1881.)

fringed along the sleeves and at the bottom. Short leggings and moccasins completed her typical attire. A man wore a shirt with fringed sleeves and a knee-length kilt belted at the waist, fringed at the bottom, and decorated with quill designs. They also wore long fringed leggings and quill-decorated moccasins.

The relative stability of community life facilitated the accumulation of varied artifact types, and flexible materials dominated in their manufactures. They favored bark for storage and maple sap containers, as trays for mixing meal, and as ladles. Woven baskets were made but had limited use. Animal skins commonly accommodated household items, and a skin bag that hung from a man's belt contained most of the artifacts required when traveling. They ate soup and hominy from wooden ladles with deep bowls. Food commonly was cooked or stored in grit-tempered and fired pottery. Surprisingly, perhaps as a technological bias, they produced relatively few artifacts from stone, despite its

Figure 12-3 | Model of an Iroquois settlement with a longhouse under construction. (Courtesy of the Rochester Museum and Science Center, Rochester, NY.)

abundance. Chipped (flaked) arrow points and ax blades represented important examples of those they did make. Stone processed by grinding and then polishing produced mortars and adz blades.

Items for transport represent a final major cluster of artifacts. Winter travel over deep snow involved the use of short, yet broad, snowshoes with hickory frames laced with babiche. Traveling along a trail with a burden led to the development of pack frames made from hickory that fitted the bearer's back; support for a load was provided by a chest strap, tumpline, or the combination. Canoes were the dominant means of water transport. A vessel could be from twenty to forty feet long with a slight upturn at the bow and stern. The rounded ribs of ash were covered with red elm or hickory bark attached to ash gunwales. They used a single-bladed paddle.

SUBSISTENCE ACTIVITIES The Iroquois diet consisted primarily of three sacred domestic plants, maize, beans, and squash, collectively termed the Three Sisters. Women, as the primary cultivators, cleared the land and thereby

Figure 12-4 | Model of one portion of a Seneca longhouse. (Courtesy of the Rochester Museum and Science Center, Rochester, NY.)

became the owners of specific plots. They planted, controlled the weeds, and harvested crops. A digging stick and a hoe with a scapula blade served as their primary tools. The singular importance of maize is indicated by the identification of at least fifteen varieties. Women likewise collected wild plant foods, including over thirty fruits and about fifty additional plant products ranging from roots to leaves. Dependence on wild plants for food became critical when the corn and bean crops failed. They also planted tobacco, which seeded itself. Following the first frost the leaves were picked and dried for use. Tobacco use was confined to the elbow pipe made from fired clay; a man often kept his tobacco supply in a weasel-skin pouch attached to his belt.

Between fall harvests and midwinter, some families dispersed over settlement lands, especially to capture deer. The most productive means to take an individual animal was with a spring-pole snare that lifted a deer into the air by its hind legs. Communal deer hunts likewise prevailed as men drove deer between converging lines of brush, at the base of which bowmen were concealed. A snare set along a bear trail included a heavy pole to pin down an animal and prevent escape. Alternatively, a bear might be tracked a long distance and killed with arrows. A big game animal killed near a residence was hauled there on an improvised bark toboggan. Otherwise, it was butchered at the kill site, the bones removed, and the meat fire-dried for transport in bark containers.

In the spring some families scattered, occupying temporary camps to collect maple sap and hunt and fish. They set nets made from shredded bark for quail and pigeons. Alternatively, as women planted crops, husbands and sons harvested birds and fish near the village. Men guided fish with sticks into cone-shaped traps set in rapids or ripples. After the spring subsistence activities, men devoted most of their time to ceremonies, council meetings, and warfare.

For a morning meal, the only one scheduled during a day, men ate before women and children. Otherwise people ate when hungry, but a woman offered food to any visitors and to her husband when he returned from a day's activities. For meals, maize dominated, with hominy gruel, called *sagamite,* an Algonquian word, as the basic staple. To prepare it a woman first boiled maize kernels in water with wood ash to remove the hulls. She then ground the kernels with a pestle and mortar, sieved the meal, and formed it into loaves to be boiled in water. Additional maize dishes included succotash, roasted corn, and boiled corn. Meat, soup, and wild plant products rounded out the standard diet.

DESCENT, KINSHIP, AND MARRIAGE A longhouse was occupied by women of a matrilineage, their in-marrying husbands, and their children (matrilineal and matrilocal). The matrilineages were joined into fifteen named matriclans; among these were the Bear, Beaver, Deer, Hawk, Turtle, and Wolf clans. The clans of the Cayuga, Onondaga, Seneca, and Tuscarora were divided into moieties. The Mohawk and Oneida had only three matriclans. The Turtle and Wolf clans formed one moiety, and the Bear the other. The matriclans cut across national lines so that members of the Wolf clan, for example, were found in each tribe, in different villages within a tribe, and in one or more households within a settlement. The moiety division once was said to have formed the exogamous unit; any combination of marriages between persons of opposite moieties was permitted. By Morgan's time only clan exogamy and matrilineal descent prevailed. Inheritances were bequeathed by a man to his brothers, his sister's children, or some other person in his matriclan. The importance of the clan cannot be overestimated in Iroquois society; not only was it the property-holding unit, but it was empowered to invest, and renew if necessary, political leaders. Members cooperated in economic and political life and judged disputes with other clans. Furthermore, each clan had a common burial ground, held religious ceremonies, and could adopt outsiders.

In the kinship terminology, a person referred to her or his father and father's brother by the same word, and called the mother the same as mother's sister. There were separate and different words for father's sister and mother's brother (bifurcate merging terms). The words for parallel cousins (father's brother's or mother's sister's children) were the same as for biological brothers and sisters, but cross-cousins (father's sister's or mother's brother's children) were called "cousins." This is a cousin terminology that has come to be known as the Iroquois type (see Figure 12-5). By extension, all individuals of one's matriclan, irrespective of their tribal affiliations, were drawn into the system as

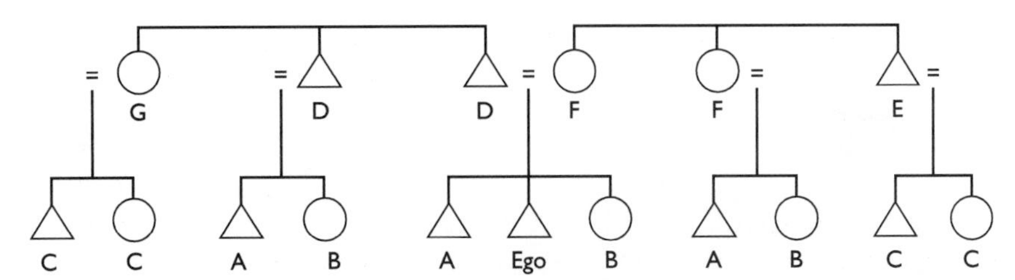

Figure 12-5 | The early historic Iroquois system of kinship terminology.

blood relatives. The basis of Iroquois political life was an extension of household and community kinship ties at the tribal and national levels.

SOCIAL DIMENSIONS The Iroquois have often been characterized, especially in older writings, as one of the best examples of a matriarchy, but this is an unfortunate label. It does not appear that they were overtly controlled by women. Because the Iroquois were matrilineal and matrilocal and because women were a very powerful political force, it certainly is appropriate to label the Iroquois as a matricentered or matrifocal society. The position of Iroquois women in the early seventeenth century, and probably for many earlier years, was well summarized by Lafitau (1974, 69): "In them [women] resides all the real authority: the lands, fields and all their harvest belong to them; they are the soul of the councils, the arbiters of peace and war; they hold the taxes and the public treasure; it is to them that the slaves [captives] are entrusted; they arrange the marriages; the children are under their authority; and the order of succession is founded on their blood."

The Iroquois clearly distinguished between the activities of men and women, and no close bonds other than family ties joined members of the opposite sex. Men sought the company of men, and women preferred to associate with other women. The primary duties of women were to care for children; to plant, cultivate, and harvest crops; to collect wild food products; and to prepare meals. Men concentrated their energies on hunting, politics, and warfare. The behavioral ideals for each sex were set forth in their oral traditions, and children were taught these values by their parents. Each person was identified with the totemic group of his or her mother but also had a personal totem, or perhaps more aptly, a guardian spirit comparable to the Algonquian manitou. A guardian spirit, or *oki,* was acquired in a dream or vision; represented by an object in a personal medicine bundle, its purpose was to aid the possessor.

When a woman died, her farmland, along with her domestic property, usually was inherited by her children, although she might will them to other

Figure 12-6 | A 1724 illustration of an Iroquois burial. (From Lafitau 1974.)

persons. A man's property normally was passed to his matrilineage, whose members disposed of his separate dwelling or apartment in a longhouse as well as his other material goods. The members might keep some items by which to remember the deceased. A man too could will his property to his wife or children if he made his desires known before a witness (see Figure 12-6).

An analysis of historical references to Tuscarora personality characteristics by Anthony F. C. Wallace (1958) provides what possibly are general traits of aboriginal Iroquois. Their "demandingness," which Wallace thought masked their extreme dependency, was best exhibited in their expectations of others; they never ceased, it seems, to expect goods and services. The same attitude was reflected in their use of intoxicants introduced by Europeans; their desire apparently knew no limits in early historic times. They blamed the difficulties resulting from intoxication on the white traders or on the rum itself but not on the person drinking it. Another striking characteristic of the Tuscarora and other Iroquois was the absence of fear of heights.

DREAMS Wallace (1958) studied early historic records about Iroquois dreams and found that the meanings they attached to dreams were in some respects similar to ideas developed by Sigmund Freud. The Iroquois in general believed that dreams expressed inner and symbolic unconscious desires, which if frustrated could cause psychosomatic illness. An individual could not always interpret his dreams properly, in which case he consulted a shaman versed in such matters. The dreamers most often mentioned in the literature were adolescent boys who embarked on vision quests, warriors who feared torture, and the ill who feared death. The young boys had dreams of the visitation form, according to the twofold Iroquois dream classification of Wallace. In these, the supernatural communicated with the dreamer, bestowing power such as good fortune in hunting or war or some other inordinate ability. One of the most important powers given was a capacity to predict the future. Symptomatic dreams told one of the desires of his soul. Wallace (1958, 244) wrote that "the only way of forestalling realization of an evil-fated wish was to fulfill it symbolically. Others were curative of existing disorders, and prophylactic only in the sense of preventing ultimate death if the wish were too long frustrated. The acting out patterns can also be classified according to whether the action required is mundane or sacred and ceremonial." It was under the compulsion of fulfilling a symptomatic dream that men were tortured by their friends, sought some material object even if it meant great hardships, held traditional but special ceremonies, or introduced a new ritual.

In summary, Wallace's (1958, 247) concluding paragraph is best quoted.

> The culture of dreams may be regarded as a useful escape-valve in Iroquois life. In their daily affairs, Iroquois men were brave, active, self-reliant, and autonomous; they cringed to no one and begged for nothing. But no man can balance forever on such a pinnacle of masculinity, where asking and being given are unknown. Iroquois men dreamt; and, without shame, they received the fruits of their dreams and their souls were satisfied.

ENTERTAINMENT Diversion in the form of games of chance and skill played an important part in Iroquois religious and social life. The contests were between individuals or teams organized within a community or beyond it, including different tribes. The teams generally seem to have been divided along clan lines. These people were avid gamblers, and betting on the outcome of a game was intense: a man might gamble all of his property on the outcome of a game. The favorite game was lacrosse, played on a field about 450 yards long. Each of the six to eight players on a team carried a crook that had netting strung from the curved end to about halfway up the stick; the ball could be moved only with this racket. The object was to drive a deerskin ball from midfield through the opposing team's goal, which consisted of two poles near each other at one end of the field. The rules allowed a variation from five to seven in the number of goals necessary to win a game. Another game was to throw a javelin through a rolling hoop or to throw it farther than an opponent.

The snow snake game was played mainly by children. The snow snake was a thin, smoothed hickory shaft some six feet in length, with the forward end increased in diameter and slightly upturned. There were up to six players, with three to a side, and each hurled his snow snake across a snow surface. The game was scored according to the distance achieved until the specified number of points had been reached by one side. The snow boat game was based on the snow snake principle. A snow boat, constructed from a solid piece of beech wood, looked like a round-bottomed vessel with an upturned bow. The boat had small feathers at the top of the stern and an oblong central opening in which was placed an arched piece of wood hung with rattles. On a hillside each player trampled a runway in the snow, iced the depression, and propelled two or three boats down the chute and as far as possible across the snow below.

POLITICAL LIFE In standard accounts about the Iroquois, they are noted for their political acumen, best reflected in the Iroquois League (League of the Longhouse). Traditionally, the League is presented as a powerful, essentially unified force in colonial and later times, but this image is a distortion. Despite the towering contributions of Lewis Henry Morgan (1851) to Iroquois studies, he did not fully understand some key developments. One reason is the nature of the evidence available. European and Euro-American accounts are uneven, and, although rich at times, they may also be poor or nonexistent at other times. Iroquois oral traditions committed to paper are relatively recent and can be contradictory. A recent study by the historian Daniel K. Richter (1992) provides a new, tightly reasoned interpretation of Iroquois political evolution. His findings dominate the following presentation.

According to Iroquois legends, the intensity of warfare within the Five Nations, and with other tribes, produced "mourning wars," a widespread Native American response to the killing of relatives. Warriors among the Iroquois, at the instigation of female relatives, raided enemies for captives who were either ritually executed, as a part of the mourning process, or adopted by a family in mourning to replace the deceased. All too often mourning wars led to ongoing feuds. After the closely spaced deaths of his daughters, an Onondaga, Hiawatha, became distraught and wandered about in a forest. Here he met Deganawida, a person of supernatural origins. Deganawida taught Hiawatha how to remove his grief, and thus eliminate mourning wars; his teaching came to be identified as the Good News of Peace and Power. Together Hiawatha and Deganawida successfully introduced the new doctrine among the Five Nations. This led to the formation of a Grand Council of some fifty leaders, sachems selected by females representing leading matrilineages within the matriclans of the Five Nations. These men were chosen based on specific qualities; each sought goodwill, peace, and harmony. The Great League of Peace and the

Grand Council gave rise to the Iroquois League, which was, and remains, largely a ritual institution in which comparatively few organizational changes have occurred.

When the League originated is unclear. Dates between A.D. 1400 and 1600 have been favored by historians; it clearly existed by the 1660s. According to Seneca oral tradition, the League was founded soon after a total eclipse of the sun. Barbara A. Mann and Jerry L. Fields (1997) propose that this eclipse occurred on August 31, 1142. It well may be, however, that the League formation was not a single event but a gradual process, irrespective of any proposed date for its creation.

At the annual Grand Council meetings, a central ceremonial involvement of the sachems, Words of Condolence, was held to honor those of their number who had died. Older women in leading matrilineages of the matriclans of deceased sachems selected the successors. The pertinent ceremonies sought to replace a mourning war with "mourning peace." In the seventeenth and eighteenth centuries, the Iroquois League did *not* represent a central government with unified policies or goals and the means to achieve them. Peace itself was a primary purpose, and they lacked institutional means to prevent raids and warfare. Sachems could only seek to dissuade potential war parties from being launched. Thus League sachems were incapable of dealing with Europeans in diplomatic or political contexts.

To obtain European trade goods on a reliable basis became an early historic Iroquois challenge, accompanied by the power struggle among European colonizers. The Mohawk began trading with the Dutch at Fort Orange (Albany) in the 1610s, and eventually all Five Nations traded there with relative security. Algonquians to the north and east obtained European goods from the French based in Quebec before the Iroquois did, which prevented full Iroquois participation in the fur trade. Nor did they have a locally abundant supply of beaver, a key item in the trade; but beaver were plentiful in Algonquian country. The Iroquois plight compounded as diseases of European origins spread among them; by the 1640s contagions had killed about half of the Five Nations people. Women who had lost family members to enemies inspired a response to these hardships. Women encouraged war chiefs and warriors to seek revenge for relatives killed. As a result the Iroquois preyed on Algonquian traders among the French along the St. Lawrence River. The Iroquois sought guns and ammunition, beaver pelts, as well as captives to satisfy mourning women. The adoption of captives, replacing dead Iroquois, became a major factor contributing to Iroquois survival. Their success by the 1650s led to attacks on neighboring tribes. The French response was to launch concerted military attacks against the Iroquois, which forced them to make peace with the French in the 1660s. All of this produced a revival of mourning wars and destruction of the Great League of Peace. The Iroquois League and its Grand Council could not cope with these developments.

The Iroquois Confederacy evolved as a political and diplomatic solution. By the mid-1600s, French and Iroquois tension began to be dealt with by councils at the village level. The grassroots male leaders included varying numbers of war chiefs, knowledgeable old men, and, secondarily, sachems. In deliberations, Great Peace rituals with an emphasis on peace, condolence, oratory, and gift exchanges became incorporated into Confederacy organization. By the 1660s village leaders met among the Onondaga to address common concerns in war councils that were not as yet distinct from the League. Unified positions among the Five Nations could not be achieved; quite to the contrary, community representatives sought to further their own particular political goals.

Following treaties with the French in 1665–1667, Jesuit priests worked among the Five Nations in a concerted effort to convert them to Catholicism. One result was the emergence of a faction favoring the French, and some of them moved to Canada. Their opposition was driven toward the English sphere in New York and to the Anglican church. By the late 1600s the Iroquois were deeply divided. The French–English factionalism produced increasing unity within the English faction, and the Confederacy formally emerged as distinct from the League, although key League rituals remained. By the 1690s the Confederacy councils met frequently. The leaders were not League sachems but Five Nation community leaders who often sought neutrality. The end result was a series of treaties with the French and their Indian allies in 1701. In the early eighteenth century the Iroquois raided widely, especially to the south, and adopted the remnants of numerous tribes to increase their core population. Confederation cohesion was destroyed by the American Revolution, in part because the Six Nations (by then the Tuscarora were included) could not achieve a unified position toward the colonists and the British. In New York State by 1797 the modern Iroquois reservations were established by treaty, although they are much smaller than originally. Illegal seizures of Iroquois land by white settlers in the nineteenth century produced the small present-day reservations and a decline of the Confederacy.

In sum, the Iroquois Confederacy emerged from the Iroquois League, in part because the latter could not meet political needs in dealing with Europeans in the seventeenth century. The League was not a political monolith. To draw attention to the League–Confederacy distinction is more than an academic exercise in understanding early Iroquois and colonial history.

Wampum played a significant role in Iroquois history. The word *wampum* is an Algonquian term for a string of white beads. Among the Iroquois wampum served as a currency and was made into belts. A convention required that one or more gifts must accompany important decisions, and wampum emerged as the most appropriate gift to bind a treaty or other agreement with foreign Indians or Europeans. An Onondaga chief was the Keeper of the Wampum. A topic of importance was "talked into" the bead pattern memorized by the keeper and learned by his successors. Iroquois wampum is known only from historic sites, usually those dating after the sixteenth century. Their wampum appears to be primarily or exclusively a historical development.

Intermittently the question is raised about the possible impact of Iroquois political organization on the origins of the U.S. Constitution. Some scholars contend there was none, because the American colonists did not really understand Iroquois political life. It also has been noted that the Iroquois system of government did not appear in written form until the 1800s, in which case they could have borrowed concepts from the U.S. Constitution. Yet Iroquois sachems were present at meetings as the Declaration of Independence was being formulated. This leads other historians to contend that the Iroquois contribution was substantial. Evidence for a causal link is inviting but not nearly as conclusive as the proponents imply. The debate is reviewed in a volume edited by José Barreiro (1992).

WARFARE It is fitting initially to examine some of the Iroquois conventions in warfare and place them in perspective. Methods of war among Europeans and Indians in eastern North America during the seventeenth and eighteenth centuries are briefly compared. The best study is by Thomas S. Alber (1992).

Scalping the dead, or sometimes the living, was a custom of the pre-Columbian Native Americans. Whites quickly learned to scalp enemies. Scalping was unknown in Europe, although decapitating enemies and exhibiting their heads was reasonably common. For Indians, scalps usually had sacred associations, but this was not true of heads taken by Europeans. Cannibalism among eastern Indians was practiced, and it usually had sacred associations (e.g., to gain the supernatural power of a slain enemy). It did not prevail in Europe, nor did Europeans adopt this Indian custom.

Torture in Europe was well known, not only to obtain confessions but also as a part of public executions to entertain English or French crowds. For example, in Paris in 1757 some prisoners to be hanged might first have their hands cut off or their tongues cut out. In this context, Iroquois torture techniques, soon to be described, may seem a little less barbaric.

Although not politically sanctioned in Europe, the rape of women was and remains a part of the European warfare complex. Indian warriors in eastern North America do *not* appear to have raped captive women. The evidence, slim as it may be, certainly suggests that the practice was unknown. One possible reason was that sex and warfare were incompatible ideas to warriors; they were considered to be separate domains. However, the rape of Indian women by whites occurred not infrequently.

It must finally be noted that on occasion the French in Canada during the latter seventeenth century tortured Iroquois prisoners as public spectacles.

Warfare was *the* paramount Iroquois interest, irrespective of the goals of the League. Accounts about their war complex postdate the introduction of European firearms, and therefore the aboriginal patterning is reconstructed. Apparently early historic war parties were large, organized by chiefs in council and led by war chiefs and shamans; these were "public wars." After about 1640 guns began to replace the bow and arrow and war clubs as weapons. The famous tomahawk apparently was not an aboriginal Iroquois weapon but was known among the eastern Algonquian, from whom it was derived. The blade was hafted in the manner of a modern hatchet. Metal tomahawks soon were manufactured in Europe for the Indian trade, and they often had a pipe integrated in their design (see Figure 12-7). Early historic war parties most often were composed of young, ambitious men who sought glory in "private wars," irrespective of the wishes of chiefs in council.

Near the center of each settlement was a war post, and a chief who sought to organize a fighting party whooped about the village, stuck a red tomahawk adorned with red feathers into the war post, and danced around it. Any man willing to join the party participated in the dance. After a band of warriors had been organized, women began preparing food for the venture. The standard fare was very dry, pulverized maize mixed with maple sugar and placed in a bearskin bag. A war chief customarily led a raiding party, and each was organized as a small contingent that might join one or more similar units. The units had no overall commander; each party leader was responsible for his group. Participants were free to act according to their personal feelings, and proper behavior could not be dictated. Before the warriors departed, at their camps, and on their return trip, they painted symbols on trees representing the number of raiders, the destination of the war party, and the outcome of the raid. When the combatants returned, the authority of the temporary leader ended. Because warfare focused the lives of men and brought them glory and prestige, the organizer of a war party could recruit a following easily. The Iroquois considered themselves at war with all Indians with whom they had no alliance; thus, there always were potential victims.

When a returning war party passed through a League village, its captives were forced to run the gauntlet naked, and according to Cadwallader Colden (1755, vol. 1, 9), "the Women are much more cruel than the Men." As the warriors approached their home village, they sounded a war whoop and danced as they led their captives. At the war post they were welcomed and praised by an elder. In reply, warriors narrated their exploits and performed the War Dance. Captives were repatriated only under extenuating circumstances. A man either was adopted into the tribe or was tortured to death. The one exception was to free an extremely brave enemy warrior. If the warriors had lost one of their number to an enemy, the Iroquois widow could adopt any male prisoner to take the place of her husband. First, however, he was obliged to run a gauntlet to his new home. The women and children lined up with whips, and the potential adoptee ran between the lines. If he stumbled and fell, he was considered an unworthy person and was killed; if he ran the lines successfully, he became a member of the tribe.

The fact that widows had first choice concerning the fate of captives has been cited as evidence that women were important in decision making. In addition, there are records of women inducing men to go on war parties or restraining them under certain circumstances. Evidence such as this has led to the generalization that Iroquois society was dominated by women. In a review of ethnohistorical writings about the status of Iroquois women, Cara B. Richards

Figure 12-7 | An aquatint of an Iroquois warrior in 1787; note the war club, ax, and tomahawk. (Courtesy of the Library of Congress.)

(1957) concluded that they gained dominance in relatively recent times. She notes that early reports state that the fate of captives was determined by the captor and the council. If a woman disagreed with their decision, she could not take effective counteraction until after the captor and council released the prisoner. Later in time the release of a prisoner by the council became an unimportant formality, indicating increased female authority. One factor leading to the expanding importance of women in decision making may have been the instability in village life after the introduction of firearms and the subsequent increase in mortality among warriors.

Nathaniel Knowles (1940, 188) reviewed the treatment of prisoners by the Iroquois. Among the techniques were: "applying brands, embers, and hot metal to various parts of the body; putting hot sand and embers on scalped head; hanging hot hatchets about neck; tearing out hair and beard; firing cords bound around body; mutilating ears, nose, lips, eyes, tongue, and various parts of the body; searing mutilated parts of the body, biting or tearing out nails; twisting fingers off; driving skewers in finger stumps; pulling sinews out of arms; etc." Only the Onondaga tortured young and old, male and female; the other tribes reserved their tortures for men. The usual practice, except for a person slated for possible adoption, was to begin abusing a captive soon after he was taken and to begin his systematic torture when he arrived in the settlement of the captor. The prisoner was forced to run around inside a longhouse as young men burned him, primarily on the legs, until he fainted. As he was slowly being tortured, he was expected to sing about his lack of fear. After a captive fainted, he was revived and the tortures repeated. Care was taken to see that he did not die from the tortures because he was to mount a platform at dawn. Here he was bound so that he could move about and was tortured more before the entire community. When the captive was very near the point of dying, he was stabbed to death or his head was smashed. Normally the body of a tortured person was cooked and eaten.

RELIGION For the Iroquois, the world was occupied by a host of invisible spirits. The most powerful deity was the Great Chief, who created people, other animals, plants, and forces for good in nature. The Great Chief indirectly guided human affairs but could not be appealed to directly. He was capable of countering the Evil Twin by applying his energies, and people passed through life between these competing fraternal deities. Among the lesser supernatural controlling forces for good was the Thunderer, who was capable of bringing rain or exacting vengeance, especially against witches. Associations of the Thunderer with productivity are reflected in prayers offered to him when crops were planted and thanks expressed after a harvest. The Spirit of the Winds commanded the winds and therefore could either help or harm people. The Three Sisters, the spirits of maize, beans, and squash, were conceived as lovely women and collectively called Our Life. Everything that aided people, including particular plants, fire, and water, had its spiritual associations. Some spirits assumed human form and were assigned specific obligations, and all bore the general name the Invisible Aids. It was possible to communicate with the lesser spirits for good by burning tobacco, as it was thought that through this medium prayers and special needs could be made known to the gods. Gratitude was expressed in thanksgiving statements.

The Evil Twin controlled a host of lesser spirit beings who brought pestilence to people and to crops, but few of these forces were systematized in the thinking of the Iroquois. One organized group of evil supernaturals was the False Faces, who were able to send death and destruction. They existed as contorted and evil-appearing faces and lived in out-of-the-way places; it was thought that anyone who chanced to see them would become paralyzed.

The most dreaded antisocial actions were believed to be performed by witches in league with the Evil Twin. Anyone could conceivably assume the form of an animal, bird, or reptile in his or her desire to do evil. Witches were supposedly difficult to detect because they transformed themselves into inanimate objects at will. Witches were thought to have a society with regular initiations; to become a member an initiate supposedly had to kill his or her closest friend by supernatural means. Anyone who saw a witch practicing was free to kill him or her, and the normal punishment for unconfessed witches was death. It was possible to establish at a council meeting whether someone was a witch; if the accused confessed and promised to reform, he or she was freed.

Religious specialists, or Keepers of the Faith, were chosen by female and male elders of the matriclans and were expected to serve when requested. Both sexes were represented in nearly equal numbers, and all members held equal rank. Each was invested by being given a new name announced at the next general meeting of the nation. Their primary duty was to arrange and conduct the main religious ceremonies; sachems and chiefs were ex officio Keepers of the Faith. Among their other duties was the censuring of antisocial behavior; the strongest form of censure was to report serious transgressions to the tribal council. A person could choose to relinquish the obligations of Keeper of the Faith by assuming his or her old name.

Major Ceremonies The Iroquois held six major religious ceremonies; in sequence of occurrence they were the Maple, Planting, Strawberry, Green Maize, Harvest, and New Year's (Midwinter) ceremonies. The first five were similar in many respects, as in sharing the common feature of public confessions prior to group observances. During these confessions, confessors held a string of white wampum as a symbol of sincerity. The audience did not pass judgment on transgressions, but it was expected that future behavior would reflect renewed purpose and intent. On the day of any ceremony, sacred rituals were held in the morning. The religious aspects included speeches by the Keepers of the Faith about the precedent and purpose of the ceremony, offerings of burnt tobacco, prayers, and thanksgiving speeches. In the afternoon and evening, social festivities included dances and feasting. One of the most popular dances was the Feather Dance, which included not only a dance but accompanying songs of thanksgiving.

The seven-day New Year's Ceremony usually was held in early February. Before the rituals began, people who had dreamed went from house to house asking the residents to guess the nature of their dreams. When someone suggested a reasonable text and meaning for a dream, the dreamer ceased his or her quest for an interpretation. If the accepted text and its meaning included statements about the future behavior of the dreamer, she or he was obligated to behave as directed. Jesuit missionaries who witnessed the dream procedure in 1656 recorded it as a violent affair, with the dreamer threatening and actually destroying a great deal of household property until he or she was satisfied with an interpretation.

The formal New Year festivities, designed to drive away evil, were launched by two Keepers of the Faith disguised in skin robes and adorned with corn husks. On the first day, they visited each household on two separate occasions to announce the purpose of the ceremony and to sing a song of thanksgiving. The same day one or two white dogs, symbolizing purity, were sacrificed and hung from a pole. On the second day the Keepers of the Faith dressed as warriors and visited each household three different times to perform rituals that included prayer and song. The third and fourth days were devoted to dancing and visiting among the people. At this time, groups of boys, accompanied by an old woman carrying a basket, visited each house. The boys danced, and, if given presents, they all moved on. If no gifts were forthcoming, they stole whatever they could. If they were caught, they returned what they had taken. On the fifth day the sacrificed dog or dogs were placed in the council house and a speech was made about their dedication to the Great Spirit; later the dog or dogs were burned in a fire to carry a message of contrition to the Great Spirit. The Thanksgiving Dance was held on the sixth day, and gambling dominated the final day. Note that midway through and at the end of the ceremonies, time was set aside for entertainment, possibly as a relief from the intensity of the religious obligations.

False Face Society The famous False Face Society was organized to counteract disease. A male became a participant by dreaming that he was a member and left the society by dreaming that he was no longer active. The only woman member was the Keeper of the False Faces, who not only kept the ceremonial paraphernalia but was supposed to be the only one who knew the identity of all the members. A False Face Society probably was represented in each village; its duties included curing illness and keeping evil spirits at bay. If someone was ill with a disease that was often treated by the society, and if he or she dreamed of false faces, it was a sign that the person could be cured by the False Face Society. The society was most noted for its ability to cure eye inflammations, nosebleeds, swellings, and toothaches. The Keeper of the False

Figure 12-8 | Two ceremonial items: a False Face mask and a cow horn rattle, shown by a dancer on his traveling rounds to private homes before a ceremony in the longhouse. (Photo by Annemarie Shimony, circa 1970.)

Faces was notified when someone hoped to be cured, and she assembled the members, each of whom covered himself with a face mask and blanket and carried a turtle-shell rattle. The members sprinkled the patient with hot ashes, performed a dance, and then withdrew. The main function of the False Face Society was to clear disease from a village at regular intervals.

The False Face Society masks were inspired by mythological beings and creatures seen during dreams. A mask was carved from a living basswood tree and portrayed one of about a dozen facial types. As the most distinguishing feature, some had crooked mouths, others a smile, some a protruding tongue, and so on (see Figure 12-8). They might be painted black, brown, red, or white. Another type of mask was made from braided and sewn corn husks. These represented important farming and hunting deities. Corn-husk masks also could be differentiated according to facial features.

The preceding chapters about specific peoples have each included sections about the life cycle, but information of comparable scope for an Iroquois tribe does not exist.

Later History

A synopsis of Iroquois history to the late 1700s, centering on League–Confederacy evolution, is presented earlier in this chapter. It briefly outlines additional colonial developments, such as the fur trade and relations between the French and British.

The final political drama in which the Iroquois participated was the American Revolution. Most Iroquois appear to have been loyal to the British, who sought their active support following the Declaration of Independence in 1776. The rebels hoped for Iroquois neutrality, but the Confederacy could not achieve a unified position. Among the Mohawk and Onondaga there were both loyalist and rebel factions, whereas the Cayuga and Seneca supported the loyalists; the Oneida and Tuscarora in theory were neutral but aided the rebels. Following early Iroquois and loyalist victories, in 1779 rebel troops destroyed Iroquois communities, crops, and grain caches to end their effectiveness. Many Iroquois fled to Canada, abandoning their traditional lands forever.

In Canada some Mohawk settled near Montreal, where they were given land. When peace was achieved, no mention was made of the Indian participants and their future. In recognition of Mohawk aid, the British granted a prominent leader, Joseph Brant, land along the Grand River that flows into Lake Erie. A portion of this area is the modern Six Nations Reserve. Separate treaties were made between the Six Nations and the United States, in which the Oneida and Tuscarora, who had remained relatively neutral in the conflict, were permitted to retain much of their land, but the other nations, who had aided the British, were forced to relinquish claim to most of their land.

THE NEW RELIGION In addition to the political influence of Iroquois tribes, a second major influence was the emergence of the "New Religion." It originated with a Seneca prophet. His revelations occurred at Burnt House in northwestern Pennsylvania, a small land grant from the Quakers where one of their missionaries recorded what happened. In 1799 Handsome Lake appeared to be near death when he had a vision. By then generations of Iroquois had become addicted to the excessive consumption of intoxicants. In an initial vision three men told Handsome Lake that the Great Chief was displeased by the drunkenness and that if he recovered he was not to consume intoxicants. In a second vision the Great Chief apparently talked with Handsome Lake, who went into a trance and was thought to have died. Yet he recovered some seven hours later to reveal what he had learned. Among the revelations was that Handsome Lake was not to consume alcoholic beverages and was to abandon all dances except the Green Corn Ceremony. Children were to respect their parents, and, if people agreed, it was proper to accept whites as teachers. Finally, Handsome Lake was told that he was to return among the living and that he would see no more of these things until he died; in death he would return to this setting if he behaved properly.

When Handsome Lake recovered, he began preaching his doctrine, which came to include the rejection of schools and a return to a subsistence-based economy. In 1802 his cause received American support when Handsome Lake went to Washington, D.C., with other Iroquois and President Thomas Jefferson condoned his teachings. Partly because of this official sanction, Handsome Lake became an acknowledged prophet. From the time of his recovery until his death, Handsome Lake visited Seneca communities to influence the behavior of others. By 1807 his fame as a prophet had spread widely among the Iroquois and to other eastern tribes. When the War of 1812 began, the Iroquois had learned their lesson, and most of them did not participate. Handsome Lake in particular preached neutrality because of his continuing close ties with the Quakers. In 1815 the prophet moved to Onondaga, and it was here that he died the same year.

As Merle H. Deardorff (1951) noted, the Handsome Lake revelations, the Good Message, came to be joined by a body of teachings that included biographical material, prophecy, law, parable, and anecdote. Believers called the entire system the New Religion. The Good Message was not the only basis for the New Religion; some of the more important changes proposed in the revelation had been initiated before Handsome Lake's trances. If the text of the revelations had been the only document to survive, Handsome Lake might have been assumed to be a great innovator; but from the diaries of the Quaker missionaries it is obvious that the revelations were in step with what were recognized and pressing problems at Burnt House. Although much of the Handsome Lake doctrine was influenced by Quaker and earlier Jesuit missionaries and although some aspects were novel, these teachings also had deep roots in Iroquois religious life of old. The emphasis on confession, the continuity in honoring traditional gods, and the prominence of the annual ceremonial round are examples. Furthermore, the Iroquois had long placed considerable emphasis on prophetic dreams, and this too was a critical element in the Handsome Lake revelations. Unlike many other Indian prophets, Handsome Lake was willing to adapt his basic ideas to accommodate Quaker beliefs and to accept certain material aspects of white culture, such as farming methods. This flexibility contributed to the stability of Iroquois life in his time and unquestionably aided the long-term survival of the Good Message. Soon after Handsome Lake's death, other Christian missionaries proselytized among the Seneca, and the Indians labored in council to establish a uniform approach to religion. The time-honored pattern of unanimity, however, could not be achieved, and by 1820 the New Religion had separated from other Iroquois religious systems.

The Good Message was not recorded systematically until 1845, and no single text became standard. By 1949 the New Religion was being taught in ten ceremonial structures, each termed a longhouse, on the meeting circuit of the

Six Nations. Most of the preachers required four days to relate the Good Message. The Tonawanda Longhouse was called symbolically the Central Fire, and here were kept the most sacred strings of wampum that had belonged to Handsome Lake.

The New Religion includes the following tenets: the prohibition of intoxicants; obedience of children toward their parents and care of aged parents; faithfulness of married couples; reproval of gossiping or boasting; killing of witches; awareness of a hell for sinners and heaven for persons who have lived good lives or repented of having lived evil lives; and the acceptance of the ways of whites save for schools. As has been noted by Edmund Wilson (1960, 87), the New Religion "has a scope and a coherence which have made it endure as has the teaching of no other Indian prophet, and it is accepted at the present time by at least half the Iroquois world as a source of moral guidance and religious inspiration."

OTHER CHANGES The course toward modern Iroquois life was set in the early nineteenth century. Many of those Iroquois who sympathized with the British had moved to Canada, and the ones in the United States had settled on small reservations. Each of these two major groups had its own chiefs, councils, and wampum, and each became increasingly involved in reservation or reserve politics and relationships with the respective governments. In the early 1800s the Iroquois in both countries continued to hunt over broad areas that reached beyond their boundaries and to plant traditional crops in old ways. However, as increasing numbers of white settlers occupied nearby land, Iroquois life began to change in basic ways.

The ability of the Indians to hunt profitably declined as the supply of game diminished; furthermore, they no longer could move from one area to another as the productivity of their farmland declined. Consequently, they turned increasingly to plow agriculture, farming in the manner of whites. In New York State, the Iroquois depended heavily on annuities derived from the sale of land to obtain items of material culture such as blankets, guns, and farming equipment. Annuity payments unquestionably eased their transition to a more sedentary lifestyle. The greatest threat to their security was continued encroachment of whites on their lands; another concern was the conflict arising from the pull of traditional Iroquois culture and the attractions of white culture. This inevitably caused factions to develop on reservations and reserves that have continued into the present.

The Six Nations Reserve

By the end of the American Revolution, Iroquois men were scattered widely in the western provinces of Canada and the western United States. Most of them worked for the North West and Hudson's Bay companies, especially as canoemen in the fur trade. Some of these Iroquois, however, were freemen as trappers and traders, and small groups have maintained their separate identity in western Canadian provinces. Other Iroquois, especially Cayuga and Seneca, who had settled in Ohio, were forced to move to Indian Territory under the Indian Removal Act of 1830 and to live on a reservation in northeastern Oklahoma. There likewise is an Oneida reservation in Wisconsin. From about 1870 to 1881 Iroquois from the Six Nations Reserve in Ontario, especially Cayuga, moved to the Oklahoma reservation and remained there. The emphasis now shifts to the Six Nations Reserve in Canada for three good reasons. The reserve is the most populous Iroquois stronghold up to the present, each tribe is represented, and an account about the reserve by Annemarie A. Shimony beginning in the 1950s is superior.

As compensation for land lost in New York State following the American Revolution, the Mohawk war chief, Joseph Brant, received an original tract of about 675,000 acres along Grand River from the British. In 1784–1785, about 1,450 Iroquois began to settle there and were accompanied by nearly 400 persons from other tribes who lived among the Iroquois.

Brant justifiably claimed that the land grant reflected British recognition of Iroquois national sovereignty, and he felt free to do as he wished with the land. Soon he had sold about half of the acreage to whites. He felt that white farmers in their midst would encourage Indian men to farm. The Mohawk, Oneida, and Tuscarora lived largely along upper Grand River and became known as the Upper Tribes. Many had been Christianized before migrating to the reserve, and they were as a group reasonably responsive to becoming more like white Canadians. Down the river were the Lower Tribes, the Cayuga, Onondaga, and Seneca, who retained a far more traditional way of life and the Good Message of Handsome Lake.

By 1956 the reserve population, most of whom were Mohawk and Cayuga, numbered about sixty-five hundred. They lived on scattered homesteads, and individual holdings were inherited by members. The stress placed by Euro-Canadians on inheritance through males confused the traditional Iroquois matrilineal descent system. Inheritance rights, like individual rights to band membership, were calculated patrilineally according to the Canadian authorities but matrilineally by the Iroquois. Another difference was that Canadians considered the nuclear family an important social unit, and their emphasis on it robbed the clans of important functions. A newly married couple on reserve land now lived either with the husband's or wife's relatives only until they could establish an independent household (neolocal residence). The exogamous nature of the matriclans continued to be observed by some people, but others felt it was acceptable to marry anyone to whom close genealogical ties could not be established. The matrilineages remained important in selecting leaders, but disputes arose over which were the leading lineages with the vested rights. Members of the leading lineages of a clan most often made an effort to retain their clan ties so that they would not lose their political and religious authority. A real difficulty, however, stemmed from the fact that even some conservative families could no longer trace their clan affiliations.

THE NEW RELIGION Four local congregations formed the organizational base for the New Religion, each centered at a different longhouse. The Central Fire was the Tonawanda Longhouse in New York State. Here preachers on the longhouse circuit were invested, but the Central Fire had no jurisdiction over the Home Fires. The rituals of the four longhouses were essentially the same. Each longhouse had wampum to validate its legitimacy, and the particular one to which a person belonged was determined by matrilineage ties and by its proximity. Longhouses were the traditional rectangular wooden buildings, usually with doors and wood-burning stoves at each end and with benches along the walls.

Longhouse leaders were Keepers of the Faith or deacons, as they more commonly were called. Each longhouse had a leading male and female Keeper of the Faith, chosen on the basis of merit. They guided all longhouse functions. With a breakdown of the clan structure, Keepers of the Faith as a group had an increased voice in community affairs. A second longhouse functionary, the Keeper of the Fire, was the guardian of the longhouse wampum. His moiety and clan affinities were unimportant, but he had to be a staunch believer in the New Religion. The wampum was symbolic of the longhouse traditions, and the people believed that Canadian officials sought to destroy the wampum and thereby eliminate the longhouses. The final longhouse leader was the Speaker, who presented traditional and extemporaneous speeches to the congregation. Such persons did not hold a formal office, nor were they usually preachers on the longhouse circuit. A Speaker was required to have a talent for public speaking and knowledge of traditional speeches.

A longhouse served many functions in the members' efforts to resist becoming like other Canadians. The organization fulfilled social, medical, economic, and political needs. Social gatherings included softball or lacrosse games, raffles, and dances. Organized social activities sponsored outside the longhouse usually were closed to longhouse members by their own dogma. The longhouse ceremonial round was rich in detail; it was based on the Handsome Lake revelations, as well as the aboriginal planting and harvest ceremonies and the old and new means for curing. An important aspect of almost any longhouse function was the recitation of a formal address of thanks to the Great Chief for the continued life of the persons attending and thanks to the participants for attending. In all longhouse activities the ritual and social language was Iroquois; speaking English was disapproved in any context. To the members, participation in longhouse events gave real purpose to life and at the same time offered a systematic philosophy for living. People were encouraged to remember the teachings of Handsome Lake and to live good lives. At times the younger members were told not to imitate such fashion extremes of whites as high-heeled shoes and low-cut dresses for girls. Neither should one listen to the radio, watch television, or drink intoxicants, for such behavior was not in keeping with the New Religion. Behind it all was the real fear that the longhouse members would become carbon copies of their white Canadian neighbors. The conflict of values seems often to have led to trauma at the time of death for those individuals who had at some time followed forbidden white ways.

For members of the New Religion and other Iroquois as well, there was a deeply rooted focus on death. Death supposedly could be caused by failure to accept a time-honored view about the spirit world, by showing a lack of respect for plants or animals, or by failing to hold rituals as directed. Furthermore, the dead had great power over the living, and to neglect them was an invitation to disease and death. In general, it was thought that souls resided in a pleasant upperworld or else suffered punishment. Souls bent on evil could assume animal forms, but ordinarily they were nonmaterial or a light vapor. All of this concern with death and the dead necessitated the proper performance of obligations to the dead.

The sachems, who were either Christians or members of the New Religion, represented traditional authority and formed the official political body of the Six Nations Reserve until 1924. The longhouse sachems considered that their Christian counterparts were not legitimate officeholders unless they had been invested at a longhouse ceremony, which was comparable to raising up a sachem in the old League. With respect to Canadian officials, the sachems were divided over whether or not they favored closer rapport. In 1924 some World War I veterans, especially those from the Upper Tribes, formed a group known as the Progressive Warriors and sought Canadian recognition of an elected council. During an ensuing investigation of Six Nations Reserve affairs, the sachems would not present their case to Canadian representatives; thus, the government heard from only the "progressive" faction, which supported elected chiefs. The Canadians decided in favor of elected leaders, since they received little cooperation from the sachems, who represented the traditional confederacy council. An elected council was installed in 1924; the New Religion sachems were locked out of the council house, and Royal Canadian Mounted Police officers enforced the government's decision. The supporters of the Confederacy were bitter against the Canadians, as well as against their factional opposites, and the bitterness continues to the present. In an ethnohistorical account about the relatively recent past on the reserve, Sally M. Weaver (1972) has noted that the confederacy council refused to disband after the elected council was instituted and continued to hold regular meetings in the hope of being reinstated as the only legitimate authority.

RECENT DEVELOPMENTS ON THE RESERVE A current major issue is the identity of a status Indian (a registered member of the reserve). In 1998 there were about 20,000 status Indians enrolled on the reserve, and about 50 percent of them lived there. Of this total, 24 percent became members as a result of the 1985 Canadian government Bill C-31; it reinstated band membership to women who had married non-native men. However, under current Canadian government policy a child with one C-31-status parent *cannot* pass membership on to his or her children, and about one-half of the children have only one status parent. If this trend continues, it will not be many generations before there are *no status Indians*. Understandably, the Six Nations government is very concerned about this possibility, and they plan to change the current status determination with Canadian government approval.

Furthermore, the elected Six Nations government passed a by-law in 1986 stating that only registered band members could live on the reserve. If a band member files a formal complaint that a non-band member lives there and the complaint proves to be valid, the person must leave the reserve within forty-eight hours. The Ontario courts have thus far accepted the Six Nations residency law. It must be emphasized that these Native Americans are legally defined as *allies* of the Crown, not *subjects* of the Crown, irrespective of Canadian law. The Six Nations own their land; it is not Crown land. To have their own residency laws on the reserve represents one effort to be more fully self-governing.

In another context, the Canadian government has transferred the funding and partial control of some programs to the Six Nations band council. By 1994 the band had received nearly $21 million from the federal government and nearly $8 million from the provincial government. Most of this money supported the band council government, infrastructure, and social services. Thus the Six Nations have gained and continue to gain greater local administrative power.

By the late 1990s, elected band council members were far less sympathetic to Canadian government policies than they had been in 1924. The traditional leaders as hereditary chiefs have maintained a "shadow government" on the reserve up to the present. In some contexts, the traditional council leaders—with considerable authority but no formal power—support the positions of the elected leaders in a more united effort to gain autonomy. One ongoing problem is that the federal, provincial, and local Canadian governments have refused to recognize the hereditary council. One instance in which the two councils are united is an effort to establish a traditional Iroquois justice system on the reserve despite Euro-Canadian opposition.

For most band members, a disturbing development emerged first in 1988 when a militant group, the Warrior Society, began patrolling the reserve as nonlegal police. The hereditary and elected chiefs alike denounced the Warriors, and the patrols soon ceased. By 1994 they had few members and sympathizers, perhaps a total of forty individuals. One major problem, however, is that the Warriors, like the hereditary chiefs, seek far greater independence from Canadian government control. Both groups seek an Iroquois government. The Warriors, however, have been involved in smuggling alcoholic beverages, guns, tobacco, and drugs from Iroquois reservations in the United States. Some smugglers on the reserve are multimillionaires. Legitimate leaders fear that Warrior activities will undermine the basis for band control and will provide the Canadian government with reasons for abrogating the rights of Six National Reserve members. In a real sense Warrior activities are compatible with the traditional Iroquois emphasis on warfare; what they do is dangerous and akin to

Figure 12-9 | Erik Bruce Isaacs, a Cayuga, won the "Typical Indian Baby" award at the Six Nations Fall Fair in 1983. (Courtesy of the *Brantford Expositor.*)

the early historic "private wars." The massive Warrior smuggling activities from the United States involved U.S. Mohawk at the St. Regis Reservation and at least $687 million U.S. dollars. In 1999 some twenty-seven participants, Indian and non-Indian, pleaded guilty to or had been convicted of felonies from investigations in the United States.

In 1997 an estimated 9,500 Iroquois lived on the reserve, and they have been increasingly concerned about the perpetuation of Iroquois culture. The Woodland Cultural Centre at Brantford includes a museum, archives, and numerous programs that stress traditional Indian life (see Figure 12-9). One major fear is that their aboriginal languages will become extinct. In 1998 at the Six Nations Reserve no one spoke Seneca or Tuscarora, and the other Iroquoian languages combined were probably spoken by fewer than 350 persons. Most important, longhouse ceremonial texts are traditionally delivered in an Iroquoian language, and about 50 percent of the reserve residents are members of a longhouse. Although a local radio station, CKRZ, includes Iroquoian-language texts and programs, these efforts do not appear to be very effective in language instruction. In 1986 concerned parents launched a language program to teach Mohawk and Cayuga at a small number of reserve schools. Mohawk and Cayuga are taught in an immersion program.

The Six Nations Reserve is among the strongest centers for the perpetuation of traditional Iroquois culture in Canada and the United States. Their sense of Indian identity, much greater than it was twenty years ago, continues to grow with each confrontation with Canadian authorities. The Six Nations willingly concede little to Euro-Canadians, not only because the reserve residents own the land they occupy but also because they continue to consider themselves "allies of the Crown," not its subjects. As the Mohawk linguist, longhouse member, and political activist Amos Keye says, "Lead, follow, or get out of the way!"

In recent years Euro-Canadians have been confronted with scandals involving residential schools for Native Americans. Beginning in 1863 strenuous efforts were made to suppress aboriginal cultures by forcing First Nations children between the ages of four and eighteen to attend a residential school. Nearly one hundred of these schools were operated by churches under contract with the federal government until the 1960s. Children routinely had their heads shaved on admission, were issued uniforms, and were closely regimented and forbidden to speak their native languages. The physical, psychological, and sexual abuse of students was widespread and was exposed in the early 1990s. In 1998 the federal government established a $350 million "Residential Schools Healing Fund."

Six Nations children, and those from other tribes, attended the Mohawk Institute Residential School operated by the Anglican Church of Canada near Brantford from 1834 to 1969. A woman who was a student there in *1968* reported that she used one word of greeting in an Iroquoian language. As punishment she was beaten with a tack-studded belt on her neck, back, and legs. In 1998 over 800 former students at this school launched a class-action suit against the church involved and the federal government for $1.7 billion. By 2000 it appeared that the Anglican Church of Canada could be bankrupt as a result of this and similar suits, especially if the federal government does not provide most of the money to settle claims by former students.

A long-term negative result of the treatment that Indian children received at residential schools over the generations is that, as adults, they raised their children, not infrequently, in the manner of residential schoolteachers and supervisors. Residential school graduates often purposefully did not teach their children an Indian language or Indian ways so that they would not suffer similar trauma in school. It also has been established that children who attended residential schools have a high rate of substance abuse, suicide, and emotional problems compared with other Canadians. By mid-2000 some 6,000 lawsuits across Canada were based on alleged abuse at government-owned schools.

SKYWALKERS The word "skywalkers" refers to Indian ironworkers, especially Mohawk, who construct skyscrapers, bridges, and other high steel structures. Since the late 1940s ethnographic and popular accounts have praised their inordinate success in this dangerous occupation. The best overview of the skywalkers is by Richard Hill (1987), an ironworker.

Traditionally, as discussed earlier in this chapter, warfare was a primary focus among Iroquois men, but warfare diminished rapidly following the War of 1812. Some of the men became canoemen in the fur trade—a dangerous occupation, especially when in enemy country. This trade, however, began to decline about 1800. Adventurous men were next drawn to the timber industry; rafting logs through fast water and rapids was hazardous work. At about the same time, other men became farmers, and still others began to travel about New England selling Indian medicines.

Reports about the Mohawk dating from colonial times suggest that at least some men did not fear heights. They were observed crossing deep creeks by walking fearlessly on small poles and had been seen casually striding along the ridges of gabled houses. Some outsiders have suggested that an absence of a fear of heights was inborn, but it seems more likely that the ability was learned. The Mohawk began to work iron systematically in 1886, when a cantilever bridge, known to them as the "black bridge," was built across the St. Lawrence River and buttressed on the Caughnawaga Reserve. In exchange for building rights, the contractor agreed to hire Mohawk for unskilled jobs. The Indians were unhappy with this arrangement and could not be kept off of the bridge as it was being built. It soon appeared that they were unafraid of heights and were pleased with the new experience. Finally a few men were hired, and they proved to be excellent workers. Three crews reportedly were trained on the black bridge. In the construction of a bridge of this nature, precut and drilled beams and girders were hoisted in place with a crane or derrick, temporarily bolted and plumbed, and then riveted. The Mohawk became members of riveting crews, both the most dangerous and the most lucrative work.

By 1907 there were more than seventy skilled Mohawk ironworkers. Thirty-eight were working on the Quebec Bridge across the St. Lawrence River near Quebec City. On August 19, 1907, while still under construction, the bridge collapsed, killing ninety-six workers, thirty-three of whom were Mohawk. Bridge work then took on a new meaning; because it obviously was dangerous, it became an attractive type of employment to Mohawk men. Mohawk women, however, insisted that the gangs of ironworkers hire out on many different projects so that another disaster could not devastate so many families at the same time (see Figure 12-10).

Over the years, some Mohawk who attempted to become ironworkers failed because they feared heights or found the work unappealing. To others, however, it was exciting work, and the comparatively high wages were especially attractive. In the early 1900s Mohawk and other Iroquois men began working on jobs in the United States and established skywalker colonies in such cities as Buffalo and Brooklyn in New York State. They were among the earliest modern urban Indian populations. Following World War II, Iroquois from each of the U.S. reservations and Canadian reserves had become skywalkers. By the late 1980s there were about 130,000 ironworkers in the United

Figure 12-10 | Stan Hill, a Mohawk ironworker in 1973. (Courtesy of Richard W. Hill, Sr.)

States and Canada, of whom about 7,000 were Indians. Although Indians, especially Mohawk, are the best known skywalkers, they obviously represent a minority of the persons, including some women, who work in high steel. (The first steel-framed skyscraper dates from 1886.) Despite their smaller numbers, it appears that Indian skywalkers are maimed or killed in accidents at about the same rate as non-Indians.

In a search for the reasons behind Mohawk success as ironworkers, Morris Freilich (1958) learned that Mohawk men were not free from fear of heights but that they concealed their fear in order to behave as warriors and prove their courage. Also, work in high steel was highly compatible with many essential features of the old Mohawk way of life. The men left home to work for extended periods as they had left to hunt and fight in aboriginal times. There was danger and possible death in what they did, just as there had been of old. When a man returned, he could boast of the tall buildings on which he had worked, just as he once had boasted of his skills in combat. The modern steelworker was subject to little authority, and if he was displeased he could quit his job, just as he formerly had been able to drop out of a war party. These and other parallels lent support to the traditional status of the male in a nontraditional setting. Yet when an ironworker retired, he was likely to return to a reservation or reserve. His adjustment to an uneventful and sedentary life was difficult.

One response was to readopt Indian ways, to the point of refusing to speak English, and to become deeply involved in local social life and politics.

Nationalism and Sovereignty

As the twentieth century progressed, the Iroquois increasingly asserted their nationalism. In World War I, the Iroquois in the United States, as a separate entity, declared war on Germany. In Canada, the people of the Six Nations Reserve had a forceful confrontation with the Royal Canadian Mounted Police in 1924 to assert their national sovereignty. In both countries, the Iroquois tend not to vote in non-Indian elections as a means of emphasizing their separate identity. In New York State, the Iroquois have forcefully resisted efforts by state officials to intervene in their affairs. Predictably, in the United States the Iroquois have avoided paying state and federal income taxes and fought varied efforts to use reservation lands for the St. Lawrence Seaway, the Power Authority of New York State, and the relocation of highways or the building of dams. These disputes have often been complicated by the fact that elected leaders cooperate with the whites, whereas hereditary leaders continue to support the Iroquois Confederacy (see Figure 12-11).

Yet times are changing! In 1976 the Seneca of the Allegheny Reservation signed an agreement with New York State *as equals*. This was the first time since the early 1800s that the state had recognized the sovereign or national status of the Seneca. To build a highway through the reservation, the state attempted to exercise its power of eminent domain, but the courts, including the U.S. Supreme Court, held that the state had no right to condemn reservation lands for the highway. As a result, the state negotiated with the Seneca and received an easement of, but not title to, 795 acres of land. In return the state agreed to pay $2 million, give the Indians *title* to 795 acres of land from the adjoining Allegheny State Park, and provide other benefits.

The Iroquois have long been adamant in asserting that the governments of Canada and the United States must acknowledge their distinct national identity and deal with them as a sovereign nation on the basis of negotiated treaties. In the recent past, the federal government of the United States had refused to entertain the concept of "nations within a nation," but as indicated in the previous paragraph, the federal courts began to be far more sympathetic to sovereignty cases in the mid-1970s (see also Chapter 2).

Among the Iroquois, other Indians, and Euro-Americans alike, Indian gaming has been and remains a divisive issue. Some Iroquois favor it, whereas others are clearly opposed. One early basis for Indian gaming was on the Oneida Reservation in New York State, and the circumstances merit review. Public bingo was launched in 1975, but the prize money awarded was in greater amounts than the state permitted. The operation was soon closed by county authorities. However, this effort initiated gaming on reservations and led to many court cases before gaming was finally sanctioned by the federal government (see also Chapter 2). In 1993 the 1100 Oneida opened another gaming facility, the Turning Stone Casino. Soon after opening, the casino was

Figure 12-11 | This statue of Joseph Brant was unveiled at Brantford, Ontario, in 1886. In a 1990 protest, the blindfold over Brant's eyes and the sign symbolized a major confrontation with the Canadian government. At the Oka Reserve, Quebec, the Mohawk contested the proposed construction of a golf course on an Iroquois burial ground. The conflict peaked in a standoff between the Iroquois and Canadian military forces. The golf course was not built. (Courtesy of the *Brantford Expositor.*)

employing about 1,500 people and beginning to attract some 7,000 visitors each day. Within a few years, gaming profits revolutionized the quality of reservation life. By 1996 some elderly people who had never dreamed of having adequate housing began to occupy up-to-date dwellings funded by gambling profits, as well as by Department of Housing and Urban Development funds. They built a new health care clinic, day care center, and recreational center for young people. Before the casino operation, only two Oneida had attended college; soon after, thirty-eight received scholarships. Furthermore, the Oneida have been buying available local farmland; as a result, the original 32-acre reservation now includes nearly 4,000 acres. As the Oneida leader Ray Halbritter said (McAuliffe 1996, 8), "Our future depends on our ability to take care of ourselves, not on our ability to get anybody else to look out for us by either giving us money or having a law that protects you. We've really got to, number one, develop our own empowerment. Gaming gives us one step in that direction."

Additional Sources

The book by Lewis Henry Morgan (1851) remains a standard Iroquois source. The first systematic study is by Joseph François Lafitau; it was translated and edited by William N. Fenton and Elizabeth L. Moore (1974, 1977) and remains an ethnographic classic. Daniel K. Richter (1987, 1992) examined the League and Confederacy in colonial times. The most comprehensive relatively recent ethnographic study about the Six Nations Reserve is by Annemarie A. Shimony (1994). Nancy Bonvillain (1992) provides a relatively brief book-length overview of the Mohawk; Barbara Graymont (1988) does the same for the Iroquois in general. The Seneca ethnohistory by Anthony F. C. Wallace (1970) is superior. Lawrence M. Hauptman (1981, 1986) examines the relatively recent past in perceptive detail. Uneven presentations about the Iroquois are included in the *Northeast* volume (15) of the *Handbook of North American Indians* edited by Bruce G. Trigger (1978) and published by the Smithsonian Institution. The writings by Fenton about various aspects of Iroquois life are superior.

Selected Bibliography

Alber, Thomas S. 1992. Scalping, torture, cannibalism and rape. *Anthropologica* 34: 3–20.

Barreiro, José. 1992. *Indian roots.* Ithaca, New York.

Biggar, H. P., ed. 1925. *The works of Samuel de Champlain,* vol. 2. Toronto.

Bonvillain, Nancy. 1992. *The Mohawk.* New York.

Colden, Cadwallader. 1755. *The history of the Five Indian Nations of Canada.* 2 vols. London.

Deardorff, Merle H. 1951. *The religion of Handsome Lake: Its origin and development.* Bureau of American Ethnology Bulletin 149, 79–107. Washington, DC.

Fenton, William N. 1940. Problems arising from the historic northeastern position of the Iroquois. *Essays in Historical Anthropology of North America.* Smithsonian Miscellaneous Collections, vol. 100, 159–251.

———. 1941. *Tonawanda longhouse ceremonies: Ninety years after Lewis Henry Morgan.* Bureau of American Ethnology Bulletin 128, 140–66.

———. 1951a. *Locality as a basic factor in the development of Iroquois social structure.* Bureau of American Ethnology Bulletin 149, 35–54.

———. 1951b. *The concept of locality and the program of Iroquois research.* Bureau of American Ethnology Bulletin 149, 1–12.

———. 1951c. *Iroquois studies at the mid-century.* Proceedings of the American Philosophical Society, vol. 95, 296–310.

———. 1957. Long-term trends of change among the Iroquois. In *Cultural stability and cultural change,* 30–35. American Ethnological Society.

———. 1998. *The Great Law and the Longhouse.* Norman, OK.

Freilich, Morris. 1958. Cultural persistence among the modern Iroquois. *Anthropos* 53: 473–83.

Graymont, Barbara. 1988. *The Iroquois.* New York.

Hauptman, Lawrence M. 1981. *The Iroquois and the New Deal.* Syracuse.

———. 1986. *The Iroquois struggle for survival.* Syracuse.

Hill, Richard. 1987. *Skywalkers.* Brantford, Ontario.

Knowles, Nathaniel. 1940. *The torture of captives by the Indians of eastern North America.* Proceedings of the American Philosophical Society, vol. 82, 151–225.

Lafitau, Joseph François. 1974. *Customs of the American Indians compared with the customs of primitive times,* William N. Fenton and Elizabeth L. Moore, eds. and trans., vol. 1, Toronto, 1974; vol. 2, Toronto, 1977.

Lydekker, John W. 1938. *The faithful Mohawks.* Cambridge.

Mann, Barbara A., and Jerry L. Fields. 1997. A sign in the sky. *American Indian Culture and Research Journal* 21(2)105–163.

McAuliffe, Dennis, Jr. 1996. For many Indian tribes, the buffalo are back. *Washington Post National Weekly Edition.* March 18–24, 8–9.

McKenney, Thomas L., and James Hall. 1933. *The Indian tribes of North America,* vol. 1. Edinburgh.

Mitchell, Joseph. (*See* Wilson, Edmund.)

Morgan, Lewis Henry. 1851. *League of the Ho-De-No-Sau-Nee or Iroquois.* 2 vols. New York. (Editions published in 1901 and 1904 were edited and footnoted by Herbert M. Lloyd and were reproduced in 1954 by the Human Relations Area Files.)

———. 1881. *Houses and house-life of the American aborigines.* Contributions to North American Ethnology no. 4.

Parkman, Francis. 1892. *A half-century of conflict.* 2 vols. Boston.

———. 1901, 1902. *The conspiracy of Pontiac and the Indian war after the conquest of Canada.* 2 vols. Boston.

Richards, Cara B. 1957. Matriarchy or mistake: The role of Iroquois women through time. In *Cultural stability and cultural change,* 36–45. American Ethnological Society.

Richter, Daniel K. 1992. *The ordeal of the longhouse: The peoples of the Iroquois League in the era of European colonization.* Chapel Hill, NC.

Shimony, Annemarie A. 1994. *Conservatism among the Iroquois at the Six Nations Reserve.* Syracuse, NY. (First published in 1961.)

Snow, Dean R. 1996. *The Iroquois.* Cambridge, MA.

Thwaites, Reuben G. 1898. *Travels and explorations of the Jesuit missionaries in New France,* vol. 13. Cleveland, OH.

Trigger, Bruce G., ed. 1978. *Northeast,* vol. 15, *Handbook of North American Indians.* Washington, DC.

Wallace, Anthony F. C. 1951. *Some psychological determinants of culture change in an Iroquoian community.* Bureau of American Ethnology Bulletin no. 149, 55–76.

———. 1958. Dreams and the wishes of the soul: A type of psychoanalytic theory among the seventeenth century Iroquois. *American Anthropologist* n.s. 60: 234–48.

———. 1970. *Death and rebirth of the Seneca.* New York.

Weaver, Sally M. 1972. *Medicine and politics among the Grand River Iroquois.* National Museum of Man Publications in Ethnology, no. 4.

Wilson, Edmund. 1960. *Apologies to the Iroquois.* (Includes a reprinting of "The Mohawks in High Steel," by Joseph Mitchell.) New York.

13 The Eastern Cherokee: Farmers of the Southeast

My companions, men of renown, in council, who now sleep in the dust, spoke the same language [antiremoval] and I now stand on the verge of the grave to bear witness to their love of country. My sun of existence is fast approaching to its setting and my aged bones will soon be laid in the bosom of this earth we have received from our fathers who had it from the Great Being above. When I sleep in forgetfulness, I hope my bones will not be deserted by you.

Woman Killer, a man reportedly over eighty years of age in 1830, argues against selling Cherokee land at the time of their pending removal from North Carolina. (Strickland 1977, 379)

HISTORICALLY IN THE Southeast culture area, the Cherokee, Chickasaw, Choctaw, and Creek tribes dominated. Along with the Seminole, who emerged in historic times, these people collectively are identified as the Five Civilized Tribes. The Cherokee occupied the largest area, whereas the Creek initially dominated in the political sphere. Choctaw and Chickasaw influence declined rather rapidly as Euro-Americans became established in the region. Each tribe held land coveted by white settlers. The Indian Removal Act of 1830 led to most of these Indians being resettled in Indian Territory (Oklahoma). The illegal seizure of their homelands and private property, accompanied by calculated cruelties, characterized the years of their displacement. Some Cherokee, however, hid in the Great Smokey Mountains and avoided removal. This chapter first concerns Cherokee life before removal and then concentrates on those who remained in North Carolina. They represent the largest aboriginal tribe that continues to live in their southeast homeland. Interestingly, the present-day Eastern Cherokee domain is *not* a reservation in the usual sense because the land was purchased for them after the removal act. The position of women in Cherokee life is emphasized. Their dominance as artifact makers and as the providers of most food is notable in combination. Women likewise play a dominant role in religious life and an influential one in political life. These aspects of Cherokee culture early in their history are vividly presented by Theda Perdue (1998).

People, Population, and Language

The archaeological record suggests that the ancestors of the Cherokee (CHER-uh-kee) occupied the Southeast culture area for thousands of years. At the time of historic contact, they may have numbered 22,000. Cherokee is a corruption of Tsalagi, the Choctaw–French term for the Cherokee, which they adopted for themselves. Originally they called themselves "the principal people," and they clustered largely in western North Carolina (see Figure 13-1). Their language belongs to the Iroquoian family, and their nearest linguistic relatives are the Iroquois. They occupied four regional groups separated by rugged terrain, which led to a certain degree of isolation that is reflected in dialectic differences. The Eastern Band of Cherokee Indians numbered nearly 12,000 in 2000, and they owned about 57,000 acres in North Carolina. (The population of the Cherokee Nation of Oklahoma was almost 130,000.)

Early Historic Life

The Cherokee were not described in reasonable detail until the mid-1700s, and since their ties with traders and other whites were well established by then, an aboriginal base line ethnography was never assembled. The description that follows therefore focuses on their early historic life.

ORIGIN MYTH The earth once was a great island of water floating on a sea of water. In primeval times animals existed above the sky vault, which

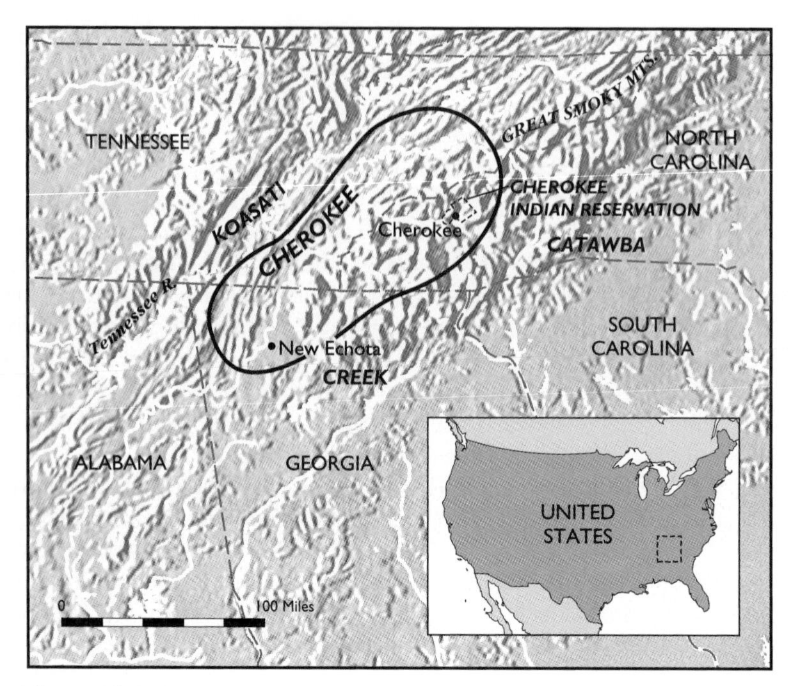

Figure 13-1 | Aboriginal range of the Eastern Cherokee Indians.

became crowded, and they wondered what was beneath the water. Water Beetle volunteered to explore the water, and after diving to the bottom it surfaced with soft mud. As the mud expanded it became the earth and was suspended to the sky and above it with four cords, one in each cardinal direction. Because the earth was soft, various birds were sent to find somewhere to land. Each failed until Great Buzzard flew low over the earth. As he tired his wings struck the earth over what would become Cherokee country, and many valleys and mountains were created. After the earth dried, animals came down from above into darkness, which led to the sun's creation.

The arrival of animals and plants on earth was followed by a human brother and sister. The brother struck his sister with a fish and told her to reproduce, and an offspring was born in seven days. She reproduced in this manner time and again until the number of people grew alarming. Then it was deemed that a fertile woman should bear one offspring a year, and this pattern continues. When the earth ages and wears out, the suspension cords holding it up will break and the earth will sink into the sea.

CLOTHING AND APPEARANCE As was true for other Indians in the Southeast, the Cherokee made most clothing of deerskins sewn with sinew thread. A man's basic garment was a breechclout, and women wore knee-length skirts. Their moccasins were of deerskin, and they wore bison-skin robes during cold

Figure 13-2 | Three Cherokee men during a visit to England in 1762. (By permission of the British Library.)

weather. (In early historic times bison were scattered throughout most of the United States and from Mexico into Canada.) Capes for summer wear had feathers attached to a fiber base. Buckskin shirts and cloth boots were added in early historic times. The most distinctive personal adornment was the ear decoration of males. A section of the outer border of each ear was cut free, stretched, and wound with wire to hold it in an expanded arc (see Figure 13-2). This aboriginal practice declined in popularity when silver jewelry became popular in the late 1700s. Wealthy persons wore collarlike bands of clamshell beads around their necks. Youthful warriors were tattooed by pricking the skin with a needle and rubbing bluish coloring in the openings. Designs of animals, flowers, and geometric forms were tattooed on the chest or muscular parts of the body. All the hair was plucked from a man's head except for a scalp lock at the back; it was decorated with beads or feathers. Women apparently drew their hair back into a very long bundle held with ribbons.

SETTLEMENTS AND MANUFACTURES In reasonably early historic times, the Cherokee lived in scattered settlements because relatively level plots of ground suitable for cultivation were scarce. They built communities near streams and rivers to have access to fish and to game that was attracted to water and also for religious reasons. A large settlement might encompass 450 acres, but a typical community covered a much smaller area. Matrilineal families owned dwellings, storage facilities, and a nearby menstrual hut. The rectangular summer house had pole framing, a gabled bark-covered roof, and walls of poles interwoven with branches and covered with mud. A large winter house was constructed much the same way. Within both types were platforms along the walls, and heat and light were provided by firewood in fireplaces; neither type had windows or a chimney. The most imposing structure was the council house used for religious, social, and political purposes; some of these buildings accommodated five hundred people. A council house was seven-sided, framed with logs, and had a roof supported by concentric circles of interior posts. The entire structure was covered with earth except for a narrow doorway and a smokehole at the center of the roof. Inside were benches and a central fireplace.

Women were the primary artifact makers. They possessed diverse craft skills combined with patience and hard work. Their superior glazed pottery included cooking pots, bowls, dishes, and food-storage vessels. It required highly technical skills and hours on end to produce baskets woven from swamp cane, food and garment containers, sieves, household mats, and additional items. Deerskins and gourds fashioned into receptacles held water, honey, or bear oil. The women appear to have made pipes from soapstone, and they were avid smokers. Women supplied their households with water and firewood. These obligations, combined with food preparation and caring for children, meant that they typically worked hard most of the year.

The physical labor of women in artifact production had no realistic counterpart among men. Men made large dugout boats, the major conveyance, from logs as long as forty feet. To hollow a log, they burned one side and chipped away the charred wood. These boats were some two feet wide, straight-sided, and flat-bottomed, and they could carry as many as twenty people. Wood-framed canoes covered with bark had far less importance. Men likewise fashioned their weapons for the hunt and warfare—bows and arrows, spears, and clubs.

SUBSISTENCE ACTIVITIES Women planted, tended, and harvested crops, the primary staples. Each matrilineal household had a field at the edge of a settlement. Men cleared and burned small trees and brush; they girdled large trees to kill them as a later source of firewood. Women planted three varieties of maize in small hills, and among the hills sowed bean, gourd, and squash seeds. The bean vines grew up the maize stalks, and the leaves of the gourds and squash helped retain moisture in the soil. Women hoed the most troublesome weeds, and throughout the growing season elderly women sat atop platforms in the fields to scare off predators, such as crows and raccoons. In addition, women gathered a wide variety of wild edibles, including berries, leaves, and seeds. Honey locust tree and sugar maple sap were processed as sweeteners.

While women farmed in the summer, men at a settlement gambled and lounged before traveling widely as warriors to confront enemies. Men hunted with self bows and reed arrows tipped with bone or fish-scale points. The most important big game included white-tailed deer and black bear, and bison and elk were available in some sectors. The most important game bird was wild turkey, hunted for its meat and, equally important, its feathers. They harvested small game and small birds with darts shot from blowguns, a widely prevailing weapon in the Southeast that probably was introduced from Mexico or the Antilles. Men fished with hooks, leisters, and traps, and traps were set for game and birds. The only aboriginal domestic animal was the dog, but Europeans introduced chickens, hogs, horses, and new crops such as potatoes and watermelons.

GENDER IDENTITY Early Western observers, meaning European men, customarily wrote that Cherokee men were lazy and that servile women slaved for them. The two previous sections of this chapter may suggest that women were subservient, but clearly this was not the case. Largely unbiased observers noted that women were willing and cheerful workers who had an advantageous position because they controlled the fruits of their labor, especially crops, for general welfare. In mythology and in fact, women played a critical role that balanced that of men. The word "balance" was, and in part remains, central to gender relations. The division of labor was theoretically rigid, but in actuality men and women consistently aided one another. Men, irrespective of their social standing, helped clear the fields that women planted. Women turned to medicine men to produce rain for crops in time of droughts. Men depended on the women who accompanied them on extended hunting trips and raids to fulfill their gender roles. Religion and social relations focused in large degree on the harvest of maize, especially the Green Corn Ceremony, in which women as the providers played a central role, as is discussed later. No remotely comparable ceremonial recognition was accorded the contributions of men for their skills as hunters and fishermen.

DESCENT, KINSHIP, AND MARRIAGE Descent was traced through females (matrilineal), and a person was prohibited from marrying a member of his or her own matriclan (clan exogamy) or father's clan. A man's preferred mate was from his father's father's or mother's father's clan. After a man married and moved to another settlement (matrilocal residence), he still was regarded as a member of the clan of his birth. The members of a localized clan segment made certain that a spouse was mourned properly and that men fulfilled familial obligations. Violations led to public whippings by the women of the clan involved. A widow was expected to marry her deceased husband's brother (levirate), and a widower was supposed to take his deceased wife's sister as a spouse (sororate).

The aboriginal Cherokee kinship terminology reportedly was of the Crow system, meaning that the cousin terms were of the Crow type and descent was matrilineal. In this cousin terminology, a father's sister's daughter and mother's brother's daughter were termed differently from each other and from sisters or parallel cousins (mother's sister's and father's brother's daughters). However, a father's sister's daughter was classed with father's sister. With respect to the words for aunts, the term for mother and mother's sister were the same, but a separate term existed for father's sister (bifurcate merging parental generation terminology). The kinship terms made it possible to distinguish precisely the four matrilineages that were most important to an individual: those of mother, father, mother's father, and father's father (see Figure 13-3).

SOCIAL DIMENSIONS Eighteenth-century Cherokee households usually consisted of a number of nuclear families related through females (matrilineal extended family). Ideally, the household included an elderly couple, their daughters, the daughters' husbands, unmarried males born into the household, and the daughters' daughters. The mutual obligations of household members and their relationship with the members of other such units were defined with precision. A father taught his son to hunt, but a mother's brother, who lived in another household, was a child's disciplinarian. An in-marrying male was respectful toward his in-laws but was expected to joke with his wife's brothers and brothers-in-law; through the jokes of others, one became aware of erring ways. In-marrying males retained close ties with their natal households and the clans of their birth, yet a household's members formed the most closely cooperating economic unit in the society.

In social and political terms, matrilineages were less important than matriclans. Members of the same clan in a band acted collectively. Apparently seven named clans (Bird, Blue Paint, Deer, Red Paint, Twister-Long Hair, Wild Potato, and Wolf) were represented in each village, and members of a clan cooper-

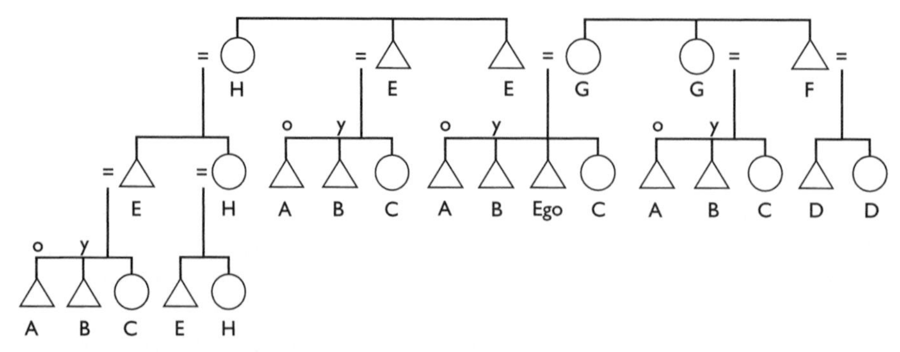

Figure 13-3 | The early historic Cherokee system of kinship terminology.

ated closely at the village level. The seven clans in a settlement allotted farmlands to member households and regulated marriage. Another important obligation of a clan was to settle disputes with the members of another clan. The most serious crime was murder. If someone killed a person in another clan, all local members of the murderer's clan were held responsible, and all males of the dead person's clan were obligated to seek revenge. Preferably the offender himself was killed in revenge, although one of his clan mates might be substituted.

In the drift of history, early and contemporary sources suggest basic continuity in the ways that individuals deal with one another. Thus the information in this paragraph is in the present tense. I begin with inappropriate behavior. Included is any form of overt and direct aggression or hostility in face-to-face contacts. Parsimony with one's property, time, and especially food are singularly undesirable. Particularly anathema are assertive and boastful persons. The reactions to undesirable behavior are powerful weapons—gossip, withdrawal, and turning to witchcraft are prime examples. In general, misfortune, such as bad luck, is anticipated for aggressive persons. The opposites of all these traits are encapsulated in the anthropological label for Cherokee behavior, the Harmony Ethic. In essence, when dealing with others a good person is friendly but not innocent in being generous, helpful, and understanding. Quite obviously, to coerce others has no place in the Harmony Ethic.

Among the Cherokee and other Indians in the Southeast, stickball, the generic game from which lacrosse is derived, was a popular sport (see also Chapter 12). Every player carried a stick that had a small loop and a pocket attached at the end. The object of the game was to carry a small ball across the goal of the opposite team. The ball could be carried in one hand, in the mouth, or in the mesh pocket of the stick. Any means, including the use of the stick, could be employed to obtain the ball; injuries, both purposeful and unintended, were difficult to prevent. They quite reasonably called the game "the little brother of war." Stickball games were social events but included many ceremonial aspects. For example, a man was not to have sexual intercourse with his wife for at least seven days before participating in a game, and if she was pregnant, he could not play. Several shamans were active for each side, and a rite was performed at running water. On the night before the game a dance was held, magic was invoked against opponents, and other rituals took place. During a game itself, each side tried to disable the best players on the other team.

POLITICAL LIFE Early in their history, Cherokee political life was well-organized, although it was localized and did not unite the tribe as a whole. This political organization changed as it was affected by both British influences and inclusion of warriors.

Early Organization A large village or a number of small ones formed a political aggregate, or band, of from 350 to 600 persons. As a group approached the larger number, the tendency was for a portion to separate and organize as a new unit. In the early 1700s some sixty settlements were represented by about thirty-five bands. Each band was politically autonomous. Control was in the hands of a council of elders, both female and male, the heads of clans, and representatives of two organizations, called the Whites and Reds, that stood in opposition to one another. The Whites symbolized peace, and members were traditionally old, passive, and mild-mannered. White chiefs achieved their goals through diplomacy and reached decisions by consensus. The Reds, by contrast, symbolized war; members were expected to be young, active, and impetuous. Reds generally were young males who had married into a village and thus occupied a marginal position within the social system. As Reds aged, they became associated with the Whites and gradually found themselves integrated into community life.

Each fall, after the Harvest Ceremony and before rekindling a sacred fire, a white flag flew over the council house to indicate that the community was in control of the Whites. At an assembly, seating arrangements were by age, gender, and clan. Deliberations were guided by a general council composed of elderly men, called Beloved Men, and by priests. There was also an inner council of seven Beloved Men, one from each clan. Topics for discussion typically included relations with other Indians and non-Indians, matters of war and peace, and trade. With the priests as arbitrators, any question put before a council was stated and restated until a consensus was achieved. Apparently the members of each clan attempted to reach a unified position, but if it became clear that a clan could not support an emerging consensus, they withdrew to avoid open conflict.

A council served one large settlement or a cluster of smaller communities, but no larger political structure united the bands or the tribe. Each village was an independent political entity that sought to live in harmonious relations with other such units. Fred Gearing (1962, 83) has reasoned that prior to 1730 the Cherokee comprised a "jural community," meaning that they were united by cultural and social ties. The members of one village might cooperate with those in another, and they appear never to have fought each other, although they were often at war with adjacent tribes. Some villages were more important than others because of their strategic location, the learning of their priests, or the importance of a secular leader, but no village appears to have been dominant for very long. Conflict between Cherokee villages most likely developed if a man killed someone from another village. This was a matter to be resolved by the members of the clans involved, and because each clan was represented by fictive brothers in every other village, these ties, and the ideals of proper behavior in times of disputes, were enough to avert open conflict.

British Influences In 1730 the village council functioned as it had in the past, but British colonial administrators, because the Cherokee spoke a common language, began to view them as a single political unit rather than an aggregate of independent villages. Thus, when a raiding party attacked a white frontier settlement, all of the Cherokee were held responsible. To avoid reprisals, a tribal government began to form. The first person with political authority beyond the village level was Moytoy, an Overhill Cherokee, who presumably was a war chief. He was crowned "Emperor" of the Cherokee in 1730 by the British. The Overhill settlements had long been influential, and they became more important as the military effectiveness of the Chickasaw declined. This placed the Overhill communities on the French frontier and led to their strategic importance to the British and Cherokee alike. The influence of Moytoy was not acknowledged among all Cherokee, but his political office was widely recognized as legitimate. A smallpox epidemic in 1738–39 seems to have killed about half of the people, which led to greater power shifting to political leaders. With the death of Moytoy in 1741, his son Amouskositte became the leader. Presumably, it was he who threatened to destroy a Cherokee village and kill all the inhabitants if they did not kill a man who had murdered a trader. The pressure to take action against the murderer had come originally from the governor of South Carolina, who threatened to cut off trade to the Cherokee. Without arms and ammunition they would have been unable to defend themselves against the French and their Indian allies. Thus the actions of any one village began to be subordinated to broader interests.

In this and other episodes, particular individuals emerged as spokesmen for the Cherokee, but only in dealing with alien powers. By 1753 a priest state was beginning to emerge, roughly paralleling the village-level organization. The capital settlement was the residence of the most notable leader and the chief priest. Other leaders from representative villages met there to deliberate. The major problem was how to prevent warriors from launching raids. The tribal council could punish raiders after the fact but had no institutionalized network to prevent raids. The inability of Amouskositte's successor to curb raids against frontier settlements led to a war with the English from 1759 to 1761. The destruction of numerous villages forced the Cherokee to sue for peace. Raids continued to be a problem, however, and as white settlers boldly began farming Cherokee land, retaliatory raids increased.

Influence of Warriors By 1768 the Cherokee had decided to include outstanding warriors among the decision makers at the tribal council meetings. Heretofore warriors had played an integral part in council decisions only during preparations for conflict and when actually at war. Although the tribal council in theory remained opposed to reprisal raids, integrating the warriors into the tribal political organization meant that any activities they undertook would be legitimate. The American Revolution and the opening of Kentucky to white settlers split the Cherokee into two factions. Most young warriors sided with the British and were armed by them; the old men only sought peace. Decades of raids by warriors such as Dragging Canoe led American military forces to destroy nearly all Cherokee settlements, but the people were not destroyed. When their villages were burned, they fled to the mountains, and after the conflict they returned to reestablish farming communities. Although they repeatedly were forced to give up land, in 1800 they still held title to about forty-three thousand square miles, about half of it in Tennessee and the remainder in adjacent sectors of Alabama, Georgia, and North Carolina.

WARFARE Among the aboriginal population, armed conflict meant primarily raids against enemies who had killed a Cherokee. The purpose was to avenge a death so that the person's soul could finally be at ease. A raiding party typically included a few warriors related to the deceased who set out to kill or capture one or more persons of the tribe responsible for the death. By the early 1700s much of Cherokee energy focused on raids and war as a direct and indirect result of white contact. When a council decided to make war, a red flag was raised over the council house, and the Reds began their preparations. Rituals by priests, fasting and dances by warriors, narrations of heroic deeds, and ritual bathing were all involved. An oration by the war speaker preceded the formal departure of a war party. When venturing forth, the warriors were elaborately painted red and black. The war club, with a projection at one end, was either hand-held or thrown. Warriors also used bows and arrows and spears when fighting. In early historic times, the metal tomahawk of European manufacture was popular, but these and earlier weapons were replaced by imported firearms and knives as they became available (see Figure 13-4).

Native American women typically did not fight tribal enemies, although exceptions are reported, especially in the Southeast culture area. Among the Cherokee, women and warfare had a well-established institutional basis. As noted earlier, obligations based on gender had become comparatively rigid; a clear exception was women and warfare. War parties could include women to perform camp chores, such as hauling water and preparing food. Yet a relatively small but distinct number fought in the manner of men and became War Women. Some ethnographic sources use this term as an alternative to Beloved Women, a good indicator that among females a War Woman occupied a unique position. If one were captured by an enemy and survived to return home, she underwent the same purification rituals as a man under like circumstances.

Relatively little is known about War Women, with the partial exception of Nan-ye-hi (Nancy Ward, d. 1822). In 1750, during a Cherokee–Creek conflict, she had accompanied her husband, and when he was killed, she fought with his gun. Her subsequent achievements as a warrior are poorly known. It is clear, however, that she achieved prominence as a diplomat, evidenced by an oration she gave during negotiations with a U.S. treaty commission in 1785.

This is a fitting context in which to report why the status of War Women declined rapidly in the early 1700s. As the Cherokee became increasingly dependent on the British for trade goods, especially guns and ammunition, they became British allies against the French and enemy Indians. One result was an expanding importance of European methods of warfare. The old pattern, for a few Cherokee warriors to seek revenge for the death of one of their number, declined. European warfare did not include females as fighters, and, when-

Figure 13-4 | Pencil drawings of Cherokee men by George Catlin. (Collection of The New-York Historical Society, neg. no. 33072.)

ever possible, battles dominated over raids, with obvious implications for War Women. Equally important, in European warfare men were killed, and women and children became captives. In the Southeast captives emerged as an asset and became marketable slaves, which led to a decline in the torturing of captives to death. The enslavement of Cherokee women, and those of other tribes in the region, led to their close contacts with African slaves. This may help to explain the prominence of women in Afro-American culture, especially when one considers the matrilineal emphasis of tribes in the Southeast. Furthermore, some contemporary residents in the Southeast culture area who are identified as blacks by outsiders stoutly maintain that their biological heritage is more Indian than black. Oral traditions about their hereditary in all likelihood have a factual basis.

RELIGION The power of blood, deeply ingrained in their belief system, found a major focus in female physiology: menstruation, childbirth, and menopause. Women were isolated during their periods, and restrictions and taboos accompanied pregnancy and childbirth. Unlike the widely held belief in Western societies, women were not considered unclean during menstruation; quite to the contrary, they possessed extraordinary qualities. In one myth, a stone-skinned cannibal approached a settlement. As he came nearer, a medicine man had menstruating women stand at intervals along the path. The cannibal became weaker and weaker. As he passed the last woman he collapsed and was killed. In this general context, menstrual blood was regarded as an unborn offspring, and with childbirth a new generation arose. In sum, the fertility of women was pivotal in life itself, embodying a combination of danger and power.

By the 1700s, as religious life began to be recorded in reasonable detail, the Green Corn Ceremony dominated. It was intimately associated with women, the maize harvest, and rebirth of the Cherokee as a people for the coming year. Preparations began in late September with feasting, extinguishing household fires, cleaning homes, and preparing the square ground (plaza) where nonconforming men could not enter. Warriors and Beloved Women fasted for a short period, and then these women prepared a sacred emetic for warriors to consume and thereby purge themselves of physical and spiritual pollution. Presentation of the new maize crop by Beloved Women was the unifying ritual. A priest received the crop, kindled a new fire symbolic of renewal, and placed maize in the flames for a feast. People confessed their transgressions since the last Green Corn Ceremony, such as unpaid debts, grudges, and adultery, which were forgiven by the onlookers. The square ground then became the center for feasting and dancing. Lastly, people painted their bodies with white clay, a symbol of peace and well-being, and ritually bathed in a river. An explicit goal was to begin life anew and thereby sustain the Harmony Ethic.

As European contacts intensified in the 1750s, traditional ceremonies were consolidated or abandoned. Following the American Revolution, families tended to occupy scattered homesteads, as towns no longer provided adequate defense. As a result of this and other conditions, clan unity diminished, along with a cohesive identity as Cherokee that previously was reinforced in collective rituals and ceremonies. The Green Corn Ceremony survived for a time, but without the unifying qualities of old.

Early History

The expedition led by Hernando de Soto may have passed through a Cherokee community in 1540, but not until the late 1600s were white intrusions relatively common. Firearms and other trade goods became available about 1700, and shortly thereafter traders settled among them. It was not long before the Cherokee were embroiled in hostilities with white colonists from the eastern seaboard, and old rivalries with other Indians intensified. In a series of conflicts with English colonists in 1759–61, many settlements were destroyed, and the Cherokee were defeated. Soon thereafter intrusions by white settlers became increasingly common, and the Cherokee were forced to give up large sectors of land. In the American Revolution, they understandably fought on the side of the British because white settlers posed the greater threat. An alliance with the British, however, led to the repeated destruction of their settlements. Peace was made in 1794, and some Cherokee decided to settle west of the Mississippi River because they felt that whites would never be satisfied in their desire for more land. Most Cherokee remained, however, and became prosperous farmers, even organizing a government modeled after that of the United States. Yet pressures by whites for land never ceased.

When George Washington initiated a policy of Indian assimilation in 1789, he expected the process to be completed within fifty years for all Indians east of the Mississippi River. Assimilation was to be achieved by teaching English to Indians, introducing the farming methods of whites, and imposing the concept of private land ownership. In 1794 the Cherokee signed a treaty of peace with white Americans. This was meant to end the bitter conflict that for twenty years had destroyed the aboriginal basis of Cherokee culture and had sapped the energies of the surviving Indians. Many of them concluded that the selective adoption of white ways was not only desirable but also essential for survival. However, the process of Indian assimilation was hampered by the anti-Indian attitude of many whites along the frontier.

Missionaries were to play a key role in Christianizing and "civilizing" the Cherokee. The first series of Protestant missionaries arrived among them in 1799. As the historian William G. McLoughlin (1984) noted in his seminal study of early missionary activities among the Cherokee, their resistance to becoming Christian was far greater than the missionaries had anticipated. Before long these Indians tried to revive their religion of old, but with little success. In the early 1800s the Cherokee were still attempting to adopt white ways on a selective basis and at their own pace, but the Jacksonian era that began in 1828 brought changes in federal policies toward Indians, and it became increasingly difficult to sustain traditional cultural ways.

ADAPTATIONS The Cherokee Nation founded in 1827 was modeled after the government of the United States, with executive, judicial, and legislative branches. A capital with buildings in the Euro-American architectural style was constructed at New Echota, Georgia, in 1825. Soon after the nation was founded, Sequoya (George Gist), who was of Cherokee and white ancestry, presented to the leaders a proposal for writing their language. In 1809 Sequoya had become impressed with the importance of writing, and he had originated a system whereby symbols represented syllables in the Cherokee language (see Figure 13-5). After the syllabary was adopted in 1821, the vast majority of the Cherokee soon became literate. The syllabary served to preserve traditions by allowing the Cherokee to transcribe their sacred formulas and to record their own history. A print shop was established at New Echota, and a bilingual newspaper appeared in 1828. By then they were numbered among the Civilized

Figure 13-5 | Sequoya (circa 1760–1843) originated the Cherokee syllabary adopted by the Cherokee Nation in 1821. (From McKenney and Hall 1933.)

Tribes. Their population was about 13,500, in addition to nearly 150 white men who had married Cherokee women and about 75 white women who had Cherokee husbands. At this time, too, they owned nearly 1,300 black slaves, which indicates that some members of the nation were succeeding in the Southern economic system.

THE TRAIL OF TEARS Of all the Indian policies enacted by the United States, none was more heartless than "removal." In 1830 the U.S. Congress passed the Indian Removal Act, which provided for the relocation of all Indians in the southeastern states and the Ohio River drainage to Indian Territory (Oklahoma). The act was strongly supported by President Andrew Jackson, whose goal, at least in part, was to prevent the inevitable destruction of these Indians at the hands of whites. Cherokee resistance was strong but largely unsuccessful. They had adopted "civilized" ways, which was disconcerting to politicians in Georgia who yearned to bring their productive lands under state control. In 1829 the Georgia legislature passed a law making much of the Cherokee Nation land into state holdings. Under terms of the law, all previous federal legislation and regulations were to be null and void. In addition, Indians were prohibited from testifying in court cases involving whites, and prohibitions were established against interference with removal plans. About this time, gold was discovered on Cherokee holdings, and the governor declared that all gold-bearing lands belonged to the state. The actions of the Georgia legislature led to the famous *Worcester v. Georgia* case, which reached the Supreme Court in 1831. The court judgment, under Chief Justice John Marshall, was that the federal government, not the state of Georgia, was responsible for the Cherokee. Illegal seizures of land and other property by whites, conflicting policies of the Indian leaders, intrigue by unscrupulous whites and Indians, and harassment by state representatives finally led to the 1835 Treaty of New Echota and Cherokee removal.

Before the Cherokee treaty leading to their "legal" removal, gross injustices were perpetrated by citizens and representatives of the state of Georgia. Indians were forced from their lands at bayonet point, they were removed in chains without due legal process, they were sold intoxicants in violation of federal regulations, and their movable property was often stolen with impunity. A state law prohibiting a Cherokee from employing a white was used as a pretext for seizing plantations; these then were distributed to whites by lottery. The Cherokee were allowed by law to transfer land only to the state. When some families finally were forced to leave Georgia, much of the property they carried with them was seized and their money extorted. Food and shelter during the forced migration often were inadequate or nonexistent, and the weakened emigrants were struck by cholera, along with other diseases. Yet, by 1838 when all of these people were supposed to be gone, only two thousand had been deported; the other fifteen thousand still believed that somehow they would not be driven from their homeland. Such was not the case. About seven thousand soldiers under General Winfield Scott moved against the Cherokee, who had previously been disarmed. Scott ordered that within a month's time every Cherokee must be moving westward. Soldiers went from house to house, forcing people to leave at once. Often the Indians were not allowed to take anything with them, and they were impounded in stockades until they could be shipped west. Their journey to Oklahoma is known to the Cherokee as the Trail of Tears; about four thousand people died as a direct result of their forced removal. This episode in American Indian history is the saddest of the sad.

Later History: The Eastern Band of Cherokee

During the forced removal by the federal government, at least one thousand conservative Cherokee successfully hid in the mountains. Nonetheless, well into the 1840s federal and state officials encouraged them to move west to Indian Territory; small numbers relocated there at that time and later. The most important white advocate for the Eastern Cherokee was William H. Thomas, a businessman, attorney, and the adopted son of a chief. He became a state legislator and helped persuade government officials to permit the remnant population to remain in the region. Yet his financial reverses and mental instability produced greater periodic turmoil. The local Cherokee could not legally own land, which was bought for them by Thomas and others. This land came to be known as the Qualla Indian Boundary. The State of North Carolina recognized the Cherokee as legal residents in 1866, and soon thereafter federal recognition was achieved. Following lengthy and complex legal battles, the title to Qualla Boundary land, some seventy-three thousand acres, was granted to the Eastern Cherokee collectively in 1874. They incorporated as the Eastern Band of Cherokee in 1889 and were acknowledged by the state. With revisions, this incorporation document remains a primary basis for their government. As their legal status evolved, it became a curious and confusing combination of state and federal jurisdictions. Band members voted and paid taxes to the state and were likewise considered wards of the federal government. A major problem was state land taxes; their inability to pay these led to the sale of some holdings. The only major band resource, timber, was harvested to pay some tax debts.

The 1887 passage of the Dawes Act and separate efforts to allot Oklahoma Indian lands led to rumors that Eastern Cherokee land was to be allotted. A long-standing complaint, and one that would recur, was that some whites used devious means to become tribal members in the hope of obtaining land. Some whites reportedly became "five-dollar Indians" by paying this amount as a bribe to be entered on the roll. The enrollment of these whites, in addition to the children of white–Indian marriages, has, over the years, meant that there are a significant number of "white Indians."

A concerted effort by the federal government to further "civilize" these people introduced schools that were managed by Quaker missionaries until 1893. The Quakers succeeded in upsetting the pattern of Indian life, but not nearly as much as did their educational successors in the BIA. The pattern of formal education under the BIA was for a child to attend a day school through the fourth grade and then attend a local boarding school through the ninth grade; his or her education was completed at a distant boarding school such as the one for Indians in Carlisle, Pennsylvania. The goal of compulsory education helped destroy traditional Indian life; children were punished for speaking Cherokee, chained to their beds if they repeatedly ran away, and forced to learn white ways.

In the late 1800s a new source of income emerged as timber companies bought large tracts of land to harvest hardwoods. Mill towns and railroads penetrated sectors to transport and process logs. Cherokee men found seasonal employment in logging and with railroad companies for relatively short-term economic gain. The old forests were cleared of timber by the 1930s, and the related jobs disappeared.

By the early 1900s, following years of trauma and uncertainty, the lives of Qualla Boundary residents became more stable (see Figure 13-6). The *gadugi,* a free labor company, became a prominent cooperative enterprise and a source of pride. It was represented in most communities as a dozen or so men who formed a company to help one another with farming and other activities; they could likewise borrow money from the treasury. As they began hiring themselves out to whites around 1910, however, these companies became taxable by the state, and they began to disappear. Subsistence farming remained the basis of the economy, but by the late 1920s stock-fencing laws and a chestnut blight led to a decline in hog production, a significant source of meat. The standard of living decreased at a time when the population was growing. An eventual positive economic factor was an expansion of the local road network to provide access to wage labor jobs, although jobs were few, and the living standard declined.

Figure 13-6 | A North Carolina Cherokee home in 1888. (Courtesy of the Smithsonian Institution, National Anthropological Archives, neg. no. 1000-B.)

Continuity with the past was provided by a wide variety of dances associated with ceremonies. Prominent among these was the Booger Dance. The word *booger* has the same root in English as the word *bogy,* meaning goblin. In its Cherokee meaning it approximated the concept of ghost and was represented on dance masks as caricatures of foreigners (see Figure 13-7). It appears as though the dance was originally performed to induce men to join war parties and to dilute the harmful spirits of foreigners. By the 1930s, the dance had lost its religious associations and portrayed whites and blacks. Performers, usually men, danced in a circle, frightened children, and joked with adults in the audience who stood in a proper joking relationship.

In retrospect, *the* most dramatic change in Eastern Cherokee life since the Trail of Tears began in the 1920s and continues relentlessly into the present. It is tourism. It began in 1914 with the annual Cherokee Indian Fair (now the Cherokee Fall Festival) attended by the local population. Then as the system of regional roads improved in the late 1920s, the fair attracted expanding numbers of tourists. Of paramount importance, in 1926 the federal government established the nearby Great Smoky Mountains National Park. Land for the park was transferred to the federal government from the states of Tennessee and North Carolina in 1934, and the park was dedicated in 1940. Before the formal dedication, tourists visited the park, and their number increased dramatically as a system of paved roads was developed following World War II.

The most important Cherokee-crafted items for sale were baskets produced by women, and this remains true into the present. It cannot be overemphasized that by the late 1800s, baskets provided the most reliable income source for innumerable families, especially during economically stressful times,

Figure 13-7 | Booger Dance mask. (Courtesy of Museum of the Cherokee Indian.)

such as when the timber industry declined. The basketry tradition slowly changed in response to the market, including widely available nontraditional materials. Most every home included basketmakers who worked throughout the year to feed and clothe family members. Eventually the Qualla Arts and Crafts Cooperative set high standards for the baskets they marketed. In response to tourist desires, baskets are usually now richly ornamented, and the small ones sell best.

The contrast between those Cherokee who followed the essence of their traditional way of life and those who were becoming more involved with Euro-American ways became especially evident in the 1950s. The differences are highlighted in the following summary, which owes a great deal to the notable presentation by John R. Finger (1991).

Indianness had become best associated with being a full-blooded Cherokee accompanied by a configuration of cultural characteristics. The dichotomy between "full-bloods" and "white Indians" was expanding. Full-bloods "looked like Indians," and they subscribed to the Harmony Ethic. Being generous and kind to others, withdrawing from potential conflict, and minding one's own business fostered harmony. For example, the officers in a surviving gadugi worked in an egalitarian manner. Decisions reflected common consent.

Because overt disagreements ran counter to their values, in a voting situation individuals ideally either cast an affirmative vote or did not vote.

People of full Cherokee heritage customarily lived in relatively remote communities. They spoke Cherokee at home but could converse in English; many children learned Cherokee as their first language. These "true Indians" represented possibly one-fourth of the population. Family heads farmed less often than they had previously and sought wage labor jobs instead. Young men sporadically worked at unskilled jobs in cities, and military service was common. Householders often lived in log cabins and had wood-burning stoves and privies; many did not have electricity; telephones were rare and automobiles few. Christian church membership represented a major involvement with the supernatural, yet shamanism continued.

The "new" Cherokee may or may not have a significant genetic heritage quantum, but among them the use of their aboriginal language was in rapid decline. Their homes usually were of frame or cinder block construction, and numerous households had electricity, television sets, telephones, and indoor plumbing. They typically lived in increasingly accessible communities in which the roads were paved and the ownership of automobiles was common.

Among both population segments, the old system of kinship terms had changed. Cherokee terms were employed in a manner compatible with English usage. In other words, the terminology that had made it possible to identify relatives based on their matrilineage and clan had been modified for bilateral application. The regulation of marriages by clans waned. Common-law marriages became a standard practice, and illegitimate offspring were not stigmatized. Notably, young adults with a minimum of Indian heritage tended to marry persons with a greater quantum to ensure the Eastern Cherokee rights for their children. Nuclear family households became more common, but a significant number of households consisted of small extended families, especially among conservative families. It may be that the larger households represented continuity with the old matrilocal residence pattern.

In the 1950s, to improve economic conditions, a concerted effort was made by the BIA and the band to attract small manufacturing plants on unused band lands. The inducements for companies included long-term leases, tax and other incentives, and the availability of an underemployed labor force. The goal was to achieve year-round employment, but many potential workers did not place an emphasis on material wealth and objected to the on-the-job discipline. The program was moderately and temporarily successful. One later major manufacturing venture by the band was the 1986 purchase of a mirror-producing company. It was not as successful as they had hoped, and in 1999 its sale was being negotiated.

Another change that had a reservation-wide impact was the program of formal education. By 1954 road access to remote communities was improving rapidly, and boarding schools were abandoned. In the 1970s the Cherokee High School opened and began to offer a comprehensive Cherokee language program. The Eastern Cherokee assumed direct control of the school system from the BIA on the Qualla Boundary, and in 1998 a language immersion program was launched for kindergarten through sixth grade.

Federal efforts, especially the "Great Society" programs of President Lyndon B. Johnson and the "War on Poverty" in the 1960s, created greater Cherokee dependency, as well as many benefits. House construction and renovation increased, day-care centers were built, and social programs expanded. The federal emphasis on tribal self-determination beginning in 1975 represented a major change in the band administration as members obtained increasing control from the BIA.

In 1972 the Eastern Cherokee met in general council for the first time since 1838. They gathered to decide whether they should accept nearly $2 million from the federal government for *25 million acres* of land lost to whites and other injustices. They agreed to receive the settlement and divided the money among the band members. Each person, some 7,200, received about $250 each. This settlement finally resolved an old grievance, and other factors were beginning to favor them as well.

The Contemporary Scene

As previously noted, tourists are a dominant factor in Cherokee life. In 1999 the Great Smoky Mountains National Park attracted more than 10 million visitors, and the town of Cherokee in the Qualla Boundary was host to many of them. Nearly sixty motels operate there, in addition to innumerable restaurants and craft shops. Initially, the white-owned Cherokee Historical Association was largely responsible for major tourist promotions in the town, including the presentation of the outdoor drama *Unto These Hills,* which began in 1950. Some Cherokee have been distressed by the manner in which their history is presented in this play. They are depicted as having been simple savages until their Great White Father, William H. Thomas, and white missionaries saved them and their land. Other major attractions are the white-owned Museum of the Cherokee Indian and Oconaluftee Indian Village, managed by the Cherokee Historical Association. Many tourist-oriented shops have an official greeter dressed in Plains Indian attire, who for a fee can be photographed next to a totem pole, a tepee, or a tourist (see Figure 13-8).

A long-standing Cherokee objection to the tourist-oriented enterprises has been to the long-term leases to non-Cherokee business owners. Although small numbers owned businesses, Indians usually held low-paying service jobs. A major band response was to launch Cherokee Bingo in 1982, which later became Tribal Bingo. Initially, Indian and non-Indian management of questionable integrity produced modest profits. By 1987 the band more fully controlled bingo, earned nearly $1 million that year, and paid for nearly one-third of band government expenses. The bingo operation, with the highest jackpots anywhere in the country, attracted busloads of players from cities throughout the eastern United States and eastern Canada. After expansion, the bingo hall held over one thousand players and employed about two hundred workers.

Figure 13-8 | Millions of families visit Cherokee, North Carolina, each year, and many enjoy taking a picture of their children with an Indian. This photograph was taken in 1984.

The success of bingo led to a far greater gaming operation. Harrah's Cherokee Smoky Mountains Casino opened in 1997, with an initial fifty thousand square feet of gaming space, soon expanded by ten thousand square feet, at a total cost of $85 million. The contract gave Harrah's a management fee of *27 percent* of net revenues. In 1999 this contract was renegotiated at a lower but undisclosed rate. By then the casino employed about fifteen hundred people, of whom about six hundred were from the Qualla Boundary. A band ordinance established that 50 percent of the net profits from gaming were to be distributed to enrolled members on a per capita basis. The remaining 50 percent supported band government and diverse social and health programs. In 2000 the casino launched a $60 million new construction program, and Tribal Bingo was absorbed by the casino.

In theory, casino revenues would provide far greater economic security for band members. However, they receive much smaller per capita payments than they had been led to expect. According to a letter to the band newspaper, *The Cherokee One Feather* (12-9-99), the payments per member in 1997 were $2200 for the year and $2462 the following year; these amounts are unverified. The letter writer appeared to share a widespread feeling that, despite the debt service to Harrah's, the payments should be significantly greater. In this instance, for whatever the reasons, band members are not becoming wealthy as a result of casino profits.

Eastern Cherokee band lands now include about fifty-seven thousand acres. They own the land, and it is held in trust by the federal government; court decisions have established that their acreage is not subject to state taxes. A major issue for about one hundred years has been, "Who is a 'real' Cherokee?" Social and political factionalism continues. Behind the factionalism is the matter of Cherokee genetic heritage; persons of full heritage are likely to be more traditionally oriented than any of the others. Enrollment has been confined to the descendants of persons who had one-sixteenth or more Cherokee heritage in a 1924 roll, some of whom now have one-thirty-second Cherokee heritage, or none at all in the case of white Indians on the 1924 roll. Membership currently is closed except to the newborn of members.

An outline of recent developments in band government helps illuminate the problem. The key governing document for the Eastern Band is the 1889 State of North Carolina charter and its amendments. As noted earlier, these Indians became responsible to both the state and federal governments, leading to jurisdictional and other disputes. For instance, in the early 1980s a band constitution was proposed that would restrict the roll and be far more progressive than the original charter. Voters defeated the proposal. At about the same time, some 60 percent of the band members had less than one-half Cherokee genetic heritage, suggesting that the proposed constitution was not acceptable to most persons of mixed heritage and white Indians. Two years later the band council proposed that the chief and vice-chief could be elected from the band membership and not be required to have at least one-half Cherokee heritage as had been provided in the original charter. In addition, a band member with insufficient Cherokee heritage for enrollment would have the same benefits as his or her enrolled parents or from the estate of parents. These proposals were accepted by voters, representing a victory for people of mixed-heritage and white Indians. The Harmony Ethic apparently led numerous traditionally oriented members not to cast ballots. Another constitution was proposed and voted on in 1999. It would negate the state jurisdiction and resolve the many administrative ambiguities, such as their court system having no jurisdiction over non-Indians. It was overwhelmingly rejected. A reasonable conclusion is that the confusion in the original charter served the best interests of mixed-heritage Cherokees, white Indians, and at least some traditionalists.

For many years, political issues had focused to a great extent on local problems confronting small communities as voting units. The Harmony Ethic of old is increasingly under pressure from new realities in tribal politics. Cooperation, consensus seeking, persuasion and compromise, fair treatment, and working together are words and phrases still used by tribal politicians. At the same time, these politicians openly, and sometimes forcibly, accuse one another of fraud, of using political office for personal gain, of political favoritism, and of similar infractions. For example, in 1997 the board appointed by the principal chief to exercise control over gaming resigned en masse to protest a tribal council decision. The council chose to reinstate the daughter of a council member who had been fired from her job at Tribal Bingo. The board members acted in terms of the Harmony Ethic—they withdrew when they could not support the council decision. The principal chief refused their resignations while at the same time unsuccessfully seeking replacements for them. Thus the give and take, compromise and openness, of this and many other decisions in the Cherokee political process reflects a vigorous vitality.

Additional Sources

The best starting place probably is the short book by Theda Perdue (1989). The best comparative study about the Cherokee and other Indians in the Southeast is by John R. Swanton (1946). The relatively early historical study by James Mooney (1900) is a standard source. The book about Cherokee women from 1700 to 1835 by Perdue (1998) is superior. The recent historical accounts by John R. Finger (1984, 1991) are excellent. William O. Steele (1977) examined early English and Cherokee relations. Fred Gearing's (1962) analysis of Cherokee political developments merits careful study. The works by Harriet J. Kupferer (1966), John Gulick (1960), and Sharlotte Neely (1991) examine continuities with the past and relatively recent culture change.

Selected Bibliography

Adair, James. *See* Williams, Samuel Cole.

Anderson, William L., ed. 1991. *Cherokee removal: Before and after.* Athens, GA.

Coe, Joffre L. 1961. *Cherokee archaeology.* Bureau of American Ethnology Bulletin 180, no. 7. Washington, DC.

DePratter, Chester B. 1991. *Late prehistoric and early historic chiefdoms in the southeastern United States.* New York.

Ehle, John. 1988. *Trail of Tears: The rise and fall of the Cherokee Nation.* New York.

Finger, John R. 1984. *The Eastern Band of Cherokees: 1819–1900.* Knoxville, TN.

———. 1991. *Cherokee Americans: The Eastern Band of Cherokees in the twentieth century.* Lincoln, NE.

Fogelson, Raymond D., and Paul Kutsche. 1961. *Cherokee economic cooperatives: The gadugi.* Bureau of American Ethnology Bulletin 180, no. 11. Washington, DC.

Gearing, Fred. 1962. *Priests and warriors.* American Anthropological Association Memoir 93.

Gilbert, William H. 1943. *The Eastern Cherokee.* Bureau of American Ethnology Bulletin 133, 169–413. Washington, DC.

———. 1965. Eastern Cherokee social organization. In *Social anthropology of North American tribes,* Fred Eggan, ed., 283–338. Chicago.

Goodwin, Gary C. 1977. *Cherokee in transition: A study of changing culture and environment prior to 1775.* Chicago.

Gulick, John. 1960. *Cherokees at the crossroads.* Chapel Hill, NC.

Hill, Sarah H. 1997. *Weaving new worlds: Southeastern Cherokee women and their baskets.* Chapel Hill, NC.

Kilpatrick, Anna Gritts, and Jack F. Kilpatrick, eds. 1966. *Chronicles of Wolfetown: Social documents of the North Carolina Cherokees, 1850–1862.* Bureau of American Ethnology Bulletin 196, no. 80. Washington, DC.

King, Duane H., ed. 1979. *The Cherokee Indian nation: A troubled history.* Knoxville, TN.

Kupferer, Harriet J. 1966. *The "Principal People," 1960.* Bureau of American Ethnology Bulletin 196, no. 78. Washington, DC.

Leftwich, Rodney L. 1970. *Arts and crafts of the Cherokee.* Cullowhee, NC.

Malone, Henry Thompson. 1956. *Cherokees of the old south: A people in transition.* Athens, GA.

McKenney, Thomas L., and James Hall. 1933. *The Indian tribes of North America,* vol. 1. Edinburgh.

McLoughlin, William G. 1984. *Cherokees and missionaries, 1789–1839.* New Haven, CT.

Mooney, James. 1900. *Myths of the Cherokee.* Bureau of American Ethnology, 19th Annual Report, pt. 1, 3–548. Washington, DC.

Neely, Sharlotte. 1971. *The role of formal education among the Eastern Cherokee Indians, 1880–1971.* M.A. thesis, University of North Carolina at Chapel Hill.

———. 1978. Acculturation and persistence among North Carolina's Eastern Band of Cherokee Indians. In *Southeastern Indians since the removal era,* Walter L. Williams, ed., 154–73. Athens, GA.

———. 1991. *Snowbird Cherokees: People of persistence.* Athens, GA.

———. 1992. Adaptation and the contemporary North Carolina Cherokee Indians. In *Indians of the Southeastern United States in the late twentieth century,* J. Anthony Paredes, ed., 29–43. Tuscaloosa, AL.

Perdue, Theda. 1989. *The Cherokees.* New York.

———. 1998. *Cherokee women: Gender and culture change, 1700–1835.* Lincoln, NE.

Reid, John Phillip. 1970. *A law of blood: The primitive law of the Cherokee nation.* New York.

Speck, Frank G., and Leonard Broom. 1951. *Cherokee dance and drama.* Berkeley and Los Angeles.

Steele, William O. 1977. *The Cherokee crown of Tanaassy.* Winston-Salem, NC.

Strickland, Rennard. 1982. *Fire and the spirits: Cherokee law from clan to court.* Norman, OK.

Strickland, William. 1977. Cherokee rhetoric. *Journal of Cherokee Studies* 2:375–83.

Swanton, John R. 1946. *The Indians of the southeastern United States.* Bureau of American Ethnology Bulletin 137. Washington, DC.

Williams, Samuel Cole, ed. 1930. *Adair's history of the American Indians.* Johnson City, TN.

14 The Natchez: Sophisticated Farmers of the Deep South

A great number of years ago there appeared among us a man and his wife, who came down from the sun. Not that we believe that the sun had a wife who bore him children, or that these were the descendants of the sun; but when they first appeared among us they were so bright and luminous that we had no difficulty to believe that they came down from the sun.

A priest described the origin of the Great Sun and his lineage. (Le Page du Pratz 1947, 312)

ALONG THE EASTERN bank of the lower Mississippi River developed the most elaborate Indian cultures reported to the north of Mexico. Nowhere else were similar heights of cultural complexity reported. In essence, the Natchez had achieved a chiefdom level of sociopolitical development. Fortunately, their aboriginal culture was recorded in considerable detail, unlike those of other Indians in the area who probably exhibited comparable complexity. Natchez political life was dominated by a royal family, and the people had inordinately complex religious and social conventions. In addition, their relations with the French passed through well-defined stages that were often similar to European–Indian historical contacts elsewhere.

The word *Natchez* is apparently derived from a French interpretation of the name of their settlement, called Naches, but these people called themselves the *Thécoel*. The language of the Natchez (NACH-uhz) is an isolate, meaning that it had no widely accepted ties with any other language. It is interesting to note that although the women spoke the same language as the men, women were said to "soften and smooth their words, whereas the speech of the men is more grave and serious" (Le Page du Pratz 1758, 312). Because the French learned the language from women, their pronunciation was feminine and ridiculed by both Natchez men and women. At the end of the seventeenth century, the Natchez numbered about thirty-five hundred, and in 1720 they could assemble twelve hundred warriors, including refugees they had absorbed and the Tiou (Tioux), who were a dependent people (see Figure 14-1).

Aboriginal Life

The Natchez clearly stand apart from all the Indians reported on in earlier chapters. Natchez social conventions, political organization, and religious institutions survived into historic times, whereas other mound-building Indians in the Southeast with similar cultures soon disappeared. It is assumed, and with good reason, that the Natchez had deep prehistoric roots in the Southeast. Fortunately, one careful observer, Antoine S. Le Page du Pratz, Dutch by birth, lived among the Natchez from 1720 to 1728 and learned to speak their language. His observations are superior and form the primary basis for the following account.

ORIGIN MYTH The mythological beginnings of the Natchez offer special insight into the form of sociopolitical structure that they developed. According to tradition, a man and his wife entered an already established community to the southwest of historic Natchez country. The newcomers were so bright in appearance that they seemed to have come from the sun. The man said he had noted that the people did not have effective means for governing themselves and that he had come from the sky to instruct them. He told the people about the Great Spirit and what they must do to please him. Among the rules of be-

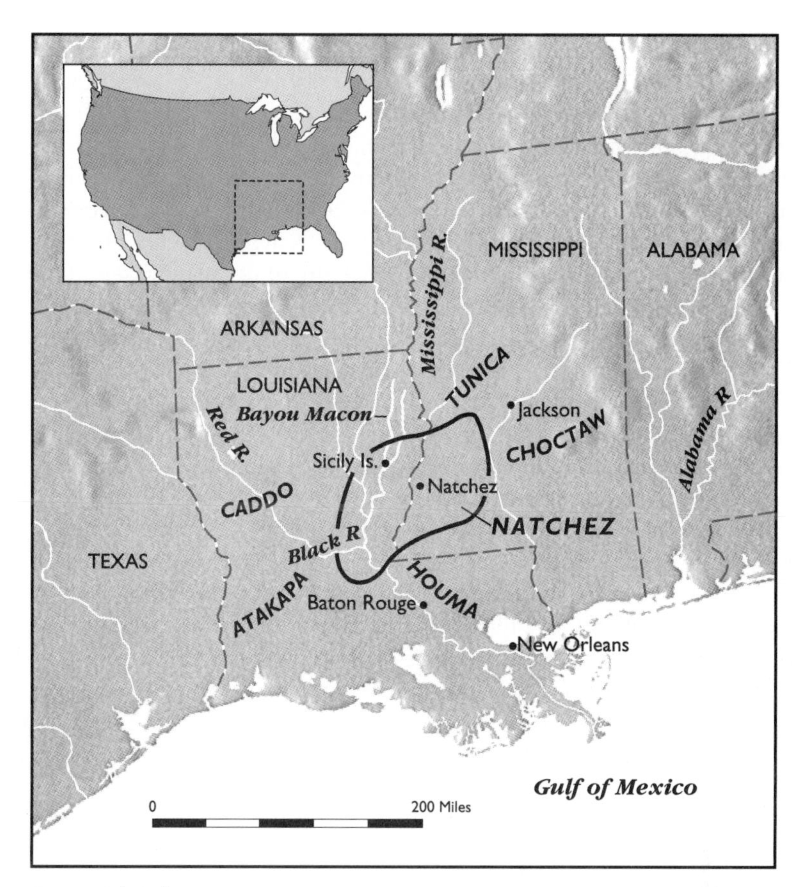

Figure 14-1 | Aboriginal range of the Natchez Indians.

havior were a series of prohibitions: do not kill except in self-defense; do not have sexual intercourse with a woman not one's wife; do not steal, or lie, or become intoxicated. (Alcoholic beverages do not appear to have existed in this area until early historical times.) Finally, he said that the people should give freely of what they had to those in need. After hearing these rules of conduct, the people agreed to their wisdom and asked the man to be their leader. He said he would do so only under certain conditions. Among these were that the people must obey him but no other and that they must move to another country, to which he would lead them; finally, he set forth the rules for selecting his successor. He said too that they should build a temple in which the leaders could communicate with the Great Spirit. In the temple would be an eternal fire that he would bring from the sun. The people agreed to these and other conditions, and the sacred fire was brought from the sun. This man then became the first Great Sun.

APPEARANCE AND CLOTHING The Natchez were striking in appearance, according to the French. Their proud air and noble bearing became the American Indian stereotype among Europeans. Le Page du Pratz (1947) described them as 5½ feet or more in height, lean, sinewy, with rectangular features, coarse black hair, and black eyes. To him they were "naturals," but to other French observers they were "savages." As infants their foreheads were flattened by the straps that held them in cradleboards. A woman wore short bangs in front and bound her long hair in a mulberry thread net with tassels at the ends. Her ears were pierced, and from each large hole hung an elongated shell ornament. Around her neck she might wear strings of small stones or perforated shell disks. Around a man's head was a band of short hair. A few hairs were allowed to grow long at the crown, and white feathers were worn in these scalp locks. Often the young Natchez dandies painted themselves red and wore bracelets made of steamed deer ribs bent in circles and then polished to a high luster. They might carry fans of turkey tail feathers, and they wore necklaces of stone beads like those of the women. The people plucked their axillary hair, and the men plucked their whiskers.

The tattoos of these people were impressive in their diversity and complexity. Youthful males and females were tattooed with lines on the face. Persons of the nobility and warriors were elaborately tattooed on the body, head, and limbs. The patterns were of serpents, suns, and other undescribed forms. Warriors who had slain an enemy were permitted to tattoo themselves as evidence of their kills, and for a brave deed a man had the right to tattoo a war club on his shoulder with a sign beneath symbolizing the people involved in his conquest. The tattooing method was to prick the skin until blood flowed freely and then rub charcoal, red pigment, or blue pigment into the openings. Warriors pierced their earlobes and expanded the holes until they would hold decorative plugs about an inch in diameter.

Males younger than twelve years and girls younger than nine went without clothing. An older girl's primary garment consisted of a short fringed skirt made from the threads of mulberry inner bark. An adult woman wore a deerskin that was fitted about the waist and reached the knees. Some high-status women wore cloaks of netting made on a loom from mulberry inner bark. The netting was covered with overlapping rows of bird feathers. In cold weather a woman wore a cape, probably of skins, that passed under her right armpit and fastened over the left shoulder. Ordinary men wore skin breechclouts that were belted and colored white; breechclouts of nobles were black. The leggings of men reached from their thighs to their ankles, but they wore skin moccasins only when traveling. In cold weather a man wore a poncholike shirt of deerskin that was sleeved and reached below the knees. In severe weather a bisonskin robe with the hair intact and facing inward was worn. Deerskin garments were sewn with sinew after an awl was used to pierce the skins. Class distinctions in dress and adornment included elaborate tattoos for the nobility, feather-covered mantles for noblewomen, and black breechclouts for the chiefs or nobles. Infants of the nobility wore two or three pearls about their necks. These ornaments were taken from the temple and were returned when a child was about ten years old.

SETTLEMENTS AND MANUFACTURES The main area of Natchez settlement was along the eastern bank of the Mississippi River near the present city of Natchez, but the Natchez also seem to have controlled adjacent land on the western bank of the river. During the French period, the main settlement area was a rolling plain of black soil covered with grasses, hickory forests, cane thickets in the low-lying areas, and adjacent pine or hardwood forests. There were reportedly five communities. Grand Village, the principal settlement and the one that may have been termed Naches, was the residence of the Great Sun and other officials. Nearby settlements included Grigras, a community of refugees among the Natchez, Hickory, Flour, and White Apple. These designations possibly were neighborhoods around Grand Village, the only site identified with certainty; it has been partially excavated.

In the center of Grand Village was an open plaza measuring 250 by 300 paces with a flat-topped mound at each end. On top of one mound was a temple, and on the other was the home of the Great Sun. The temple mound was about eight feet high, relatively steep on three sides, and sloped gently to form a ramp on the side toward the open plaza. The temple on top probably was about thirty feet long and somewhat narrower. This structure was built of thick logs ten feet in height and plastered on the outside with mud. The roof was ridged, and three large wooden figures of birds adorned the peak. Entered through a rectangular doorway, the temple was divided into two rooms. A perpetual fire burned in the larger outer room, and on a nearby platform was a cane coffin containing the bones of the most recently deceased Great Sun. In the inner room were two special boards with unidentified items attached. The wooden box that contained the stone statue of the first Great Sun probably was kept here. Reportedly, he turned himself into stone because he feared that his remains would be tainted if placed in the ground. The bones of other persons probably were stored in this room.

The home of the Great Sun was on an earthen mound some eight feet high, and the house itself was twenty-five feet wide and forty-five feet long. All other houses were at ground level, but the eight homes nearby were larger than the other houses. At the death of a Great Sun his house was burned, and the same mound probably was increased in size and used as a foundation for the home of his successor. The houses in general appear to have been square, rectangular, or, less often, round. Their straight walls were not less than fifteen feet high, and they had rectangular doorways but no windows. Hickory timbers were embedded in the ground at the four corners; they were bent over at the tops and tied to form a dome. Along the sidewalls similar poles were embedded in the earth, bent, and tied to the primary dome branches. Poles forming the inner walls were tied in place, and the inner as well as outer walls were spread with a clay and moss plaster and covered with split cane mats. The roof was covered with a mixture of sod and grass and topped with cane mats. In the winter the inhabitants built a fire for warmth. Recent experiments in a reconstructed Natchez dwelling suggest that the fire drew air *into* the building, and the smoke filtered out through the roof. It appears that the houses may have been scattered widely. Somewhere near a village were raised platforms on which the bodies of deceased persons were placed. A woven mat smeared with mud covered the body; the head of the individual was left uncovered so that food offerings might be placed beside it. After the flesh had decayed, the bones were moved to the temple.

A number of household artifacts were reported among the Natchez, and others were excavated from a historic site. Within the cane-walled dwellings were household goods not usually reported north of Mexico. The most prominent furnishings were beds made from poles and cane with bearskins over the frame, a bison skin cover, and log pillow. When relaxing during the day, the people sat either on the beds or on short-legged wooden stools. Pottery vessels were commonly used, including some with shallow bowls decorated with incised scrolls or meanders. Some large pots held up to forty pints of bear oil. A wide variety of cane basketry included sieves of various grades for sifting maize, containers for small items of adornment, and hampers for maize. Knives were made from split sections of hard cane, and stone-bladed axes served for heavy woodworking.

For water transportation, they used both rafts and canoes. Rafts were used to carry relatively light loads and were made from bundles of cane lashed together. For transporting heavy loads, large canoes were made from hollowed-out cypress or poplar logs. The interior of the log was removed by controlled burning, after which the charred wood was chipped away. These dugout canoes were some forty feet long, had three-foot beams, and could carry up to twelve tons.

SUBSISTENCE ACTIVITIES Cultivated crops were the most important source of food; hunting and fishing clearly were secondary. A farm plot was cleared of cane, which was dried and burned, and the ground was broken up with an L-shaped mattock of hickory. Maize was planted by making holes in the ground with a digging stick and dropping a few grains of corn into each hole. The Natchez probably cultivated their crops with a hoe made by hafting a bison scapula blade at right angles to a wooden handle. The principal cultigen was maize, and from two varieties some forty named dishes were prepared in the Natchez area. Maize was mixed with beans, smoke-dried, ground into meal, prepared as hominy, or parched. Ground meal was made into cakes that were roasted in ashes, baked, or boiled in water. Additional crops included squash and beans, while two species of wild grass were cultivated along riverbanks. The Natchez consumed walnuts, chestnuts, and acorns, but these were not important dietary items. There were no set mealtimes except for feasts. When an ordinary meal was served, the males, including those who were very young, ate before the females.

A primary reason the French established plantations in the Natchez region was for the cultivation of tobacco. The Indians had raised tobacco in aboriginal times, and the people were described as avid smokers. They smoked pipes of unknown form and inhaled the smoke. Smoking was not merely a pleasant activity; pipes and smoking played an important part in events surrounding war and peace.

Hunting was most important in the fall, and deer sometimes were pursued by about a hundred men at a time as a sport. Once they had located and surrounded a deer, men forced the animal to run back and forth until it was exhausted. It was taken alive to the Great Sun or his representative, who killed it and divided the meat among the leaders of the hunt. In ordinary hunting a man wore a deer disguise when animals were cautious and imitated the deer's call to attract an animal. Hunters used self bows of locust wood strung with plant fiber or twisted sinew. Arrows of cane or wood had feather vanes and heads made from splinters of bone, garfish scales, stone, or a fire-hardened shaft tip. Cane-shafted spears were tipped with flint points and used when hunting large game such as bear, bison, and deer. When a kill was made near a settlement, the hunter returned with the choice parts and sent his wife to retrieve the remainder of the animal. Meat was either cooked or smoke-dried for future use. They ate bear meat only if it was lean, but bears were killed when they were fat to obtain the oil. These animals were smoked out of their holes in trees, and if a cub was found, it was sometimes taken alive to the village and tamed. The only domestic animal of the Natchez was the dog. It was used to tree turkeys so that they could be killed with arrows. Fishing was a less important means of obtaining food than either farming or hunting. Among the fishing devices were gill nets made from organic fibers and fish arrows that had pointed bone tips and wooden floats attached by a cord to the shaft. They also used hooks, and the species they took most often were suckers and catfish.

SOCIOPOLITICAL DIMENSIONS For years the accounts of Natchez sociopolitical life had been confused and contradictory. Thanks to Douglas R. White, George P. Murdock, and Richard Scaglion (1971), particulars about their descent and ranking system have been clarified. The Great Sun ruled as a divine king and administered Grand Village. He appointed administrative officers, including the Great War Chief, a supervisor of public works, the leader of temple ceremonies, and others. The Great Sun also appointed the War Chief in each of the other major villages.

The Suns constituted a royal family, and in 1700 they numbered seventeen individuals. Members of the royal family were obligated to seek a commoner as a spouse. Inheritance was through the matrilineal line for the royal family; it was extended to only three collateral generations. The fourth generation of collaterals became Nobles, and three generations after that they became Stinkards (commoners). Furthermore, the male children of Noble men became Honored men; women could only achieve Honored status as the wives of Honored men. The Honored title could not be passed on to either male or female children; thus there were no Honored women by birth. The summary of descent and rank provided by White, Murdock, and Scaglion (1971, 373) follows:

Parent(s)	*Offspring*
Sun mother	Sun rank, Noble class
Sun father	Noble class
Noble mother	Noble class
Noble father	sons: Honored rank, commoner class daughters: Stinkard (commoner) class
Honored father	Stinkard (commoner) class
Stinkard parents	Stinkard (commoner) class

The sons of highest rank, from oldest to youngest, held the key political offices. Noble men in turn filled subordinate offices, and Honored men also appear to have served in lesser offices. As will later become apparent, under special conditions, a male commoner could be elevated to the rank of an Honored person.

WARFARE Judging by the respect the French gave the Natchez, it is apparent that their military power was considerable. A Great War Chief was in charge of warfare. Ideally, it appears, warfare was controlled at the tribal level. The rationale for aggression might be real—for instance, another tribe may have been hunting on Natchez land—or an offense might be fabricated. Subordinate to the Great War Chief were three grades of combatants: apprentices, warriors, and old warriors. Old warriors played a critical role in military matters, and one of these men led a delegation to confront a potential enemy. They carried a peace calumet but offered no gifts so that they would not be thought of as appeasers. A delegation of this nature was usually well received, gifts were presented to them, and the matter was closed. If this effort failed, the Natchez prepared for war.

To prepare for combat, the military hierarchy performed numerous formal rites and ceremonies that lasted for three days. A pole with a war calumet attached, representing the enemy, was raised near the house where the plans were being formulated. The Great Sun, lesser war chiefs, warriors, and old warriors met, and the Great War Chief described the grounds for launching an attack. The opinions of the old warriors were decisive. If the presentation was accepted as valid, they proceeded with preparations for combat. Each warrior painted his body in different colors and carried a bisonskin shield and war club into combat. A meal was prepared of coarse food to remind warriors that they did not require dainty edibles, and later a dog was roasted for ceremonial

Figure 14-2 | The plan of a fort and illustration of methods of torture. (From Le Page du Pratz 1947, vol. 2.)

consumption. Subsequently, as an act of purification, a war drink that was a powerful emetic was drunk by each man, who then vomited violently. The three-day ceremony also included dances, recitations of personal achievements in warfare, and the singing of death songs.

A war party could include as many as three hundred warriors, who traveled only by night. If they interpreted any sign as an ill omen for an attack, the men returned to their villages, despite all of the preparations. Similarly, if they met an unanticipated enemy party, they withdrew. Attacks were launched at daybreak. The intent was to kill and scalp as many men as possible and to take one male captive, along with all of the women and children. If an enemy had been forewarned and had prepared a defensive position, the Natchez searched for hunting parties to attack. Whenever possible, a Natchez killed in combat was scalped by his comrades to prevent an enemy from obtaining a Natchez scalp. The raiders returned home in honor if they had taken a living enemy man as a captive. On their return, the Great War Chief would compensate the families of any warriors lost in battle.

Back in their own village, the warriors planted two poles in the ground if a male captive had been taken; on them a crosspiece was lashed near the ground and another somewhat higher than a man's head. The captive was stunned with a blow at the base of the skull and was scalped by his captor. The victim's naked body was tied in spread-eagle fashion on the pole frame (see Figure 14-2). The young persons in the assembled throng gathered canes and lighted them; the first flaming cane was applied to the captive by his captor. The torturer was free to apply the cane anywhere he chose, and it was most likely to be on the arm with which the victim had best defended himself. The victim was then burned by the others as he sang his song of death. Some sacrificial victims were reported to have sung for seventy-two hours without pause before dying. However, not all captive males were dealt with in this manner; if a young woman whose husband had been killed claimed the captive, he was given to her as a husband. Captive women and children had their hair cut short and became the servants of their captors.

When an attack was anticipated, the Natchez usually decided in council to defend themselves rather than appease the aggressors. They warned outlying families to join the main group and posted guards at the approaches to their settlements. Another defensive move was to build palisaded fortifications. Forts were rather complex structures built around a tall tree that served as a watchtower. The trunks of trees were stripped of branches and were set in the ground to reach a height of about ten feet. The palisades were arranged in a roughly circular form with an overlap at the ends. Inside were structures to protect the women and children from arrows. The entrance was protected by towers, and in the passage to the outside were placed brambles and thorns. When an attack was imminent, emissaries carrying a peace calumet were sent to enlist the aid of friendly peoples. In the meantime the Great War Chief cited in council the reasons for defending themselves. He sought the support of warriors by reminding the older ones of their honor and pointing out the vengeance they could obtain and by holding out for youths the hope of glory.

Warriors who had distinguished themselves were given new names by the Great War Chief. These denoted particular levels of achievement in warfare. For example, the name Great Man Slayer could be claimed by a warrior after he had taken twenty scalps or ten prisoners. A warrior also might tattoo his body to commemorate an achievement and might be elevated to Honored status.

RELIGIOUS SYSTEM The Natchez religious system was a formalized network of beliefs, ceremonies, and dogma maintained by specialists who devoted all their time to supernatural matters. They were priests in a generic sense and served as guardians of the major temple. One of these men explained Natchez religion to Le Page du Pratz. The latter recorded that they believed in an all-powerful Great Spirit who created all things good and was surrounded by lesser spirits that did his bidding. A particularly malignant spirit led the spirits of evil, but because it was tied up forever by the Great Spirit, it could do no great harm. The Great Spirit reportedly molded the first man from clay, and the figure grew to the proportions of a normal man. It was believed that woman probably was created in the same manner, but because man was created first, he was stronger and more courageous.

The reigning Great Sun, the highest authority on earth, combined the qualities of a god and a king. His power and authority over things religious were paramount, and his decisions were very important in secular matters. In

Figure 14-3 | The Great Sun being carried on a litter. (From Le Page du Pratz 1947, vol. 2.)

this theocratic state, all religious, social, and political control was, in theory, in the hands of this individual. The Great Sun was surrounded by warriors and retainers wherever he went. When he traveled about, he was carried on a litter by eight warriors (see Figure 14-3); in his dwelling he sat on a small wooden throne. The Great Sun was distinguished in his dress from others; for example, his normal headdress was a net covered with black feathers and bordered in red decorated with white seeds; hanging from the top of the headdress were long white feathers in front and shorter ones behind. Lesser Suns appear to have worn similar headpieces.

The core of religious life was a sacred temple fire tended by eight elders; two of them cared for the fire continually, and they were killed if they permitted the fire to go out. When ordinary persons walked in front of a temple, they put down any load that they might be carrying and extended their arms toward the temple as they wailed loudly. The same type of behavior was followed when they passed before the Great Sun. The Great Sun visited the temple daily to make certain that the fire still burned, and each morning at sunrise he faced the east, bowed to the ground, and wailed three times. With a special calumet he blew smoke first toward the rising sun and then in each of the other cardinal directions. Thus the Great Sun venerated the sun and was in turn venerated by all other persons in the tribe. What we see is a direct line of continuity from the past functionally linked to the Great Spirit, the Great Suns, and an eternal fire.

Ceremonies

The annual ritual calendar focused on edibles, the temple, and the Suns. A new year began in March, and each of the thirteen months was named for the most important food identified with the previous month. Seeds were blessed at the temple before they were sown, and family heads presented the first harvest of edibles (first fruit ceremony) to temple guardians for the Great Sun to distribute at his discretion. A feast was celebrated at the beginning of each month by a person of Sun rank, and following ceremonies and ritual acts, the Great Sun received gifts while on his throne.

The seventh month, Great Corn, celebrated the first harvest of maize and climaxed their annual celebrations. Warriors had planted ceremonial corn in virgin soil, tended the crop, and stored it in a granary some distance from the settlement. Villagers assembled at the cache for the arrival of the Great Sun on his litter adorned with flowers. For the prolonged ceremonies, a special dwelling on a raised platform was built for the Great Sun, and other temporary housing accommodated the other assembled families. A new fire was kindled by rubbing sticks together, and corn was presented first to a Sun woman and then to the others. After cooking the sacred crop people feasted, heard orations, and danced to torch light throughout the night to the accompaniment of music played on a drum and gourd rattles. Women danced in the opposite direction to men (see Figure 14-4), and individuals from the audience replaced tired dancers. A violent and highly competitive ball game highlighted the next day's activities; the purpose was to drive a ball to an opposite goal. One team of warriors, led by the Great Sun, wore headdresses of white feathers, and their opposites, led by the Great War Chief, wore red feathers. The winning team received gifts from the captain of the losing team and could wear their headdresses until the game was played again. Following the contest warriors performed a war dance, and the festivities concluded after all of the maize had been consumed.

Apart from the temple cult, a host of spirits prevailed, possibly as lesser agents of the Great Spirit. The honey locust tree, for example, represented supernatural power, and beneath one such tree near the Grand Village temple sacred firewood was cached. Lightning appears to have had religious associations, and a deep-seated fear of snakes was common. Because moisture was all important for crops, the Suns and all others fasted for rainfall.

Shamans These specialists appear to have functioned independently of the Sun-centered theocracy. A man or woman who aspired to become a shaman went into isolation for nine days and consumed only water until a spirit aid appeared. During the power quest, the seeker reportedly acquired particular skills. Subsequently, the practitioner filled a small basket with objects such as owl heads, animal teeth, small stones, and spirit aids. A shaman who did not cure a patient might be killed, but successful treatment brought material gain.

Figure 14-4 | A dance scene. (From Le Page du Pratz 1947.)

One cure included making an incision at the locus of an illness and sucking blood from the wound. When the shaman spit blood into a container, he or she spit not only blood but also a foreign object such as a piece of wood, straw, or leather; the illness was attributed to this item.

The more mundane treatment of illness, possibly by other practitioners, likewise prevailed, with plant products making up at least some medicines. In this context Le Page du Pratz cited repeated examples in which French physicians were unsuccessful, whereas their Natchez counterparts cured either the same or other patients.

LIFE CYCLE Soon after babies were born, they were tied to a cradleboard, and strips of deerskin were bound over their foreheads to flatten them. The cradleboard was placed in a bed beside the baby's mother. Infants were smeared with bear oil to keep flies off and to make them supple. When nearly a year old, infants were encouraged to walk; they were nursed until they weaned themselves or until the mother again became pregnant. As children grew they came under the influence of an elder male in their extended family; this man counseled all the nuclear families within his group. A child termed this man father, but he might be a great-grandfather or even a great-great-grandfather. Children were discouraged from fighting with the threat that they would be sent away from the Natchez. Boys were encouraged to exercise and gradually acquire adult skills from about the age of twelve, and the gender division of labor was instilled at this time. Hunting, fishing, fighting, some farming, and the manufacturing of most artifacts were male activities. Carrying home game or fish, most of the farming, preparing food, and manufacturing clothing, baskets, or pottery were female responsibilities, along with raising children.

Following puberty, youths were free to have sexual intercourse, and girls apparently did not bestow sexual favors without material gain. A potential husband was proud of the amount of property his bride-to-be might accumulate in this manner. Males did not marry until they were about twenty-five, but females appear to have been somewhat younger. Once the couple decided to marry, the man went before the heads of their respective families to be questioned. If no close blood ties existed and if the pair loved each other, the elders sanctioned the marriage. On the wedding day the woman was led by the elder of her family, and followed by the remainder of her family, to the home of the man. Here they were greeted and invited into the house, where, after a pause, the elders of both families asked the couple whether they loved each other and were willing to be husband and wife. The ideals of domestic harmony were set forth, the couple exchanged vows, and a gift was made to the bride's father. The bride's mother handed her a laurel branch to hold in one hand and an ear of corn to hold in the other hand. She gave the corn to her husband, and he said, "I am your husband," to which she answered, "I am your wife." Finally the husband told his wife, "There is our bed, keep it tight," which was an injunction against committing adultery. After a special meal the couple and their guests danced from early evening through the night. This description of a marriage by Le Page du Pratz does not specify whether or not these customs were observed by everyone. The need for such clarification is evident, because other descriptions of Natchez marriages differ from this form.

Most marriages were monogamous, and a couple established an independent household (neolocal residence). Yet plural marriages prevailed among the nobility, and sororal polygyny was the most common form. A man with many wives lived with one or two of them and visited the others at their natal homes. In polygynous households, the wife who bore the first offspring supervised the other wives. Divorce was extremely rare for most persons, but an upper-class woman married to a common man was free to take other husbands (polyandry). Furthermore, such a woman could have her husband put to death if he committed adultery. This is an unusual form of the double standard of morality. Berdaches (transvestites) were reported, but their position in the society is not clear.

The writings of Le Page du Pratz and a few others convey the essence of the ideals that guided adult life. Tribal unity did not prevail during the brief historical era, and there is good evidence of a power struggle among leading upper-class persons that influenced intervillage affairs. Some communities were friendly to the French, whereas others were hostile, suggesting that the Great Sun could not, or did not, effectively control all the members of his lineage. Yet it appears that villagewide harmony existed and that the upper class did not abuse its power. The people in general were honorable in their dealings with each other and with the French. Recall that in the myth about the acceptance of the first Great Sun, certain specific rules of behavior were stated; they were maintained insofar as possible by the priests and the upper class in general.

One of the most vivid descriptions by Le Page du Pratz was of the funeral for the Great War Chief, Tattooed Serpent, who was the brother of the Great Sun and nearly as powerful. When he died everyone was greatly distressed because each brother had vowed to kill himself at the death of the other. The temple guardians urged Le Page du Pratz, who was influential among the Natchez and a friend of the Great Sun, to avert the leader's potential suicide. Le Page du Pratz and other whites went to the home of the Great Sun and talked with him. The Great Sun was deeply grieved over the death of his brother but was successfully restrained from committing suicide.

At the house of Tattooed Serpent, his corpse lay on the bed he had occupied while alive. His face was painted red, and he was clothed in his finest garments, including a feather headdress. Beside the bed were his weapons and the peace calumets he had received during his life. From a pole stuck into the ground hung forty-six linked sections of red-painted cane representing the number of enemies he had killed. Gathered around the body were his "chancellor," physician, chief domestic, pipe bearer, two of his wives, some old women, and a volunteer from among the noblewomen, all of whom were to be killed as a part of the funeral ceremony. The next day included a Dance of Death and two rehearsals for the deaths of persons to be killed. At about this time, two commoner parents strangled one of their offspring out of respect for Tattooed Serpent; by doing so they were raised to noble standing and would not be killed when the Great Sun died. Some warriors also had apprehended a common man who had been married to a Sun woman but had fled at her death to avoid being killed. His capture once again slated him for death, but three old women related to him offered themselves to be killed in his place. The man in turn was elevated to the upper class by the women's sacrifice.

On the day of the funeral, the "master of ceremonies" was painted red above the waist and wore a garment about his waist with a red and white feather fringe. On his head was a crown of red feathers, and he carried a red staff with black feathers hanging from the upper part and a crosspiece near the top. When this impressively arrayed individual approached the house of the deceased, he was greeted with "hoo" and by wailing indicating death. A procession formed behind the master of ceremonies; he was followed by the

Figure 14-5 | The burial of Tattooed Serpent, brother of the Great Sun. (From Le Page du Pratz 1947.)

oldest warrior carrying the staff from which hung the red cane rings and a war pipe that reflected the honor of the dead man. These men were in turn followed by six temple guardians who carried the body on a litter (see Figure 14-5); then came those who were to be killed, each accompanied by eight relatives who served as executioners. Each of these relatives was subsequently freed from the probability of being killed at the death of the Great Sun and seemingly was raised to Honored status. The procession circled the house of the deceased three times, and then the litter bearers walked in intersecting circles to the temple. The dead child was thrown repeatedly in the path of the bearers and retrieved by its parents. After the body of Tattooed Serpent was placed in the temple, the sacrificial victims, their hair covered with red paint, were drugged with tobacco and strangled. Within the temple the two wives of

Tattooed Serpent and two men were buried in the grave with him. The other victims were buried elsewhere, and the funeral ended by burning the home of Tattooed Serpent.

With a great man's death, pomp, pageantry, and human sacrifice unrolled; the death of a Sun was a tragic highlight to life. The number of persons killed at the funeral of Tattooed Serpent unquestionably was fewer than would have been considered fitting before the French arrived. For other people to die was of lesser moment, and yet any death was surrounded with further deaths. When an outstanding female Sun died, her husband, a commoner, was strangled by their eldest son. Then the eldest surviving daughter ordered twelve small children killed and placed around the bodies of the deceased couple. In the plaza fourteen platforms were erected, and on each was a man who was to die during the funeral. These men danced before the house of the deceased every fifteen minutes and then returned to their platforms. It was said that after four days the March of the Bodies ritual took place. The dead children previously had been placed outside the dead woman's home, and with them were the live victims. The woman was carried out on a litter, and the small bodies were dropped repeatedly before the procession so that by the time the litter reached the temple the corpses of the children were in pieces. After the woman's body was inside the temple, the fourteen victims were strangled, but not before they had received water and wads of tobacco that drugged them into unconsciousness. The living mourned for an important deceased person by weeping for four days. In general, mourners cut their hair but did not paint their faces, and they avoided public gatherings. The temporary grave was on a raised platform. A shelter of branches formed a vault over the body, and there was an opening at the end near the head where food was placed. The mourners grieved at the grave each day at dawn and at sunset for a month. After the flesh had decayed, the bones were placed in a basket in a temple.

The custom of executing persons at the death of the Suns and other upper-class individuals may seem barbaric and senseless, but they believed that it had very real advantages to the individuals involved. In their belief system, one's spirit under such circumstances would accompany the deceased upper-class person to the world of the dead and serve him or her there in perennial happiness. The same future awaited all others who observed the rules of the society during their lifetimes. It was thought that a person who had broken the rules of the people would go to a place covered with water; naked, she or he would be bitten by mosquitoes and have only undesirable foods to eat.

Tattooed Serpent's Oration

Only a few short years following the dramatic burial ceremonies for Tattooed Serpent, the Natchez were nearly extinct. It seems fitting to record a speech that Tattooed Serpent made to Le Page du Pratz (1947, 40–41) after a war with the French and shortly before the Natchez were destroyed.

I did not approve, as you know, the war our people made upon the French to avenge the death of their relation, seeing I made them carry the *pipe of peace* to the French. This you well know, as you first smoked in the pipe yourself. Have the French two hearts, a good one to-day, and to-morrow a bad one? As for my brother and me, we have but one heart and one word. Tell me then, if thou art, as thou sayest, my true friend, what thou thinkest of all this, and shut thy mouth to everything else. We know not what to think of the French, who, after having begun the war, granted a peace, and offered it of themselves; and then at the time we were quiet, believing ourselves to be at peace, people come to kill us, without saying a word.

Why . . . did the French come into our country? We did not go to seek them: they asked for land of us, because their country was too little for all the men that were in it. We told them they might take land where they pleased, there was enough for them and for us; that it was good the same sun should enlighten us both, and that we would walk as friends in the same path; and that we would give them of our provisions, assist them to build, and to labour in their fields. We have done so; is not this true? What occasion then had we for Frenchmen? Before they came, did we not live better than we do, seeing we deprive ourselves of a part of our corn, our game, and fish, to give a part to them? In what respect, then, had we occasion for them? Was it for their guns? The bows and arrows which we used, were sufficient to make us live well. Was it for their white, blue, and red blankets? We can do well enough with buffalo skins which are warmer; our women wrought feather-blankets for the winter, and mulberry-mantles for the summer; which indeed were not so beautiful; but our women were more laborious and less vain than they are now. In fine, before the arrival of the French, we lived like men who can be satisfied with what they have; whereas at this day we are like slaves, who are not suffered to do as they please.

Natchez History

Andrew C. Albrecht (1946) identified six phases of Natchez history, a framework that I have followed. The *first phase* is represented by contacts with European explorers. Initial exploration of the region in 1542 was by the Spanish under the command of Hernando de Soto, who died that year. The next year the expedition survivors rafted down the Mississippi River and were attacked by Native Americans, quite possibly by the Natchez. Far more important was a French expedition in 1682 led by Sieur de La Salle. The Natchez graciously hosted these explorers but were not overawed by them. La Salle smoked a peace calumet with the Natchez and was cautious in dealing with them.

A *second phase* began as missionaries and fur traders from Canada in 1698 launched the era of European exploitation. French colonials arrived from the south in 1700 under the leadership of Pierre de Iberville. He established friendly relations with the Natchez at Grand Village and wrested political control of the region from the French Canadians to establish a separate French colony. English traders from the Carolinas, however, soon began to influence the Natchez at some of their settlements. Competition between European nations produced discord among the Natchez.

The *third phase* began in 1713 with the establishment of a French trading post in Natchez country. A wealthy speculator, Antoine Crozat, was granted a monopoly of all the trade in Louisiana, with the stipulation that he bring slaves from Africa and settlers from France. A trading post was built, but intrigue by English traders led Natchez sympathizers to attack the fort, plunder, and destroy it. As a result the French found themselves in a tenuous position. Their solution was to subjugate the Natchez.

The *fourth phase,* military control, began in 1716 when Jean de Bienville, with a small force, tricked the Natchez and was able to seize and kill those who had murdered Frenchmen and plundered the trading post. The Natchez agreed to peace with the French and aided in the construction of the stockaded Fort Rosalie, built to the west of their villages and overlooking the Mississippi River. Relations temporarily stabilized, with the Natchez controlling their settlements and a small French garrison representing the outpost of an empire.

The *fifth phase* began with the arrival of French colonists in 1720 under the sponsorship of John Law, a Scottish businessman. He obtained the right from the French government to colonize and trade in the region. The colonists established small, scattered plantations, a good indication that Natchez relations were congenial. The colonist to whom we are most indebted for our knowledge about the Natchez was, as mentioned earlier, Antoine S. Le Page du Pratz. From him we learn that the French were provided land and food by these Indians. In turn they received guns, powder, lead, intoxicants, and cloth, a satisfactory arrangement for both parties. Then in 1723 at Fort Rosalie an old Natchez warrior was killed needlessly by a soldier, and his murderer went unpunished by the fort commander. In retaliation the Natchez killed some French settlers. Peace was reestablished within a few days, but a course toward further hostilities had been set. After the peace the French attacked White Apple, demanding and receiving the head of a leader who had been hostile to them. The Natchez could not understand this deception by the French and subsequently avoided contact with them.

At this crucial point in Natchez–French relations two Natchez deaths occurred that quite possibly led to temporary Indian disorganization. In 1725 the younger brother of the Great Sun, Tattooed Serpent, died, and three years later the Great Sun died. Thus, in 1728 a young and inexperienced Great Sun was in power. In the next year, 1729, a new commander of the Fort Rosalie garrison decided quite arbitrarily that he required the land of White Apple for settlement. When he told the Natchez leader of the community to forfeit the village, the Noble refused, and the commander became furious. The Natchez parleyed to decide a course of action. They concluded that because the French were becoming more numerous, were corrupting the Natchez youth, and were breaking their promises, the French should be destroyed.

The *sixth phase,* the final one, was the Natchez revolt and their destruction as a tribe. In 1729 the pro-English Natchez faction attacked Fort Rosalie and the French plantations. They may have killed two hundred colonials and took women, children, and black slaves hostage. The next year the French

Figure 14-6 | Nancy Taylor, one of the last Natchez speakers, in 1908. (Courtesy of Smithsonian Institution, National Anthropological Archives, Swanton Book IV 180-A.)

attacked two Natchez forts in which hostages were held. In the conflict neither side prevailed, and a truce was arranged. The Natchez release their captives, and the French moved back to the Mississippi River from Grand Village. Then the Natchez slipped across the Mississippi River, ascended the Red River to the Black River, and built a fort at Sicily Island. In 1731 a French and Indian force was sent against them, and about two hundred, including the Great Sun, were forced to surrender. These Natchez were sold into slavery in the West Indies.

The Indians captured by the French at Sicily Island were primarily women and children. The main body of warriors escaped and intermittently raided French settlements for the next five years. Eventually they became refugees among the Chickasaw, Cherokee, and Creek. With the Indian Removal Act of 1830 the majority of Native Americans in the Southeast were forced to relocate in Indian Territory, including most Natchez survivors. In 1907 Swanton located some Natchez near Braggs, Oklahoma, in the southwestern part of the Cherokee nation; five of the individuals he found still knew some of the language (see Figure 14-6). In 1934, when Mary R. Haas worked among the Natchez liv-

Figure 14-7 | Matthew Creel and Andy Spell, Edisto-Natchez-Kusso Indians, at their festival in 1992. (Photo by Gene Joseph Crediford, © 1999.)

ing near Braggs, she found that only two Natchez speakers had survived among the postremoval Oklahoma Cherokee. Today a few rituals are preserved in Cherokee and Creek communities into which Natchez survivors intermarried. The descendants of these Natchez identify themselves as Cherokee or Creek and no longer perform these rituals in the Natchez language (Moore 1994, 371). Today in Natchez, Mississippi, the Grand Village of the Natchez has been reconstructed as a state park.

In 1747 Natchez survivors living among the preremoval Cherokee petitioned the colonial government in Charleston, South Carolina, to become "settlement Indians." They were given land near Charleston along the Edisto River. Today in South Carolina the 450 people in the communities of Four Holes and Creeltown are petitioning for federal acknowledgment as the Edisto-Natchez-Kusso Indians (see Figure 14-7). As an independent tribe, however, the Natchez are extinct, like so many Native American tribes.

| Additional Sources

The best comparatively brief and insightful account of Natchez ethnography and ethnohistory is by Jim Barnett (1998). The most worthwhile firsthand account is by Le Page du Pratz (1947), the primary source for this chapter. For additional details and a comparative view of the Natchez and other Indians in the Southeast, the best source is the 1946 publication by John R. Swanton.

Selected Bibliography

Albrecht, Andrew C. 1946. Indian–French relations at Natchez. *American Anthropologist* n.s. 48:321–54.

Barnett, Jim. 1998. *The Natchez Indians.* Mississippi Department of Archives and History. Natchez, MS.

Blumer, Thomas J. 1994. Edisto. In *Native America in the twentieth century: An encyclopedia,* Mary B. Davis, ed., 181–82. New York.

Crediford, Gene Joseph. 1993. *Those who remain: Native Americans in South Carolina 500 years after Columbus.* Columbia, SC.

Fogelson, Raymond D., ed. (forthcoming). *Southeast,* vol. 14, *Handbook of North American Indians.* Washington, DC.

Ford, James A., and Clarence H. Webb. 1956. *Poverty Point, a Late Archaic site in Louisiana.* Anthropological Papers of the American Museum of Natural History, vol. 46, pt. 1. New York.

Haas, Mary R. 1939. Natchez and Chitimacha clans and kinship terminology. *American Anthropologist* n.s. 41:597–610.

Le Page du Pratz, Antoine S. 1947. *The history of Louisiana.* Paris. (Published in London, 1758; reprinted at New Orleans, 1947.)

Moore, John H. 1994. Natchez. In *Native America in the twentieth century: An encyclopedia,* Mary B. Davis, ed., 370–71. New York.

Neitzel, Robert S. 1965. *Archaeology of the Fatherland site.* Anthropological Papers of the American Museum of Natural History, vol. 51, pt. 2. New York.

Swanton, John R. 1946. *The Indians of the southeastern United States.* Bureau of American Ethnology Bulletin 137. Washington, DC.

Taukchiray, Wesley DuRant, and Alice Bee Kasakoff. 1992. Contemporary Indians of South Carolina. In *Indians of the Southeastern United States in the late twentieth century,* J. Anthony Paredes, ed., 72–101. Tuscaloosa, AL.

White, Douglas R., George P. Murdock, and Richard Scaglion. 1971. Natchez class and rank reconsidered. *Ethnology* 10:369–88.

15 Current Realities: Fears and Hopes

This sign, photographed in 1997, was at the entrance to the Pass Cahuilla Reservation in California.

> *Survival = Anger × Imagination. Imagination is the only weapon on the reservation.*
>
> *The Lone Ranger and Tonto Fist Fight in Heaven,* Sherman Alexie, 1994, 150. (Courtesy of The Atlantic Monthly Press.)

THE INTRODUCTORY CHAPTERS survey the background to modern Native American life north of Mexico, and the twelve tribal chapters examine specific lifestyles, past and present. The accounts about particular tribes have one clear limitation: generalizations are usually of restricted scope. Thus the previous chapters about tribes beg for a discussion that focuses not so much on the past as on the present and the future. As a general introduction, recent news reports and their background are informative.

Indians in the News

Coverage of Native Americans in national and regional newspapers is intermittent, and television news focuses largely on confrontational situations. Although written and visual accounts are varied, the topic commanding the greatest newspaper attention is gaming.

GAMING Indian casinos in the United States dominate newspaper articles for good reasons. First, these enterprises are both a comparatively recent development and clearly dramatic. Second, their casinos attract record numbers of non-Indians to reservations. The best measure of Indian gaming success is reflected in total earnings. Between 1988 and 2000, the revenues increased from $212 million to $9.6 billion. The Foxwoods Resort Casino in Connecticut is reportedly the most profitable casino in the country. In 1999 an Indian casino in North Carolina and another in Oregon were the leading tourist attractions in these states.

Indian gaming casino-style has been called the "new buffalo." It likewise has been termed "Indian catch-up," with all that this phrase suggests. Tribes with reasonably successful casinos have been able to provide members with unprecedented health and social services, greater fire protection, and other positive benefits (see Figure 15-1). A few tribes have become extremely wealthy. However, most of the nearly 310 casinos do not appear to be highly profitable. (Federal legislation prohibits the official release of detailed public information about their gaming profits.) We do know that by 1999, about 5 percent of the tribes with casinos earned about 90 percent of the total Indian gaming profits. Tribes that do not have casinos because of their location or attitudes toward gambling typically remain poor.

Indian gaming is by far the most regulated form of legal gambling in the United States, and the 1988 congressional act to control their operations is flawed. The act gave partial control to states without tribal consent. Thus an aspect of Indian sovereignty was relinquished to the states. Tribes face varied hurdles in developing casinos. If a new casino is to be located on trust land set aside for Indians prior to 1988, then, in theory, negotiations with a state are relatively straightforward. If Indians seek to open a casino on land recently purchased by a tribe, negotiations are far more complex. The primary reason why a tribe seeks this alternative is that its reservation is not readily accessible to

Figure 15-1 | The Chinook Winds Casino of the Confederated Tribes, Siletz Indians, in Lincoln City, Oregon, one of the most popular tourist attractions in the state in 2000.

large numbers of potential patrons. State governors have the capacity to accept or reject such proposals and seldom have concurred. In addition, tribes with established casinos typically oppose the construction of new ones on nontrust lands by other tribes.

Tribes have begun to cooperate to develop gaming. Recent efforts in California provide a dramatic example of newfound Native American political action that received considerable attention in newspapers. For years the State of California obstructed tribal efforts to establish or to expand and control their casinos, largely as a result of successful lobbying by Nevada gambling interests. Reportedly, in recent years one-third of all Nevada casino patrons have been from California, and they spend over $7 billion each year. In 1998, California tribes collectively put forth Proposition 5, the Indian Self-Reliance Initiative, and spent over $60 million on behalf of the measure. Tribes sought the authority to run their gaming operations, about forty in number at the time, without gross state interference. Opposition to the initiative came largely from Nevada gambling interests, which spent more than $22 million in their effort. Although the initiative passed, the California Supreme Court ruled that it violated the state constitution, which prohibits Nevada-style casinos.

As a result of this court ruling, the governor of California, Gray Davis, negotiated an agreement, and the state legislature approved new compacts with fifty-seven California tribes that required passage of a state constitutional amendment. It became Ballot Proposal 1A, the Indian Self-Reliance Initiative, in 2000. The tribes spent at least $21 million to promote 1A, but there was no formal opposition from Nevada gambling interests. The constitutional change was approved by 65 percent of the voters and received federal approval in 2000. Highlights of 1A include sanctioning casino-style gambling, including two thousand, possibly more, slot machines for each casino. The tribes with casinos will share their profits with tribes without casinos. There is "revenue sharing" with the state for state goals, including grants to aid addicted gamblers. The compacts also allow unions to organize casino workers. Objections to 1A include the probability that Nevada gambling companies will be operating California casinos under contracts with tribes, as already is the case in some other states. In addition, California will have far less control over Indian casinos than is the case in some other states, especially with reference to the number of slot machines, which are extremely profitable. Indian gaming in California is expected to expand and to be second only to gambling in Nevada within a relatively few years.

Senator Slade Gorton (R-Wash.), chair of the Senate Interior Appropriations Subcommittee, launched a direct attack on tribal sovereignty as a result of their casino earnings. In 1998 he advocated allocating federal funds to Indians according to the wealth of a tribe. This proposal would punish tribes for economic development and represents a not-so-subtle effort to "tax" tribes with successful gaming operations. Gorton also sought to require tribes to waive sovereign immunity as a condition of BIA funding. The Senate rejected both proposals, but Gorton continued to advocate withholding federal funds from tribes based on casino profits; he was defeated in his 2000 reelection bid.

In Canada casino-style gambling is a contentious issue for First Nation bands and tribes. One problem is that casinos operated by provinces are quite profitable, and thus there is resistance to First Nations casinos. By 2000, there were no Indian casinos in Manitoba, although they were operating in Saskatchewan.

HUMAN REMAINS AND ARTIFACTS Archaeologists have excavated countless Native American graves, on and off tribal lands, and shipped the bones with their accompanying grave goods to museums for study and storage. Collectors for museums, knowingly and unknowingly, bought artifacts from individual Indians who were not their rightful owners; ceremonial garments and wampum belonging to clans are examples. Museum purchases usually were legitimate, although examples of stolen artifacts may occur in collections. In addition, exceptional archaeological and ethnographic artifacts have long been sought by private collectors willing to pay high prices. Some tribes consider the excavation of graves sacrilegious and believe that the bones and artifacts recovered are tribal property and should be returned.

In 1990 the U.S. Congress enacted the Native American Graves Protection and Repatriation Act. It established a process for public and private museums, colleges, and universities that receive federal funds to repatriate Native American skeletal remains and artifacts. The attitudes of collection curators ranged from sympathetic and cooperative to hostile and obstructionist. At the same time, some curators often faced the daunting task of not only compiling appropriate inventories but also, and equally important, identifying the tribe of origin; early museum records may not be clear. Unquestionably, the rightful tribal owners of archaeological finds that are thousands of years old may be impossible to identify, although this problem is not addressed in the federal act. This issue has produced conflicts among Indians, archaeologists, and other interested parties.

The return of human remains for appropriate reburial is a major issue. An important repatriation with considerable press coverage occurred in 1999. The remains of nearly two thousand individuals from the now abandoned Pecos Pueblo in New Mexico were returned by Harvard University and Phillips Academy to Jemez Pueblo, where the Pecos descendants now live. Reburial was at the Pecos National Historical Park, New Mexico.

The Navajo response to the repatriation act is revealing. The tribe was contacted by about 350 institutions concerning pertinent human remains and artifacts in their collections. The enduring ambivalence of many Navajo about the dead posed a problem for the tribal leadership, especially because the collections included thousands of skeletal remains. Tribal leaders concluded that reburial should be at the place a body originally was interred, which would be difficult if not impossible in many instances. They therefore did not seek the return of skeletal remains nor the accompanying grave goods. Regarding most other artifacts, such as rugs and jewelry, they felt that these items were purchased legally and need not be returned. Medicine bundles, however, represented a major concern. It was considered desirable to return them if similar items continue to be used by medicine men; they would be reintegrated into appropriate ceremonies. The return of religious objects associated with abandoned ceremonies was not desirable, nor did they feel it was fitting for the tribe to curate them.

What does all of this mean in terms of present-day realities? First, it demonstrates in yet another context that the federal government continues to acknowledge the sovereign status of tribes. The repatriation act fosters tribalism. Second, museums and tribes have become integrated in an unprecedented manner. Human bones and artifacts represent invaluable biological and cultural assets for everyone. The new dialogue has produced far greater mutual understanding among the parties most directly concerned.

Finally, some museum curators in foreign countries and private collectors in this country appreciate the deep symbolic significance of particular artifacts for specific tribes. The voluntary return of historically important artifacts is a reasonably common and praiseworthy practice.

KENNEWICK MAN The discovery of human remains along the Columbia River in Kennewick, Washington, by two college students in 1996 receives continuing and reasonably intense coverage in newspapers and other publications. A nearly complete skeleton was recovered, and it is among the most complete early skeletons known in the Americas. Radiocarbon dates indicate that it is about ninety-four hundred years old. The find is especially noteworthy because experts initially identified the bones as Caucasoid (resembling or related to Caucasians), or, more strikingly, as Caucasian. The plot thickens.

The bones were on Army Corps of Engineers land. Under the federal Repatriation Act of 1990, the bones of Native Americans can be claimed by the tribe with which they are identified. The local Umatilla and other nearby Indian groups claimed the bones and planned to rebury them as soon as possible in a secret place. The Corps was prepared to turn the skeleton over to the Indian claimants. Eight anthropologists launched a suit against the Corps, insisting that the bones be studied systematically, not only because they were old but also because the modern tribes claiming ownership could not prove that the bones are those of a local Indian group. Following a legal tug-of-war, a federal judge gave anthropologists the right to perform DNA tests to clarify the racial background of the person involved. Insufficient DNA existed in the available bones to make the tests. Curiously, the femurs, which may contain enough DNA for testing, had disappeared before the tests. In October 2000, the FBI was attempting to locate the femurs. In late September the secretary of the Department of the Interior ruled that the bones are to be returned to the Umatilla and other local tribes. However, in October a federal judge reactivated the suit filed by anthropologists. Thus the status of Kennewick Man is unresolved.

Studies of the bones themselves appear to confirm that Kennewick Man shares numerous Caucasian racial characteristics and cannot be clearly associated with any particular Native American group. To complicate his identity, the tip of a stone spearhead is embedded in the pelvis. The weapon point is similar to those identified with Native American cultures in the area from about nine thousand to forty-five hundred years ago.

If the morphology of the skeleton does represent a person of Caucasian background, the question of how the Americas were populated becomes a far more complex puzzle. Two major possibilities have been suggested. Perhaps they entered the New World from the Bering Strait region, either on foot or by boat. More controversial is the suggestion that at least some early migrants to North America arrived by boat across the north Atlantic Ocean. This is an inviting alternative for a number of prominent archaeologists. They reason that Clovis cultural remains are among the earliest finds in North America and that their technology has numerous significant parallels with finds from the Solutrean culture of Spain and France dating between twenty thousand and sixteen thousand years ago. Archaeological finds in northeastern Asia do not appear to share a technological affinity with Clovis artifacts.

Were Caucasians among the earliest migrants to the New World? Perhaps. Yet many physical anthropologists have long contended that present-day "racial" differences among peoples of the world are a relatively recent evolutionary development and may date from ten thousand to fifteen thousand years ago. Is Clovis derived from Solutrean? Maybe. However, similar and sometimes identical technological developments clearly have occurred totally independent of one another in different parts of the world. Then too the current dating of Clovis and Solutrean is troublesome.

WORDS ASSOCIATED WITH INDIANS Native American names for sports teams are widely considered negative and have received sporadic press coverage. By 1999, at least six hundred high school and college teams had, under pressure from Indians and others, dropped their Indian-associated names. More than twenty-five hundred other institutions retain such names or other symbols. In the same year, the Washington Redskins football team name was challenged as a racial slur. The basis for the complaint is the 1946 Lanham Act; it prohibits registered trademarks that are contemptuous, disparaging, or scandalous. The trademark panel of judges cancelled the Redskins' trademark. An appeal is planned in federal court contending that the name honors Native Americans.

The word "squaw," with its negative associations, is a widespread word in place names and is considered racist and derogatory. The State of Montana, for example, passed a bill in 1999 to eliminate the seventy-four "squaw" names from maps, signs, and markers, to the satisfaction of Montana and other Indians.

MAKAH INDIAN WHALING A revival of gray whale hunting by the Makah became an important story in 1999, at least in part because of the avid opposition of some environmental groups. The hunt lent itself to presentation on television news programs.

The Makah have a small reservation in the extreme northwestern corner of Washington state. Aboriginal whaling played a significant part in their economic and religious lives. With the 1855 Treaty of Neah Bay, they ceded most of their land to the United States in return for benefits, including the right to hunt whales. In the 1860s commercial seal hunting became highly profitable for the Makah, and they temporarily abandoned whaling, only to return to the pursuit of whales as the market for sealskins declined. By the 1920s the gray whale population had become dangerously low from overhunting by non-Indians; the Makah then stopped whaling. The gray whale eventually was placed on the Endangered Species list, but the gray whale population made a dramatic comeback, and it was removed from the list in 1994. The International Whaling Commission, founded in 1946, had been granting Eskimos and others the right to harvest a limited number of whales, including the gray whale. The Makah obtained a permit in 1997 and sought to follow aboriginal whaling patterns, with some exceptions. They built traditional canoes and harpoons and revived whaling rituals. They successfully harpooned a gray whale in 1999 and killed it with firearms to ensure a quick death. Environmentalists harassed the whalers as they hunted, until the whalers were stopped by the U.S. Coast Guard. In the television news reports the hunt was filmed at various stages.

THE SACAGAWEA COIN A one-dollar U.S. coin, issued in 2000, honors this woman, and the coin's release drew press reports. As a young woman Sacagawea (Sacajawea) helped guide the 1804–1806 expedition led by Meriwether Lewis and William Clark to the Pacific Ocean. As the modern feminist movement emerged early in the twentieth century, Sacagawea gained widespread recognition and stature. Her role as a guide for Lewis and Clark was far more modest than her symbolic importance. Little is known about her. She usually is considered to have been a Northern Shoshone, although this tribal identification is not certain. She probably died in 1812, although Indian oral traditions report her death in 1884. A Shoshone–Bannock woman posed for the portrait on the coin.

PRESIDENT CLINTON VISITS A RESERVATION An official visit by a sitting president obviously receives press attention and television coverage, at least for a few days. So it was in 1999 with the visit by President Clinton to the Pine Ridge Indian Reservation, South Dakota, as he toured impoverished communities. The Pine Ridge Reservation is the second largest in the United States and has about thirty-eight thousand residents. It is the home of the Oglala and Lakota (Sioux), who receive periodic press attention because of the depressed reservation conditions. The poverty rate is about five times the national average, the unemployment rate is about 70 percent, and the scope of alcoholism is alarmingly high. Their housing is grossly substandard, and shortly before the Clinton tour, a tornado had destroyed about 160 buildings.

Ironically, in 1927 the *last* official reservation visit by a sitting president took place at the same reservation, by President Calvin Coolidge. Clinton stopped there for about three hours. He promised new housing and water projects for this and other reservations, plus additional commitments by the federal government. Clinton also visited the Navajo Reservation in 2000.

GEORGE W. BUSH COMMENTS ON THE STATUS OF INDIANS During his 1999 Republican campaign for president, Bush is quoted as follows: "My view is that state law reigns supreme when it comes to the Indians, whether it be gambling or any other issue." The Native American response was incredulity. For instance, the Navajo Nation President Kelsey Begaye characterized the Bush statement as "appallingly inaccurate," saying that it "either demonstrated his ignorance of 200 years of his country's constitutional and judicial structure, or a shocking display of political cynicism" (*Navajo Times,* 11/24/99).

Indians as Environmentalists

The "Noble Savage" concept as a characterization of Native Americans living north of Mexico gained prominence in the late 1700s, especially in its artistic and literary expressions. In recent years, this "good Indian" image has gained greater stature, and Indians are widely characterized as "the first American environmentalists."

Examples of conservation practices among aboriginal Indians are widely reported in ethnographic accounts. For fishermen to leave openings in weirs for the escapement of fish is one example. Another is for beaver trappers to leave a few animals in a lodge to reproduce. Concurrently, and in varied contexts, aboriginal Americans might not have the technological capacity to disrupt the balance in nature. For instance, their relatively short gill nets, made from rawhide or plant fibers, produced comparatively modest harvests, especially when compared with the long modern nets made from synthetic fibers.

Environmentalists today forcefully and avidly condemn the burning of tropical rain forests throughout the world to produce farmlands. In eastern North America, however, indigenous Americans typically and systematically burned vast areas to produce arable land. The same was true for Euro-American pioneers, whether they were settling in Ohio or Oregon. Furthermore, it was commonplace for Indians to burn grasslands to drive out animals that could be killed for food. Native Americans were thorough vegetation burners, just as are many other peoples throughout the world.

Most Euro-Americans today probably think that Indians harvested only enough fish, game, and birds to provide necessary food and raw materials. For some tribes this was true beyond doubt. But not for others. Justifiably, we condemn white hunters in the 1870s who killed countless bison for "pleasure." But did some Indians also kill animals needlessly? The answer is a clear "yes." However, we must step back and place such killings in their context. Although not everyone would agree, a good argument can be made that killing per se is learned behavior. Assuming this is so, the sooner a child in a society of hunters learned to kill nonhuman species, the greater the person's survival potential. Thus, when a small child found a nest of ducklings and systematically pulled live birds apart, the process became a learning experience. The child was praised, not reproved, by adults. In sum, among hunters killing became a way *to* life and a way *of* life.

It is not difficult to document the destruction of game by Native Americans in early historic times. A Chipewyan example will suffice. Samuel Hearne (1958), on his travels from Churchill along western Hudson Bay to the Coppermine River and the Arctic Ocean, reported Chipewyan wastefulness soon after their first contact with the British. He reported that caribou were so abundant that Indians "frequently [killed] great numbers merely for the fat, marrow, and tongues" (p. 75); "[i]ndeed, they were so accustomed to kill every thing that came within their reach, that few of them could pass a small bird's nest, without slaying the young ones, or destroying the eggs" (p. 76); and caribou "were very plentiful on the whole way [south]; the Indians killed great numbers of them daily, merely for the sake of their skins" (p. 127). Despite these quotes, it must be added that the Chipewyan believed, based on their creation myth, that game would always be abundant (see also Chapter 4).

Not only was the reckless destruction of animals reasonably widespread in aboriginal times among some Indians, but the practice expanded exponentially as they received firearms in the emergence of the European fur trade. Indians contributed to the near extinction of sea otter and greatly reduced the beaver and musk ox populations. Furthermore, destructive harvests have continued into the present. Why is this practice, as selective as it might be, not generally known? One answer is that modern ethnographers do not publish information about overkills, of which they are fully aware. Their rationale is to protect Native Americans from law enforcement agents and others. As Shepard Krech III (1999) suggests in his study of Indians as environmentalists, it may be that the prevailing contemporary view of Indians as ecologically caring was *borrowed from* Euro-Americans in the recent past.

Tribalism

Tribalism refers to a unique sense of ingroup identity, which distinguishes the lifeway of one tribe from another. In early historic times, the Indian sense of tribal identity ranged from strong to weak and essentially nonexistent, depending on economic, political, and other factors. Tribal identity sometimes gave way to tribal alliances in unsuccessful attempts to avoid Euro-American domination. Following the establishment of reserved lands for Native Americans, tribalism often grew stronger as relations with whites stabilized. Indian identification with a particular tribe, whether weak or strong, represents the modern face of tribalism, irrespective of how similar or different their culture may be from its early historic configuration.

By the early 1900s ethnographers and many older Indians alike lamented the decline in traditional tribalism. This remains true at present, with a far greater sense of cultural losses. Modern expressions of tribalism are highly varied. At one extreme are tribal members who have abandoned their tribal identity by "going white." In the 1980 federal census, about one-fourth of Native American respondents did not list any tribal affiliation. An opposite extreme is represented by traditionalists, the "real" Indians, who usually live on or near their reserved lands and seek to retain or to revitalize their distinct identity. Between these extremes are innumerable alternatives suggested by the following examples. An Indian family might move to an urban area but retain close ties with their reservation, returning often to participate in social and religious activities. Alternatively, a young adult raised on a reservation might abandon tribal conventions. Later in life, he or she might begin to identify primarily with his or her tribe, especially in religious aspects. Another common pattern is for an individual or family to leave a reservation or region repeatedly to obtain work and periodically return home.

An additional gauge of a decline in tribalism is the number of aboriginal languages that continue to be spoken north of Mexico. By 1995 about half of the four hundred aboriginal languages were extinct, as previously noted (see Chapter 1). The same year forty-six tribal languages continued to be spoken by many adults and substantial numbers of children. They include Cherokee, Cree, Hopi, Inuit (Eskimo), Navajo, and Yuit (Eskimo). Traditional cultural ways are likely to persist among tribes with the greatest language vitality.

Tribal cultures possibly have their greatest strength among relatively isolated populations that have retained their indigenous languages and that depend heavily on local food resources and in tribes for which Euro-American control is a comparatively recent development. Some modern Eskimos meet these criteria. For instance, in the early 1990s at Holman, an Inuit community in the Northwest Territories of Canada, the aboriginal language continued to be spoken, but with declining proficiency by younger residents, especially those raised in nontraditional households. In general, most children were more fluent in English than in Inuit. Some twenty years previously, little English was spoken there. The material culture at Holman was dominated by imported manufactures, including television sets, washing machines, dryers, and freezers. Likewise, decreasing numbers of settlement youth were interested in traditional subsistence pursuits. Why? Some of them lacked the essential hunting skills or the economic ability to purchase the required equipment. Wage labor jobs had greater appeal, and store-bought foods were preferred by some youth over traditional edibles. Then, too, introduced sports, such as basketball and hockey, represented compelling interests. Somewhat similar studies exist about Eskimo high school students in northwestern Alaska and in the Bristol Bay sector. In the early 1990s most of these students living in towns, and nearly half of the villagers sampled, expected to leave their communities *permanently*. Students typically characterized life in their home settlements as "boring." Anticipated out-migration by students who expected to attend college was higher than for other students. I suspect that these responses of modern youthful Eskimos in Canada and Alaska are similar to those of most other relatively isolated Native Americans.

Although physical isolation unquestionably is a significant factor contributing to the relative vitality of Native American cultures, other variables demand recognition. Especially prominent is the impact of the electronic age and its potential in fostering tribal *and* intertribal identity. This influence is in part reflected in the television programs received by isolated households. Some videos, especially those made by Indians or reproduced from public television, encourage Native Americans in the United States to learn more about what is happening among the First Nations in Canada and vice versa. It appears, too, that the Internet is becoming a prominent means for Indians to communicate with members of their own and other tribes for a personal exchange of information. Additionally, and possibly just as important, individuals may access information on the Internet that is far more difficult to obtain by other means. As younger Native Americans in particular acquire the required skills, the Internet may have a lasting impact on their lives.

Being Native American Today

Historically, race and culture emerged as key identifiers of aboriginal Americans, with race as paramount. In the United States a widespread historic definition of an Indian, with reference to biology, requires one-fourth or more Native American genetic heritage. Federal regulations defined and required this quantum, or a lesser amount, incorporated in tribal constitutions as a continuing basis for membership. For a tribe to require irrefutable proof of 100 percent indigenous American genetic background would reduce membership dramatically. A liberal interpretation of who is biologically eligible obviously diminishes the meaning of tribal membership.

Lawrence R. Baca (1988, 230) suggests that a working legal definition of an Indian is "a person, some of whose ancestors lived in America before the arrival of Whites, who is generally considered to be an Indian by the community in which he lives or from which he comes, and who holds himself to be an Indian." While acknowledging a genetic factor, this definition reasonably places far greater emphasis on sociocultural identification as an aboriginal American. Note in particular that self-identification as an Indian is fully recognized and makes legal determinations more individualistic.

Qualifications for tribal membership are irregular. As mentioned, genetic quantum is often one-fourth Indian, but it varies. For instance, the Confederated Tribes of the Grand Ronde of Oregon require a one-sixteenth minimum genetic quantum for someone in their group combined with that of a person of any other federally recognized tribe. The Cherokee Nation of Oklahoma emphasizes descent from persons eligible for a 1906 roll. The Tohono O'odham (Papago) of Arizona place primary emphasis on residence; an offspring born to a reservation member is automatically a tribal member.

The most troublesome issue, one of seismic magnitude, is the genetic quantum requirement, especially if it is relatively low *and* if marriages to non-Indians are common. Within a few generations there may be no tribal members unless the genetic quantum for membership is reduced or is ignored and membership is based on descent from a particular roll. It appears that at present about half of Native American marriages are to non-Indians. (This problem in Canada is addressed in Chapter 12.) For tribes with membership based on genetic heritage who have few "full bloods," or "heavy bloods," the problem is especially pressing.

Another issue surrounding Native American identity in the United States centers on tribes unrecognized by the federal government. Recognition is *not* essential to be considered a tribe, but obtaining formal federal acknowledgment has innumerable advantages (e.g., education, health, and other benefits). Unrecognized tribes or bands usually have few members and either continue to occupy their original historic homeland or more often live elsewhere; they are concentrated largely in the eastern states and in California. Typically, they have been ignored by the federal government because of their size, location, or historical background. Unrecognized groups number about 130, and their population exceeds 130,000. Most federally acknowledged tribes gained recognition by treaty, agreement, statute, or an executive order to create a tribal land base. In 1978 the Department of the Interior created the Federal Acknowledgment Project to establish a formal procedure for a group to gain federal recognition. A major requirement is that they demonstrate historical continuity as a tribe or subtribe, a long and involved process. The Little Shell Ojibwa (Chippewa) provide an example. They were living at the Turtle Mountain Reservation, North Dakota, in 1892 when an Indian agent arrived there. At the time Chief Thomas Little Shell, accompanied by more than one hundred families, was away hunting. The agent dropped them from the tribal roll, and their land was sold. Despite protests by the chief, they became landless, and in 1896 some six hundred Little Shell Indians were captured by soldiers, put into railroad boxcars, and deposited at the Canadian border. They wandered south during the winter. Some of them received land allotments from the public domain by 1920, but in 1953 the band was terminated by the federal government under House Concurrent Resolution 108. After the Federal Acknowledgment Project was launched, a lawyer began to press their claim, which has been judged as valid, and their formal recognition is likely in 2001. The four thousand Little Shell are to receive $2.2 million that the federal government holds for them, plus ongoing benefits received by other federally recognized tribes.

The legal status of Hawaiians as an aboriginal population, which is not comparable with that of federally recognized tribes in the United States, has become an issue. In 2000, some two hundred thousand persons were considered as descendants of the indigenous population. They benefit directly from many state and federal programs, which are widely regarded as inadequate. Bills before the U.S. Congress would treat eligible Hawaiians much the same as other Native American groups with federal recognition. It appears that Hawaiians may achieve a more equitable settlement than obtained by Indians, and the deliberations will produce a framework for actual "government-to-government" recognition.

Tribal Administration

In the United States each federally recognized tribe, band, village, or other political unit is beholden to the federal government with its administrative labyrinth. To receive federal funds, these Indians must accept the accompanying management procedures. Federal requirements became daunting, especially after the Indian Reorganization Act in 1934. One eventual result was that in 1975 the federal government began to encourage tribes to assume far greater direct administrative responsibilities. Yet tribes have had little voice in establishing policies. With block grants, tribal involvements have expanded further. Non-Indians generally are unaware of the complexities in the tribal and federal government relationship.

The Hopi serve as an example. By 1999 their enrollment was about twelve thousand, some nine thousand of whom lived on their reservation. The number of administrative units requiring local management was forbidding, and most residents were either quite young or old and not eligible for positions. The basic organization, grounded in the Hopi Tribal Constitution, included an election board, enrollment department, tribal council, judicial branch, budget committee, tribal management department, and housing authority. Social service units were concerned with the elderly, behavioral health, and law enforcement. Programs dealt with water resources, abandoned mines, and nutrition. Offices included mining and mineral resources, research and planning, and construction. Diabetes treatment, woodland management, and maintenance of the Hopi language were among the projects. This list, although far ranging, is *not* complete. Irrespective of how capable and devoted administrators may be, each aspect of government is complex. Many Hopi have made careers of working for the tribal government, the primary employer on the reservation. In sum, the Hopi increasingly have learned to deal with Euro-American bureaucrats, and many have themselves become bureaucrats. This is a major factor in modern Hopi life. At the same time, the typical Hopi probably distrusts the tribal leaders in general. To a greater or lesser extent, the same is likely true on many other reservations.

Factionalism is often a further impediment to tribal development. One group is often identified as "conservative" (traditional, hostile) and their opposition as "progressive" (friendly, acculturated), irrespective of the many gradations. The dichotomy is most evident in political life and reminds one of the differences between the Democrats and Republicans. Just as with these political parties, one Indian faction, correctly or not, accuses the other of nepotism, favoritism to allies, corruption, or fraud. Furthermore, as one faction replaces another in tribal government, the patterning seems to be more of the same with different actors. A constructive opposition capable of conceiving and developing innovative programs to break the cycle seldom seems to emerge. In brief, tribal political factionalism endures along well-established lines.

Urban Indians

Only recently have urban Indians become a focus of ethnographic studies. The concentration of Native Americans in towns and cities is a comparatively recent development, and the modest interest in them by ethnographers dates largely from the 1960s. About 60 percent of indigenous Americans in the United States, and 50 percent in Canada, currently live off of their reserved lands. Nonetheless, this book concentrates almost entirely on Indians who live in their aboriginal homeland or on land set aside for them in historic times. It also is essential to note that reservations and reserves have produced racial segregation, federal paternalism, and depressed living standards.

A brief overview of the emergence of urban Indians is instructive. First, the Indian population reached an all-time low between 1890 and 1900, when the population total was about 250,000 in the United States and 100,000 in Canada. Thus small numbers survived, especially compared with an estimated two to four million some five hundred years previous. In 1900 urban Indians in the United States represented about 0.4 percent of their total population. By then Indians represented a remnant population, and years of exploitation by Westerners and intermarriages with non-Indians had reoriented the lifestyles of most tribes as they sought accommodations with whites for survival. Working indirectly (e.g., the fur trade) and directly (e.g., wage labor) for whites became common responses. Second, intense daily contacts with non-Indians in the United States did not become commonplace until World War II; some twenty-five thousand Native Americans became members of the armed services, and many thousands moved to urban areas for war-related employment. In either instance, when this war was won, their experiences made them far more capable of dealing with whites. Third, soon after World War II, the U.S. federal government was determined to "get out of the Indian business" by terminating the status of some reservations and establishing a timetable to abolish *all* reservations. Fourth, the Relocation Program in the 1950s was designed to assimilate Indians rapidly into the American "melting pot" by providing job training, economic support, and jobs in urban areas. The program failed in most respects, but it did introduce many Native Americans to city living. Fifth, the civil rights movement of the 1960s and the beginning of the war in Vietnam, in which some forty-five thousand Indians served, introduced a greater sense of their unique identity as "Indian Americans." At this time the federal government largely abandoned its assimilation policies (see also Chapter 2). Sixth and last, in the 1970s the federal governments in the United States and Canada began to encourage Native Americans to become their own tribal administrators; this continues to be policy.

Before turning to urban Indians per se, it is fitting to recognize that since colonial times, some Native Americans have become integrated into the Euro-American melting pot. Clearly, a significant but largely unknown number of persons who technically qualify as Indians have abandoned their aboriginal identity. They are the "invisible" Indians. Persons judged as white in their community may report that in family history or lore they have near or distant Indian relatives, or they may identify a particular tribe, such as the Cherokee.

Why do so many Native Americans now live in urban areas? A prominent reason is to achieve greater economic success. Reservation unemployment rates typically are high, often in the 50 percent range. The poverty rate for Indian families is far higher than for any minority group in the United States. A common response is for individuals or families to relocate to towns or cities, sometimes to Indian neighborhoods, and hope to earn enough money to move back home. Typically, however, they obtain low-paying jobs and do not receive social and health benefits comparable to those on reservations. Then, too, they are likely to be laid off when the general economy takes a downturn, and they return home. Commonly, these people move back and forth in a circular residence pattern, especially when urban areas are relatively near reservations. Another reason why Indians return to their reservations is that they often encounter racism away from home. On reservations they more fully realize the satisfactions of being different and being Indian.

Many Native Americans have permanent homes in urban areas, accept many aspects of Euro-American life, maintain comparatively close cultural ties with their tribe, and visit their reservations or reserves for extended periods. In other words, they participate in two distinct cultures, an adaptive process identified as *biculturation*. Another alternative is for urban Indians essentially to lose their tribal identity even while being proud of their Indian heritage, as attenuated as it might be. For them participation in Pan-Indian activities, especially powwows, often is personally satisfying. Finally, the American "melting pot" model is best represented by Indians born in urban settings, whose parents speak only English, and who have no formal reservation or reserve ties. They represent various stages of assimilation into the greater society, but they are a relatively small percentage of modern urban Indians.

The identification of Indians with urban settings appears to be increasing steadily for reasons cited previously. Then, too, urban developments are now encompassing previously rural reservations, especially in sectors of Arizona, California, and New Mexico. Some of the more isolated reservations and reserves have become retirement communities for older Indians; younger Indians in the United States may return there because of jobs and economic security provided by casinos.

Diabetes and Native Americans

In 1999 some ten million cases of diabetes were diagnosed in the United States, and an estimated six million more cases were undiagnosed. Two primary forms of diabetes are generally identified. Type 1 usually, but not always, develops in young people whose bodies have stopped producing insulin, which is required to metabolize blood sugar. They must rely on insulin shots to stay alive. (Two Canadians, Frederick G. Banting and Charles Best, first produced insulin from beef pancreases in 1922.) Type 1 is rare, possibly about 8 percent of all cases, and it may not exist among Native Americans. Type 2 diabetes victims are not insulin dependent but may require injected insulin to remain healthy. It typically appears among adults, although Type 2 is increasingly common among youthful Indians. Individual lifestyle is critical in the development of Type 2, although a genetic factor is involved.

Unusual among diseases, diabetes requires daily monitoring, which can only be realistically accomplished by the person affected. Failure to test one's blood sugar level day to day and to take appropriate measures (i.e., diet, exercise, insulin, pills) may rapidly or eventually produce dire consequences (e.g., amputations, blindness, kidney failure, heart attacks).

Among Native Americans before the 1950s, the diabetes rate was low, but it has become an epidemic. In the late 1980s the age-adjusted Indian death rate from diabetes was 2.7 times the rate for the general U.S. population. Among the Pima Indians in Arizona in the 30–64 age bracket, the death rate in the 1980s was about 500 per 1,000, one of the highest rates recorded. A longitudinal study suggests that the Pima incidence may be attributed to their high-caloric diet, lack of exercise, and subsequent obesity that prevails as their traditional lives have been affected increasingly by Euro-American culture.

In 1996 an estimated 9 percent of Native Americans in the United States who were age twenty or older were diagnosed as diabetic, compared with 4.2 percent for non-Hispanic whites. The U.S. Indian Health Service and tribes now have prevention and treatment programs, including classes and health fairs designed to aid in diagnosis and treatment. One major difficulty is to identify and treat high-risk individuals, such as pregnant women, who do not routinely receive medical treatment. It is imperative for Native Americans to learn more about the behavioral patterns that have produced these high percentages. New centers for the study and treatment are being established, with trained Native Americans interpreting the needs and methods best suited for diabetics in particular localities.

From Tribal Sovereignty to ?

Before the arrival of Europeans in what is now the United States, it was all "Indian Country." Non-Indians now own over 97 percent of this land. At first the international sovereignty of tribes was recognized by the federal government, resulting in government-to-government relations. By the 1830s tribes became identified as "dependent nations." They increasingly ceded powers to the federal government in exchange for benefits in treaties and agreements. They also were subject to congressional measures without tribal consultation. Restricted tribal rights continue to be recognized. Tribes may set their own membership standards, and they have limited judicial powers and the right to regulate property use and to tax (see also Chapter 2). Federally recognized tribes may not make treaties with foreign powers or alienate land without federal approval, nor do they have jurisdiction over major crimes. Likewise, tribes have a limited capacity to deal with non-Indians who live on, work on, or visit Indian lands.

With Public Law 280 in 1953, Congress unilaterally terminated some reservations and gave select states control over such matters as the jurisdiction over major crimes, water rights, and land use. This was a major anti-Indian effort by Congress because it gave states far greater control over tribes. Again in 1953 Congress established a timetable to terminate all reservations. Likewise, in the 1950s the BIA launched a "relocation" program to encourage, or force,

Indians to move to urban areas; the goal was to integrate them into the American "melting pot" (see also Chapter 2). One reaction to these developments by a small minority of Indian leaders in the 1960s was to advocate a return to "tribal sovereignty," but this effort had few supporters among Indians and was not seriously considered by the federal government. By the early 1990s tribal sovereignty became prominent among tribes and the federal government, in part as a result of federal court rulings to support the sovereign status of tribes based largely on treaties.

Related to sovereignty is "self-determination," a phrase and policy that gained prominence in the 1970s. The focus was largely on the development of tribal governments for economic betterment and greater self-sufficiency. By the 1990s the catch phrase became "self-governance" to achieve essentially the same goals. So far, so good. Yet the BIA is the federal agency that provides most direct services to reservations. Largely as a result of congressional actions, the general approach of the bureau is that "one size fits all," which is unrealistic considering the tremendous tribal variability. The poor reputation of the bureau is partially responsible for its typically being underfunded by Congress, and there are periodic rumblings to do away with the bureau. As inadequate as the BIA may be, it remains the major advocate for Indians at the federal level. Indians justifiably fear that "self-governance" and underfunding the bureau will lead to renewed efforts, such as those in the 1950s, to terminate federal obligations to all tribes. This fear is justified by the hostile positions toward Native Americans in recent sessions of Congress. However, the bureau budget for 2001 was increased 15 percent, which partially compensates for years of relative neglect. It even appears as though Congress was impressed by bureau efforts to improve their management practices.

Native Americans have been criticized by non-Indians because they seek more land and greater sovereignty, while at the same time insisting on continuing protection and financial aid from federal governments. Partial sovereignty and special status are not, in my view, contradictory goals. With fleeting exceptions, ever since foreigners began to encounter aboriginal Americans, European legal concepts and political ground rules have prevailed. Treaties, laws, compacts, and so on with Indians are based on Western institutions. Indian traditions, conventions, and their customary laws seldom are seriously considered. Western cultural imperialism endures with vigor. As Marc G. Stevenson (1997, 336) pointed out in this general context, Native Americans are forced to play by the rules of someone else. This is a compelling reason why they should continue to receive federal protection and financial aid.

Native Americans are not cultural imperialists; they do not seek to make outsiders into Indians. History shows, however, that many Euro-Americans, racial prejudice aside, have tried for various reasons to re-form Indians in a white image, though not all have done so. For example, anthropologists and ethnohistorians have worked to preserve Native American oral traditions. Archaeologists excavate sites to reveal and preserve the Indian past. Physical anthropologists identify their biological characteristics, and ethnographers have recorded old and new information about life among Indians. There is no moral justification for not helping and working with Indians in a humane and respectful manner. Above all else, we all should strive to do Native Americans no more harm.

Additional Sources

As noted for Chapter 2, the best widely available and authoritative source about Native American relations with Euro-Americans is volume 4 of the new *Handbook of North American Indians,* edited by Wilcomb E. Washburn (1988) and published by the Smithsonian Institution.

The most comprehensive reports about current issues confronting indigenous Americans appear in tribal newspapers. Prominent examples include the *Navajo Times* (Window Rock, AZ), *News from Indian Country* (Oneida, NY, published in Hayward, WI), *Tutuveni* (Hopi, Kykotsmovi, AZ), and *Tekanwennake* (Six Nations, Ohswekan, Ontario, Canada).

Major studies about youthful Eskimos are by Richard G. Condon, Peter Collings, and George Wenzel (1995) and by Lawrence Hamilton and Carole L. Seyfrit (1993, 1994). Pioneering studies about urban Indians are by John A. Price (1968, 1978). Robert Jarvenpa (1985) provides an excellent historical review of Native American adaptations in Canada and the United States. Sharon O'Brien (1989) examines the development of tribal governments in the United States. Carole Goldberg (1997) presents the background to tribes unrecognized by the federal government, with emphasis on California Indian groups.

Selected Bibliography

Baca, Lawrence R. 1988. The legal status of American Indians. In *History of White–Indian relations,* Wilcomb E. Washburn, ed., vol. 4, 230–37. *Handbook of North American Indians.* Washington, DC.

Condon, Richard G. 1981. *Inuit behavior and seasonal change in the Canadian Arctic.* Ann Arbor, WI.

———, Peter Collins, and George Wenzel. 1995. The best part of life. *Arctic* 48(1): 31–46.

Goldberg, Carole. 1997. Acknowledging the repatriation claims of unacknowledged California tribes. *American Indian Culture and Research Journal* 21(3): 183–190.

Hamilton, Lawrence C., and Carole L. Seyfrit. 1993. Town-village contrasts in Alaskan youth aspirations. *Arctic* 46(3): 255–63.

———. 1994. Coming out of the country. *Arctic Anthropology* 31(1): 255–63.

Hearne, Samuel. 1795. *A journey from Prince of Wales's Fort in Hudson's Bay to the Northern Ocean.* London. (Other editions: Dublin, 1796; Toronto, 1911; Toronto, 1958)

Jarvenpa, Robert. 1985. The political economy and political ethnicity of American Indian adaptations and identities. In *Ethnicity and race in the U.S.A.,* Richard D. Alba, ed., 29–47. Boston.

Krech, Shepard, III. 1999. *The ecological Indian: Myth and history.* New York.

O'Brien, Sharon. 1989. *American Indian tribal government.* Norman, OK.

Price, John A. 1968. The migration and adaptation of American Indians to Los Angeles. *Human Organization* 27:168–75.

———. 1978. *Native studies, American and Canadian Indians.* Toronto.

Stevenson, Marc G. 1997. *Inuit, whalers, and cultural persistence.* Toronto.

Washburn, Wilcomb E., ed. 1988. *History of White–Indian relations,* vol. 4, *Handbook of North American Indians.* Washington, DC.

Wunder, John R., ed. 1996. *Native American sovereignty.* New York.

Appendix A
Tools, Weapons, Nets, and Traps

TOOLS

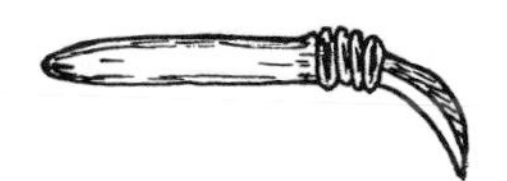

The RODENT TOOTH KNIFE was widely used. It was commonly made from a beaver incisor because of the durable, chisel-like cutting surface of the tooth. The tooth typically was inserted into a wooden handle and lashed into place. This knife type served primarily to hollow out wooden artifacts or to cut grooves in their surfaces. The back of the tooth could be used to make the final polish on a wooden artifact, and the tooth sides could be used to sharpen the blades of other knives. Like the adz and the crooked knife, the rodent tooth knife was drawn toward the user when cutting.

A SEMILUNAR KNIFE blade usually was made from flaked or ground stone and wedged into an antler or wooden handle. An Eskimo form, called an *ulu* by some Eskimos, is becoming a generic term for the type. The Eskimo ulu was a woman's knife and varied widely in size according to its purpose (e.g., sewing, butchering big game). The type occurred commonly in the Arctic and Subarctic and sporadically elsewhere. For example, in the Lake Superior region, the blade was fashioned from cold-hammered copper. In historic times metal saw blades were remade into ulu blades.

The CROOKED KNIFE apparently originated after heat-treated metal was obtained from exotic sources, especially from European traders. The narrow bent iron or steel blade, from which the knife receives its name, might be made from a barrel hoop, imported trap, or scrap metal. The blade was riveted, lashed, or wedged into a handle of wood, antler, or other material. The type became a widespread woodworking tool for finishing wooden artifacts after they were blocked out with an adz. This knife type continues to be used by Native American craftspersons.

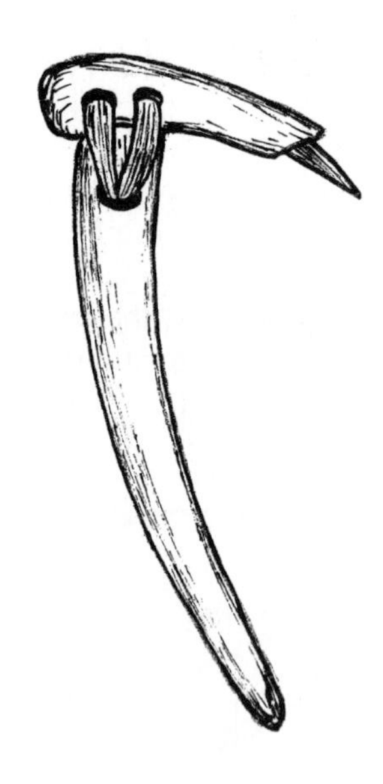

The ADZ dominated as a woodworking tool. Contrasting with an ax, whose blade is set parallel to the handle, an adz blade is set at right angles to the handle. In a typical wooden or antler adz handle, the blade was either lashed directly on top of the handle or, as in the illustration, held in a separate socket. Depending on the shape, which varied widely, adzes produced coarse to relatively fine woodwork and could also be used to fell trees. The latter purpose usually was avoided, although standing dead trees might be burned at the base and the charred sections chipped away with a heavy adz. Logs were preferably obtained as fallen trees or as driftwood. In colonial American the adz once was a primary woodworking tool. One advantage of an adz for careful woodwork is that it is drawn toward the user, and the blows can be more precise than those of an ax. Contemporary Native American craftspersons typically continue to use adzes with metal blades for woodwork.

WEAPONS

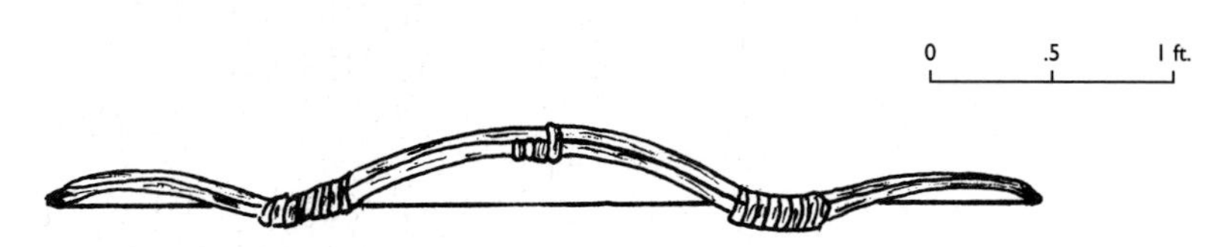

Surprisingly perhaps, the BOW AND ARROW appear to have been invented only once in prehistory. The earliest secure evidence is from Europe, some 10,500 years ago. The combination was introduced to the Arctic culture area about 4,000 years ago and to the contiguous states during the Christian era. At the time of historic contact, the bow and arrow were nearly universal north of Mexico. The earliest bows had wooden shafts (self bow) with attached bowstrings. The earliest composite bow, like the one in this illustration, arrived in the Arctic from Asia around A.D. 800. This type usually was fashioned from sections of antler or wood that were tied or glued together; lengths of sinew were sometimes tied on the back of the bow (composite, sinew-backed bow) or added to the back of a self bow (sinew-backed self bow).

Arrowheads typically were made from antler, stone, or bone and attached to either a foreshaft or directly to the shaft. The base (nock) of an arrow usually included feathers (fletching).

In general, ethnographic accounts report that an archer's target usually was quite close; thus great skill was required when approaching prey on foot or waiting at a concealed location. The advantage of the composite or sinew-backed bow was that it typically had greater thrust than a self bow.

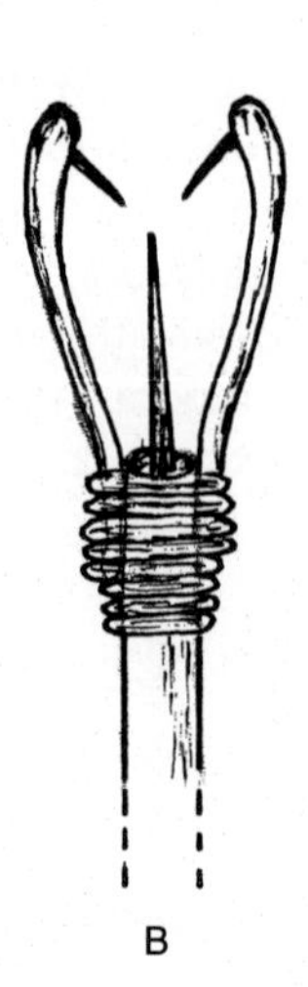

The FISH SPEAR (leister) was widely used except in desert and semidesert areas. Two basic types were common, each with a long handle. One form had two or more similar barbed points (a). After a fish was struck, the barbs held it fast for retrieval. Multiple points increased the likelihood of striking the prey. Another form had a central point and two flexible prongs, each with a separate point (b). After a fish was impaled on the central point, the lateral points held it in place for retrieval. In the far north fish spears often were used at holes in ice where the water was clear and still. In the eastern and western sectors of North America, but not in the far north, leisters were used from boats at night, and fish were speared by torchlight.

The TOGGLE HARPOON, used primarily by Eskimos, held but did not kill aquatic species (e.g., seals, walrus, whales). It was the most technologically complex weapon in aboriginal North America; a Greenland type included more than thirty parts. The illustrated example to the left was for taking seals on sea ice. The stone-pointed ivory harpoon head (a) was joined to the foreshaft (b) and tied to the shaft (c); an icepick (d) was bound at the shaft base. The line (e) attached to the harpoon head was handheld or, for other harpoon styles, attached to flotation devices. As a seal entered a breathing hole (illustration on right), the harpoon was thrust (B), and the head cut into the animal's flesh and toggled (A) as the seal attempted to escape (C). The hunter played the seal with the line until it was exhausted and then pulled it to the ice hole to kill with a knife. Figure D shows narwhal hunting from a kayak. The harpoon head was attached to a sealskin float and drag anchor (E) to tire the whale, which was eventually killed with a lance. (Original drawings by Patrick Finnerty.)

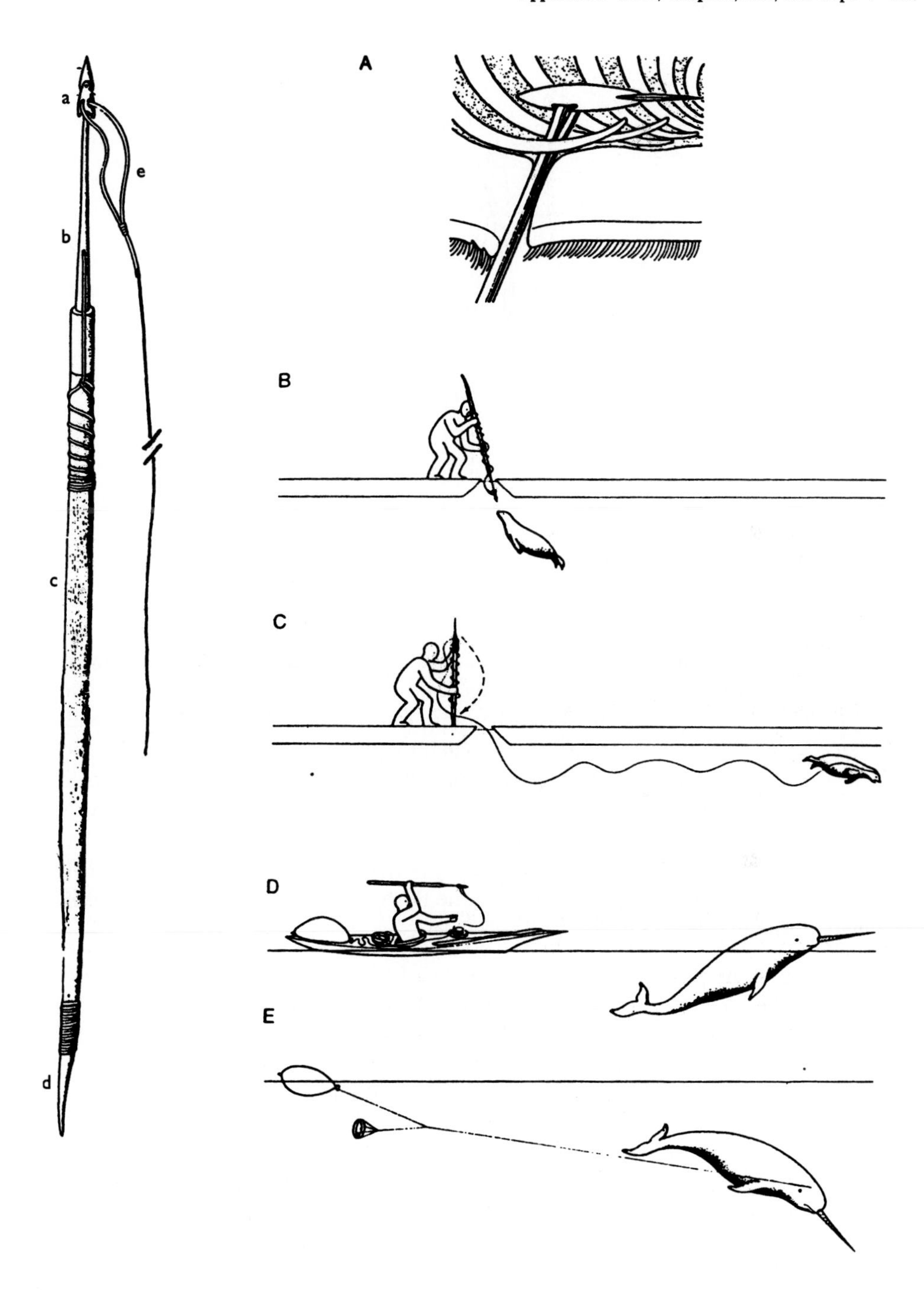
a
b
c
d
e
A
B
C
D
E

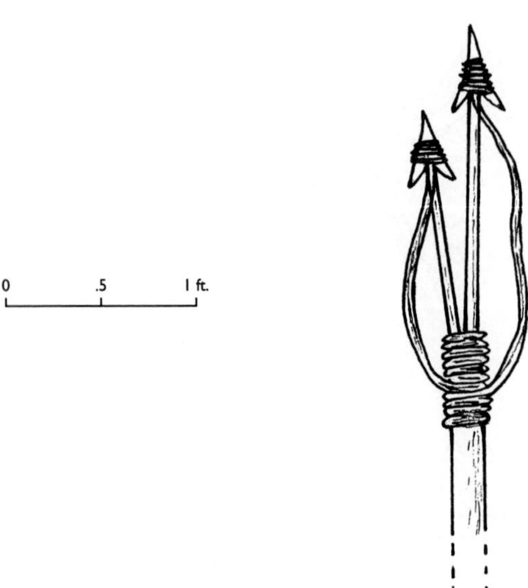

The DOUBLE-HEADED TOGGLE HARPOON was widespread along the Northwest Coast and western California and was used primarily to take salmon. At the top of a long wooden shaft were diverging foreshafts of different lengths with a toggle head at the end of each one. Each toggle of bone or horn was bound as a unit and tied to the shaft with a short line. This harpoon often was used at river eddies in which fish congregated to rest or feed. A harpooned fish was landed by raising the shaft. The use of diverging heads increased the probability of striking a fish. A barbed spear was not as effective against large fish because the barbs often tore free from the flesh; this occurrence was less likely with a toggling harpoon.

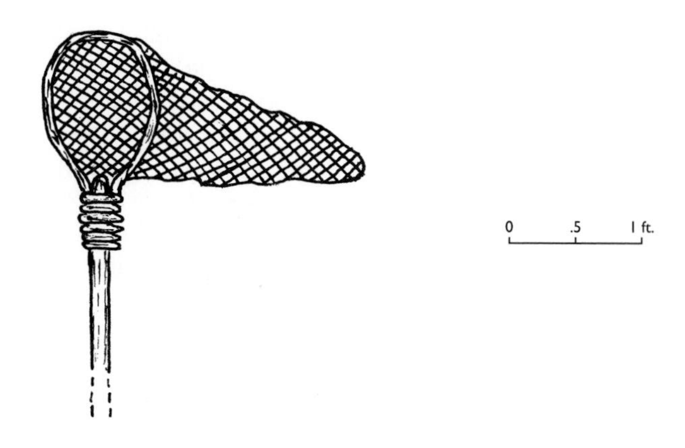

NETS

A DIP NET for fish was widely used by aboriginal North Americans. The cone-shaped net was usually attached to a wooden hoop that kept the netting open at the mouth. Made from thong or fiber lines, the mesh size depended on the species sought. These nets were typically employed directly in streams or rivers, at weirs, or from platforms built at an eddy or other spots where fish congregated. With a migrating species such as salmon, hundreds of fish could be harvested in a single day.

The GILL NET had a relatively limited distribution and was probably most popular in the Northwest Coast culture area. The netting, of thongs or fiber, looked like a modern tennis net and had wooden floats and stone sinkers. Small fish swam through the netting, and large fish would bump against the netting and back off. A fish of the proper size, however, could not swim through the netting and was held fast by its gills. These nets typically were short and fragile, and they required careful maintenance. Gill nets also might be set from boats and drifted down a river; they are termed drift nets. Somewhat similar to a gill net were the nets used on land in British Columbia for deer or elk. Seines are similar to gill nets but have very small mesh. They were usually manipulated by two or more persons along a shoreline or riverbar and drawn to the shore or bank where the catch was collected.

TRAPS

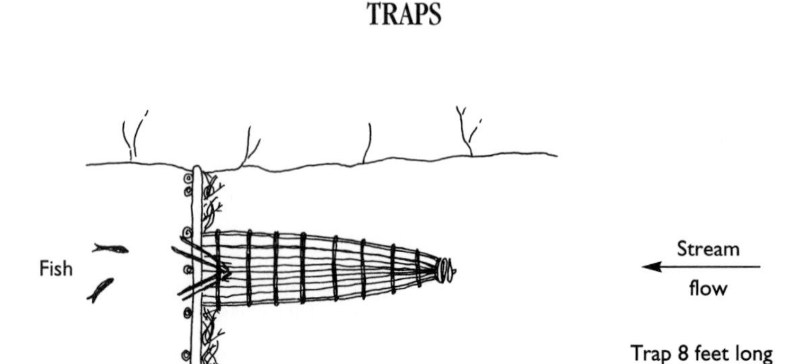

The FISH WEIR AND TRAP dominated along the Northwest Coast and was most effective for taking migratory species, especially salmon. A trap was fashioned from wooden splints bound in place with fiber lines. This trap for salmon faced downstream in a waterway; at right angles to it was constructed a weir (fence-like arrangement) of poles and brush. Fish ascending the waterway swam into the trap, and a funnel-shaped opening to the trap prevented most fish from escaping. This type of trap could be set beneath ice. They were sometimes made in sections and reached an overall length of about fifteen feet. The obvious advantage of a trap of this nature was that it harvested most fish ascending a stream or river.

Numerous varieties of SNARES were widely used, depending on environmental conditions and the potential quarry. It was desirable to set snares across a game

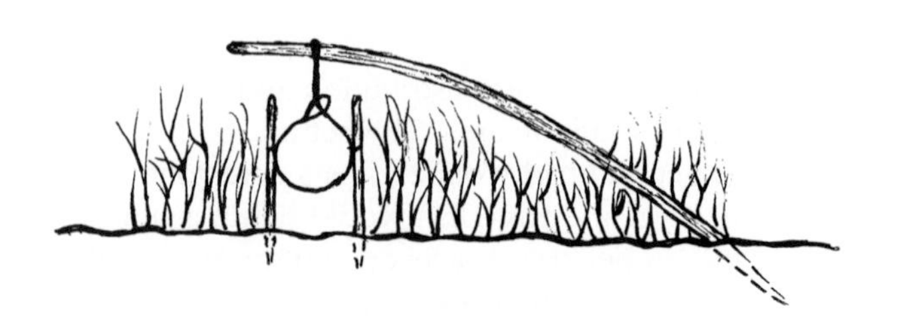

trail, as in the illustration. This type was made from thong or fiber, with a noose at one end and an attachment at the other end. The noose opening size and height depended on the species sought, for example, rabbit or ground squirrel. As the prey stuck its head into the opening, the noose tightened and choked the animal to death. In still water another variety might be used for waterfowl. Multiple snares floated in a wooden, hooplike frame and held the feet of prey, such as ducks. Alternatively, stout and more elaborate snares trapped big game, such as bears. Snares usually were not tended by a person and thus operated all of the time, an advantage for capturing nocturnal species or potentially dangerous animals.

Appendix B
Resources about Native Americans

At the close of each chapter, "Additional Sources" provide an initial guide to further information about the topics and tribes presented. However, the range of subjects pertaining to Indians is so vast that your particular interests may not be accommodated. This guide to sources is more expansive but overlaps with the chapter listings.

ENCYCLOPEDIAS For an introduction to most topics, encyclopedias concentrating on Native Americans may be the best place to begin, although the quality of particular entries varies widely. Some of them are: *Native America in the Twentieth Century: An Encyclopedia,* Mary B. Davis, ed., 1994, New York; *Encyclopedia of North American Indians,* Frederick E. Hoxie, ed., 1996, New York; *Native American Tribes,* Sharon Malinowski and Anna Sheets, eds., 1998, New York; *American Indians,* Harvey Markowitz, ed., 1995, Pasadena, CA.

SOURCE BOOKS These works concentrate largely on present-day organizations, such as museums, tribal governments, libraries, and federal agencies: *Native Americans Information Directory,* Julia C. Furtaw, ed., 1993, Detroit, MI. *The Native American Almanac,* Arlene Hirschfelder and Martha Kreipe de Montaño, eds., 1993, New York.

ARCHAEOLOGY The best overview about the prehistory north of Mexico is the college textbook *Ancient North America,* Brian M. Fagan, 1995, New York. For details the following sources are especially recommended: *Archaeology of Prehistoric Native America: An Encyclopedia,* Guy Gibbon, ed., 1998, New York; *Historical Dictionary of North American Archaeology,* Edward B. Jelks, ed., 1988, Westport, CT.

TRIBAL ETHNOGRAPHIES The best published bibliographic source by far about specific tribes is *Ethnographic Bibliography of North America,* George Peter Murdock and Timothy J. O'Leary, 4th ed., 1975, New Haven, CT, and the supplement, 1973–1987, by M. Marlene Martin and Timothy J. O'Leary, 1990, New Haven.

ETHNOLOGICAL COMPARISONS If you are interested in the regional cultural variability among aboriginal North Americans, including those in Middle America, a key source is *Indians of North America*, Harold E. Driver, 1961, Chicago. Among the subjects examined are house types, garments, crafts, music, art, warfare, social life, and religion.

IN-DEPTH REGIONAL AND TOPICAL STUDIES The new multivolume *Handbook of North American Indians*, William C. Sturtevant, gen. ed., Smithsonian Institution, Washington, DC, is an excellent source. Not all twenty volumes of this monumental work have yet appeared. The published volumes are as follows: v. 4, *History of Indian-White Relations*, 1998; v. 5, *Arctic*, 1984; v. 6, *Subarctic*, 1981; v. 7, *Northwest Coast*, 1990; v. 8, *California*, 1978; vols. 9, 10, *Southwest*, 1979, 1983; v. 11, *Great Basin*, 1986; v. 12, *Plateau*, 1998; v. 15, *Northeast*, 1978; and v. 17, *Languages*, 1996.

THE INTERNET For U.S. Federal Government sources, consult the *Internet Blue Pages*, Laurie Androit, 1998, Medford, NJ. A more general source is *The Internet Directory*: version 2.0, Eric Braun, ed., 1996, New York.

Key U.S. Government web sites are as follows:

Department of Commerce—Census Bureau—American Indian Data—
http://www.census.gov/population/www/socdemo/race/indian.html

Department of Interior—Bureau of Indian Affairs—
http://www.doi.gov/bureau-indian-affairs.html

Department of Interior—Bureau of Land Management—Guidance for Native American Consultation—
http://www.blm.gov/nhp/efoia/wo/handbook/h8160-1.html

Department of Interior—Office of American Indian Trust—
http://www.doi.gov/oait

Department of Interior—Office of the Special Trustee for American Indians—*http://www.ost.doi.gov*

Department of Justice—Office of Tribal Justice—
http://www.usdoj.gov/otj/otj.html

Department of Labor—Indian & Native American Programs—
http://www.wdsc.org/dinap

Environmental Protection Agency—American Indian Environmental Office—*http://www.epa.gov/owindian*

Federal Emergency Management Agency—Draft American Indian and Native Alaska Policy—*http://www.fema.gov/library/frgn019.htm*

U.S. Representatives Internet Law Library—Indian Nations and Tribes—
http://law.house.gov/31.htm

U.S. Senate—Committee on Indian Affairs—
http://www.senate.gov/~scia

An informed nongovernment web site is the National Congress on American Indians at *www.ncai.org*

VIDEOS The account about "the last wild Indian in North America," discovered in California in 1911, is widely acclaimed and titled *Ishi, the Last Yahi.* A classic documentary, released first in 1922 and filmed by Robert Flaherty, is about Eskimos (Inuit) along the eastern shore of Hudson Bay and titled *Nanook of the North*. A comprehensive guide to films and videos about Native Americans is *Films for Anthropological Teaching,* Karl G. Heider and Carol Hermer, 1995, American Anthropological Association.

FEATURE FILMS Two comparatively recent films are especially notable and widely available in video stores. Each is a poignant, sad, and humorous account of modern Indian life. *Pow Wow Highway,* is regarded by many Indians as the best film about the contemporary scene. Sherman Alexie, of Spokane and Coeur d'Alene ancestry, wrote and coproduced *Smoke Signals,* released in 1998, which has received numerous awards.

NOVELS The key source is *The Native American in Long Fiction, An Annotated Bibliography,* by Joan Beam and Barbara Brandstad, 1993, Walnut Creek, CA.

Glossary

acculturation (culture contact, transculturation) represents the changes in the culture of a people resulting from contacts with other peoples; the Native American response to Euro-Americans is an example

agriculture the cultivation of field crops with the aid of plows and draft animals

Anglo (Anglo-American) English-speaking whites; the term is used most commonly in the Southwest

artifact (artefact) any object of human workmanship

babiche thin, dehaired strips of animal skins; used primarily as binders

Bahana the Hopi word for the mythological older brother of the Hopi, whose descendants would someday return when the Hopi were in desperate need

band a small, family-oriented group of aboriginal foragers; the word is now used in Canada and the United States to identify some federally recognized groups of Native Americans, for example, the Six Nations Band

bannock (fry bread, Indian bread) in Native American context, refers to white flour and baking powder mixed with water and fried in grease

baseline ethnography the description of a tribe before the members had significant contact with representatives of a literate society; thus the time frame varies widely by geographical area

berdache traditionally identified as a physiological male who assumes the behavior, dress, and status of a woman; more recently defined as a physiological male *or* female who assumes the behavior, dress, and status of the opposite sex; the terms "man-woman," and "woman-man" appear to be gaining favor

biculturation combining the traits of one culture with those of the members of another culture; for example, a modern Crow Indian shares in both Crow and Euro-American culture at the same time

bifurcate collateral kinship terms (for parents and their siblings) an uncle, aunt, mother, and father are each given separate terms

bifurcate merging kinship terms (for parents and their siblings) father and father's brother are called by one term, mother and mother's sister by another term, but mother's brother and father's sister terms are distinct

bilateral descent relatives are traced through both the male and female lines; the descent system used in the United States today

bilocal residence the establishment of residence by a married couple with or near either the husband's or the wife's parents

booger mask a Cherokee term, with the same root as the English word "bogey"; refers to enemies depicted on dance masks

bow, composite *See* composite bow

bow, self *See* self bow

bow, sinew-backed *See* sinew-backed bow

bride price an alternative term for bridewealth

bridewealth material property presented by a man, or a man and his kin group, to reward a woman's family for the loss to her natal group and to legitimize a marriage

bull-roarer usually a piece of wood tied to the end of a cord that is twirled to make a roaring sound; the sound produced may have supernatural implications

calumet a Native American ceremonial pipe smoked in religious contexts or on state occasions, such as to validate a treaty

cariole a French word to refer to a toboggan with side panels and stanchions at the back; the cariole is a French innovation. *See also* toboggan

cat's cradle a string tied at the ends and looped around the fingers of both hands to form a cradlelike pattern; as the string is manipulated different patterns emerge; may involve two persons

charismatic person an individual with an inordinate personal capacity for leadership

Chilcat robe a woven woolen dance robe made by Chilkat (Tlingit) women

clan a unilineal descent group in which relatives are traced primarily along the male or female line to a presumed common ancestor; thus matriclans and patriclans

Code Talkers Navajo in the U.S. Marine Corps during World War II who used Navajo words as a code in frontline radio transmissions in the Pacific campaign

composite bow sections of antler or horn glued together to form a bow; it may be backed with strands of sinew as one type; *see* Appendix A for an example

count coup a means of exhibiting bravery in warfare by striking or touching a live enemy; associated primarily with Plains Indians

cousin terms *Crow type:* father's sister's daughter and mother's brother's daughter are termed differently from sisters and parallel cousins, but father's sister's daughter is termed the same as father's sister and/or mother's brother's daughter is termed the same as brother's daughter

Eskimo type: parallel and cross-cousins are termed the same but with a separate term from those used for siblings; this is the cousin terminology used in the United States

Hawaiian type: parallel and cross-cousins are termed the same as siblings; thus "uncles" and "aunts" are termed the same as "mother" and "father"

Iroquois type: father's sister's daughter and mother's brother's daughter are called by the same terms, but different terms are used for parallel cousins and for sisters

Omaha type: father's sister's daughter and mother's brother's daughter are called by terms different from each other and different from those used for parallel cousins and sisters; however, father's sister's daughter is termed the same as sister's daughter and/or mother's brother's daughter the same as mother's sister

cross-cousins the children of siblings of the opposite sex; father's sister's children and mother's brother's children

Crow-type cousin terms *See* cousin terms, Crow type

cultural blindness a trait that appears to be illogical in its cultural context; for example, the long, slim olive jars in the United States today that make it difficult to remove the olives

cultural relativism the view that any human behavior occurs in the context of a particular culture and should be considered within that framework; for example, societies have different cleanliness standards

culture area a geographical sector of the world whose occupants exhibit more cultural similarities with each other than with the peoples in other culture areas

deadfall a trap with a baited and triggered entry and a weight above that falls on an animal when it attempts to take the bait; especially useful against bears

descent, bilateral *See* bilateral descent

descent, unilineal *See* unilineal descent

Dinetah the Navajo word for their traditional homeland in the Southwest

dip net a bag-shaped net with rigid support around the mouth and a long handle used to scoop fish or other aquatic species from the water; broadly similar to a butterfly net used in the United States; *see* Appendix A for an example

dumaiya the Hopi word applied to a young man who secretly visits a young woman in her home at night to have sexual intercourse

encomienda a land grant in the Southwest given to Spanish colonists as a reward for services rendered; included control over resident Indians

endogamy marriage to someone within a defined group, for example, band or village

Eskimo-type cousin terms *See* cousin terms, Eskimo type

ethnocentrism the attitude that one's own culture is superior compared with all others; an example is to regard your own religion as superior to all others

ethnographic present the use of the present tense when describing past forms of behavior; a literary device to convey the vitality of an ethnographic account

ethnography a descriptive framework for behavioral information about a population at a particular point in time, usually a year

ethnography, baseline *See* baseline ethnography
ethnohistory the presentation and interpretation of ethnographic information in historical context
ethnology the systematic comparison of cultures to establish how and why they are similar or dissimilar
ethos the guiding beliefs, standards, or ideals that characterize a people; the Harmony Ethic of the Cherokee is an example
extended family the families of two or more siblings that are joined over two or more generations
False Face Society an Iroquois sodality whose members were primarily curers
first fruit (first harvest) the ceremonial distribution of an initial harvest for a plant product or an animal species
First Nations a designation in Canada for their Eskimo (Inuit), Indian, and Métis populations
fish trap an arrangement of stones or wooden splints, often funnel-shaped, set in conjunction with a weir to capture and hold, but not kill, fish; *see* Appendix A for an example
Five Civilized Tribes the Cherokee, Chickasaw, Choctaw, Creek, and Seminole
foragers people who depend on wild species for food; they hunt, fish, and collect plant products for a living
gadugi the Cherokee term for a free labor company, a sodality
generational kinship terms (for parents and their siblings) the father term is extended to uncles and the mother term is extended to aunts
gill net a fishing device that looks somewhat like a tennis net with floats attached at the top and weights at the bottom; as a fish of appropriate size attempts to swim through the mesh, it is caught by its gills; may be used to entangle other species, such as beaver; *see* Appendix A for an example
Harmony Ethic the Cherokee ideal for people to be nonaggressive and generous with one another
harpoon, toggle-headed *See* toggle-headed harpoon
Hawaiian-type cousin terms *See* cousin terms, Hawaiian type
hogan the Navajo word for their pole-framed and earth-covered types of dwellings
hominy from an Algonquian word that now refers to a food prepared from kernels of corn whose shells have been removed
hooch a distilled alcoholic beverage originally made by Indians
hopi a Hopi term for a person who is good, honorable, and nonaggressive
horticulture the small-scale cultivation of domestic plants with a hoe and digging stick
hozho the Navajo word that means balance, beauty, goodness, happiness, harmony, and health
Indian an aboriginal or indigenous (as opposed to an immigrant) inhabitant of the Americas; an American Indian or Native American

infanticide the killing of a newborn offspring, or sometimes a young child

Iroquois-type cousin terms *See* cousin terms, Iroquois type

kachina doll the small-scale representation of mythological, ancestral, or historical figures; the figures are not "dolls" as toys but are designed to teach children the differences among the many types of kachinas

kahopi a Hopi word for a person who is dishonorable and aggressive

kayak a skin-covered Eskimo vessel with an enclosed deck designed to accommodate one person; the boat is framed with wood and/or antler

kinaalda the Navajo word for the ceremony that a girl underwent at her menarche

kindred close bilateral relatives along the male and female lines; a kindred is ego-centered, meaning that a particular kindred is shared only by biological siblings; the kindred is an important kin group in the United States today

kiva a Pueblo Indian ceremonial structure that is often beneath the ground

kueex the Tlingit term for a potlatch

kwaan a major geographical area identified by the Tlingit; comparable in many ways to a "tribe"

labret (lip plug) an artifact, often made from wood, worn in a perforation above, below, or at the sides of the lips; multiple labrets may be worn

leister (fish spear) often with multiple barbed heads; *see* Appendix A

levirate the marriage of a woman to her deceased husband's brother

lineage a consanguineal kin group with descent traced along either the female or male line from a known common ancestor

lineal kinship terms (for parents and their siblings) father's brother and mother's brother are given one term, father's sister and mother's sister are given a different term; both terms are different from those for parents; this is the "uncle" and "aunt" classification used in the United States today

lip plug *See* labret

Long Walk the forced removal beginning in 1863 of Navajo to Fort Sumner (Bosque Redondo) by the U.S. military; the captives remained there under military control until 1868

manitou an Algonquian word for a supernatural force

mano *See* milling stones

material culture the physical objects made and used by a people; the products of technology; examples include tools, weapons, garments, dwellings, and art objects

matriclan relatives traced through the female line to a presumed common ancestor

matrilineal descent relatives traced through the female line

matrilocal residence the establishment of residence by a married couple within or near the wife's mother's household

medicine bundle (sacred or spirit bundle) a packet of sacred objects for an individual or for a group such as a clan

menarche the initial menstruation of a female

metate *See* milling stones
Métis the term widely used in Canada to refer to a person of mixed Indian and non-Indian ancestry
milling stones used to pulverize seeds or animal materials in the preparation of edibles; the base stone may be termed a milling stone, metate, or quern; the hand-held stone may be termed a hand stone, mano, or rubbing stone
mnemonic to aid memory; for example, tying a string around a finger
moiety a social group that is one of two larger groups; for example, one moiety within a tribe comprises clans A, B, and C, and the second moiety is represented by clans D, E, and F
moiety exogamy the convention that an individual must marry someone from the opposite moiety
money a medium of exchange with a standardized value
neolocal residence the establishment of a separate residence by a married couple apart from the husband's or wife's parents
neonate a newborn human offspring less than twenty-eight days of age
net the male leader of a Cahuilla clan
nuclear family same as the basic or elementary family; a person, the person's spouse, and their dependent offspring
oki an Iroquois term for a personal guardian spirit
Omaha-type cousin terms *See* cousin terms, Omaha type
paha a male ceremonial leader among some groups of Cahuilla
Pan-Indianism or pantribalism; a sharing of traits among the members of different tribes, for example, apparel, dances, foods, and ceremonies
parallel cousins the children of siblings of the same sex; father's brothers' children and mother's sisters' children
patriclan a group of families related primarily through males to a presumed common ancestor
patrilineage a family line that is traced primarily through males to a known common ancestor
patrilineal descent relatives traced through the male line
patrilocal residence the establishment of residence by a married couple within or near the husband's family's household
pemmican a Cree word that refers to dried pulverized meat and fat used mainly as food for travelers
peon a guessing game played by the Cahuilla
personal kindred blood relatives of a person of his or her generation, as well as junior and senior generations; the convention that prevails in the United States at present
phratry an exogamous group of clans
piki a Hopi word for finely ground cornmeal mixed with water and ashes and cooked on a heated stone slab
polyandry a form of marriage in which a woman has two or more spouses at the same time

polygamy a form of marriage in which the participants have two or more spouses at the same time

polygyny a form of marriage in which a man has two or more wives at the same time

potlatch from the Nootka word "gift"; a ceremonial occasion in which wealth is displayed and gifts presented to honor a person and validate the claim to a title

powwow a Narraganset word originally referring to the activities of shamans; presently used to refer to a public Indian gathering that focuses on feasting, dancing, other performances, and the sale of Indian craft items

primogeniture preferential inheritance by the firstborn male or, less often, by the firstborn female

religion a minimal definition proposed by Edward B. Tylor in 1871 is "the belief in Spiritual Beings"; a more detailed definition by Melford E. Spiro in 1966 is "an institution consisting of cultural patterned interaction with culturally postulated superhuman beings"

sachem based on an Algonquian word and used widely to refer to a hereditary male leader; the head of a matriclan among the Iroquois is called a sachem

sacred bundle (medicine or spirit bundle) a packet of sacred objects of an individual or a group, such as a clan

sagamite an Algonquian word applied to corn porridge; a hominy gruel

seine a small-meshed net the ends of which are drawn together to enclose fish

self bow a bow made from a wooden shaft

shaman a word from the Tungus in Russia; a part-time specialist in the supernatural; "shaman" does not mean sha*man,* a shaman may be male or female; the plural is shamans

sinew-backed bow a wooden bow shaft or composite bow strengthened with strips of sinew along the back; *see* Appendix A for an example

skywalker a term used to refer to Indians, especially Mohawk, who work in high steel

slave the subordinate status of a person that is passed on to his or her descendants; a captive in warfare, an individual purchased, or the child of an indebted person often were slaves

sliding historical baseline the beginning of history on a regional basis; for example, in area A historic contact with Euro-Americans may have taken place in A.D. 1600, whereas in area B it came in A.D. 1800; the time difference is ignored when establishing the beginnings of written history in the respective areas

snare a running noose of babiche or other strong material, firmly anchored (e.g., to a bush or tree) to hold a bird or other creature that is caught in the noose; *see* Appendix A for an example

sodality a secondary, special-purpose association with either voluntary or involuntary membership

sorcery the use of power gained with the assistance or the control of evil spirits; witchcraft is the use of sorcery

sororal polygyny a form of marriage in which a man marries two or more women who are sisters

sororate the marriage of a man to the sister of his wife, either while he is married to or after the death of his first wife

surround a structure often made from stone or poles and brush into which big game was driven to become impounded and killed by other means

sweat bath bathing in the heat produced by coals from a fire or fire-heated stones for pleasure and/or for a supernatural purpose; often a small structure; water may be placed on stones to produce a steam bath

taboo (tabu) a Polynesian word meaning "sacred"; it commonly refers to something that is both sacred and forbidden

taiga a moist subarctic forest dominated by conifers

teknonymy naming a parent after a child, often the firstborn; for instance, if the child's name is Alfred, his mother is called "Alfred's mother"

throwing stick (boomerang, rabbit-killing stick) used to hurl at birds or small game to stun or kill; the self-returning boomerang did not exist in North America

toboggan an Algonquian word; a flat-bottomed conveyance usually made from thin strips of wood bound together and bent upward at the front; *see also* cariole

toggle-headed harpoon a weapon, typically associated with Eskimos, designed to pierce the skin of an aquatic species and then to toggle (somewhat in the manner of a button passing through a buttonhole); a harpoon usually holds but does not kill prey; *see* Appendix A for an example

tolache from a Nahuatl word adopted by the Spanish; among the Cahuilla it refers to a narcotic, jimsonweed, used by some Cahuilla in a male initiation ceremony

tomahawk an Algonquian word for a light stone ax used as a weapon; following European contact a tomahawk head was manufactured from metal as a trade item and could include a pipe bowl at the head

totem pole a pillar facing or pole with carved and painted symbols representing a clan and based on mythological or historical events

Trail of Tears the Cherokee term for the removal of most Indians from the Southeast to Indian Territory in the 1830s

trait an act, object, or thought identified with a specific culture; examples include shaking hands (an act), a pencil (an object), and doomsday (a thought)

transhumance the seasonal movement of livestock by herders from one altitude to another

transvestite a person who adopts the clothes of the opposite sex and often behaves in the manner of the opposite sex; *see also* berdache

travois a French Canadian word for a conveyance consisting of two trailing poles with a platform for a load; a travois was initially pulled by a dog and later by a horse

tribe in general, a small-scale society with a name, dialect, and a territory, but without central political authority

tunraq protective spirits that Eskimo (Inuit) shamans attempt to control

tupiliq dangerous Eskimo (Inuit) spirits that were especially hostile toward people and capable of causing illness or death

umiak a large open wood-framed and skin-covered Eskimo boat

unilineal descent relatives are traced through the female line (matrilineal) or the male line (patrilineal)

universalism the approach to human behavior based on the acceptance of value categories applicable to all cultures

value a shared concept of what is desirable or undesirable

village endogamy marriage to someone within one's own community

wampum based on an Algonquian word for a string of white beads; the bead patterns of a wampum belt were "talked into" as a means of keeping records; for example, a particular bead pattern might refer to a tribe, whereas a second bead pattern might refer to the place of a treaty arrangement

weir an obstruction of stone, brush, or other material across a stream or river to block the progress of fish; it may form a dam and be used with fish spears or have openings for fish traps; *see* Appendix A for an example

witchcraft employing sorcery; sorcery is the use of power gained with the assistance or control of evil spirits

Yei the Navajo word for their mythological Holy People

Pronunciation Guide*

Aleut AL-ee-oot
Algonquian al-GON-kin
Amouskositte (early Cherokee leader) ah-mos-ko-SIT-tee
Anasazi (archaeological tradition in the Southwest) Ah-nuh-SAH-zee
Apache uh-PATCH-ee
Apsáalooke (Crow name for themselves) ap-SOO-laa-ka
Arapooish (Crow leader) AARLA-push
Auke (Tlingit geographical unit) AA-kay
babiche (strip of skin used as a binder) bah-BEESH
Bannock ("Indian bread") BAN-uck
berdache (transvestite, "man-woman" or "woman-man") BEHR-dash
Blackfoot BLAK-fůt
Cahuilla kuh-WEE-uh
calumet (ceremonial pipe) KAL-u-meht
cariole (type of toboggan) KAHR-ee-ool
Caughnawaga (Iroquois reserve) gon-na-WAH-ga
Cayuga ki-YOO-guh
Cherokee CHER-uh-kee
Chickasaw CHICK-uh-saw
Chinook shi-NOOK
Chipewyan chip-uh-WI-uhn
Chippewa CHIP-uh-wah
Coeur d'Alene kur-duh-LANE
coup (touching an enemy in warfare) koo
Crow KRO
Daganawida (cofounder of the League of the Iroquois) da-gon-na-WEE-dah
Dine (the Navajo's name for themselves) di-NAY
Dinetah (Navajo homeland) di-NAY-tah
dumaiya (Hopi courting practice) doo-MIY-yuh
gadugi (Cherokee free-labor company) gah-DOO-gee
Gros Ventre grow-VAHN-truh
Haida HI-duh

*AUTHOR'S NOTE: Some Aboriginal languages have sounds that are quite different from those of American English.

Hiawatha (cofounder of the League of the Iroquois) hi-uh-WAW-ta
Hidatsa he-DOT-suh
hogan (Navajo dwelling) HO-hwahn in Navajo; HO-gon in English
hooch (distilled alcoholic beverage) hootch
Hopi ho-PEE in their language; HO-pee in English
Hupa HOOP-uh
Huron HYUR-on
Inuit IN-yoo-it
Iroquois IR-uh-kwoi
kachina (Hopi mythical, ancestral, or historical supernatural) kaht-SEE-nuh in Hopi; ka-CHE-na in English
kahopi (Hopi word for a dishonorable person) kah-HOH-pee
Karok KAH-ruke
Kepel (former Yurok village) kep-EL
kinaalda (Navajo term for a girl's puberty ceremony) ki-nahl-DAH
Klukwan (Tlingit village) KLUCK-ahn
Kootenai KOOT-nee
kueex (Tlingit word for potlatch) qu-EEX
kwaan (major Tlingit geographical unit) QU-aan
Kwakiutl KWAH-kee-oo-tel
Maasaw (Hopi god of death) maah-SAHW
Manitou (a supernatural force) MAN-i-too
Mohawk MO-hawk
Moytoy (early Cherokee leader) MOY-TOY
Mukat (one of the twin Cahuilla creators) MU-kat
Naa Ka Hidi Theater (Tlingit performance group) naa-kah-HIDI
Nampeyo (Hopi woman) naum-PEH-yoh
Nan-ye-hi (Cherokee name for Nancy Ward) nan-YEE-hee
Natchez NATCH-is
Navajo NAV-uh-ho
net (a Cahuilla clan leader) net
Netsilik NET-silik
Oconaluftee (reconstructed Cherokee settlement) oh-KOE-nah-LUF-tee
Ojibwa o-jib-WAY
Oraibi (Hopi village) oh-zhiy-VHEE in Hopi; oh-rye-be in English
pah (a Cahuilla leader) PA-ha
parfleche (container made of folded skin) PAHR-flehsh
Passamaquoddy pah-suh-muh-KWOD-ee
pemmican (dried meat as food for travelers) PEHM-i-kehn
Penobscot puh-NOB-scot
peon (Cahuilla guessing game) pe-ON in Cahuilla
piki (a Hopi ground cornmeal "bread") PEE-kee
poncho (garment) PAHN-choh
potlatch (ceremonial wealth display and gift giving) POT-lach
Powamu (Hopi ceremony) poh-WAH-moo

Powhatan pow-HAT-un
Requa (Yurok village) req-WAH
Saa or **Sa'a** (Yurok place-name) SAAH
Seneca SEN-uh-kuh
Sioux SUE
Soyal (Hopi ceremony) soh-YAHL
Tamaiot (one of the twin Cahuilla creators) tim-a-YO-hwit
Tekakwitha, Kateri (Mohawk, became a Roman Catholic saint) de-ga-GWEE-ta, ga-de-LEE
Tlingit THLING-kuht
Tododaho (Onondaga sachem) ta-do-DAH-hoe
Tuscarora tusk-uh-ROAR-uh
Weitspus (Yurok village) WEET-puss
Wuwuchim (Hopi secret society) woo-WOO-thim
Wuya (Hopi clan ancestors) WOO-yuh
Yei (Navajo mythological Holy People) yay
Yupik (Eskimo linguistic group) YOO-pik
Yurok YUR-ahk
Zuni ZOO-nee

Name Index

Subject Index

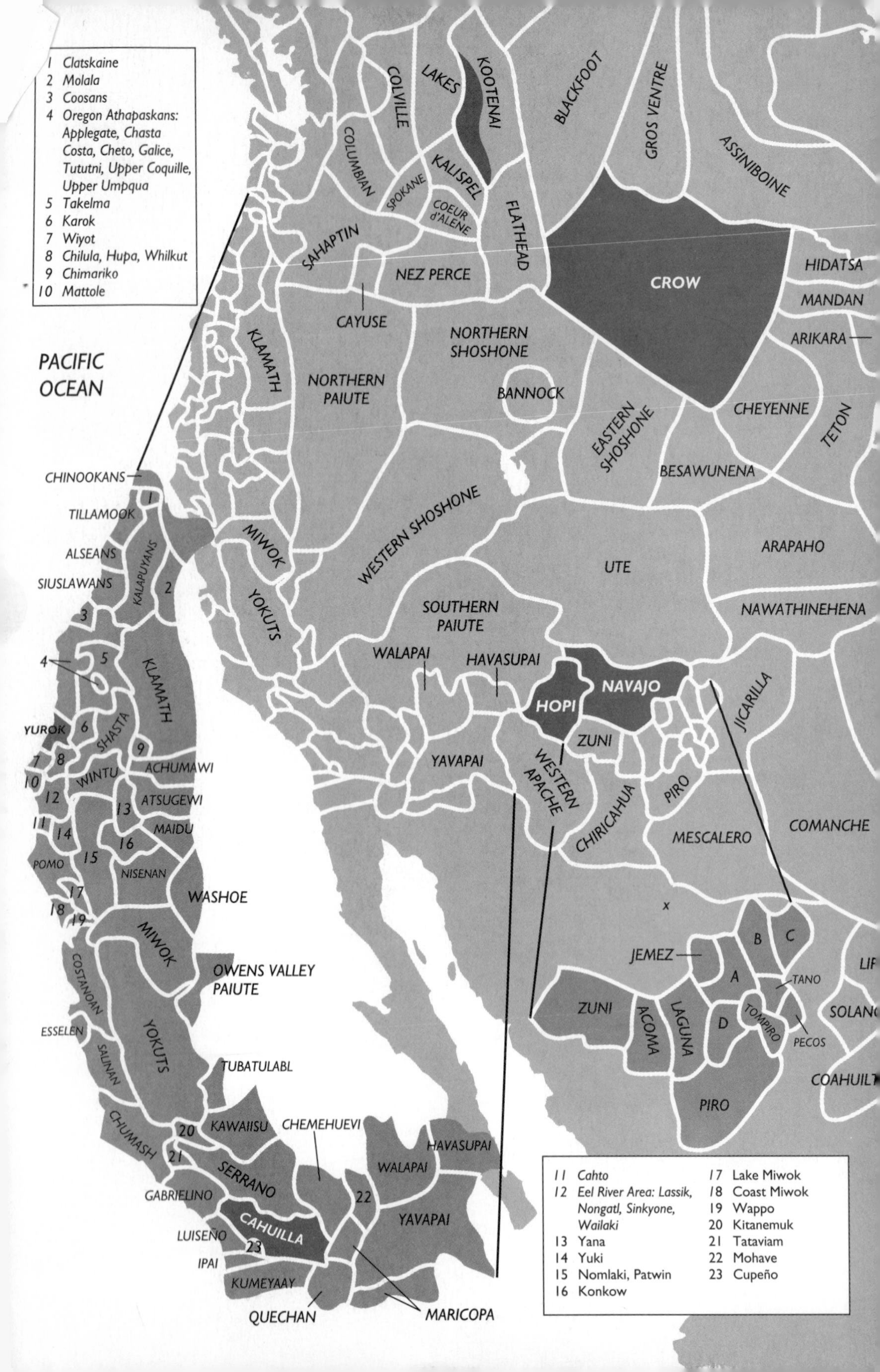
1 Clatskaine
2 Molala
3 Coosans
4 Oregon Athapaskans: Applegate, Chasta Costa, Cheto, Galice, Tututni, Upper Coquille, Upper Umpqua
5 Takelma
6 Karok
7 Wiyot
8 Chilula, Hupa, Whilkut
9 Chimariko
10 Mattole
PACIFIC OCEAN
KOOTENAI
LAKES
COLVILLE
BLACKFOOT
GROS VENTRE
ASSINIBOINE
COLUMBIAN
KALISPEL
SPOKANE
COEUR d'ALENE
FLATHEAD
SAHAPTIN
NEZ PERCE
CROW
HIDATSA
MANDAN
ARIKARA
CAYUSE
NORTHERN SHOSHONE
KLAMATH
NORTHERN PAIUTE
BANNOCK
EASTERN SHOSHONE
CHEYENNE
TETON
BESAWUNENA
WESTERN SHOSHONE
MIWOK
YOKUTS
UTE
ARAPAHO
SOUTHERN PAIUTE
NAWATHINEHENA
WALAPAI
HAVASUPAI
HOPI
NAVAJO
JICARILLA
ZUNI
YAVAPAI
WESTERN APACHE
PIRO
CHIRICAHUA
MESCALERO
COMANCHE
CHINOOKANS
TILLAMOOK
ALSEANS
KALAPUYANS
SIUSLAWANS
KLAMATH
YUROK
SHASTA
ACHUMAWI
WINTU
ATSUGEWI
MAIDU
POMO
NISENAN
WASHOE
MIWOK
COSTANOAN
OWENS VALLEY PAIUTE
ESSELEN
SALINAN
YOKUTS
TUBATULABL
CHUMASH
KAWAIISU
CHEMEHUEVI
HAVASUPAI
WALAPAI
SERRANO
GABRIELINO
CAHUILLA
YAVAPAI
LUISEÑO
IPAI
KUMEYAAY
QUECHAN
MARICOPA
JEMEZ
A
B
C
D
TANO
TOMPIRO
PECOS
ZUNI
ACOMA
LAGUNA
PIRO
SOLANO
COAHUILTECAN
11 Cahto
12 Eel River Area: Lassik, Nongatl, Sinkyone, Wailaki
13 Yana
14 Yuki
15 Nomlaki, Patwin
16 Konkow
17 Lake Miwok
18 Coast Miwok
19 Wappo
20 Kitanemuk
21 Tataviam
22 Mohave
23 Cupeño